*Metallic Materials in*

# ENGINEERING

# Metallic Materials in
# ENGINEERING

**CARL H. SAMANS, Ph.D.**

*Division Director, Engineering Materials,*
*Whiting Laboratories, American Oil Company*

The Macmillan Company, New York
Collier-Macmillan Limited, London

*To*

DERC, SCOTT, AND BRIAN

Fifth Printing, 1967

Previous edition, entitled *Engineering Metals and Their Alloys,* copyright 1949 by The Macmillan Company

Library of Congress catalog card number: 63-11808

The Macmillan Company, New York
Collier-Macmillan Canada, Ltd., Toronto, Ontario

Printed in the United States of America

# Preface

$L$ike its widely used predecessor, *Engineering Metals and Their Alloys,* this book gives a background of metallurgical information intended primarily for engineers—the principal users of metallic materials. In the extensive rewriting and reorganizing incident to bring this volume up to date, the size of the book has been reduced to be consistent with the one-semester course generally given to engineering students. Many sections of the earlier edition have been condensed or eliminated entirely, and new sections have been added wherever they would assist in understanding fundamentals from a metallurgical viewpoint. Numerous references for further reading are given to assist the student in delving more deeply into specific aspects, and a series of questions appear at the end of each chapter to encourage further thinking and the application of text material to various types of engineering problems.

Engineering progress today often is restricted by the materials available. Because of this, considerable attention and financial support has been directed in recent years toward the material science approach for developing new materials to solve these existing and anticipated problems. Ultimately this approach should lead to significant progress. However, it is the author's opinion that the field of materials science is still far too undeveloped to be used as a basis for teaching engineering students. They will soon become significant users rather than developers of materials and hence should have a different type of preparation. This preparation should be directed primarily toward metals because, for many years to come, the vast majority of applications still will be filled by the eight tonnage engineering metals, and all of the basic engineering materials will continue to be metallic. No other known materials have the same combination of properties and general characteristics. Consequently, it is important that the engineer know how the useful characteristics of these metallic materials can be modified by alloying, by mechanical deformation, and by heat treatment.

Alternative materials, both nonmetals and other metals, always have been available and new ones will continue to be announced daily. However, these are alternatives for specific applications rather than for general replacement, so they cannot be covered adequately on any useful basis. Instead, each must be considered on its own merits, in direct competition with the metallic material that usually would be the original choice based upon sound engineering analysis.

The time when tailor-made materials will be practical is well in the future. In fact, a surprising number of the more-or-less conventional new materials being announced these days are far from being ready for industrial use—particularly for competitive consumer items. The reasons for this lie both in stage of development and in cost. However, the two usually are not interrelated, as might normally be expected and has so often been the case in the past. In fact, real breakthroughs still must be achieved if many of these announced developments are ever to be economically competitive for other than a few highly specialized applications.

As with the earlier edition, little or nothing in this text is new. The author's sole contribution has been to present a logical development of the information—with brief discussions where it seemed desirable—concerning pertinent alloys available to industry today and used for various reasons. It is inevitable that many will object to this approach, if only because so much of the material is generally considered to be well established and of the handbook type. However, it must not be forgotten that this information is not known by the student who is seeing most of it for the first time, and is no longer remembered by many graduate engineers who find need to refresh their knowledge. Such information will provide a firmer background for appreciating and for using the fund of information given in the literature and in such complete sources as the *Metals Handbook* of The American Society for Metals.

My sincere thanks are given to those who assisted in supplying information used in this text, as well as to those who contributed the many photomicrographs used in the original text and now carried over to this revision. The number is so large that it is impossible to be assured of proper individual acknowledgement. I am grateful also to Standard Oil Company (Indiana) and to American Oil Company, its operating subsidiary in the refining field, for making it possible for me to complete this revision.

CARL  H.  SAMANS

*Chicago, Illinois*

# Table of Contents

## 1. General Characteristics of Metallic Materials    1

METALS · PHYSICAL STATES OF A METAL · ATOM RELATIONSHIPS IN THE STABLE STATES · THE THERMAL METHOD FOR DETERMINING ENERGY CHANGES · COOLING CURVES · GRAIN SIZE PRODUCED DURING SOLIDIFICATION · HEATING CURVES · METALLIC CHARACTERISTICS · STRUCTURE OF METALS · MECHANICAL STABILITY OF METALS · SPACE LATTICES · BODY-CENTERED CUBIC LATTICE · FACE-CENTERED CUBIC LATTICE · CLOSE-PACKED HEXAGONAL LATTICE · ALLOTROPY · ALLOTROPIC METALS · THE METAL IRON · THE CURIE POINT · ENERGY CHANGES CONNECTED WITH ALLOTROPY · SOLID SOLUTIONS · METALLOGRAPHY · ETCHING · MEASUREMENT OF GRAIN SIZE · LATTICE IMPERFECTIONS · POINT IMPERFECTIONS · SURFACE IMPERFECTIONS · IMPERFECTIONS PRODUCED BY IRRADIATION · LINE IMPERFECTIONS OR DISLOCATIONS · EDGE DISLOCATIONS · SCREW DISLOCATIONS · DISLOCATION PICTURE OF GRAIN BOUNDARIES · DIFFUSION

## 2. Mechanical Deformation and Fracture    38

ENGINEERING EFFECTS OF WORK-HARDENING · MECHANICAL PROPERTIES · HARDNESS OR RESISTANCE TO PENETRATION · STRENGTH OR RESISTANCE TO DEFORMATION · TENSILE STRENGTH · MODULI OF ELASTICITY · YIELD STRENGTH · ULTI-

MATE STRENGTH · ELONGATION AND REDUCTION IN AREA ·
CRYSTALLOGRAPHIC PLANES · CLOSE-PACKED PLANES · CLOSE-
PACKED DIRECTIONS · THEORETICAL YIELD STRENGTH OF
METALS · COLD WORK · EFFECTS OF GRAIN SIZE ON COLD WORK-
ING · THE GEOMETRICAL DEFORMATION PROCESS · SLIP · SLIP
LINES · GLIDE OF DISLOCATION · FRANK-READ SPIRALS AND
SOURCES · CLIMB OF DISLOCATIONS · DISLOCATION EXPLANA-
TION OF WORK-HARDENING · GRAIN-BOUNDARY DEFORMATION
IN A METAL AGGREGATE · TWINNING · MECHANICAL TWINNING ·
FRACTURE · SHEAR FRACTURE · CLEAVAGE FRACTURE · INTER-
GRANULAR FRACTURE · DUCTILE-BRITTLE FRACTURE TRANSI-
TIONS · IMPACT TESTS · IMPACT STRENGTH · FATIGUE STRENGTH

### 3. *Softening by Heat* 91

ANNEALING BY HEATING AFTER COLD WORKING · STRESS-RELIEF
OR RECOVERY · POLYGONIZATION · PRIMARY STRAIN RECRYSTAL-
LIZATION · EFFECT OF TIME, AND PERCENTAGE REDUCTION BY
WORKING, UPON RECRYSTALLIZATION · GRAIN GROWTH AFTER
RECRYSTALLIZATION · IMPURITY INHIBITED GRAIN GROWTH ·
ABNORMAL GRAIN GROWTH · SECONDARY RECRYSTALLIZATION ·
EFFECT OF RATE OF COOLING FOLLOWING STRAIN RECRYSTAL-
LIZATION UPON GRAIN SIZE · ALLOTROPIC RECRYSTALLIZATION ·
PROPERTY CHANGES RESULTING FROM ALLOTROPIC RECRYSTAL-
LIZATION IN IRON · EFFECT OF RATE OF COOLING AFTER ALLO-
TROPIC RECRYSTALLIZATION · RECRYSTALLIZATION OF CAST
STRUCTURES · STRUCTURAL CHANGES DURING FUSION WELDING ·
HOT WORK · EFFECT OF HOT WORK ON GRAIN SIZE · ANNEALING
FOR MAXIMUM DUCTILITY · THE ERICHSEN AND OLSEN DUC-
TILITY TESTERS · ANNEALING OR RECRYSTALLIZATION TWINS ·
CREEP · STRESS RUPTURE · RELAXATION · PARAMETERS FOR
EXTRAPOLATING STRESS RUPTURE AND CREEP DATA

### 4. *Common Engineering Metals* 128

CHARACTERISTICS OF ENGINEERING METALS IN INDUSTRIAL
USE · INDUSTRIAL ALUMINUM · ALUMINUM FOR ELECTRICAL
CONDUCTIVITY PURPOSES · INDUSTRIAL COPPER · OXYGEN-FREE
HIGH-CONDUCTIVITY COPPER · TOUGH-PITCH COPPER · EMBRIT-
TLEMENT OF COPPER BY HYDROGEN · DEOXIDIZED COPPER ·
FREE-MACHINING COPPER · ELECTRODEPOSITED COPPER · PURE
IRON · MAGNETIC PROPERTIES OF IRON · INGOT IRON · WROUGHT

IRON · MECHANICAL PROPERTIES OF INDUSTRIAL IRON · SOFT
LEAD · HARD LEAD · LEAD AND TERNE COATINGS · MAGNESIUM ·
NICKEL · ELECTRODEPOSITED NICKEL · TIN AND TIN PLATE ·
ROLLED ZINCS · ZINC COATINGS

## 5. *Simple Alloy Systems* 157

LIMITATIONS OF EXISTING KNOWLEDGE ABOUT ALLOYS · LIQUID
SOLUTIONS · COMPONENTS · METHODS OF ALLOYING · POWDER
METALLURGY · PHASES · THE GIBBS' PHASE RULE · PHASE DIA-
GRAMS · TYPES OF SOLID PHASES IN BINARY ALLOYS · PRIMARY
OR TERMINAL SOLID SOLUTIONS · INTERMETALLIC COMPOUNDS ·
SECONDARY OR INTERMEDIATE SOLID SOLUTIONS · MECHANICAL
MIXTURES · LIMITATIONS IN THE USE OF PHASE DIAGRAMS ·
ALLOYS WITH COMPLETE SOLID SOLUBILITY IN BOTH THE SOLID
AND LIQUID STATES · CHANGES OCCURRING DURING THE NORMAL
SOLIDIFICATION OF SOLID SOLUTION ALLOYS · THE LEVER RULE ·
NORMAL SOLIDIFICATION AT NONEQUILIBRIUM RATES · LIQUA-
TION · ZONE MELTING · INDUSTRIAL COPPER-RICH ALLOYS WITH
NICKEL · INDUSTRIAL NICKEL-RICH ALLOYS WITH COPPER ·
ALLOYS WITH PARTIAL SOLID SOLUBILITY · THE EUTECTIC ·
CONSTITUTIONAL DIAGRAM FOR ALLOYS WITH PARTIAL SOLID
SOLUBILITY · CHANGE OF SOLID SOLUBILITY WITH TEMPERA-
TURE · OCCURRENCE OF THE EUTECTIC CONSTITUENT · THE
SIMPLE EUTECTIC DIAGRAM · THE $1:2:1$ RULE · TIN-LEAD
ALLOYS · SILVER-LEAD ALLOYS · LEAD-ANTIMONY ALLOYS ·
ALUMINUM-SILICON ALLOYS · ALUMINUM-ZINC ALLOYS · ZINC-
BASE DIE-CASTING ALLOYS WITH ALUMINUM · MAGNESIUM-LEAD
ALLOYS · COPPER-MAGNESIUM ALLOYS · ANTIMONY-TIN ALLOYS:
THE PERITECTIC REACTION · PERITECTIC REACTIONS UNDER
NONEQUILIBRIUM CONDITIONS · TIN-BASE BEARING ALLOYS ·
ALUMINUM-BASE ALLOYS WITH MAGNESIUM · MAGNESIUM-
BASE ALLOYS WITH ALUMINUM

## 6. *More Complex Alloys* 234

COPPER-ZINC AND COPPER-TIN ALLOYS · COLOR CHANGES OF
BRASSES WITH INCREASING ZINC CONTENT · WROUGHT BRASSES ·
DEZINCIFICATION OF BRASSES · LEADED BRASSES · ALLOY
BRASSES · WROUGHT MANGANESE BRONZES · NICKEL SILVERS ·
SEASON CRACKING OF BRASS · WROUGHT BRONZES · MICRO-
STRUCTURES OF CAST BRASSES AND BRONZES · CAST RED

BRASSES · CAST YELLOW BRASSES · STEAM AND STRUCTURAL
BRONZES · HIGH-LOAD BEARING BRONZES · LEAD BRONZES ·
GRAPHITE BRONZES · HIGH-STRENGTH CAST NICKEL BRONZES ·
CAST MANGANESE BRONZES · EFFECT OF ALLOYING ELEMENTS
ON THE ALLOTROPIC TRANSFORMATIONS IN PURE IRON · IRON-
CARBON ALLOYS · THE EUTECTOID · REACTION TO ETCHING OF
CONSTITUENTS IN IRON-CARBON ALLOYS · TRANSFORMATION
NOMENCLATURE IN IRON ALLOYS · MICROSTRUCTURAL CHANGES
AS A HYPOEUTECTOID STEEL COOLS SLOWLY · MILD AND LOW-
CARBON STEELS · USE OF LOW-CARBON STEELS AT ELEVATED
TEMPERATURES · GRAPHITIZATION OF LOW-CARBON STEELS ·
ELEVATED-TEMPERATURE HYDROGEN ATTACK ON LOW-CARBON
STEELS · NOTCH-BRITTLENESS OF LOW-CARBON STEELS · CAR-
BON-STEEL CASTINGS · MICROSTRUCTURAL CHANGES AS EUTEC-
TOID STEEL COOLS SLOWLY · MICROSTRUCTURAL CHANGES AS
A HYPEREUTECTOID STEEL COOLS SLOWLY · PROPERTY CHANGES
WITH PERCENTAGE CARBON IN SLOWLY-COOLED STEELS · THE
EFFECTS OF ALLOYING ELEMENTS UPON IRON-CARBON ALLOYS ·
THE EFFECTS OF CARBON ON IRON-BINARY ALLOYS · ALLOY DIS-
TRIBUTION IN HEATED STEELS · IRON-NICKEL ALLOYS · NICKEL
STEELS · IRON-NICKEL ALLOYS OF CONTROLLED THERMAL EX-
PANSION · MAGNETIC ALLOYS OF IRON AND NICKEL · IRON-SILI-
CON ALLOYS · THE STABLE IRON-GRAPHITE DIAGRAM · CAST
IRON · WHITE CAST IRON · MALLEABLE CAST IRON · GRAY CAST
IRON · MOTTLED AND CHILL CAST IRON · SUPERHEATING AND
INOCULATION · NODULAR (SPHEROIDAL) CAST IRON · WEAR-
RESISTANT CAST IRONS · HEAT-RESISTANT CAST IRONS · CORRO-
SION-RESISTANT CAST IRONS

7. *Principles Affecting Reactions Under Nonequilibrium
   Conditions*                                                    330

TRANSFORMATIONS UNDER NONEQUILIBRIUM CONDITIONS · THE
PRECIPITATION PROCESS · FORCES OPPOSING NUCLEATION ·
DRIVING FORCE FOR PRECIPITATION · SIGNIFICANCE OF REAC-
TION TEMPERATURE · CONTROL OF QUENCHING RATE · DIFFU-
SIONLESS OR SHEAR TRANSFORMATIONS · ENERGY REQUIRE-
MENTS FOR TRANSFORMATION · EQUILIBRIUM VERSUS TRANSI-
TION PRECIPITATES · EFFECT OF COLD DEFORMATION ON
PRECIPITATION · PRECIPITATION AT INTERNAL SURFACES ·
HOMOGENEOUS VERSUS HETEROGENEOUS PRECIPITATION

## 8. *Heat-Treatment of Steels* 347

COMMERCIAL HEAT-TREATMENTS FOR STEELS · TRANSFORMA-
TION OF AUSTENITE AT A CONSTANT SUBCRITICAL TEMPERA-
TURE · AUSTENITE TRANSFORMATION PRODUCTS · PEARLITE ·
BAINITE · MARTENSITE · THE HARDNESS OF THE PRODUCTS OF
AUSTENITE TRANSFORMATION AT CONSTANT TEMPERATURE ·
THE EFFECT OF CARBON CONTENT ON THE TRANSFORMATION
OF AUSTENITE · AUSTENITE STABILIZATION · EFFECT OF ALLOY-
ING ELEMENTS ON AUSTENITE TRANSFORMATION · AUSTENITIC
STEELS · EFFECT OF GRAIN SIZE ON AUSTENITE TRANSFORMA-
TION · AUSFORMING · TRANSFORMATION OF AUSTENITE DURING
CONTINUOUS COOLING · EFFECT OF RATE OF COOLING ON AUS-
TENITE TRANSFORMATION · CRITICAL COOLING RATE · INTER-
RUPTED QUENCHING · MARTEMPERING · FACTORS AFFECTING
COOLING RATE DURING HEAT TREATMENT OF PLAIN-CARBON
STEELS · INTERNAL STRESSES AND CRACKING DURING QUENCH-
ING · RELATIONSHIP BETWEEN MICROSTRUCTURE AND PROPER-
TIES OF HEAT-TREATED STEELS · HARDENABILITY · THE CRITICAL
DIAMETER · THE JOMINY END-QUENCH TEST · EFFECTS OF
ALLOYING ELEMENTS ON HARDENABILITY · REHEATING OR
TEMPERING · DECOMPOSITION OF MARTENSITE DURING REHEAT-
ING · CHANGE IN ALLOY CONTENT OF CARBIDES DURING TEM-
PERING · EFFECT OF CARBON CONTENT ON THE HARDNESS OF
TEMPERED STEEL · COMPARATIVE PROPERTIES OF LAMELLAR
AND SPHEROIDAL STRUCTURES · EFFECT OF CARBON CONTENT
ON MACHINABILITY · CARBURIZING · AUTOMOTIVE STEELS · CAR-
BURIZING GRADES OF AUTOMOTIVE STEELS · HEAT-TREATMENT
AFTER CARBURIZING · THE MCQUAID-EHN TEST · HEAT-TREATING
GRADES OF AUTOMOTIVE STEELS · ALLOYING ELEMENTS IN TOOL
STEELS · GENERAL PURPOSE TOOL STEELS · DIE STEELS · HIGH-
SPEED TOOL STEELS

## 9. *Chromium Steels and Stainless Steels* 417

IRON-CHROMIUM ALLOYS · SIGMA PHASE IN FERRITIC ALLOYS ·
EFFECT OF CARBON ON IRON-CHROMIUM DIAGRAM · HARDEN-
ABLE IRON-CHROMIUM STEELS · EFFECT ON WELDING OF THE
AIR-HARDENING OF CHROMIUM STEELS · LOW- AND INTERME-
DIATE-CHROMIUM STEELS · THE 12%-CHROMIUM STEELS · NON-

HARDENABLE 12%-CHROMIUM STEELS · CUTLERY-TYPE STAIN-
LESS STEELS · UNHEAT-TREATABLE STAINLESS IRONS · HIGH-
TEMPERATURE DISABILITIES OF FERRITIC STAINLESS ALLOYS ·
,IRON-CHROMIUM-NICKEL ALLOYS · SIGMA PHASE IN AUSTENITIC
ALLOYS · COMMON AUSTENITIC STAINLESS STEELS · EFFECT OF
CARBON AND NITROGEN ON STRUCTURE OF AUSTENITIC STAIN-
LESS STEELS · SOLUTION AND PRECIPITATION OF CARBIDES IN
AUSTENITIC STAINLESS STEELS · EFFECT OF CARBON CONTENT
ON THE PROPERTIES OF 18:8 STAINLESS STEELS · SENSITIZA-
TION · PREVENTION OF SENSITIZATION · WORK-HARDENING
CHARACTERISTICS OF 18:8 STAINLESS STEELS · SHOT-WELDING
OF 18:8 STAINLESS STEELS · EFFECT OF LOW TEMPERATURE ON
MECHANICAL PROPERTIES OF 18:8 STAINLESS STEELS · STRESS-
CORROSION CRACKING OF AUSTENITIC STAINLESS STEELS · AUS-
TENITIC CHROMIUM-MANGANESE STAINLESS STEELS · SURFACE
HARDENING OF STAINLESS STEELS · PRECIPITATION-HARDENING
STAINLESS STEELS

## 10. *Aging and Precipitation-Hardening*     460

AGING IN IRON AND LOW-CARBON STEELS · DISLOCATION EX-
PLANATION OF AGING IN IRON AND STEELS · BERYLLIUM-COPPER
ALLOYS · ALUMINUM-COPPER ALLOYS · ALUMINUM BRONZES ·
ALUMINUM ALLOYS CONTAINING COPPER · PRECIPITATION-
HARDENABLE ALUMINUM STRUCTURAL ALLOYS · ALUMINUM-
COPPER-MAGNESIUM ALLOYS · ALUMINUM-MAGNESIUM-SILICON
ALLOYS · ALUMINUM-COPPER-MAGNESIUM-ZINC ALLOYS · PRE-
CIPITATION-HARDENABLE MAGNESIUM-ALUMINUM ALLOYS ·
MAGNESIUM-ZINC ALLOYS · ALLOYS OF MAGNESIUM AND RARE-
EARTH METALS · MAGNESIUM-THORIUM ALLOYS · PRECIPITA-
TION-HARDENABLE NICKEL-BASE ALLOYS · AGE-HARDENABLE
NICKELS · AGE-HARDENABLE NICKEL-COPPER ALLOYS · AGE-
HARDENABLE NICKEL-CHROMIUM ALLOYS · AGE-HARDENABLE
IRON-NICKEL ALLOY

*Appendixes*     504

*Index*     511

# 1 General Characteristics of Metallic Materials

## METALS

O F THE ONE HUNDRED AND THREE [1] KNOWN CHEMI-
cal elements in the periodic table (Figure 1.1), approximately eighty are
metallic, and a few are borderline cases between the metals and the nonmetals. More than three-quarters of these metals are used industrially to
some extent, but only eight are available at a low enough cost and in
sufficient quantity to serve as bases for common engineering materials.[2]
Four of these eight—copper, iron, lead, and tin—have been used for thousands of years in various metallic forms. The remaining four—aluminum,
magnesium, nickel, and zinc—are relatively new additions. Their commercial uses as metals date only to the latter part of the nineteenth century,
even though the brasses, which contain copper and zinc, have been used
for centuries, and nickel has been a useful component of many irons,
especially those of meteoric origin. All the remaining metals seem to be
excluded at present from this group of basic engineering metals either
because of inadequate sources of supply or because of economically un-
feasible methods of production.

At least fourteen other metals—antimony, beryllium, cadmium, chromium, cobalt, columbium, manganese, mercury, molybdenum, tantalum,
titanium, tungsten, vanadium, and zirconium—are of secondary industrial

---

[1] Eleven transuranium metallic elements, the best known of which is plutonium,
have atomic numbers greater than ninety-two. These have been produced in limited
quantities by special procedures and are shown in the periodic table, but they are not
discussed in this text.

[2] See H. G. Bachmann, *Scientific American,* **202** (1960), 146–56.

*1*

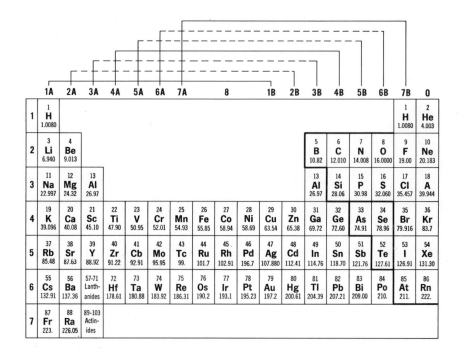

| | 1A | 2A | 3A | 4A | 5A | 6A | 7A | 8 | | | 1B | 2B | 3B | 4B | 5B | 6B | 7B | 0 |
|---|---|---|---|---|---|---|---|---|---|---|---|---|---|---|---|---|---|---|
| 1 | 1<br>H<br>1.0080 | | | | | | | | | | | | | | | | 1<br>H<br>1.0080 | 2<br>He<br>4.003 |
| 2 | 3<br>Li<br>6.940 | 4<br>Be<br>9.013 | | | | | | | | | | 5<br>B<br>10.82 | 6<br>C<br>12.010 | 7<br>N<br>14.008 | 8<br>O<br>16.0000 | 9<br>F<br>19.00 | 10<br>Ne<br>20.183 |
| 3 | 11<br>Na<br>22.997 | 12<br>Mg<br>24.32 | 13<br>Al<br>26.97 | | | | | | | | | 13<br>Al<br>26.97 | 14<br>Si<br>28.06 | 15<br>P<br>30.98 | 16<br>S<br>32.060 | 17<br>Cl<br>35.457 | 18<br>A<br>39.944 |
| 4 | 19<br>K<br>39.096 | 20<br>Ca<br>40.08 | 21<br>Sc<br>45.10 | 22<br>Ti<br>47.90 | 23<br>V<br>50.95 | 24<br>Cr<br>52.01 | 25<br>Mn<br>54.93 | 26<br>Fe<br>55.85 | 27<br>Co<br>58.94 | 28<br>Ni<br>58.69 | 29<br>Cu<br>63.54 | 30<br>Zn<br>65.38 | 31<br>Ga<br>69.72 | 32<br>Ge<br>72.60 | 33<br>As<br>74.91 | 34<br>Se<br>78.96 | 35<br>Br<br>79.916 | 36<br>Kr<br>83.7 |
| 5 | 37<br>Rb<br>85.48 | 38<br>Sr<br>87.63 | 39<br>Y<br>88.92 | 40<br>Zr<br>91.22 | 41<br>Cb<br>92.91 | 42<br>Mo<br>95.95 | 43<br>Tc<br>99. | 44<br>Ru<br>101.7 | 45<br>Rh<br>102.91 | 46<br>Pd<br>196.7 | 47<br>Ag<br>107.880 | 48<br>Cd<br>112.41 | 49<br>In<br>114.76 | 50<br>Sn<br>118.70 | 51<br>Sb<br>121.76 | 52<br>Te<br>127.61 | 53<br>I<br>126.91 | 54<br>Xe<br>131.30 |
| 6 | 55<br>Cs<br>132.91 | 56<br>Ba<br>137.36 | 57-71<br>Lanth-<br>anides | 72<br>Hf<br>178.61 | 73<br>Ta<br>180.88 | 74<br>W<br>183.92 | 75<br>Re<br>186.31 | 76<br>Os<br>190.2 | 77<br>Ir<br>193.1 | 78<br>Pt<br>195.23 | 79<br>Au<br>197.2 | 80<br>Hg<br>200.61 | 81<br>Tl<br>204.39 | 82<br>Pb<br>207.21 | 83<br>Bi<br>209.00 | 84<br>Po<br>210. | 85<br>At<br>211. | 86<br>Rn<br>222. |
| 7 | 87<br>Fr<br>223. | 88<br>Ra<br>226.05 | 89-103<br>Actin-<br>ides | | | | | | | | | | | | | | | |

| Lanthanides | 57<br>La<br>138.92 | 58<br>Ce<br>140.13 | 59<br>Pr<br>140.92 | 60<br>Nd<br>144.27 | 61<br>Pm<br>147. | 62<br>Sm<br>150.43 | 63<br>Eu<br>152.0 |
|---|---|---|---|---|---|---|---|
| | 64<br>Gd<br>156.9 | 65<br>Tb<br>159.2 | 66<br>Dy<br>162.46 | 67<br>Ho<br>164.94 | 68<br>Er<br>167.22 | 69<br>Tm<br>169.4 | 70<br>Yb<br>173.04 | 71<br>Lu<br>174.99 |

| Actinides | 89<br>Ac<br>227.05 | 90<br>Th<br>232.12 | 91<br>Pa<br>231. | 92<br>U<br>238.07 | 93<br>Np<br>237. | 94<br>Pu<br>239. | 95<br>Am<br>241. |
|---|---|---|---|---|---|---|---|
| | 96<br>Cm<br>242. | 97<br>Bk<br>243. | 98<br>Cf<br>244. | 99<br>E<br>253. | 100<br>Fm<br>234. | 101<br>Mv<br>256. | 102<br>No<br>(254.) | 103<br>Lw<br>(257.) |

**Figure 1.1** The periodic table of the chemical elements. All the elements to the left of the heavy line are metallic. Arsenic, selenium, and tellurium are borderline elements. Note: The name niobium (Nb) now is used in chemistry whereas the name columbium (Cb) is used more frequently in metallurgy for element 41. [Adapted from B. S. Hopkins, *Chapters in the Chemistry of the Less Familiar Elements.*]

importance tonnage-wise although their use for specific applications often is vital because of particular properties or characteristics.[3]

Finally, there are the noble or precious metals—gold, platinum, silver, iridium, osmium, palladium, rhodium, and ruthenium—which have a somewhat greater permanence than the other metals because they resist the action of many chemicals and hence, in a few instances like gold and silver, have enjoyed some prominence as monetary standards and as media for international exchange. In addition, materials containing the noble

[3] The properties of many of these metals are given in Refs. 34 and 35 at the end of this chapter.

metals sometimes are used for special engineering applications in which their comparatively high cost is not too important a factor.

The other metals find only limited industrial use at present, and some of them still must be classed as almost laboratory curiosities.[4]

Materials based on the metal iron are known as ferrous whereas those based on any of the other metals are called nonferrous. The ferrous materials are made and used in quantities greater than all of the nonferrous materials together.

## PHYSICAL STATES OF A METAL

There are three states in which a metal may exist: solid, liquid, and vapor. These are stable at ascending temperatures at a given pressure. From an engineering viewpoint, the solid state is of greatest interest. In any of these states, the energy content varies in a definite manner with temperature, determined by the specific heat. Furthermore, in the transition from one state to another, there is a discontinuous change in energy because of the change in the binding forces between atoms. This change in energy is called the latent heat of transformation. It may be termed, specifically, a latent heat of vaporization if the transformation is between the liquid and vapor states, or a latent heat of fusion if the transformation is between the solid and liquid states. Near room temperature, most of the metals are solid; but four of them—mercury, gallium, rubidium, and cesium—can be liquid; and one element—hydrogen, which behaves like a metal chemically—is a gas.

## ATOM RELATIONSHIPS IN THE STABLE STATES

Different relationships exist between the atoms in each of these physical states. In the highest energy state, the gaseous or vapor state, metals are known to be monatomic, each atom moving independently and with a high energy content. Gases have no definite shape, and occupy no definite volume.

In the medium energy or liquid state, the fact that some association exists between the atoms can be shown by X-ray and electron diffraction.[5]

---

[4] Nevertheless, the space and missile programs have caused considerable interest in some of them; see, for example, E. R. Parker, *Trans. A.S.M.*, **42** (1950), 399–404.

[5] This subject was reviewed by B. R. T. Frost in *Progress in Metal Physics*, **5** (New York: Interscience Publishers, 1954), 96–142. See also D. Turnbull, *Trans. A.I.M.E.*, **221** (1961), 422–38.

Liquids have no definite shape, but they do occupy a definite volume; this is evidence that there is some sort of binding between the individual atoms.

In the lowest energy or solid state, the geometrical relationships between atoms are better known because of X-ray, neutron, and electron diffraction studies.[6] These indicate that the atoms are bound to and vibrate about mean positions on or in the three-dimensional geometric pattern, called a space lattice, that characterizes the metal. The vibration of the atom and the dimensions of the space lattice vary with the temperature. Because of these factors, solids not only have a definite volume but also occupy a definite shape.

## THE THERMAL METHOD FOR DETERMINING ENERGY CHANGES

Information on the transitions of a metal from one state to another during heating and cooling is given by measurements of temperature and time while it passes from the liquid to the solid state, or vice versa.[7] This can be done most simply, as indicated in Figure 1.2, by melting the metal in a crucible, inserting a protected thermocouple or some other suitable temperature-measuring device, and then taking simultaneous measurements of temperature and time as the metal cools. The plot of such data is called a cooling curve, and the plot of similar data taken during a heating cycle is termed a heating curve. The discussion that follows is devoted largely to cooling curves.

### COOLING CURVES

A typical simple cooling curve for a pure metal, either in the solid or the liquid state (the two could differ somewhat in slope and curvature), is shown in Figure 1.3*a*.

When a transformation, such as freezing (solidification) for example, is encountered, the curve becomes more complex (Figure 1.3*b*). The liquid metal first cools with an instantaneous rate determined by its specific heat and thermal diffusivity and by the experimental conditions. If a very pure metal is cooled very slowly and outside disturbances are kept to a minimum, the liquid often may be cooled to a temperature below its true freezing point before any solidification occurs. This phenomenon is known

---

[6] See, for example, Refs. 3, 30, and 31 at the end of this chapter.

[7] See also R. M. Evans, E. O. Fromm, and R. I. Jaffe, *Trans. A.I.M.E.*, **194** (1952), 74–75. Other properties, such as electrical resistivity, may be used in some instances; see R. Hultgren and S. A. Lever, *Trans. A.I.M.E.*, **185** (1949), 67–71.

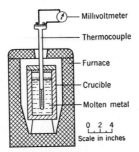

Millivoltmeter

Thermocouple

Furnace

Crucible

Molten metal

0 2 4
Scale in inches

**Figure 1.2** Diagrammatic cross section of simple apparatus suitable for determining heating and cooling curves. [After *Tech. Paper 170*. Nat. Bur. Stand., 1921.]

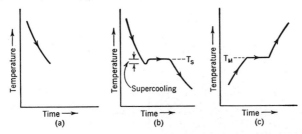

(a)

(b)

(c)

**Figure 1.3 a.** Cooling curve of a liquid metal. The cooling curve for a solid metal would be similar, but might differ somewhat in slope. **b.** Solidification of a liquid metal as indicated on a cooling curve. $T_S$ is the solidification temperature for the cooling conditions used. Some supercooling is indicated, although it does not always occur. **c.** Melting of a solid metal as indicated on a heating curve. $T_M$ is the melting temperature for the heating conditions used.

as supercooling. Regardless of whether supercooling takes place or whether solidification begins when the freezing temperature is reached, at some instant the first minute particle of a solid—that is, a solidification nucleus—will form either spontaneously or because of the disturbing presence of some foreign material.[8] Generally, more centers of solidification are found in impure than in pure metals.

In changing from the liquid to the solid state, the latent heat of fusion is liberated, and the temperature drop is arrested—that is, solidification takes place at such a rate that the latent heat evolved just balances the heat lost by radiation. If the temperature falls even slightly, there is an increase in the rate of formation of solid, either as new nuclei or by growth of the old ones into larger grains, and the energy so released restores the temperature to its equilibrium value. This process continues at a constant

[8] An excellent survey of this subject is given in Ref. 4 at the end of this chapter; see also W. C. Winegard, *Metallurgical Reviews,* **6** (1961), 57–99.

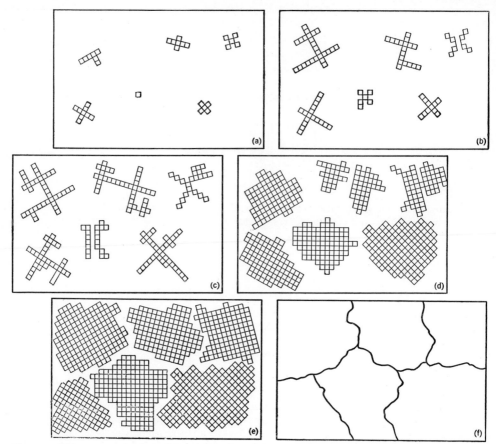

**Figure 1.4** Schematic representation of various stages in the process of solidification of a molten metal. [After W. Rosenhain, from W. H. Clapp and D. S. Clark, *Engineering Materials and Processes.* Courtesy International Text-book Company.]

temperature, as illustrated schematically in Figure 1.4, until solidification is complete, that is until the new and old crystallization nuclei have grown, as grains, to the point that all the volume available is filled. For most metals, the final volume is smaller than the initial volume occupied by the liquid metal.

Once solidification is complete, there is no further latent energy to be released, and the temperature of the solid metal falls steadily at a rate determined, as for the liquid, by its thermal diffusivity and by the experimental conditions. Grains formed in this manner, the external shape of which is determined by chance external conditions, are said to be allotriomorphic and equiaxed if all three dimensions are nearly the same, Figures 1.5a and d, or columnar if one dimension is more elongated than the others, Figures 1.5b, c, and e. In the irregularly shaped grains, the atomic arrangement is just as regular as it is in a crystal which grows without external interference, and thus is able to develop its characteristic crystal faces.

6

**Figure 1.5** Macrostructure of typical cast ingots. **a** (*top left*). A 2-in. square experimental ingot of stainless steel (0.10% carbon, 13% chromium, remainder iron). The fine grain size probably results from the presence of some oxide which assists the formation of crystallization nuclei. [Courtesy The Carpenter Steel Company.] **b** (*top right*). Similar ingot cast after adding 1% aluminum to the molten steel. A normal commercial addition is 0.15 to 0.20% aluminum. Note the coarse grains after the oxide is removed. [Courtesy The Carpenter Steel Company.] **c** (*middle*). End-poured copper wire bar. [Courtesy Anaconda Wire and Cable Company.] **d** (*bottom left*). Horizontal-cast copper wire bar. Rapid cooling from the mold on three sides results in a fine grain size, but in the region last to solidify the grain size is much coarser. [Courtesy Anaconda Wire and Cable Company.] **e** (*bottom right*). "Sunburst" structure in cast copper billet (end-poured). [Courtesy Research Department, Chase Brass and Copper Company.]

**Figure 1.6** Idiomorphic crystals of the compound SbSn in an alloy of 70% tin, 30% antimony. Etched with nital (×100). [Photomicrograph by J. Caum.]

Under some conditions, however, grains which do possess regular geometrical shapes, such as those shown in a bearing metal in Figure 1.6, are formed within a solid alloy. These grains are said to be idiomorphic.

## GRAIN SIZE PRODUCED DURING SOLIDIFICATION

The slow solidification of a pure metal in some sort of container or mold generally results in an extremely large grain size,[9] Figures 1.5c, d, and e. The presence of foreign material, either metallic or nonmetallic, tends to give a much smaller grain size because more crystallization nuclei are formed, and the average grain size thus is smaller; for example, compare Figures 1.5a and b.

Should the rate of cooling be increased, the tendency to form additional nuclei, which serve as centers of crystallization growth, also is increased so that a large number of grains per unit volume would be expected, giving a structure comparable with Figure 1.5d. In addition, increasing the rate of cooling gives less time for the grains to grow in size. This process is known to proceed [10] in a geometrical manner and to require a measurable time.

Hence, the general statement may be made that, under normal conditions, when crystallization nuclei are formed during cooling, the slower the rate of cooling the larger the resulting grain size is; and the more rapid the rate of cooling, the smaller the resulting grain size is. Some modification of this statement must be made whenever conditions are not normal,

[9] Measurement of grain size is discussed later in this chapter.
[10] See, for example, U. M. Martius in *Progress in Metal Physics,* **5** (New York: Interscience Publishers, 1954), 279–309; also B. Chalmers, *Trans. A.I.M.E.,* **200** (1954), 519–32.

for example, if they should result in an abnormally large number of nuclei or an abnormally slow rate of solidification.

It must be remembered, also, that metallic grains are rigid structures. They can grow in size when sufficient energy is available but then must remain at this size if the energy is held constant or is decreased. They cannot grow smaller unless some new reaction takes place to cause crystallization nuclei to form and new grains to grow. Some of these recrystallization reactions are discussed in a later chapter.

## HEATING CURVES

Similar discontinuities occur in heating curves except that the process is reversed, and marked superheating does not occur. Melting usually tends to occur first at the grain boundaries. The absorption of the latent heat of fusion at the melting point keeps the temperature constant until melting is complete (Figure 1.3c).

## METALLIC CHARACTERISTICS

The metals which are important in engineering possess certain unique characteristics. They conduct electricity and heat well. They can be formed readily into the particular shapes called for by engineering designs and, in those shapes, have a satisfactory combination of strength properties with which to resist overload and failure. Different metals possess these and other characteristics, such as the manner in which they reflect light, sometimes called metallic luster, in different degrees.

The properties of pure metals can be modified, within limits, in various ways. Mechanical deformation increases strength but usually with some sacrifice of workability. The intimate admixture of other metals or nonmetals with a metallic base, usually while it is molten to form an alloy, alters its properties. It is customary to refer to such additional metals or nonmetals as impurities if they are present unintentionally, and as alloying elements if they are added deliberately. The general effects of the two may differ only in degree. Alloys have their own metallic characteristics which can be modified, if desired, by mechanical deformation and, in some instances, by heat treatment as well.

In general, nonmetallic materials do not behave chemically like metals, they do not conduct heat or electricity so readily, and they are not workable like metals. These differences are related to the energy levels occupied by the electrons in the outer shell of each atom, to the geometrical arrangements of the atoms relative to each other, and to the nature of the binding forces between atoms. In some characteristics, such as strength, especially per unit of weight, and resistance to specific chemicals, some of the non-metallics, such as certain ceramic and plastic materials, may be superior to the metals even though they may possess other properties which are not so desirable.

## STRUCTURE OF METALS

In the solid state, all metallic materials are crystalline. However, the individual crystals or grains usually are too small to be distinguished by the unaided eye. The engineering characteristics of metallic materials are determined either by the nature and condition of these minute crystals or by the manner in which they are aggregated into larger masses.

Each grain of a metal is made up of a three-dimensional array of atoms comprising what is called a space lattice. When free, or as separate entities with no near neighbors, each of these atoms is composed of a nucleus made up of positively charged particles called protons and uncharged particles, called neutrons, outside of which are negatively charged particles, called electrons, each of which acts as though it were spinning about an axis through itself. The electrons exist, statistically, at various energy levels with respect to the nucleus, some of them being tightly bound to an individual atom while others apparently are relatively free to move throughout the crystal as a whole. Metals can be considered conveniently as an array of positive ions (composed of the nucleus and the tightly bound electrons) through which free electrons are in motion.[11]

The atomic number of an element is given by its position in the periodic table (Figure 1.1). This number is equal in magnitude to both the positive charge of the nucleus and the equal total negative charge of the electrons related statistically to each nucleus. The physical and chemical properties of metals, in general, are controlled by the geometrical arrangement of the atoms relative to each other and by the number and energetic nature of the free electrons.[12]

Isotopes are different varieties of the same element which have the same number of positive and negative charges, and hence the same atomic number and chemical properties, but have different atomic weights because of additional mass-increasing neutrons in their nucleus.

---

[11] The present state of knowledge in this aspect of the metallic state is covered well in Refs. 6, 7, and 8 at the end of this chapter.

[12] See, however, C. Zener, *Trans. A.I.M.E.,* **203** (1955), 619–30, for some further factors of importance.

## MECHANICAL STABILITY OF METALS

The mechanical stability of metals, and in fact that of any solid, results from the existence of two sets of forces which normally are balanced. Cohesive forces, which apparently are largely electrostatic in nature, hold the metal atoms together while short-range repulsive forces prevent them from approaching too closely. The point of balance determines the interatomic distance.[13] If an external force is applied, this balance is upset. To restore equilibrium, the atoms must move slightly relative to each other in order to establish a new balance between the attractive, the repulsive, and the external forces.

In addition to the distance between the atoms, the symmetry of their regular arrangement on a space lattice is important.[14]

If the crystal structure is known, it sometimes is possible to arrive theoretically at a reasonable approximation for the binding energy and the interatomic distance. However, this binding energy is merely a measure of the extra stability of the crystal with respect to the free atom and does not correlate quantitatively with the mechanical strength of metals. In fact, it has not yet been found possible to apply the methods of electron physics to the problem of strength or of mechanical properties of metals with any success.

## SPACE LATTICES

The space lattice is an idealized representation of the regular arrangement of atoms in the solid state. In general, the metallic space lattices are highly symmetrical in nature, although those of antimony, manganese, plutonium, tin, and uranium ($\alpha$, $\beta$) are complex and of lower symmetry. Complex lattices also are found in certain alloys. Two of the commonest types are cubic lattices, although no metal crystallizes in the simple cubic system.

As illustrated in Figure 1.7, in a simple cubic lattice each corner of each unit cube is occupied by a single atom. Each of the eight corners is shared by seven other unit cubes, so only one-eighth of each corner atom can be considered as belonging to any specific unit cell. By examination it can be seen, therefore, that each unit cube contains but one atom.

[13] Refs. 9 and 24 at the end of this chapter give values for most metals and many alloys.
[14] Many of these factors are discussed in Ref. 8 at the end of this chapter.

## BODY-CENTERED CUBIC LATTICE

If two simple cubic lattices are so arranged that the corners of one fall exactly in the centers of the cubes of the other, as shown in Figure 1.8, the first of the common metallic lattices, body-centered cubic, results. Each cube now contains two atoms, one in the center and one from the simple cubic structure—that is, eight corners with one-eighth of an atom from each.

At room temperature, many of the stronger common metals, such as chromium, columbium, iron, molybdenum, tantalum, tungsten, and vanadium crystallize in this lattice. Manganese has a somewhat similar, but much more complex, structure.

## FACE-CENTERED CUBIC LATTICE

If an atom is placed in the center of each face of a simple cubic lattice, or if two simple cubic lattices are expanded in one dimension until their height is 1.414 times the side of their base and then arranged as in the body-centered cubic lattice, the face-centered cubic lattice shown in Figure 1.9 results. The unit cube now contains four atoms—namely, one from the simple cubic lattice and one-half of an atom from each of the six faces of the cube.

At room temperature, many of the more ductile metals, such as aluminum, copper, gold, iridium, lead, nickel, palladium, platinum, rhodium, and silver, crystallize in this type of space lattice. The arrangement of atoms in this lattice is one of the two ways in which spheres can be packed together most closely (Figure 1.9$b$).

## CLOSE-PACKED HEXAGONAL LATTICE

The second method for close-packing spheres is based upon the hexagonal arrangement illustrated in Figure 1.10. The unit hexagonal cell contains six atoms—namely, one-sixth from each of the six corners of the basal faces, one-half from the centers of each of these basal faces, and the three atoms in the interior of the unit cell. The axial ratio in a close-packed hexagonal structure—that is, the ratio between the unit cell dimension, $c$, perpendicular to the basal plane and the distance, $a$, between the atoms on the basal plane, may be the same as for face-centered cubic metal, 1.633, or larger or smaller depending on the metal.

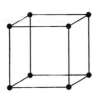

(a) Atom Positions
Represented By Points

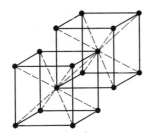

(b) Atoms Represented By Spheres

**Figure 1.7** The simple cubic lattice.

(a) Atom Positions
Represented By Points

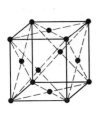

(b) Atoms Represented By Spheres

**Figure 1.8** The body-centered cubic lattice.

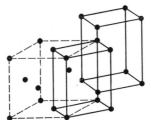

(a) Atom Positions
Represented By Points

(b) Atoms Represented By Close-Packed Spheres.
Note the relationship between successive close-packed planes as compared with the hexagonal lattice below

**Figure 1.9** The face-centered cubic lattice.

(a) Atom Positions
Represented By Points

(b) Atoms Represented By Close-Packed Spheres.
Note the relationship between successive close-packed planes as compared with the face-centered lattice above

**Figure 1.10** The close-packed hexagonal lattice.

At room temperature, some of the more common metals crystallizing in this lattice are beryllium, cadmium, cobalt, magnesium, osmium, ruthenium, titanium, zinc, and zirconium. Mercury, when solid, also crystallizes in it.

## ALLOTROPY

The atoms of some chemical elements, both metallic and nonmetallic, crystallize on different space lattices under different conditions of temperature or pressure. Such materials are said to be allotropic. Practically, this term is used interchangeably with the term polymorphic, although, strictly, polymorphic transformations are nonreversible.

## ALLOTROPIC METALS

The principal allotropic metals are chromium, cobalt, iron, manganese, plutonium, tin, titanium, uranium, and zirconium. Of these, the most important is the metal iron. All of the major changes which take place in steel, and many other iron alloys, are related either directly or indirectly to the allotropic changes occurring in iron. Without these changes, iron and its alloys would not be nearly so important as they are today because their properties could not be modified so drastically by heat treatment.

## THE METAL IRON [15]

The allotropic changes occurring in pure iron are shown schematically in Figure 1.11a. Below its freezing point, at approximately 2800 F (1535 C), iron crystallizes in a body-centered cubic arrangement called delta ($\delta$) iron. This form persists, perfectly stable, until a temperature of 2570 F (1410 C) is reached. Here there is a spontaneous rearrangement of the atoms into a face-centered cubic form known as gamma ($\gamma$) iron. No further change occurs until 1670 F (910 C) is reached. The most important change takes place at this temperature, the change from the face-centered cubic gamma form back to the body-centered cubic arrangement, now termed alpha ($\alpha$) iron.[16] No atomic rearrangement has been found at any lower temperature in iron of any purity that has been studied.

[15] See Ref. 10 at the end of this chapter.

[16] Common usage refers to gamma iron as austenite and to alpha iron as ferrite, although, as will be discussed in a later chapter, these terms apply, strictly, only to alloys.

## THE CURIE POINT

Although the change from gamma to alpha is the last change known to involve an atomic rearrangement, there is another change, at about 1415 F (768 C), known as the Curie point, at which alpha iron starts to behave ferromagnetically. This change develops over a temperature range and is caused by a rearrangement of the electron spins of each atom and not by a change in the grouping of the atoms.

## ENERGY CHANGES CONNECTED WITH ALLOTROPY

Just as there is an evolution of a latent heat of fusion when liquid iron solidifies, there is an evolution of a heat of transformation when each of the allotropic changes occurs. If the rate of cooling is sufficiently great to undercool the reaction, the energy evolved at the change from the gamma to the alpha form causes the temperature of the metal to increase noticeably, a phenomenon known as recalescence.

As with solidification, the energy changes during allotropic transformations cause discontinuities in heating and cooling curves, either as a constant temperature halt or arrest, or as a change in slope of the curve. These

**Figure 1.11 a** (*left*). Schematic representation of allotropic transformations in iron. **b** (*right*). Schematic cooling and heating curves for iron, showing nomenclature customarily employed.

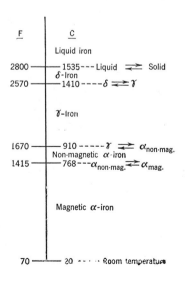
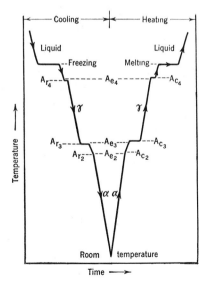

arrests were determined first in iron by the French scientist, LeChatelier, so his original terminology always has been used in designating them, as indicated in Figure 1.11$b$. The occurrence of an arrest is indicated by the letter $A$ (from the French *arrêt*). If the change occurs on heating, the subscript $c$ is used (from the French *chauffage*), whereas if it occurs on cooling, the subscript $r$ is employed (from the French *refroidissement*). For practical cooling and heating rates, $A_c$ and $A_r$ are not identical because most transformations initiate or nucleate at different rates depending upon whether the temperature is rising or falling. If the heating or cooling rates were infinitely slow, $A_c$ and $A_r$ should coincide at $A_e$, the equilibrium transformation temperature.

For iron, these changes then are designated individually by number, the highest temperature one (delta $\rightleftharpoons$ gamma) being $A_{c_4}$ or $A_{r_4}$ as the case might be, the next (gamma $\rightleftharpoons$ alpha) $A_{c_3}$ or $A_{r_3}$ and the magnetic change $A_{c_2}$ or $A_{r_2}$. In a general reference to one of these transformations, the letter subscript usually is eliminated, and it is referred to simply as $A_4$, $A_3$, $A_2$, etc. The $A_1$ change occurs only in the presence of carbon, and hence is not found in pure iron.

## SOLID SOLUTIONS

Even the purest of the metals used industrially contains foreign atoms,[17] usually dissolved in the parent metal, forming what is called a primary solid solution. In such cases the characteristic space lattice of the parent metal is retained with a small change in size. Each dissolved atom, depending on its size and characteristics, either replaces one of the parent atoms in the space lattice, forming a substitutional solid solution, or takes up a position between the atoms in the space lattice, forming an interstitial solid solution. To a given base metal some atoms can be added only in concentrations of a fraction of a per cent. On the other hand, other atoms might be added in any amounts so that a continuous solid solution is formed which can vary in composition from 100% of metal A to 100% of metal B. Many of the factors involved in making these solid solutions are fairly well understood.[18] In general, the solute atoms must be quite similar to those of the solvent, both in size and in characteristics, if they are to form a substitutional solution; and they must be very small, such as those of hydrogen, nitrogen, and carbon, to form an interstitial solution.

---

[17] Foreign elements which occur as nonmetallic inclusions often are not counted as impurities.

[18] This has been discussed well by W. Hume-Rothery and G. V. Raynor in Ref. 8 at the end of this chapter.

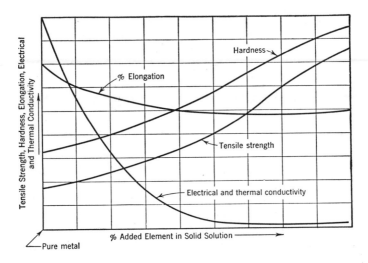

**Figure 1.12** Schematic illustration of the general change of properties with composition in alloys which are solid solutions.

In substitutional solid solutions, the solute atoms can take up any site on the solid-solution lattice with complete freedom of choice. This is called a random arrangement of atoms. Because solute and solvent atoms are "mixed" on the atomic scale of the space lattice, they cannot be distinguished under the optical microscope. The alloy may be statistically homogeneous and often appears to be perfectly so. Detailed studies, however, indicate that "microsegregation" (nonuniformity of composition on a microscopic scale) often is present and it may well be that no solid solution is truly homogeneous if judged on a scale such as that of an X-ray microscope with high resolving power.

Because the space lattice of a pure metal changes continuously in dimensions as solute atoms are introduced,[19] the properties of the solid solution change continuously from those of the pure metal, depending upon the nature of the added alloying elements and the relative concentrations of the two types of atoms on the space lattice. In general, the addition of elements in solid solution results in an increase in strength and hardness,[20] and a decrease in workability (elongation) and in electrical and thermal conductivity, as indicated schematically in Figure 1.12. Properties like corrosion resistance depend on the metal, sometimes increasing and sometimes either decreasing or remaining nearly unchanged as the solute is changed in nature and amount.

[19] R. S. Busk, *Trans. A.I.M.E.,* **188** (1950), 1460–64, has shown this with considerable data for magnesium alloys, for example.

[20] Solid-solution hardening and electrical resistivity are discussed by W. R. Hibbard, *Trans. A.I.M.E.,* **200** (1954), 594–602; and *ibid.,* **212** (1958), 1–5.

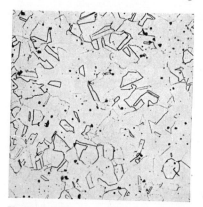 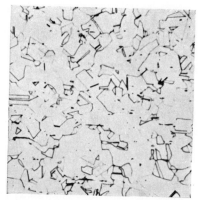

**Figure 1.13   a** (*left*). Metallographic structure of Monel metal, a primary solid solution containing approximately 70% nickel, 30% copper. Etched with nitric and acetic acids (×100). [Photomicrograph by L. Litchfield.] **b** (*right*). Metallographic structure of commercially pure nickel. Etched with nitric and acetic acids (×100). [Photomicrograph by L. Litchfield.]

Under the microscope it often is impossible to differentiate with certainty between a primary solid solution and the pure metal upon which it is based. This can be seen readily by comparing the photomicrographs shown in Figure 1.13. Only high-precision X-ray diffraction studies show the change in the size of the pure metal space lattice as foreign atoms "dissolve" in it.[21]

## METALLOGRAPHY

A solid alloy does not necessarily consist of a single solid solution. In many instances, only a limited amount of a foreign element can be added to a given base metal to form either a substitutional or an interstitial solid solution. Once this solubility limit is exceeded, the excess foreign atoms appear in some new form. If only two kinds of atoms are involved, this new form may be characteristic of the second metal, of a solid solution based on the second metal (containing the original metal in solution), or it may be of some intermediate composition characteristic of what is called an intermetallic compound. These compounds are not like the usual chemical compounds because the well-known laws of chemical valence seldom apply. Instead they are composed of two (or more) metals or metals and nonmetals, often, but not necessarily, in simple stoichiometric proportions and usually are characterized by metallic characteristics.[22] Explana-

[21] Ref. 9 at the end of this chapter.
[22] See J. H. Westbrook (ed.), *Mechanical Properties of Intermetallic Compounds* (New York: John Wiley & Sons, 1960).

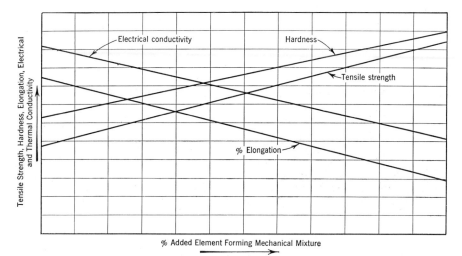

**Figure 1.14** Schematic illustration of the nearly linear change of properties with composition in alloys which are mechanical mixtures ot two phases. The changes shown assume substantially no solid solubility of either metal in the other.

tions of why such compounds do, or do not form, have been given only for some of the simpler types.[23] These regions of new atomic arrangement are, in effect, mechanically mixed with the original primary solid solution phase. They can be distinguished readily from it and often can be separated from it by chemical or mechanical means. In such mechanical mixtures the change in properties is nearly linear, as shown schematically in Figure 1.14 (which assumes a pure metal with substantially no solid solubility because no initial curvature is shown).

The branch of science which relates the constitution and structure of metals and alloys to their properties and characteristics is known as metallography.[24] Most metallographic examinations are made under the microscope at relatively high magnifications.[25] For convenience, the specimen to be examined usually is mounted in a thermosetting plastic or a low melting material and then is polished to a perfectly flat, scratch-free, mirror surface by the successive use of a series of graded abrasives.[26]

---

[23] See W. Hume-Rothery and G. V. Raynor in Ref. 8 at the end of this chapter.
[24] C. S. Smith, *Trans. A.S.M.,* **45** (1953), 533–75, gives an excellent discussion of microstructure.
[25] See J. R. Vilella, *Trans. A.I.M.E.,* **191** (1951), 605–19.
[26] Methods for preparing metallographic specimens are outlined completely in *A.S.T.M. Tentative Standard E3-T.* See also Ref. 24 at the end of this chapter and the *1954 Supplement,* 164–77. Specific etchants, in particular, are well covered.

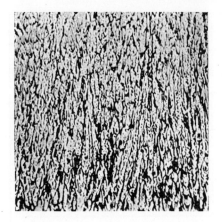

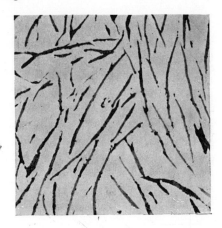

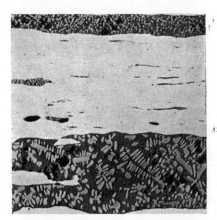

**Figure 1.15  a** (*upper left*). Cross section of strip-cast copper-lead automotive bearing alloy (65% copper, 35% lead). Unetched (×100). The thin, needle-like, light-colored regions are copper. [Photomicrograph courtesy The Cleveland Graphite Bronze Company.] **b** (*upper right*). Appearance of coarse graphite flakes (1 to 2 in. in length) in gray cast iron. Unetched (×50). **c** (*lower left*). Structure within slag particle in wrought iron. Unetched (×250). The light-colored areas are probably an iron phosphate and the dark gray areas an iron silicate.

## ETCHING

In order to make a metal structure visible, some method must be used to differentiate between the different grains of which it is composed.[27] If certain of the grains vary markedly in hardness, as is often the case with alloys which are mechanical mixtures of several constituents of different hardnesses, such as lead and copper, or graphite or slag and iron, the polishing operation alone may suffice by producing a difference in level between them, as illustrated in Figure 1.15. Usually, however, some form

[27] The method of stereoscopic microradiography, which can be used with some alloys to give a three-dimensional view of the grain structure, has been described by W. M. Williams and C. S. Smith, *Trans. A.I.M.E.*, **194** (1952), 755–65.

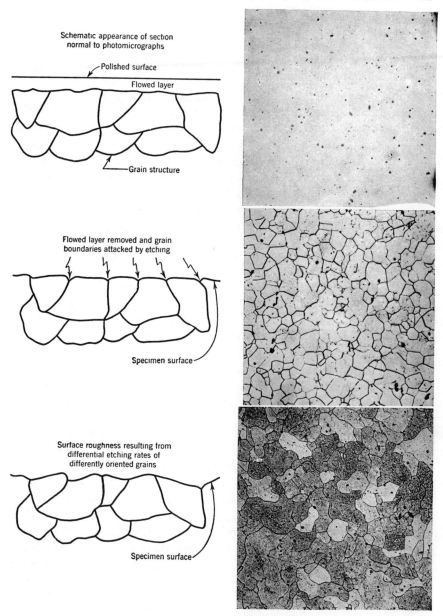

**Figure 1.16** Stages in the etching of a metallographic specimen of commercially pure iron. **a** (*top*). Specimen "as polished." Dark spots are largely oxide inclusions. **b** (*middle*). Polished specimen after light etch. Dark lines are grain boundaries. **c** (*bottom*). Polished specimen after heavy or contrast etch. All grains have essentially the same composition but etch at different rates because of differences in orientation.

of chemical attack is required. Such an attack, when properly controlled, is called etching.

In some alloys, polarized light can be used advantageously to delineate metal structure. Even in the absence of etching, different constituents often reflect polarized light differently and hence can be distinguished readily.

Except for cases such as those already mentioned, a polished metallic surface is completely lacking in detail (Figure 1.16a) because of the presence of a flowed surface layer, even though many grains, differing either in composition or in orientation, may be cut by it. For a metal or single solid solution, light etching tends first to dissolve this flowed layer and to attack the grain boundaries (Figure 1.16b), revealing them as thin lines. As etching continues, these boundaries thicken somewhat and the grains themselves are attacked to an extent dependent, at least partially, on their orientation. Hence, a heavy or contrast etch (Figure 1.16c) not only may result in appreciable differences in level between neighboring grains, but also frequently produces markedly different shadings, because of the reflection or lack of reflection of light from the surface to the eye of the observer, for the reason illustrated in Figure 1.17. This can result from variations in orientation, with corresponding differences in etching rates, even though all the grains are identical in composition. If the grains differ in composition, as well as in orientation, the contrast may be even more striking (Figure 1.18).

Occasionally, in alloys with two microconstituents,[28] such as that in Figure 1.18, etching may be so much concentrated on one constituent, or on the interface between the two, that features such as grain boundaries are not revealed.

The rate of etching depends not only on the solution employed, and the composition of the material, but also on the uniformity of the material. Inhomogeneity, resulting from strain, impurity, or a difference in composition, tends to produce accelerating conditions. In general, although there are many exceptions, pure metals are more difficult to etch than either impure metals or alloys of the same type. Also, because of imperfections that exist there, grain boundaries and other internal surfaces tend to etch more rapidly than the parent metal within the grains. Depending to a considerable extent on the degree of misfit, this accelerated grain boundary etching may vary between a series of etch pits, for boundaries across which the orientation difference is small, to a continuous groove-like region for boundaries across which the orientation difference is large. The reasons for this are discussed later.

---

[28] This phrase often is used to describe the separable entities of solid solutions, compounds, etc., seen microscopically.

**Figure 1.17** Schematic illustration of reflection of parallel rays of light from the surface grains of a specimen given a contrast (heavy) etch. [After W. Rosenhain.] The more nearly the reflected rays are parallel to the incident rays, the brighter the surface of the grain will appear under the microscope.

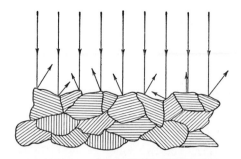

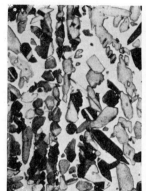

**Figure 1.18** Variations in metallographic structure of an extruded brass of the 60% copper, 40% zinc type. The light-colored, relatively unetched, background is the beta, and the different-colored etched grains are the alpha solid solutions of zinc in copper. Three different structures resulting from position in a 1.37 in. diameter bar extruded at a low temperature. (*left*) Specimen taken 6 in. from front end. (*center*) Specimen taken from middle of bar, from 1 ft from front end to two-thirds of length. (*right*) Specimen taken from extreme back end. Extrusion direction vertical. Extrusion is forcing the metal through a small diameter or shaped opening under pressure while it is at a temperature somewhat below its melting point. Etched with $NH_4OH + H_2O_2$ (originally ×75; reduced somewhat in reproduction). [Photomicrographs courtesy Research Department, Chase Brass and Copper Company.]

## MEASUREMENT OF GRAIN SIZE

Some knowledge of the size of the grains of which metals and alloys are composed often is desirable because it can be determined readily and has been found to correlate well for many metals with hardness, tensile strength, workability, and other significant engineering properties, such as machinability and reaction to heat treatment. Such correlations as can be established, however, hold only for the one particular metal.

Three general methods for determining grain size from a polished and etched metallographic specimen are in common use today.[29]

## Direct Comparison with Standards

Direct comparison with standard micrographs, similar to those shown in Figures 1.19 and 1.20, prepared by the American Society for Testing and Materials, is used to determine grain size for ferrous and nonferrous materials. The two differ in the nomenclature used. Ferrous alloys are rated on a logarithmic scale based on the expression

$$a = 2^{n-1}$$

where *n* is the A.S.T.M. grain size and *a* is the number of grains per square inch when viewed at a magnification of 100 diameters. Nonferrous grain sizes generally have been based upon a linear diameter scale and have been expressed as average grain diameter in inches or in millimeters. This difference in ratings is arbitrary and the mathematical scale used for ferrous metals could be used with equal convenience for both.

## Measurement of Average Grain Diameter

Actual measurement of the average diameters of a large number of grains, either by means of a graduated eyepiece or by projection upon a ground glass screen, is a method frequently used, although it is apt to be somewhat tedious.

## The Jeffries Method

In the Jeffries method, the number of grains falling within, and on, a circle 79.8 mm in diameter (5,000 mm² area) drawn on a ground glass screen, is measured and is used to determine the grain size. This method gives the most accurate data, but is extremely tedious to carry out successfully, and the greater precision seldom is worth the additional trouble involved.

All three methods are apt to give similar results, so the simplest one generally is used industrially. It always must be remembered, however, that such a count is two dimensional, even though the actual grains involved are three dimensional. Therefore, unless there is strong evidence that the

---

[29] All of these are discussed in considerably greater detail in *A.S.T.M. Standards* or *Tentative Standards* (Philadelphia: American Society for Testing and Materials, published triennially).

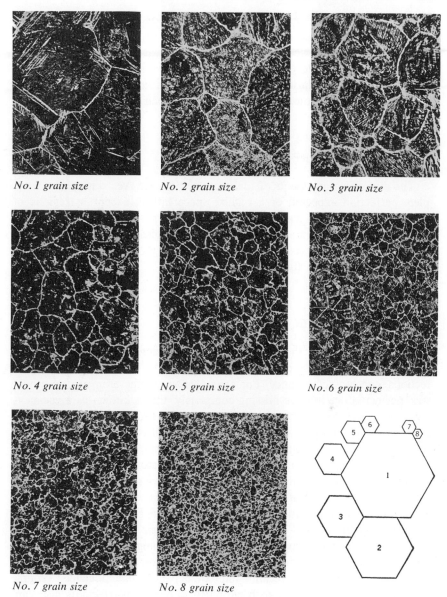

*No. 1 grain size*        *No. 2 grain size*        *No. 3 grain size*

*No. 4 grain size*        *No. 5 grain size*        *No. 6 grain size*

*No. 7 grain size*        *No. 8 grain size*

**Figure 1.19**  Typical standards for estimating the (austenitic) grain size of steel. [Courtesy American Society for Testing and Materials.] **a.** Photomicrographs of samples carburized at 1700 F (930 C) for 8 hours and slowly cooled to develop the cementite network. Etched with nital (×100). [Photomicrographs courtesy The Timken Roller Bearing Company.] **b** (*bottom right*). Standard grain sizes idealized as uniform hexagonal areas. [Courtesy Heppenstall Company.]

grains are equiaxed, a large number of readings on three mutually perpendicular faces should be taken, regardless of the method used, in order to secure a proper statistical average of the actual grain size or actual grain diameter. With a little experience it is relatively simple to pay attention only to grain boundaries, ignoring subgrain structures, annealing twin bands and other microfeatures which are described later.

## LATTICE IMPERFECTIONS

The atomic arrangements of real metals seldom if ever achieve the complete perfection expected of a regular space lattice, except in regions of limited extent. Several types of imperfections are possible and each of these is important in understanding certain metallurgical phenomena.[30] These imperfections add a certain amount of energy to the crystal because of the local distortions which they introduce.

## POINT IMPERFECTIONS

Once the nature of the array of atoms in a single metal crystal is appreciated, the possibility of certain types of defects, known as point imperfections, can be seen at once. For example, one of the atoms in an otherwise perfect lattice may be missing completely; this is known as a vacancy. In a sense, both substitutional and interstitial solid solutions also are defect structures. Even though a substitutional atom still is in its proper position on the space lattice the binding forces between it and the neighboring atoms must be different from those between the parent atoms themselves. Consequently, a substitutional imperfection results. Likewise, those smaller atoms which occupy positions in the holes between the atoms on the normal space lattice are interstitial imperfections. Here too, the binding forces between the atoms on the normal lattice are changed by the presence of the interstitial atoms and the properties of the material change also. There are also Frenkel defects [31] in which a missing lattice site atom takes up an interstitial position, thus forming a "vacancy-interstitial pair." Other localized groups and associations of these three basic types of point imperfections also can exist.

[30] Ref. 13 at the end of this chapter gives a well-rounded discussion of this general subject; see also W. Shockley, *Trans. A.I.M.E.,* **194** (1952), 829–42; and W. M. Lomar in *Progress in Metal Physics,* **8** (New York: Pergamon Press, 1959), 255–320.
[31] J. Frenkel, *Zeit. f. Physik,* **35** (1926), 652; see also R. Maurer in Ref. 13 at the end of this chapter.

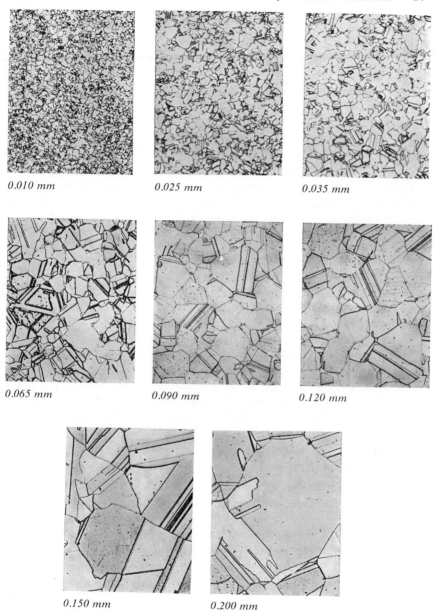

0.010 mm        0.025 mm        0.035 mm

0.065 mm        0.090 mm        0.120 mm

0.150 mm        0.200 mm

**Figure 1.20** Typical standards for estimating grain size of annealed non-ferrous materials such as brass, bronze, and nickel silver (×75). Actual diameter of average grain is noted. [Courtesy American Society for Testing and Materials.]

## SURFACE IMPERFECTIONS

When it is recalled that all solid metals are crystalline, the likelihood of additional imperfections becomes clear because of variations in crystal growth, mechanical deformation and thermal history. The most obvious of these is the surface imperfection which results from the fact that the array of atoms is not the same on both sides of a surface, either external or internal. These differences automatically result in complexities in the force fields surrounding the surface atoms. Such complexities disturb the regular array in which the surface atoms exist. Complicated imperfections of related types occur at the grain boundaries of polycrystalline aggregates and at interfaces between microconstituents.

## IMPERFECTIONS PRODUCED BY IRRADIATION

Most metallic materials undergo some small but observable changes when exposed to the various radiations which occur in atomic reactors.[32] The metallic materials retain their properties better, and the changes which occur in metals are less harmful and are less persistent at a given temperature than is true for nonmetallic materials. Aluminum seems to be affected less than any other of the engineering metals. Usually the effects of irradiation reverse as rapidly as they are induced when the materials are held well above room temperature during irradiation. Near room temperature the reversal may be quite slow.

The effects of irradiation have been studied by the empirical method of exposed prototypes or by the research method of using beams of nuclear particles from various accelerators to bombard laboratory samples.[33] Particles with energies of about 10 million electron volts have been used most commonly. Neutrons (uncharged) react with the nuclei of the solid atoms and transfer energy by knocking atoms out of their normal positions in the lattice.[34] The primary atom displaced by this means then has, in its turn, sufficient energy to knock many others out of position. At the present time, there is evidence only that vacant lattice sites or normal atoms in interstitial positions can be produced by these displacements. It requires less

[32] See D. O. Leeser, *Nucleonics,* **18** (1960), 68–73; also Ref. 23 at the end of this chapter.

[33] Work on this aspect has been summarized by F. Seitz, *Trans. A.I.M.E.,* **215** (1959), 354–67.

[34] D. R. Harries, *Journ. Iron and Steel Inst.,* **194** (London: 1960), 289–304, has studied these effects on irons and steels.

energy to produce a vacancy (that is, to remove an atom from the lattice surface) than to produce an interstitial (that is, to bring in an atom from the outside and add it to the lattice) so more vacancies than interstitials should be generated. In general, when the solid is composed of light atoms, the individual displaced atoms are not close together. However, when the solid is composed of heavy atoms, a number of nearly neighboring atoms are displaced at the same time by the primary atom and its secondaries so a highly disorganized spherical region containing possibly 1,000 atoms is produced. Such regions, called displacement spikes, may be the real cause of most of the property changes noted.

When charged particles, such as protons, deuterons, alpha particles, or electrons, are used to bombard metals, there is a strong interaction with the electrons moving about the nuclei. Most of the energy lost by the particles is lost to these electrons. Such excited electrons do not have sufficient energy to knock atoms out of place by direct impact and have no more effect on typical metals than that which would be produced by mild local heating. However, there probably is a highly localized region, sometimes called a point thermal spike, which is heated by the energy of the collision.

## LINE IMPERFECTIONS OR DISLOCATIONS

There are also line imperfections, known as dislocations, which can extend for relatively large distances, either into the lattice of a single crystal or into that of the individual crystals in a polycrystalline aggregate. Any dislocation can be regarded as consisting of two basic types known, respectively, as edge dislocations and screw dislocations. The nature of each of these is now well established.[35] These line imperfections do not necessarily have to be present in crystals at all times. However, if they are not always present, it must be possible to generate them readily at either internal or external surfaces.

## EDGE DISLOCATIONS

The nature of a pure edge dislocation is shown schematically in two dimensions in Figure 1.21. It can be seen that this type of dislocation basically is formed by deforming and displacing two portions of a crystal

[35] For a more extensive discussion see E. R. Parker, *Trans. A.S.M.,* **50** (1958), 52–104; J. B. Newkirk, *Trans. A.I.M.E.,* **215** (1959), 483–97; P. B. Hirsch, *Metallurgical Reviews,* **4** (1959), 101–40; also Refs. 17, 18, and 19 at the end of this chapter.

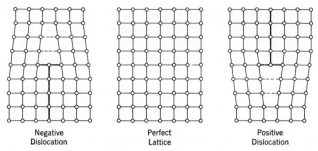

Negative          Perfect          Positive
Dislocation       Lattice          Dislocation

**Figure 1.21**   Schematic two-dimensional representation of edge dislocations. The negative dislocation contains the extra plane of atoms in the lower portion, and the positive dislocation contains the extra plane in the upper portion. [After G. I. Taylor.]

in such a way that there is one less vertical plane of atoms in the lower portion than in the upper portion [36]—that is, this dislocation characterizes the edge of an incomplete atomic plane. Some distance above and below the dislocation, the two lattices are substantially strain-free. In the vicinity of the edge dislocation, however, there must be considerable distortion because the two lattices apparently are bonded together on either side of the extra plane. A crystal containing only an edge dislocation always is made up of parallel planes of atoms perpendicular to the dislocation.

Striking evidence of the existence of a simplified form of edge dislocations has been found in two-dimensional bubble rafts.[37] In fact, most of the initial experimental observations on the characteristics and movements of dislocations were made and were studied by this means.

SCREW DISLOCATIONS

A screw dislocation is shown in Figure 1.22. Note that with this type of dislocation the planes of a crystal which are normal to the dislocation no longer are parallel and one above the other. Instead, these planes, in the entire region containing the screw dislocation, now constitute a single atomic plane in the form of a spiral ramp.

The nature of a screw dislocation provides a particularly favorable situation, under some conditions, for the growth of the grains in metallic materials, substantially in one direction, by continuous deposition of atoms

[36] This is known arbitrarily as a positive dislocation (symbol ⊥). In a negative dislocation (symbol ⊤) the missing plane of atoms is in the upper portion. Clearly, two dislocations of opposite signs will neutralize or destroy each other.

[37] See W. L. Bragg and J. F. Nye, *Proc. Roy. Soc.*, **A190** (London: 1947), 474; and W. L. Bragg and W. M. Lorner, *Proc. Roy. Soc.*, **A196** (London: 1949), 171.

on the single spiral plane which results from the dislocation. There are numerous experimental observations to indicate that this type of growth actually occurs when a crystal is formed directly from the vapor or from dilute solution.

**Figure 1.22** Nature of a screw dislocation. [After A. H. Cottrell.]

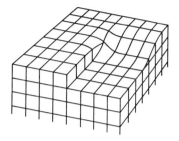

## DISLOCATION PICTURE OF GRAIN BOUNDARIES

Some evidence has been presented [38] about the nature of the regions at which adjacent grains come in contact which indicates that many of these regions differ in chemical activity and that they may differ in composition from the remainder of the grain. Because each grain grows independently, in a manner determined largely by chance, it ordinarily is oriented completely at random with respect to its neighbors. Each atom is subjected to a series of forces from its individual neighbors. Hence, in regions near grain boundaries where these differently oriented regions meet (compare Figure 1.4), atom arrangements should be distorted drastically because of the complexity of the forces acting on them. These are, in fact, typical examples of surface imperfections, each grain boundary constituting an internal surface. The effects of such imperfections account to a large extent for the different physical and chemical properties of the grain boundary material.

The exact nature of the grain boundary regions probably is largely a question of the extent of misfit between the two grains. As indicated in Figure 1.23, when the angle of misfit, $\theta$, between two grains is small, the nature of the boundary can be pictured readily as a series of dislocations, the distance, $D$, between dislocations being given by $D = a/\theta$ where $a$ is the interatomic spacing and $\theta$ is in radians.

[38] See, for example, G. R. Dean and W. P. Davey, *Trans. A.S.M.,* **26** (1938), 267–76; E. H. Dix, Jr., *Trans. A.I.M.E.,* **137** (1940), 11–40; F. Weinberg in *Progress in Metal Physics,* **8** (New York: Pergamon Press, 1959), 105–46.

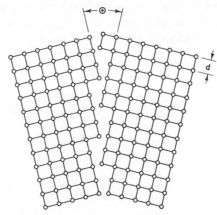

**Figure 1.23** Schematic representation of a low-angle grain boundary by a series of line dislocations. In an actual grain boundary, the distortions probably would be more complex than those shown. [After J. M. Burgers.]

Observations on small angle metal bicrystals, in which dislocations are shown up because of the etch pits they produce under certain conditions, are quite consistent with this explanation. However, as the angle of misfit increases, the dislocations required to compensate become closer together until eventually they would have to be no less than one or two interatomic spacings apart. Under these conditions, grain boundaries are considered more conveniently as continuous interfaces along which the grains do not fit together well, thus leading to more complex types of surface imperfections. Under such conditions, there is no obvious reason why any one point in the grain boundary should nucleate an etch pit rather than any other point. Hence, a uniform groove results when a grain boundray is etched.

### DIFFUSION

Although in the solid state the atoms commonly are said to oscillate around certain mean positions in a geometrical space lattice, it must not be assumed that the mean position of each atom remains fixed in these positions except on a statistical basis. The various point imperfections— vacancies, substitutional atoms, and interstitial atoms [39]—all have a certain mobility and are known to be in a continuous, although usually slow, motion through the lattice. One simple mechanism by which this could occur

[39] A. G. Guy, *Trans. A.S.M.*, **44** (1952), 382–96, 397–403, analyses interstitial diffusion.

is by a vacancy and a solvent atom or a substitutional solute atom moving in opposite directions by simple positional interchange. This motion of atoms through a space lattice is known as diffusion.[40] Related processes also occur in the liquid and gaseous states. If motion of only one type of atom is involved, as in a pure metal, the term self-diffusion is used. If more than one type of atom is involved, the term interatomic diffusion is more common. Parent atoms and foreign atoms frequently diffuse independently, each at its own rate.

Knowledge of diffusion largely is based on analogy with heat flow. Two laws commonly are used, known as Fick's [41] laws. The first law concerns steady-state diffusion and states that the mass of diffusing substance, $m$, which passes per unit time, $t$, through a unit area, $A$, of a plane at right angles to the direction of diffusion, $x$, is proportional to the concentration gradient,

$$\frac{dc}{dx},$$

of the diffusing substance.[42] This may be written as

$$dm = -D \cdot A \cdot \frac{dc}{dx} \cdot dt$$

The proportionality factor, $D$, known as the diffusion coefficient, has the dimensions of $(length)^2/(time)$ but it may or may not be a constant. The units square centimeters per second are common.

Fick's second law concerns diffusion with a changing concentration gradient and is derived from the first by using the simple consideration that the difference between the amount of material flowing in and that flowing out is the amount accumulating in a given volume element. This may be written as

$$\frac{dc}{dt} = \frac{d}{dx}\left(D\frac{dc}{dx}\right)$$

These equations can be solved like any other differential equations provided suitable boundary conditions are known. Many of the more common

[40] See R. F. Mehl, *Trans. A.I.M.E.*, **122** (1936), 11–56; A. D. LeClaire in *Progress in Metal Physics*, **1** (New York: Interscience Publishers, 1949), 306–79; also Refs. 20, 21, and 22 at the end of this chapter.

[41] Adolf Fick, *Pogg. Ann.*, **94** (1855), 59.

[42] For simplicity, this has been limited here to one direction, $x$; there is no other reason why this restriction should be imposed.

cases have been worked out and are in the literature.[43] Volume diffusion ($D_v$), grain boundary diffusion [44] ($D_{gb}$), and surface diffusion ($D_s$) all have characteristic diffusion coefficients, often differing greatly in magnitude.

Increasing the temperature increases atomic mobility. This results not only in an increase in the amplitude and frequency of atomic vibrations, but also in an increase in the rate of interdiffusion of the atoms present. The effect of temperature on diffusion coefficient can be represented by the Arrhenius relationship

$$D = Ae^{-Q/RT}$$

where $R$ is the gas constant, $T$ the absolute temperature, $A$ the frequency factor, and $Q$ the activation energy. It readily can be seen that, if this equation holds, a plot of log $D$ (or of any of the comparable factors which can be derived from it) against the reciprocal of the absolute temperature, $1/T$, should give a straight line, the slope of which is $Q/R$.

In general, diffusion is more rapid the greater the difference in characteristics between the two kinds of atoms, the greater the concentration gradient, and the higher the temperature. In alloys, the diffusion coefficients of the various alloying elements may vary independently with concentration [45] as well as with temperature. In every case, diffusion takes place in such a manner as to approach equilibrium—that is, to decrease thermal, strain, and concentration gradients, and in general to approach the state of lowest over-all free energy.

## QUESTIONS

1. What would you expect to be the effect of increasing pressure on the three physical states of a metal? Under suitable conditions, could different states be indistinguishable? What would be the latent heat of transformation under such conditions?

2. When liquid metals solidify under the conditions given in Figure 1.2, would solidification nuclei be expected to occur at random or in a definite pattern? Why? Why would the type of solidification shown schematically in Figure 1.4 be more apt to occur as metals solidify from a liquid than the formation of roughly spherical grains?

---

[43] See, for example, E. M. Baroody, *Trans. A.I.M.E.,* **209** (1957), 819–22; A. S. Yue and A. G. Guy, *ibid.,* **212** (1958), 107–12; also Refs. 20 and 21 at the end of this chapter.

[44] S. Yukawa and M. J. Sinnott, *Trans. A.I.M.E.,* **203** (1955), 996–1022, give an example of this.

[45] D. E. Thomas and E. E. Birchenall, *Trans. A.I.M.E.,* **194** (1952), 867–73, discuss this and E. E. Birchenall and co-workers cover other cases in subsequent publications.

3. What effect will the number of crystallization nuclei formed in the liquid have on the final grain size of the solidified material? Can you suggest any ways to make this final grain size smaller? or larger?

4. What are the three main ways of changing the properties of pure metals? Must these be used independently or can they be combined to give further increase in properties? Give some examples.

5. What are the two main properties whose existence together in metals but not in nonmetals makes the former of greater engineering importance? Why are isotopes not used more as engineering materials?

6. In two-dimensional sketches, can you show the differences between the simple cubic, body-centered cubic, and face-centered cubic space lattices? Also, in two-dimensional sketches, what are the differences between the face-centered cubic and close-packed hexagonal methods of close-packing spheres. By using three-dimensional sketches can you illustrate some simple lattice deformations which should transform a face-centered cubic space lattice into a body-centered cubic lattice?

7. As pure iron cools slowly from the liquid state to room temperature, how many times and at what temperatures will the grain structure of the metal change completely? Will this affect the grain size also? Why? Why are there energy changes during allotropic transformations?

8. In what manner would you expect the atom positions in a pure metal to change with increasing amounts of atoms: (1) much larger (25%) than the original, (2) moderately (5 to 10%) larger than the original, (3) approximately the same size as the original, (4) moderately smaller than the original, (5) much smaller than the original?

9. Why do most intermetallic compounds retain metallic properties whereas few chemical compounds possess these properties?

10. Can you point out any examples of etched metal structures which you have observed in your everyday world rather than in the laboratory? Grains in metals are three dimensional but the methods used to measure grain size metallographically generally are two dimensional. How may the three-dimensional existence affect the two-dimensional measured size?

11. Why is a perfect lattice so unlikely in actual metals? Would the various types of imperfections have equal likelihoods of occurrence? Why is neutron irradiation more apt to damage a metal than proton irradiation? than deuteron irradiation?

12. Show schematically by a series of sketches the interaction between a positive dislocation and negative dislocation. What would be the angle of misfit in the grain boundary of an aluminum bicrystal if the dislocations were two atomic distances apart? four atomic distances apart?

13. Would diffusion of interstitial atoms be expected to be faster than diffusion of substitutional atoms? Why? Should diffusion in the liquid state be faster than diffusion in the solid state? Why?

14. What complications arise in applying Fick's laws for diffusion to actual

diffusion systems? What can be done to facilitate application and, thus, quantitative measurements of diffusion?

15. On semilogarithmic paper, using any convenient units, draw a straight line to represent a log $D$ vs. $1/T$ Arrhenius plot. From this line, can you show how to compute a value for the frequency factor $A$ and the activation energy $Q$? From these values, can you recompute two points on the line as a proof of correctness?

## FOR FURTHER STUDY

1. *Man, Metals and Modern Magic* by J. G. Parr. Cleveland: American Society for Metals, 1958.

2. *Chemistry of the Solid State* by W. J. Dunning. New York: Academic Press, 1955.

3. *Structure of Metals* by C. S. Barrett. New York: McGraw-Hill, 1952.

4. *Liquid Metals and Solidification.* Cleveland: American Society for Metals, 1958.

5. *Growth and Perfection of Crystals.* New York: John Wiley & Sons, 1958.

6. *An Introduction to the Electron Theory of Metals* by G. V. Raynor. London: The Institute of Metals, 1953.

7. *Atomic Theory for Students of Metallurgy* by W. Hume-Rothery. London: The Institute of Metals, 1955.

8. *The Structure of Metals and Alloys* by W. Hume-Rothery and G. V. Raynor. London: The Institute of Metals, 1954.

9. *A Handbook of Lattice Spacings and Structures of Metals and Alloys* by W. B. Pearson. New York: Pergamon Press, 1958.

10. *The Metal Iron* by H. E. Cleaves and J. G. Thompson. New York: McGraw-Hill, 1935.

11. *Relation of Properties to Microstructure.* Cleveland: American Society for Metals, 1954.

12. *Imperfections in Nearly Perfect Crystals.* New York: John Wiley & Sons, 1952.

13. *Impurities and Imperfections.* Cleveland: American Society for Metals, 1955.

14. *Defects in Crystalline Solids.* New York: The Physical Society, 1955.

15. *Vacancies and Other Point Defects in Metals and Alloys.* London: The Institute of Metals, 1958.

16. *Metal Interfaces.* Cleveland: American Society for Metals, 1952.

17. *Dislocations and Plastic Flow in Crystals* by A. H. Cottrell. Oxford: The Clarendon Press, 1953.

18. *Dislocations in Crystals* by W. T. Read, Jr. New York: McGraw-Hill, 1953.

19. *Dislocations in Metals.* New York: American Institute of Mining and Metallurgical Engineers, 1954.

20. *Diffusion In and Through Solids* by R. M. Barrer. New York: Cambridge University Press, 1941.

21. *Diffusion in Solids, Liquids and Gases* by W. Jost. New York: Academic Press, 1952.

22. *Atom Movements.* Cleveland: American Society for Metals, 1951.

23. *Reactor Handbook, Vol. I, Materials.* New York: Interscience Publishers, 1960.

24. *Metals Handbook,* 7th ed. (1948) and *Supplements,* and 8th ed., Vol. I (1961). Metals Park, Ohio: American Society for Metals.

25. *Strengthening Mechanisms in Solids.* Metals Park, Ohio: American Society for Metals, 1961.

26. *Physical Metallurgy* by Bruce Chalmers. New York: John Wiley & Sons, 1959.

27. *Microscopical Techniques in Metallurgy* by Henry Thompson. New York: Pitman Publishing Corp., 1954.

28. *Procedures in Experimental Metallurgy* by A. U. Seybolt and J. E. Burke. New York: John Wiley & Sons, 1953.

29. *Introduction to Solids* by L. V. Azaroff. New York: McGraw-Hill, 1960.

30. *X-ray Metallography* by A. Taylor. New York: John Wiley & Sons, 1960.

31. *X-ray Microscopy* by V. E. Cosslett and W. C. Nixon. New York: Cambridge University Press, 1960.

32. *Rare Metals Handbook* by C. A. Hampel. New York: Reinhold Publishing Corp., 1954.

33. *Photomicrography of Metals,* Publication No. 9-39. Rochester, N. Y.: Eastman Kodak Co., 1959.

34. *Metals for Supersonic Aircraft and Missiles.* Cleveland: American Society for Metals, 1957.

35. *Symposium on Newer Metals, S.T.P. No. 272.* Philadelphia: American Society for Testing Materials, 1960.

36. *The Structure and Properties of Solid Solutions* by J. M. Sivertsen and M. E. Nicholson. New York: Pergamon Press, 1961.

# 2 *Mechanical Deformation and Fracture*

## ENGINEERING EFFECTS OF WORK-HARDENING

$A$T NORMAL ATMOSPHERIC TEMPERATURES, MOST metals and nearly all engineering alloys are hardened and strengthened by mechanical deformation.[1] It is largely because of this characteristic of work-hardening that metals are of such great engineering importance.[2] Many engineers still seem to believe that once metal in a structure undergoes any permanent set, it becomes useless. Actually, so long as any structural member continues to function satisfactorily, and remains in stable equilibrium under the stresses to which it is subjected, it still is undamaged for that application,[3] even if some plastic deformation was needed to reach the new condition of equilibrium.

If a sufficiently large load is applied to a nonmetallic material in which any defect exists, it generally is found that the stress tends to concentrate at the defect and causes it to propagate until fracture occurs.[4] Some metallic materials which work-harden only slightly, if at all, behave similarly, failing rapidly and with little or no deformation. Such materials are said to be

[1] N. F. Mott, *Trans. A.I.M.E.,* **218** (1960), 962–68; also E. H. Edwards, J. Washburn, and E. R. Parker, *Trans. A.I.M.E.,* **197** (1953), 1525–29.

[2] L. M. Clarebrough and M. E. Hargreaves in *Progress in Metal Physics,* **8** (New York: Pergamon Press, 1959), 1–103.

[3] H. F. Moore, *Proc. A.S.T.M.,* **39** (1939), 549–70, discusses this further.

[4] This is not true, however, of certain ionic crystals, like silver chloride for example, which deform much like a metal crystal; see R. D. Moeller, F. W. Schonfeld, C. R. Tipton, Jr., and J. T. Waber, *Trans. A.S.M.,* **43** (1951), 39–66.

brittle. In brittle materials the front of the defect tends to become sharper as the defect propagates. This increases the stress concentration and the ease of propagation until failure finally results. Brittle materials, or ductile materials which for some reason behave in a brittle manner, are those which should cause greatest concern from an engineering viewpoint.

On the other hand, many metals which work-harden are said to be tough because they first resist the deformation by work-hardening instead of failing at once. In tough materials, the front of the defect tends to become more rounded as the defect propagates. This decreases the stress concentration at this point and makes it more difficult for propagation to occur. Thus, a defect in such a material is protected, in a sense, by the work-hardening and strengthening of the metal around it so that further propagation does not proceed until the material has undergone the maximum amount of work-hardening. Because of this, in practically all applications in which work-hardening is possible, a slight overload actually strengthens the material and makes it more resistant to further deformation than it was before. This statement does not imply, in general, that such overloading is desirable. Rather, it emphasizes that metallic materials can, and frequently do, withstand appreciable overloading without harmful effect. The picture, of course, changes as the stress system becomes more complicated because plastic flow of the metal under the stress must be possible if work-hardening is to result. Under the extreme case, if a metal were to be subjected to equal triaxial tension forces, there could be no flow and hence any such metal should behave as if it were completely brittle. Also, a material which is severely work-hardened may behave like a brittle material.

It is known that work-hardening is affected by several factors, among which are (a) the dominant metal, (b) the alloying element or elements and their concentration, (c) the temperature, and (d) the type, rate,[5] and amount of deformation. In any given alloy, the rate of work-hardening decreases as the percentage reduction in thickness or area increases. Thus, in the typical curves shown in Figure 2.1, the slope decreases as the percentage reduction increases.

## MECHANICAL PROPERTIES

The mechanical properties most frequently referred to and used in connection with metallic materials are (a) the hardness or resistance to penetration, (b) the strength when subjected to axial tension, and (c) the

[5] Under explosive shock loading some very peculiar effects occur. See, for example, C. S. Smith, *Trans. A.I.M.E.,* **212** (1958), 574–89.

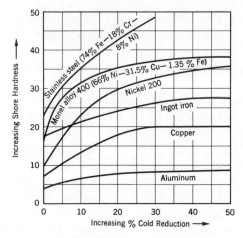

**Figure 2.1** Increase in Shore hardness of various metals and alloys with cold working. [Courtesy The International Nickel Company.]

amount of deformation at fracture in tension. As discussed more fully below, tensile tests often are made with equipment which gives information on the progress of longitudinal strain during the test. Although, for many engineering designs, it would be desirable to know more about the strength and deformation characteristics under various combinations of stresses, relatively little work of direct value has been done in this field and few data are available.

In general, most mechanical property tests are conducted at ambient or normal atmospheric temperatures, usually called, arbitrarily, room temperature. In those cases which concern applications of materials at higher or lower temperatures, suitable corrections, based on experience, are applied to the room temperature data or special tests are run simulating the actual conditions under which the metal is to be used. As will be shown later by some typical examples, new phenomena sometimes appear at sub-atmospheric temperatures or at elevated temperatures which cannot be predicted from room temperature tests but are significant in controlling the behavior in service.

## HARDNESS OR RESISTANCE TO PENETRATION

Hardness is measured in a number of different ways.[6] Many of these are based on the Meyer hardness analysis [7] which involves the measurement

[6] For a more complete discussion see H. O'Neill, *The Hardness of Metals and Its Measurement* (Cleveland: The Sherwood Press, 1934); also see S. R. Williams, *Hardness and Hardness Measurements* (Cleveland: American Society for Metals, 1942).

[7] J. H. Frye, Jr. and W. Hume-Rothery, *Proc. Royal Soc.,* **A181** (London: 1942–43), 1–14; also several papers by J. H. Frye, Jr., and co-workers in *Trans. A.I.M.E.* (1943–45).

of the variation, with load, of the diameter of the impression left by a ball indenter. For many materials, the applied load, $L$, and the diameter of the impression, $d$, are related by the expression

$$L = ad^n$$

where $a$ and $n$ are material constants, known, respectively, as the index of relative hardness and the index of resistance to deformation or the index of strain hardening. This expression plots linearly on log-log coordinates, which facilitates securing the values of the two constants. Although $n$ is a constant in relating the applied load to the diameter of the impression, it varies with the prior deformation of the metal, ranging from roughly 2.7 for metallic materials in their softest condition, to approximately 2.0 for work-hardened materials.

The Meyer hardness itself is the ratio of the applied load to the projected area of the impression and thus varies with the load employed as well as with the ball diameter. However, if conditions are such that the diameter of the impression is the same as the diameter of the ball indenter, the hardness varies only slightly with the ball diameter. This value, which may be obtained from the log-log plot of the relationship between $L$ and $d$, is known as the ultimate Meyer hardness.

Three of the most common methods used today are the Rockwell, Brinell, and Vickers diamond pyramid hardness tests. In these, a diamond cone, a hardened steel ball, or a carefully ground diamond pyramid is impressed into the material being tested, under a definite load and for a definite time or until the penetration reaches equilibrium. The general nature of these three types of tests is illustrated in Figures 2.2, 2.3, and 2.4.[8] The hardness number either is read directly on a dial gauge, or else is determined by reference to tables based upon the diameter, depth, or depth increment of the impression for the test conditions used.

A fourth method, the Shore scleroscope, Figure 2.5, purports to measure the amount of energy that is expended in deforming the specimen elastically, as indicated by the rebound of a small hammer of definite weight when dropped from a definite height on to the specimen surface. Other hardness testing machines act on a similar principle but none of them have been used too widely. This is, therefore, more nearly a dynamic hardness test and probably measures a somewhat different type of penetration hardness than the other three tests. The relative size of the impressions made by these hardness tests is indicated in Figure 2.6.[9]

[8] The Vickers test with a light load is one form of microhardness test. For other forms, of which the Tukon test is one, see V. E. Lysaght, *Metal Progress,* **78** (August 1960), 93–97, 122, 124; *ibid.* (September 1960), 121–25.

[9] In the Monotron test, mentioned in Figure 2.6, the load required to press a 0.75 mm diam diamond indenter into the test specimen to a depth of 0.045 mm is measured on a dial gauge.

(*left*) The Rockwell hardness tester. (*above left*) Brale and (*above right*) ball penetrators.

(*below*) Principle of operation of the Rockwell hardness tester (*B* scale).

Note: The scale of the dial is reversed so that a deep impression gives a low reading and a shallow impression a high reading, in this way a high number means a hard material.
The "set" position is at 30 on the "B" (red) scale which is used with the ball penetrator.

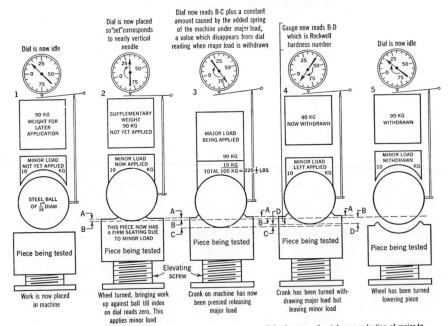

Dial is now idle

**1**

90 KG WEIGHT FOR LATER APPLICATION

MINOR LOAD NOT YET APPLIED 10 KG

STEEL BALL OF $\frac{1}{16}$" DIAM

Piece being tested

Work is now placed in machine

---

Dial is now placed so "set" corresponds to nearly vertical needle

**2**

SUPPLEMENTARY WEIGHT 90 KG NOT YET APPLIED

MINOR LOAD NOW APPLIED 10 KG

THIS PIECE NOW HAS A FIRM SEATING DUE TO MINOR LOAD

Piece being tested

Wheel turned, bringing work up against ball till index on dial reads zero. This applies minor load

Elevating screw

---

Dial now reads B-C plus a constant amount caused by the added spring of the machine under major load, a value which disappears from dial reading when major load is withdrawn

**3**

MAJOR LOAD BEING APPLIED

90 KG 10 KG TOTAL 100 KG = 220$\frac{1}{2}$ LBS

Piece being tested

Crank on machine has now been pressed releasing major load

---

Gauge now reads B-D which is Rockwell hardness number

**4**

90 KG NOW WITHDRAWN

MINOR LOAD LEFT APPLIED 10 KG

Piece being tested

Crank has been turned withdrawing major load but leaving minor load

---

Dial is now idle

**5**

90 KG WITHDRAWN

MINOR LOAD WITHDRAWN 10 KG

Piece being tested

Wheel has been turned lowering piece

---

A-B = Depth of hole made by minor load of 10 kg

A-C = Depth of hole made by major load of 100 kg

B-D = Difference in depth of holes made = Rockwell hardness number

D-C = Recovery of metal upon reduction of major to minor load. This is an index of the elasticity of metal under test and does not enter the hardness reading

*42*

**Figure 2.2** The Rockwell hardness test. [Courtesy Wilson Mechanical Instrument Division, American Chain & Cable Company, Inc.] In the normal "Rockwell" hardness tester, the minor load is 10 kg, the major loads are 60, 100, or 150 kg, and either a Brale (diamond-pointed cone) or a ball penetrator may be used. The reference point for all readings is at the point on the scale marked "Set." This point is at 30 on the $B$ (red) scale, rather than at 0 as on the $C$ (black) scale, in order to avoid negative readings on the softer materials for which the ball penetrator is intended. The combinations used most frequently are

| Rockwell Scale | Major Load, kg | Penetrator | Scale Color |
|----------------|----------------|------------|-------------|
| A | 60 | Brale | C (black) |
| B | 100 | $\frac{1}{16}$ in. Ball | B (red) |
| C | 150 | Brale | C (black) |
| D | 100 | Brale | C (black) |
| E | 100 | $\frac{1}{8}$ in. Ball | B (red) |
| F | 60 | $\frac{1}{16}$ in. Ball | B (red) |
| G | 150 | $\frac{1}{16}$ in. Ball | B (red) |
| H | 60 | $\frac{1}{8}$ in. Ball | B (red) |

Thus a reading of 68 on the $B$ (red) scale secured with a 60 kg load and a $\frac{1}{16}$ in. ball penetrator would be reported as Rockwell hardness $F68$; and a reading of 65 on the $C$ (black) scale secured with a 150 kg load and a Brale penetrator would be reported as Rockwell hardness $C65$.

For thin specimens or metal with a shallow, hard surface a special Superficial hardness tester, having a 3 kg minor load, major loads of 15, 30, or 45 kg, and using either a Brale ($N$) or a $\frac{1}{16}$ in. ball ($T$) penetrator, is used. A reading of 40 secured with a 30 kg load and a Brale penetrator would be reported as Rockwell Superficial hardness 40 ($30N$). The gauge scale on both machines is reversed so that, in conformity with custom, high hardness numbers mean a shallow indentation and thus a hard material.

The greatest hardness that can be tested is limited only by the ability of the diamond penetrator to withstand the stress. For very low hardnesses the larger diameter balls frequently must be used and constant test times also are often necessary to limit material flow. Specimens to be tested must be smooth on both sides, clean, and thick enough so that no impression, called the anvil effect, shows on the underside.

When testing curved surfaces greater than $\frac{1}{2}$ in. in diameter little error is introduced by the curvature, but for smaller rounds the diameter always should be specified as well as whether the test was made on a flat or a round surface. When close hardness tolerances are important and must be related to readings on flat surfaces, a correction should be applied, if necessary, after standard calibration blocks for that hardness range have been measured.

Great care must be used in trying to relate differences in hardness on any of the scales because one point near the high side of any scale signifies a hardness difference considerably greater than one point near the middle or low range of the scale. Different scales may overlap in certain regions, but outside of such regions they cannot be compared satisfactorily. Hardness conversions between different scales also are not always the same for different materials.

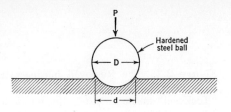

(*left*) Manual and (*middle*) air-operated Brinell hardness testers. (*above right*) Impression made in specimen by Brinell ball.

**Figure 2.3**  The Brinell hardness test. [Courtesy Tinius Olsen Testing Machine Company.] For ferrous materials $P/D^2 = 30$, with $P = 3000$ kg and $D = 10$ mm, applied for 30 sec in the standard test. For nonferrous materials $P/D^2 = 5$, with $P = 500$ kg and $D = 10$ mm, applied for 60 sec in the standard test.

$$\text{Bhn} = \frac{\text{Load in Kg}}{\text{Area of spherical impression in sq mm}}$$

$$= \frac{P}{\frac{\pi D}{2}(D - \sqrt{D^2 - d^2})}$$

Specimens, preferably, should be at least ½ in. thick and fairly large.

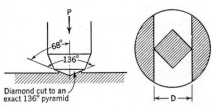

(*left*) The Vickers hardness tester. (*above left*) Cross section and (*above right*) surface of Vickers hardness impression (schematic).

**Figure 2.4**  The Vickers hardness test. [Courtesy Riehle Testing Machines, a Division of Ametek, Inc., East Moline, Ill.]

$$\text{Vhn} = \frac{\text{Load in Kg}}{\text{Lateral area of pyramidal impression in sq mm}}$$

$$= (2 \sin 68°)\frac{P}{D^2} = 1.854 \frac{P}{D^2}$$

Vickers hardness numbers are practically independent of the load, which may have any value from 1 to 120 kg and is applied for 10 sec. The test, therefore, may be used successfully with almost any type or thickness of material. A polished surface is preferable, however.

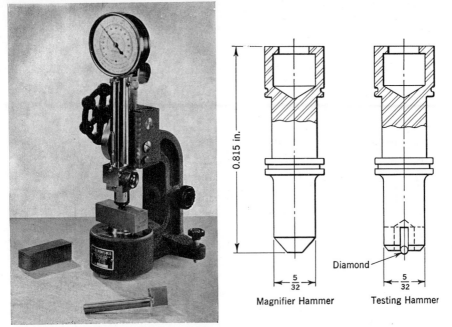

Magnifier Hammer | Testing Hammer

0.815 in.

Diamond

**Figure 2.5** The Shore Scleroscope hardness test. [Courtesy Shore Instrument Manufacturing Company.] The height of rebound of a small diamond hammer, of definite weight and falling from a definite height, is measured either by visual observation or on a recording dial. The constants involved depend on the model instrument used but the principle of all of them is identical. The scale used is arbitrary, determined by considering the rebound from quenched pure high-carbon steel to be 100 and dividing it into 100 equal divisions. Almost any thickness specimen may be used, but a smooth surface is essential. Practically no mark is made on the specimen. For soft materials, a special magnifier hammer is used. The instrument can be used in a portable manner provided the clamping pressure on the specimen is kept constant, and the mass of the specimen is at least as large as that of the usual anvil.

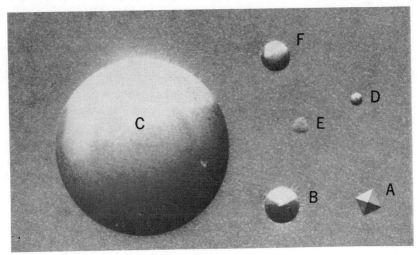

**Figure 2.6** Hardness-test impressions of six different hardness testers. Enlarged to approximately 6½ diameters. (A) Vickers, (B) Rockwell "C," (C) Brinell, (D) Monotron, (E) Scleroscope, (F) Rockwell "B." [From H. B. Pulsifer, courtesy American Society for Metals.]

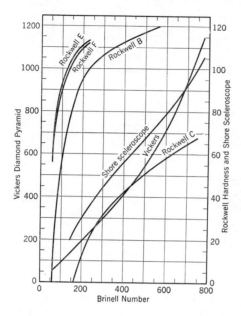

**Figure 2.7** Approximate relationships between several of the commonly used hardness scales.

Still other methods of hardness testing use various systems of scratch hardness, either relative or in comparison with arbitrary standards.

A comparison of some of the commonly used hardness scales is shown in Figure 2.7. These relationships are only approximate, and should not be used on any other basis.[10]

Hardness seldom is determined for its own sake and usually is an index of some other more complex and elusive property such as strength or workability. Sometimes even such widely different properties as wear or abrasion resistance, cutting ability and machinability, are referred to as "hardness."

In all of these tests, work-hardening causes the properties of the material being tested to change to some extent during the test, even though much effort has been directed toward eliminating or minimizing such changes by modifications in penetrator design. Consequently, no values so secured can be absolute and, in reality, they measure some combination of the actual hardness and the hardness increase during the test.

Care must be taken, however, to make all hardness tests on appropriate specimens, and to limit interpretation of results to comparable materials.

As a simple, easily made test, especially for control purposes, hardness tests have a definite and important place in industry.

[10] More accurate relationships are given in *A.S.T.M. Standard E140* and in Ref. 18 at the end of this chapter.

## STRENGTH OR RESISTANCE TO DEFORMATION

The strength of metals and alloys generally parallels their hardness. With proper treatment, wires of some metals, such as tungsten, have developed a longitudinal tensile strength as high as 500,000 psi, but even this is far below the strengths found in other materials such as certain glass fibers, for example. Practically, strengths of the order of 1,000,000 psi now seem to be the maximum presently attainable in industrial metallic materials. Even such values can be achieved only in a few materials.

For many applications the strength:weight ratio may be more important than the strength itself. The reasons for this can be appreciated better if it is remembered that the total design load is composed of a dead load, the weight of the structure, and a live or pay load, the load which the structure can carry. It is the latter load which justifies the structure economically.

Of the major engineering materials, alloys based upon iron or nickel generally are the strongest; those based upon copper, aluminum, or magnesium occupy intermediate positions; and those based upon lead, tin, or zinc are of comparatively low strength. Where weight or load-carrying capacity is important, the relative positions of the alloys of the light materials, aluminum and magnesium, are improved markedly because their lower specific gravities give them higher strength:weight ratios. Likewise, the moderately low specific gravity of titanium makes some of its higher strength alloys of interest for particular applications up to 800 F (425 C) for which its higher cost can be justified. For applications at very high temperature, alloys based upon some of the minor engineering metals such as cobalt have shown excellent properties. Such alloys usually are available only in modest quantities, however.

## TENSILE STRENGTH

The ordinary axial tensile test [11] is used to secure information on both the elastic and the plastic properties of a material. Such tests normally are made on standardized test pieces, with gauge lengths appropriate to the diameter of the parallel portion and to that of the thickened ends. Extensometers or strain gauges may be provided, so that longitudinal strain readings can be made throughout the application of load, and load versus elongation or stress versus strain curves can be drawn or recorded.

[11] See, for example, C. W. McGregor, *Proc. A.S.T.M.,* **40** (1940), 508–34; also *A.S.T.M. Standard E8.*

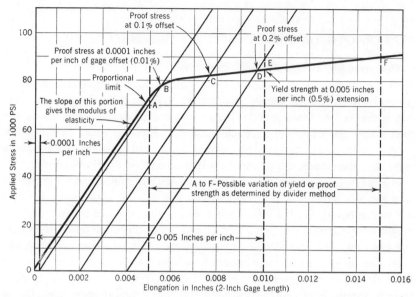

**Figure 2.8** Initial portion of typical stress-strain curve for cold-drawn steel showing method of determining various values. Because the elastic limit, by definition, depends on the permanent set after successive reloadings, with complete release of load each time, it cannot, strictly, be shown on such a diagram.

When a specimen is stressed in tension it tends to deform by shear and to elongate. While it remains elastic, the strain is proportional to the stress, as shown by the first portion of the curves in Figure 2.8; that is, the material obeys Hooke's law. Actually, a perfect straight-line relationship between stress and strain probably never occurs, but the law is a very close approximation for many materials in the correct ranges of stress, and early deviation from a straight line can be detected only with the most precise instruments.

As the load is increased, a stress is reached which is no longer proportional to the strain. If the specimen is stressed somewhat above this point, and the load then is released, it is found that the specimen has suffered a permanent set or deformation. This point, therefore, is above the primitive elastic limit, by definition, the maximum unit stress that can be developed in a material without causing a permanent set. To avoid possible later confusion, it must be emphasized that, strictly, the true elastic limit can be determined only by successively loading and unloading a specimen until a load is reached for which a permanent measurable set results. As this procedure is extremely laborious to carry out, the true elastic limit seldom is secured, although the term elastic limit sometimes is used loosely in referring to other points on a load-extension or stress-strain curve.

With accurate devices for measuring strain, it is possible to detect a point close to but below the true elastic limit at which there is a deviation from Hooke's law, but no apparent set. This point is called the primitive proportional limit, the maximum unit stress for which the unit strain increases at the same rate as the unit stress [12] for the material in its initial condition. In a strict sense, neither the elastic limit nor the proportional limit is used industrially. The exact value of either of them depends, to a large extent, on the accuracy of the measuring instruments used to determine the unit strain, and on the stress intervals at which readings are taken.

## MODULI OF ELASTICITY

The four common constants of elastic theory are: (1) Young's modulus, $E$, (2) shear modulus, $G$, (3) Poisson's ratio, $v$, and (4) bulk modulus, $K$.

Within the range of stress for which Hooke's law is valid, the slope of the stress-strain curve, that is, the ratio of the unit stress to the unit strain, gives what is called Young's modulus of elasticity in tension (or in compression if a compression test is run) of the material being tested. This may be expressed as

$$E = \frac{P/A}{e/L} = \frac{PL}{Ae} = \frac{\sigma}{\epsilon} = \frac{\text{stress}}{\text{strain}}$$

Where $E$ is Young's modulus,[13] $P$ the load, $A$ the cross-sectional area, $e$ the elongation or the change in length produced by the application of the load, and $L$ the original length.

Similarly, the shear modulus of elasticity, $G$, sometimes called the modulus of rigidity, is given by the ratio of the shearing unit stress to the shearing unit strain as measured in a torsion test. This may be expressed as

$$G = \frac{\tau}{\gamma} = \frac{\text{shear stress}}{\text{shear strain}}$$

The shear modulus, $G$, is smaller than the elastic modulus, $E$, the relationship between the two being given by the expression

$$G = \frac{E}{2(1 + v)}$$

[12] See R. L. Templin, *Proc. A.S.T.M.*, **39**, II (1929), 523.
[13] $E$ generally is stated in pounds per square inch.

Poisson's ratio, $v$, is the ratio between the unit transverse contraction and the unit axial elongation which occurs when a body made of elastic material is subjected to a tensile load (for compressive loads, the contraction is axial and the elongation is transverse.) [14]

The bulk modulus of elasticity, $K$, is the resistance to change in volume under pressure

$$\frac{-dP}{dV/V}$$

It thus is the reciprocal of the compressibility

$$-\frac{1}{V}\frac{dV}{dP}$$

However, because it is comparatively difficult to measure, advantage usually is taken of the fact that the bulk modulus is related to Young's modulus and the shear modulus by the expression

$$K = \frac{E}{3 - \dfrac{E}{G}}$$

and direct measurements of bulk modulus seldom are encountered, most experimental data being designed to determine the other three elastic constants. [15]

Moduli of elasticity are of importance in engineering design because they determine the stiffness of a given material, and hence influence strongly the section shapes, the unsupported spans, and various other parameters. The value of the modulus of elasticity is determined almost entirely by the dominant metal in the alloy. It is changed somewhat by alloying but only to a small extent by mechanical or thermal treatment. All these moduli, however, are strongly temperature sensitive, especially in low melting point materials. Approximate values of Young's modulus for the major engineering metals at room temperature are, in millions of pounds per square inch: nickel, 30; iron, 28.5; copper, 16; aluminum, 9; magnesium, 5.8; tin, 6; and lead, 2; in zinc this modulus is not clearly defined. These values also

[14] A good review of this, with numerical values for many metals, is given by W. Koester and H. Franz, *Metallurgical Reviews,* **6** (1961), 1–55.

[15] For a more complete discussion see "Symposium on Determination of Elastic Constants," *S.T.P. No. 129* (Philadelphia: American Society for Testing Materials, 1952).

are reasonable approximations for most of the engineering alloys of these metals.

## YIELD STRENGTH

In a ductile material, increasing the load above the elastic limit results in permanent deformation of the specimen in shear. The weakest section, naturally, is the first to yield or deform plastically. It strain hardens and is strengthened as a result of its deformation until it can sustain the load. The next weakest section then has to help bear the load, so it deforms and is work-hardened, in a similar manner, until it can sustain the load also. As this progressive strengthening continues, the specimen elongates continuously.

Except for those materials (such as low-carbon steels) which have a clearly defined point (load) on their stress-strain curves at which yielding or initial plastic deformation occurs, the definition of yield strength is empirical and arbitrary because the departure from proportionality is slow and progressive. For such materials, a preferred practice is to define a value of proof stress or yield strength in terms of a specified degree of departure from the modulus line. Thus, the 0.5% proof stress or yield strength, is the stress causing an offset of 0.5% from the modulus line, as indicated in Figure 2.8.

For the class of materials mentioned above as having a more clearly indicated change from elastic to plastic deformation, the yield point may be defined as the unit stress at which the material continues to deform without an increase in load. In many materials, this is manifested by an apparent decrease in the load measured by the testing machine, the so-called drop of the beam, as shown in the curve for annealed steel in Figure 2.9. However, it must be remembered that the testing machine is imposing a strain on the specimen at a definite rate, and if the load indicated suddenly decreases, it simply means that the specimen momentarily is yielding

**Figure 2.9** Initial portion of stress-strain curves for aluminum, copper, and steels in various conditions. Note that the higher moduli of elasticity give steeper initial slopes to the curves.

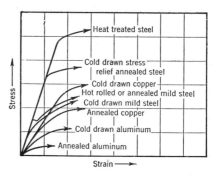

at a faster rate and under a lower stress than the machine is applying to it by its steady movement. With a dead load there could be no decrease in the load although a sudden increase in the rate of elongation would be noted.

Relatively few materials exhibit a true yield point. Hence, the proportional limit and yield strength are much more significant values, even though the actual magnitude of the former depends on the sensitivity of the measuring device used to record the elongation, and that of the latter depends on a more or less empirical elongation value. Values of yield strength are the ones quoted most widely although they may be labeled incorrectly.

## ULTIMATE STRENGTH

In a ductile material, continued application of the load causes further elongation and accompanying work-hardening until a load is reached at which some section is unable to strain-harden rapidly enough to support the load. All of the load then is concentrated on this section, which elongates rapidly, decreasing in cross-sectional area by necking down, until fracture occurs.

In the usual stress-strain or load-extension curve, stress is calculated in terms of the initial cross-sectional area, as though this remained essentially unchanged throughout the test. As soon as the section begins to neck down, therefore, the stress so defined decreases. The magnitude of the unit stress at this maximum point is known as the ultimate tensile strength of the material.

If the actual cross-sectional area is used instead of the original value, as in Figure 2.10, the true unit stress is found to increase continually as fracture is approached. The ratio between the ultimate tensile strength as determined from the original cross-sectional area and the maximum true stress as determined from the actual cross-sectional area, gives a satisfac-

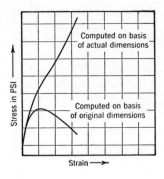

**Figure 2.10** Comparison stress-strain curves for mild steel in which the stress is plotted, both from original specimen dimensions and from actual specimen dimensions during test, against the strain (elongation). [From C. W. MacGregor, *Trans. A.I.M.E.,* **124** (1937), 208–26.]

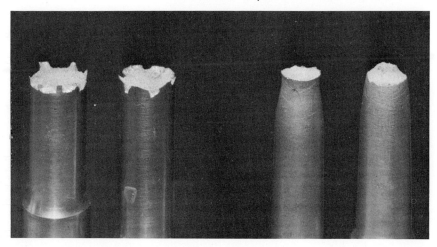

**Figure 2.11** (*left pair*) Typical brittle and (*right pair*) ductile fractures secured in tensile tests of 0.5 in. diameter brass rod. [Photograph courtesy Technical Department, the American Brass Company.]

tory method for evaluating the work-hardening capacities of different
metals. However, a better value can be secured from the power relationship which exists,[16] beyond the point of ultimate tensile strength, between
the true stress $\sigma$, and the true strain, $\epsilon$

$$\sigma = \kappa \epsilon^n$$

$\kappa$ and $n$ are materials constants, usually called the strength coefficient and
the strain-hardening exponent,[17] respectively.

### ELONGATION AND REDUCTION IN AREA

Even without making detailed strain measurements under load, some
idea of the workability of the material, in certain deformation processes
at ambient temperatures, can be secured from the tensile test [18] by measuring the percentage elongation and the percentage reduction in area at
the fracture. For low-ductility materials (generally classed, loosely, as
brittle) which have a fracture similar to that shown at the left in Figure
2.11, both of these values are low, of the order of a few per cent at most.

[16] Originally observed by P. Ludwik over 50 years ago, but a more modern discussion is given by G. V. Smith in Ref. 8 at the end of this chapter.

[17] Note particularly that this is not the same $n$ as was used in the Meyer hardness
analysis discussed earlier in this chapter and also that it is not the rate of strain
hardening, a factor that decreases in the early stages of deformation but reaches
a substantially constant value later.

[18] See H. W. Gillett, *Proc. A.S.T.M.*, **40** (1940), 551–78.

However, for materials which are tough and workable, values of 50% or higher are common, sometimes accompanied by a cup and cone fracture similar to that shown at the right in Figure 2.11.

Two terms are used commonly in speaking of workability: ductility, the ability to be drawn into fine wires; and malleability, the ability to be beaten or compressed into thin foil. Although the two are not identical (because ductile materials must have a certain ability to work-harden that malleable materials need not necessarily possess), they both are used loosely in the same sense.

Workability is a property which generally opposes hardness and strength. Thus, pure metals, which tend to have lower hardnesses and strengths, usually are quite workable, and a simple qualitative test for purity can be based upon the excellence of workability. The workability of many metals, however, is decreased to a low value if small amounts of certain specific impurities are present, even though the hardness is not increased greatly. Likewise, alloys which are very strong and hard are apt to be brittle or to have little, if any, workability. The majority of the engineering alloys are intermediate in nature, with varying combinations of the two properties.

A better understanding of what some of these mechanical properties really mean in terms of the basic structure of a metal can be secured by looking more closely at space lattices and the defects which exist in them.[19]

## CRYSTALLOGRAPHIC PLANES

Because of the approximately regular spacing of the atoms in solid metals upon a space lattice, it usually is possible, from purely geometrical considerations, to pass through that lattice families of equidistant parallel planes upon which the atoms are regularly, but more or less densely, distributed.[20] For a two-dimensional lattice, such as that illustrated in Figure 2.12, this can be illustrated schematically by parallel lines which are traces of the crystallographic planes in a three-dimensional space lattice. These planes are characterized in two further ways: (1) the number of families is limited by the fact that no plane with irrational or large integral indices is recognized as a crystallographic plane, and (2) each family may include more than one set of parallel planes—for example, in a cubic lattice there are three sets of equivalent planes parallel to each of the three cube faces, each pair of which is separated by another plane of the same set which

[19] C. H. Mathewson, *Trans. A.S.M.,* **32** (1944), 38–87, has summarized well the basic structural factors involved in strain-hardening.

[20] In alpha-uranium and similar low-symmetry structures, such planes sometimes are corrugated.

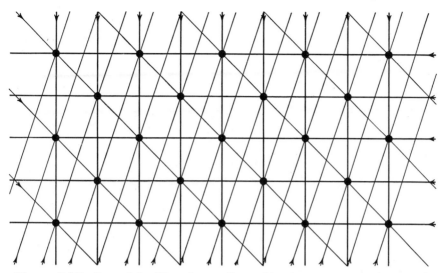

**Figure 2.12**  Several families of crystallographic planes represented as parallel-line traces on a two-dimensional projection of a face-centered cubic space lattice.

includes the face-centered atoms or the body-centered atom, depending on the symmetry of the structure.

### CLOSE-PACKED PLANES

The density of packing on any plane of a given family is determined by the arrangement of atoms on the space lattice. Clearly, if the atoms are packed most densely on each of a given family of planes, then successive planes of that family also must be spaced most widely. Planes of this type are known as close-packed planes. In other families of planes, the members are spaced more closely and the density of packing on each is lower.

A typical series of close-packed planes for each of the three simple metal space lattices is indicated in Figure 2.13. In the hexagonal system, there is only one set of such planes, called the basal planes, because they are parallel to the base of the hexagon; but in both of the cubic lattices, there are several sets. Only one set of a family is illustrated, although the locations of the others should be readily apparent from symmetry considerations. In the face-centered cubic system, the close-packed planes are called the octahedral or body-diagonal planes. In the body-centered cubic system, at least three families are nearly equally close-packed; the planes shown are the face diagonals, also called dodecahedral planes because there are twelve of them.

55

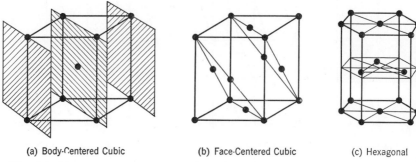

(a) Body-Centered Cubic          (b) Face-Centered Cubic          (c) Hexagonal

**Figure 2.13** Examples of close-packed planes for the three simple metal space lattices.

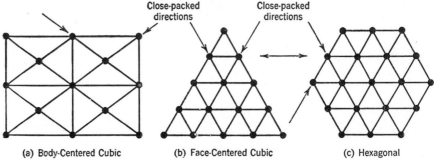

Close-packed directions          Close-packed directions

(a) Body-Centered Cubic          (b) Face-Centered Cubic          (c) Hexagonal

**Figure 2.14** Atom arrangements on typical close-packed planes for the three simple metal space lattices. Note that the closest approach of the atoms is along the close-packed directions, and that the atom positions on any one close-packed plane are identical for both the face-centered cubic and the hexagonal lattices. The latter two lattices, however, differ in the relative displacements of the planes of atoms above and below, respectively, the plane shown (compare Figures 1.9 and 1.10).

## CLOSE-PACKED DIRECTIONS

The arrangement of the atoms on a typical close-packed plane of each of the three lattices is shown in Figure 2.14. The atoms are packed more closely along certain lines in these planes than along others. These are the close-packed directions which lie in the close-packed planes. Both the close-packed planes and the close-packed directions are significant in explaining the deformation of metals.[21] In the body-centered cubic structure, in fact, the close-packed direction may be the more significant factor

[21] See, for example, *Distortion of Metal Crystals* by C. F. Elam (New York: Oxford University Press, 1935); R. Maddin and N. K. Chen in *Progress in Metal Physics*, **5** (New York: Interscience Publishers, 1954), 53–95; and Ref. 9 at the end of this chapter.

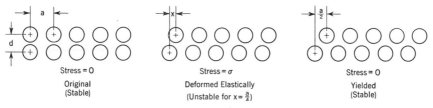

**Figure 2.15** Successive positions of planes of atoms in perfect crystal showing elastic deformation and yielding schematically.

because there are at least three families of planes of nearly the same denseness of packing that contain the close-packed direction.

## THEORETICAL YIELD STRENGTH OF METALS

Until the significance of the various types of imperfections in space lattices became appreciated, one of the most troublesome questions about metals was not why they were so strong but why they were so weak. The theoretical stress at which a metal crystal will undergo shear or slip can be estimated in a relatively simple manner.[22] In a perfect crystal, this value is very high because strong interatomic forces must be overcome. Consider, as in Figure 2.15, two planes of atoms spaced a distance $d$ apart with $a$ the distance between any two adjacent atoms in the close-packed direction. Next, shear these two planes past each other. If, for a shear stress, $\sigma$, the upper row is displaced a distance $x$ relative to the lower row, there should be an elastic deformation of somewhere between 3% and 10%. Also, there is a relationship between the shear stress and the displacement. Although this function is not known specifically, various possibilities can be considered, all of them, however, subject to the limitation that the stress be zero at positions corresponding to the normal lattice sites and also, for reasons of symmetry, at those positions half-way between. In other words, initially, the deformation is elastic because each atom is attracted toward its nearest position in the normal lattice by the interatomic forces and tends to return to it if the stress is released.

At first approximation, this required function of $x$ which has the period $a$ can be assumed to be sinusoidal so that

$$\sigma = k \sin\left(\frac{2\pi x}{a}\right)$$

[22] J. Frenkel, *Zeit. f. Physik,* **37** (1926), 572; E. Orowan, *Proc. Phys. Soc.,* **52** (1940), 8; N. J. Petch in *Progress in Metal Physics,* **5** (New York: Interscience Publishers, 1954), 1–52.

The constant $k$ must be chosen so as to make the initial slope correspond to the shear modulus of the crystal. For small displacements not greatly removed from the equilibrium condition, the value of the sine of the angle does not differ greatly from the value of the angle so the stress can be approximated closely by

$$\sigma = k\frac{2\pi x}{a}$$

From Hooke's law, this stress also is given by

$$\sigma = \frac{Gx}{d}$$

These two values for the stress can be equated, giving

$$k\frac{2\pi x}{a} = \frac{Gx}{d}$$

So

$$k = \frac{Ga}{2\pi d}$$

And

$$\sigma = \frac{Ga}{2\pi d}\sin\left(\frac{2\pi x}{a}\right)$$

Therefore, the critical elastic shear stress, $\sigma_c$, at which the lattice becomes unstable and the two planes should slip over each other, assumed to be when the displacement, $x$, is equal to $a/4$, is given by

$$\sigma_c = \frac{Ga}{2\pi d}$$

This is roughly equal to $G/2\pi$ because both $a$ and $d$ are of comparable magnitudes. The shear modulus of most engineering metals is above a million pounds per square inch so this critical elastic stress should have a value of the order of a million pounds per square inch whereas its measured value is some orders of magnitude smaller.

Admittedly, the assumptions made, particularly the one involving the sinusoidal relationship and the critical elastic stress at which the lattice becomes unstable, have been overly simplified. However, even with the greatest refinements possible on the basis of existing knowledge, this estimated value has only been reduced to about $G/30$, still much larger than the values of the critical shear stress for yield of single crystals found experimentally.

Independent work, with perfect two-dimensional rafts of bubbles [23] which are believed to act much like perfect crystals, indicates that slip takes place along close-packed rows of bubbles at a critical stress which is roughly $\dot{G}/30$. Thus, in this type of a perfect lattice-like arrangement, the observed and estimated stresses agree. However, when imperfections, especially of the line imperfection or dislocation type, exist in these bubble rafts, slip can be made to take place under relatively minor stresses.

It also has been found [24] that, under certain circumstances, extremely fine metal whiskers about 0.001 in. in diameter and several millimeters long can be grown which can support (in bend tests) stresses of the order of magnitude of the shear modulus and an elastic deformation of the order of 3% without deforming plastically. Whiskers are probably as close to being structurally perfect as any metallic materials known today.

These two pieces of evidence indicate still further that, in the real crystals of which metals are composed, the known imperfections must be sources of mechanical weakness of such a nature that slip can start at relatively low applied stresses, yet without altering the elastic moduli or making it possible for slip to occur on different crystallographic planes or in new directions. The theory of defects predicts, also, that the shear strength should decrease as the density of the defects decreases, so long as the total number of defects is not zero.

## COLD WORK

Under the action of external forces, each crystal of an aggregate tends to deform or to change its shape in a manner which depends on its own lattice orientation as well as upon the directions in which the applied stress is transmitted to it by its neighbors. If the deformation takes place in a temperature range in which work-hardening occurs, the deformation is known as cold-work regardless of the actual temperature involved.

Cold work always results in a distorted and disrupted grain structure and in a marked increase in the mechanical properties related to strength and hardness, with an accompanying decrease in those properties related to workability. These changes in structure and properties are illustrated in Figure 2.16 for an oxygen-free copper.

[23] See various papers by W. L. Bragg and/or co-workers—for example, *Proc. Roy. Soc.*, **A190** (London: 1947), 474; *ibid.*, **A196** (1949), 171; *ibid.*, **A196** (1949), 182.
[24] See, for example, the initial work on tin of C. Herring and J. K. Galt, *Phys. Rev.*, **85** (1952), 1060; and the article by H. K. Hardy in *Progress in Metal Physics*, **6** (New York: Pergamon Press, 1956), 45–73.

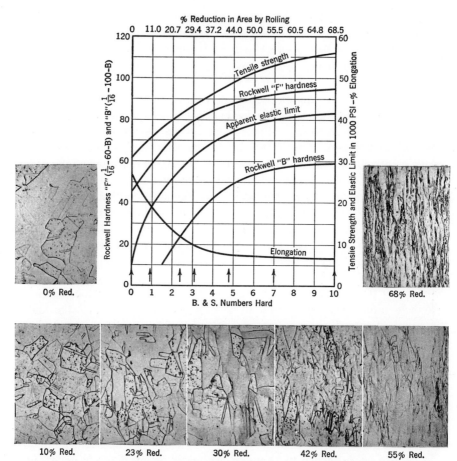

**Figure 2.16** Changes in microstructure and properties resulting from cold-working oxygen-free copper. [From R. A. Wilkins and E. S. Bunn, *Copper and Copper Alloys*. New York: McGraw-Hill, 1943. Photomicrographs by L. Litchfield.]

Most impurities and alloying elements cause a metal to work-harden more readily and to a greater extent than a pure metal would. This is illustrated in Figure 2.17 for some of the commercial grades of copper.

## EFFECTS OF GRAIN SIZE ON COLD WORKING

In general, the finer the grain size of the material, the greater is the increase in strength and hardness produced by cold work (Figure 2.18), and the greater is the energy required to produce a given deformation. A coarse grained material has a rough appearance when bent because

*60*

of the movements between the grains at the free surface (Figure 2.19). Therefore, grain size control influences not only the characteristics and appearance of the metal after working, but also the energy that must be expended in working it.

## THE GEOMETRICAL DEFORMATION PROCESS

Two alternative mechanisms appear to explain adequately the geometrical deformation of the space lattices of individual crystals. These are

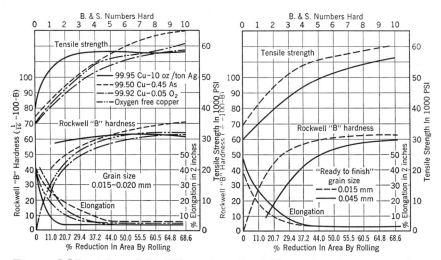

**Figure 2.17** (*above left*) Effect of small additions of various elements on the work-hardening characteristics of copper. [From Wilkins and Bunn, *Copper and Copper Alloys*.]

**Figure 2.18** (*above right*) Comparative effects of grain size on the work-hardening characteristics of oxygen-free copper. [From Wilkins and Bunn, *Copper and Copper Alloys*.]

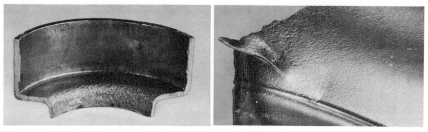

**Figure 2.19** "Orange peel," caused by coarse grains, on the surface of drawn steel. [Photographs courtesy American Rolling Mill Company.]

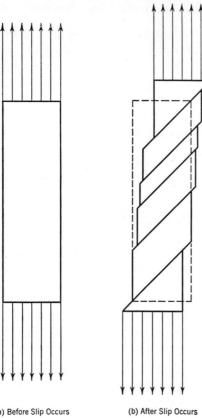

**Figure 2.20** Schematic representation of the process of slip in metallic deformation of a single crystal. (A third stage, not shown, consisting either of rotation or of slip in another direction, would be required to realign the tensile forces acting on each end.)

(a) Before Slip Occurs     (b) After Slip Occurs

called slip and twinning.[25] However, work-hardening can be explained satisfactorily only by utilizing the complexities which arise because of the presence of the various types of lattice imperfections.

### SLIP

A simple idealized shear mechanism which explains slip in a single crystal geometrically [26] is illustrated in Figure 2.20. Under the action of a suitable stress, the magnitude of which depends on the temperature and

[25] Much of the understanding of deformation in metals was secured by studying single crystals. Methods of preparation of crystals in usable sizes are given by A. N. Holden, *Trans. A.S.M.*, **42** (1950), 319–46.

[26] This mechanism of slip is discussed in *The Distortion of Metal Crystals* by C. F. Elam (New York: Oxford University Press, 1935); and by R. Maddin and N. K. Chen in *Progress in Metal Physics,* **5** (New York: Interscience Publishers, 1954), 53–95; see also Ref. 9 at the end of this chapter. A thorough discussion of deformation in single crystals of zinc is given by D. C. Jillson, *Trans. A.I.M.E.*, **188** (1950), 1009–18.

on the rate of straining as well as on several structural characteristics of the crystal, blocks of crystalline material slide over their neighbors along planes which are usually the close-packed planes, and in directions which are almost invariably the close-packed directions. In the close-packed metal structures, face-centered cubic and hexagonal, there is only one family of close-packed planes, with three possible close-packed directions in each. However, in body-centered cubic metals, only the close-packed direction, the body diagonal, is defined clearly. At least three families of planes, containing this close-packed direction, have nearly the same density of packing. Hence, any of them can serve as slip planes depending upon the specific conditions. This makes the deformation of body-centered metals more complicated than that of the close-packed metals. The thickness of these slipped blocks will vary, depending upon the metal and the specific conditions existing when the deformation takes place. However, the usual glide distance of a single slip process is of the order of hundreds or thousands of atomic distances and the blocks which slip as a unit are of the order of 1,000 atoms thick (minimum).

As can be seen from Figure 2.20, simple slip in tension alone will not maintain alignment of the tensile loading. In addition, there must be a rotation of the slip planes in such a way that they tend to become parallel to the tensile force.[27] In a polycrystalline material this rotation causes the grains to slide over one another at the grain boundaries.

Deformation by slip seems to be independent of the stress normal to the slip plane; it proceeds only along certain planes and in certain directions; it is self-stopping; and it results in definite work-hardening, which affects not only the specific plane upon which it occurs but also inactive planes. Furthermore, as the crystal deforms by slip, it hardens and becomes stronger as a whole rather than only in the regions of the active slip planes.

## SLIP LINES

If a metal test piece with a polished surface is deformed, the effects of the block movement, which has been called slip, can be seen readily. Relatively straight lines appear, running across each crystal, as illustrated in Figure 2.21. Sometimes, also, there is actual displacement of the crystal with respect to neighboring grains (Figure 2.22). The reasons for these slip lines easily can be understood from the diagram of Figure 2.23. Simple repolishing of the surface removes the difference in level and thus eliminates the slip lines.

[27] This was shown originally for single crystals of zinc, in which the basal plane (hexagonal structure) is the only active slip plane, by H. Mark, M. Polanyi and E. Schmid, *Zeit. f. Physik,* **12** (1927), 58.

**Figure 2.21** (*above left*) Slip lines in a coarsely crystalline brass. Etched with $NH_4OH + H_2O_2$ (×200). Most of the area shown is occupied by a single crystal within which two sets of slip lines appear. Notice how the secondary slip lines have produced a displacement of the primary slip lines in certain regions, and how the secondary slip lines change direction on passing through the annealing twin bands. [Photomicrograph courtesy R. M. Brick.]

**Figure 2.22** (*above right*) Displacement of grain boundaries by slip in an alloy of 90% aluminum, 10% magnesium. Etched with ½% HF (×500). The specimen was given a solution heat-treatment, cold-rolled, and then given a precipitation treatment of ½ hr at 400 F (205 C). The black slip lines, showing a clear-cut boundary displacement in several places, can be seen here because of the fine precipitate produced by the last heat-treatment. [Photomicrograph courtesy R. M. Brick.]

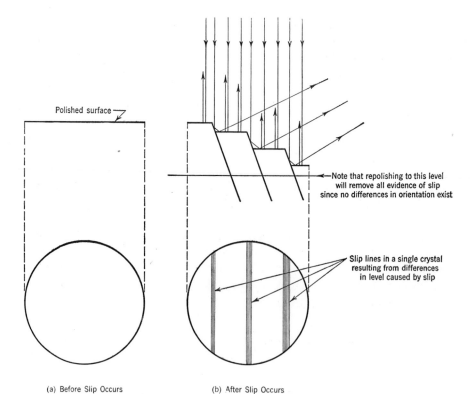

Polished surface

Note that repolishing to this level will remove all evidence of slip since no differences in orientation exist

Slip lines in a single crystal resulting from differences in level caused by slip

(a) Before Slip Occurs          (b) After Slip Occurs

**Figure 2.23** Schematic explanation of the formation of slip lines in a metal crystal.

## GLIDE OF DISLOCATIONS

So long as there are imperfections in a crystal there is distortion present because of the elastic stress fields which surround them. When stress is applied, this distortion simply moves through the crystal, a process which requires a relatively small stress. The motion of any dislocation under an applied stress can be resolved into a component in the slip plane, called glide, and a component normal to the slip plane, called climb. The motion of a screw dislocation, however, always is glide.

The manner in which an edge dislocation propagates through a crystal is shown schematically in Figure 2.24. It is apparent that the glide of one

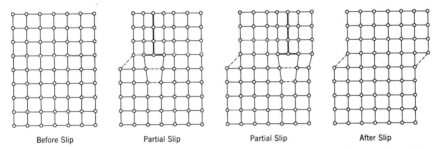

| Before Slip | Partial Slip | Partial Slip | After Slip |

**Figure 2.24**  Schematic illustration of slip in a crystal lattice as the glide of an edge dislocation.

dislocation across the crystal results in a movement of atoms equivalent to slip over a distance of one atomic distance. Hence, any explanation by this means of the process of slip over thousands of atomic distances, as has been observed experimentally, requires (a) the existence in each crystal of very large numbers of dislocations, (b) some process for producing dislocations within each crystal spontaneously in large numbers during the deformation process, and (c) some method by which one dislocation can produce large amounts of slip before it becomes ineffective.[28]

## FRANK-READ SPIRALS AND SOURCES

A method of producing large amounts of slip from a single dislocation was found when dislocations were considered as three dimensional rather than two dimensional. This was the so-called Frank-Read [29] spiral mechanism by means of which a bent pure edge dislocation which does not lie

[28] See Ref. 5 at the end of this chapter.
[29] Those interested in pursuing this mechanism further should read Refs. 7 and 10 at the end of this chapter and the original paper by F. C. Frank and W. T. Read, Jr., *Phys. Rev.*, **79** (1950), 722–23.

entirely in a single plane parallel to the slip plane becomes anchored at one end within the crystal and, in its future motion under the action of a favorably oriented stress, rotates around its anchor, producing one unit of slip in the area swept out or moved over. This is illustrated schematically in Figure 2.25. A dislocation is not rigid and can change both its length and its shape. This dislocation, anchored at one end, can continue to rotate indefinitely, winding itself up into a spiral, so it can produce an unlimited number of dislocations.

As an improvement on this means of producing unlimited dislocations, which involves the same principle, a straight line dislocation was envisaged which was entirely within a single crystal and was anchored at each end. In the operation of this so-called Frank-Read source, Figure 2.26, the dislocation first bulges outward in the slip plane from its original location, thus becoming curved between its two anchors even though it still is an-

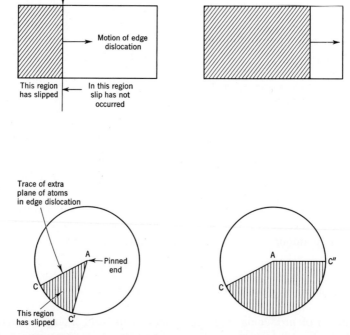

**Figure 2.25**  Schematic views from above of motions of edge dislocations leading to slip. (*upper group*) Linear motion, compare Figure 2.24. (*lower group*) The Frank-Read single-ended source, running to a free surface. Rotational motion about central point that remains pinned or fixed in position. The motion of the part *AC* causes one unit of slip for each complete rotation it makes around point *A*. This can continue indefinitely. [After F. C. Frank and W. T. Read, Jr.]

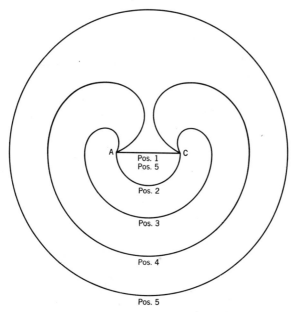

**Figure 2.26** Schematic views from above of motion of dislocation, $AC$, which has both ends pinned so they cannot move. This is the Frank-Read double-ended source, acting inside a crystal rather than at an edge. When subjected to a proper critical shear stress, $AC$ first will curve or bow until it forms approximately a semicircular arc (Position 2). The loop then expands without restraint through typical positions (3, 4, and 5) ultimately reforming both a new double-ended source like the original one, to start over again, and a closed dislocation loop which passes outward. All of the material within the successive positional loops has undergone one unit of slip. [From F. C. Frank and W. T. Read, Jr., *Phys. Rev.,* **79** (1950), 722–23.]

chored at its ends in the same slip plane. In this bulging process it changes from a pure line dislocation to a complex dislocation that has both line and screw components. Because the length of the dislocation, $L$, has been increased by this bulging, the total energy is greater and an applied stress, $\sigma$, is needed to maintain the radius of curvature, $R$. If the stress is removed at this stage the curved dislocation will tend to straighten and shorten. The tension required, $\tau$, is roughly equal to $Gb^2/2$ where $G$ is the shear modulus and $b$ is the Burgers vector.[30]

The condition for equilibrium is $\sigma b = \tau/R$ or, approximately, $\sigma = Gb/2R$. As the stress increases, the curvature increases until the dislocation line becomes a semicircle—that is, $2R = L$. Therefore at the critical

[30] Burgers vector, $b$, is a lattice vector which specifies the direction and distance by which atoms within the slipped region on one side of the slip plane have moved with respect to those on the other (unslipped) side. Its minimum magnitude is one lattice spacing because this is the minimum slip that can make the initial and final configurations the same.

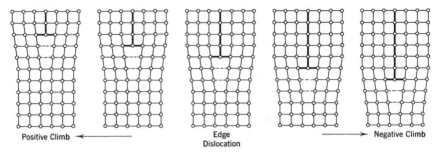

**Figure 2.27** (*left*) Positive and (*right*) negative climb of an edge dislocation (*schematic*).

stress, $\sigma_c = Gb/L$, the curved dislocation becomes unstable and expands indefinitely, ultimately doubling back on itself and breaking up into (a) a region within a closed dislocation loop that has undergone one unit of slip and now continues to expand, and (b) a dislocation identical with the original source which is ready to bulge again to produce a second closed loop. This process can continue indefinitely, producing expanding loops of dislocations, each loop producing unit slip in the area traversed as it expands over the slip plane. It stops only if the dislocations start to pile up and the resulting internal stress fields become too great to be overcome by the external stress acting.

### CLIMB OF DISLOCATIONS

In climb there must be mass transport (diffusion). The extra row of atoms which comprises the edge dislocation moves upward one atomic spacing, Figure 2.27, thus ending on the next higher slip plane and leaving one less atom in the row. One such atom must be removed for every atomic plane in which the dislocation climbs up one atomic spacing. It is called positive climb when the atom must be taken away from the extra plane. On the other hand, if the extra plane increases in length, requiring an atom to be added to it on each atomic plane in which it grows one atomic spacing, it is called negative climb.

There are at least two ways in which positive climb can occur (negative climb occurring by the reverse process).[31] First, a lattice vacancy could diffuse to the dislocation and interchange with the end atom, thus filling the vacancy with the atom and causing the dislocation to climb one unit. Second, the atom at the end of the dislocation could break loose, become

[31] An explanation of the actual three-dimensional case is much more complicated than the two-dimensional simplification shown in Figure 2.27.

an interstitial atom and diffuse away. Presumably, however, the possibility of this type of interstitial transport would be limited to certain types of atoms. In any case, it is apparent that an edge dislocation is both a source and a sink for vacancies and interstitial atoms. Furthermore, an excess of vacancies is a driving force to climb. Climb also can be affected by macroscopic strain. From Figure 2.27 it can be seen readily that, when atoms are removed from the end of the extra plane, the effect locally is similar to that of a compression strain, that is, the crystal decreases in volume locally. Likewise, when atoms are added here the crystal increases in volume locally, an effect similar to a tensile strain. Consequently, an applied compressive stress tries to squeeze out the extra plane of atoms and an applied tensile stress tries to make it grow, just as an applied shear stress encourages a slipped area to expand.

## DISLOCATION EXPLANATION OF WORK-HARDENING

Work-hardening, basically, is a combination of two distinct factors. The first of these is structural in nature and is the direct result of cold-working. The resistance to slip in a metal crystal increases with increasing amounts of plastic deformation, primarily because it becomes more difficult to move the dislocations, not because it becomes more difficult to produce them. It is the elastic stress fields around existing dislocations which oppose further motion. These internal stresses are built up around each dislocation on an active slip plane, so succeeding dislocations pile up and become fixed within the crystal rather than continuing through to a free internal or external surface.[32] In polycrystalline materials there are other restraints to slip introduced by the neighboring grains. These also result in dislocation pile-ups. Very large forces are required to drive dislocations past each other, even when they are on neighboring planes, so either these stress values are attained or the dislocations remain fixed, thereby effectively preventing slip on all planes passing through or near them. Experimental observations are consistent with values for density of dislocations of about $10^8$ per sq cm in a fully soft crystal and of about $10^{12}$ per sq cm in fully cold-worked material. Consequently, as deformation increases, the density of dislocations increases steadily, causing higher interaction forces and requiring a higher stress to cause further plastic deformation.

The second factor arises from the fact that, in any array of dislocations, those which can be moved most readily start to move at the lowest stress and move until they pile up or are destroyed (as by meeting a dislocation

[32] J. D. Meakin and H. G. F. Wilsdorf have found evidence of this in alpha brass, *Trans. A.I.M.E.,* **218** (1960), 737–52.

of opposite sign). With increasing amounts of hardening, therefore, all dislocations approach an equal difficulty of movement so the hardening rate decreases of necessity.

### GRAIN-BOUNDARY DEFORMATION IN A METAL AGGREGATE

It frequently has been observed that there is some movement between the grains themselves in addition to the deformation within the grains. This results often in the roughening of the surface of a deformed piece of poly-crystalline metal, especially when it has a large grain size. In formed metal sheets, such an effect gives what often is called an orange-peel surface (Figure 2.19).

The significance of this grain boundary deformation, compared to that within the grains, varies both with the rate of deformation and with the temperature. Only the middle of crystals in an aggregate deform by the simple slip process because of these complicating effects of grain boundaries.[33]

The combination of very slow rates of deformation and increased testing temperatures tends to result in intercrystalline rather than in transcrystalline fracture. In some materials, low temperatures and high rates of deformation produce comparable results. Consequently, under some conditions at least, the movement between the grains must be relatively important.

### TWINNING

Twinning also occurs in metal crystals. Twins are mirror images, with respect to lattice orientation, produced on either side of a neutral plane called the composition plane (Figure 2.28). The composition plane may or may not be a close-packed plane. Geometrical descriptions of mechanism of twin formation have been adequate in most instances.[34] Twins may be produced either by deformation, known as mechanical twins, or by heat-treatment, called annealing twins. The latter will be discussed in a later chapter.

[33] Many of these effects of crystal boundaries are discussed by R. King and B. Chalmers in *Progress in Metal Physics,* 1 (New York: Interscience Publishers, 1949).
[34] See, for example, C. H. Mathewson, *Trans. A.I.M.E.,* 78 (1928); also C. S. Barrett in Ref. 8 at the end of this chapter.

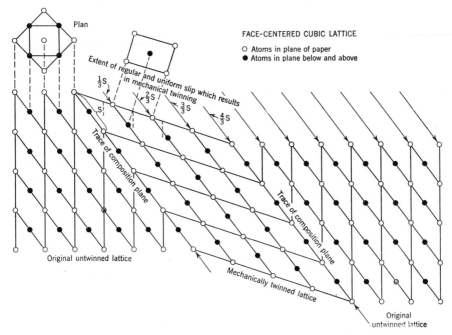

**Figure 2.28**  Schematic explanation of the formation of a twinned orientation in a face-centered cubic lattice by a process of regular and uniform slip. [From C. H. Mathewson and K. R. Van Horn, *Trans. A.I.M.E.,* **89** (1930).]

## MECHANICAL TWINNING

Mechanical twins, such as those in zinc (Figure 2.29*a*) or the Neumann bands in iron (Figure 2.29*b*) may or may not be perfectly straight depending to a large extent on the method by which they were produced. The deformation lines in copper and brass (Figure 2.29*c*), although somewhat similar in appearance to mechanical twins, probably are clusters of slip bands instead. Mechanical twinning often displaces the grain boundary (Figure 2.30). A definite relationship in orientation exists between the twinned and the untwinned portions which requires that many atoms are in places which are quite "wrong" in respect to the untwinned lattice [35] (compare Figure 2.28). Hence, a simple repolishing of the specimen does not remove the bands (Figure 2.31), although subsequent etching may be required to show them up distinctly.

[35] These have been discussed in detail for cubic symmetry by W. C. Ellis and R. G. Treuting, *Trans. A.I.M.E.,* **191** (1951), 53–55.

**Figure 2.29** Various forms of mechanical twinning in metals. **a.** Mechanical twins in commercial zinc. Etched with nitric and chromic acids (×100). [Photomicrograph by B. S. Norris.] **b.** Neumann bands in electrolytic iron. Etch with nital (×250). [Photomicrograph courtesy Research Laboratory, General Electric Company.] **c.** Deformation lines in a bronze. These are similar in appearance to mechanical twins in other metals and are so classed by some although they probably are clusters of slip bands. Etched with $NH_4OH + H_2O_2$ (×200). [Photomicrograph by L. Litchfield.]

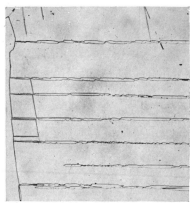

**Figure 2.30** Displacement of grain boundary *(left)* by Neumann bands in electrolytic iron. Etched with nital (×250 originally, reduced approximately one-half in reproduction). [Photomicrograph courtesy Research Laboratory, General Electric Company.]

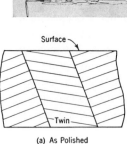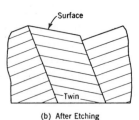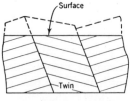

(a) As Polished

Twinned region not visible

(b) After Etching

Twinned region shown by difference in etching characteristics

(c) After Etching and Repolishing

Twinned region still present but not visible until re-etched

**Figure 2.31** Diagrammatic representation of effect of etching and repolishing on twins in a metal crystal.

Mechanical twins are usually of little significance with respect to deformation except for metals crystallizing in the hexagonal and some of the more complex lattices where, because of the relatively small number of possible slip planes, they may be an important factor in facilitating the deformation of some orientations. In the cubic metals, they serve to distinguish the body-centered metals (in which they occur) from the face-centered metals, and also afford an indication that mechanical deformation has taken place under conditions unfavorable to slip—for example, in ferrite they occur at low temperatures and high velocities, especially with ballistic impact. The twin bands probably exert some strengthening effect upon the aggregate, comparable to that of a smaller grain size. Because the orientations of a grain and its twins are different, even though related, they reflect light differently when heavily etched (Figure 2.29) and sometimes when illuminated with polarized light.

From an energetic viewpoint, the process of mechanical twinning is even more difficult to rationalize than the process of slip is. The geometrical explanation requires a fixed amount of shear on each successive twinning plane, and would require very high stresses to break the necessary interatomic bonds. It is recognized that the process is made much more feasible by the introduction of line or screw dislocations and several rather incomplete explanations have been offered on this basis.[36]

## FRACTURE

Fracture of any metallic material always is preceded by some plastic deformation even though, in some instances, evidence of this plastic deformation may be difficult to detect.[37] Most of the important engineering metallic materials are primary solid solutions, or mechanical mixtures in which primary solid solutions predominate, so they undergo considerable plastic deformation before they fracture. It appears likely that fracture in metal is initiated by deformation itself. One method of initiating a crack is the sudden stopping of a slip band at a corner where three grains meet. At such corners the stress system is largely hydrostatic and cannot be relieved by plastic flow. Local cracks apparently can be nucleated also as the result of stress concentrations resulting from the pile-up of dislocations at an obstruction. In addition, there are some metallic materials which are truly brittle and hence fracture after undergoing only elastic deformation, but they are special cases.

[36] See Refs. 7 and 10 at the end of this chapter.
[37] See N. J. Petch in *Progress in Modern Physics,* **5** (New York: Interscience Publishers, 1954), 1–52; also Clarence Zener in Ref. 12 at the end of this chapter.

Fundamentally, there are only three ways in which engineering materials fracture: (1) by shear, (2) by cleavage, or (3) by intergranular separation. However, some confusion has arisen because of the fact that some of these materials are notch sensitive—that is, they have much less ductility when fracture starts under the restraints imposed by a notch or other similar stress concentrator than they have in the unnotched condition. The notches may be internal, built-in in a sense, instead of external and readily apparent, so their existence and effects often may be overlooked.

## SHEAR FRACTURE

Because both of the principal modes of plastic deformation—slip and twinning—are basically shear processes, it is inevitable that shear-type fractures are the predominant types.[38] Dislocations and other types of lattice defects normally only serve to decrease the stress at which the shear occurs, not to change the manner of fracture. However, in solid materials each composition and condition has a limited capacity for plastic deformation, so dislocations and other lattice defects may exert an important effect on the amount of plastic deformation that can occur. The usual ductile fracture propagates at a relatively slow rate—for example, about 20 feet per second in an impact test.

There are two types of shear fractures: high-ductility and low-ductility. High-ductility fractures are characterized by a relatively localized flow which in some instance may become unstable. Low values of the strain-hardening coefficient encourage instability and presumably high-ductility fractures. Low-ductility fractures, sometimes called fibrous, develop relatively slowly and are particularly apt to occur in the presence of hydrostatic tensions, as in the necked region of a tensile specimen. Smaller grain sizes also lead to this type of fracture. The tensile fracture stress is inversely proportional to the square root of the grain size.

Pure face-centered cubic metals, particularly in the form of single crystals, have a minimum of restraints because of the absence of grain boundaries. These often elongate so much that fracture occurs as a line because too little metal is left in the cross section to support any load.[39] However, if impurities are present, either in solid solution or mixed mechanically in the solid metal structure, the ability to deform before fracture decreases and the fracture of a single crystal becomes more like that of a polycrystalline material.

[38] Tensile fractures of ductile metals are discussed by H. C. Rogers, *Trans. A.I.M.E.*, **218** (1960), 498–506.

[39] Some prefer to call this rupture rather than fracture.

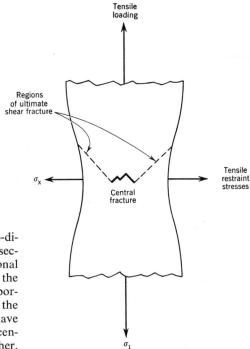

**Figure 2.32** Schematic two-dimensional projection of cross section of necked zone in conventional tensile test specimen just before the specimen breaks. The central portion already has fractured and the edge regions, which previously have acted as restraints to keep the central portion from reducing further, are about to fracture in shear.

Some hexagonal metal single crystals, such as zinc crystals of proper orientation for example, also show very high ductilities for many orientations, although they will fracture in a brittle manner if the basal plane is parallel to or perpendicular to the tensile stress. However, single crystals of other hexagonal metals, either because of impurities or because the orientation is unfavorable, may undergo only limited deformation before fracturing parallel to the slip planes. One of the key factors is the ease with which these crystals can twin mechanically to reorient their slip planes more favorably with reference to the applied stress.[40]

A ductile cup-and-cone fracture of the type shown at the right in Figure 2.11 usually results whenever the material can resist the tendency to neck sufficiently to support transverse or radial tensile stresses. Such resistance can result from the strengthening effects of certain impurities or alloying elements, of previous deformation, or of increased diameter of the test specimen. The presence of these transverse tensile stresses subjects the center of the bar to a complex tensile stress as indicated schematically in Figure 2.32. This complex tension subjects the specimen to a smaller shear stress, for example $(\sigma_1 - \sigma_x)/2$, instead of the shear stress produced by

[40] Ref. 9 at the end of this chapter discusses this.

the axial tension, $\sigma_1$. At the same time the ability of the specimen to deform also is decreased because the metal is less able to contract laterally as it is elongated axially. Thus, fracture takes place first at the center of the necked region. Usually this initial fracture is of the low-ductility shear type and it can propagate only by an increase in strain. Therefore, as the strain increases the crack opens up gradually, roughly at right angles to the tensile force as indicated in Figure 2.32. Ultimately, the solid metal remaining around the periphery of the specimen becomes too thin to support the transverse stress. This periphery metal then fails in shear, giving the typical cup-and-cone fracture. Although this usually is described as a ductile fracture it really is a combination of a low-ductility shear failure in the central region and a shear failure near the periphery, between the edges of the internal crack and a circle of high stress concentration in the neck of the specimen. In some instances, by the time the central crack propagates enough to free the peripheral metal from its restraints, the load may be so great, or the ability to deform plastically in the peripheral metal may be so small, that it fails immediately without stretching at all. Such a fracture may show little or no transverse contraction and generally would be classed as a brittle fracture even though it is of the low-ductility shear type. If the test specimen is made of material whose ability to deform further already has been exhausted somewhat by prior work-hardening, or which inherently has a low ability to deform because of its composition or structure, the final fracture of the peripheral material might be started by small surface defects in the material which cause it to tear. The appearance of such fractures may be like that of the left-hand specimen in Figure 2.11.

In general, engineering materials with a face-centered cubic structure deform plastically quite readily. However, alloying either may decrease the capacity to deform plastically or, what may be the same thing, may increase the rate of work-hardening to the point where fracture becomes of the low-ductility type. The specific base metal, and the alloying element added, both are important in this respect, and commercial alloys usually are formulated to secure as much ductility as possible consistent with the strengths required.

Engineering materials with a close-packed hexagonal structure may have either high ductility or relatively low ductility depending on whether or not the crystals are oriented favorably for slip initially. If they are not oriented favorably, ductility depends upon whether the twinning mechanism is able to operate to provide new orientations favorable for deformation by slip. In many hexagonal materials, each crystal has only one parallel family of slip planes, the basal planes. If these planes are not oriented favorably for slip with reference to the applied stress, and cannot be reoriented favorably by mechanical twinning, fracture occurs readily.

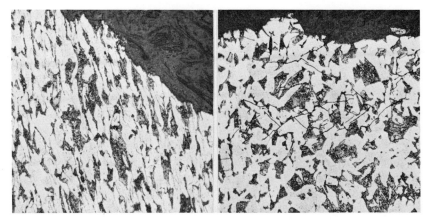

**Figure 2.33**  Metallographic cross sections typical of (*left*) ductile and (*right*) cleavage-type brittle fractures in low-carbon steel. Both structures etched with nital (×100).

In the engineering body-centered cubic metals, plastic deformation occurs readily by shear, but yielding may not be homogeneous. These metals frequently display an upper and lower yield point. The stress first builds up elastically to a relatively high value before certain regions yield preferentially and deform a considerable amount, forming what are known as Lueder's lines. These are discussed in more detail in a later chapter. Fractures are of either the low-ductility or the moderately high-ductility type, Figure 2.33 (*left*), depending on the purity, on the general characteristics of the material, and on the temperature of testing. If the temperature is high enough, and for many of these materials even subzero temperatures are sufficiently high, these metals generally fail in shear. If it is too low, they fail by an entirely different mechanism called cleavage, usually preceded by very little plastic deformation, Figure 2.33 (*right*), or by intercrystalline fracture.

## CLEAVAGE FRACTURE

Cleavage fractures, as close to brittle failures as occur in most engineering metallic materials,[41] follow crystallographic planes which may be the same as or may differ from those operating during slip. In the body-centered cubic materials, the cube planes, which parallel the faces of the unit cube

[41] See A. H. Cottrell, *Trans. A.I.M.E.*, **212** (1958), 192–203; see also D. C. Drucker, *Mechanisms of Brittle Fracture* (Washington, D. C.: National Academy of Sciences, 1954).

in the space lattice, are the usual cleavage planes. In close-packed hexagonal materials, the basal planes, which usually are the slip planes as well,
often are the cleavage planes, although there may be others. Cleavage has
not been observed in face-centered cubic materials, or in one body-centered
cubic metal, tantalum.

In body-centered cubic metals, alternative deformation mechanisms exist
and the deformation occurs by the mechanism which takes the least energy
(not necessarily the least stress).

Apparently, any changes in the material which increase its yield strength
or decrease its ability to deform plastically, such as lowering the temperature, previous cold-work, or the presence of very finely dispersed
regions which differ in some way from the matrix, increase the likelihood
of cleavage failure, provided that the metal can fracture in this manner.

With high stress, cleavage is highly localized. It is the only mode of
failure at very high velocities, although it may change to shear as the
velocity decreases. In Izod impact test failures of steels, where cleavage
is the main mechanism, the initial crack is formed by shear and the first
crack is behind, not at, the notch.

The presence of a notch, or a marked increase in the rate of straining,
particularly in ferrous metals which have a high velocity dependence of
the yield stress-strain curve, can impose sufficient restraints on the deformation to cause multiaxial loading. Likewise, superimposing a hydrostatic tension restricts the ability of the material to deform plastically and,
hence, encourages cleavage failure. Strangely enough there seems to be
no pronounced size effects in unnotched specimens, although notched
specimens have shown large size effects.[42] Inhomogeneous specimens, for
example those containing welds, also sometimes show marked size effects.

Much of the rationalization of brittle cleavage fractures in metals has
been based on the Griffith [43] theory, a two-dimensional case developed
originally to explain brittle fracture in truly brittle materials like glass.[44]
The basic principle of this theory is that a crack propagates when, and only
when, the free energy of the system is being continually lowered by this
propagation. Accordingly, the crack propagates only when the strain energy of the system, which decreases as the crack spreads, is more than
enough to take care of the increase in the surface energy of the growing
crack. The crack can grow, therefore, only when it is larger than a certain

[42] See the article by E. R. Parker in Ref. 12 at the end of this chapter.

[43] A. A. Griffith, *Phys. Trans., Roy. Soc.,* **A221** (London: 1920), 163; see also
*Proc. First Int. Cong. for Appl. Mech.* (Delft: 1924), 55. This is summarized well
by O. L. Anderson in Ref. 13 at the end of this chapter.

[44] Another explanation, somewhat similar except that a shear crack is taken as
the initiation point rather than the Griffith crack, has been proposed by C. Crussard,
R. Borione, J. Plateau, Y. Morillon, and F. Maratray, *Journ. Iron and Steel Inst.,*
**183** (London: 1956), 146–77.

critical size. The relationship between crack size and the tensile strength, $\sigma$, of a brittle body with a Young's modulus, $E$, is

$$\sigma = \sqrt{\frac{2\alpha E}{\pi c}}$$

if the plate is thin compared with the length of the crack, $c$, and

$$\sigma = \sqrt{\frac{2\alpha E}{(1 - \nu^2)\pi c}}$$

if the plate is thick compared with the length of the crack. In these equations, $\alpha$ is the specific surface energy of the crack and $\nu$ is Poisson's ratio.

In general, the Griffith theory can be applied only if no plastic deformation occurs during the fracture process. Hence, in metals, where some plastic deformation always precedes fracture, the fundamental problem of crack initiation is: how can cracks arise, in the interior, of sufficient size that their propagation will be attended by a continuous decrease in free energy? Orowan [45] has assumed that, for metals, the tensile strength should be given by

$$\sigma = \sqrt{\frac{2(\alpha + \rho)E}{\pi c}}$$

where $\rho$ is the plastic surface work per unit of area of crack surface. Because $\rho$ is about three orders of magnitude larger than $\alpha$ this equation can be simplified to

$$\sigma = \sqrt{\frac{2\rho E}{\pi c}}$$

This fracture stress is that required to start the crack under static loading, not to accelerate it. It is equivalent, therefore, to a stress concentration condition which is satisfied if the elastic energy released during the crack propagation is just sufficient to supply the work required to enlarge the walls of the crack. The initial crack cannot start propagating in a typical brittle manner under static load because it has no velocity and, without velocity to raise the yield strength, the metal yields before the stress can build up to the magnitude of the fracture strength. Hence, local plastic deformation takes place first until the ensuing plastic constraint develops a triaxiality of tension high enough to change the initial fibrous crack into

[45] See D. K. Feldbeck and E. Orowan, *Welding Res. Suppl.*, **XX** (1955), 570s–75s.

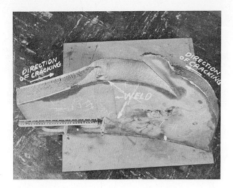

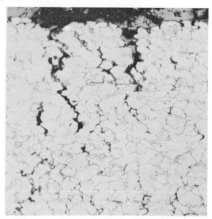

**Figure 2.34** (*left*) Cleavage fracture in thick steel plate showing shear lip at edges, chevron markings pointing back toward origin of fracture and the shift to shear fracture, with ultimate stopping, as velocity decreases.

**Figure 2.35** (*right*) Typical intergranular fractures produced by testing a steel under constant stress in tension at 1000 F (540 C) until failure occurred. Etched with nital (×150).

a brittle one. Once the brittle crack is started, it accelerates rapidly until the velocity effect takes over, making further plastic deformation unnecessary to raise the maximum tensile stress to the level of the brittle fracture stress. The high velocity of a cleavage crack in steel, of the order of magnitude of the transverse velocity of sound in steel—namely, several thousand feet per second—requires that the energy fed into it from the surface work, $\rho$, be obtained from the elastic energy released during propagation, or from a very high velocity of loading.

At a free surface no triaxiality can exist. Hence, some shear fracture must occur if the stress raising effect of velocity is insufficient. This produces a shear lip near the free surface (Figure 2.34), essentially the same phenomenon that causes a cup-and-cone fracture in a necked tensile specimen. The width of this shear lip gives some measure of how much the velocity effect falls short of being able to produce brittle fracture. Triaxiality alone cannot produce really brittle fracture, except at low temperatures where only a relatively small amount of plastic constraint is necessary, because there must be appreciable plastic deformation before it can lead to cleavage.

## INTERGRANULAR FRACTURE

Intergranular fracture (Figure 2.35) results whenever these boundaries are weaker or otherwise more susceptible to fracture than the material within the grains.[46] Sometimes this weakness arises from the formation of

[46] H. C. Chang and N. J. Grant, *Trans. A.I.M.E.,* **206** (1956), 544–51, have proposed a mechanism for this type of fracture.

foreign particles at the grain boundaries. Materials with such intergranular particles often are notch-sensitive also. Under these circumstances, even face-centered cubic engineering materials have been known to fracture by high-ductility shear under some conditions and by low-ductility inter-granular fracture under others.

## DUCTILE-BRITTLE FRACTURE TRANSITIONS

In between the conditions which produce high-ductility or low-ductility shear fractures and those which produce brittle fractures of either the transgranular cleavage or the intergranular types there usually is found a region of mixed fractures. This region is called the ductile-brittle transition range (Figure 2.36). Ordinarily, these brittle transition ranges are determined as a function of temperature, largely because knowledge about any tendencies of a given material to behave in a ductile or a brittle manner depending on the temperature may be of considerable practical importance. However, it must be emphasized that these transition temperatures depend on the test conditions and may vary considerably depending on the specific criteria or test procedure used. Furthermore, the results secured with relatively small test specimens do not necessarily correlate

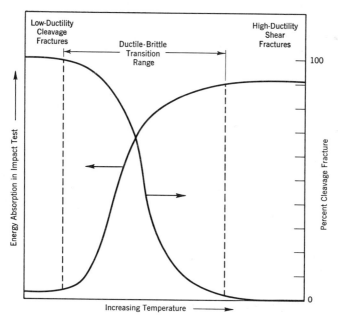

**Figure 2.36** Schematic ductile-brittle transition curve typical of notched-bar impact test on carbon steel.

with the results which can be expected for larger specimens or for full-size engineering structures.

## IMPACT TESTS

Because of this tendency of some materials to fail in a ductile or a brittle manner depending on the rate of loading, impact tests are used both to determine resistance to impact loading and to determine notch sensitivity. Because notch sensitivity also is a function of temperature, these tests usually are run over a range of temperatures in order to determine the brittle transition temperature (really temperature range) of the material.

As a general rule, impact testing of full-size specimens is impractical and such tests must be confined to relatively small specimens. The actual value of these tests depends on how well correlations can be established with actual service results. With many fairly tough materials the use of the notch is necessary to produce a fracture. The use of a notch likewise decreases the value of the results so far as design work is concerned because in engineering design it invariably is desired to get as far away from notch effects as possible. However, in structures fabricated by welding, even the best welded joints probably contain numerous defects which, in effect, act like notches in service but which cannot be avoided in fabrication. Consequently, evaluating the notch sensitivity of structural material to be used in a welded structure may be quite desirable.

## IMPACT STRENGTH

The impact test assumes that the resistance of a material to shock loading depends on its ability to equalize concentrated stresses safely and rapidly. Usually, such data can be measured and recorded only in terms of the energy absorbed in causing fracture, simply because the intensity and distribution of the stress during the test are too complex to be analyzed satisfactorily. On this basis, a brittle material would, as a rule, tend to absorb appreciably less energy than a tough one. However, if there is also a distinct change in mode of fracture, as between shear and cleavage for example, useful information about the characteristics of the material can be determined by visual estimates of the two components of the fractured surface.

Two methods of impact testing, the Charpy or simple beam, and the Izod or cantilever beam, are used most widely. No complete standardiza-

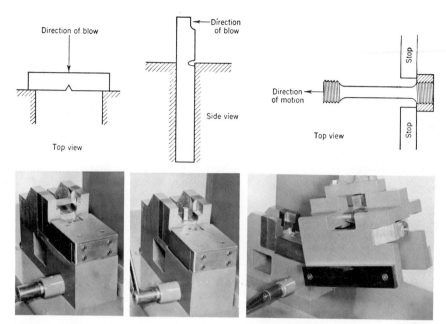

**Figure 2.37** Principle of the (*left*) Charpy, (*center*) Izod, and (*right*) tensile impact tests. [Photographs courtesy Tinius Olsen Testing Machine Company.]

tion has been made yet but the trend in recent years has been toward a V-notch Charpy test. The differences between the two are indicated in Figure 2.37. In both tests, a single blow is struck by a falling pendulum. Because this pendulum has a definite weight, is released from a fixed height, and swings downward in a vertical plane, its energy, when it strikes the specimen at a definite position as it passes through the lowest point in its travel, is quite reproducible. The energy remaining in the pendulum after it strikes and breaks the specimen is used in carrying the pendulum up a certain distance in its swing. Consequently, by measuring the difference in the angle of rise when the pendulum swings free and when it has broken a specimen, the energy absorbed in breaking the specimen may be determined.

The Charpy test employs a specimen which is a simple horizontal beam supported at the ends. The specimen originally was notched in a characteristic keyhole shaped manner to concentrate the stress; today a V-notch is used more often for simplicity. In the Izod test, on the other hand, the specimen is clamped on one end in a vertical position, and acts as a cantilever beam. Izod specimens usually are V-notched.

Most modern Charpy and Izod machines, such as the one shown in Figure 2.38, also are equipped for tensile impact testing (Figure 2.37).

**Figure 2.38** A modern impact testing machine readily adaptable for Charpy, Izod, or tensile impact testing. The hammer is set for an Izod test. [Courtesy Tinius Olsen Testing Machine Company.]

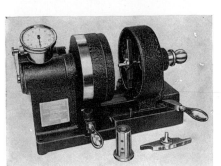

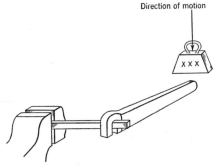

Direction of motion

x x x

The Principle of Torsion Impact

**Figure 2.39** A Carpenter (Luerssen-Greene) torsion impact tester (*left*) for use with hard steels. [Courtesy of Wiedemann-Baldwin Testing Machine Division, Wiedemann Machine Company.] (*right*) Schematic sketch illustrating the basic principle of torsion impact. [From F. R. Palmer, *Tool Steel Simplified,* courtesy The Carpenter Steel Company.]

In tensile impact, a pure tensile loading is applied suddenly by stopping one end of the specimen at the bottom of the pendulum.

The Carpenter or Luerssen-Greene torsion impact tester [47] (Figure 2.39) which was developed primarily for testing hard steels and brittle materials such as tool alloys, is another type of impact test. In the torsion impact test, the specimen is clamped at one end and the other is engaged with a head, rotating at a definite speed, which twists it until it breaks. The change of speed of the rotating head is used to compute the energy ab-

[47] G. V. Luerssen and O. V. Greene, *Proc. A.S.T.M.,* **33,** II (1933), 315–33.

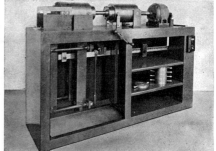

**Figure 2.40** Some typical fatigue-testing machines. (*top left*) R. R. Moore rotating beam machine. (*top right*) Large-size R. R. Moore fatigue machine. (*bottom right*) Wiedemann-Baldwin universal fatigue machine for tension-compression, torsion, and flexure. [Courtesy Wiedemann-Baldwin Testing Machine Division, Wiedemann Machine Company.]

sorbed. In the usual impact tests on brittle materials, with either notched or unnotched specimens, results tend to be inaccurate and misleading. Torsion impact, by loading the entire cross section at the same time, gives more significant data.

### FATIGUE STRENGTH

Parts subjected to a large number of stress reversals sometimes fracture at stresses within the elastic range which otherwise would produce no permanent deformation. This type of failure, known as fatigue,[48] has become increasingly important since the development of high-speed rotating and reciprocating equipment and the emphasis, in design, on high strength-weight ratios.

Three types of commonly used fatigue-testing machines are illustrated in Figure 2.40. In the R. R. Moore machine, a common type, a rotating specimen is bent elastically, thereby imposing alternate tensile and com-

[48] See *Proceedings of the International Conference on Fatigue of Metals* (London: The Institution of Mechanical Engineers, 1956); also Refs. 21, 22, and 23 at the end of this chapter.

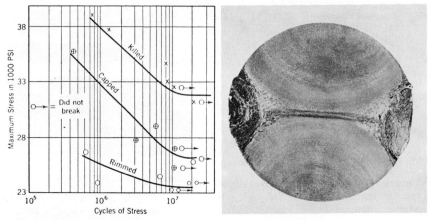

**Figure 2.41** (*above left*) Stress-cycle diagram for killed, capped, and rimmed steels. [Courtesy *Materials in Design Engineering*.]

**Figure 2.42** (*above right*) A typical fatigue fracture of a steel part. [Photograph courtesy Bethlehem Steel Company.]

pressive stresses on the surface fibers. Many fatigue tests also are run under simulated service conditions.

The number of cycles to cause failure varies with the applied stress; the higher the stress, the fewer the cycles to fracture. As the stress is decreased, the number of cycles to fracture increases, as illustrated in the semilogarithmic plot of Figure 2.41 for steels made by three different techniques.[49] For some metals, a fatigue limit ultimately is reached below which there is a very low probability that fracture will occur within the limits of a standard test.[50] Other metals do not appear to exhibit such a leveling off and, instead, fracture at a lower and lower stress as the length of the test is extended.

A typical fatigue fracture (Figure 2.42) has an appearance different from that of a static shear failure. The fracture starts at a point of high stress concentration and propagates slowly until it weakens the part so much that it can fail by simple shear. Even in ductile metals the fracture frequently has a brittle appearance because there is no significant plastic deformation of the part as a whole. The statement frequently is heard that

[49] These involve making additions, such as silicon and aluminum, to the bath of molten steel, in a steelmaking process, in order to control gas evolution during ingot solidification. Killed steels have little if any gases, capped steels are solidified in such a way that gases given off build up a back pressure in a closed mold, and rimmed steels solidify with a selective type of gas evolution which gives a very clean surface and subsurface porosity.

[50] Customary standard test periods are of the order of 500,000 cycles for hard steel; 5,000,000 for soft steel; 10,000,000 for cast steel and cast iron; and from 1,000,000 to 50,000,000 for the nonferrous metals depending upon the metal.

the metal failed because it crystallized under the action of the repeated stress and thus became embrittled. This statement is erroneous because all solid metals are crystalline and no change in their inherent crystallinity occurs because of the action of the repeated stress. This apparent difference in behavior under repeated loading results from the initial nature of fatigue damage and from the progressive manner in which the damage accumulates under each repetition of loading.

Any imperfection, such as a notch, inclusion, or other defect, may act as a stress raiser to initiate a fatigue crack. Likewise, discontinuities introduced by the design should be kept to a minimum, especially if they involve abrupt changes in section or in direction. Usually, defects in the surface are the most significant ones because the stresses are highest at the surface, but internal defects also can be important if the general stress level is high enough. The better the surface finish, the greater the precautions which must be taken to prevent defects. For example, perspiration from handling polished parts without gloves may cause minute corrosion pits on the surface; these may decrease the fatigue strength by 10 to 15%. When corrosion and fatigue occur simultaneously, called corrosion fatigue, reductions in the fatigue limit as high as 65% have been noted because both the corrosion and the fatigue damage are accelerated.

The initial crack is the result of a combination of factors. First, local stress can reach very high values in the vicinity of defects. Second, the design stress is only a nominal or average stress so the actual stress acting to produce plastic deformation in individual crystals may be much higher than the average because of their favorable orientation. Furthermore, under static loads, slow plastic deformation of the highly stressed region would tend to redistribute the stress over a larger volume and thus to eliminate concentrations. Under rapid cycle conditions there may not be time for this readjustment to occur. Therefore, the plastic deformation tends to concentrate in specific structural discontinuities such as the initial deformation bands, for example, until minute cracks appear. Initially, these cracks are so small that they can be detected only by such devices as the electron microscope but, as the damage progresses, they grow to micro- and macroscopic sizes.

The metal as a whole usually is not deformed at all, and only those regions in which stress concentrations of sufficient magnitude exist undergo damage. In a sense, therefore, the development of fatigue damage is a statistical process determined by the chance distribution of the weaker crystals in the highly stressed zone.

Fatigue strength is affected by factors such as the size of the part, the rate of cycling, the temperature, the presence of residual stresses, the strength of the material, and the metallurgical structure. The first three of these will have different effects depending on the particular metal or alloy. However, because cracks do not initiate except under a tensile stress, the presence of residual compressive stresses in the surface delays crack initiation, if it does not prevent it entirely, depending on the service conditions. Cold-working, tumbling, or shot peening [51] produces plastic deformation in the surface layers and therefore leaves the surface in compression. A residual tensile stress in the surface layers has the opposite effect. Other means, such as surface hardening by heat-treatment [52] also can be used to increase the tensile strength of the surface layers and thus raise fatigue strength. Likewise, surface treatments that weaken the surface layers decrease fatigue strength. In utilizing these surface effects, however, complications of various types may arise so it is well to service test such parts thoroughly before depending upon them.

## QUESTIONS

1. Why does severe work-hardening tend to make a metal behave like a brittle material? Why is the Meyer hardness of lesser industrial importance than some of the other hardness methods? Why are Brinell hardnesses used so frequently in industry?

2. Solid electrical conductors of aluminum and of copper have tensile strengths of 27,000 psi and 57,000 psi respectively. What are their strengths for equal volumes? for equal weights? (The specific gravity of aluminum is 2.70 and of copper is 8.94.)

3. Draw a sample stress-strain curve on graph paper. On it, can you differentiate between proportional limit, yield strength for 0.2% elongation, yield strength for 0.02% elongation, yield point, and elastic limit?

4. What are the values of the shear modulus, $G$, and the bulk modulus, $K$, for iron if the value of the elastic modulus, $E$, is $28.5 \times 10^6$ psi and that of Poisson's ratio is 0.25?

5. On one or more three-dimensional sketches of a face-centered cubic lattice can you indicate all the octahedral (body diagonal) slip planes and show mathematically that these planes are closer together than the cube planes?

6. If the lattice parameter for body-centered cubic iron is 2.876 A.U., compute, for the case of slip on dodecahedral (face diagonal) planes, the approximate value of the critical elastic sheer stress, $\sigma_c$, at which the lattice of a single crystal should become unstable and slip should initiate. Should this value change with different directions of application of the shear force?

7. Give some reasons why the effect of work-hardening would be expected to be different in fine-grain than in coarse-grain materials. Should it be greater or smaller? If the metals were not cubic would any differences be expected?

---

[51] Impinging round metallic shot on the surface of the part, under relatively high velocity. See J. O. Almen, *Product Engineering*, **21** (1950), 117–40.

[52] See Chapter 8.

8. Can you show by simple three-dimensional sketches why there are more slip planes in a face-centered cubic structure than in the nearly equivalent close-packed hexagonal structure of equal axial ratio $(c/a)$?

9. On the basis of dislocation theory, why might solid solutions be expected to work-harden more rapidly than pure metals? What is meant by an edge dislocation being a sink for interstitial atoms? What does the term "atmosphere of interstitial atoms around a dislocation" mean?

10. What is your picture of the movement of atoms in the original end-anchored line dislocation as a Frank-Read source develops?

11. Why do dislocations tend to pile up at discontinuities in the structure? What kind of discontinuities might be particularly effective in this way? Why is dislocation climb probably much more important in the deformation of high-melting metals at elevated temperatures—for example, creep—than in the deformation of the same metals at room temperature?

12. Why is it so difficult to apply to polycrystalline materials basic information on the deformation process found out by studying single crystals? Can twinning in metal crystals be produced, in theory at least, by rotation on the composition plane as well as by definite slip on planes parallel to it? If such rotation worked, how could it compare with slip as a possible mechanical twinning mechanism?

13. How does cleavage fracture differ from shear fracture? Why does it occur only in certain types of metals? Why are shear fractures the predominant types? What determines whether a shear fracture shows high ductility or low ductility?

14. A plot of Charpy impact energy absorption versus test temperature shows a sudden drop to low energies at lower temperatures over a relatively small range of temperature. Does the metal undergo a ductile-brittle transition? Is the low-energy fracture necessarily of a cleavage type? Why do you believe this? Carbon steel is known to fail by cleavage under certain conditions. A 15 ft-lb minimum energy absorption (Charpy) at the lowest expected temperature of use generally is considered to be safe. A certain high-strength aluminum alloy had an energy absorption (Charpy) of only 10 ft-lb. Is the likelihood of cleavage failure of this material greater or less than that of the steel? Why?

15. In a fatigue failure, which would be the more time-consuming stage: the formation of the initial fracture or its propagation? Why are standard test periods different for different metals, from this viewpoint? Why is it commonly said that the metal has crystallized when it fails by fatigue? Is this correct?

## FOR FURTHER STUDY

1. *Structure of Metals* by C. S. Barrett. New York: McGraw-Hill, 1952.
2. *The Structure of Metals.* New York: Interscience Publishers, 1959.

3. *Elements of X-ray Diffraction* by B. D. Cullity. Reading, Mass.: Addison-Wesley Publishing Co., 1956.

4. *X-ray Diffraction Procedures* by H. P. Klug and L. E. Alexander. New York: John Wiley & Sons, 1954.

5. *The Role of Dislocations in Plastic Deformations* by John C. Fisher. Philadelphia: American Society for Testing Materials, 1959.

6. *Dislocations and Mechanical Properties of Crystals.* New York: John Wiley & Sons, 1957.

7. *Dislocations and Plastic Flow in Crystals* by A. H. Cottrell. Oxford: The Clarendon Press, 1953.

8. *Cold Working of Metals.* Cleveland: American Society for Metals, 1949.

9. *Plasticity of Crystals with Special Reference to Metals* by E. Schmid and W. Boas. London: F. A. Hughes & Company, 1950.

10. *Dislocations in Crystals* by W. T. Read, Jr. New York: McGraw-Hill, 1953.

11. *Dislocations in Metals.* New York: American Institute of Mining and Metallurgical Engineers, 1954.

12. *Fracturing of Metals.* Cleveland: American Society for Metals, 1948.

13. *Fracture.* New York: John Wiley & Sons, 1959.

14. *The Problem of Fracture.* New York: American Welding Society, 1946.

15. *Behavior of Metals at Low Temperatures.* Cleveland: American Society for Metals, 1953.

16. *Brittle Behavior of Engineering Structures* by E. R. Parker. New York: John Wiley & Sons, 1957.

17. *Fundamentals of the Working of Metals* by G. Sachs. New York: Pergamon Press, 1954.

18. *Metals Handbook,* 7th ed. (1948) and *Supplements,* and 8th ed., Vol. I (1961). Metals Park, Ohio: American Society for Metals.

19. *Elasticity and Anelasticity of Metals* by Clarence Zener. Chicago: University of Chicago Press, 1948.

20. *Imperfections in Crystals* by H. G. VanBueren. Amsterdam: North-Holland Publishing Co., 1960.

21. *Fatigue of Metals and Structures* by H. J. Grover, S. A. Gordon, and L. R. Jackson. Washington, D. C.: Bureau of Naval Weapons, Department of the Navy, 1960.

22. *Metal Fatigue,* G. Sines and J. L. Waisman (eds.). New York: McGraw-Hill, 1959.

23. *Fatigue of Metals* by R. Cazaud. New York: Philosophical Library, 1953.

24. *The Effect of Temperature and Alloying Additions on the Deformation of Metal Crystals* by R. W. K. Honeycombe. New York: Pergamon Press, 1961.

# 3 *Softening by Heat*

## ANNEALING BY HEATING AFTER COLD WORKING

WHEN SEVERAL SAMPLES ARE CUT FROM A COLD-worked material, and each is exposed to a different elevated temperature and then is cooled to room temperature, hardness tests yield data similar to those plotted in Figure 3.1.[1] For simplicity, the holding time at temperature is kept constant although comparable results can be secured with many metals and alloys by increasing the holding time at a lower temperature. Heating below a certain temperature range produces essentially no change in properties. The strength and hardness both remain high, the ductility low, and stresses produced by the deformation persist within the metal. As the exposure temperature increases, however, the greater atomic mobility resulting from this larger intensity of energy results in a series of structural changes which are known, successively, as: recovery, polygonization,[2] primary strain recrystallization, grain growth, and secondary recrystallization. This type of heat treatment, broadly, is known as annealing.

[1] See, for example, R. F. Mehl in Ref. 1 (7th ed., pp. 259–63) at the end of this chapter; see also J. E. Burke and D. Turnbull in *Progress in Metal Physics,* **3** (New York: Interscience Publishers, 1952), 220–92.

[2] Polygonization may be a phenomenon of only limited occurrence.

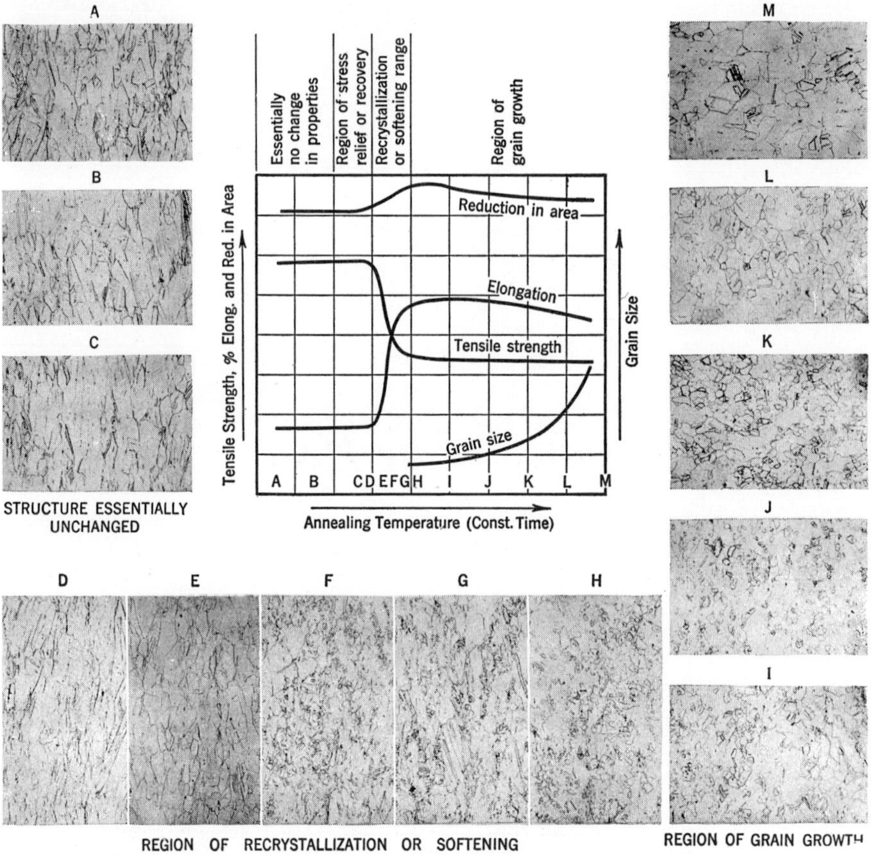
A
B
C
STRUCTURE ESSENTIALLY UNCHANGED
Essentially no change in properties
Region of stress relief or recovery
Recrystallization or softening range
Region of grain growth
Reduction in area
Elongation
Tensile strength
Grain size
Tensile Strength, % Elong. and Red. in Area
Grain Size
A B CDEFGH I J K L M
Annealing Temperature (Const. Time)
M
L
K
J
I
D
E
F
G
H
REGION OF RECRYSTALLIZATION OR SOFTENING
REGION OF GRAIN GROWTH

| Metal | Temperature F | Temperature C |
|---|---|---|
| *Lead* | Below room temperature | |
| *Tin* | Below room temperature | |
| Cadmium | About room temperature | |
| *Zinc* | About room temperature | |
| *Aluminum* | 300 | 150 |
| *Magnesium* | 300 | 150 |
| *Copper* | 390 | 200 |
| Gold | 390 | 200 |
| Silver | 390 | 200 |
| *Iron* | 840 | 450 |
| Platinum | 840 | 450 |
| *Nickel* | 1110 | 600 |
| Molybdenum | 1650 | 900 |
| Tantalum | 1830 | 1000 |
| Tungsten | 2190 | 1200 |

APPROXIMATE LOWEST RECRYSTALLIZATION TEMPERATURES OF VARIOUS METALS

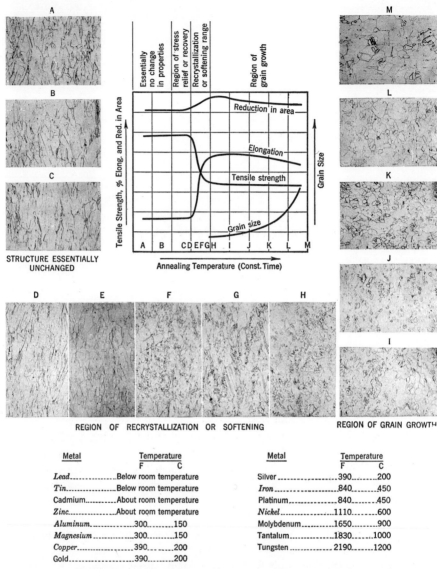

**Figure 3.1** Typical changes in microstructure and properties of a cold-worked metal resulting from heating to elevated temperatures for a constant time. [Photomicrographs courtesy R. H. Harrington. Table after Z. Jeffries and R. S. Archer, *Science of Metals*. New York: McGraw-Hill, 1924.]

## STRESS-RELIEF OR RECOVERY

At the lowest temperatures of the annealing range, called the region of stress-relief or recovery, the internal stresses are decreased markedly. They also become distributed more uniformly, and thus are less significant.

Stress-relief heat treatments generally are believed to be advantageous from an engineering viewpoint because they increase the effective factor of safety. Any engineering structure is designed to withstand a certain type and magnitude of stress. If, because of the methods of fabrication, treatment, or construction, internal stresses of appreciable magnitude remain in the structure, its effectiveness may be changed considerably, being either reduced or increased from that for which it was designed originally. This is especially significant when the internal stresses are not distributed uniformly and, therefore, are more likely to lead to overloading in one particular portion of the structure. It is this possible concentration of stresses that may become dangerous rather than the actual presence of the internal stresses, because any engineering structure in use contains some of the latter even though they may not attain a magnitude that is harmful.[3]

Artificially produced internal stresses, in fact, may be of considerable value if they can be distributed uniformly and can be controlled properly, both in magnitude and in direction—that is, made to be either tensile or compressive as desired. In the production of certain structures, such as large guns, car wheels, and the like, outer layers have been shrunk on, thus producing a uniformly distributed compressive stress in the inner layers. This process, known as autofrettage, also can be applied by expanding an inner section, by hydraulic means, against an outer one.[4] Any bursting force acting from the inside of this inner layer then must overcome not only the compressive force superimposed by the outer shrinkage or the inner expansion, but also the yield strength and ultimate strength of the material itself before failure can occur. Usually this advantageous use of internal stresses only can be employed if very symmetrical structures are involved. It was pointed out in Chapter 2, also, that a markedly greater fatigue strength invariably results when the residual stress in the most highly stressed portions is compressive in nature and that a residual tensile stress in these regions tends to have a weakening effect.

During recovery there is substantially no change in the structure that can be detected either microscopically or by X-rays. X-ray diffraction patterns do tend to become sharper, however, because of the decrease in elastic distortion of the lattice. In particular, during recovery there is no migration of grain boundaries which were there prior to the deformation.

At recovery temperatures only limited atomic displacements can take place. However, dislocations can diffuse along the slip planes, so dislocations of opposite sign probably destroy each other. This is the major factor in relieving internal stresses and also may result in small increases in mechanical properties. This destruction of dislocations leads to a state

[3] For a discussion of residual stresses, see G. Sachs and K. R. Van Horn, *Practical Metallurgy* (Cleveland: American Society for Metals, 1946), Chap. VI; see also K. R. Van Horn, *Trans. A.I.M.E.,* **197** (1953), 405–22.

[4] See, for example, N. E. Woldman, *Trans. A.S.M.,* **25** (1937), 206–28.

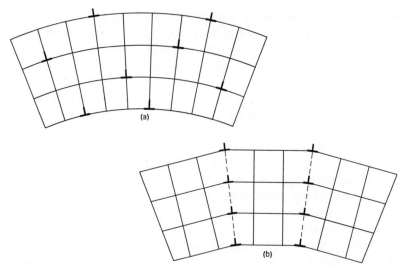

**Figure 3.2** Two-dimensional representation of some possible distributions of dislocations of the same sign on slip planes. **a.** Randomly located, causing bent planes. **b.** Aligned by annealing, at boundaries of zones which are undistorted but differ slightly in orientation. [After R. W. Cahn and A. H. Cottrell.]

of lower energy and consequently is the real reason why there is a stage of recovery. Recovery has no incubation period, it starts as soon as a suitable temperature is reached. The rate of recovery decreases as the process continues because it then takes longer for the smaller number of dislocations of opposite sign to get together to destroy each other.

## POLYGONIZATION

In any process of deformation it would be very unusual if the deformation were completely homogeneous. Consequently, there always is some bending and an excess of dislocations of one sign over those of the other sign. This is shown schematically for a single crystal in Figure 3.2a. In a suitable temperature range these excess dislocations diffuse along the slip planes and line up at intervals, as illustrated schematically in Figure 3.2b. When this occurs the slip planes between these lines of dislocations tend to straighten, thus making, in the crystal, a series of zones differing slightly in orientation and hence detectable both microscopically and by X-ray diffraction. This process is known as polygonization.[5]

[5] See also "Symposium on Polygonization" in *Progress in Metal Physics,* **2** (New York: Interscience Publishers, 1950), 151–202.

This change from bent slip planes to slip planes composed of substantially undisturbed zones set at small angles, often in the order of minutes of arc, to each other leads to a decrease in elastic energy even though the opposite might be expected because of the known tendency of dislocations of the same sign to repel each other. If these dislocations align themselves in a boundary plane perpendicular to the slip direction, the elastic field associated with each dislocation is decreased because it is restricted to the immediate location of this boundary rather than being spread over a much larger volume. This decrease in elastic energy which makes polygonization possible is greatest if the aligned dislocations are spaced at uniform intervals and if the lattices on either side are completely unstrained.

The net result of polygonization, then, is to produce a set of subgrain boundaries which are very mobile. Because of their relatively small energies, as compared with the usual high-energy grain boundaries, these subboundaries may be difficult to reveal in some metals. In fact, if the two adjacent regions have almost the same orientation there are so few dislocations in the subboundary that it may not be revealed by etching.

There is a close relationship between the new structure and the old structure and polygonization usually is accompanied by marked softening. The lines of dislocations which separate the polygonized blocks can be displaced readily, so blocks can grow at the expense of their neighbors. Polygonization thus may progress to the point that only a few subgrains remain from the original crystal although, in general, polygonized subgrains have dimensions of the order of $10^{-3}$ to $10^{-5}$ cm.

If the amount of prior deformation is small, recovery and polygonization together may give such a stable structure that no further changes in microstructure take place until quite high temperatures are reached.

## PRIMARY STRAIN RECRYSTALLIZATION

When heating is carried to temperatures higher than those at which recovery and polygonization occur, the metal recrystallizes,[6] and most of the dislocations in the lattice disappear, provided the deformation is more than a certain minimum value. The deformed structure is replaced by a new undistorted grain structure. Also, as indicated schematically in Figure 3.1, both the strength and the hardness decrease markedly, and the ductility increases. The approximate lowest temperature at which recrystallization will occur for several common metals also is given in Figure 3.1. The time of holding at these temperatures is important because, within limits, in-

[6] E. C. W. Perryman, *Trans. A.I.M.E.,* **203** (1955), 1053–64, discusses the relationship between recovery and recrystallization in superpurity aluminum.

Influence Of Small Amounts Of Foreign Elements on the Recrystallization Temperature Of Copper Previously Reduced 98% by Working.

| Element | Weight % added to copper | Recrystallization temperature F | C |
|---|---|---|---|
| Copper (Electrolytic) | — | 390 | 200 |
| Aluminum | 0.12 | 300 | 150 |
| Iron | 0.21 | 375 | 190 |
| Bismuth | 0.027 | 390 | 200 |
| Zinc | 0.33 | 430 | 220 |
| Silicon | 0.06 | 475 | 245 |
| Gold | 0.20 | 480 | 250 |
| Nickel | 0.28 | 480 | 250 |
| Arsenic | 0.14 | 480 | 250 |
| Sulfur | 0.21 | 525 | 275 |
| Antimony | 0.06 | 535 | 280 |
| Cadmium | 0.19 | 570 | 300 |
| Manganese | 0.23 | 610 | 320 |
| Phosphorus | 0.36 | 615 | 325 |
| Lead | 0.15 | 615 | 325 |
| Silver | 0.24 | 645 | 340 |
| Tin | 0.24 | 705 | 375 |

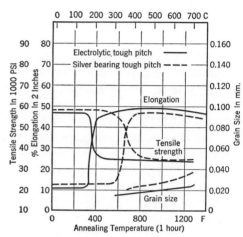

**Figure 3.3** (*left*) Influence of foreign elements on the recrystallization temperature of copper. [After H. Widmann, *Zeit. Physik,* **45** (1927), 200.] (*right*) Effect of silver on the annealing characteristics of copper rod. [Courtesy Bridgeport Brass Company.]

creasing the holding time lowers the recrystallization temperature.[7] Alloying elements in solid solution raise these minimum recrystallization temperatures appreciably, depending on the type and amount of alloying elements present.[8] The order of magnitude of these changes is shown for copper in Figure 3.3.

Recrystallization is dependent on the formation of nuclei which are produced with a certain probability determined by the amount of prior deformation, by the temperature of heat-treatment, and by the time of holding at that temperature. These recrystallization nuclei apparently are formed in substantially a random manner and the orientations of many of the recrystallized grains are quite different from, although related to, those of the parent grains.

As illustrated in Figure 3.4 for a brass, there is first an incubation period during which little evidence of reaction can be detected by most techniques. After this, new, substantially strain-free, grains nucleate at a finite number of sites, usually found at internal boundaries of various types. The number of nucleation sites increases with time. The difference in mean free energy

[7] Illustrative of this, A. L. Simmons, *Trans. A.S.M.,* **41** (1949), 1440–51, gives data for many copper-base alloys.

[8] For some of these effects in iron, see E. P. Abrahamson II and B. S. Blakeney, Jr., *Trans. A.I.M.E.,* **218** (1960), 1101–04; also R. L. Rickett and W. C. Leslie, *Trans. A.S.M.,* **51** (1959), 310–33.

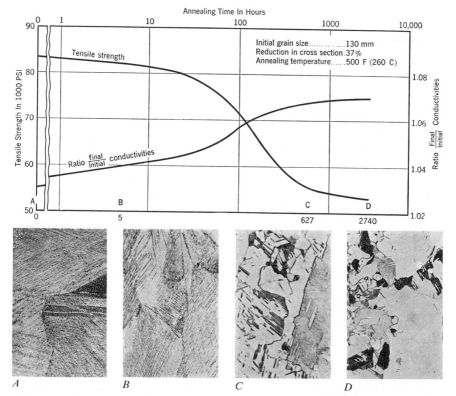

**Figure 3.4** Changes in microstructure and properties at various stages of recrystallization of an alloy containing 70% copper, 30% zinc when heated for varying times at a constant temperature. Initial grain size, 0.130 mm; reduction in area by drawing, 37%; annealed at 500 F (260 C) for times shown. Etched with $NH_4OH + H_2O_2$ (original magnifications: *A, B, C,* ×500; *D,* ×250; reduced approximately one-half in reproduction). [Courtesy Research Department, Chase Brass and Copper Company.]

between cold-worked and annealed material is relatively small so the driving force for nucleation is not great. However, the magnitude of the potential energy barrier between the two states probably is more important than the over-all free energy change in controlling the incubation period.

The most likely explanation for the formation of recrystallization nuclei in deformed material seems to be by a uniform transformation of the material in a volume larger than that actually needed to form a stable nucleus.[9] As the interior portion of this nucleating region changes from a deformed to a strain-free structure, and dislocations are eliminated, the free energy released is made available to increase the surface energy around the

[9] This is discussed in Ref. 3 at the end of this chapter.

periphery of the region. The local release of free energy is increased if the nucleation occurs preferentially in the more highly strained regions— for example, at internal surfaces, as usually is the case. The surface energy then gradually increases and the strain-free region grows until, ultimately, an interface is established between the new grain and the deformed matrix.

## EFFECT OF TIME, AND PERCENTAGE REDUCTION BY WORKING, UPON RECRYSTALLIZATION

Recrystallization is a rate process, as are nearly all the other reactions in the solid state. It should be possible to describe it, therefore, in terms of a nucleation frequency, $N$, per unit volume. The lower the temperature at which it occurs, or the lower the intensity of the available energy, the more slowly it takes place. This rate function probably is a complex one.[10] Heavy reductions in thickness by cold-working before heat-treatment increase the ease of recrystallization, probably by increasing the number of available nuclei and the rate of nuclei formation. Hence, it may be stated that, in general, the greater the amount of previous cold-work, the lower is the recrystallization temperature range for a constant annealing time, and the longer the annealing time, the lower is the recrystallization temperature range for a constant amount of cold-work.[11] These statements are illustrated for high-purity copper by the plots of Figures 3.5 and 3.6. In Figure 3.7 the combined relationship between grain size, reduction in thickness, and annealing temperature is shown for commercially pure iron and for cartridge brass. These graphical relationships show that the final grain size depends, somewhat differently for each material, on the amount of deformation as well as on the annealing temperature. The effect of deformation is somewhat more complicated than it might appear because the actual magnitude of deformation is not uniform but varies somewhat from point to point. In general, the greater the deformation and the lower the annealing temperature, the smaller the grain size is. This is the result of a combination of heavy nucleation, because of the prior deformation, with limited grain growth rate because of the low temperature. It also is true, although not shown specifically in these plots, that the larger the grain size before deformation, the greater is the amount of cold-work required to give a comparable recrystallization temperature and time.

---

[10] For a thorough review of this see J. E. Burke and D. Turnbull in *Progress in Metal Physics,* **3** (New York: Interscience Publishers, 1952), 220–92. The kinetics for low-carbon steel are discussed by S. F. Reiter, *Trans. A.I.M.E.,* **194** (1952), 972–79; and for nickel, by G. W. Wensch and H. L. Walker, *Trans. A.S.M.,* **44** (1952), 1186–98.

[11] See S. E. Maddigan and A. I. Blank, *Trans. A.I.M.E.,* **137** (1940), 170–92.

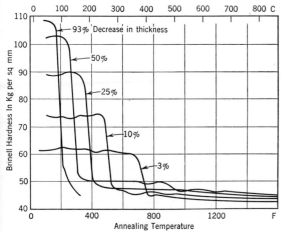

**Figure 3.5** (*left*) Influence of reduction in thickness on the softening temperature of cold-rolled high-purity copper. [After W. Koester.]

**Figure 3.6** (*right*) Influence of annealing time on the softening temperature of copper wire reduced 93% by cold-drawing to a diameter of 0.0105 in. (0.26 mm). [After W. E. Alkins and W. Cartwright.]

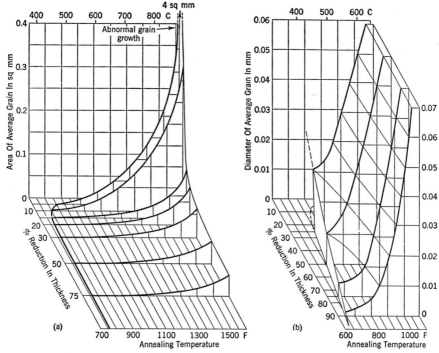

**Figure 3.7** Recrystallization diagrams for **a.** iron [after P. Oberhoffer and W. Oertel] and for **b.** cartridge brass, 70% copper, 30% zinc [from R. S. French, *Trans. A.I.M.E.*, **156** (1944), 195–209].

## GRAIN GROWTH AFTER RECRYSTALLIZATION

Once recrystallized, grains tend to grow in size at a linear rate, $G$, by absorbing any adjacent deformed material as well as recrystallized but less stable neighbors, so long as the available intensity of energy is sufficiently large and is maintained. However, when growing grains start to impinge on one another grain growth decreases.

This growth is by a process of discontinuous grain boundary migration.[12] The rate and direction of migration may change, but a curved boundary usually migrates toward its center of curvature, because in this way energy is gained by the decrease in grain boundary surface area and curvature. It is quite possible, therefore, for a grain to be consuming another grain on one side at the same time that it is being consumed itself on the other side by a neighboring grain. The net result, however, is toward a uniform increase in grain size and hence to fewer grains. The basic factor involved is a change toward a structure for which the grain boundary energy is a minimum. In general, in a metal or an alloy with only one type of grain—that is, not mechanical mixtures—the tendency is for grains to grow in such a way that, at their corners, grains come together in threes and meet at angles approaching $120°$.[13]

For every temperature above the strain recrystallization range, there should be an equilibrium grain size for a given metal, which cannot be exceeded in any reasonable time. Both the magnitude and the rate of attainment of this size are functions of the heat-treating temperature. In general, the higher the annealing temperature, the larger the equilibrium grain size is, and the more rapidly it is attained (compare Figure 3.14). The over-all changes occurring in a 70% copper, 30% zinc cartridge brass are illustrated in Figure 3.8 (compare Figure 3.1).

## IMPURITY INHIBITED GRAIN GROWTH

The addition of certain impurities to a metal or alloy often gives a fine-grained recrystallized structure, as illustrated in Figure 3.9b for lead.[14] Such impurities may increase the rate of nucleation, decrease the rate of grain growth, or both. Cases are known where grain growth apparently is inhibited largely because of an increase in grain boundary energy, which makes migration more difficult, and where growth is inhibited by the pres-

---

[12] D. Turnbull, *Trans. A.I.M.E.*, **191** (1951), 661–65.

[13] The subject of grain size and shape, called topology, has been studied thoroughly by C. S. Smith. See, for example, the discussion in Ref. 4 at the end of this chapter.

[14] See also, D. L. Wood, *Trans. A.I.M.E.*, **209** (1957), 406–08.

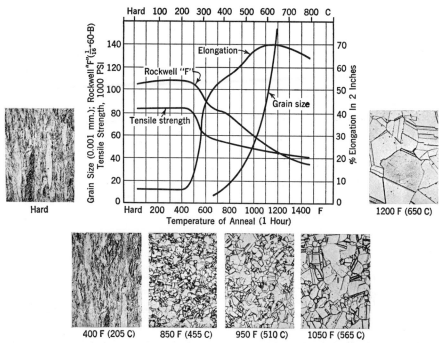

Hard

1200 F (650 C)

400 F (205 C)    850 F (455 C)    950 F (510 C)    1050 F (565 C)

**Figure 3.8** Progress of recrystallization in the annealing of cold-worked cartridge brass (70% copper, 30% zinc) showing the changes that occur in both properties and metallographic structure. Etched with $NH_4OH + H_2O_2$ ($\times 75$). Compare Figure 3.1.

**Figure 3.9** Effect of impurities on the grain size of lead. Etched with acetic acid $+ H_2O_2$ ($\times 50$). **a** (*left*). Pure (coarse grain) 99.999 + % lead, recrystallized after deformation. **b** (*right*). Impure (fine grain), 0.02% calcium, 0.02% magnesium, 0.25% tin, remainder lead, partially recrystallized after cold-rolling 90%. The "bands" are probably remnants of the original coarse grains which were elongated during rolling. [Photomicrographs courtesy Research Department, American Smelting and Refining Company.]

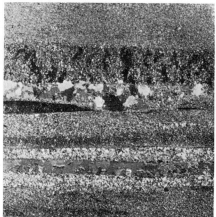

ence of a grain boundary precipitate or of concentrations of dissolved foreign elements at grain boundaries. The grain growth inhibiting effect of impurities usually persists only to a temperature high enough to overcome the effect or to dissolve the precipitate. The grains, therefore, remain small only up to some limiting temperature known as the coarsening temperature. If this temperature is exceeded, the grains become larger, just as though the impurities were not present. Increasing the annealing time also may cause fine grains to coarsen. The terms "fine grain" and "coarse grain," therefore, refer only to the results of certain more or less definite treatments. In the so-called coarse-grain materials, grain growth generally proceeds in a more regular manner than in the fine-grain materials. These effects are illustrated in Figures 3.10 and 3.11*b*.

## ABNORMAL GRAIN GROWTH

The grains of an aggregate also may coarsen far more than would be expected for a given annealing temperature or treatment. If the reduction by cold-work is relatively small, generally less than 2%, few if any nuclei for recrystallization form, and the main effect of the deformation seems to be a partial rupturing of the material at the grain boundaries. Consequently, when the specimen is heated to an appropriate temperature range, some of the existing grains grow by absorbing their less stable neighbors, but without passing through any real stage of recrystallization. This effect is indicated in the low-deformation regions of the diagram in Figure 3.7*a*, and is illustrated for pure aluminum by the photomicrographs in Figure 3.11*a*. It naturally leads to the formation of abnormally large grains; and by heat-

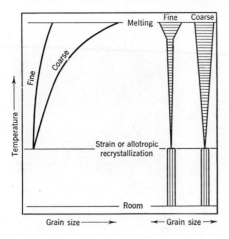

**Figure 3.10** Various methods of illustrating the effects of temperature on grain size. The figure at left shows graphical plots in two different ways. In the left-hand example the coarsening of the fine-grain material is indicated as being much less than in the right-hand example.

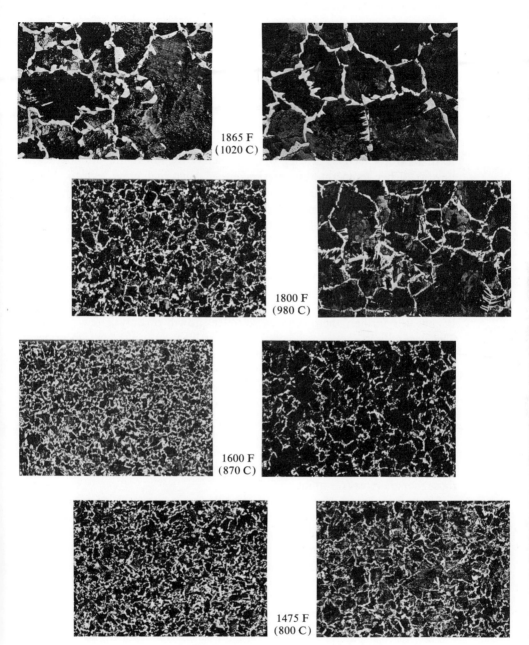

1865 F
(1020 C)

1800 F
(980 C)

1600 F
(870 C)

1475 F
(800 C)

**Figure 3.10** (*cont.*)   Composite micrographs showing the actual grain sizes of (*left*) coarse- and (*right*) fine-grain steels after air cooling from the temperatures shown (normalizing). Etched with 1% nital (×100). [Photomicrographs courtesy T. G. Digges and S. J. Rosenberg.]

ing to the proper temperature range, comparatively large specimens of some metals, notably aluminum, have been converted into single crystals by this method.[15] In industrial operations, however, abnormal grain growth generally is avoided by all means available; an exception is in silicon iron transformer sheets where large grain gives favorable magnetic properties.

In some cases, furnace atmospheric conditions—for example, reducing, oxidizing, or neutral—have been known to exert a pronounced effect upon grain growth [16] because of their influence on factors which normally inhibit it. In allotropic metals, alloying which preserves the low-temperature structure to higher temperatures may encourage abnormal grain growth. Because of the effect of large grains in producing an orange-peel surface, Figure 2.19, the conditions that produce such effects must be known and kept under careful control if consistent results are to be secured.

## SECONDARY RECRYSTALLIZATION

When a material that already has undergone primary recrystallization is annealed further, there often is selective growth of only a few grains. This generally is known as secondary recrystallization [17] although no prior deformation is required and nucleation probably is not involved. Instead, grain growth occurs by the migration of grain boundaries that were present prior to annealing so secondary grain growth probably would be a more accurate name. The kinetics of secondary recrystallization appear to be quite similar to those of abnormal grain growth in lightly deformed specimens. Secondary recrystallization also can be described in terms of a nucleation frequency per unit volume, $N$, and a linear rate of grain growth, $G$. It is possible that only the most perfect of the grains grow in this way, that is, those that are most free of internal stress.

There probably is some dependence of the grain boundary migration on the relative orientations of the growing grains and the remaining primary grains. A few grains become very large because of the ease with which they can grow rather than because of any positive tendency to grow. In rolled copper, for example, grains oriented in such a way that the cube plane in the space lattice is parallel to the sheet surface, the so-called cube

[15] See H. C. H. Carpenter and C. F. Elam, *Proc. Roy. Soc.,* **A100** (London: 1921), 329, for the pioneer work in this field.

[16] See, for example, A. Phillips and M. J. Weldon, *Trans. A.S.M.,* **23** (1935), 886–905, and discussion.

[17] A tertiary recrystallization to still a differently oriented structure has been reported for silicon irons by J. L. Walter and C. G. Dunn, *Trans. A.I.M.E.,* **215** (1959), 465–71. See also M. L. Kronberg and F. H. Wilson, *ibid.,* **185** (1949), 501–4; and J. E. May and D. Turnbull, *ibid.,* **212** (1958), 769–81.

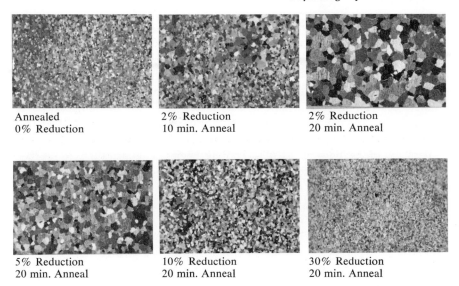

Annealed
0% Reduction

2% Reduction
10 min. Anneal

2% Reduction
20 min. Anneal

5% Reduction
20 min. Anneal

10% Reduction
20 min. Anneal

30% Reduction
20 min. Anneal

**Figure 3.11** Examples of the effects of preliminary cold-working and time of annealing on grain coarsening. **a** (*above*). The macrograin structure (×0.6) of pure aluminum sheet resulting from rolling different reductions and then annealing at 950 F (510 C) for 10 or 20 min. [Macrophotographs courtesy Aluminum Company of America.] **b** (*right*). Effects of time on the coarsening of austenitic grains in an iron-carbon alloy. [From J. Johnston, *Trans. A.I.M.E.*, **150** (1942), 1–29.]

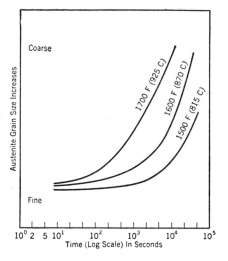

texture, will grow to quite large sizes, of the order of several millimeters in many instances.[18] The mechanical properties of such a texture approximate those of a single crystal of the same orientation and thus are different in different directions and inferior to those of a finer-grained polycrystalline aggregate.

[18] See, for example, Paul A. Beck, *Trans. A.I.M.E.*, **191** (1951), 474–75; also M. L. Kronberg and F. H. Wilson, *ibid.*, **185** (1949), 501–14.

## EFFECT OF RATE OF COOLING FOLLOWING STRAIN RECRYSTALLIZATION UPON GRAIN SIZE

After strain recrystallization has occurred in a previously deformed material, the final grain size is determined both by the temperature to which the strained material is heated, and by the time it is held at that temperature. Even if equilibrium has not been attained at the actual temperature of heating, as soon as cooling begins a temperature is reached for which the grain size is as large as it can grow in a given time with the intensity of energy available; and for which it is, therefore, in essential equilibrium. The grains so produced are rigid structures, and the only way their size can decrease is by deforming them and subsequently recrystallizing to a smaller size. Hence, cooling alone involves simply decreasing the intensity of energy to a level such that no further changes can occur in the time available. As a result, rate of cooling has no effect upon the grain size and no effect upon the properties unless the thermal strains produced by rapid cooling are sufficiently large to produce some deformation or significant residual stresses.

After ordinary strain recrystallization, therefore, it should make little difference, so far as structure is concerned, whether the metal is cooled slowly or is quenched.

## ALLOTROPIC RECRYSTALLIZATION

In addition to the strain recrystallization which allotropic metals undergo after cold-working, when heated to appropriate temperatures—for example, approximately 1200 F (650 C) or higher for pure iron—another type of recrystallization is possible, which under the proper conditions occurs spontaneously and without any necessity for strain or other complicating conditions. This is the recrystallization accompanying the allotropic change —for example, that occurring at $A_3$ for pure iron. When an allotropic metal is heated through the temperature of allotropic transformation, regardless of its previous physical condition, it recrystallizes spontaneously because of the allotropic rearrangement of the atoms into the new crystallographic structure. This is illustrated schematically in Figures 3.12 and 3.14 for iron. The grain size resulting depends upon the purity, and upon the temperature and the time,[19] in a manner quite similar to the case of strain recrystallization. Thus, if only a relatively low intensity of energy is sup-

---

[19] This has been shown by O. O. Miller, *Trans. A.S.M.*, **43** (1951), 260–87, for the austenitic (gamma iron) grain size of steel.

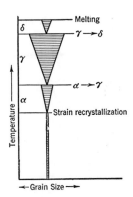

**Figure 3.12** Schematic representation of strain recrystallization and allotropic recrystallizations when cold-worked iron is heated. See also Figure 3.14.

plied, as by heating just above the transformation temperature, a small grain size results. On the other hand, a large grain size can be produced by heating to a high temperature—for example, just below $A_4$ for iron—and thus supplying a comparatively high intensity of energy. As before, also, the lower the temperature the longer is the time required to attain a grain size that is in essential equilibrium, although in the higher temperature ranges all of these times are rather short.

A similar recrystallization takes place in iron on heating through $A_4$, but this is not a normal industrial procedure.

When the metal cools again through the allotropic transformation there is another complete recrystallization of the structure, this time forming strain-free grains of the phase stable at lower temperatures.

The change from alpha iron to gamma iron that occurs on heating is completely reversible in cooling. However, this means only that a specimen that consisted of alpha iron before heating also consists of alpha iron after the cycle is complete. It says nothing about the size, shape, or orientation of the alpha iron groups in the two cases.

Allotropic changes take place by a combination of block movements proceeding by a process of nucleation and growth. Although there are definite crystallographic relationships between the orientations of the original and the final grains there are several possible paths, particularly with the cubic structures, along which the transformation can proceed. The one selected by any particular transforming region is determined by chance. Thus one alpha grain could transform into several gamma grains of different orientations depending on the number of nucleation points and the transformation path for each point. Likewise, during cooling, several alpha grains, probably all differing in orientation, nucleate within one gamma grain. The net structural effect of either heating or cooling through an allotropic transformation, therefore, is a complete refinement of the grain structure into crystals which usually differ completely in orientation from the grains from which they formed.

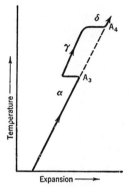

**Figure 3.13** Schematic representation of the thermal expansion and contraction of iron during heating.

The ferrite grain size, or the grain size of the room-temperature stable alpha iron, is one referred to most frequently in commercially pure irons,[20] whereas the grain size of the gamma iron, known usually as the austenitic grain size, is the important one in most industrial iron alloys, including the steels, even though the gamma form usually is not the stable form at ambient temperatures.

## PROPERTY CHANGES RESULTING FROM ALLOTROPIC RECRYSTALLIZATION IN IRON

The allotropic changes in commercially pure iron (ferrite) are important because they permit the production of either a relatively weak coarse-grain or a stronger fine-grain alpha-ferrite structure at will, merely by varying the heat treatment used. All of the mechanical properties of the iron depend on its grain size to some extent. In addition, there is a pronounced contraction in volume at $A_{c_3}$ and a comparable expansion at $A_{c_4}$, because of the fact that the face-centered cubic arrangement is more closely packed than the body-centered cubic one. These volume changes are reversed on cooling. This is illustrated in Figure 3.13 and is of some importance commercially.

## EFFECT OF RATE OF COOLING AFTER ALLOTROPIC RECRYSTALLIZATION

In allotropic recrystallization of iron, in direct contrast with strain recrystallization, the rate of cooling affects the final grain size of the alpha ferrite markedly, even though it has no influence upon the grain size of the gamma iron produced by heating. With alpha ferrite, nuclei for starting

[20] G. Wiener, *Trans. A.S.M.*, **44** (1952), 1169–84, discusses grain growth in pure iron.

the recrystallization are produced spontaneously by the allotropic transformation, which takes place on cooling as well as on heating. Because nuclei are produced on cooling, the effects resulting are comparable to those occurring during the solidification of a liquid metal. This is true even though, in this instance, the changes take place entirely within the solid state instead of in the transition between the liquid and solid states.

When iron is cooled slowly through $A_3$, therefore, comparatively few alpha-ferrite nuclei are formed. In addition, the decrease in the intensity of energy is so gradual, and the rate of growth of the new grains is so rapid, that a coarse alpha-ferrite grain size almost invariably results unless impurities exist to modify one or more of the controlling factors.

On the other hand, as the rate of cooling is increased, the number of available alpha-ferrite nuclei tends to increase, the decrease in the intensity of energy becomes more marked, and the time available for grain growth decreases. All of these factors combine to give a fine alpha-iron grain size.

In some allotropic metals and alloys, where the allotropic change cannot be initiated without crossing a potential energy barrier, the allotropic transformation may be suppressed partially or entirely by cooling rapidly enough, and the higher temperature form may be retained at room temperature even though it is not stable. However, in pure iron, rapid cooling has little effect and, regardless of the rapidity of cooling, the allotropic change takes place. Only after slowing down the transformation markedly by alloying can it be suppressed by rapid cooling, and the gamma form be retained at room temperature.

### RECRYSTALLIZATION OF CAST STRUCTURES

As a rule, castings solidify comparatively slowly from the liquid state so they normally have a coarse-grained structure. Comparatively poor mechanical properties generally accompany such structures, and hence it would be desirable to refine them by recrystallization if it could be done. Unfortunately, however, this is rarely possible unless the metal or alloy undergoes an allotropic transformation and, hence, can recrystallize spontaneously. Industrial use is made of this for certain iron alloys. In other metals and alloys some cold-working is required before recrystallization can take place. Such cold-working of a casting would be difficult if not impossible, because castings are poured directly to their final shape. Also, they frequently are made of compositions which are not amenable to mechanical working.

This inherently coarse grain size restricts the application of many nonferrous castings. With these materials, the initial cast structure is the final structure, and no further grain refinement is possible, even though the properties of some alloys may be improved by proper heat-treatment without modifying the grain structure.[21] With most ferrous castings, on the other hand, a grain refinement results from every heating or cooling through the allotropic transformation range and hence, appreciable improvement of both structure and properties can be secured by simple heat-treatments.

## STRUCTURAL CHANGES DURING FUSION WELDING

Fusion welding is a process for joining metals either by melting them together or by fusing them with a filler metal deposited in the joint. During welding, part of the base metal and all of the filler metal are molten. The heat required can be produced by mixing and burning gases such as oxygen and acetylene in a welding torch, but techniques for heavy sections generally use an arc struck either between the work and an electrode which also serves as the filler metal or between two independent electrodes, with external filler metal added as needed.

The soundest welds are made with some sort of protective environment provided by a flux or a nonoxidizing atmosphere around the molten metal. This inert atmosphere may be formed by the decomposition of coatings on the welding electrodes or may be provided separately. The processes used most widely today are shielded metal-arc welding with coated electrodes, or with bare-wire passing through a separately maintained flux pool (submerged arc welding), consumable metal-arc inert-gas welding (MIG) and tungsten-arc inert-gas welding (TIG). These processes can be used manually or in semiautomatic or automatic equipment. For welding steels, precautions are required to minimize the pick-up of hydrogen by the weld metal and heat-affected zone as this impurity tends to embrittle the steel and to produce cracking underneath the deposited weld bead.

Regardless of the process, however, the good thermal conductivity of metals results in a temperature gradient extending from the melting point of the metal, at the fusion zone, to the ambient temperature at a distance from the weld zone. The sharpness of this gradient depends on the type of metal, its thickness, the method of cooling used, and whether or not any extra heat is supplied before or during welding.

The metallographic structure and properties of a fusion weld, for the relatively simple case of a cold-worked metal which undergoes no allotropic transformation (Figure 3.14), are those of a casting in the weld zone, and those of the recrystallized base metal, with grain growth where this is possible, in the heat-affected zone. This zone runs parallel to the line of weld and includes all the metal which, during welding, reached the recrystallization temperature for the base metal. That is, beyond this there is no change in structure for lower temperatures. The maximum temperatures attained at and alongside a typical fusion weld, are illustrated diagrammati-

[21] This is discussed in Chapter 10.

cally in Figure 3.15. This means that the weld zone, and a region an appreciable distance on either side of it, has very much poorer properties than the unrecrystallized work-hardened base metal, and hence is more susceptible than it to overload and failure. The fusion zone itself usually is thickened somewhat during welding. Consequently, in a tensile test, failure is most likely to occur in that part of the heat-affected zone, usually immediately adjacent to the fusion zone, which has the largest grain size.

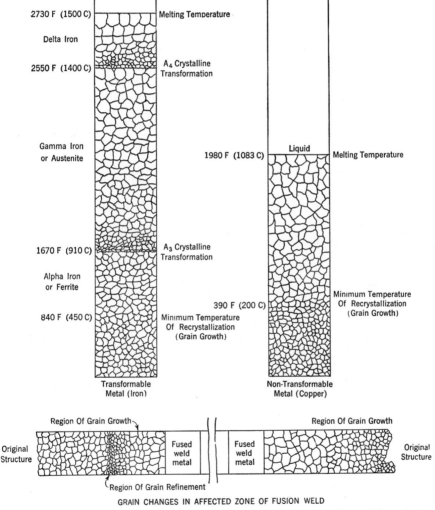

GRAIN CHANGES IN AFFECTED ZONE OF FUSION WELD

**Figure 3.14** (*top*) Schematic changes in grain size on heating cold-worked metals (*left*) with and (*right*) without allotropic transformations. (*bottom*) Schematic illustration of the manner in which these changes affect the grain size in a fusion weld. [Courtesy American Welding Society.]

In annealed nonferrous metals, fusion welding often results in no marked change in structure or properties because, at worst, a cast structure merely is substituted for an annealed one. However, there usually are enough residual strains to cause some grain coarsening adjacent to the fusion zone so failure in a tensile test still occurs in this region. In addition, the partially melted metal at the edge of a weld bead has low-strength properties. Therefore, it fractures, called hot-tearing, if subjected to stress before it is cooled sufficiently. Such stresses can be produced, for example, by restraints in the engineering structure being welded.

For a weld in iron, the $A_3$ allotropic critical temperature is in the neighborhood of 1670 F (910 C), and there is grain refinement of the metal which has reached this temperature, followed by progressive coarsening as the line of weld is approached, until the $A_4$ transformation is reached, when there is another band of grain-refined iron, and further coarsening at the edge of the fusion zone. Where the temperature reached is below $A_3$, the base metal structure is unchanged unless it is subject to strain recrystallization. This is indicated schematically in Figure 3.14. The grain size of the alpha-iron formed from the gamma-iron as the metal cools depends on a variety of factors. Other metals which undergo allotropic transformations behave similarly but have different critical ranges. Similar changes will occur with steels, but with additional complications that will be appreciated better after studying Chapters 6 and 8.

Similarly, deposited beads in fusion-welded iron or steel can be recrystallized by permitting each bead, after it is deposited, to cool below the critical range and to transform before the next bead is laid down. Thus, each bead recrystallizes as it is reheated above the critical range by the

**Figure 3.15**  Diagram showing the maximum temperatures generally attained at and alongside a typical fusion weld. [Courtesy American Welding Society.]

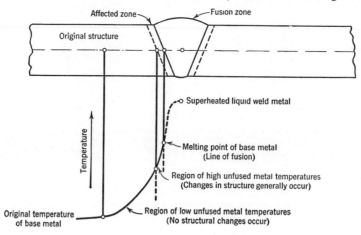

subsequent welding operations. In Figure 3.16, the macrographic structure of such a weld is shown. Because the various beads have somewhat different chemical compositions and physical properties, it is comparatively simple to distinguish between them.

## HOT WORK

When a metal is deformed above its strain recrystallization temperature it recrystallizes spontaneously as it is deformed mechanically. Hence, it cannot work-harden because any effects of stress are removed as soon as they are produced. Deformation of this nature is known as hot work. It must be emphasized that reference is to a temperature which is characteristic for the metal concerned and is related roughly to its melting point. For example, lead or zinc would be hot worked at 68 F (20 C) or less, whereas iron and nickel could be cold worked at 1000 F (540 C) or even higher, especially for rapid types of deformation.

Hot work has other advantages. It requires a much smaller amount of energy than cold work because metals are more plastic in the hot-working range than in the cold-working range. In addition, the metal can be deformed hot to a greater extent, and in larger steps than by cold work because it remains soft throughout, and does not work-harden, so that the energy requirements do not increase as the process goes on.

Hot work also has certain disadvantages, however. The comparatively high temperature at which it can be done in most metals usually make accurate dimensions difficult, if not impossible, to attain; surface oxidation is apt to be heavy; and the metal cannot be hardened or strengthened by working.

Hot working is used more frequently for early and intermediate stages of working than for the final ones, especially for impure metals and alloys

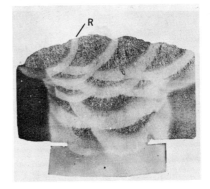

**Figure 3.16** Micrograph of a 15-bead butt weld in mild steel, revealing two types of structure, the darker areas representing unrecrystallized weld metal, and the lighter areas (*R*) representing recrystallized weld metal (×2 originally, reduced somewhat in reproduction). [From L. C. Bibber and H. C. Ellinger, *Welding Symposium*. London: The Iron and Steel Institute, 1935. Photomicrograph courtesy U. S. Steel Research Laboratory.]

with coarse cast structures which probably would fail during cold working. In other cases, the finish, the accuracy of dimensions, and the properties desired are the real determining factors on the choice of hot- or cold-working procedures.

## EFFECT OF HOT WORK ON GRAIN SIZE

Hot working reduces the size of the grains that are stable at working temperature. If a piece of metal (Figure 3.17) is worked, starting at a temperature, $T_3$, at which it has a relatively coarse grain size, strain re-crystallization occurs at once. The grains in the new structure immediately start to grow toward their equilibrium size. However, this equilibrium size is smaller than that existing before deformation, because the metal has cooled to a lower temperature, $T_2$. Further working and cooling produces still smaller grains. The limiting size is reached at the strain recrystallization range itself. If working is stopped just above this range, the resulting unstrained grains have the smallest possible size. If, on the other hand, working is continued below this range, the existing grains are strained and cold worked. In some instances, an increase in the strain recrystallization temperature resulting from alloying makes the temperature at which an allotropic change occurs, rather than that of the strain recrystallization range, the lowest at which it is desirable to hot work. The principle is the same in either case.

## ANNEALING FOR MAXIMUM DUCTILITY

In most metals, maximum ductility is secured with a small grain size.[22] In steel, the shape of the grains also is significant. Carbon acts as a deterrent to grain growth in steels so it usually is kept above 0.03%. These low-carbon steels are predominantly ferrite and are susceptible to grain coarsening under proper circumstances both below and above the $A_3$ critical so considerable care must be taken during heat-treatment if the grain size is to be kept small. If the grain size gets too large the carbon tends to form, as an iron carbide, in continuous films around the grains instead of as discrete particles distributed at random in the structure. If the material is finished by a cold reduction in excess of 15% it softens significantly if heated to a temperature in the range 1000 to 1600 F (550 to 870 C) as indicated in Figure 3.7. In general, the lower the temperature, provided recrystalliza-

---

[22] R. L. Rickett, S. H. Kalin, and J. T. Mackenzie, Jr., *Trans. A.I.M.E.*, **185** (1949), 242–51, discuss some of the grain size and shape factors.

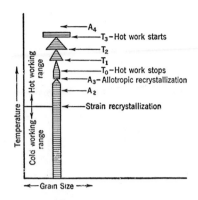

**Figure 3.17** Schematic representation of the change in grain size of pure iron during hot-rolling to a temperature just above $A_3$.

tion occurs, the smaller the grain size. However, it is important to have the material both completely recrystallized and as uniform as possible. Bright annealing in a nonoxidizing atmosphere and annealing in closed steel containers frequently are used to achieve this without excessive surface oxidation.

Hardness and tensile test results are, unfortunately, not too good criteria of how well a given steel will deform by the process of deep drawing, one type of which is typified by an automobile body or fender and another is illustrated in Figure 2.19. The draw itself, or the manner in which it is made, is frequently much more significant.

## THE ERICHSEN AND OLSEN DUCTILITY TESTERS

A measure of the ability of a metal to draw and the general appearance of its surface after drawing to various depths can be secured by applying either the Erichsen or the Olsen cupping test.[23] These two tests are similar and essentially consist of clamping a piece of metal between two flat faces and then forcing a round-headed steel ball or punch into the piece until fracture occurs. The gauge and depth of the cup, which the Erichsen machine measures in millimeters and the Olsen test measures in thousandths of an inch, and the character of the surface all are important in judging the formability of the material. Under certain conditions the location and type of fracture when the test is carried to breaking also may give worthwhile information. The general principles of the two tests are illustrated in Figure 3.18.

The Erichsen and the Olsen tests are used in both the ferrous and nonferrous industries although the methods of application and interpretation may vary.

[23] Considerable information on Olsen tests on low-carbon sheet steel is given in Ref. 1 (8th ed., Vol. I, pp. 82–86) at the end of this chapter.

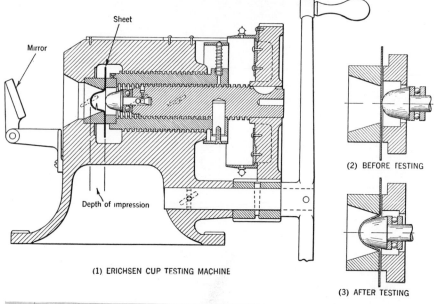

Sheet

Mirror

Depth of impression

(1) ERICHSEN CUP TESTING MACHINE

(2) BEFORE TESTING

(3) AFTER TESTING

**Figure 3.18** Two common types of cupping tests used on sheet metal to determine grain size and ductility. (*upper*) The Erichsen test, most commonly used on nonferrous metals, with examples of cups made in high brass sheet. The grain size becomes coarser successively from left to right. [Courtesy the Bock Machine Company and the American Brass Company.] (*left* and *bottom*) The Olsen test, most commonly used on ferrous metals, with examples of cups made on mild steel sheet; (*bottom left pair*) fine grain, (*bottom right pair*) coarse grain. [Courtesy Tinius Olsen Testing Machine Company, and Research Laboratories, The American Rolling Mill Company.]

## ANNEALING OR RECRYSTALLIZATION TWINS

Annealing twins form to some extent during recrystallization in all face-centered cubic metals and their alloys although they are relatively rare in aluminum. Some examples are shown in Figure 3.19. The straight-sided bands, either dark or light in color depending on how incident light is reflected (compare Figures 1.17 and 2.23), are the twins. They provide a simple method for identifying most metals of this type qualitatively from their microstructure. These twins often are straight sided and are much wider than mechanical twins (compare Figure 2.29), although the orientation relationship with the matrix (Figure 2.28) is comparable in the two cases. The twinning or composition plane, common to both the twinned and untwinned material, is a close-packed octahedral plane in face-centered cubic metals. The atomic match across the composition plane is perfect so there is no strain. Boundaries across which atomic matching can be maintained, either with or without strain, are called coherent and are relatively low-energy boundaries. However, there is considerable mismatch at other boundaries such as at the ends of twin bands. These boundaries, which have higher energies, are called incoherent.

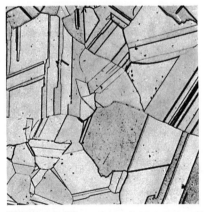

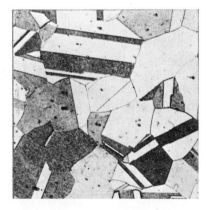

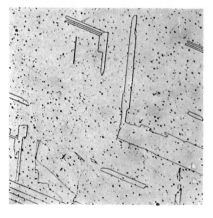

**Figure 3.19 a** (*top left*). Annealing twins in soft brass. Etched with $NH_4OH + H_2O_2$, lightly ($\times100$). **b** (*top right*). Annealing twins in soft brass. Etched with $NH_4OH + H_2O_2$, heavily ($\times100$). **c** (*bottom right*). Annealing twin bands in single crystal of pure copper to which 0.2% phosphorus and 0.005% sulfur had been added. Sample was cold-rolled 40% and annealed 30 min at 1650 F (900 C). Etched with $NH_4OH + H_2O_2$ ($\times75$). [Photomicrograph courtesy Research Department, American Smelting and Refining Company.]

**Figure 3.20** Change in direction of slip lines in brass on passing through annealing twin bands. Etched with $NH_4OH + H_2O_2$ ($\times 50$). See also Figure 2.21. [Photomicrograph courtesy R. M. Brick.]

**Figure 3.21** Stacking sequences in close-packed metal structures. The letters A, B, C, indicate successive close-packed planes—for example, the octahedral planes for face-centered cubic structures and the basal planes for hexagonal structures.

```
    A B C A B C A B C ----A B C
(a) Face-centered cubic (cf. Fig. 1.9)

    A B A B A B A B ----A B
(b) Close-packed hexagonal (cf. Fig. 1.10)

    A B C A C B A C B A B C ----A B C
         →|  Twinned  |←
(c) Twinned face-centered cubic (cf. Fig. 2.28)

    A B C A C B C A B C A B C A C B C A B C ----A B C
       |←—↑—→|              |←—↑—→|
       Stacking              Stacking
        fault                  fault
(d) Face-centered cubic with stacking faults
```

As might be expected from the twinned orientation, slip bands change direction when they pass through an annealing twin band (Figures 2.21 and 3.20). Thus twin-band boundaries probably exert some strengthening effect upon the aggregate, comparable in many respects to a grain boundary. The orientations of a grain and its annealing twins are different, even though related, so they reflect light differently when heavily etched (Figure 3.19*b*). Like mechanical twins, annealing twins cannot be removed by repolishing. Because of the difference in orientation, a subsequent etch will disclose them exactly as they were before polishing, Figure 2.31.

Several explanations have been given for the formation of annealing twins.[24] Annealing twins are rarely, if ever, found in cast metals so it appears that either the process of recrystallization or the process of grain-boundary migration, which occurs during grain growth, must be essential to their formation. Annealing twins do not grow by migration of their coherent boundaries, that is, in width, but they do grow in length within a grain by migration of their noncoherent boundaries. The mechanism of formation presently accepted proposes a change in stacking sequence whenever a properly oriented grain boundary migrates. Various stacking sequences are shown schematically in Figure 3.21. Such a change in se-

[24] See, for example, J. E. Burke, *Trans. A.I.M.E.*, **188** (1950), 1324–28.

quence would be relatively simple from an energy point of view because coherent interfaces have very low surface energies and the number of nearest neighbors would not be changed, merely their orientation.[25] It must be assumed, however, that the grain then grows in the reverse or twin sequence, until a later time when a similar stacking accident on a parallel octahedral plane restores the original orientation. This explanation leaves many questions unanswered.

## CREEP

For engineering applications involving elevated temperatures, the creep and stress-rupture characteristics of a material are frequently of major importance. This importance has increased directly with the increase in operating temperatures and pressures in both mechanical and chemical equipment. In turbine blades, autoclaves, unfired pressure vessels, high-pressure boilers, steam lines, and similar applications, failure can result readily from creep or stress rupture unless the proper factors are considered in the original design, and the proper alloys are used.

Creep [26] is plastic elongation of a material with time, when subjected to a constant stress. From a practical viewpoint, however, most creep tests are run under a constant load because it is simpler. The differences are minor so long as the strains are small, but they become significant for large strains. Clearly, as elongation increases, the cross-sectional area must decrease and consequently, in a constant load test, the stress increases.

Tests usually are conducted at a constant temperature. The temperature range in which creep is an important phenomenon depends on the material being tested. For example, lead or soft solder creeps dangerously at temperatures far below those at which most steels creep. Some soft metals, in fact, creep significantly at subzero temperatures.

When a specimen is subjected to a fixed dead load greater than its elastic limit at the testing temperature, it elongates fairly rapidly, initially. This first stage of creep is a combination of both elastic and plastic deformation, the former occurring largely during loading and the latter over a significant period of time. If the test is made in a temperature range in which work-hardening occurs, this initial deformation work-hardens the specimen until it can support the applied load without further deformation. The elongation-time curve under these conditions tends to become horizontal,

---

[25] C. S. Barrett, *Trans. A.I.M.E.,* **188** (1950), 123–35, has shown that stacking faults are more common than had been expected. See also B. E. Warren in *Progress in Metal Physics,* **8** (New York: Pergamon Press, 1959), 147–202.

[26] For more complete discussions of various aspects of this subject see Refs. 9 and 10 at the end of this chapter; and A. H. Sully in *Progress in Metal Physics,* **6** (New York: Pergamon Press, 1956), 135–79.

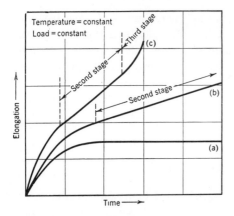

Temperature = constant
Load = constant

Elongation →

Time →

**Figure 3.22** Idealized creep curves for metals held under a constant load at a constant temperature. **a.** Curve taken in range in which work-hardening occurs tends to become horizontal as the metal strengthens and supports the load. **b.** Curve taken above work-hardening range frequently tends to attain a steady state which may persist for a very long time. **c.** Curve taken above work-hardening range may tend to pass relatively quickly into a third stage in which rapid elongation occurs.

as in curve (*a*) in Figure 3.22, but even so, the total elongation which occurs may be too great for some critical engineering applications. If, however, the alloy is tested in a temperature range above that in which considerable work-hardening occurs, this rapid deformation decreases to a steady rate of elongation known as the second stage of creep. This nearly constant rate, indicated by the straight line portion of curve (*b*) in Figure 3.22, may persist for very long periods of time; but eventually it passes into a third stage during which the specimen elongates more rapidly, as shown in curve (*c*) in Figure 3.22, sometimes necking down until fracture occurs. These three stages occur in this manner only when the microstructure is stable, a condition that often can be produced by a preliminary heat-treatment at a higher temperature than the test temperature. If the structure is not stable and changes during the test, creep results are unpredictable and can vary over a wide range depending on the changes that occur. From an industrial viewpoint this is an undesirable condition which is avoided if at all possible. As an example, long-time creep failures in the temperature range in which secondary creep rather than work-hardening becomes the controlling process often are intercrystalline and occur with very low elongation.

From a dislocation viewpoint the first stage of creep is a combination of an elastic deformation, slip caused by the movement of dislocations, and the eventual slowing down of this movement as the dislocations pile up at barriers. The second stage, then, is diffusion dependent as the dislocations climb and either rearrange themselves into a more stable configuration by a process similar to polygonization or else permit further slip by what amounts essentially to the movement of one dislocation at a time. The activation energy for the second stage of creep correlates quite well with that for self-diffusion, as would be expected if the diffusion of dislocations, that is, climb, were the rate controlling step. Very rapid creep differs from slow creep in that the stresses applied during rapid creep are sufficient to produce plastic deformation and often recrystallization as well. It thus approximates hot-work rather than a process controlled by self-diffusion. Because of the recrystallization, fractures in such tests are transcrystalline and seldom, if ever, are intercrystalline.

The general expression for secondary creep is the form

$$\dot{\epsilon} = \frac{d\epsilon}{dt} = At^{-n}$$

where $A$ and $n$ are constants, $n$ varying between 0 and 1. If this portion of the creep curve is linear, $n = 0$; curves corresponding to values of $n = 1$ (logarithmic creep) and $n = 2/3$ also are known, depending on the metal, the stress, and the test temperature. Under some conditions the data are fitted best by an equation combining two types of creep, particularly when structural changes also occur.

The better explanations of the third stage of creep assume a segregation of vacant lattice sites at grain boundaries, leading first to the formation of microcracks and ultimately to the formation of intercrystalline fissures. However, these fissures also may be the result of exhaustion of ductility or ability to deform further.

Creep data, of course, are of the greatest importance in applications where a given dimensional change must not be exceeded within the life of the equipment. In fact, from an industrial viewpoint, it is important that secondary creep continues throughout the life of the equipment and that tertiary creep is avoided. Unfortunately, no short-time test has been found yet which assists materially in predicting the results which would be secured under long-time creep loading. This means that it is an extremely time-consuming job to secure reliable creep data, and that, even at best, only the results of relatively simple loadings can be studied. Consequently, where creep is important, a conservative position must be taken. For this reason, a safe design stress often is considered to be one which will cause a creep rate of 1% in 100,000 hr even though nearly all such data are extrapolated from rates found in tests of less than 10,000-hr duration.

## STRESS RUPTURE

Even though the secondary creep rate often is substantially linear, the time at which the third stage starts and is followed by rupture is difficult to predict. Because of this, for many applications, tests to determine the time at which rupture occurs under a given loading may be of even greater importance than the actual elongation of the specimen, or its rate of elongation by creep, because the time-for-rupture indicates tendencies under overloads not called for by the design. Such data are secured, most simply, merely by applying a constant load to a specimen and determining the time required for rupture to occur in a constant temperature test. Indications are that the rupture time at any temperature is some function of the applied load, as indicated in the log-log plot of Figure 3.23. Oxidation of the alloy appears to affect the rupture time markedly, so for best results oxidation should be minimized.

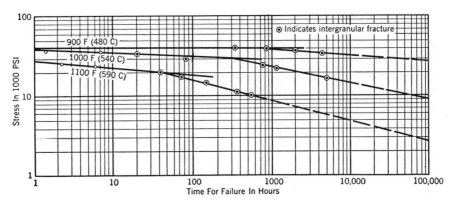

**Figure 3.23**    Stress versus time-for-rupture curves for a carbon-molybdenum steel. The initial straight-line relationship is followed so long as the steel is stable under the temperature and atmosphere used. More rapid deterioration (instability) is marked by a steeper slope of the lines (dashed). [From R. H. Thielemann, *Proc. A.S.T.M.*, **40** (1940), 791. Courtesy American Society for Testing and Materials.]

For shorter rupture times, fracture is transgranular and the specimen shows considerable ductility. However, as the rupture time increases, usually starting at about the break in the curve, the fracture becomes intergranular and the ductility decreases progressively with the increase in rupture time. If nonoxidizing atmospheres are used, the break in the curve either can be eliminated or delayed to longer times. Behavior in an accelerated stress-rupture test may be fundamentally different from that in creep. However, there has been some success in correlating the two types of data by use of the Monkman-Grant relationship [27]

$$\log t_r + m \log \epsilon_c = K$$

where $m$ and $K$ are constants for a given alloy system, $t_r$ is the rupture time, and $\epsilon_c$ is the secondary creep rate.

[27] F. C. Monkman and N. J. Grant, *A.S.T.M.*, Preprint No. 72 (1956), 1–13.

## RELAXATION

Relaxation is a phenomenon somewhat similar to creep, the main difference being that instead of length changes being measured at constant load,
stress changes are measured at constant length.[28] Relaxation tests are particularly significant for structural elements which are deformed a prede-
termined amount and then are expected to carry a load at this deformation.
Thus, a tightened bolt may relax at certain temperatures by elongating to
such an extent as to remove its tension. Under such conditions, the bolt no
longer fulfills its function, and becomes useless simply because it was employed in the wrong temperature range. A considerable amount of work on
relaxation still needs to be done.

## PARAMETERS FOR EXTRAPOLATING STRESS-RUPTURE AND CREEP DATA

In an effort to aid the design engineer in estimating the long-time stress-
rupture strength of possible alloys from the usual short-time test results,
various parameters have been proposed.[29] All of these parameters are
functions of stress, and incorporate time and temperature test data into
a single expression which then can be plotted as a "master curve." Such
correlations, however, do not apply in the region of major metallurgical
transformations.

The Larson-Miller parameter [30] used most commonly is

$$P_{L-M} = T_R(\log t_r + C)$$

where $T_R$ = absolute temperature, $°R(= °F + 459)$
$t_r$ = time to rupture, hr
$C$ = constant

The best value of $C$ is determined from a constant-stress plot of $\log t_r$
versus $1/T_R$, which should give a series of straight lines converging at the
point, $1/T_R = 0$, at which $\log t_r = C$. The optimum value for $C$ may
range from 15 to 27, depending on the material, but for a wide range of

---

[28] See C. L. Clark, Ref. 11 at the end of this chapter.

[29] This subject has been treated extensively by R. M. Goldhoff, *Trans. A.S.M.E., Journal of Basic Engineering,* Paper No. 58-A-121 (1958), 1–15. See also S. S. Manson, G. Succop, and W. F. Brown, Jr., *Trans. A.S.M.,* **51** (1959), 911–25; and W. Betteridge, *Journ. Inst. Metals,* **86** (London: 1958), 232–37.

[30] F. R. Larson and J. Miller, *Trans. A.S.M.E.,* **74** (1952), 765–71.

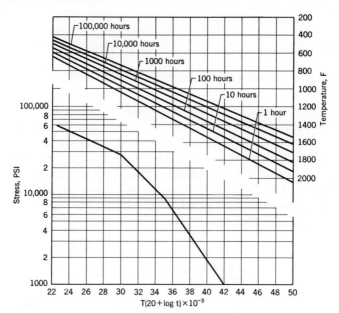

**Figure 3.24** Larson-Miller master rupture curve for low-carbon steel ($T$, absolute temperature in $°R$; $t$, time in hours). The curve shown summarizes data for short-time tensile strength and for stress-rupture tests at 1000, 1200, 1300 and 1400 F. [After F. R. Larson and J. Miller.]

materials it is approximately 20 so this value often is used. A master curve for low-carbon steel, plotted for $C = 20$, is shown in Figure 3.24. In general, better extrapolations are secured, however, if the best value of $C$ as determined above, is used instead of $C = 20$.

Two other parameters have been proposed but have not been used as widely as that of Larson-Miller:

(a) Orr, Sherby and Dorn: [31]

$$P_D = t_r \exp \frac{-\Delta H}{RT_K}$$

where $R$ = gas constant; $T_K$ = absolute temperature, $°K(= °C + 273)$; $t_r$ = time to rupture, hr; and $\Delta H$ = constant. This should give a series of parallel straight lines on a plot of log $t_r$ versus $1/T_K$ whose slope represents $\Delta H$. This parameter has been quite useful in correlating data on pure metals and on several nonferrous alloys. However, values of $\Delta H$ for structural steels have not been available so there has been only limited engineering use of this parameter thus far.

[31] R. L. Orr, O. D. Sherby, and J. G. Dorn, *Trans. A.S.M.*, **46** (1954), 113–28.

(b) Manson-Haferd: [32]

$$P_{M-H} = \frac{T - T_a}{\log t - \log t_a}$$

where $T$ = temperature, °F; $t$ = time, hr; and $T_a$ and $t_a$ are constants.

In a constant-stress plot of log $t$ versus $T$ this should give a series of straight lines converging to a point $T_a$ and log $t_a$. This sometimes is called the "linear parameter." This parameter, with its two constants, has been most useful in correlating data for high-strength materials.

Similar parameters may be used to correlate creep rates. For example, the Larson-Miller parameter for creep rates becomes $T_R(C_1 - \log \epsilon_c)$ where $\epsilon_c$ is the creep rate and $C_1$ is a constant different from the constant, $C$, in the stress-rupture parameter.

## QUESTIONS

1. Give some examples of ways in which a fabricated part or an engineering structure might acquire residual stresses. How can these stresses be relieved? What effects would such variables as heating rate, maximum temperature, holding time, and cooling rate be expected to have on stress relief by heat-treatment? Should it be possible to relieve stresses to some extent by mechanical treatment as well as by heat treatment? Why?

2. What is meant by a subgrain boundary and how does it differ from a grain boundary? How can subgrain boundaries be produced and under what conditions can they move?

3. Why do dislocations disappear during primary strain recrystallization? Why must a minimum deformation be exceeded before recrystallization occurs? What effect does this deformation have on grain size? Why do recrystallized metals not continue grain growth during recrystallization until they become a single crystal? Inasmuch as grains grow with increasing temperature after recrystallization, will they then decrease in size as the temperature decreases below the maximum value?

4. Why do most solid state reactions, such as recrystallization, start with an incubation period? What would be the nature of such an incubation period if the sensitivity of measurement is increased for whichever property is being studied?

5. Why does recrystallization tend to start at the more highly strained regions? Give some examples of such regions. What is meant by surface energy in the case of recrystallization?

6. What general type of annealing treatment, namely, prior deformation, annealing temperature, holding time, rate of cooling, etc., should be used if

[32] S. S. Manson and A. M. Haferd, *N.A.C.A., T.N. 2890* (March 1953).

a uniform grain size is desired? Would the grain size be expected to be more uniform if such controls were used for more than one cycle of deformation and annealing instead of only the final one?

7. If the basic change during grain growth following recrystallization is toward a structure for which the grain boundary energy is a minimum, why is the final structure not a collection of spheres, the ideal form for minimum surface energy? If not a sphere, what shape does the grain in the final equilibrium structure tend to have? Would this final structure be expected to differ if it were a secondary part of the structure (nonmatrix) rather than a primary part (matrix)? Must grains be approximately equiaxed if they are strain free?

8. Why will the coarsening temperature depend on the nature of the impurity causing it? If finely dispersed nonmetallic particles are present, which do not dissolve at any elevated temperature, what effect would this be expected to have on grain size and coarsening temperature? Discuss two ways in which furnace atmosphere during annealing could affect the grain size of at least the surface layers. Would these effects be expected to increase or decrease with longer annealing times at the same temperature?

9. Why does the rate of cooling following allotropic recrystallization affect the grain size of the lower temperature phase whereas it does not affect the grain size following strain recrystallization? Suppose a relatively low melting metal like lead were cooled drastically after strain recrystallization; could the grain size be affected? Why?

10. Disregarding any major structural changes which might take place during cooling, give some reasons why the austenitic (gamma iron) grain size might affect the room temperature properties even though the structure at room temperature is substantially all alpha-ferrite. Would the presence of impurities be apt to affect this? Would the type of impurity be important? Why?

11. What methods of grain size control can be used for castings? Does it make any difference whether or not the metal or alloy undergoes any allotropic changes? If the grain size of a casting can be controlled by heat-treatment, should two successive heat-treatments give a more uniform structure than a single heat-treatment? Why?

12. Point out the similarities between the grain structure of a fusion weld and that of a casting or annealed wrought material. If an engineering structure is built of a cold-rolled alloy to take advantage of its higher strength, should a lower allowable stress be used if fabrication is by fusion welding? Why? Why is it commonly said that a weld is stronger than the parent metal? Can this be shown experimentally? Is the statement correct?

13. Is a pure metal or simple alloy hardened by hot work? Why? Can a hot-worked material contain residual stresses after it cools to room temperature? Why? Would knowledge of this, one way or the other, be of any practical importance? If laboratory tests indicate that a metal requires the same energy to deform it at, say, 1300 F and at 1800 F, at which tempera-

ture would it be preferable to hot-work it? Why? Which temperature would be more apt to be used industrially?

14. Give some examples of applications for which secondary creep rate data should be more important than creep-rupture life and vice versa. How would the results of creep tests under constant stress be expected to differ from those under constant load? How does relaxation differ from creep and of what importance is it?

15. Why do elevated temperature failures tend to occur at grain boundaries as the time of failure increases? Does this mean that the metal failed because it crystallized? Why is so much attention devoted to finding parameters for extrapolating stress-rupture and creep data? What objections can you find to the use of Larson-Miller plots (for example, Figure 3.24) for extrapolating creep-rupture values?

## FOR FURTHER STUDY

1. *Metals Handbook,* 7th ed. (1948) and *Supplements,* and 8th ed., Vol. I (1961). Metals Park, Ohio: American Society for Metals.

2. *Thermodynamics in Physical Metallurgy.* Cleveland: American Society for Metals, 1950.

3. *Dislocations in Metals.* New York: American Institute of Mining and Metallurgical Engineers, 1954.

4. *Metal Interfaces.* Cleveland: American Society for Metals, 1952.

5. *The Physical Chemistry of Metallic Solutions and Intermetallic Compounds,* Vols. I and II. London: Her Majesty's Stationery Office, 1959.

6. *The Annealing of Low-Carbon Steel, A.S.M.* Cleveland: Lee Wilson Engineering Company, 1960.

7. *Creep and Recovery.* Cleveland: American Society for Metals, 1957.

8. *Symposium on Strength and Ductility of Metals at Elevated Temperatures, S.T.P. No. 128.* Philadelphia: American Society for Testing Materials, 1952.

9. *Metallic Creep and Creep Resistant Alloys* by A. H. Sully. London: Butterworth's, 1949.

10. *Creep of Engineering Materials* by Iain Finnie and William R. Heller. New York: McGraw-Hill, 1959.

11. *High Temperature Alloys* by Claude L. Clark. New York: Pitman Publishing Corp., 1953.

12. *Creep and Fracture of Metals at High Temperatures.* New York: Philosophical Library, 1957.

13. *The Strength of Wrought Steels at Elevated Temperatures, S.T.P. No. 100.* Philadelphia: American Society for Testing Materials, 1950.

14. *Digest of Steels for High Temperature Service.* Canton, Ohio: The Timken Roller Bearing Co., 1957.

15. *Seamless Steel Tubing.* Beaver Falls, Penna.: The Babcock & Wilcox Co. 1959.

# 4 *Common Engineering Metals*

## CHARACTERISTICS OF ENGINEERING METALS IN INDUSTRIAL USE

Some engineering metals as pure as 99.999% are available in at least moderate quantities. Others have been made in smaller amounts with impurity contents in the range of parts per billion. Various methods of refining, some of which are discussed in Chapter 5, and various methods of melting and casting into ingots under a vacuum, or a suitable controlled atmosphere depending on the metal, have made these improvements possible.

A brief survey of the industrial types of the eight engineering metals will give a reasonable picture of their characteristics.[1]

## INDUSTRIAL ALUMINUM

There are three commercial grades of aluminum, differing in purity: 1100 (99% aluminum min), EC (99.45% aluminum min) and 1060 [2] (99.6% aluminum min). An even purer grade, 99.99% aluminum min, also can be purchased in moderate amounts. The hardness, strength, and

---

[1] Properties of many of the less common metals are reviewed in Refs. 2 and 3 at the end of this chapter.

[2] The meaning of the alloy and temper designations for aluminum and its alloys is given in the Appendix.

electrical resistivity decreases as the purity increases.[3] All of these grades have a tensile strength of 10,000 to 12,000 psi in the soft (-O) condition, increasing to 19,000 to 24,000 psi, depending on the purity, in the commercial full-hard (-H18 or -H19) temper. The accompanying elongations range from about 40% in 2 in. for the soft material to about 10% in 2 in. for the hardest temper depending also on the form in which the material is tested. Brinell hardness (10 mm–500 Kg) is between 20 and 45 depending on the amount of cold work, although in these soft materials Brinell hardness is not too significant.

The 1100 alloy is used widely for applications involving severe drawing, stamping or spinning operations but not requiring a great deal of strength. Typical properties are given in Table 5.8. A temperature of about 650 F (345 C) is used industrially for full annealing this material regardless of the amount of previous cold-work. Metallographic specimens do not etch readily to show the crystal structure clearly because of the numerous inclusions (see Figure 4.1). These inclusions are various intermetallic compounds formed by the impurities present, principally silicon and iron.

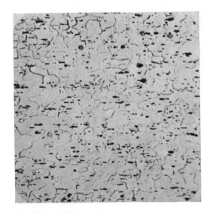

**Figure 4.1** Metallographic structure of annealed commercially pure aluminum, 1100-O. Etched with ½% HF (×100). [Photomicrograph courtesy Aluminum Research Laboratories.]

Aluminum is used to make cans and other containers both in the solid form and as a coating on steel, paper, or cardboard. It also is used to a limited extent as a coating on steel for resistance to some oxidizing media such as air, sulfur, and sulfides. However, if the aluminum was molten at any stage in its application the intermediate layers of brittle iron-aluminum compounds formed may decrease the usefulness of the coating. Aluminum can be deposited electrolytically only from certain molten salts or organic baths, not from aqueous media. Vapor deposition in a vacuum is quite feasible, however.

[3] The effect of alloying elements on electrical resistivity has been reported by A. T. Robinson and J. E. Dorn, *Trans. A.I.M.E.*, **191** (1951), 457–60.

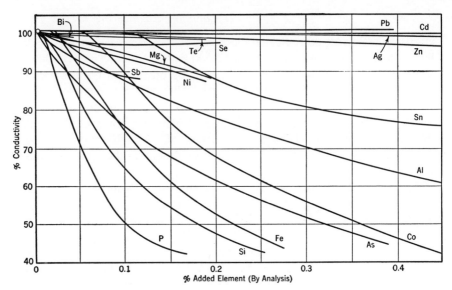

**Figure 4.2** Effects of small amounts of various elements, when present alone, on the electrical conductivity of copper. [From unpublished data of S. Skowronski, International Smelting and Refining Company.]

## ALUMINUM FOR ELECTRICAL CONDUCTIVITY PURPOSES

When measured by the customary method of equal cross-sectional areas, EC alloy has about 61% the conductivity of copper. However, it has a density only one-third that of copper, so an aluminum conductor is about one-third the weight of a copper conductor of equal cross section and length. For conductors of equal length and weight, therefore, aluminum has more than 201% the (mass) conductivity of copper, and a considerably greater strength, even though the mechanical properties of annealed aluminum are appreciably lower than those of annealed copper. Aluminum electrical conductor wire generally is used in a full-hard temper (-H19) with a tensile strength of 23,500 to 29,000 psi depending on the diameter, and an elongation of approximately 1.5% in 10 in.

Usage of aluminum or copper for electrical conductivity purposes at any particular time depends upon an economic balance between the cost of the two metals in the form to be used and the conductivity and strength properties required. At the present time indications are that any advantage in the immediate future will favor aluminum. The addition of any elements in solid solution to harden and strengthen aluminum results in a marked decrease in conductivity. Strengthening can be secured with least damage to conductivity by using alloys which precipitate "keying" phases [4] without leaving appreciable residual elements in solid solution—for example, an alloy which contains 98.8% aluminum, 0.4% magnesium, 0.5% silicon,

[4] See Chapters 7 and 10 for a more complete discussion.

and 0.3% iron has been used extensively in Europe for overhead transmission lines.

To overcome difficulties arising from the comparatively low strength of aluminum cables which have the same conduction as copper, the commonest method has been to use a steel wire in the center of a stranded conductor to strengthen and stiffen it. Other methods, taking advantage of the various principles of engineering design, such as built-up sections and special shapes, also have been used to some extent to increase the effective stiffness.

## INDUSTRIAL COPPER

Three principal commercial types of copper are used today, largely for conductivity or corrosion-resistant purposes: (a) oxygen-free copper, (b) tough-pitch copper, and (c) deoxidized copper. Even small amounts of most of the common impurities, with the exception of lead, oxygen, and silver decrease the conductivity of copper, as illustrated in Figure 4.2. Cold-work has a similar but somewhat less marked effect, usually resulting in a maximum decrease in the conductivity of about 3%.[5]

## OXYGEN-FREE HIGH-CONDUCTIVITY COPPER

Oxygen-free high-conductivity copper, copper alloy No. 102, contains at least 99.95% copper [6] and is the purest form of an engineering metal in direct industrial use today. It usually is made by melting and casting under conditions which prevent absorption of oxygen, or by continuous casting in rod form. Typical properties are given in Figures 2.16, 2.17, 2.18, and 4.3. The conductivity of the best grades may be as high as 102% of the International Annealed Copper Standard (I.A.C.S.), which represents the highest quality attainable fifty years ago. As would be expected because of the purity, the microstructure is quite clean, Figures 2.16 and 4.4.

## TOUGH-PITCH COPPER

Tough-pitch copper, copper alloy No. 110, contains 99.90% min copper and 0.01 to 0.07% oxygen (as $Cu_2O$). If it is also a "lake" copper, it may contain as much as 0.1% silver (10 oz silver per ton is equivalent to 0.034%), copper alloy Nos. 113, 114, 116. In these amounts, neither

---

[5] See D. K. Crampton, H. L. Burghoff, and J. T. Stacy, *Trans. A.I.M.E.,* **143** (1941), 228–45.
[6] Often 99.999% copper.

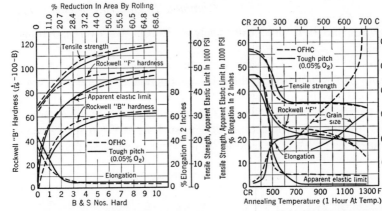

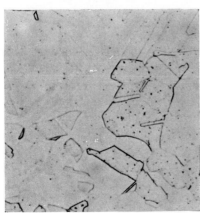

**Figure 4.3** Comparison between the mechanical properties of tough-pitch and O.F.H.C. coppers (*above left*) during cold-rolling to various reductions and (*above right*) during annealing. [From R. A. Wilkins and E. S. Bunn, *Copper and Copper Alloys.* New York: McGraw-Hill, 1943.]

**Figure 4.4** (*left*) Metallographic structure of O.F.H.C. copper. Etched with $NH_4OH + H_2O_2$ ($\times200$). The dark spots are etching pits resulting from the long time required to etch this relatively pure material. [Photomicrograph by L. Litchfield.]

**Figure 4.5** Metallographic structures of two tough-pitch coppers containing (*left*) 0.025% and (*right*) 0.075% oxygen (as $Cu_2O$), as cast. Etched with $NH_4OH + H_2O_2$ ($\times100$). [Photomicrographs by M. Brezin.]

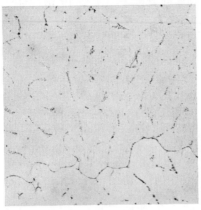 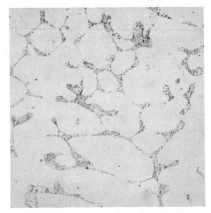

oxygen nor silver reduce the electrical conductivity appreciably, and values of 101% I.A.C.S. are common. Silver also increases the rate of work-hardening (Figure 2.17) and increases the recrystallization temperature from near 390 F (200 C), or lower, for pure copper to as high as 645 F (345 C) (Figure 3.3).[7]

In tough-pitch copper, any silver is in solid solution, but oxygen appears in the microstructure either as small globules of cuprous oxide or as the copper-cuprous oxide eutectic, which can be seen readily at the dendritic and grain boundaries (Figure 4.5) in typical photomicrographs. After working and annealing, the oxide is distributed throughout the structure as small particles in a background of twinned polyhedral grains of copper (Figure 4.6a). The mechanical properties of tough-pitch copper (Figures 2.17 and 4.3) tend to fall somewhat below those of the oxygen-free types. Although data are not shown, the reduction in area, in particular, is decreased by the presence of copper oxide in the cross section.

## EMBRITTLEMENT OF COPPER BY HYDROGEN

The most serious difficulty encountered with any of the oxygen-bearing coppers is their tendency to embrittle at temperatures above approximately 750 F (400 C) when exposed to reducing gases, especially those containing hydrogen,[8] or to conditions involving moisture or oil plus heat plus iron.

Under these conditions, atomic hydrogen diffuses into the metal and reacts internally with the oxygen in solid solution (or possibly with the copper oxide) to form steam and sponge copper. The pressure caused by this steam formed internally literally blows the copper apart, causing a separation at the grain boundaries and consequent lack of cohesion between the grains. The effect on the microstructure is illustrated in Figure 4.6b for wrought material and in Figure 4.6c for a casting. Although both the hydrogen and the steam formed would occupy equal volumes if they were present as gases, the hydrogen is dissolved in the copper until the steam is formed. The steam, being insoluble, is liberated as a gas under high pressure and thereby causes most of the difficulty.

$$Cu_2O + \underset{\substack{\text{(dissolved in} \\ \text{copper)}}}{H_2} = 2Cu + \underset{\text{(gas)}}{H_2O}$$

Oxygen dissolved in copper might be the active component also.

[7] Additional information on properties of these alloys is given by W. Hodge, *Trans. A.I.M.E.*, **209** (1957), 408–12.

[8] See L. L. Wyman, *Trans. A.I.M.E.*, 1931 Preprint; **104** (1933), 141–51; **111** (1934), 205–13; **137** (1940), 291–96.

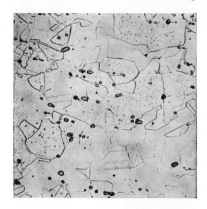
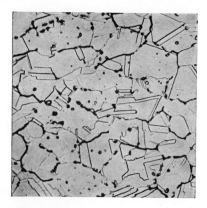
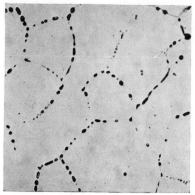

**Figure 4.6** Metallographic structures of electrolytic tough-pitch copper (×500). **a** (*top left*). Typical annealed wrought tough-pitch copper. The gray particles are cuprous oxide. Etched with $NH_4OH + H_2O_2$. **b** (*top right*). After embrittling by heating in hydrogen for 2 min at 1560 F (850 C). The copper oxide appears to have migrated to the grain boundaries and largely has been reduced by the hydrogen. Etched with $NH_4OH + H_2O_2$. **c** (*bottom*). Cast copper embrittled by heating in hydrogen. Again the copper oxide appears to have migrated to the grain boundaries and largely has been reduced. Unetched (×500 originally; reduced approximately one-third in reproduction). [Photomicrographs courtesy Research and Works Laboratories, General Electric Company.]

## DEOXIDIZED COPPER

By using various deoxidizing agents, such as phosphorus, carbon, calcium or lithium,[9] in a carefully controlled manner, the oxygen content of

---

[9] These deoxidizers are added to the liquid metal just before it is cast into a mold to form an ingot for further working. Their purpose is to react with dissolved oxygen and form solid compounds. The oxygen then is not evolved as a gas when the metal solidifies.

copper can be reduced to a low value without any appreciable amount of residual deoxidizer remaining in the metal. For example, phosphorus can be kept below 0.012% without difficulty, copper alloy No. 120. The microstructure of these alloys is identical with that of pure copper (compare Figure 4.4), although sometimes they are not so free of inclusions as some of the other grades. However, conductivities of up to 100% I.A.C.S. still can be secured with very little change in the mechanical properties.

If a larger amount of phosphorus is used as a deoxidizer, so that the residual is 0.015 to 0.040%, copper alloy No. 122, the conductivity is somewhat lower, about 80 to 90% I.A.C.S., but with no commensurate increase in strength and no noticeable change in microstructure. The electrical applications of this material are limited because of its lower conductivity, but it makes up an appreciable proportion of the copper used industrially, for example, as water tubing to resist mild corrosion.

## FREE-MACHINING COPPER

The toughness of pure copper makes it difficult to machine even in the hard-drawn form. However, for many applications in electrical machinery, forgings and screw-machine parts are required which have high conductivity and at least fair machinability. Machinability can be improved markedly by adding elements which are practically insoluble in copper and appear in the structure as small chip breakers.

The addition of lead, the element most commonly used for this purpose, is undesirable because it tends to give the metal low ductility at elevated temperatures, called hot-shortness. However, in spite of this difficulty, free-machining high-conductivity coppers containing 1% lead are made. They have a conductivity of 95 to 98% I.A.C.S. and a machinability about 80% that of free-machining brass, with about the same tensile strength and somewhat lower ductility than the nonleaded coppers. Marked improvement in machinability also can be secured by the addition of 0.5% sulfur (copper alloy No. 147), 0.5% selenium, or 0.5% tellurium (copper alloy No. 145).[10] Typical microstructures are shown in Figures 4.7 and 6.9c. These nonleaded alloys are not hot-short, and may be worked equally well either hot or cold. A 0.5% tellurium alloy, for example, has a machinability rating of approximately 80%, with a conductivity of 85% I.A.C.S. when deoxidized normally with phosphorus or as high as 98% I.A.C.S. when high conductivity is specified.

[10] See C. S. Smith, *Trans. A.I.M.E.,* **128** (1938), 325–34; H. L. Burghoff and D. L. Lawson, *ibid.,* 315–24.

## ELECTRODEPOSITED COPPER

Pure copper also is electrodeposited, both for ornamental purposes and to build up thickness in applications such as electrotyping and electroforming. Typical structures are shown in Figure 4.8. Both the structure and the properties of the deposit can be varied considerably by changing the nature of the electrolytic bath and the plating conditions. Copper frequently is used also on steel as a heavy undercoat for nickel and chromium (compare Figure 4.8*d*). Such deposits either must be smooth and bright enough as plated or must be buffed or polished to produce a suitable finish before the surface layers are deposited.

**Figure 4.7**   Metallographic structures of longitudinal sections of some commercial free-machining high-conductivity copper-base rod alloys in the annealed condition. Etched with $NH_4OH + H_2O_2$ ($\times 75$). **a** (*top left*). Leaded copper (0.94% lead, 0.03% phosphorus, remainder copper). **b** (*top right*). Tellurium copper (1.05% tellurium, remainder copper). **c** (*bottom left*). Selenium copper (0.90% selenium, remainder copper). **d** (*bottom right*). Sulfur copper (0.78% sulfur, remainder copper). Structure of the *b* alloy in the hard-drawn condition is illustrated in Figure 6.9*c*. [Photomicrographs courtesy Technical Department, The American Brass Company.]

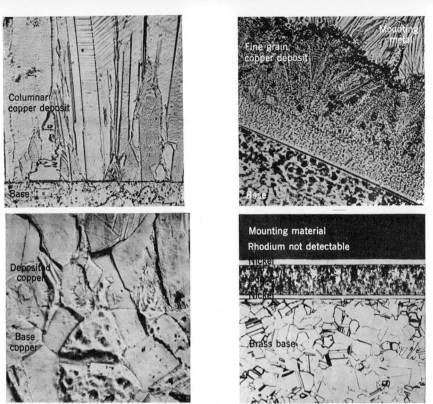

**Figure 4.8** Metallographic structures of various types of electrodeposited copper. **a** (*top left*). Copper deposited from an acid solution, showing reproduction of the structure of the base metal by a columnar deposit which apparently is twinned (×1000). **b** (*top right*). Copper deposited with a grain so fine it has barely been resolved metallographically (×1000). The nodular-type growth is caused by the presence of metallic impurities in the copper-plating solution. **c** (*left*). Almost perfect reproduction of the copper base by copper electrodeposited from an acid solution on a base deeply etched with nitric acid (×1000). [Photomicrographs courtesy Walter Meyer, The Enthone Company, New Haven, Connecticut.] **d** (*right*). Brass, plated with successive deposits of nickel, copper, nickel, and rhodium. Etched with $NH_4OH + H_2O_2$ (×200). This illustrates how little of the structure of even relatively thick electrodeposits can be seen at low magnifications.

## PURE IRON

Very pure carbonyl iron (99.90+% iron), made by the decomposition of iron carbonyl, a gas, and reasonably pure electrolytic iron (99.90% iron) are available industrially in moderate amounts.[11] These irons sometimes are purified further by elevated temperature treatments in wet hydrogen or by vacuum remelting. Even purer irons (99.99+% iron) can be

[11] G. A. Moore, *Trans. A.I.M.E.*, **197** (1953), 1443–48, gives a method for preparing high-purity iron.

made by chemical decomposition of purified iron compounds if cost is of little importance.

### MAGNETIC PROPERTIES OF IRON

The magnetic properties of these purer irons often are the important ones. A typical magnetization curve is shown in Figure 4.9. If the magnetizing force, or the magnetic field intensity $H$ (in oersteds or $0.4\pi$ times the ampere turns per centimeter), applied to a previously unmagnetized ferromagnetic material (that is, the center of coordinates in Figure 4.9) is increased, the magnetic induction or the flux density $\beta$ (in gauss or lines of force per square centimeter) increases to the magnetic saturation point at $+\beta_{max}$, where it becomes almost horizontal. If the magnetizing force then is decreased gradually from its maximum value $H_{max}$ to zero, the value of $\beta$ is greater while $H$ is being diminished than it was while $H$ was being increased. Even when $H$ is reduced to zero, $\beta$ still has an appreciable magnitude known as residual or remanent magnetism, $\beta_r$. If a magnetizing force in the reverse direction then is applied and increased gradually, $\beta$ continues to diminish until it becomes zero at a negative magnetizing force, the numerical value of which is the coercive force $H_c$ of the material. Both the remanent magnetism $\beta_r$ and the coercive force $H_c$ increase in magnitude with the maximum magnetizing force $H_{max}$ being used, but they approach limiting values very rapidly. These limiting values, known as the remanence and the coercivity, are specific properties of the material.

If the negative magnetizing force then is increased to a negative maximum value equal to the previous positive maximum—that is, to $-H_{max}$, reduced again to zero, reversed, and increased to the original positive maximum value, a cyclic process is carried out which, when $\beta$ is plotted against $H$ (Figure 4.9), is represented by a symmetrical loop called the hysteresis loop. Such a loop shows that the magnetic behavior of the material is dependent on its previous magnetic history, and its area represents the energy which must be expended to carry the material through the corresponding cycle of magnetization.

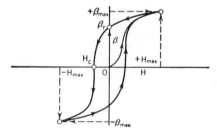

**Figure 4.9**  Typical magnetization curve and hysteresis loop. Coordinates represent magnetizing force $H$ in oersteds (1 oersted = $0.4\pi$ amp turns per cm) and magnetic flux density $\beta$ in gauss (1 gauss = 1 line of force per sq cm).

For magnetically soft materials it is desirable to have a high permeability, a high value of magnetic saturation ($\beta_{max}$) and a minimum hysteresis loss (a hysteresis loop of minimum area). Conversely, the magnetically hard, permanent-magnet alloys should have a high value of $H_c$, a high value of $\beta_r$, and a wide hysteresis loop.

If alternating-current magnetization is used, a further energy loss occurs in magnetic materials because of induced eddy currents. The energy so expended is transformed into heat, and its magnitude is the principal factor in determining the temperature rise in electrical machinery and transformers which are subject to alternating magnetization.

The ratio of the flux density $\beta$, or the magnetic induction, to the magnetic field strength $H$, or the applied magnetizing force, is called the permeability $\mu$. In practical measurements, however, it is more customary to refer to the relative permeability $\mu_r$, which is the ratio of the permeability of the metal $\mu$ to the permeability of a vacuum (or of air) $\mu_o$.

The permeability is the magnetic conductivity of a material and, except for the ferromagnetic alloys, for which the relative permeability may be as high as 100,000, it is usually about 1. Metals whose permeability is slightly less than 1 are said to be diamagnetic, and those for which it is slightly greater than 1, paramagnetic.

Pure iron is, in many respects, the ideal ferromagnetic material except for its comparatively low electrical resistance [12] which makes it unsuitable for use with alternating currents because of the necessity of restricting the eddy currents. This can be done, partially, by using magnetic cores built up of thin laminations. However, it also is customary to alloy silicon [13] with the iron to increase the electrical resistivity.

INGOT IRON

The purest tonnage industrial grade of iron today, ingot iron, is used more for corrosion resistance than for its magnetic properties. A typical analysis is: 0.012% carbon, 0.017% manganese, 0.005% silicon, 0.005% phosphorus, 0.025% sulfur, remainder iron. The total impurity content usually is less than 0.16%, but the material also may contain some nitrogen and as much as 0.10% oxygen, an element not considered as an impurity in this material. Hence the actual iron content is about 99.75%.

Most of the elements present are in solid solution in the ferrite so a metallographic structure (Figure 4.10) shows little except a polyhedral

---

[12] The effects of single trace alloy additions on the properties of pure iron are given in *PBO 71045* (Washington, D. C.: U. S. Dept. of Commerce, 1960).

[13] See Chapter 6. Aluminum additions have comparable effects but have not been used industrially to any extent because of manufacturing difficulties.

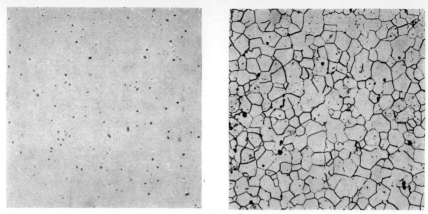

**Figure 4.10** Metallographic appearance of ingot iron with numerous iron oxide inclusions (×100), **a** (*left*). Unetched. **b** (*right*). Etched with nital.

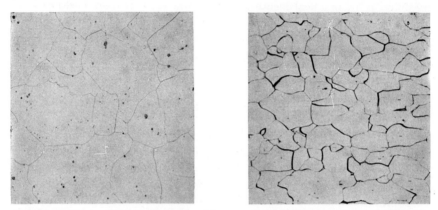

**Figure 4.11 a** (*left*). Metallographic structure of high-purity iron (Puron). Etched with picral (×100). [Photomicrograph courtesy Research Laboratory, Westinghouse Electric Corporation.] Oxygen is not considered as an impurity in this material. **b** (*right*). Metallographic structure of sheet steel that has been decarburized drastically by annealing in moist hydrogen. Etched with nital (×250). [Photomicrograph courtesy Research Laboratory, General Electric Company.] Both photomicrographs reduced approximately one-half in reproduction.

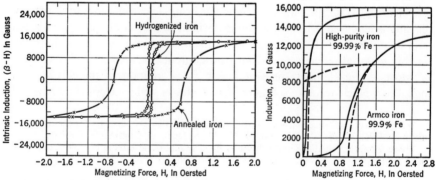

**Figure 4.12** (*left*) Hysteresis loops for annealed ingot iron and for hydrogenized iron. [After P. P. Cioffi.] (*right*) Magnetization curves for ingot iron and for high-purity iron. [After T. D. Yensen.]

ferrite structure with numerous small inclusions of iron oxide. The much cleaner structure of a commercial high-purity iron is shown in Figure 4.11*a* along with that of an industrial low-carbon steel from which all the carbon has been removed, called decarburizing, by annealing in an atmosphere of wet hydrogen, Figure 4.11*b*. Typical differences in the hysteresis loops and the $\beta$ versus $H$ curve for these irons are illustrated in Figure 4.12.

## WROUGHT IRON

The time-tested material, wrought iron, also is used extensively because of its resistance to corrosion by various types of water and atmospheres and to fatigue. A typical wrought iron analysis will show the data in Table 4.1.

**TABLE 4.1**

| | | % C | % Mn | % P | % S | % Si | % Slag (wgt.) |
|---|---|---|---|---|---|---|---|
| Total Analysis | | 0.02 | 0.03 | 0.12 | 0.02 | 0.15 | 3.00 |
| Separate Analysis | Base metal | 0.02 | 0.01 | 0.10 | 0.02 | 0.01 | — |
| | Slag | — | 0.02 | 0.02 | — | 0.14 | — |

The phosphorus content, which may run higher than 0.25%, is largely responsible for the good corrosion resistance of the material.

At the time wrought iron first was made it was impossible to remove the slag because temperatures high enough to melt large quantities of iron could not be produced on an industrial scale. Consequently, after hot-working, a characteristic structure was produced (Figure 4.13). The slag usually appears as stringers in a longitudinal section and as the more regular cross sections of those stringers in a transverse section. In either section the ferrite grains usually are essentially equiaxed. Greater detail of the slag structure is shown in Figure 1.15*c*.

## MECHANICAL PROPERTIES OF INDUSTRIAL IRON

Mechanical properties of all of these grades of iron may vary widely depending on the exact composition and the grain size. Typical values are shown in Table 4.2. When heavily cold worked, ingot irons recrystallize near the range 390 to 575 F (200 to 300 C). At higher temperatures grain growth is apt to be extensive.

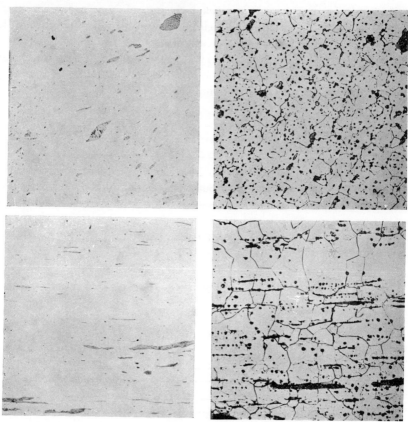

**Figure 4.13** Metallographic structures typical of wrought iron (×100 originally, reduced approximately one-half in reproduction). Transverse section (*top left*) unetched and (*top right*) etched with nital. Longitudinal section (*bottom left*) unetched and (*bottom right*) etched with nital. [Photomicrographs courtesy A. M. Byers Company.]

**TABLE 4.2**

| Property | Pure Iron | Ingot Iron | Wrought Iron |
|---|---|---|---|
| Tensile strength (psi) | 28,000–40,000 | 40,000–45,000 | 48,000 |
| Yield strength (psi) | 15,000–24,000 | 25,000–30,000 | 29,000 |
| Elongation (% in 2 in.) | 30–40 | 40 | 25 |
| Reduction in area (%) | 50–55 | 50 | 40 |
| Brinell hardness (10 mm–500 Kg) | 60 | 85 | 97–105 |
| Rockwell hardness ($\frac{1}{16}$-100-*B*) | — | — | *B*55–*B*60 |

Several materials similar to ingot iron but containing small amounts of various alloy elements are available commercially. A small amount (up to 0.25%) of copper seems particularly beneficial for increasing corrosion resistance to industrial atmospheres and to mildly acidic waters. Strength properties of these varieties usually are somewhat higher than those of the unalloyed types.

Ingot iron materials of all of these types often are covered with zinc or tin to increase corrosive resistance. Thin aluminum coatings also are used for some purposes.

## SOFT LEAD

Chemical or soft lead contains less than 0.1% of other impurities, chiefly copper.[14] Other grades, containing up to 0.25% impurities and known as corroding leads are used for a variety of applications. Typical mechanical properties are:

| | |
|---|---|
| Tensile strength | 2,100–2,900 psi |
| Yield strength | |
| (0.5% elong.) | 1,100–1,400 psi |
| Maximum tensile load | |
| for indefinite time | 410–690 psi |
| Elongation | 30–70% in 2 in. |
| Reduction in area | 88–100% |
| Brinell hardness | |
| (10 mm–500 Kg) | 3–5.5 |

These are very sensitive to the amount of impurity present; the presence of only a few hundredths of a per cent produces marked changes. The purer leads have the lower strengths and hardnesses and the higher workabilities. The strength properties are so low that soft lead can be used satisfactorily only if it is supported properly. A typical microstructure is shown in Figure 3.9. Metallographic specimens of pure lead are extremely difficult to prepare except by special techniques, such as the microtome [15] or electrolytic polishing. Lead flows so easily and recrystallizes so readily that ordinary mechanical polishing methods are practically out of the question.

Chemical lead is used chiefly because of its corrosion resistance. This is particularly good under conditions, such as exposure to neutral or acid solutions, which favor the formation of protective carbonate or oxide coatings. Highly corrosion-resistant surface layers also are developed in

---

[14] See E. E. Schumacher, *Trans. A.I.M.E.*, **188** (1950), 1097–1110.
[15] This is a sharp-edged knife which removes a thin layer from the surface without work-hardening it significantly.

strong sulfuric and phosphoric acids. The joining of lead alloys by fusion, either with or without added lead, is known as lead burning, an art requiring considerable skill.

### HARD LEAD

The addition of about 0.06% tellurium, to form a eutectic [16] mixture, improves the physical properties, and raises the temperature of rapid recrystallization well above room temperature, thus permitting the alloy to be hardened by cold-work. The metallographic structure of a cold-worked alloy is shown in Figure 4.14. Hardening produced in this manner de-

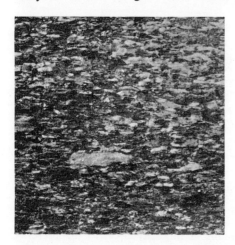

**Figure 4.14** Metallographic structure of tellurium lead (0.05% tellurium, 0.06% copper, remainder lead), cold-rolled 50%. Etched with HAc + $H_2O_2$ (×50). [Photomicrograph courtesy Research Department, American Smelting and Refining Company.]

creases gradually with time, however, because recrystallization proceeds slowly even at room temperature. Even this softening with time has certain advantages because it is accompanied by a definite increase in ductility. The average properties of tellurium lead, in the form of rolled commercial sheet, are shown in Table 4.3. The alloy also tends to have a finer grain size than the pure metal, which gives increased resistance to fatigue stresses.

**TABLE 4.3**

|  | Tested After 1 Day | Tested After 90 Days |
|---|---|---|
| Ultimate tensile strength (psi) | 4,030 | 3,800 |
| Elongation (% in 2 in.) | 8 | 23 |

[16] The eutectic alloy is discussed in Chapter 5.

Hard leads also are produced by additions of approximately 0.10% each of arsenic, tin and bismuth, of up to 1% antimony [17] or of 0.025 to 0.04% calcium.

The antimony alloy, used widely for electrical cable sheathing, can be age-hardened somewhat by heat-treatment.[18] After extruding [19] and aging one month at room temperature the tensile strength is 2,750 to 3,050 psi, with an elongation of 30 to 40% in 2 in.

The calcium alloys are used for storage batteries, for telephone and power-cable sheathing, and for bearings. In a storage battery they behave like pure lead, both anodically and cathodically, but are appreciably stronger and stiffer, and sulfatize more slowly than lead-antimony alloy plates. These alloys also age-harden at room temperature after being quenched. Their properties depend on the calcium content (Table 4.4). Castings, as-cast, can be aged to comparable strengths.

TABLE 4.4

| % Ca | Tensile Strength (quenched *), psi | Tensile Strength (quenched and aged †), psi |
|---|---|---|
| 0.04 | 3,000 | 5,300 |
| 0.12 | 4,600 | 8,200 |
| 0.20 | 5,400 | 6,500 |

* Quenched from 400 F (205 C).
† Quenched and aged 7 days at room temperature and 16 hr at 210 F (100 C).

## LEAD AND TERNE COATINGS

Lead coatings also are applied to steel by hot dipping and adhere well if the steel is perfectly clean. They can be soldered readily, take paint well, and do not embrittle the steel because lead does not form compounds with iron.

Lead coatings may be of chemical or low-antimonial lead but are more apt to contain as much as 2.5% tin or 2% antimony. One of the most common types, terne plate, is a 75% lead, 25% tin alloy. Hot-dipped lead coatings have a much greater tendency to pinhole than terne coatings

[17] Alloys containing considerably more antimony, up to 6%, are known commercially as "hard lead" and are covered in Chapter 5.
[18] The principles involved are discussed in Chapter 7.
[19] Extrusion is forming by pushing through a die at a temperature not far below the melting point.

so they usually are more than twice as thick as terne coatings. A common coating of lead is 20 lb per double base box,[20] whereas terne coatings are usually about 8 lb per double base box.

The protection accorded by lead coatings (including terne plate) is purely mechanical, and sheets exposed to corrosion must be kept painted, preferably with an acid-resisting paint.

## MAGNESIUM

Magnesium of commercial purity (99.80% min) is available in a variety of forms but it finds little engineering application. Major uses are for alloy additions, deoxidation, pyrotechnics, dry electric current rectifiers and as sacrificial anodes for corrosion protection.[21] Corrosion resistance is very sensitive to the amount and nature of the impurities present. Heavy metals like iron, nickel, and copper are particularly bad.

Magnesium has a Young's modulus of elasticity of 6,500,000 psi and develops fair strength properties (Table 4.5). After a 30% cold reduction the 99.85% magnesium alloy recrystallizes in 1 hr at 350 F (175 C) and the 99.99% magnesium alloy in 1 hr at 200 F (90 C).

**TABLE 4.5**

|                          | Sand Cast * | Annealed * | Hard-Rolled * |
|--------------------------|:-----------:|:----------:|:-------------:|
| Tensile strength (psi)   | 12,000      | 27,000     | 37,000        |
| Yield strength (psi) †   | 3,000       | 14,000     | 27,000        |
| Elongation (%)           | 6           | 16         | 9             |
| Brinell hardness (10 mm–500 Kg) | 30   | 40         | 50            |

\* ½ in. diameter for the castings, sheet specimens for the wrought metal.
† 0.2% offset.

The simplest industrial magnesium alloy [22] (M1A) contains a minimum of 1.20% manganese and 0.09% calcium, with closely controlled impurity content. It has good formability and good resistance to salt water. A typical

[20] Lead- and terne-coated plate are measured and sold by the double base box, that is, 112 sheets 20 in. by 28 in., or 62,720 sq in. of any size and 125,440 sq in. of surface to be coated.
[21] Magnesium is more active electrochemically than most other metals. Hence, it dissolves in preference to the other metal if connected to the other metal electrically and exposed to the same corroding solution.
[22] Other magnesium alloys are discussed later, in Chapters 5 and 10.

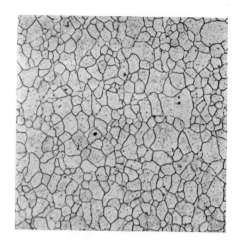

**Figure 4.15** Metallographic structure typical of magnesium alloy M1A (1.5% manganese, 0.09% calcium, remainder magnesium) sheet, rolled and annealed. Etched 10 sec with acetic-glycol etchant (×250). [Photomicrograph courtesy the Dow Chemical Company.]

microstructure is shown in Figure 4.15. Most of the manganese is in solid solution. Any excess precipitates as alpha-manganese particularly if silicon is present as an impurity. Strength properties of sheet at room temperature (Table 4.6) are somewhat higher than those of pure magnesium. Extrusions and forgings have comparable properties.

**TABLE 4.6**

|  | Annealed | Hard-Rolled |
|---|---|---|
| Tensile strength (psi) | 33,000 | 35,000 |
| Yield strength (psi) * | 18,000 | 26,000 |
| Elongation (%) | 17 | 7 |
| Brinell hardness |  |  |
| (10 mm–500 Kg) | 48 | 54 |

* 0.2% offset.

After a cold-work reduction of 20%, a 1-hr anneal at 500 F (260 C) recrystallizes the alloy.

## NICKEL

Two commercially pure nickels [23] have the nominal percentage compositions shown in Table 4.7.

[23] Other varieties, Duranickel alloy 301Ⓣ and Permanickel alloy 300Ⓣ, which contain small amounts of alloying elements are age-hardenable by heat-treatment and hence are discussed in Chapter 10.

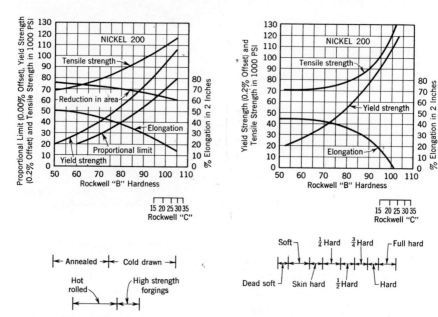

**Figure 4.16** Relationships between average tensile properties of Nickel 200 ⑲ and Rockwell hardness. (*left*) Hot-rolled, forged, and cold-drawn rods. (*right*) Cold-rolled sheet and strip. [From *Engineering Properties of Nickel 200*⑲, courtesy The International Nickel Company.]

**TABLE 4.7**

| | % Ni * | % Mn | % C | % Cu | % Fe | % Si |
|---|---|---|---|---|---|---|
| Nickel 200⑲ | 99.5 | 0.25 | 0.06 | 0.05 | 0.15 | 0.05 |
| Nickel 201⑲ | 99.5 | 0.20 | 0.01 | 0.05 | 0.15 | 0.05 |

\* Including cobalt.
⑲ Registered trade-marks.

Both Nickel 200⑲ and Nickel 201⑲ are strongly magnetic at room temperature and retain their magnetism to 680 F (360 C).

The general relationship between tensile properties and Rockell hardness for Nickel 200⑲ is indicated in Figure 4.16 for several different treatments. In all except the fully work-hardened condition, the combination of strength and ductility is excellent. The retention of these properties at elevated temperatures is good. Nickel 201⑲ is appreciably softer than Nickel 200⑲, and does not work-harden so rapidly.[24] Its elastic and strength properties

[24] The effects of trace elements on high-purity nickel has been reported by K. M. Olsen, *Trans. A.S.M.*, **52** (1960), 545–58.

also are somewhat lower than those of the regular variety, and its ductility is somewhat higher.

Nickel 200⑰ has high energy absorption in notched impact tests. Probably because of its face-centered cubic crystal structure, room temperature energy absorption is retained to temperatures below $-310\,F$ ($-190\,C$). Unfortunately, this toughness also makes the metal difficult to machine so low cutting speeds, light feeds, and high-speed steel tools must be used as considerable heat is generated during machining. High-sulfur oils assist materially, but must be removed completely before the material is heated.

Nickel 200⑰ is very resistant to many types of corrosive media. In general, oxidizing conditions attack it more severely than reducing conditions, although sometimes even the rate of attack under oxidizing conditions is less than expected because of the formation of a tightly adherent oxide coating or of a passivated film. The chief advantage of Nickel 201⑰ is its ability to withstand oxidizing furnace atmospheres at temperatures up to 2000 F (1100 C). It also can be used for anodes in electroplating.

Nickel 200⑰ hot-works readily, especially in the range 1600 to 2300 F (850 to 1250 C), although it can be hot-worked, with somewhat more difficulty than steel, as low as 1200 F (650 C). The metal also can be cold-worked readily if allowance is made for its fairly high elastic limit, which necessitates the use of somewhat greater power than for mild steel. After cold work, it may be box annealed in 2 to 6 hr at 1350 to 1450 F (730 to 790 C), or open annealed in 2 to 5 min at 1600 to 1750 F (870 to 950 C). Full softening, however, requires times about 50% longer. Lower temperatures may be used for annealing, but they are somewhat uncertain because of possible variations in the amount of cold work and the carbon content. Quenching, in water containing about 2% of denatured alcohol, following annealing helps to prevent oxidation. In annealing nickel or its alloys, sulfur-bearing and highly oxidizing furnace gases *must* be avoided.

The metallographic structure of worked and annealed nickel of either type is a typical twinned structure similar to that shown in Figure 4.17.

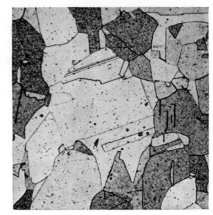

**Figure 4.17** Metallographic structure of worked and annealed Nickel 200⑰ with a fairly coarse grain size. Etched with Marbles reagent (4 g $CuSO_4$, 20 ml HCl, 20 ml $H_2O$) to produce contrast ($\times100$). The appearance of nickel of smaller grain size, when etched with a flat solution, can be seen in Figure 1.13*b*. [Photomicrograph by L. Litchfield.]

A cast form, Nickel 210®, is made containing 95.6% nickel, 0.9% manganese, 0.8% carbon, 0.3% copper, 0.5% iron, and 1.60% silicon. Because it is cast, it usually has a large grain size and, because of its greater percentage of impurities and slow rate of solidification, it usually exhibits some lack of homogeneity, known as coring.[25]

## ELECTRODEPOSITED NICKEL

Electroplated nickel finishes are used widely because of their desirable combination of physical, mechanical and chemical properties. Nickel also is the best undercoat for chromium, with which it is used most commonly, as well as for palladium and rhodium. Depending on the type of bath used and the controls exercised, nickel deposits can be either ductile and dull to moderately bright or bright with, at most, moderate ductility. The very fine and characteristically banded structure of a hard bright nickel deposit is shown in Figure 4.18. Softer deposits of nickel frequently have coarser grain structures comparable with those for copper, Figure 4.8.

## TIN AND TIN PLATE

Commercially pure tin rarely is used except as a coating material on steel (tin plate) or copper. Tin coatings have an excellent appearance, resist corrosion, and give a surface which is soldered readily. This surface usually is uniform in color and appearance but etching discloses the coarse grain structure of the tin, Figures 4.22b and c. Both hot-dipping and electrolytic deposition are used to make tin plate. The usual base metal is steel plate or strip 0.006 to 0.015 in. thick and containing up to 0.12% carbon and usually up to 0.20% copper.

Hot-dipped tin generally carries from 1 to 2.5 lb of tin per base box,[26] that is, a thickness of 0.000059 to 0.000146 in. The structures of two types of hot-dipped coatings are illustrated in Figure 4.19. Under a surface layer of relatively pure tin is a layer, about 0.00002 in. thick, of rectangular crystals of the iron-tin compound $FeSn_2$ (80.9% tin).

Steel plate also is coated continuously with tin by electrolytic deposition (electrotin). These coatings, illustrated in thickness by Figure 4.20 (although the subsequent melting stage frequently is not used so the alloy layer is not present), are much thinner; 0.5 lb per base box (0.00003 in.) is a common thickness which still seems to meet tin plate requirements for

[25] Coring is discussed in Chapter 5.
[26] A base box, the usual measure for tin plate, consists of 112 sheets of 14 in. by 20 in. plate, or 31,360 sq in. of any size plate, and 62,720 sq in. of surface to be coated.

**Figure 4.18** Metallographic structure of bright-nickel deposit, illustrating characteristic banded structure (×1000). This structure also is very fine and nearly unresolved.

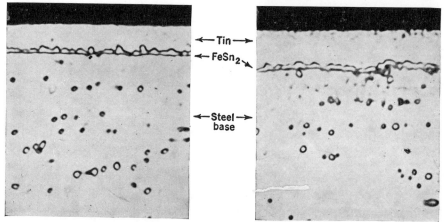

**Figure 4.19** Metallographic structure of cross sections through hot-dipped tin plate. (*left*) Coke tin plate, average weight of coating 1.46 lb per base box. Double-etched first with nitric and hydrofluoric acids in glycerine, and then with 5% picral, to reveal FeSn$_2$ alloy layer (×2500). (*right*) Charcoal tin plate, average weight of coating 3.75 lb per base box. Double-etched first with weak alcoholic hydrofluoric acid and then with 5% picral, to reveal FeSn$_2$ alloy layer (×2500). [Photomicrographs courtesy O. E. Romig.]

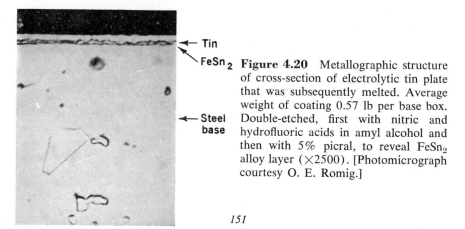

**Figure 4.20** Metallographic structure of cross-section of electrolytic tin plate that was subsequently melted. Average weight of coating 0.57 lb per base box. Double-etched, first with nitric and hydrofluoric acids in amyl alcohol and then with 5% picral, to reveal FeSn$_2$ alloy layer (×2500). [Photomicrograph courtesy O. E. Romig.]

most applications, and coatings down to 0.25 lb per base box have been used. Electrotin deposits frequently are made thicker on the side of the sheet which will become the inner surface of the can than they are at the outer surface.

Tinned copper and copper alloys also are used. In this case the tin should protect the copper electrochemically as well as physically. However, with hot-dipped coatings a very thin layer of copper-tin alloy which is cathodic to copper usually forms between the copper and the tin. If both this layer and the copper are exposed to a corrodant simultaneously, chemical attack on the copper may be accelerated.

## ROLLED ZINC

Zinc of very high (99.99+%) purity is readily available commercially but it finds little use except as an alloying element. The purest commercial rolled zincs, usually containing small amounts of lead, find a variety of applications where formability is required but not stiffness. Metallographic structures of hot-rolled and hard-rolled commercial zinc under polarized light are shown in Figure 4.21a. Mechanical twinning is apparent in the hard-rolled structure but the hot-rolled material is free from it. Commercial rolled zincs have tensile strengths of 21,000 to 27,000 psi hard-rolled and 19,000 to 23,000 psi hot-rolled or annealed, with corresponding elongations of 50 to 40% and 50 to 65%, respectively. Both types of material usually have the lower strength and the higher ductility in a direction parallel to the rolling direction and the opposite values perpendicular to the rolling direction.

Generally, small amounts of alloying elements, such as copper (to 1%), lead (0.3%), cadmium (0.3%), magnesium (0.02%), and titanium (0.15%) are added to increase the strength of the matrix or to form dispersed particles of a second phase which increase the resistance to sagging. The hot-working temperature range is determined by the alloy content. Above this range hot-shortness or brittleness appears, below it the alloy work-hardens.

These hardened zincs can be cold-rolled to tensile strengths of 26,000 to 50,000 psi with elongations of 60 to 20% depending on the composition and the orientation with reference to the rolling direction. Subsequent annealing, by heating at 480 F (250 C) reduces the strength to 18,000 to 30,000 psi and the elongation to 50 to 20% depending on the composition. Metallographic structures of the 1% copper, 0.02% magnesium, 0.08% lead alloy are illustrated in Figure 4.21b. In this alloy the copper is largely in solid solution in the zinc-rich matrix, but the magnesium occurs as very fine particles of the intermetallic compound $MgZn_5$ scattered throughout

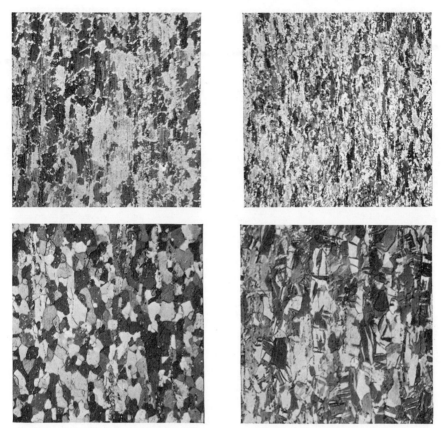

**Figure 4.21** Metallographic structures typical of commercial rolled-zinc alloys. **a** (*top pair*). Commercial rolled-zinc. (*top left*) Hot-rolled and (*top right*) hard-rolled. Etched with solution containing 20 g $CrO_3$, 1.5 g $Na_2SO_4$, 100 ml $H_2O$. Polarized light ($\times$200). **b** (*bottom pair*). 1%-copper alloy. (*bottom left*) Hot-rolled and (*bottom right*) hard-rolled. Etched with solution containing 20 g $CrO_3$, 0.75 g $Na_2SO_4$, 100 ml $H_2O$. Polarized light ($\times$200). [Photomicrographs courtesy Research Division, Technical Department, the New Jersey Zinc Company.]

the structure. It is this constituent which gives the alloy its superior resistance to sagging.

## ZINC COATINGS

Zinc is applied, usually to steel, as hot-dipped coatings by a process called galvanizing, or as electroplated coatings. Galvanized coatings have a characteristically spangled appearance because of their coarse grain size, Figure 4.22a. In zinc coatings, 1 oz per sq ft corresponds approximately to a

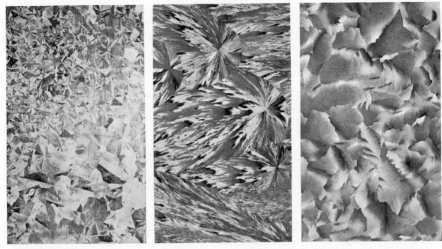

**Figure 4.22  a** (*left*). Surface appearance of galvanized iron sheet. Natural size originally; reduced somewhat in reproduction. **b** (*center, right*). Surface appearance of etched tin plate. Etched with alcoholic acid ferric chloride ($\times\frac{3}{4}$ originally, reduced approximately one-half in reproduction). (*center*) Coke tin plate, 1.51 lb per base box. (*right*) Charcoal tin plate, 6 lb per base box. [Photographs courtesy O. E. Romig and D. H. Rowland.]

thickness of 0.002 in. Zinc coatings are good for general purposes but are considered unsuitable for the storage of foods.

Galvanized coatings on iron, Figure 4.23, usually are composed of at least two layers. The outer layer is substantially pure zinc and the sub-surface layers are relatively hard and brittle iron-zinc compounds, probably $FeZn_7$ (10.9% iron) and $FeZn_3$ (22.16% iron). Zinc coatings give

**Figure 4.23** Metallographic structure of cross sections through hot-dipped zinc (galvanized) coatings on steel after polishing with pH-controlled abrasive. (*left*) Commercial coating, average weight 1.58 oz per sq ft. Etched with nitric acid in amyl alcohol ($\times1000$). (*right*) Coating containing approximately 0.20% aluminum, average weight 1.44 oz per sq ft. Etched with nitric acid in amyl alcohol ($\times500$). [Photomicrographs courtesy D. H. Rowland and O. E. Romig.]

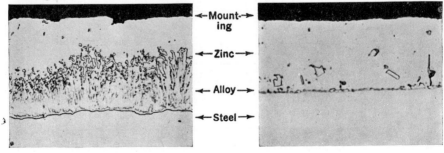

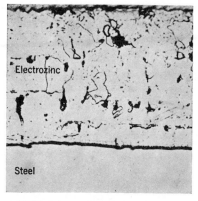

**Figure 4.24** Metallographic structure of cross section through an electrozinc coating on steel wire. Etched with 5% HCl (×1000). [Photomicrograph by L. Litchfield.]

better protection to steel than lead coatings do because zinc is more active than iron, so its protection is electrochemical as well as physical, whereas lead is not. In case of a break in the coating the zinc tends to corrode preferentially, leaving the iron bright. This protection is effective for areas up to roughly 0.25 in. in diameter.

Zinc also is electrodeposited on steel, Figure 4.24, especially wire and wire products, although sheet also is coated in this manner. Electrodeposited zinc coatings are appreciably more ductile than hot-dipped coatings because there are no layers of hard and brittle iron-zinc compounds between the zinc and the steel. This improves adherence to the steel base also. Electrozinc coatings seldom are thicker than 0.0005 in., much thinner than the usual galvanized coating.

## QUESTIONS

1. With the present market price of the conductivity grades of aluminum and copper, what would be the relative cost for conductors of (a) the same electrical conductivity, and (b) the same strength?

2. List in some detail the various stages in the reaction of hydrogen gas with the oxide in tough-pitch copper causing embrittlement. Which one of these steps will control the rate of the reaction?

3. Why do free-machining coppers which contain 1% to 1.5% of alloying element have a higher electrical conductivity than phosphorus-deoxidized copper in which the phosphorus content is only 0.02%?

4. In general, the machinability of a metal or an alloy can be improved in several ways. What are some of them? From their nature why would you expect the machinability to be increased?

5. In alternating current equipment, why do induced eddy currents in a magnetic material cause the material to heat up? How can these eddy currents be minimized?

6. How do wrought iron and ingot iron differ in metallographic structure from high-purity iron? What causes these differences?

155

7. How would you expect the decarburization of iron in wet hydrogen to resemble and to differ from the embrittlement of tough-pitch copper in hydrogen?

8. Various alloying additions to lead affect its hardness in different ways. From a general (not specific) viewpoint, what basic types of hardening occur if no heat-treatment is involved?

9. Why is terne plate preferable to lead-coated steel from the coating viewpoint? Why are terne coatings usually thinner than lead coatings? How does hot tin plate compare with the other two?

10. What are some of the advantages of Nickel 201Ⓣ over Nickel 200Ⓣ? How could the Curie temperatures for the two materials differ from each other and from the Curie temperature of iron?

11. Nickel is difficult to machine. Why? What can be done to increase machinability? High-sulfur oils assist materially in machining nickel but must be removed completely before heating. Why?

12. In a copper-nickel-chromium three-layer electroplate on steel, it is customary to polish (buff) the copper before nickel plating and the nickel before chromium plating. Why do you think this is done? What ways can you see by which the cost of such coatings might be reduced? Would these tend to decrease the protection given by the coating, or to affect its appearance?

13. Why have efforts been made to make aluminum-coated steel and thinner electrotin plate for use in the can industry? Why is the coated metal usually heated after the coating is deposited? How high a temperature would you expect to be desirable?

14. What is the difference between galvanized corrugated sheet and rolled zinc corrugated sheet? What are some advantages and disadvantages of each?

15. What are the advantages and disadvantages from the general use viewpoint of electrozinc steel and galvanized steel? How do zinc coatings, lead coatings, and aluminum coatings on steel compare in corrosion resistance? How about usage for canning food?

### FOR FURTHER STUDY

1. *Metals Handbook,* 7th ed. (1948) and *Supplements,* and 8th ed., Vol. I (1961). Metals Park, Ohio: American Society for Metals.

2. *Metals for Supersonic Aircraft and Missiles.* Cleveland: American Society for Metals, 1957.

3. *Symposium on Newer Metals, S.T.P. No. 272.* Philadelphia: American Society for Testing Materials, 1960.

4. *The Structure of Metals.* New York: Interscience Publishers, 1959.

5. Publications of the producers and fabricators of these metals, most of which can be secured on request.

# 5 *Simple Alloy Systems*

## LIMITATIONS OF EXISTING KNOWLEDGE ABOUT ALLOYS

THE ADDITION OF OTHER ELEMENTS TO ENGINEERING metals, to form alloys, is the most effective way of improving their properties to make them into more useful engineering materials. However, to utilize this method properly there must be a clear understanding of the various types of alloys which can be formed and of the advantages and limitations of each type.

Although certain broad principles connected with the formation of alloys are known [1] most of the knowledge in this field still is on an empirical basis. Even experts can do little more than guess about the results that can be expected when two or more metals are alloyed together. Consequently, predictions are all but impossible for the average user of metals. Experimental studies are necessary whenever new combinations of metals are to be tried.

Fortunately, the work which already has been done by others [2] can be interpreted readily and can be used if certain fundamentals are understood. Such an understanding is all that reasonably can be expected of an engineer, because his problem is one of application rather than of alloy development.

---

[1] See, for example, Ref. 1 at the end of this chapter. W. Hume-Rothery has discussed this well for copper alloys in *Journ. Inst. Metals,* **90** (London: 1961–62), 42–51.

[2] For an excellent compilation see Refs. 2 and 9 (7th ed.) at the end of this chapter.

These fundamentals first will be explained and then will be applied to binary alloy systems of increasing complexity. The basic concepts can be applied to any alloy system, whether it be ferrous or nonferrous. However, the ferrous alloys are complicated to some extent by the allotropic transformations of iron so they are discussed in Chapter 6.

## LIQUID SOLUTIONS

The concept of a liquid solution usually is not too difficult to grasp because it is encountered so frequently. When one or more pure solids dissolve in a pure liquid solvent, or when two or more pure liquids dissolve in each other, the resulting liquid solution (a) must contain both solvent and solute, (b) has properties differing from those of any of the pure materials to an extent which is dependent on the nature and amount of each present, and (c) readily becomes quite uniform because of the comparatively rapid diffusion and the ease of mixing of liquids. If the solute used is a solid, it is found, in addition, that it dissolves at temperatures well below its own melting point. Therefore, it must exist in a new form in solution. There also are many cases of two (or more) liquid solutions which are immiscible, or not compatible, and thus separate into distinctly different layers even after thorough mixing.

These general statements concerning liquid solutions are independent of the temperature, and hence are as valid for molten metals as for substances like water, which are more familiar because they are liquid at room temperature.

## COMPONENTS

In discussing alloys, it is useful to refer to the different atomic types involved as the components of the alloy, a definition which usually means that each component is a different chemical element. Although this is not in strict accord with customary usage in physical chemistry,[3] which defines a component as the least number of independently variable substances required to express the composition of each phase of a system, it is somewhat more convenient for use with alloys, in which the exact nature of compounds is not always so clearly defined as it is in chemistry. However, in some cases it also is convenient to consider intermetallic compounds

[3] See, for example, *The Phase Rule and Its Applications* by A. Findlay, 9th ed., revised by A. N. Campbell and N. O. Smith (New York: Longmans, Green, 1939); *Principles of Phase Diagrams* by J. S. Marsh (New York: McGraw-Hill, 1935); and Ref. 3 at the end of this chapter.

as components and thus be consistent with the physical chemistry definition. If two chemical elements are components, the alloy is known as a binary alloy; if three, a ternary alloy; if four, a quaternary alloy, etc. The binary alloys will receive the most attention in the following discussion.[4]

## METHODS OF ALLOYING

There are three general methods of alloying by forming a liquid solution as the first step:

1. The components each can be melted and then mixed.
2. The higher melting components can be melted, and the lower melting ones added as solids.
3. The lower melting components can be melted, and the higher melting ones added as solids (this includes the case in which all the components are put in the same container and heated until a molten alloy is formed).

In each case some adjustment of the temperature may be required to keep the alloy in the liquid state until complete solution occurs. The reasons for this will be clearer after further discussion. As has been pointed out, not all metals form liquid solutions with each other in all proportions. However, they generally do for at least some ranges of composition.

The last two are the methods preferred for convenience. Any choice between them depends upon the general characteristics of the dominant metal present.

With some metals it also is possible to form alloys by having one as a solid and the other as a vapor. Alloying then occurs by diffusion inward from the surface of contact.

## POWDER METALLURGY

In addition to the methods of alloying by first forming a liquid solution or by diffusion from a vapor into a solid there is another method, developed in the 1930's although it was known much earlier, for making solid alloys at temperatures which may be well below their melting points.

By molding properly proportioned mixtures of suitable metal powders under pressure and then sintering these compacts,[5] for the correct time in

---

[4] The multicomponent alloys have been discussed in detail by F. N. Rhines in Ref. 3 at the end of this chapter; see also Ref. 5 at the end of this chapter.

[5] See A. J. Shaler, *Trans. A.I.M.E.*, **185** (1949), 796–804, for a good discussion of sintering; also Refs. 13 and 14 at the end of this chapter.

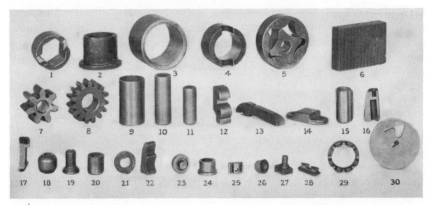

**Figure 5.1**   Miscellaneous parts made from pressed powders (less than one-third actual size). *1, 3, 9, 10, 11, 18, 19, 20,* and *24:* Bronze bearings and bushings of the self-lubricating type. *2* and *4:* Self-lubricating bushings made from iron powder. *5* and *7:* Automatic oil-pump parts made from iron powder. *6:* Block composed of alternate layers of compressed iron and bronze. *8:* Self-lubricating iron gear used in electric washer. *12, 21, 23, 25, 27,* and *30:* Miscellaneous parts made from mixtures of copper and tin powders. *13, 14, 16, 17,* and *22:* Iron dovetails and brackets, chiefly automotive. *15:* Self-lubricating spline bearing made from iron powder. *26:* Porous bronze cone used as an oil filter, to replace one made of ceramic material. *28:* Cutter for Disposall unit—made of Carboloy powder. *29:* Bronze bearing race. [Photograph courtesy General Electric Company.]

the correct temperature range and, preferably, in a controlled atmosphere, coherent parts can be produced with characteristics which sometimes are impossible to secure by other means and which are suited particularly well to certain types of applications. The molded compact is homogenized by intermetallic diffusion.[6] Numerous small parts made by this process, the techniques of which now are known as powder metallurgy,[7] are illustrated in Figure 5.1.

Ductile tungsten wire for lamp filaments, cemented metal carbides for tools, self-lubricating and "oil-less" bearings, diamond-impregnated grinding and cutting wheels, porous metal filters for oil and gasoline, metal powder reinforced brake bands and clutch plates, light-weight metal gears, new and strong permanent magnets, and numerous types of electrical contacts all have been made possible through this method of fabrication.

By using the methods of powder metallurgy any metals can be "alloyed" to some extent. However, intermetallic diffusion [8] is the essential factor so

[6] G. C. Kuczynski, *Trans. A.I.M.E.,* **185** (1949), 169–78, discusses the role of self-diffusion in the sintering process.

[7] See Refs. 13 and 14 at the end of this chapter; also Ref. 9 (7th ed.).

[8] The theory is given by P. Duwez and C. B. Jordan, *Trans. A.S.M.,* **41** (1949), 194–211.

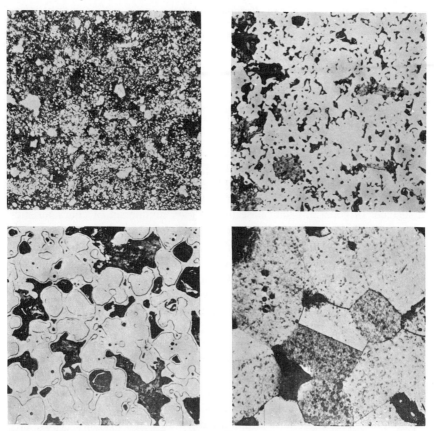

**Figure 5.2** Metallographic structure of a porous bronze bushing made by powder-metallurgical methods. Composition 88% copper, 10% tin, 2% carbon (graphite). Etched with $NH_4OH + H_2O_2$ ($\times100$). [Photomicrographs by L. Litchfield.] The phases mentioned below are discussed in detail in Chapter 6. **a** (*top left*). As compacted under 50 tons pressure. The fine particle size of the powder is apparent. **b** (*top right*). After heating compact in hydrogen for 1 hr at 1400 F (760 C). Some free tin and graphite in an $\alpha$-bronze matrix. The dark areas are largely porosity. **c** (*bottom left*). After heating compact in cracked gas for 15 min at 1600 F (870 C) and oil-quenching. Diffusion of tin at higher temperature has produced an $\alpha$-$\beta$ bronze matrix. The dark regions are largely porosity. This structure is rather abnormal because the $\beta$ phase is unstable at room temperature and tends to transform to $\alpha$ and $\delta$ during cooling. The cooling rate used was probably too rapid to permit this transformation to occur. **d** (*bottom right*). After heating compact in cracked gas for 15 min at 1600 F (870 C) and furnace cooling. The structure shows $\alpha$ bronze containing particles of $\delta$ precipitated during cooling.

the resulting mass may require rather complicated treatments to make it even approximately homogeneous. Three stages in this process are illustrated in Figure 5.2 for a commercial bearing-alloy, which was not sintered in strict accord with common practice.

*161*

Probably the most important characteristic of parts made by powder metallurgy methods is their ability to combine certain physical and mechanical properties with almost any density desired, merely by controlling the composition and the conditions of manufacture.

## PHASES

A phase is an equilibrium state of a substance, of definite composition, which exists at a defined temperature and pressure. In principle at least, a phase should be homogeneous, mechanically separable, and bounded by a surface. In general, each phase has its own unique set of characteristics.

In a single-component system such as a pure metal, or the chemical compound water ($H_2O$) which may be more familiar, there are three different states: vapor (compare steam), liquid (compare water), and solid (compare ice [9]), all of identical composition.

Over wide ranges of temperature and pressure the pure metal (or water) is entirely in one of these states, but under special conditions two states can coexist in equilibrium, and for one specific set of conditions all three can coexist. Thermodynamic concepts require that all parts of a system be at the same temperature and pressure for the system to be in equilibrium, that is for different states or phases to coexist.

If the system has more than one component, for example a binary alloy, it becomes possible for different phases, each with its own composition, to be in equilibrium while at a common temperature and pressure. Thus, such a system could have two (possibly more) liquid or solid phases but only one vapor phase, because all vapors will mix in all proportions.

Each phase in a multicomponent system is continuously variable into phases of the same broad type but of different temperatures, pressures, and compositions. In the case of solids these phases of variable composition, called solid solutions, have the same type of crystallographic structure but with lattice dimensions characteristic of their individual compositions and temperatures (see Chapter 1) and with properties which also vary continuously.

## THE GIBBS' PHASE RULE

Consider the completely generalized case of an alloy system with any number of components, $C$, and any number of phases, $P$. Under equilibrium conditions the chemical potential of each component is the same in all the

---

[9] There are several allotropic forms of ice depending on the temperature and pressure, just as there are with some metals.

phases in which this component occurs. The chemical potential of any phase, even though it may not be possible to compute it or to determine it otherwise, depends on the composition of the phase, on the temperature and on the pressure. The composition of a unit mass of each of $P$ phases can be determined, therefore, if the masses of all but one of the $C$ components are known for each phase; the mass of the other component can be determined by difference. Each phase then has $(C-1)$ variables in composition and the entire system of $P$ phases has $P(C-1)$ variables in composition. There also are two other variables, temperature and pressure, unrelated to composition, so the total number of variables needed to define the system is equal to $P(C-1) + 2$.

The state of any system can be determined completely if there are as many equations as there are variables. If there are fewer equations, values for some of the variables cannot be defined specifically but must be assigned arbitrarily before the system can be determined completely. These undefined variables comprise what is known as the degrees of freedom of the system, that is, the number of variables which can be changed without disturbing the equilibrium.

In order to determine how many equations can be written for any system, use is made of the fact that, under equilibrium conditions, the chemical potential of each component is the same in all the phases in which this component occurs. Any phase in which all $C$ components occur can be selected as a standard even though the exact value of the chemical potential for this phase is not known. Then each component in any other phase in equilibrium with this arbitrary standard must have the same chemical potential as it has in the standard phase. Thus, for each of these other phases there will be a definite equation of state for each component in the phase. Consequently, if there are $P$ phases, including the standard phase, there must be $(P-1)$ equations for each component, because one phase always must be used as a standard to establish each equation. For $C$ components, therefore, there is a total of $C(P-1)$ equations.

The number of undefined variables, called the degrees of freedom, $F$, then, is given by the difference between the $P(C-1) + 2$ variables and the $C(P-1)$ equations. Thus

$$F = P(C\text{-}1) + 2 - C(P\text{-}1) = C + 2 - P$$

Or, rearranging

$$P + F = C + 2$$

This is the phase rule, first deduced by Willard Gibbs,[10] which rationalizes the conditions of equilibrium in a system of any number of components.

[10] See Ref. 6 at the end of this chapter.

This rule is essentially geometrical in its nature, that is, for a system which is described by the phase rule the possibility exists of drawing a single diagram or building a single model which would represent the equilibrium state of every member of the system.

In most phase-equilibrium work in engineering metallurgy the vapor pressure is low.[11] Hence the vapor phase is of little importance, and the pressure is held substantially constant so temperature, $T$, and composition, $x$, are the only significant degrees of freedom. Consequently, plots of equilibrium phase relationships generally are $T$-$x$ diagrams. If any of the alloy components has an appreciable vapor pressure in the temperature range of interest, a simple $T$-$x$ equilibrium diagram may be misleading, and it may be necessary to use the relatively complicated pressure-temperature-concentration ($p$-$T$-$x$) diagrams,[12] relatively few of which have been worked out; gas-metal systems are typical examples.

For the substantially vapor-free, or condensed, systems, therefore, it is convenient to use another variable $P_{sl} = P\text{-}1$ to represent only the solid and liquid phases. Substituting this in the original statement of the phase rule

$$F = C + 2 - (P_{sl} + 1) = C + 1 - P_{sl}$$

Or, rearranging

$$P_{sl} + F = C + 1 \qquad (p = \text{constant})$$

For a pure metal with negligible vapor pressure, $C = 1$ and $x = $ constant; hence $P_{sl} + F = 2$ and temperature is the only variable under normal conditions. If there is one degree of freedom, that is, if the temperature can be varied without changing the equilibrium, only one phase can be stable. This can be either a solid phase or a liquid phase, within the temperature limits of their stability. If there are no degrees of freedom, two phases, either a solid and a liquid phase, as at the melting point, or two solid phases, as at an allotropic transformation, can be in equilibrium at the same time but only if the temperature is held constant. At sufficiently high pressures the other possibility also has been proven experimentally for several metals,[13] that is, at a constant temperature a phase change can be produced in a pure metal by changing the pressure. Hence, all such solid-liquid (melting or freezing) transformations must take place at a constant temperature as pointed out in Chapter 1.

---

[11] R. Speiser and H. L. Johnston, *Trans. A.S.M.*, **42** (1950), 283–306, give methods for determining the vapor pressure of metals.

[12] The principles of these are given in Ref. 3 at the end of this chapter.

[13] See, for example, the numerous papers by P. W. Bridgman in *Proc. Amer. Acad. Arts and Sciences* between 1935 and 1954; also Ref. 3 at the end of this chapter.

For a binary-alloy system $C = 2$, so

$$P_{sl} + F = 3 \qquad (p = \text{constant})$$

Within the limits of a single-phase field, there are two degrees of freedom so both the temperature and the composition of the single phase present can be defined independently and changed independently without disturbing the equilibrium. This is true regardless of whether the single phase is a solid or a liquid.

Within the limits of a field in which two phases are stable, there can be only one degree of freedom. Thus, if the temperature is defined, the compositions of both stable phases, regardless of their nature, is fixed also. If either composition is changed, the equilibrium is disturbed unless the temperature is changed simultaneously. Likewise, if the composition of either phase is fixed, this fixed composition only can be stable at a fixed temperature; at any other temperature this composition cannot be stable in a two-phase field. At this fixed temperature the composition of the other stable phase also is fixed. It should be noted that the phase rule as such tells nothing about the relative amounts of the phases in such a case. These must, of course, vary from alloy to alloy at a given temperature. The manner of variation can be determined, from an established phase diagram, by using the lever rule, as discussed later.

When three phases are stable simultaneously in a condensed binary system, there are no degrees of freedom. Therefore, in a binary-alloy system three phases are stable simultaneously only at a fixed temperature and when the compositions of the three phases in equilibrium also are fixed. Thus, if the temperature is changed or if the composition of one (or more) of the phases is changed, the equilibrium is disturbed and one of the three phases must disappear.

## PHASE DIAGRAMS

The diagrams which are used to express the relationships between phases under conditions of equilibrium are known as phase or equilibrium diagrams.[14] However, if the strictest terminology is not adhered to, and it need not be in engineering metallurgy, the more general term of constitutional diagram may be preferable.

For binary alloys, these $T$-$x$ diagrams are two-dimensional plots of temperature as ordinate versus composition as abscissa as indicated in Figure 5.3. It is customary to draw binary diagrams with the alphabetically earlier

[14] See Refs. 3 and 4 at the end of this chapter.

chemical symbol as the left axis. However, there are exceptions, particularly where the diagram has long been used in the reversed form.

For ternary alloys, phase diagrams are three dimensional, the temperature axis usually being plotted vertically either from an equilateral-triangular base, each corner of which indicates 100% of one of the components as shown in Figure 5.4; or from a right-triangular base as in Figure 5.5.

More complex alloy systems, obviously, can be represented in three dimensions only by fixing certain of the variables. Sections through a ternary or more complex alloy system which can be treated as though they are binary systems, because one or both of the terminal components are compounds, are called pseudobinary or quasibinary systems.

The composition axis may be plotted in a number of different ways although weight percentage is most common as well as most convenient from a practical viewpoint. For scientific work atomic percentage often is used. The relationship between these two percentages is relatively simple.

Atomic % $A$

$$= \frac{(\text{Weight } \% \ A/\text{Atomic weight } A)}{(\text{Weight } \% \ A/\text{Atomic weight } A) + (\text{Weight } \% \ B/\text{Atomic weight } B)}$$

Weight % $A$

$$= \frac{(\text{Atomic } \% \ A \cdot \text{Atomic weight } A)}{(\text{Atomic } \% \ A \cdot \text{Atomic weight } A) + (\text{Atomic } \% \ B \cdot \text{Atomic weight } B)}$$

Data from which to plot equilibrium diagrams can be secured by any method which indicates changes in the equilibrium state of alloys belonging

**Figure 5.3**   Schematic method of plotting $T$-$x$ constitutional diagrams. The pressure is considered to be constant. The chemical symbol for Metal I usually precedes that for Metal II, alphabetically.

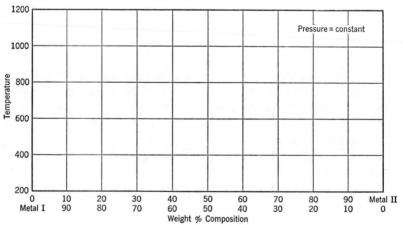

**Figure 5.4** Schematic method of plotting ternary constitutional diagrams from an equilateral-triangular base. In a two-dimensional representation, as shown, both the temperature and the pressure are considered to be constant. In three dimensions, the temperature usually is plotted normal to the base, and the pressure is considered to be constant.

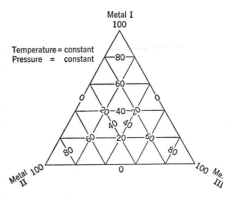

**Figure 5.5** Schematic method of plotting ternary constitutional diagrams from a right-triangular base. In a two-dimensional representation, as shown, both the temperature and the pressure are considered to be constant. In three dimensions, the temperature usually is plotted normal to the base, and the pressure is considered to be constant.

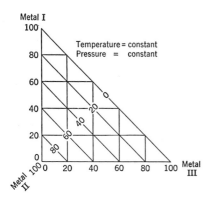

to the system. Determinations of the variation with temperature of the physical properties, for example, electrical conductivity, heat content, specific heat, or thermal expansion, are used most frequently, although methods involving microscopic examination or X-ray structure analysis are common also.

The general methods for securing simple thermal data already have been mentioned in Chapter 1.

## TYPES OF SOLID PHASES IN BINARY ALLOYS

There are only four basic types of solid phases known to exist in binary alloys. These have the general group names.

1. Commercially pure metal (substantially no range of solid-solubility).
2. Primary or terminal solid solution (appreciable solid-solubility).
3. Intermetallic compound (substantially no range of solid-solubility).
4. Secondary or intermediate solid solution (appreciable solid-solubility).

Two components can combine to form more than one example of a given type, but only the four general types are known. It must be realized, however, that this is merely a convenient method of classification. If some other basis were used, such as type of atomic binding, for example, a different grouping probably would result.

## PRIMARY OR TERMINAL SOLID SOLUTIONS

Both the commercially pure metal and the primary or terminal solid solution are modifications of the pure metal, produced by introducing foreign atoms into the pure metal space lattice either in substitutional or interstitial positions. The commercially pure metal, therefore, is only a limiting case of the primary solid solution in which the solid solubility is of limited extent. A pure metal would be represented as one edge of a conventional *T-x* diagram, a commercially pure metal as an area of limited

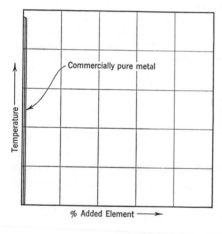

**Figure 5.6**  Schematic representation of a commercially pure metal on a binary constitutional diagram.

**Figure 5.7**  Schematic representation of a primary or terminal solid solution on a binary constitutional diagram. The line limiting the solid solution need not have a constant composition as it is drawn.

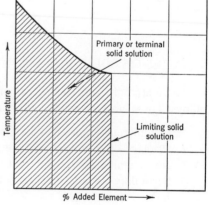

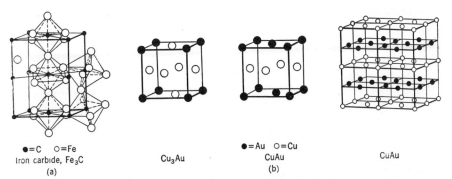

●=C  ○=Fe
Iron carbide, Fe₃C
(a)

Cu₃Au

●=Au  ○=Cu
CuAu
(b)

CuAu

**Figure 5.8**  Possible atom arrangements in three typical intermetallic compounds. **a.** Iron carbide, Fe₃C. [After S. B. Hendricks.] **b.** The copper-gold compounds, Cu₃Au and CuAu.

extent, Figure 5.6, adjacent to such an edge, and a primary solid solution as a terminal area of considerable extent, Figure 5.7.

## INTERMETALLIC COMPOUNDS

Many intermetallic compounds are similar in nature to chemical compounds. These have definite compositions, definite and individual properties and characteristics, and melt or decompose at definite temperatures, either congruently, to a single-liquid phase, or incongruently, to a mixture of two phases.[15] However, even these intermetallic compounds differ from chemical compounds in one very important respect. They rarely obey the laws of chemical valence, whereas chemical compounds invariably do. A certain amount of theoretical study on intermetallic compounds [16] has indicated that the structure of at least some of them can be correlated empirically by the ratio of the sum of the valence electrons of the atoms involved to the number of atoms in a unit cell. Such structures sometimes are called electron compounds, and the ratio referred to is termed the electron concentration. It has not been possible, however, to rationalize many compounds on this basis.

Intermetallic compounds have characteristic, and frequently unique, space lattices which usually are complex in nature. Research has indicated that it is common, in these space lattices, to find certain positions occupied by certain types of atoms. As a result, under this definition not only com-

[15] The incongruent decomposition usually is referred to, in metallurgy, as a peritectic reaction. It is discussed later.

[16] For a further discussion see *The Structure of Metals and Alloys* by W. Hume-Rothery (London: The Institute of Metals, 1960); also *Journ. Inst. Metals,* **90** (London: 1961–62), 42–51.

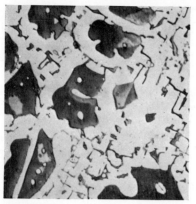

**Figure 5.9**   Metallographic structures of a typical intermetallic compound and a secondary solid solution. **a.** Crystals of the intermetallic compound $Mg_2Si$ in an alloy of 68% aluminum, 20% magnesium, 12% silicon. Etched with ½% HF ($\times$500). [Photomicrograph by L. H. Houtz.] **b.** Crystals of the $\beta$ secondary solid solution in an alloy of 55% copper, 45% zinc after quenching from 1475 F (800 C). Etched with $NH_4OH + H_2O_2$ ($\times$100). [Photomicrograph by A. J. Calpaxis.]

pounds with complex structures, such as iron carbide, $Fe_3C$, shown in Figure 5.8*a*, but also structures such as the copper-gold phases corresponding to $Cu_3Au$ and $CuAu$ (Figure 5.8*b*) would be classed as intermetallic compounds. These copper-gold phases differ from a primary solid solution only in the regularity of arrangement of their atoms, and hence sometimes are called ordered solid solutions in contrast to the disordered or random [17] arrangement of a true primary solid solution in which the positions of the atoms on the space lattice are determined by chance.

Their complex structures, and the forces between the unlike atoms whose positions are interrelated so definitely, cause intermetallic compounds generally to be characterized by a high hardness and brittleness at atmospheric temperatures,[18] and by a high melting point, when they melt congruently. Compounds whose melting points are higher than those of either of their components frequently are found, although this is by no means general. Because of their high hardness and brittleness, intermetallic compounds themselves seldom are found in engineering alloys except as minor constituents. In many alloys, however, such minor constituents are responsible for important engineering properties. Knowledge concerning the actual strength of most compounds is inconclusive. Although the strengths are

[17] For a further discussion of this subject see F. C. Nix and W. Shockley, *Rev. Mod. Physics,* **10** (1939), 1; H. Lipson in *Progress in Metal Physics,* **2** (New York: Interscience Publishers, 1950), 1–52. F. N. Rhines and J. B. Newkirk, *Trans. A.S.M.,* **45** (1953), 1029–46, view the order-disorder transformation as a classical phase change.

[18] J. H. Westbrook (ed.), *Mechanical Properties of Intermetallic Compounds* (New York: John Wiley & Sons, 1960).

believed to be comparatively high, brittleness prevents accurate measurement. The electrical resistance of intermetallic compounds is frequently surprisingly low.

Under the microscope, intermetallic compounds appear as an aggregation of uniform crystallites, each exactly like the others and, except for variations in shape and size, indistinguishable from them. This is typified by the large dark particles in Figure 5.9a. By metallographic examination alone, therefore, it might be practically impossible to distinguish between a pure metal, a primary solid solution, and an alloy which was composed completely of an intermetallic compound.

The resistance of intermetallic compounds to the corroding effects of certain reagents is frequently exceptional, but they rarely are used industrially to resist corrosion because of other difficulties, usually connected with fabrication, although casting can be used in some instances.

In a constitutional diagram, an intermetallic compound would be indicated by a vertical line as in Figure 5.10—that is, a definite composition containing both components. However, all vertical lines need not designate compounds, as will be seen shortly.

**Figure 5.10** Schematic representation of two intermetallic compounds on a binary constitutional diagram.

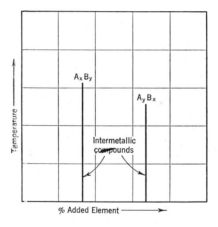

## SECONDARY OR INTERMEDIATE SOLID SOLUTIONS

The space lattice of an intermetallic compound, like that of a pure metal and of some chemical compounds, frequently can accommodate, in altered proportions, one or both of the components. The space lattice of the definite compound, which is characteristic of a separate phase, then is stable over a range of compositions. Such a phase, possessing a range of homogeneity and based upon the space lattice of an intermetallic compound, is called a secondary or intermediate solid solution. An intermetallic compound, then, really is a limiting case of a secondary solid solution, that is, a secondary solid solution which is stable only over a very re-stricted range of compositions.

Instances even are known in which the intermetallic compound is not stable except in the form of a secondary solid solution in which one component is in excess. An example is ferrous oxide, or Wuestite, which approaches but does not reach, the stoichiometric composition FeO.

The secondary solid solution may melt over a range of temperatures, like a primary solid solution, or, like an intermetallic compound, it may melt or decompose at a constant temperature for some one composition, although this composition may not be exactly stoichiometric, or at an expected electron concentration.

Some secondary solid solutions also are quite hard and brittle, and of little engineering importance by themselves. This applies particularly to the members of phase fields in the middle of multiphase systems. Under the microscope, they are similar in appearance to any other single-phase alloy, as illustrated in Figure 5.9*b*.

In a constitutional diagram, a single-phase field in which a secondary solid solution is stable is represented by an area within the diagram, as shown in Figure 5.11.

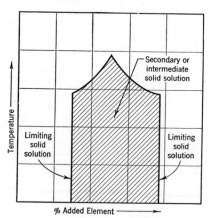

**Figure 5.11** Schematic representation of a secondary or intermediate solid solution on a binary constitutional diagram. The lines limiting the secondary solid solution need not indicate a constant composition as they have been drawn.

## MECHANICAL MIXTURES

Within a binary constitutional diagram, two-phase fields always are adjacent (in composition) to single-phase fields. In such two-phase fields, at a particular temperature, two phases of fixed compositions exist as a mechanical mixture, just as in the case of salt and water, for instance. As salt is added to water, it dissolves until the limit of solubility is reached. Any salt added subsequently is merely mechanically mixed with the saturated solution. Other chemicals may form hydrates first—that is, compounds with the water, which then mix mechanically with the aqueous solution when their solubility is exceeded. They still are separable.

Thus, in binary alloys, any two liquid or solid solutions, or any other mixture of any two phases of like or different types, may coexist in complete stability over a definite range of composition provided the temperature is suitable. Several examples for solid alloys are illustrated metallographically in Figure 5.12. As pointed out in the discussion of the phase rule,

**Figure 5.12** Photomicrographs typical of solid binary alloys which are composed of mechanical mixtures of two phases. **a** (*top left*). Two commercially pure components: needles of silicon in an aluminum matrix in an alloy containing 87.5% aluminum, 2.5% silicon. Etched with ½% HF (×100). [Photomicrograph by L. A. Rodecker.] **b** (*top right*). Two primary solid solutions: plates of antimony-rich solid solution in a lead-rich solid solution matrix in an alloy containing 87% lead, 13% antimony. Etched with 5% nital (×100). [Photomicrograph by L. Wysocki.] **c** (*bottom left*). A primary and a secondary solid solution: β secondary solid solution between the grains of twinned α primary solid solution in a bronze containing 85% copper, 15% tin which was quenched from 1100 F (600 C). Etched with Grard's No. 1 (×100). [Photomicrograph by C. M. Campbell.] **d** (*bottom right*). A commercially pure metal and an intermetallic compound: spheroids of iron carbide in a matrix of iron in a 1.24% carbon steel. Etched with picral (×500). [Photomicrograph by M. C. Fetzer.]

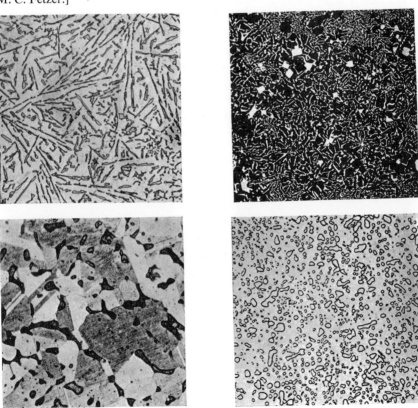

three phases can exist in equilibrium in condensed binary alloys only at a definite temperature and composition. No more than four phases can be present in equilibrium in any binary alloy; even then the temperature, pressure, and composition all must be fixed and one of the phases must be a vapor. Any change in the conditions, in these special cases, causes the excess phase or phases to disappear.

## LIMITATIONS IN THE USE OF PHASE DIAGRAMS

Strictly, the phase relationships shown in constitutional diagrams are valid only when pure components achieve equilibrium conditions. These conditions almost never occur completely in industrial alloying. The validity of the relatively simple binary or ternary diagrams for the interpretation of the metallographic structures found in engineering alloys might be questioned, therefore. However, the simple diagrams, when properly and intelligently used, permit predictions of what might be expected in alloys corresponding approximately to the compositions shown on the diagram. This usually is all that is needed for engineering purposes.

The specific conditions required to produce a given set of properties almost never can be arrived at without a certain amount of preliminary experimentation. The greater the familiarity of the engineer with metallic materials, the more will he realize the truth of this statement. Constitutional diagrams enable him to find an approximate starting point and thus to keep the required experimental work to a minimum. A simple way to acquire the familiarity needed is to examine several typical diagrams.

## ALLOYS WITH COMPLETE SOLUBILITY IN BOTH THE SOLID AND LIQUID STATES

If the heating and cooling curves mentioned in Chapter 1 are used to determine the thermal changes occurring in alloys of the two metals copper and nickel, it is found that the curves differ considerably from those of either pure metal. For simplicity, further discussion is confined to cooling curves, because heating curves are essentially the reverse of the cooling curve, with probably some temperature displacement.

The typical cooling curve for these alloys shown in Figure 5.13, consists of three branches: (a) the liquid solution cools uniformly, exactly as in the case of a pure liquid metal; (b) there is a change in slope to another uniform curve within the limits of which both a solid and liquid phase coexist in equilibrium; (c) there is a second change in slope, below which

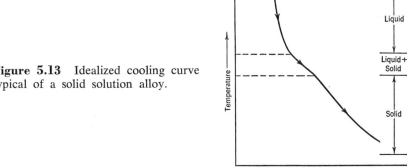

**Figure 5.13** Idealized cooling curve typical of a solid solution alloy.

the solid metal cools uniformly. All alloys with varying proportions of copper and nickel give similar curves, differing only in the temperatures at which the changes in slope occur and, to a lesser degree, the slope between these points. Microscopic examination of the completely solidified alloys, cooled slowly enough to establish essential equilibrium shows that in every case the microstructures consist of similar crystals of a single phase which is, therefore, a solid solution. Furthermore, because the change from either pure metal to a solid solution is continuous, this must be a primary solid solution. In the copper-rich members of the series, the pink color of copper is whitened progressively as nickel is added, thus giving visual evidence of progressive composition change within the phase field.

If a temperature-composition ($T$-$x$) diagram now is made by plotting the freezing points of the pure metals, copper and nickel, and the two transformation points of each of the alloys studied, the diagram shown in Figure 5.14$a$ results. Above the upper line, called the liquidus line, only one liquid solution exists; below the lower line, called the solidus line, only one solid, a solid solution, exists.

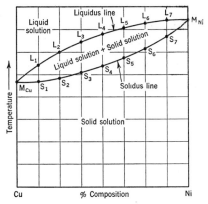

**Figure 5.14 a.** Idealized binary constitutional diagram in which complete liquid and complete solid solubility occurs, as plotted from cooling-curve data.

175

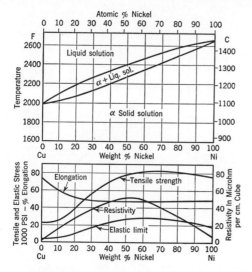

**Figure 5.14** (*cont.*) **b** (*top*). Constitutional diagram typical of binary alloys in which complete liquid and solid solubility occur: the alloys of copper and nickel. [After M. Hansen.] **c** (*bottom*). Change of properties with composition in the alloys of copper and nickel. [After A. Krupkowski.]

These two metals, therefore, are completely soluble in both the liquid and solid states, but their alloys, during solidification, consist of mixtures of solid and liquid solutions, in the lenticular region between the liquidus and solidus lines on the diagram. The property changes shown in Figure 5.14c are in general agreement with those discussed already for the solid-solution type of alloy phase.

The fields on the diagram above the liquidus and below the solidus in which only one phase is stable—that is, exists under equilibrium conditions—are single-phase fields. The area on the diagram separating these two single-phase fields, in which two phases, one liquid and one solid in the diagram shown, coexist in equilibrium, is a two-phase field.

In the two single-phase fields, the phase rule requires that there be two degrees of freedom, and it can be seen that both the temperature and the composition can be varied as desired. If either variable is fixed, the other one is not fixed automatically.

In the two-phase field, the phase rule requires that there be only one degree of freedom. Consequently, if the temperature is fixed, the compositions of the two phases in equilibrium must be fixed, or if the composition of either stable phase is fixed, both the temperature and the composition of the other phase is fixed automatically.

## CHANGES OCCURRING DURING THE NORMAL SOLIDIFICATION OF SOLID-SOLUTION ALLOYS

The validity of these deductions from the phase rule can be shown experimentally by following the changes which occur in one composition in this binary system as it solidifies normally—that is, by melting the entire volume and then allowing it to solidify continuously starting at the free surfaces. Approximate equilibrium can be maintained by cooling very slowly or by holding the temperature constant at successive temperature levels for a sufficiently long time for intermetallic diffusion to keep the solid and liquid phases homogeneous. The liquid and solid then may be separated completely at each temperature and each weighed and analyzed. The results of several of these analyses can be followed better by reference to Figure 5.15.

At and above a temperature $T_0$, the alloy of composition $X$ is entirely a liquid solution. At temperature $T_1$, however, the composition of the liquid in equilibrium with solid is $L_1$, whereas that of solid is $S_1$. The compositions $L_1$ and $S_1$ are the intersections of the temperature isotherm, $T_1$, with the liquidus and solidus curves, respectively. This result is verified by repeating the test at other temperatures such as $T_2$ and $T_3$. Thus, the composition of the liquid and the solid in equilibrium in any two-phase field at any temperature is secured by drawing an isotherm at that temperature, and determining its intercepts with the liquidus and solidus lines or, more generally, with the boundary lines at either limit of that two-phase field. This composition rule can be used to determine the stable compositions in any two-phase field for any constant temperature. The validity of the phase rule thus is confirmed because a definite relationship has been established between the compositions of the two phases which are in equilibrium at any constant temperature. Hence, defining the temperature or the composition of either phase automatically defines the entire relationship so long as the pressure is kept constant.

It can be understood readily from these results that, even though solid-solution-type alloys form homogeneous liquid solutions before solidification and homogeneous solid solutions after complete equilibrium solidification,

**Figure 5.15** Schematic representation of the changes in composition of the liquid and solid-solution phases during the solidification of the alloy under equilibrium conditions.

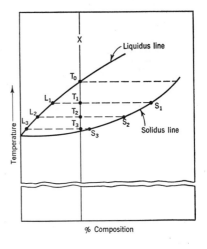

both the liquid and the solid phases change markedly in composition and relative amount during the course of solidification.

During solidification, the process of diffusion is extremely important because the first crystals that separate from the liquid are always rich in the higher melting component, nickel in the example selected, whereas the last liquid to freeze is always rich in the lower melting component, copper in this example. So long as the liquid remains homogeneous and continues to solidify or freeze slowly under conditions of equilibrium, new solid crystals continue to form and to grow in size. In addition, each existing crystal must change its composition continuously as the temperature falls, and must approach the equilibrium composition as indicated by points on the solidus line. Simultaneously, the liquid must vary in composition continuously as indicated by points along the liquidus line. This continuous change in composition by diffusion requires an appreciable time even at relatively high temperatures.

The apparent anomaly of both liquid and solid solutions becoming richer in the lower melting component at the same time is, of course, only possible because the relative amounts of the two change markedly during solidification. This can be shown best by drawing any diagram of this type on graph paper, and then following quantitatively the changes occurring during solidification by using the lever rule.

## THE LEVER RULE

The relative weights of the two phases in equilibrium also can be determined in a simple manner from the binary constitutional diagram. For

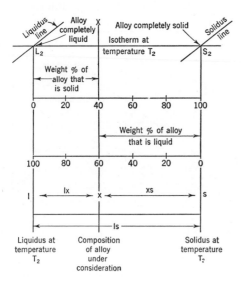

**Figure 5.16** Diagrammatic representation of various methods of applying the lever rule to a two-phase alloy in order to determine the relative amounts of the two phases that will be in equilibrium at any temperature, $T_2$ (See Figure 5.15).

any constant composition it should be apparent that, if the temperature corresponds to that of the liquidus, the alloy will be completely (100%) liquid, whereas if it corresponds to that of the solidus, it will be completely (100%) solid. The amount of either phase (the sum of the two, obviously, always must be 100%) existing at temperatures in between these two points, such as temperature $T_2$ in Figure 5.15, for example, can be determined by drawing a horizontal line equal in length to the distance between the liquidus and the solidus at the desired temperature, and marking on it the average composition of the alloy being studied. This procedure is indicated in Figure 5.16. If this line then is divided into 100 parts starting with zero at the liquidus end, as indicated, the intercept indicates the weight per cent of the total which is solid. If, on the other hand, it is divided into 100 parts starting with zero at the solidus end, the intercept indicates the weight per cent of the total which is liquid. However, identical results can be secured without going to all this trouble merely by using the simple relationships

$$\frac{\text{Percentage liquid}}{100\%} = \frac{\text{distance } xs}{\text{distance } ls}$$

$$\frac{\text{Percentage solid}}{100\%} = \frac{\text{distance } lx}{\text{distance } ls}$$

What these say, of course, is that the two phases only can be present in proportions which do not disturb the average composition of the alloy.

This simple rule is known as the lever rule because of its similarity in principle to the simple lever, namely, the greater percentage (weight) is on the opposite side of the composition studied, $x$ (the fulcrum), from the longer lever arm.

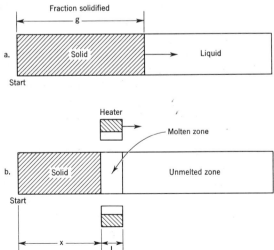

**Figure 5.17** Idealized representations of **a** (*upper*) normal solidification and **b** (*lower*) zone melting. [From W. G. Pfann, courtesy American Society for Metals.]

It must be emphasized specifically that the lever rule tells nothing about the compositions or the nature of the phases involved, and only deals with their relative amounts. Their compositions must be secured by using the composition rule already described, and their nature can be deduced quite simply, once the phase diagram is known.

## NORMAL SOLIDIFICATION AT NONEQUILIBRIUM RATES

Normal solidification can be idealized, as in Figure 5.17a, by a rod of metal which is completely molten initially and then solidifies progressively toward the right. This has the additional advantage that it does not require that shrinkage be considered. Shrinkage is a common difficulty in castings because of the higher density of the solid in comparison with the liquid alloy. If addition of solute raises the melting point, as in Figure 5.15 or at the copper end of the diagrams in Figures 5.14a and b, the concentration of solute in the solid that separates out, $C_s$, always is greater than its concentration in the main body of the liquid, $C_x$. If addition of solute lowers the melting point, as in Figure 5.18, or at the nickel end of the diagrams in Figures 5.14a and b, the concentration of solute in the solid that separates out, $C_s$, is less than its concentration in the main body of the liquid, $C_x$. For simplicity, major attention will be devoted to the latter case although similar reasoning can be applied to either case.

Nonequilibrium rates of solidification can be considered in addition to the equilibrium solidification, already discussed, in which diffusion maintains the compositions of both the solid and the liquid uniform at all times. Consider first that freezing is rapid compared with diffusion or other mass-transport processes which would equalize the composition of the liquid. The phase diagram, Figure 5.18, indicates that the solute concentration in the solid freezing initially, composition $O$, is lower than that of the bulk liquid, composition $X$. The excess solute enriches the liquid layer at the solid-liquid interface. As this layer becomes richer in solute and thicker, the solute concentrations of the solid freezing out of it increase. Ultimately, a thickness and related composition is reached for which the amount of solute removed from this layer on one side in the solid equals exactly the amount passing into it on the other side from the liquid, Figure 5.19a. From then on, solidification proceeds toward the right forming a solid of uniform composition, that is, with substantially no segregation. The final liquid to solidify of course contains more solute than the mean concentration. However, regardless of the manner of solidification, the average composition of the liquid before and the solid afterward must be the same, and the temperature must decrease during solidification by an amount corresponding to the temperature range between the liquidus and solidus lines on the diagram.

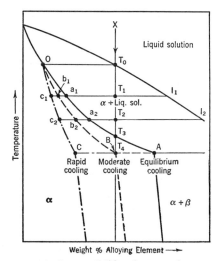

**Figure 5.18** (*above*) Effect of nonequilibrium solidification on the apparent position of the solidus line as indicated on a constitutional diagram. The alloy $X$ begins to solidify at temperature $T_0$ by the formation of crystals of composition $O$. As the temperature falls to $T_1$ the crystals should grow and change by diffusion to composition $a_1$. However, because the cooling rate is too rapid to permit complete diffusion, they actually have an average composition, such as $b_1$ or $c_1$, which is richer in the dominant metal than $a_1$. As the temperature continues to fall the lack of sufficient time for complete diffusion causes the average composition of the solid crystals to follow an apparent solidus line, such as $OB$ or $OC$ instead of the equilibrium solidus line $OA$. Thus, even though, during equilibrium solidification, the alloy should be a homogeneous solid solution at temperature $T_3$, during more rapid, nonequilibrium, cooling solidification might not be complete until temperature $T_4$ is reached and alloy $X$ even might solidify as a two-phase instead of a single-phase alloy.

**Figure 5.19** (*below*) Changes in solute concentration of solid phase during normal solidification, *a*, if freezing is rapid compared to mass transport processes in the liquid (and solid), and *b*, if freezing is slow enough for mass transport processes to remove all concentration gradients in the liquid. [From W. G. Pfann, courtesy American Society for Metals.]

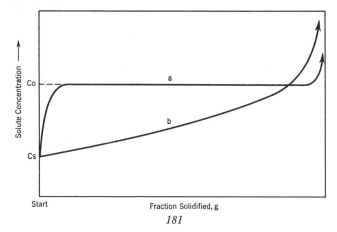

*181*

Generally, it is found that, although diffusion may not be too effective in homogenizing the solid, the combined action of diffusion and other mass-transport methods, such as, for example, turbulence, convection, or stirring, is at least partially effective in homogenizing the liquid. Under these conditions the liquid layer at the solid-liquid interface still may be enriched in solute but it does not become thick enough for its concentration to build up to the necessary equilibrium value. The concentration of the solid then increases gradually as solidification progresses (Figure 5.19*b*).

Figure 5.18 illustrates such a condition diagrammatically on a typical phase diagram. The apparent solidus line is shifted further toward the left end of this diagram as the rate of cooling is increased. When the alloy, *X,* which crosses the liquidus at temperature $T_0$, begins to solidify, solid crystals of composition *O* begin to form. As the temperature falls to $T_1$ these crystals should grow in size and change by diffusion to the equilibrium composition $a_1$ (the liquid meanwhile acquiring the composition $l_1$). How-ever, if insufficient time is given for complete diffusion to occur, the crystal does not become homogenized and instead has an average composition intermediate between *O* and $a_1$, such as $b_1$ or $c_1$, for example. The solidus for cooling under nonequilibrium conditions thus appears to follow lines as *OB* or *OC* instead of *OA*, and the alloy becomes completely solid at a somewhat lower temperature than normally would be expected.

This is the normal segregation pattern frequently found in metallurgical castings. It can be a macrosegregation which occurs, for example, between the surface and the center of an ingot or casting or between one end and the other, depending on the shape of the casting and the exact nature of the solidification. In general, however, the segregation is greatest if there is sufficient time during solidification for concentration gradients in the liquid to be removed without affecting those in the solid.

If intermetallic diffusion is slow, it also is possible to get significant differences in composition between the first portions of the individual crystals that solidify and those portions which solidify later. This type of microsegregation is known as coring or dendritic crystallization;[19] the degree of the layer-to-layer variation of composition depends on the alloy and the conditions of solidification. There also are cases, as might be expected, for which these segregation effects result in particles of a second phase being formed under conditions for which, with equilibrium solidification, there should be complete solubility.

Cored crystals can be detected metallographically because of the different etching characteristics of the various layers, Figure 5.20*a*. Before working many such alloys to any extent they must be homogenized carefully to structures similar to that shown in Figure 5.20*b*. Otherwise the strain gradients which often accompany the concentration gradients may cause

[19] See B. H. Alexander and F. N. Rhines, *Trans. A.I.M.E.,* **188** (1950), 1267–73.

**Figure 5.20** Metallographic structures of 70:30 cupronickel (70% copper, 30% nickel). **a** (*left*). As cast (×50). **b** (*right*). Worked and annealed (×100). Etched with Grard's No. 1 (0.5 g FeCl₃, 50 ml HCl, 100 ml H₂O).

cracking. From a practical viewpoint, the homogenizing may require a soaking heat treatment at a high temperature before working or it may only mean smaller reductions during the early stages of working, for example, until diffusion and recrystallization can homogenize the alloy and permit heavier reductions.

Macrosegregation can be detected by extensive chemical analysis, as for carbon segregation in steel ingots, and by various chemical tests, such as the sulfur print (Figure 5.21) used for steel. These prints are made by placing firmly in contact with the clean, flat, ground metal surface a piece of photographic paper which has been soaked in dilute (1 to 2%) hydrochloric acid. The acid reacts with iron sulfide or manganese sulfide in the steel, liberating hydrogen sulfide gas. This, in turn, attacks the silver salts in the paper, precipitating dark silver sulfide. Photographic fixing then prevents general darkening with time. Similar tests are available for determining

**Figure 5.21** Sulfur prints made on the (*left*) longitudinal section and the (*right*) transverse section of two steel bars. The white spot is the result of a lathe-centering hole.

phosphorus segregation in steel. Micro- and macrosegregations also can be studied by microradiographs (which then are enlarged for viewing), by spectrographic traverses or by the electron microprobe, in which a very fine electron beam analyzes a specific location in the specimen using the X-ray fluorescence technique.

Segregation curves can be calculated from the expression

$$C = kC_o(1 - g)^{k-1}$$

where $C$ is the concentration of solute in the solid, $g$ is the fraction of the liquid which has solidified, $C_o$ is the original concentration of the solute in the liquid, and $k$ is a constant distribution coefficient, defined as the ratio of the solute concentration in the freezing solid to that in the main body of the liquid; $k$ has a value less than unity for phase diagrams like Figure 5.18 and a value between unity and possibly 15 or more, depending on the alloy system, for diagrams like Figure 5.15.

For a diagram of the type in Figure 5.15, the solid which freezes initially is enriched in solute in comparison with the over-all liquid so the liquid layer at the solid-liquid interface must be impoverished. The net result, therefore, gives distribution diagrams for normal solidification which are the inverse of those given in Figure 5.19.

## LIQUATION

When a homogeneous solid solution alloy is heated just above the solidus temperature a small amount of liquid forms, usually at the grain boundaries. This is called liquation. When this liquid is susceptible to oxidation, the bond between the grain is destroyed and the material thus becomes useless, salvagable only by remelting. This sometimes is called burning.

When the solid solution has a cored structure, the composition of some of the cored regions may be such that melting starts at a temperature lower than the equilibrium value. Hence, liquation or burning may occur in these cases at temperatures appreciably below the solidus temperature indicated on the constitutional diagram.

## ZONE MELTING

In the process of zone melting only a limited zone in a bar or ingot is melted at one time.[20] This melted zone of constant volume then is moved progressively along the bar as illustrated schematically in Figure 5.17*b*.

[20] See Ref. 15 at the end of this chapter; also W. G. Pfann, *Metallurgical Reviews,* **2** (1957), 29. A mathematical analysis has been given by L. Burris, Jr., C. H. Stockman, and I. G. Dillon, *Trans. A.I.M.E.,* **203** (1955), 1017–23.

Multiheater modifications, which permit passing several such molten zones successively along the bar, also are used.

The process of zone melting has simplified greatly the production of materials of high purity, by zone refining, or of materials with no segregation, by zone leveling. It also is possible by this means to form sharp interfaces between zones of different compositions.

Zone refining depends on the fact that each molten zone of constant volume which moves along a bar of constant mean composition, $C_o$, causes a redistribution of solute. Solid of concentration $C_o$ enters the zone at the melting surface and solid of concentration $C_s$, impoverished in solute leaves the zone at the freezing interface. For a diagram of the Figure 5.18 type, solute accumulates in the liquid zone as it travels until a steady-state concentration is reached such that the concentration of the liquid in the zone equals the concentration of the solid leaving the zone (Figure 5.19). From then on, a uniform concentration of solid is frozen out, except that the freezing process is normal, of necessity, in the last zone to freeze. When repeated crystallizations are used, by passing a series of zones along the rod one after the other, solute is moved continuously to the far end of the ingot and almost any degree of purity desired can be secured. The ultimate solute distribution is represented, reasonably accurately, by $C = Ae^{Bx}$. Where $C$ is again the concentration of solute in the solid, $A$ and $B$ are constants, and $x$ is the distance along the bar.

In zone leveling, segregation is removed in a similar manner except that some extra solute must be supplied in the initial zone to replace that which goes into the molten region as steady-state conditions are being produced initially. In other words, the composition of the first zone must be so adjusted that the solid freezing from it is of the same composition as the liquid formed at its leading edge. Under these conditions the solid can be made uniform in composition throughout its length with no segregation.

Other distributions of solute can be secured by varying the composition of the melt, the dimensions of the melt, or the growth conditions. These techniques are particularly valuable when working with low-solute concentration.

## INDUSTRIAL COPPER-RICH ALLOYS WITH NICKEL

The copper-rich alloys of copper and nickel are known as cupronickels; the 95% copper, 5% nickel (copper alloy No. 704), the 90% copper, 10% nickel (copper alloy No. 706), the 80% copper, 20% nickel (copper alloy No. 710), the 70% copper, 30% nickel (copper alloy No. 715), and the 60% copper, 40% nickel (copper alloy No. 720) compositions are most common. All of these alloys can be worked readily and heavily if comparatively small percentage reductions per pass are given. Nickel diffuses relatively slowly so homogenization rates are low and it is difficult to eliminate severe coring found in "as cast" structures (Fig. 5.20*a*). During annealing, care must be used because too rapid heating can lead to fire cracking.[21] Bright annealing is definitely preferable, also, to control possible attack by furnace gases.

The cupronickels are much more resistant than copper to corrosion by most types of atmospheres, natural and industrial waters, and sea water, as well as many mineral and organic acids. Because of their nickel contents they show good resistance to attack by alkalies also.

A cast form of the 70% copper, 30% nickel alloy contains, in addition to the major elements, 0.5% silicon, 1% manganese, and 1% iron. It develops a tensile strength of 63,000 to 66,000 psi, with a yield strength (0.2% offset) of 30,000 to 34,000 psi, and an elongation of 35 to 40% in 2 in.

The addition of 1% iron to the standard wrought cupronickel alloys refines the grain size and gives improved alloys for sea-water service. Likewise, the addition of 1% tin to the 70:30 composition gives an alloy which has slightly better corrosion resistance and mechanical properties than straight cupronickel. The tin is in solid solution so the microstructure of the alloy is similar to that of the cupronickels.

The substitution of zinc for 5% of the copper in either 80:20 or 70:30 cupronickels produces no change in the metallographic structure and little change in the mechanical properties, but makes the alloys easier to cast and work, thus increasing the range of applications somewhat. Cast alloys containing about 5% lead and 3% tin, in addition to the copper, nickel, and zinc, also are made. They have, in general, somewhat lower mechanical properties than the wrought alloys.

Because of their high electrical resistivities, three compositions are used as "standard resistances" or, at moderate temperatures, in specific applications such as rheostats, speed regulators, and d-c starters (Table 5.1).

These resistance alloys usually contain about 1% manganese to facilitate casting and working and small amounts of iron and carbon as impurities. All of these elements are in solid solution. Tensile strengths of the order of 50,000 psi annealed or 100,000 psi cold-worked are usual.

## INDUSTRIAL NICKEL-RICH ALLOYS WITH COPPER

Monel alloy 400®, the only industrial nickel-rich alloy with copper, originally was reduced metallurgically from a natural mixture of nickel and

---

[21] Fire cracking is a form of thermal shock. The combination of internal stresses from compositional differences and from thermal gradients produced by too rapid heating becomes large enough to cause cracking. The situation is made worse if the material passes through a zone of low ductility during heating.

copper ores. It was found to have very valuable corrosion-resisting properties so it was marketed in its natural composition instead of separating the nickel and copper further, a separation which, at the time, was extremely difficult. Today, both wrought and cast monels with the nominal compositions shown in Table 5.2 are available, as well as certain special and "strong" grades.

TABLE 5.1

| | | Resistivity at 68 F (20 C) | |
| | | Ohms per | |
| % Ni | % Cu | circ mil-ft | Microhm-cm |
| --- | --- | --- | --- |
| 7–7.5 | Rem. | 60 | 10 |
| 22–23 | Rem. | 180 | 30 |
| 44–46 * | Rem. | 294 | 49 |

* This composition is sold under several names. It has practically a constant resistance in the range 68 to 900 F (20 to 480 C), and also is used in thermocouples and for heating elements which do not operate over 800 F (425 C).

TABLE 5.2

| | % Ni | % Cu | % Fe | % Si | % Mn | % C |
| --- | --- | --- | --- | --- | --- | --- |
| Monel alloy 400Ⓣ | 66 | 31.5 | 1.35 | 0.15 | 0.90 | 0.12 |
| Monel alloy 410Ⓣ | 66 | 30.5 | 1.00 | 1.60 | 0.80 | 0.20 |
| Monel alloy 506Ⓣ | 64 | 30.0 | 1.50 | 3.20 | 0.80 | 0.10 |
| Monel alloy 505Ⓣ | 64 | 29.0 | 2.00 | 4.00 | 0.80 | 0.08 |

A free-machining grade Monel alloy R-405Ⓣ,[22] running somewhat higher in sulfur (as inclusions of nickel sulfide) than the regular wrought variety and a grade which can be hardened by heat-treatment, Monel alloy K-500Ⓣ and its free-machining modification Monel alloy 501Ⓣ,[22] are also available.

The three cast Monel alloys 410Ⓣ, 506Ⓣ, and 505Ⓣ differ chiefly in their silicon content. Silicon improves the foundry properties and also makes the cast alloy stronger and harder, as well as increasing its resistance to galling. Both sand and centrifugal castings are made.

The general relationship at room temperature between properties and Rockwell hardness for wrought Monel alloy 400Ⓣ sheet, strip, and rod of

[22] Registered trademarks. Monel alloy K-500 Ⓣ is discussed further in Chapter 10.

various tempers is indicated in Figure 5.22. As judged by short-time tensile tests, the alloy retains its properties reasonably well at elevated temperatures up to about 575 F (300 C) (Figure 5.23). The creep strength, determined in long-time tests, also is relatively high. Below room temperature (Figure 5.23*b*) the yield strength, tensile strength, and hardness all increase; but the fact that the ductility and impact values remain essentially unchanged shows that this increase is accompanied by no tendency toward brittleness.

The comparatively high elastic limit and toughness of Monel alloy 400ⓣ make it difficult to machine, and necessitate the use of cutting speeds that are somewhat slower and feeds that are somewhat lighter than those used for mild steel. The free-machining grade, Monel alloy R-405ⓣ, is somewhat better. The use of a sulfurized oil as a lubricant is beneficial.

Monel alloy 400ⓣ resists most acids fairly well, unless they are either air-saturated, hot, or inherently oxidizing, and most salt solutions, unless they are acid or strongly oxidizing. The attack of most alkaline solutions is slight, unless ammonia is present. In addition, most waters and atmospheric environments have little effect unless the corroding conditions are particularly harmful to copper, in which case a typical copper corrosion product may form on the surface of the alloy. It is attacked seriously by highly oxidizing acids, ferric, stannic, and mercuric salts, sulfur-bearing gases, especially above about 700 F (370 C), and molten metals.

**Figure 5.22**   Relationships between average tensile properties of Monel alloy 400ⓣ and Rockwell Hardness. **a** (*left*). Sheet and strip. **b** (*right*). Hot-rolled and cold-drawn rod. [Courtesy The International Nickel Company.]

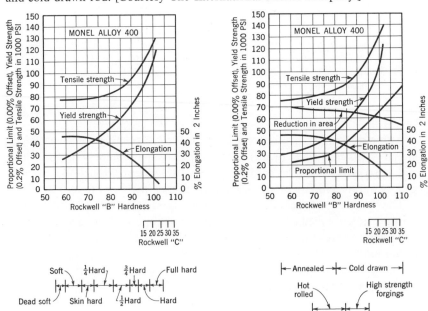

Monel alloy 400Ⓡ is readily hot-worked between 1600 and 2150 F (870 and 1170 C). However, in the range 1200 to 1600 F (650 to 850 C), the alloy has reduced hot ductility and a comparatively high elastic strength, so hot-working in this range should be avoided. Sulfur-bearing fuels form harmful atmospheres at these temperatures, and must be avoided.

## ALLOYS WITH PARTIAL SOLID SOLUBILITY

If silver, instead of nickel, is selected as a metal to be alloyed with copper, somewhat different results are secured, as indicated schematically in Figure 5.24. The cooling curves of the pure metals, (*a*) for silver and (*i*) for copper, are similar to those found previously. Also, the cooling curves of alloys containing only small amounts of copper (*b*), as well as those containing only small amounts of silver (*h*), are similar to those of the copper-nickel system. This indicates that there is some tendency for silver to dissolve copper and for copper to dissolve silver in the solid state.

**Figure 5.23** Variation of mechanical properties of Monel alloy 400Ⓡ with temperature. **a** (*left*). Elevated temperature short-time properties and creep characteristics. Curves *A* and *B* tensile and yield strengths at elevated temperatures on 1-in. diameter hot-rolled and annealed bar (tests made in the Research Laboratories of The International Nickel Company). Curves *C* and *D* from creep tests made by Clark and White at the University of Michigan on hot-rolled and annealed bars. Curve *E* limiting creep on hot-rolled bar (Tapsell and Bradley). Tapsell defines limiting creep as "the load per unit of original area which will just not break the bar when allowed to remain on the material for a very long time." Curve *F* safe working stress suggested by Tapsell as one-third the limiting creep. **b** (*right*). Percentage change in mechanical properties as temperature drops to that of liquid air. [Courtesy The International Nickel Company.]

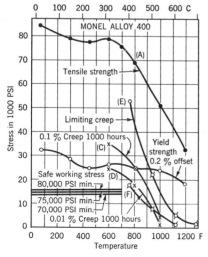
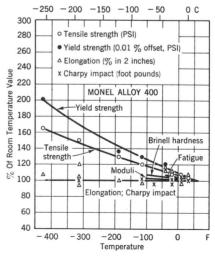

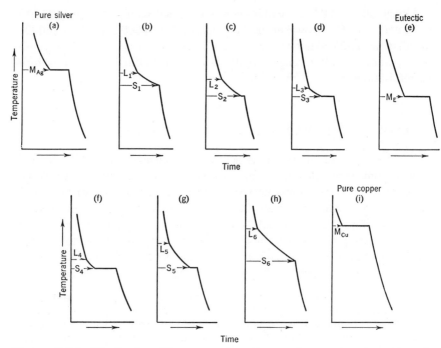

**Figure 5.24** Idealized cooling curves for silver and copper and a series of seven of their alloys.

However, as the concentrations of either element are increased, the cooling curves assume the shape shown in (c) through (g). A portion of the alloy solidifies over a range of temperature, whereas the remainder, indicated by the flat portion of the curves, always solidifies at a constant temperature. In addition, the flat portion of the curve increases in length, indicating a a longer time at this constant temperature, as the amount of silver in copper or copper in silver increases. Finally, for the alloy 71.5% silver, 28.5% copper (by weight) solidification of the entire alloy occurs at a constant temperature; and the shape of the curve (e) is exactly the same as that of a pure metal or of an intermetallic compound. This temperature, 1435 F (780 C) is much lower than the freezing point of either copper or silver, however.

Is this composition indicative of an intermetallic compound? It obviously cannot be a pure metal because it includes both copper and silver. Its fixed composition and definite, although low, melting point clearly suggest the other alternative. Were it a compound, it would be a single phase and, therefore, would be composed of homogeneous crystals. Metallographic examination of this alloy, using a high magnification to resolve the structure, shows definitely that it is composed of two distinct phases (Figure

5.25*a*) and establishes in this manner that it cannot be a compound. At low power, however, the two phases might not be separated because of inadequate optical resolution, so the structure might appear to be uniform. Because of this fact, this type of structure frequently is considered to be a separate microconstituent, termed a eutectic.

## THE EUTECTIC

The eutectic may be defined as the lowest transforming (that is, in this case, freezing) liquid solution. The comparable case of the lowest transforming solid solution is known as a eutectoid. The reaction, which occurs at constant temperature, may be expressed by the equation

$$\text{Liquid I} \underset{\text{heating}}{\overset{\text{cooling}}{\rightleftharpoons}} \text{Solid II} + \text{Solid III}$$

The structure of the eutectic in a binary system consists of a finely dispersed mixture of two phases. However, eutectics also may occur in ternary or more complex systems, and may be made up of more phases.

Three types of eutectic structures commonly are found in alloys as

**Figure 5.25** Photomicrographs illustrating three common types of eutectic structures. **a** (*left*). Lamellar: the alloy 71.5% silver, 28.5% copper. Etched with $NH_4OH + H_2O_2$ ($\times500$). [Photomicrograph by L. Litchfield.] **b** (*center*). Granular: the ledeburite eutectic of iron and iron carbide, 95.75% iron, 4.25% carbon, produced by melting commercially pure ingot iron under graphite. Etched with nital ($\times500$). [Photomicrograph by M. C. Fetzer.] **c** (*right*). Chinese script: eutectic (dark) in an aluminum casting alloy. Etched with ½% HF ($\times100$). Other constituents also can be seen because the alloy is complex. [Photomicrograph by O. G. Morgan.]

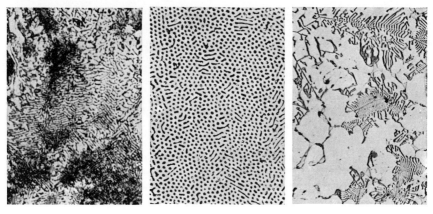

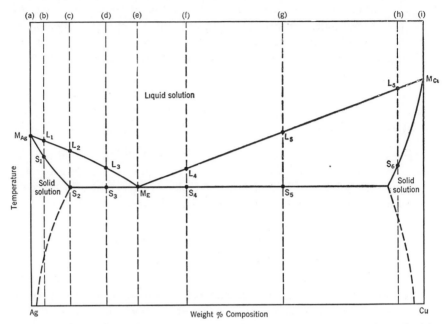

**Figure 5.26** A binary constitutional diagram in which complete liquid solubility and partial solid solubility occur, as plotted from the cooling curve data of Figure 5.24.

solidified: (1) the lamellar or layerlike type of eutectic, in which the structure is composed essentially of alternate layers of the phases involved; (2) the granular eutectic, in which the structure is composed of more or less regular fine particles of one phase dispersed in the other; (3) the so-called Chinese script type of structure, which is characteristic of certain alloys. Each of these structures indicates the mechanism of formation (or morphology) of the particular eutectic.[23] Typical examples of these three types are shown in Figure 5.25. Strictly, these structures are not in equilibrium because if they are held at high temperatures, below the melting point, the fine particles slowly become spheroidal as they approach their equilibrium condition.

## CONSTITUTIONAL DIAGRAM FOR ALLOYS WITH PARTIAL SOLID SOLUBILITY

If the thermal data which have been secured for the system silver-copper are plotted on the usual temperature-composition diagram, the solid lines

[23] H. W. Weart and D. J. Mack, *Trans. A.I.M.E.*, **212** (1958), 664–70, discuss these structures more thoroughly.

indicated in Figure 5.26 are secured. The dashed lines, which indicate the limits of solid solubility and are required to complete the diagram, usually must be determined by other methods because, in general, the heat effects of the reactions they represent are too small to be detected by the simpler methods of thermal analysis. By comparison with the copper-nickel diagram, it should be clear that, in the silver-copper system (Figure 5.27), there are three single-phase fields: (1) the liquid solution of silver and copper, existing for all compositions at temperatures above the uppermost —that is, liquidus, line; (2) a primary solid solution rich in silver, here designated $\alpha$, which is stable for compositions and temperatures falling in the left-hand area; (3) a primary solid solution rich in copper, here designated $\beta$, which is stable for compositions and temperatures falling in the right-hand area.

In each of the other three fields, mechanical mixtures of two phases are stable, the compositions of each phase being determined by the intersections of the appropriate isotherm with the adjacent phase boundaries. Knowing the composition and temperature, the relative amounts of the two phases can be computed by means of the lever rule.

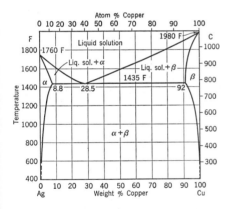

**Figure 5.27** (*left*) Constitutional diagram typical of binary alloys in which complete liquid and partial solid solubility occur: the alloys of silver and copper. [After M. Hansen.]

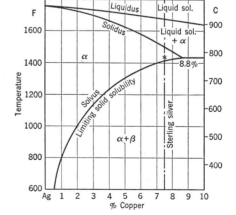

**Figure 5.28** (*right*) Silver-rich portion of silver-copper constitutional diagram plotted on an enlarged composition scale in order to illustrate the structural changes occurring within the solid alloys on cooling.

 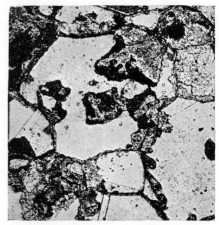

**Figure 5.29**   Metallographic structures illustrating typical examples of precipitation from a supersaturated solid solution. **a** (*top left*). Sterling silver (92.5% silver, 7.5% copper). Quenched from $\alpha$ solid-solution field. Etched with $NH_4OH + H_2O_2$ ($\times 300$). Reduced approximately one-half in reproduction. **b** (*top right*). Sterling silver (92.5% silver, 7.5% copper). Slowly cooled from $\alpha$ solid-solution field, showing copper-rich solid solution precipitated at grain boundaries. Etched with $NH_4OH + H_2O_2$ ($\times 300$, reduced approximately one-half in reproduction). **c** (*opp. page, top left*). Sterling silver (92.5% silver, 7.5% copper). Quenched, and aged 1 hr at 550 F (290 C), showing copper-rich solid solution precipitated both at grain boundaries and within the grains, particularly at the edges of annealing twin bands. Etched with $NH_4OH + H_2O_2$ ($\times 300$, reduced approximately one-half in reproduction). [Photomicrographs *a*, *b*, and *c* by L. Litchfield.] **d** (*opp. page, top right*). An 18% chromium, 8% nickel type stainless steel. Quenched from 1950 F (1065 C) and heated 15 min at 1720 F (940 C), just below the limiting solid solubility temperature, showing coarse precipitate occurring predominantly at the grain boundaries. Etched electrolytically with 2.5% oxalic acid ($\times 750$). **e** (*opp. page, bottom*). The 96% aluminum, 4% copper alloy, showing fine

---

## CHANGE OF SOLID SOLUBILITY WITH TEMPERATURE

Particularly to be noted in these diagrams (compare Figure 5.27) is the slope of the lines, sometimes called the solvus lines, which indicate the limits of solid solubility. For example, maximum solubility of copper in silver (8.8% copper) and of silver in copper (8.0% silver) occurs at the eutectic temperature; and, as the temperature falls, the solubilities decrease steadily to the room-temperature values of less than 0.3% copper (in silver), and somewhat less silver in copper. Consequently, when an alloy falling within either of these ranges, such as the sterling silver composition (92.5% silver, 7.5% copper) indicated in Figure 5.28, is heated above the solid solubility line, it is a completely homogeneous solid solution. If this alloy then is cooled slowly back to room temperature, it no longer can

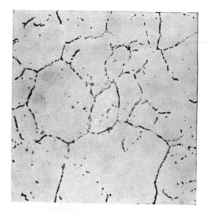
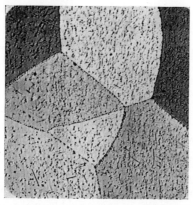

precipitate predominantly within the grains and aligned somewhat on a geo-
metrical pattern, but with some grain-boundary precipitate also. Etched with
Keller's reagent (×100). [Photomicrograph *e* courtesy Aluminum Research
Laboratories.]

remain a stable solid solution because the solubility of copper in silver
decreases. This excess copper separates out or precipitates, not as a pure
metal but as a solid solution, rich in copper and containing as much of the
silver as it can hold in solid solution—that is, its composition at room
temperature under equilibrium conditions is given by the intersection of
the room-temperature isotherm with the solid solubility limit of silver in
copper. This precipitate, depending on the alloy, may be localized, usually
preferentially at the grain boundaries, nonuniform or discontinuous, again
usually at the grain boundaries, or scattered uniformly and continuously
throughout the grains. These possibilities are illustrated schematically in
Figure 7.1 and metallographically in Figure 5.29.[24]

[24] For a further discussion, see R. F. Mehl and L. K. Jetter in *Age Hardening
of Metals* (Cleveland: American Society for Metals, 1940).

## OCCURRENCE OF THE EUTECTIC CONSTITUENT

Two other facts concerning the occurrence of the eutectic constituent must be noted. First, in order for the eutectic to appear at all in the solidified alloy, some liquid of eutectic composition must solidify, that is, the composition of the alloy must lie between the limits of the eutectic horizontal. If this condition is not satisfied, any second phase which appears was formed by crossing the solvus and is present as a dispersed solid solution rather than as part of the eutectic. Second, the solid solubilities of both solid solutions generally decrease with decreasing temperature, so the eutectic constituent in these alloys is fixed in average composition at the eutectic temperature, but the compositions and amounts of the two phases in equilibrium should change with falling temperature. Thus it is possible, although rather difficult to observe because of the fine degree of dispersion, to have a sterling silver alloy consist of three constituents: primary solid solution rich in silver, primary solid solution rich in copper which has precipitated from the silver-rich solution during cooling, and eutectic; yet there are only two phases present—namely, the two primary solid solutions. Actually, the equilibrium diagram gives information only about the number and nature of the phases existing under equilibrium conditions. It says nothing directly about the state of aggregation or the method of dispersion of these phases. This information can be inferred to some extent from the diagrams for equilibrium conditions, but only after a certain amount of experience and familiarity with them. The ability to read the constitutional diagrams in this way is valuable, because the relative amounts and degrees of dispersion of the various phases are the specific points which are of the greatest value in determining the probable characteristics of the alloy and therefore its possible engineering uses.

## THE SIMPLE EUTECTIC DIAGRAM

As the mutual solubilities of the two metals become smaller and smaller, the widths of the two solid solution areas on the equilibrium diagram also decrease. It should be clear, therefore, that the limiting case of the partial solid solubility diagram is a diagram like the one shown in Figure 5.30, in which the width of the respective areas is smaller than the diagram can resolve, and each area, therefore, is represented by a line. This simple eutectic diagram is interpreted exactly the same as diagrams showing partial solid solubility, except that, because the single-phase regions are now lines, they are, by definition, commercially pure metals instead of primary solid solutions. Although this ideal case never has been found, the tin-zinc system

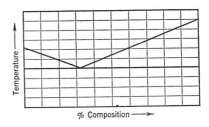

**Figure 5.30** (*right*) An idealized simple eutectic diagram, a limiting case of alloys in which solid solubility is only partial.

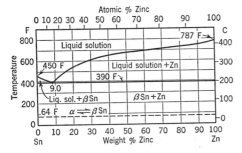

**Figure 5.31** (*left*) Typical simple eutectic constitutional diagram: the alloys of tin and zinc. [After M. Hansen.]

(Figure 5.31) is probably a close approximation. In such a system, no change in the composition of the phases takes place on cooling, so the constituents formed at the eutectic temperature persist unchanged.

## THE $1:2:1$ RULE

A study of the three simple diagrams already discussed discloses two interesting facts which can assist materially in interpreting and understanding more complex binary diagrams. First, there is usually considerable, if not complete, solubility of the two liquid metals in each other. This liquid solution constitutes a single phase at any temperature and composition. Second, by proceeding across the diagram at a constant temperature, the sequence of the number of phases stable in the successive fields is normally $1:2:1$, etc., each colon indicating a line on the diagram and each number indicating the number of phases that is stable in each corresponding field on the diagram. Apparent exceptions may arise when the path passes along a reaction line or through a singular point (liquidus maximum or minimum).

The application of these two observations eliminates any uncertainty as to whether, in a given area adjacent to a pure metal or to a compound on a constitutional diagram, a simple solid solution or a mechanical mixture of two phases is stable. By starting with a single (liquid) phase in the field above the liquidus line and proceeding horizontally (at a constant temperature) back and forth across the diagram, every field can be labeled im-

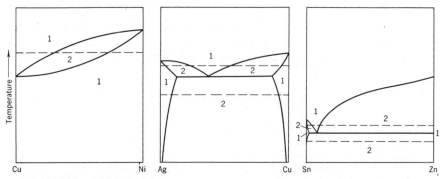

**Figure 5.32** Application of 1:2:1 rule to the three simple types of binary constitutional diagrams.

mediately as a single- or a two-phase field. As a check, in order to detect single-phase fields of zero width—that is, lines designating definite compositions—it is advisable to work from both directions instead of from one only. This method has been applied to the three simple diagrams in Figure 5.32.

Once the diagram has been labeled in this manner, it is only necessary to determine, by deduction, the nature of the phases stable in the single-phase regions. In the two-phase regions, mechanical mixtures of the saturated solid solutions belonging to the two adjacent fields occur at each temperature.

If the single-phase field is an area, it must be a solid solution. If it is a vertical line, it can be either a pure metal or an intermetallic compound according to position. If the area or line occurs at the end or terminus of the complete diagram—that is, adjacent to either of the pure metals—it indicates a primary solid solution if it is an area, or a commercially pure metal if it is a line. If the area or line is separated from the pure components by one or more two-phase fields, it must indicate a secondary solid solution (area) or an intermetallic compound (line). The characteristics of phases of these types already have been discussed. The relative amounts of any phases existing in a given binary alloy under conditions of equilibrium can be computed readily either from the lever rule or from the nature of the diagram so a satisfactory qualitative or semiquantitative estimate of the properties of the alloys under equilibrium conditions can be made.

If conditions other than equilibrium exist, the problem becomes much more complicated. Sometimes the properties of the alloys can be deduced fairly well from the nature of the diagram, but more frequently than not, this leads to misleading results. In any case, it should be applied with extreme caution.

Much of the study of metals is carried out with the aid of the microscope, and the separate and distinct types or groupings of crystals which can be recognized under the microscope are known as the metallographic constituents. These constituents must be unique, both as regards their appearance and their properties, because it is the size, shape, and arrangement of the constituents with respect to one another that determines the specific properties of a metallic aggregate.

Any of the phases of a system, either solid or liquid, also may appear as constituents, with the restriction previously stated that, in a binary alloy, no more than two phases (solid or liquid) can exist in equilibrium except under very special conditions—for example, at singular points of constant composition and temperature such as the eutectic point. In addition to the phases, as already noted, certain mechanical mixtures of two phases occasionally occur which, under conditions of equilibrium, have definite compositions, transformation temperatures, and properties. Sometimes, it is convenient to consider these specific mixtures as constituents also. Usually, but not necessarily, these constituents are apparently uniform at low magnification, although at high magnification they are resolved into their separate phases. The eutectic is an example of such a constituent, particularly in a simple eutectic type of diagram.

In the application of the lever rule to the simple eutectic system, the eutectic constituent can be treated, if desired, like a separate phase, as indicated in Figure 5.33. The two-phase area under the eutectic line thus can be considered either as a mechanical mixture of two commercially pure metals, *A* and *B*, or as subdivided into three regions, in which occur, respectively, metal *A* + eutectic, eutectic, and eutectic + metal *B*, as shown. This method of analysis, when any solid solubility occurs, as in the silver-copper system (Figure 5.27), is complicated by the two facts which already have been mentioned: first, that both the relative amounts of the two phases comprising the eutectic and their compositions may vary with

**Figure 5.33** Application of 1:2:1 rule to the simple eutectic diagram. The eutectic is considered to be a separate constituent, and is treated as a phase purely as a matter of convenience.

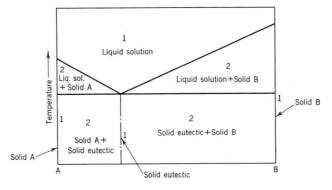

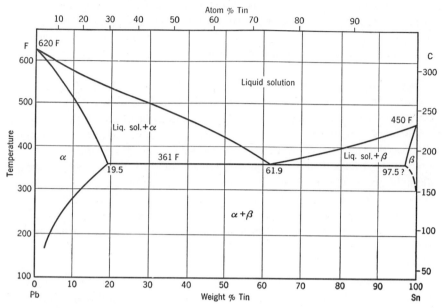

**Figure 5.34** Constitutional diagram for the alloys of lead and tin: the soft solders. [After M. Hansen.]

the temperature, depending on the slopes of the solid solubility lines; and, second, that eutectic only can be found in the solid alloy if liquid of eutectic composition solidifies. These facts, of course, make the quantitative use of constituents troublesome unless little or no solid solubility exists, or unless the solid solubility does not change appreciably with temperature. If the solid solubilities are essentially constant with temperature, as with certain ranges of compositions in the iron-carbon alloys to be discussed in Chapter 6, the constituents can be treated as though they were separate phases without any difficulty.

## TIN-LEAD ALLOYS

Tin-lead alloys, the standard soft solders for many years, are characterized by a eutectic at 61.9% tin, 38.1% lead, melting at 361 F (183 C), and a solid solubility at the eutectic temperature of 19.5% tin in lead and approximately 2.5% lead in tin. Solid solubility at room temperature is very low in both instances. The constitutional diagram is shown in Figure 5.34.

The compositions used most commonly for solders applied with an iron or torch, for dip soldering in a bath of molten solder, or for "sweating"

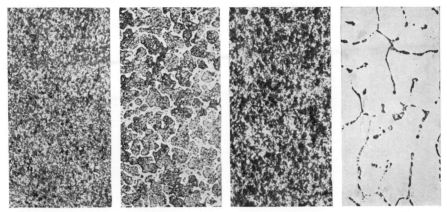

**Figure 5.35** Metallographic structures of tin-lead alloys (×100). [Photomicrographs by L. Litchfield.] **a** (*left*). 10:90 solder. Etched with glacial acetic acid. Tin-rich solid solution precipitated in finely divided form in lead-rich solid-solution matrix. Note that no eutectic forms during the solidification of this alloy. **b** (*left center*). 30:70 solder. Etched with 5% nital. Eutectic (light) at boundaries of lead-rich solid solution within which tin-rich solid solution has precipitated as the alloy cooled. **c** (*right center*). 50:50 solder. Etched with 5% nital. Eutectic (light) at boundaries of lead-rich solid solution. **d** (*right*). 90:10 alloy. Etched with 5% nital. Eutectic (dark) at boundaries of tin-rich solid solution.

are 50:50 and 40:60,[25] with onset of melting (solidus temperature) at 361 F (183 C) and of flowing (liquidus temperature) at approximately 420 F (215 C) and 460 F (240 C), respectively. These compositions can be applied more easily and have a greater fluidity than the lower tin alloys. The 30:70 and 20:80 compositions, flowing at 495 F (255 C) and 545 F (285 C), respectively, can be used entirely satisfactorily for most applications but require much more care in preparing the surfaces to be soldered and an entirely different soldering technique because of their higher flow temperatures and lower fluidity.[26] In addition, the lower-tin solders are difficult to use for joining large assemblies because of the long freezing range during which dimensional changes tend to destroy the joint. The high-lead alloys are essentially wiping solders.

The photomicrographs in Figure 5.35 illustrate the metallographic structures of the tin-lead alloys, and those in Figure 5.36 illustrate cross sections through lap joints soldered with the 30:70, 40:60, and 50:50 alloys.

[25] The conventional nomenclature usually adhered to in the industry refers to the weight per cent tin first, the weight per cent lead second, and the weight per cent antimony, if present, third. Thus a 40:60 solder means 40% tin, 60% lead, and 38:60:2 means 38% tin, 60% lead, 2% antimony.

[26] These are discussed thoroughly in *Tin Solders,* 2nd ed., by S. J. Nightingale (revised by O. F. Hudson) (London: British Non-Ferrous Research Assoc., 1942).

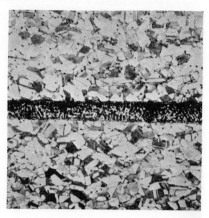

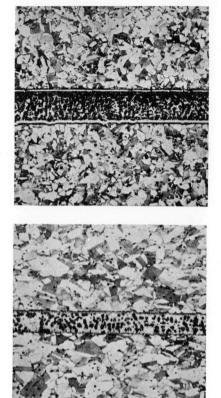

**Figure 5.36** Cross sections through soft-soldered joints between leaded high-brass sheets. Etched with $NH_4OH + H_2O_2$ and 2% HCl ($\times 200$ originally, reduced somewhat in reproduction). **a** (*upper left*). 30:70 solder. **b** (*upper right*). 40:60 solder. **c** (*lower left*). 50:50 solder. [Photomicrographs by L. Litchfield.]

Wiping solders,[27] used for joining sections of lead pipe or lead cable sheathing in preference to lead burning (the common name for torch welding lead using lead as a filler rod), or for connecting lead pipe to copper-alloy fittings, generally contain 42 to 37% tin and 58 to 63% lead, although up to 2% antimony sometimes is added for solid-solution strengthening. If the solder is used to fill joints in automobile bodies, 30:70 usually is preferred. For this type of application the solder is manipulated or wiped over the joint by hand while it is in a pasty condition—that is, between the liquidus and solidus temperatures—so a fairly extended range of partial liquefication without too high a flow temperature is desirable. In recent years various plastics have been used for much of this work.

[27] The properties of these are discussed by D. A. McLean, R. L. Peek, Jr., and E. E. Schumacher, *Journ. Rheology,* **3** (1932), 53.

## SILVER-LEAD ALLOYS

The silver-lead alloys also form an eutectic system and can be used as substitute solders if tin is not available. The eutectic of lead with 2.5% silver, to which about 0.25% copper has been added, Figure 5.37, is the commonest alloy. The more expensive 95% lead, 5% silver alloy is almost as good although it flows at a higher temperature than the alloy containing less silver.

The big disadvantages of the lead-silver solders are their low fluidity and their high melting range. The melting (eutectic) temperature is about 580 F (305 C) and the flow (liquidus) temperature about 660 F (350 C), both appreciably higher than those of the tin-lead solders. When cold-worked copper is soldered with these lead-silver alloys it is annealed because of the relatively high temperatures required. This is often undesirable. However, even the 50:50 tin-lead solders anneal copper, although to a much lesser degree.

In addition, joints made with the lead-silver alloys have neither the room-temperature strength nor the bright appearance of those made with the tin solders. They do differ in one respect which generally is not realized. When a 50:50 solder joint starts to fail, it fails suddenly and with a brittle fracture, as in opening a sardine can, for example. Joints made with a lead-silver solder, however, are just about as resistant to tearing after failure starts as they are initially. This is largely the result of the failure of the

**Figure 5.37**   **a** (*left*). Metallographic structures of 97.25% lead, 2.5% silver, 0.25% copper solder. Etched with 2% nital (×300). **b** (*right*). Cross section through soldered joint between leaded high-brass sheets made with 97.25% lead, 2.5% silver, 0.25% copper solder. Etched with 2% nital (×200 originally, reduced approximately one-half in reproduction). [Photomicrographs by L. Litchfield.]

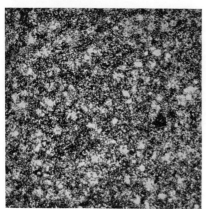 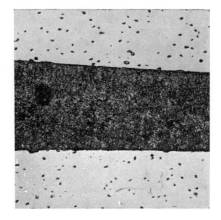

lead-silver alloys to form intermetallic compounds with either copper or iron, the usual materials soldered.

The creep strength of the lead-silver solders in shear is much higher than that of the 50:50 solder, and this strength is retained well up to at least 325 F (160 C). Furthermore, because of the low alloying tendency between lead and copper there is practically no deterioration of the bond with time. When solders with constituents, like tin, which tend to diffuse readily into copper alloys are used in this temperature range, deterioration of the bond with time often has been a serious matter.

## LEAD-ANTIMONY ALLOYS

The lead-antimony alloys also form an eutectic system, Figure 5.38. These are well-known bearing alloys which are still entirely satisfactory for many uses. The eutectic of this binary system occurs at approximately 11.7% antimony. Consequently, the alloys in the usual bearing range of 10 to 15% antimony either are predominantly eutectic or else contain a small amount of excess antimony-rich primary solid solution, as illustrated in Figure 5.39c. Ultimate strengths generally run between about 13,000 psi at room temperature and 5,000 psi at 210 F (100 C) with accompanying Brinell hardnesses (10 mm–500 Kg) of 14 to 17 and 6 to 9, respectively.

**Figure 5.38**   Constitutional diagram for the alloys of lead and antimony: early bearing alloys. [After E. E. Schumacher and G. M. Boaton.]

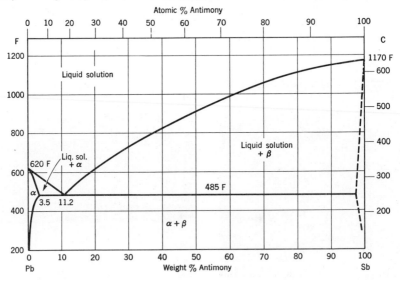

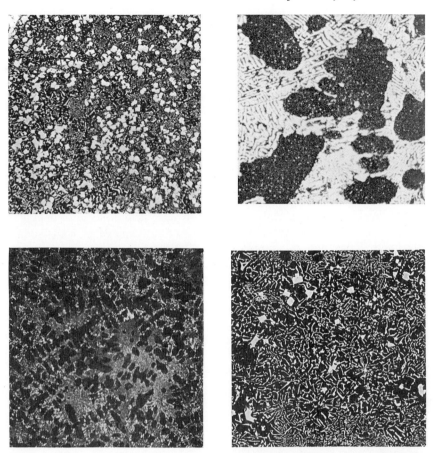

**Figure 5.39** Metallographic structures of lead-base babbitts. **a** (*top left*). High-tin type containing approximately 74% lead, 10% tin, 15% antimony, 0.5% arsenic, 0.25% copper. Etched with nital (×100). [Photomicrograph courtesy The Cleveland Graphite Bronze Company.] **b** (*top right and bottom left*). Low-tin type, containing approximately 85% lead, 5% tin, 10% antimony. Etched with nital. Chill cast (×100, left; ×500, right). [Photomicrograph by L. Litchfield.] **c** (*bottom right*). Lead-antimony type, containing approximately 87% lead, 13% antimony. Etched with nital (×100).

A modified composition used widely for heavy-duty lead-base babbitt bearings contains, nominally, 82.5% lead, 15% antimony, 1% tin, 1% arsenic, 0.5% copper. A maximum of 0.005% is set for impurities of aluminum and zinc. Other impurities are less important and are held within 0.35%. The main advantage of this alloy, other than its low cost and availability, is its fatigue resistance, which is at least equal to that of the tin-base babbitts. In addition, this alloy shows a better retention of mechanical properties at elevated temperatures than the tin babbitts (Table 5.3).

**TABLE 5.3**

| Tensile Strength (psi) | | | Elongation (%) | | | Brinell Hardness (10 mm–500 Kg) | | |
|---|---|---|---|---|---|---|---|---|
| 80 F | 210 F | 300 F | 80 F | 210 F | 300 F | 80 F | 210 F | 300 F |
| 9,600 | 6,500 | 4,100 | 1.2 | 4.8 | 15.5 | 20.8 | 14.2 | 9.8 |

This lead-base alloy usually is bonded to steel strip either in a thickness of 0.010 to 0.0625 in., for conventional bearings capable of withstanding maximum mean unit pressures of about 1,200 psi, or in a thickness of 0.002 to 0.005 in., for microbearings which give satisfactory service under maximum mean unit pressures of about 1,800 psi.

**Figure 5.40** Metallographic structure of a heavy-duty lead-base babbitt, containing 82.5% lead, 15% antimony, 1% tin, 1% arsenic, 0.5% copper, as strip cast for automotive service. Etched with dilute HCl (×500). [Photomicrograph courtesy The Cleveland Graphite Bronze Company.]

The metallographic structure of the alloy, shown in Figure 5.40, consists of primary particles rich in antimony in a background composed of lead-antimony pseudobinary eutectic and a complex eutectic.[28] The minor components occur in solid solution in one or the other of these constituents.

In addition, various combinations of lead, tin, and antimony are used for bearing materials, even though the use of tin lowers the melting point significantly, as would be expected from the lead-tin diagram. The alloys low in tin contain 5% tin, 9 or 15% antimony, 80 to 86% lead, and a

---

[28] A complex eutectic means one with three or more phases instead of the more usual two.

maximum of 0.5% copper. The properties of these alloys at room temperature are much the same as those of the higher tin group but at 210 F (100 C) they are somewhat softer and weaker. A typical microstructure will consist of varying amounts of ternary eutectic (84% lead, 4% tin, 12% antimony) and either excess lead-rich primary solid solution (Figure 5.39*b*) or cubes of SbSn, depending upon the exact composition.

The alloys with 10 or 20% tin, 12.5 or 15% antimony, 63.5 or 75% lead, and 0.2 or 1.5% copper, are typical of the lead-base bearing alloys which contain comparatively high amounts of tin.[29] Their ultimate strength generally is close to 15,000 psi at room temperature and about half that at 210 F (100 C). Brinell hardnesses are 21 to 22 at room temperature and 10 to 11 at the higher temperature. With these alloys, the ultimate strength is taken as the stress necessary to produce a deformation of 25% the length of the specimen. A typical structure in which the constituents are readily recognized is shown in Figure 5.39*a*.

### ALUMINUM-SILICON ALLOYS

The alloys of aluminum and silicon, Figure 5.41*b*, are characterized by relatively low solid solubilities and by excellent fluidity. The low solid solubility is reflected in the properties, Figure 5.41*c*, which are nearly linear with increasing silicon content. The alloys containing 3 to 12% silicon are the basis for many important casting alloys and for welding rods (silicon brazing) for both wrought and cast products, and castings containing as much as 21% silicon are being developed.

The 13% silicon alloy, 47, contains slightly more silicon than the equilibrium eutectic composition (11.7% silicon) and, if cooled in the normal manner, is coarsely crystalline and brittle, with a structure similar to that shown in Figure 5.41*a* (*left*). However, either by cooling the alloy rapidly or by adding so-called modifiers such as sodium, the apparent eutectic temperature may be decreased from 1070 F (575 C) to as low as 1050 F (565 C), as shown in Figure 5.41*b*, with a marked change in the structure (Figure 5.41*a—right*), characterized by the absence of large particles of free silicon. This is called the modified structure. In this condition, average tensile strengths of 26,000 psi are secured, with yield strengths (0.2% offset) of 11,000 psi, elongations of 8% in 2 in., and Brinell hardnesses (10 mm–500 Kg) of 45 to 60, appreciably better than those secured in the normal condition, as indicated in Figure 5.41*d*.

[29] See also A. J. Phillips, A. A. Smith, Jr., and P. A. Beck, *Proc. A.S.T.M.*, **41** (1941), 886–93.

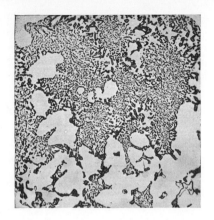
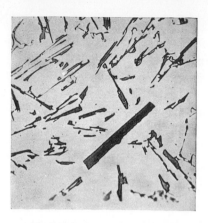

**Figure 5.41** **a** (*top left, right*). Metallographic structures typical of the aluminum-silicon casting alloy, 47 (13% silicon, remainder aluminum). (*left*) Normal structure as sand cast. (*right*) Modified structure as chill cast. Etched with ½% HF (×250). [Photomicrographs courtesy Aluminum Research Laboratories.] **b** (*bottom left*). Aluminum-silicon constitutional diagram (*upper*) and enlarged diagram of eutectic region (*lower*) illustrating depression of eutectic temperature and shift in apparent eutectic composition as a result of "modification." [After M. Hansen; also E. H. Dix, Jr. and A. C. Heath, Jr., *Trans. A.I.M.E.,* **78** (1928), 164.] **c** (*bottom right—upper*). Mechanical properties of aluminum-silicon sheet alloys. **d** (*bottom right—lower*). Tensile properties as determined from ½-in. diameter sand-cast test bars. [Figures 5.41c and d from *Metals Handbook,* courtesy American Society for Metals; and R. S. Archer and L. W. Kempf, *Trans. A.I.M.E.,* **73** (1926), 581.]

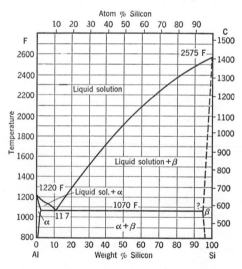

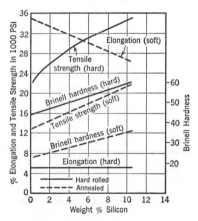

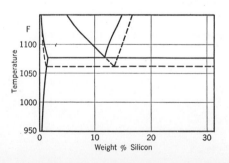

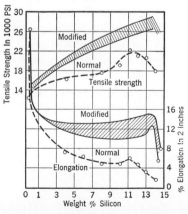

The 13% silicon alloy cannot be improved by heat-treatment so it is used primarily when heat-treating equipment is not available to treat the newer alloys. It makes good pressure-tight castings which have a satisfactory corrosion resistance, strength, and ductility, and are well suited for general purposes such as marine and automotive water-jackets and manifolds. Because of the free silicon, however, difficulties may be encountered in machining.

A modernized version, the 7% silicon, 0.1% magnesium alloy, 356, when made and heat-treated properly, develops properties comparable with those of the heat-treated aluminum-copper alloys,[30] and still retains casting

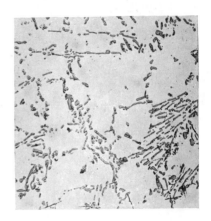

**Figure 5.42** Metallographic structure typical of the aluminum-magnesium-silicon sand-casting alloy 356-T6 (0.3% magnesium, 7% silicon, remainder aluminum), after heat-treatment. Etched with ½% HF (×100). [Photomicrograph courtesy Aluminum Research Laboratories.]

characteristics comparable with those of the aluminum-silicon alloys. Permanent-mold castings give better properties than sand castings because of the more rapid solidification. Depending on the heat-treatment used, average tensile strengths in the range 28,000 to 40,000 psi can be produced, with yield strengths (0.2% offset) of 20,000 to 30,000 psi, elongations of 9 to 2% in 2 in., and a Brinell hardness (10 mm–500 Kg) of 55 to 90. This alloy is particularly suitable for pressure-tight castings, both sand and permanent mold, such as for diesel engine crankcases and engine bases, various pneumatic tools and air compressor parts, as well as, in aircraft, for small piston-engine parts and structural fittings or for castings of intricate design. A metallographic structure typical of the 356 alloy in the heat-treated condition, similar to that shown in Figure 5.42, shows, principally, particles of free silicon in a background of an aluminum-rich primary solid solution.

The permanent-mold casting alloy, A 132 (12% silicon, 0.8% copper, 1.0% magnesium, 0.8% iron, 2.5% nickel, remainder aluminum) is used for cast pistons because it has a much lower coefficient of expansion than

[30] These are discussed in Chapter 10.

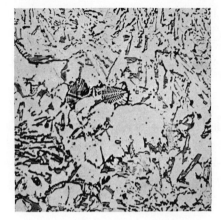

**Figure 5.43** (*left*) Metallographic structure of permanent-mold cast aluminum alloy A132 (12% silicon, 0.8% copper, 1.0% magnesium, 0.8% iron, 2.5% nickel, remainder aluminum). Etched with ½% HF (×100). [Photomicrograph by G. A. Fisher.]

**Figure 5.44** (*right*) Metallographic structure of aluminum alloy 43 (5% silicon, remainder aluminum) as sand cast. Etched with ½% HF (×100). [Photomicrograph courtesy Aluminum Research Laboratories.]

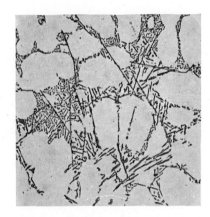

other alloys of this type. However, a special casting technique is required because of the great tendency toward internal shrinkage. The alloy has a high hardness and excellent wearing properties which can be increased still more by coating the surface anodically to a depth of about 0.0005 in. This anodized layer absorbs oil, and thus keeps a lubricant on the bearing surface at all times. The mechanical properties fall off rapidly with temperature but remain relatively stable at about 60% of their room-temperature values in the range 250 to 500 F (120 to 260 C). The metallographic structure, Figure 5.43, shows chiefly the aluminum-silicon eutectic with a few small patches of $NiSi_3$. The other elements are in solid solution in the aluminum, although they could form minor constituents with any impurities present.

Several other casting alloys also are of this type. In addition to 43 (5% silicon), Figure 5.44, 360 (9.5% silicon, 0.5% magnesium), 45 (10% silicon), and 13 (12% silicon) are used commonly.[31] The structures of

[31] See also the work on the aluminum, 21% silicon casting alloy by M. G. Urdea and Y. P. Telay, *Metals Engineering Quarterly,* **1** (1961), 54–67.

all of these are roughly similar to those shown in Figures 5.41*a* and 5.44, the relative amounts of primary aluminum-rich solid solution and aluminum-silicon eutectic varying with composition as has been discussed already.

## ALUMINUM-ZINC ALLOYS

The constitutional diagram for aluminum-zinc alloys, shown in Figure 5.45, is characterized largely by a region of partial solid immiscibility in which two solid solutions different in composition and in lattice parameters, but not in their basic crystal structure (face-centered cubic), exist as a mechanical mixture in the range 527 to 660 F (275 to 350 C). Above approximately 660 F (350 C) no miscibility gap exists and the two solid solutions merge continuously. The miscibility gap also leads to a eutectoid decomposition at 78% zinc but the remainder of the diagram is of the relatively simple eutectic type with partial solid solubility.

Engineering alloys based on this system are confined almost entirely to the zinc-base die-casting alloys. The wrought 1% zinc, remainder aluminum alloy, 7072, has a general corrosion resistance comparable with that of commercially pure aluminum, 1100, although it has an electrode potential appreciably more anodic than pure aluminum. Hence, it is used as a thin integral coating (called Alclad) to protect electrolytically those alloys

**Figure 5.45** Constitutional diagram for the alloys of aluminum and zinc. [After G. V. Raynor.]

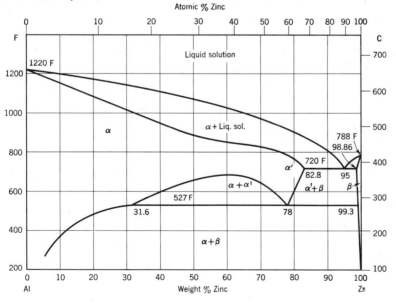

which have themselves an electrode potential too anodic to be protected by pure aluminum. The high strength aluminum-rich alloys containing zinc and magnesium, discussed in Chapter 10, are much more complicated.

## ZINC-BASE DIE-CASTING ALLOYS WITH ALUMINUM

The zinc-base die-casting alloys are used widely because of their low cost. The two commonest analyses are shown in Table 5.4.

**TABLE 5.4**

| Composition * | AG40A Alloy | AC41A Alloy |
|---|---|---|
| % Cu | 0.25 max | 1.0 |
| % Al | 4.0 | 4.0 |
| % Mg | 0.04 | 0.04 |

* Maximum limits are set for iron (0.100%), lead (0.007%), cadmium (0.005%), and tin (0.005%) in order to limit undesirable intercrystalline corrosion and growth in the A.S.T.M. standard test of exposure for 10 days to an atmosphere saturated with water vapor at 205 F (95 C). The remainder of each alloy is zinc. Special high-grade zinc (99.99+% zinc) must be used as the base material in making these alloys.

In tests on ¼ in. diameter die-cast specimens the average as-cast mechanical properties approximate those shown in Table 5.5.

**TABLE 5.5**

|  | AG40A | AC41A |
|---|---|---|
| Tensile strength (psi) | 41,000 | 47,600 |
| Elongation (% in 2 in.) | 10 | 7 |
| Compressive strength (psi) | 60,000 | 87,000 |
| Charpy impact * (ft-lb) | 43 | 48 |
| Brinell hardness (10 mm − 500 Kg) | 82 | 91 |

* ¼ in. by ¼ in. by 3 in. unnotched specimens.

These properties change significantly after aging indoors for 10 years. Hardness tests are not considered to be reliable in these materials. The alloys creep readily at room temperature so they do not have recognized elastic moduli or yield strengths although instantaneous values can be secured which apply only for one particular load and one particular time at the temperature specified.

The copper content governs the specific application to a large extent, the three most important factors to be considered being (a) the permanency of dimensions required, (b) the tensile strength and hardness, and (c) the impact strength both at room and at elevated temperatures.

The low-copper alloy, AG40A, is the more permanent with respect to dimensional changes, the maximum change to be expected being 0.001 in. per in., and even this can be reduced by proper heat-treatment. A typical stabilizing anneal is 3 to 6 hr at 212 F (100 C), followed by an air cool or by 4 to 5 weeks of natural aging. Alloy AC41A, with intermediate copper, is as good as AG40A at room temperature but is poorer at elevated temperatures. Alloy AC41A has the advantage of a better corrosion resistance than AG40A.

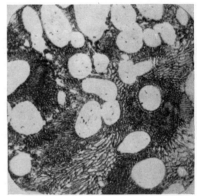

**Figure 5.46** Metallographic structure of S.A.E. 925, AC41A alloy, as die cast. Etched with solution containing 5 g $CrO_3$, 0.4 g $Na_2SO_4$, 100 ml $H_2O$ ($\times$1000). [Photomicrograph courtesy Research Division, Technical Department, the New Jersey Zinc Company.]

In Figure 5.46 a metallographic structure typical of both alloys is shown. Relatively large white particles of the $\alpha$ primary solid solution of copper and aluminum in zinc can be seen in a matrix of the eutectic formed by the zinc-rich and aluminum-rich primary solid solution phases, $\alpha$ and $\beta$. The zinc-base die-casting alloys are machinable although threads, etc., often are die-cast directly.

## MAGNESIUM-LEAD ALLOYS

The magnesium-lead diagram, Figure 5.47, is an illustration of a more complex eutectic system in which both metals are partially soluble in each other and, in addition, form an intermetallic compound, in this case $Mg_2Pb$. For purposes of interpretation, a diagram such as this one may be considered in either of the two ways shown. According to the first method, it is treated as though it were two diagrams placed side by side, one between magnesium and the compound $Mg_2Pb$, and the second between the com-

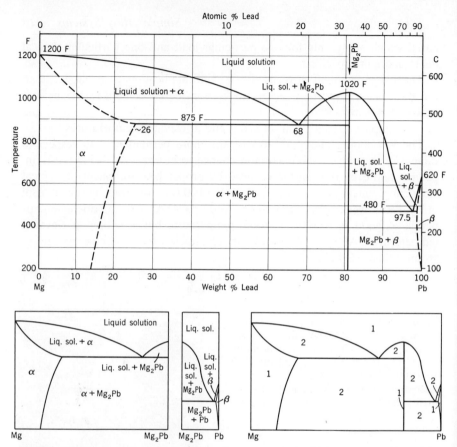

**Figure 5.47** **a** (*top*). Constitutional diagram typical of binary alloys in which one intermetallic compound is formed: the alloys of magnesium and lead. [After M. Hansen.] **b** (*bottom*). Alternate methods for interpreting diagram: (*left*) by division into two simpler diagrams and (*right*) by use of the 1:2:1 rule.

pound $Mg_2Pb$ and lead. Each of these diagrams is clearly a eutectic diagram with partial solid solubility in the metal such as has been discussed already. By the alternate method the diagram is considered as a whole, and the 1:2:1 rule is applied to assist in interpretation. Which of these methods, if either, is selected by the student is largely a matter of personal choice.

The beneficial effects of finely dispersed particles of hard intermetallic compounds, such as are formed in lead-rich alloys of this type, are utilized in the alkaline-earth lead-base bearing alloys made both in Europe and in this country. These particles account, to a great extent, for the retention of properties at elevated temperatures because of the precipitation-hardening characteristics which they produce.[32] The American alloy contains 97.5% lead, with the remainder calcium, tin, and magnesium. The impor-

[32] See Chapter 7 for a more complete discussion of this point.

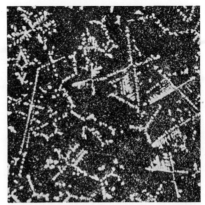

**Figure 5.48** Metallographic structure typical of a lead-alkali or -alkaline earth type bearing, containing small amounts of calcium, tin, and magnesium. Etched with nital (×100). [Photomicrograph courtesy National Lead Company, Research Laboratory.]

tant structural constituents are the intermetallic compounds, such as $CaPb_3$ and $Mg_2Pb$, which are present in the alloy (Figure 5.48) because of the small solid solubility of both calcium and magnesium in lead.

## COPPER-MAGNESIUM ALLOYS

As another example of a diagram of this general type, the copper-magnesium system shown in Figure 5.49, has four single-phase regions

**Figure 5.49** Constitutional diagram typical of binary alloys in which two intermetallic compounds are formed: the alloys of copper and magnesium. [After M. Hansen.]

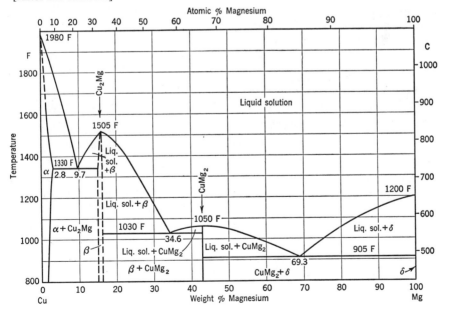

1. A primary solid solution, $\alpha$, of magnesium in copper.
2. The intermetallic compound, $Cu_2Mg$.
3. The intermetallic compound, $CuMg_2$.
4. Commercially pure magnesium (containing a maximum of 0.4 to 0.5% copper in solid solution).

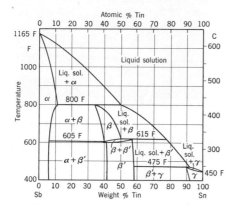

**Figure 5.50** Constitutional diagram typical of binary alloys in which peritectic reactions occur: the alloys of antimony and tin. The $\beta$ secondary solid solution frequently is referred to as SbSn. [After M. Hansen.]

## ANTIMONY-TIN ALLOYS: THE PERITECTIC REACTION

The system antimony-tin (Figure 5.50) [33] has two secondary solid solutions and two primary solid solutions. Both secondary solid solutions melt incongruently at constant temperatures—that is, each decomposes to a mixture of liquid and solid solutions at a definite temperature rather than melting completely, like a normal compound, or over a range of temperatures, like a normal solid solution.

The incongruent melting of a compound or, as occurs here, a solid solution, at a constant temperature takes place by what is known as a peritectic reaction.[34] This type of reaction is, in a way, the reverse of the eutectic reaction, the homogeneous-solution phase occuring below rather than above the constant reaction temperature. It may be expressed, therefore, by the general equation

$$\text{Liquid II} + \text{Solid III} \underset{\text{heating}}{\overset{\text{cooling}}{\rightleftharpoons}} \text{Solid I}$$

Consider, for example, the cooling under equilibrium conditions of an alloy containing equal parts of antimony and tin. Solidification begins by formation of crystals of the $\beta$ solid solution containing approximately 65% antimony, 35% tin. This continues, with changing composition of the solid

[33] The more recent diagram given by E. C. Ellwood in *Annotated Equilibrium Diagram Series No. 23* (London: The Institute of Metals, 1956), differs from this somewhat in specific temperatures and compositions.

[34] A similar but completely solid-state reaction, called a peritectoid reaction, also is known. See R. D. Reiswig and D. J. Mack, *Trans. A.I.M.E.,* **215** (1959), 301–07.

and liquid phases, until the temperature falls to 615 F (325 C). Here the reaction

$$\text{Liquid} + \beta \xrightarrow{\text{cooling}} \beta'$$

begins, and should continue, for equilibrium, at this constant temperature, until complete transformation and solidification have occurred.[35] The alloy at room temperature then consists entirely of uniform and homogeneous crystals of the $\beta'$ secondary solid solution.

It must be noted that the direct reaction between the liquid solution and the solid $\beta$ can take place only at their surface of contact. Once the first protective coating of $\beta'$ has formed, the rate of further reaction is determined by the diffusion of the two components through this layer. This naturally slows down the reaction appreciably.

## PERITECTIC REACTIONS UNDER NONEQUILIBRIUM CONDITIONS

When an alloy cools through a peritectic reaction too rapidly for conditions of true equilibrium to be maintained, the product of the peritectic reaction forms a rim, more or less isolating the two original phases. From this stage, the separated parts may constitute individual systems and each move toward an "independent" equilibrium. For the example cited the three constituents are (a) solid III, (b) the "chilled" form of liquid II, and (c) a "reaction zone" of solid I which will envelop the solid III crystals.

To illustrate this further consider, as before, the specific example of an alloy containing equal amounts of antimony and tin. Solidification again begins by the formation of crystals of $\beta$ solid solution. However, cooling is now so rapid that there is no time for the peritectic reaction at 615 F (325 C) to proceed to completion. Some $\beta'$ is formed at the surface of the $\beta$ crystals as the temperature passes through that of the peritectic reaction, but likewise some liquid has no opportunity to react and, therefore, solidifies and appears as a finely dispersed mixture of $\beta'$ and $\gamma$ solid solutions.

The structure of the alloy cooled under these nonequilibrium conditions is shown in Figure 5.51a. The unetched cores of the crystals are the initially formed $\beta$, the lightly etched boundary regions the $\beta'$ formed by interaction of $\beta$ with the remaining liquid, and the dark regions a finely dispersed mixture of $\gamma$ and $\beta'$ formed from the solidified residual liquid.

If the alloy is reheated for several hours at a temperature just below that of the peritectic horizontal, or if the original solidification is sufficiently

[35] B. L. Eyre, *Journ. Inst. Met.*, **88** (London: 1959–60), 223, considers this to be an order-disorder transformation rather than a true phase change.

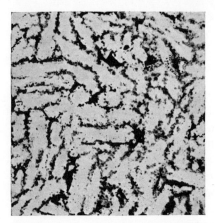 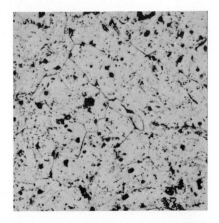

**Figure 5.51** Metallographic structure of an alloy of 50% antimony, 50% tin. Etched with ferric chloride (×200). [Photomicrographs by L. Litchfield.] **a** (*left*). After chill casting. The white crystals are $\beta$ solid solution, the darker edges of which have reacted with liquid to form $\beta'$. The dark etching regions are either voids or small patches of rapidly cooled liquid (now a finely dispersed mixture of $\beta'$ and $\gamma$ solid solutions). **b** (*right*). Crystals of $\beta'$ after heating for several hours at 525 F (275 C) and slowly cooling. The dark areas are largely voids, inclusions, and etching pits.

slow to permit the peritectic reaction to proceed to completion, the completely uniform and homogeneous $\beta'$ secondary solid solution shown in Figure 5.51*b* results.

## TIN-BASE BEARING ALLOYS

The tin-base babbitts, probably the most widely used bearing metals before World War II, are essentially alloys of tin, antimony, and copper, although lead also is added in some of the cheaper and poorer alloys. In general, there are three common constituents in the structures of these alloys

1. A secondary solid solution based on the intermetallic compound, SbSn, which appears in the form of white cubes, and has the general characteristics typical of such compounds, even though it is softer than most of them. As indicated by the phase diagram (Figure 5.50), this constituent should not be found in tin babbitts containing less than approximately 8% antimony.

2. A needlelike constituent which is much harder than SbSn and is probably the intermetallic compound $Cu_6Sn_5$ or a secondary solid solution based upon it.

3. A primary solid solution of copper and antimony in tin which, probably because of decreasing solid solubility with decreasing temperature,

always contains a fine precipitate of SbSn and probably also of $Cu_6Sn_5$. Therefore, it may appear light or dark depending upon the exact structure and the etching technique used.

These alloys conform to the general concepts of ideal bearing structures with hard compounds in a relatively soft solid-solution matrix. The presence of the needlelike $Cu_6Sn_5$ phase tends to inoculate the SbSn, and thus gives many more and smaller particles of this constituent than would be found in the lower copper alloys. It is claimed by some that the copper also prevents the gravity separation of the SbSn, because the copper compound, having the higher freezing point, is present in the solidifying alloy before the SbSn. Needles of $Cu_6Sn_5$ frequently are found within the SbSn cubes as illustrated in Figure 5.52*a*. Rapid cooling, such as in chill casting,

**Figure 5.52** Metallographic structure of a tin-base babbitt containing approximately 86% tin, 10% antimony, 4% copper. Etched with nital (×100). **a** (*top left*). Cast from 1200 F (650 C) into a heated mold. [Photomicrograph by R. P. Stemmler.] **b** (*top right*). Cast from 840 F (450 C) into a heated mold. [Photomicrograph by R. C. Altman.] **c** (*bottom*). Cast from 840 F (450 C) into a chill mold. [Photomicrograph by J. Caum.]

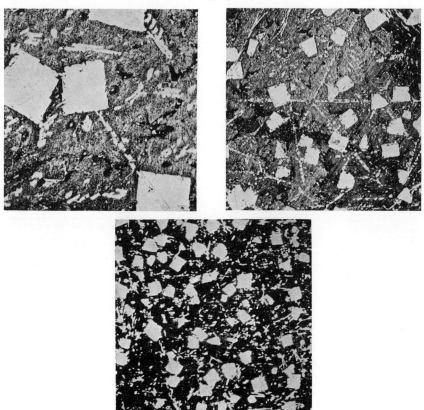

tends to retain the antimony in solid solution and thus to suppress the separation of SbSn. This gives alloys whose structures may show either no SbSn cubes or else relatively small ones, depending on the exact composition. The shape and general distribution of both the $Cu_6Sn_5$ and the SbSn particles can be influenced by controlling the cooling rate and the pouring temperature. This is illustrated by a comparison of the three photomicrographs shown in Figure 5.52. Impurities are controlled carefully in these alloys because of their effect on microstructure and hence on properties. Aluminum and zinc are eliminated completely, if possible. Bismuth is limited because it forms a tin-bismuth eutectic which melts at 280 F (137 C), and thus would lower the strength of the bearing appreciably at temperatures above this. Lead is kept low in the high-tin alloys because it forms a lead-tin eutectic which melts at 360 F (183 C), and thus decreases the strength above this temperature seriously. In the higher lead alloys, in fact, the formation of this eutectic is the main factor which limits their use, and for this reason the highly-leaded tin-base babbitts definitely are not to be recommended as a means of conserving tin.

Typical soft babbitts have a nominal composition of 91% tin, 4.5% antimony, 4.5% copper, although some variation is permitted. Impurities are limited to maximum values of 0.35% lead, 0.08% iron, 0.10% arsenic, 0.08% bismuth, and no zinc or aluminum. Structures are roughly similar to that shown in Figure 5.53a even though this alloy is of a different type. The alloy is used for both bronze-backed and die-cast bearings. It melts at 435 F (225 C), and has the approximate mechanical properties shown in Table 5.6. The soft babbitts have the lowest hardness and strength of any of the tin-base babbitts.

**Figure 5.53**   Metallographic structures of tin-base babbitts. **a** (*left*). 89% tin, 7.5% antimony, 3.5% copper, from an automotive bearing. Etched with $FeCl_3$ in alcohol (×500). [Photomicrograph courtesy The Cleveland Graphite Bronze Company.] **b** (*right*). 87% tin, 6.5% antimony, 6.5% copper. Etched with nital (×500). [Photomicrograph by L. Litchfield.]

**TABLE 5.6**

| Tensile Strength (psi) | | Yield Strength (0.125% Elongation) (psi) | | Johnson's Apparent Elastic Limit * (psi) | | Brinell Hardness (10 mm–500 Kg) | |
|---|---|---|---|---|---|---|---|
| 70 F | 210 F | 70 F | 210 F | 70 F | 210 F | 70 F | 210 F |
| 12,850 | 6,950 | 4,400 | 2,650 | 2,450 | 1,050 | 17 | 8 |

* The unit stress at the point where the tangent to the stress-strain curve is 1.5 times its slope at the origin.

The hard babbitts contain more copper and antimony than the soft babbitts; a typical alloy has a nominal composition of 89% tin, 7.5% antimony, 3.5% copper with impurities as specified for the soft babbitt. This corresponds closely to the patented analysis of the original babbitt alloy. Alloys of this type are used, in particular, for connecting-rod bearings and shaft bearings in applications requiring somewhat higher pressures than those for which the alloys lower in copper and antimony are used. They are suitable for die casting also. Typical mechanical properties are shown in Table 5.7. Figure 5.53 shows metallographic structures of typical compositions. The starlike $Cu_6Sn_5$ constituent is readily recognizable in a tin-rich solid-solution background. Any SbSn present is in the form of fine particles precipitated from solid solution.

**TABLE 5.7**

| Tensile Strength (psi) | | | Elongation (%) | | | Brinell Hardness (10 mm–500 Kg) | | |
|---|---|---|---|---|---|---|---|---|
| 80 F | 210 F | 300 F | 80 F | 210 F | 300 F | 80 F | 210 F | 300 F |
| 10,900 | 5,700 | 3,100 | 11.5 | 31.2 | 53.0 | 25.5 | 14.0 | 9.2 |

## ALUMINUM-BASE ALLOYS WITH MAGNESIUM

The constitutional diagram for the alloys of aluminum and magnesium (Figure 5.54) has three secondary solid solutions. Note particularly the δ phase, one composition of which melts at a constant temperature but is a good example of a secondary solid solution in which both components are soluble.

The common wrought aluminum-rich alloys contain less than about 5.5% magnesium, and can be hardened only by cold working. The three

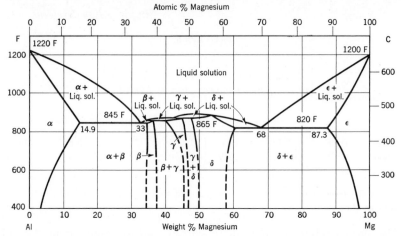

Atomic % Magnesium

**Figure 5.54** Constitutional diagram for the alloys of aluminum and magnesium. [After W. L. Fink and L. A. Willey.] The secondary solid solution phases sometimes are referred to, respectively, as $Al_3Mg_2$ ($\beta$), AlMg ($\gamma$), and $Al_{12}Mg_{17}$ ($\delta$).

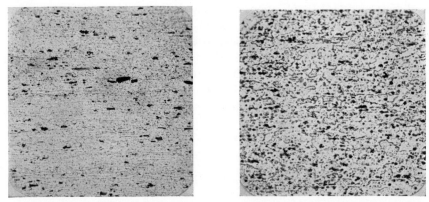

**Figure 5.55** Metallographic structures of annealed aluminum alloys (*left*) 3003 (1.2% manganese, remainder aluminum) and (*right*) 5052 (2.5% magnesium, 0.25% chromium, remainder aluminum) in the sheet form. Etched with ½% HF ($\times$100). [Photomicrographs courtesy Aluminum Research Laboratories.]

most important are 5052 (2.5% magnesium, 0.25% chromium), 5154 (3.5% magnesium, 0.25% chromium), and 5083 (4.5% magnesium, 0.75% manganese, 0.25% chromium) although others also are made. Typical properties for 5052 [36] in comparison with commercially pure aluminum, 1100, are shown in Table 5.8. The 5154 alloy has strengths about 20% higher than 5052, with somewhat lower elongation. The higher magnesium alloy, 5083, is still stronger, reaching a tensile strength of 42,000

[36] See also G. H. Boss, *Trans. A.S.M.*, **43** (1951), 122–40.

psi, with a yield strength of 21,000 psi and an elongation of 22% in the annealed condition. The alloy 3003 is a stronger form of 1100 which contains 1.2% manganese for solid-solution strengthening.

Metallographic structures of these alloys (Figure 5.55) are basically similar to that of 1100 (Figure 4.1), because the alloying elements are in solid solution or are present as submicroscopic inclusions. The amount of inclusions present depends on the impurity content, particularly silicon and iron.

The temperature for full annealing is approximately the same as for the 1100 alloy, 650 F (340 C); the preferable holding time is not longer than is necessary to bring the entire furnace load to temperature.

There are also several aluminum-rich casting alloys containing magnesium which have an excellent combination of mechanical properties and corrosion resistance. The nominal compositions of the most important of these, with the alloy designation used commonly are shown in Table 5.9.

**TABLE 5.8**

| Temper * | Tensile Strength (psi) | | Yield Strength (0.2% Offset) (psi) | | Elongation † (% in 2 in.) | | Brinell Hardness (10 mm– 500 Kg) | |
|---|---|---|---|---|---|---|---|---|
| | 1100 | 5052 | 1100 | 5052 | 1100 | 5052 | 1100 | 5052 |
| -O | 13,000 | 28,000 | 5,000 | 13,000 | 35 | 25 | 23 | 47 |
| -H12 | 16,000 | 33,000 | 15,000 | 28,000 | 12 | 12 | 28 | 60 |
| -H14 | 18,000 | 38,000 | 17,000 | 31,000 | 9 | 10 | 32 | 68 |
| -H16 | 21,000 | 40,000 | 20,000 | 35,000 | 6 | 8 | 38 | 73 |
| -H18 | 24,000 | 42,000 | 22,000 | 37,000 | 5 | 7 | 44 | 77 |

* The tempers given are -H1x for 1100 and -H3x for 5052. The -H2 temper designation also is used with alloy 1100, and the -H1, -H2 and -H3 temper designations all are used with 5052. Different tempers have somewhat different properties. For the significance of these temper symbols see the Appendix.

† These elongation values are for $\frac{1}{16}$ in. sheet. Thicker material and round bars have higher elongations, thinner material has lower.

**TABLE 5.9**

| | No. | % Mg |
|---|---|---|
| Sand castings | 220 | 10 |
| Die castings | 218 | 8 |
| Sand castings | 214 | 3.8 |

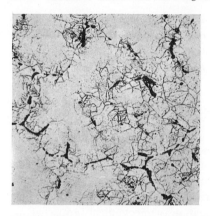 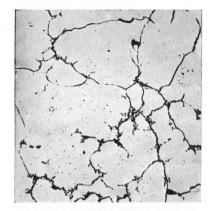

**Figure 5.56   a** (*left*). Metallographic structure typical of the aluminum-magnesium sand-casting alloy, 220-T4 (10% magnesium, remainder aluminum), after heat-treatment. Etched with Keller's reagent (×100). [Photomicrograph courtesy Aluminum Research Laboratories.] **b** (*right*). Metallographic structure of aluminum alloy 214 (3.8% magnesium, remainder aluminum) as sand cast. Etched with Keller's reagent (×100). [Photomicrograph courtesy Aluminum Research Laboratories.]

Metallographic structures of 220 and 214 in the sand cast condition are shown in Figure 5.56. Alloy 220, in the naturally aged condition (that is, aged by standing at normal atmospheric temperatures, known as -T4 temper) combines the highest strength, elongation, and shock resistance of any of the aluminum-alloy castings with a low specific gravity, excellent machining characteristics and resistance to corrosion. However, the alloy tends to oxidize during melting so it has to be cast by the techniques ordinarily used only for magnesium-base alloys. Hence, many foundries cannot handle it. When this alloy is heated into the primary solid-solution field, quenched (solution treated), and aged, either naturally or artificially (that is, at an elevated temperature where reactions are more rapid), particles of $Al_3Mg_2$—also known as $\beta(Al\text{-}Mg)$ secondary solid solution, Figure 5.54—precipitate at the grain boundaries of the aluminum-rich primary solid solution. If the precipitate forms a continuous network, the alloy becomes susceptible to stress-corrosion cracking. However, this takes years of natural aging so the alloy normally is used in this condition. Quenching into boiling water or oil at 210 to 300 F (100 to 150 C) also is used customarily instead of quenching into cold water, to increase resistance to stress-corrosion cracking by minimizing any effects of quenching stresses on accelerating precipitation.[37]

The tensile strength of 220 alloy at room temperature averages 46,000 psi, with a yield strength (0.2% offset) of 25,000 psi, and an elongation

---

[37] These effects are discussed in more detail in Chapter 10.

of 14% in 2 in. The tensile strength of 214 alloy, which is not heat-treatable, is lower, averaging 25,000 psi, with a yield strength (0.2% off-set) of 12,000 psi, and an elongation of 9% in 2 in. Brinell hardnesses (10 mm–500 Kg) of 75 for alloy 220 and 50 for alloy 214 are typical. These alloys are used for castings where a white highly-polished finish and stain resistance are required. However, none of them is really suitable for castings which are intricate, are required to be pressure-tight, or are intended for use at elevated temperatures. For permanent mold castings, a modified form of the 3.8% magnesium alloy, A214, which contains 1.8% zinc, is used.

## MAGNESIUM-BASE ALLOYS WITH ALUMINUM

At the eutectic temperature of 820 F (435 C), magnesium holds up to 12.7% aluminum in solid solution (Figure 5.54). This decreases to 1.6% at 390 F (200 C). Magnesium-rich wrought alloys are used to some extent in sheet form to resist atmospheric corrosion, chiefly because of their light weight.[38] However, magnesium alloys are somewhat difficult to roll satis-factorily so structural members usually are extruded or are forged. Mag-nesium is only two-thirds the weight of aluminum and about one-quarter the weight of brass or iron so its use results in appreciable weight reduction.

**TABLE 5.10**

| *A.S.T.M.* *Designation* | *% Al* | *% Zn* *(max)* | *% Mn* *(min)* |
|---|---|---|---|
| AZ80A | 8.5 | 0.5 | — |
| AZ61A | 5.5 | 1.0 | 0.20 |
| AZ31B | 3.0 | 1.0 | 0.20 |

Three magnesium alloys with aluminum commonly are used in the wrought or extruded form. These have the nominal compositions shown in Table 5.10, the remainder being magnesium in each case. The zinc dissolves in both the magnesium-aluminum solid solution and the compound $Al_{12}Mg_{17}$, $\delta$(Al-Mg) in Figure 5.54. The manganese forms compounds with some of the aluminum. Limitations usually are placed on the maximum amounts of silicon (0.05%), copper (0.05%), nickel (0.005%), and iron (0.005%) to minimize corrosion. Other grades of lower purity also are

[38] General tensile properties of these alloys are discussed by J. C. McDonald, *Trans. A.I.M.E.,* **137** (1940), 430–41; **143** (1941), 179–81.

made. Increasing the aluminum over 5% noticeably lowers the ductility so only the AZ31B alloy normally is cold-rolled into sheet. The AZ80A alloy can be hardened by heat treatment and is discussed briefly in Chapter 10.

Typical properties are given in Table 5.11 for AZ31B sheet up to 0.250 in. thick; heavier material has somewhat lower properties. The modulus of elasticity averages about 6,500,000 psi and the specific gravity 1.77.

**TABLE 5.11**

| Temper | Tensile Strength (psi) | Yield Strength (0.2% Offset) (psi) | Elongation (% in 2 in.) | Brinell Hardness (10 mm–500 Kg) |
|--------|------------------------|-------------------------------------|-------------------------|----------------------------------|
| -H24 | 42,000 | 32,000 | 15 | 73 |
| -F | 38,000 | 29,000 | 15 | 49 |
| -O | 37,000 | 22,000 | 21 | 56 |

The AZ61A alloy is used primarily for bars, rods, shapes, tubing and forgings. In the -F temper, the usual form, its properties are comparable to those of AZ31B-H24.

None of these alloys has a very high strength although strengths are adequate when considered on a strength-weight basis. The alloys usually are not recommended for applications subjected to high stresses, and the cold-rolled tempers should not be used where subject to shock loads because the Charpy impact strength is only 2 to 3 ft-lb. The cold-working properties of these materials are not too good and some form of hot working in the range 550 to 600 F (285 to 315 C) is used almost entirely.

Although the alloys are resistant to atmospheric corrosion, they tend to darken and to become dull in appearance. Hence, they usually are protected by painting, especially when exposed to salt atmospheres, as they are particularly susceptible to this form of attack.

Three structures of alloy AZ80A are shown in Figure 5.57 and of alloys AZ61A and AZ31B, are shown in Figure 5.58. The manganese, added to improve corrosion resistance, is largely in solid solution, any excess appearing as metallic manganese or as an aluminum-manganese intermetallic compound. The aluminum is partly dissolved in the magnesium-rich solid solution matrix and partly precipitated as the $\delta$(Al-Mg) secondary solid solution, $Al_{12}Mg_{17}$, which usually is found at the grain boundaries. Any zinc present is dissolved in the primary and secondary solid solutions. Cold working produces prominent mechanical twinning as can be seen readily from the rolled structures. These wrought alloys are susceptible to stress-corrosion cracking if tensile working stresses exceed about 30% of the tensile yield strength.

The five most common magnesium-rich casting alloys with aluminum are listed in Table 5.12, the remainder being magnesium in each case. Iron, copper and nickel are kept as low as possible to improve corrosion resistance. The first three alloys are used primarily for pressure-tight sand- and permanent-mold castings. The other two are general sand-casting alloys. The maximum properties secured in these casting alloys after heat-treatment is about 40,000 psi tensile strength, and 26,000 psi yield strength. Frequently much lower values are found. However, for castings, such properties are quite satisfactory because of the large sections usually involved and the low specific gravity of the alloy.

**Figure 5.57** Metallographic structures typical of the wrought magnesium alloy AZ80A (8.5% aluminum, 0.5% zinc, 0.2% manganese, remainder magnesium). [Photomicrographs courtesy The Dow Chemical Company.] **a** (*top left*). Extruded. Etched 10 sec with glycol etchant ($\times$250). **b** (*top right*). Extruded and heat-treated. Etched 5 sec with glycol etchant ($\times$250). **c** (*bottom*). Press-forged. Etched 5 sec with acetic-glycol etchant ($\times$250).

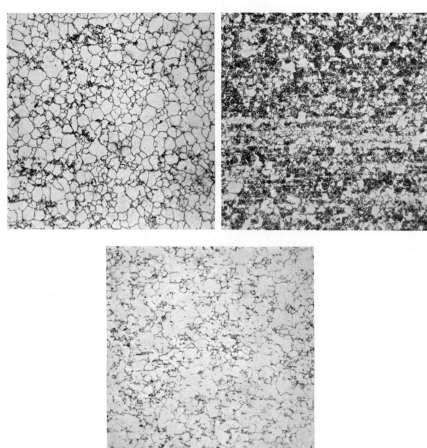

For die casting, the AZ91C alloy is modified by the addition of up to 0.5% silicon (max). A typical microstructure of an AZ91C die casting is shown in Figure 5.59*a*. The dendritic matrix of magnesium-rich solid solution contains patches of the δ(Al-Mg) secondary solid solution, $Al_{12}Mg_{17}$, in which any zinc is dissolved also. In a chill casting, like a die

**TABLE 5.12**

| A.S.T.M. Designation | % Al | % Zn | % Mn |
|---|---|---|---|
| AM100A | 10.0 | 0.3 max | 0.10 |
| AZ91C | 9.0 | 0.7 | 0.20 |
| AZ92A | 9.0 | 2.0 | 0.10 |
| AZ81A | 7.5 | 0.7 | 0.15 |
| AZ63A | 6.0 | 3.0 | 0.20 |

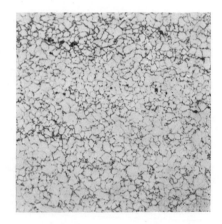

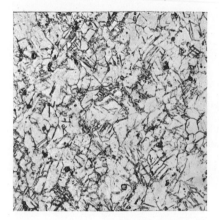

**Figure 5.58** Metallographic structures of longitudinal sections of rolled and annealed magnesium alloy sheet. **a.** AZ61A (5.5% aluminum, 1.0% zinc, 0.20% manganese, remainder magnesium), hard-rolled (*top left*) and annealed (*top right*). Etched 5 sec with acetic-glycol etchant (×250). **b.** AZ31B (3.0% aluminum, 1.0% zinc, 0.20% manganese, remainder magnesium), hard-rolled (*bottom left*) etched 5 sec with acetic-picral etchant (×250). Annealed AZ31B is similar to AZ61A. [Photomicrographs courtesy The Dow Chemical Company.]

**Figure 5.59** Metallographic structures typical of some cast magnesium alloys. [Photomicrographs courtesy The Dow Chemical Company.] **a** (*top right*). Die cast AZ91C (9% aluminum, 0.6% zinc, 0.2% manganese, remainder magnesium). Etched 5 sec in glycol etchant (×250). **b** (*middle left*). AZ92A (9% aluminum, 2% zinc, 0.10% manganese, remainder magnesium), as sand cast. Etched 5 sec with glycol etchant (×250). Sand cast AZ63A (6% aluminum, 3% zinc, 0.2% manganese, remainder magnesium) and permanent-mold castings of both alloys would have similar structures. **c** (*middle right*). AZ92A, sand cast and solution heat-treated. Etched 10 sec with glycol etchant (×250). Cast AZ63A would be similar. **d** (*bottom left*). AZ92A, sand cast, solution heat-treated and aged. Etched 5 sec with glycol etchant (×250). **e** (*bottom right*). AZ63A, sand cast, solution heat-treated and aged. Etched 5 sec with glycol etchant (×250).

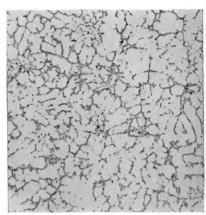

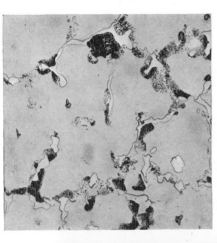
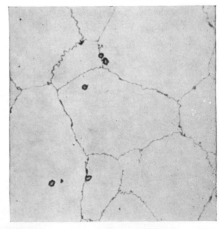

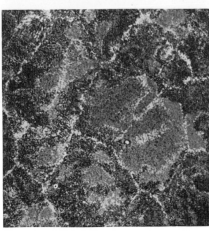
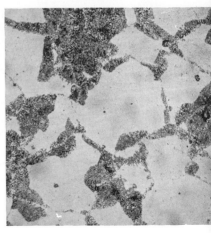

casting, the secondary solid solution appears as a lamellar constituent; in a sand casting it would be a massive constituent. Magnesium silicide ($Mg_2Si$) also may be present, depending on the silicon content, varying in color from a powder blue to an iridescent blue-green. As die castings, such alloys can be machined at more than twice the speed of free-cutting brass and at more than four times the speed of cast iron.

Probably the biggest disadvantage of magnesium alloys is their notch sensitivity—that is, sensitivity to local concentrations of stresses. This generally is shown by a low (2 to 5 ft-lb) Charpy impact strength. However, they have good resistance to fatigue particularly when subjected to large numbers of cycles at low stress. Although notch sensitivity also depends on both the magnitude and nature of the stress, sharp corners must be avoided in magnesium castings and shapes wherever possible, notches and scratches of all kinds must be eliminated, and liberal fillets should be provided, especially when stresses are apt to be high.

Metallographic structures typical of cast AZ92A, in various conditions, and of aged AZ63A also are shown in Figure 5.59. They consist essentially of a magnesium-rich solid solution containing particles of massive compound ($Al_{12}Mg_{17}$ + zinc), plus, in all but the solution heat-treated [39] structure (Figure 5.59c), a lamellar form of the compound precipitated either by holding at atmospheric temperature (aging) or else by cooling at sufficiently slow rates. A few small particles of metallic manganese or of an aluminum-manganese compound also can be seen.

## QUESTIONS

1. If it is possible to form alloys by having one metal as a solid and the other as a vapor, do you think the reverse reaction would be possible also? In other words, can one component of an alloy be removed preferentially as a vapor or gas? How could this be done, if it is possible, and what conditions should be favorable for it? If done, would there be any real difference between removing the component by vaporizing at the free surface or by reacting it with something to form a gas at the free surface? Why? In making powder-metal alloys, must the "intermetallic diffusion" required be solid-state diffusion? What difference will it make whether it is or is not solid state?

2. What are the two basic statements upon which the Gibbs' Phase Rule depends? Does the phase rule tell anything about the amounts of the various phases which are present? What does zero degrees of freedom mean?

---

[39] Cooled rapidly from the $\epsilon$-solid solution field, Figure 5.54, to preserve the primary solid solution structure. See Chapter 7.

3. Why do intermetallic compounds differ so much from chemical compounds? Would you expect these differences to be clear cut and sharp or to cover all intermediate stages depending upon the chemical elements involved? Why? A pure body-centered cubic metal $A$ is miscible in all proportions with an intermetallic compound $AB$, that is, $A$ will take another metal $B$ into solid solution up to the limiting composition $AB$. What do you think would happen to the size, symmetry and distribution of $A$ and $B$ atoms in the space lattice of $A$ as the concentration of $B$ increases?

4. From the viewpoint of physical and mechanical properties, what are some of the differences between what has been called a mechanical mixture of two phases in a solid alloy and a simple physical mixture of fine powders of these two phases without any further treatment? Assume a binary alloy, not of copper and nickel, in which both metals are soluble in each other in all proportions in the solid state. Do you think it likely that these two new metals would not be completely soluble in the liquid state also? Do you have any reasons for this? Under these conditions, how could the cooling curves of Figure 5.13 be changed?

5. Does the 1:2:1 rule work if motion on the constitutional diagram is vertical (changing temperature) instead of horizontal (changing composition)? Can you give any reasons for this?

6. In a binary alloy, what is the maximum number of phases which can coexist in equilibrium? How many degrees of freedom are there in such alloy? Which can be changed without changing equilibrium, composition or temperature? Illustrate such a region on a binary diagram. In copper-tin alloys why is it possible for the $\delta$-$Cu_{31}Sn_8$ phase to be found in castings when the composition of the alloy would indicate it to be entirely in the alpha field? What methods can you suggest for securing a casting without this $\delta$-$Cu_{31}Sn_8$ phase? Why might it be desirable to eliminate it?

7. Castings of many complex alloys are difficult to make because they tend to crack during cooling. Likewise, ingots, the first stage for making forgings or other wrought parts, may crack unless given the proper sequence of reduction by hot working (often cold working is impossible at this stage) and annealing. Can you suggest any reasons for this behavior and what to do to avoid or minimize it?

8. When a supposedly homogeneous solid alloy is heated, why does initial melting tend to start at the grain boundaries? Would this be expected to be true in a high-purity metal also? Why do these regions of initial melting tend to oxidize, leading to burning? Long time creep-rupture failures usually are intergranular, and the grain boundaries are oxidized also. Is this evidence that melting is occurring at these grain boundaries?

9. By using the principle of zone leveling, do you think a single crystal of pure copper would be converted into a single crystal of, say, an 80:20 brass merely by adding zinc? Why? Can you suggest any other way of accomplishing the same result?

10. Inasmuch as the eutectic composition freezes at a constant temperature, how is it possible to vary the size of the constituents in it—for example, the thickness of the lamellae or the size of the granules? In a lamellar eutectic, how would you expect strength to vary with lamellae thickness?

11. What reasons can you give to account for the solid solubility of one metal in another tending to increase with increasing temperature? Can you think of any reasons why solid solubility might tend to decrease with increasing temperature? Show how a constitutional diagram for alloys of partial solid solubility—for example, copper-silver alloys—should be divided if cognizance is taken of the various constituents which can be found microscopically. How does this differ from the simple eutectic diagram? Does it violate or form an exception to Gibbs' Phase Rule?

12. Why are "off-eutectic" soft solders preferred to eutectic alloys? Why are wiping solders easier to use than "lead burning"? What is the difference between the melt point and the flow point of a solder (as judged by visual appearance during soldering)? Why is a flux used during soldering? Why is tin objectionable in lead-base babbitts and lead objectionable in tin-base babbitts? Give some reasons why lead-base babbitts have displaced tin-base babbitts for most applications.

13. Compare aluminum-base and zinc-base alloys for die castings. What are the advantages and disadvantages of each? What are the objections to die castings of copper-base, nickel-base, and tin-base alloys?

14. Phases like SbSn and $Cu_6Sn_5$ occur in tin-base babbitts as fairly regular geometrical crystals. Can you suggest any reasons why these compounds appear in this form instead of as spheres or some similar shape? Under what conditions would the geometric shapes tend to become more rounded?

15. A fusion-welded tank is to be built out of an aluminum-magnesium alloy such as 5052. It is very important that this tank be kept as thin as possible by using as high-strength material as possible (strength is a factor in determining the allowable design stress). What temper material would you suggest? Why select this one? Could the tank be made thinner, do you think, by selecting another alloy of the same general type? Why?

## FOR FURTHER STUDY

1. *Theory of Alloy Phases.* Cleveland: American Society for Metals, 1956.

2. *Constitution of Binary Alloys* by M. Hansen and K. P. Anderko. New York: McGraw-Hill, 1958.

3. *Phase Diagrams in Metallurgy* by F. N. Rhines. New York: McGraw-Hill, 1956.

4. *Metallurgical Equilibrium Diagrams* by W. Hume-Rothery, J. W. Christian, and W. P. Pearson. London: The Institute of Physics, 1952.

5. *Ternary Systems* by G. Masing (translated by B. A. Rogers). New York: Reinhold Publishing Corp., 1944.

6. *The Collected Work of J. Willard Gibbs.* New Haven, Connecticut: Yale University Press, 1948.

7. *The Structures of Metals.* New York: Interscience Publishers, 1959.

8. *A Handbook of Lattice Spacings and Structures of Metals and Alloys.* New York: Pergamon Press, 1958.

9. *Metals Handbook,* 7th ed. (1948) and *Supplements,* and 8th ed., Vol. I (1961). Metals Park, Ohio: American Society for Metals.

10. *Physical Chemistry of Metallic Solutions and Intermetallic Compounds,* Vols. I and II. London: Her Majesty's Stationery Office, 1959.

11. *Relation of Properties to Microstructure.* Cleveland: American Society for Metals, 1954.

12. *Properties and Microstructure* by J. R. Low, Jr. Cleveland: American Society for Metals, 1954.

13. *Powder Metallurgy.* Cleveland: American Society for Metals, 1942.

14. *Fundamental Principles of Powder Metallurgy* by W. D. Jones. London: Edward Arnold, Ltd., 1960.

15. *Zone Melting* by W. G. Pfann. New York: John Wiley & Sons, 1958.

16. *Liquid Metals and Solidification.* Cleveland: American Society for Metals, 1958.

17. *The Annealing of Low-Carbon Steel, A.S.M.* Cleveland: Lee Wilson Engineering Company, 1960.

18. *Tin and Its Alloys.* London: Edward Arnold, Ltd., 1960.

19. *The Making, Shaping and Treating of Steels.* Pittsburgh: United States Steel Co., 1951.

# 6 *More Complex Alloys*

## COPPER-ZINC AND COPPER-TIN ALLOYS

THE BINARY ALLOY DIAGRAMS: COPPER-ZINC (FIGURE 6.1) and copper-tin (Figure 6.2), indicate the constitution of two groups of important engineering alloys, the brasses and bronzes, respectively. These diagrams are somewhat more complex than those seen before because of the numerous intermetallic phases which form. In such complex binary diagrams, accepted conventions plot at the left the element with the earlier symbol, alphabetically, and designate single-phase areas, from left to right, by the Greek letters $\alpha$, $\beta$, $\gamma$, $\delta$, etc.[1] However, many important diagrams were well established before these conventions were adopted and have not been changed to conform.

All the copper-base engineering alloys in these two systems fall in the limited portions shown in Figure 6.3.[2] These important regions consist essentially of only three fields, the copper-rich primary solid solution ($\alpha$), the two-phase field in which mechanical mixtures of the primary and secondary solid solutions ($\alpha$ and $\beta$) are stable, and the secondary solid solution ($\beta$).[3] The $\delta$-phase in the copper-tin system is an intermetallic com-

---

[1] The American Society for Testing and Materials proposed an entirely different system in 1961 but it has not yet been adopted widely.

[2] The rolled zinc alloys containing 1% copper were mentioned in Chapter 4 (see Figure 4.21*b*).

[3] The $\beta'$-phase stable at lower temperatures is an ordered form of $\beta$, often considered to be similar to it for simplicity.

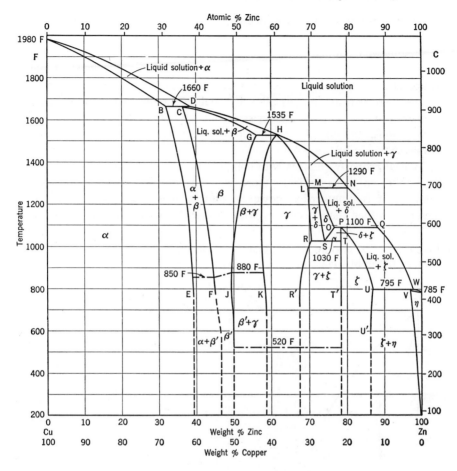

**Figure 6.1** Constitutional diagram for the alloys of copper and zinc: the brasses. [After M. Hansen.] Later work by G. V. Raynor has shown that the solubility of copper for zinc decreases below approximately 750 F (400 C) so the dotted line limiting the $\alpha$ field should curve to the left.

pound, $Cu_{31}Sn_8$,[4] which has undesirable properties and is avoided, if possible, in industrial alloys.

In each of these diagrams the primary solid solubility of either zinc or tin in copper increases as the temperature decreases, although in the copper-tin system this persists only down to approximately 970 F (570 C). In the brasses, therefore, it is quite possible to have an alloy, such as the one containing approximately 62% copper, 38% zinc, which is composed entirely of the secondary $\beta$ solid solution immediately after solidification

[4] For simplicity the formula $Cu_4Sn$ often is used.

and yet, at room temperature, is composed entirely of the primary $\alpha$ solid solution.

A somewhat similar set of conditions exists for the alloy containing approximately 58% copper, 42% zinc, which is completely $\beta$ at high temperatures and a mixture of $\alpha$ and $\beta$ at low temperatures. The structural changes which result in this alloy by cooling rapidly to preserve a high-temperature structure, and then reheating at various lower temperatures to reestablish the equilibrium structure, are indicated by the photomicrographs shown in Figure 6.4.

Typical property changes with composition also are given in Figure 6.3. The trends in the $\alpha$-field are those which would be expected of a solid solution. It is noteworthy, however, that in these alloys the elongation increases rather than decreases with increasing alloy content. Partly be-

**Figure 6.2**   Constitutional diagram for the alloys of copper and tin: the bronzes. [After M. Hansen.]

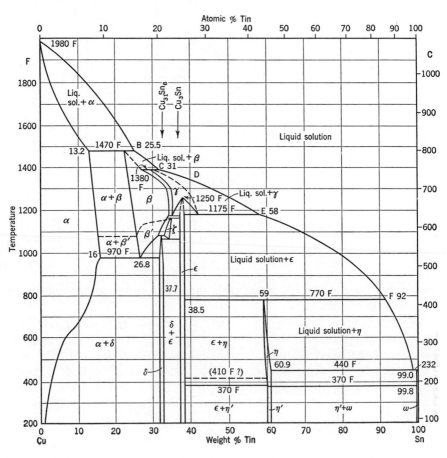

cause of this high ductility, the cold-workability of these alloys, especially those of copper and zinc, is high over the entire α-range. Ductility decreases markedly as the percentage of the brittle β-phase increases in the two-phase field.

**Figure 6.3** (*top pair*) Industrially important portions of the copper-zinc and copper-tin constitutional diagrams. The temperatures indicated by points on the constant composition line, 58% copper, 42% zinc, refer to the treatments used to produce the structures shown in Figure 6.4. (*bottom pair*) Generalized effects of composition on the properties of the engineering brasses and bronzes. [Courtesy Bridgeport Brass Company.]

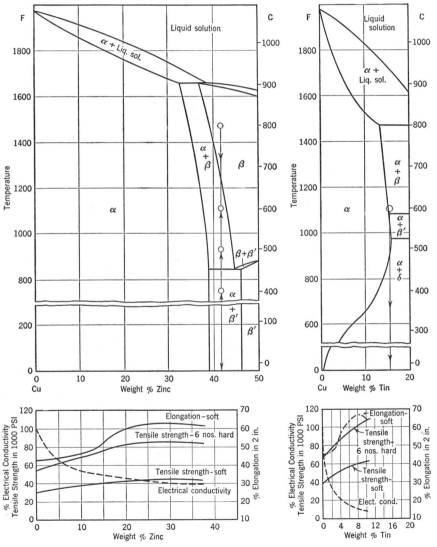

**Figure 6.4** Photomicrographs illustrating the effects of heat-treatment on the microstructure of the alloy 58% copper, 42% zinc (×100). **a** (*top left*). As quenched from 1470 F (800 C). Etched with $NH_4OH + H_2O_2$. [Photomicrograph by A. J. Calpaxis.] The structure is completely $\beta$ secondary solid solution. **b** (*top right*). Quenched and reheated ½ hr at 390 F (200 C). Etched with $NH_4OH + H_2O_2$. [Photomicrograph by J. Caplan.] Very small particles of dark etching $\alpha$ have started to precipitate within the $\beta$ grains. **c** (*middle left*). Quenched and reheated ½ hr at 570 F (300 C). Etched with $NH_4OH + H_2O_2$. [Photomicrograph by L. C. Cavalier.] The number and size of the dark etching $\alpha$ particles have increased so the rate of etching increases also. **d** (*middle right*). Quenched and reheated ½ hr at 750 F (400 C). Etched with Grard's No. 2 to darken the $\beta$. [Photomicrograph by J. W. Fissel.] The light etching $\alpha$ precipitate is coarsening and assuming a definite geometrical pattern. **e** (*bottom left*). Quenched and reheated ½ hr at 930 F (500 C). Etched with Grard's No. 2 to darken the $\beta$. [Photomicrograph by G. H. Ebbs.] The light etching $\alpha$ continues to coarsen and conforms to the regular geometrical pattern even more markedly. Photomicrographs *d* and *e* are examples of the Widmannstaetten type of structure. **f** (*bottom right*). Quenched and reheated ½ hr at 1110 F (600 C). Etched with Grard's No. 2 to darken the $\beta$. [Photomicrograph by R. Stemmler.] The light etching $\alpha$ particles are now very coarse although remnants of their geometrical arrangement still can be seen. The background is probably a finely dispersed mixture of $\alpha$ and $\beta$.

## COLOR CHANGES OF BRASSES WITH INCREASING ZINC CONTENT

All of the $\alpha$-brasses have substantially the same microstructure (see Figures 3.8 and 3.19) but their color changes markedly with zinc content as indicated in Figure 6.5. Small percentages, up to approximately 5% zinc, have little effect on the red copper color. At 5 to 10% zinc a bronze color appears which merges into a red-gold color at 15% zinc and a yellow-gold at about 20% zinc. From approximately 25 to 38% zinc, the alloys have the typical greenish-yellow brass color, and from 38 to 45% zinc, they again take on a somewhat reddish cast, passing through ochre into another series of gold hues.

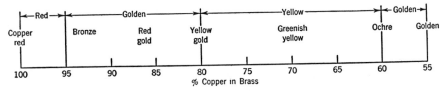

**Figure 6.5** Schematic representation of the change of color with zinc content in the commercial brasses.

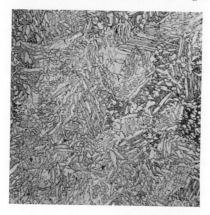 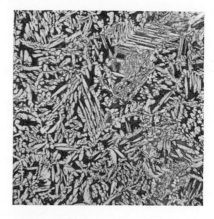

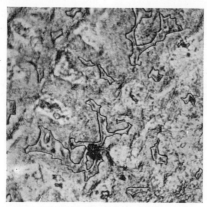

**Figure 6.6   a** (*top left*). Photomicrograph of $\alpha$-$\beta$ brass, Muntz metal (60% copper, 40% zinc). Etched with $NH_4OH + H_2O_2$ ($\times$75). **b** (*top right*). Photomicrograph of $\alpha$-$\beta$ brass, Muntz metal (60% copper, 40% zinc). Etched with $NH_4OH + H_2O_2$ and followed by acid ferric chloride to darken the $\beta$ ($\times$75). **c** (*bottom*). Photomicrograph of $\delta$-bronze constituent ($Cu_{31}Sn_8$) in an $\alpha$-bronze matrix in an alloy of 90% copper, 10% tin. Etched with $NH_4OH + H_2O_2$ ($\times$500). [Photomicrograph by C. L. McVicker.]

## WROUGHT BRASSES

The commercial wrought brasses usually are classified, according to their zinc content, into seven groups

1. Gilding metal (95% copper, 5% zinc), copper alloy No. 210
2. Commercial bronze (90% copper, 10% zinc), copper alloy No. 220
3. Rich-low, or red brass (85% copper, 15% zinc), copper alloy No. 230

4. Low brass (80% copper, 20% zinc), copper alloy No. 240
5. High, or cartridge brass (70% copper, 30% zinc), copper alloy No. 260
6. Common-high, high-yellow, or drawing brass (66% copper, 34% zinc), copper alloy Nos. 268 (sheet) and 270 (rod and wire)
7. Muntz metal (60% copper, 40% zinc), copper alloy No. 280

The corrosion resistance of all the brasses is good, particularly for many aqueous media, but the optimum resistance seems to lie in the vicinity of 85% copper, 15% zinc. The wrought brasses contain only small amounts of iron so they do not "rust." [5] However, they form a greenish-blue corrosion product with certain waters and this often may discolor the water ("green water trouble") or else give a blue stain or deposit wherever dripping occurs.

Typical microstructures of the $\alpha$-$\beta$ two-phase brass alloys are shown in Figures 1.18 and 6.6. The $\beta$ constituent is a light lemon-yellow color when etched with a mixture of ammonium hydroxide and hydrogen peroxide, the usual reagent, but darkens appreciably when etched with ferric chloride. These alloys can be hot worked readily in the range 1150 to 1400 F (625 to 750 C) but have only fair cold-working characteristics because of the influence of the relatively brittle $\beta$ constituent. However, because of the $\beta$ constituent they machine appreciably better than the non-leaded $\alpha$-brasses.

Typical properties of the wrought brasses are given in Figure 6.7. [6] The strength properties are increased and the grain structure is deformed by cold working to an extent comparable with that shown in Figure 3.8 for a cartridge brass.

## DEZINCIFICATION OF BRASSES

Those brasses that contain less than about 80% copper are particularly susceptible to dezincification, so-called because this type of corrosive attack has the general appearance of selective removal of zinc. Actually the entire portion attacked dissolves and the copper immediately reprecipitates in a spongy porous mass. In the yellow $\alpha$-brasses this attack frequently is of a plug type, Figures 6.8a and b, sometimes affecting only a small region in a long length of pipe. In the lower-cost two-phase Muntz metal, dezincification is usually of a general or uniform type, Figure 6.8c.

Small amounts (0.02 to 0.10%) of arsenic, antimony, or phosphorus are added to modern brass alloys to inhibit dezincification, but it still may

[5] Rust is a hydrated red oxide of iron, $Fe_2O_3 \cdot xH_2O$.
[6] The effects of grain size on the properties of deep-drawing brass are discussed by H. L. Walker and W. J. Craig, *Trans. A.I.M.E.,* **180** (1949), 42–51.

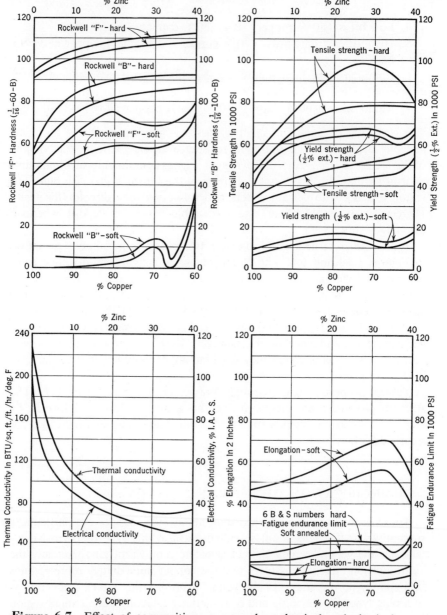

**Figure 6.7** Effect of composition on several mechanical and physical properties of copper-zinc alloys in various tempers.

occur if the alloys are exposed to water while the metal temperature is greater than approximately 130 F (55 C) or to water containing sizable amounts of dissolved oxygen and carbon dioxide. Many alloy brasses also are subject to this type of selective attack. Depending on the alloy it may be called dezincification, dealuminification, denickelification, etc.

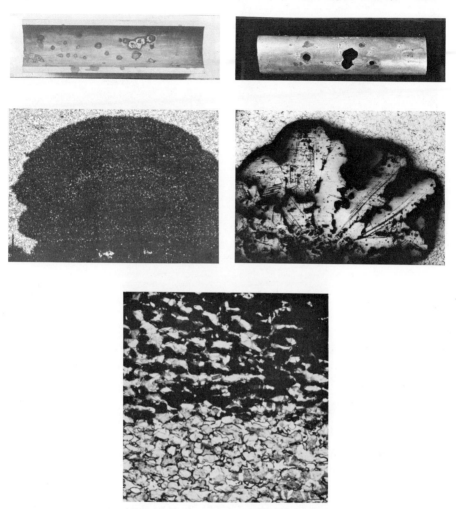

**Figure 6.8** Typical examples of dezincification in copper alloy condenser tubes. **a** (*top pair*). Macrographic appearance of plug-type in two pieces of yellow brass (2 and 1) pipe ($\times$1). **b** (*middle pair*). Metallographic structure of two corroded sections in admiralty metal condenser tubes. Etched with $NH_4OH + H_2O_2$ ($\times$75). [Courtesy Research Department, Chase Brass and Copper Company.] **c** (*bottom*). Dezincification of Muntz metal (60% copper, 40% zinc) showing preferential attack on the less noble (anodic) $\beta$ constituent.

## LEADED BRASSES

Up to 0.5% lead may be added to brasses and many other copper-base alloys to facilitate machining, without interfering seriously with general workability. The lead is insoluble and appears as small particles of a sepa-

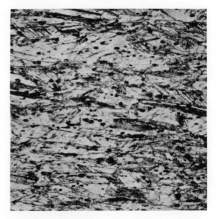

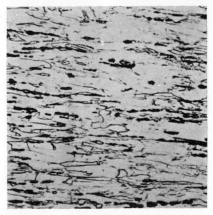

**Figure 6.9**  Metallographic structures of longitudinal sections of a leaded brass and a free-machining copper. Etched with $NH_4OH + H_2O_2$. [Photomicrograph *a* by L. Litchfield; *b* and *c* courtesy Research Department, Chase Brass and Copper Company.] **a** (*top left*). Leaded high-brass sheet—65% copper, 0.9% lead, remainder zinc ($\times 200$). **b** (*top right*). Cold-drawn free-cutting brass rod—62% copper, 3.25% lead, remainder zinc ($\times 75$). **c** (*bottom*). Cold-drawn tellurium-copper—1.05% tellurium, remainder copper ($\times 75$).

rate phase. Larger amounts of lead, up to 3.5% (Figure 6.9), are added to give free-machining characteristics, but decrease workability and other mechanical properties.

### ALLOY BRASSES

Various alloy brasses have been developed for special applications, particularly condenser tubing for use in salt water. Many of them are sold under proprietary names. The most common of these alloy brasses are modifications of the 70:30 composition in which the additional alloying elements are in solid solution so the microstructure is not changed. In general, the alloy additions increase strength and corrosion resistance.

In admiralty metal, copper alloy Nos. 442 (uninhibited), 443 (arsenical), 444 (antimonial), and 445 (phosphorized), 0.90 to 1.20% tin is added, along with, as a rule, 0.02 to 0.10% of arsenic, antimony or phosphorus to inhibit dezincification. Likewise, aluminum brasses, copper alloy No. 687, are made, which contain 1.8 to 2.5% aluminum and a maximum of 1.25% tin, and 1.25% nickel, along with one of the dezincification inhibitors. The aluminum forms a thin self-healing film of aluminum oxide on the surface; this increases resistance to air impingement attack. These two alloy brasses are satisfactory in sea water service only if the velocity is below 6 ft per sec. At higher velocities one of the cupronickel alloys mentioned in Chapter 5 generally is used instead.

The solid solution of approximately 1% tin in Muntz metal (60% copper, 40% zinc) gives an alloy known as naval brass, copper alloy Nos. 462 and 464, which has improved corrosion resistance, particularly to salt water, and mechanical properties. Naval brass also is made with dezincification inhibitors, copper alloy Nos. 465, 466, and 467.

## WROUGHT MANGANESE BRONZES

The addition of small amounts of tin, iron, manganese, and aluminum to the 60:40 alloy gives still better strengths and hardnesses, along with a finer grain size and a reduced tendency toward dezincification. These alloys are known as the wrought manganese bronzes. Typical alloys contain the metals shown in Table 6.1.

**TABLE 6.1**

| Type | Copper Alloy No. | % Cu | % Sn | % Fe | % Mn | % Al | % Zn | % Pb |
|------|------|------|------|------|------|------|------|------|
| A | 675 | 57–60 | 0.5–1.5 | 0.8–2.0 | 0.50 * | 0.25 * | Rem. | 0.20 * |
| B | 670 | 63–68 | 0.50 * | 2.0–4.0 | 2.5–5.0 | 3.0–6.0 | Rem. | 0.20 * |

* Maximum

Tensile strengths of these alloys, in the hot-rolled condition, average 55,000 to 85,000 psi, depending on the type, with yield strengths (0.5% elongation) of 22,000 to 45,000 psi and elongations of 25% or more in 2 in. By cold working, the tensile strength can be increased to 80,000 to

115,000 psi, with a yield strength of 45,000 to 68,000 psi, and an elongation of 10 to 20%. The usual annealing range is 800 to 1100 F (425 to
595 C). The manganese bronzes have excellent hot-working properties,
especially in the range 1150 to 1450 F (625 to 750 C), but they cold work
relatively poorly like the other alpha-beta brasses. Their machinability is
about 30% that of free-cutting brass.

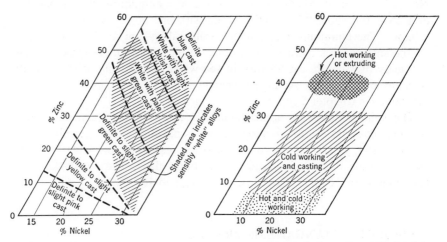

**Figure 6.10    a** (*left*). Color trends of copper-nickel-zinc alloys. **b** (*right*).
Composition ranges of nickel silvers with reference to working characteristics.
[After T. E. Kihlgren, N. B. Pilling, and E. M. Wise, *Trans. A.I.M.E.,* **117**
(1935), 279–309.]

## NICKEL SILVERS

A somewhat different modification, the nickel silvers, is made by adding
7 to 30% nickel to alloys containing 60 to 65% copper and the remainder
zinc. The colors and general working characteristics of the nickel silvers are
shown in Figure 6.10 and some properties of a common type—18% nickel
silver,[7] copper alloy No. 752—in Figure 6.11. The strength properties are
higher than those of the brasses (compare Figure 6.7). The machinability
of the nickel silvers can be improved by adding up to 1% lead, but this
decreases the deep-drawing characteristics and also makes them more apt
to fire crack because of overstressing from the combination of residual
stresses and thermal stresses produced during annealing or any sudden
application of heat.

---

[7] It is customary to designate the nickel silvers by the nickel content regardless of
their copper and zinc content.

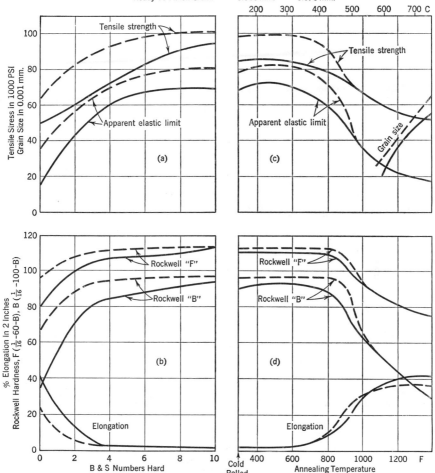

**Figure 6.11   a. and b.** Mechanical properties of 18% nickel silver sheet cold rolled from metal of two different ready-to-finish grain sizes. **c.** and **d.** Mechanical properties of 18% nickel silver sheet cold rolled from metal of two different ready-to-finish grain sizes then finish annealed. [From *Metals Handbook,* courtesy American Society for Metals.]

## SEASON CRACKING OF BRASSES

Brasses and alloy brasses, particularly those containing less than 85% copper are apt to crack spontaneously when exposed to corrosion while under stress.[8] In alpha brasses these cracks are intercrystalline. Ammonia and its compounds are active promoters, particularly in the presence of

[8] D. H. Thompson and A. W. Tracy, *Trans. A.I.M.E.,* **185** (1949), 100–109.

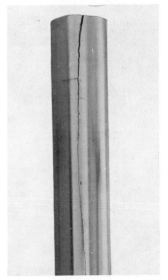

**Figure 6.12   a** (*left*). Brass bowl which failed by season cracking. **b** (*right*). Brass tubing which cracked in standard mercurous nitrate test. [Courtesy Research Department, Chase Brass and Copper Company.]

oxygen and water vapor. This phenomenon is known generally as stress-corrosion cracking, although the term season-cracking also is used.[9] Typical failures are shown in Figure 6.12. If the stresses are residual, rather than service, a stress relief anneal of 30 to 60 min at 300 to 575 F (150 to 300 C), depending on the particular part, removes the cracking tendency in most cases. Full annealing also removes the cracking tendency but softens the material as well.

### WROUGHT BRONZES

The wrought copper-tin bronzes generally are known commercially as phosphor bronzes although the phosphorus remaining, after it serves its function of deoxidation during casting, never is greater than 0.5% and often is much less. Three grades are used commonly (Table 6.2). Metallographic structures of all of these phosphor bronzes are similar to those of the brasses.

[9] A thorough review is given by A. R. Bailey, *Metallurgical Reviews,* **6** (1961), 101–42; see also A. L. Jamieson in Ref. 1 (1948 ed.) at the end of this chapter.

TABLE 6.2

| Grade | Copper Alloy No. | % Sn | % P | % Zn * |
|-------|-------------------|----------|------------|--------|
| A | 510 | 3.8–5.8 | 0.03–0.35 | 0.30 |
| C | 521 | 7.0–9.0 | 0.03–0.35 | 0.20 |
| D | 524 | 9.0–11.0 | 0.03–0.35 | 0.20 |

* Maximum

Typical mechanical properties as a function of tin content are shown in Figure 6.13 for various degrees of cold work. The cold-worked phosphor bronzes were the established nonferrous material for springs until alloys such as beryllium bronze (see Chapter 10) became available. The effect of annealing the three standard grades is given in Figure 6.14. Only alloys containing less than 2% tin can be hot worked satisfactorily. The higher alloys must be cold worked. Free-machining modifications of Grade A, containing up to 4.5% lead, are made for antifriction applications.

## MICROSTRUCTURES OF CAST BRASSES AND BRONZES

Microstructures typical of copper-zinc and copper-tin alloys in the as-cast condition are shown in Figure 6.15 with some indication of how the various phase boundaries are displaced by nonequilibrium solidification. In general, the displacement is greater and coring is more pronounced in the copper-tin alloys than in the copper-zinc alloys.

The $\delta$-constituent ($Cu_{31}Sn_8$), in the copper-tin system is bluish in color under the microscope and usually occurs in rather small particles which require a fairly high magnification to resolve (Figure 6.6c).

## CAST RED BRASSES

The most commonly used cast brass alloy is known as composition brass, ounce metal (because the earliest mixture was 1 oz each of tin, lead and zinc to 1 lb copper), cast red brass, or eighty-five three fives (85:5:5:5). It contains 85% copper, 5% tin for strength, 5% lead for machinability, and 5% zinc for ease of casting, and may be deoxidized with phosphorus.

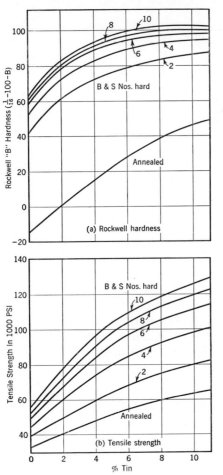

(a) Rockwell hardness

(b) Tensile strength

**Figure 6.13** (*left side*) Change in the mechanical properties of annealed and cold-rolled phosphor bronze sheet with tin content. Average grain diameter 0.050 mm, minimum gauge of sheet 0.040 in. In each case, bottom curve represents annealed material, other curves same material but rolled as indicated. **a.** Rockwell hardness. **b.** Tensile strength. [From *Metals Handbook*, courtesy American Society for Metals.]

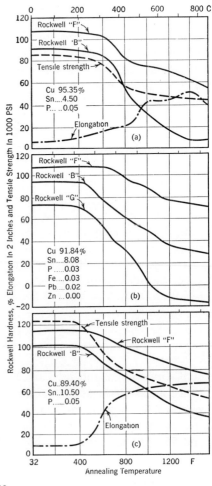

**Figure 6.14** (*right side*) Mechanical properties of 0.040-in. thick phosphor bronze sheet. Reduced 50% in thickness by rolling and annealed ½ hr at temperature noted. **a.** Grade A. **b.** Grade C. **c.** Grade D. [From *Metals Handbook*, courtesy American Society for Metals.]

Iron is kept below 0.25% to minimize hard spots, and nickel below 1% to improve fluidity. Specified minimum properties are 30,000 psi tensile strength, 14,000 psi yield strength, and 20% elongation in 2 in. The microstructure, Figure 6.16a, is similar to that of a typical cored 7 to 8% tin bronze containing many small globular particles of lead.

Modifications of the 85:5:5:5 composition, which have been used for a wide variety of brass castings in which it is desired to secure a red color at a low cost, are the alloys containing, nominally (a) 83% copper, 4% tin, 6% lead, 7% zinc, known as commercial red brass; (b) 81% copper, 3% tin, 7% lead, 9% zinc, commonly known as medium red brass or valve composition; (c) semired brass, 76% copper, 3% tin, 6% lead, 15% zinc.

## CAST YELLOW BRASSES

Lower cost brass castings, which have high allowable impurity limits and hence can be made from miscellaneous yellow brass scrap, are the yellow or plumber's brasses. In these alloys 1% tin, for somewhat better strength and corrosion resistance, and 3% lead, to improve machinability, are added to a base containing 60 to 71% copper, depending on the grade, with the remainder zinc. The metallographic structure is comparable with that of cast red brass (Figure 6.16a), with particles of insoluble lead in a cored $\alpha$ solid-solution of tin and zinc in copper.

## STEAM AND STRUCTURAL BRONZES

The highest quality cast bronzes are copper-base alloys high in tin and low in lead. These also are the highest in cost, not only because of the tin content but also because virgin metal or carefully selected scrap must be used to make them. These steam and structural bronzes are important because they combine properties of strength and toughness with bearing and antigalling [10] qualities, good casting characteristics and resistance to sea water corrosion. The commonest composition, known variously as 88:10:2, government bronze, composition "G", and zinc bronze, contains 87 to 89% copper, 9.5 to 10.5% tin, and 1.5 to 2.5% zinc, with close control of possible impurities.

For castings of large cross section an 88:8:4 modification may be used. This composition, however, is difficult to machine after it has been cooled

---

[10] Antigalling materials resist localized welding when mating surfaces become heated because of friction from limited lubrication.

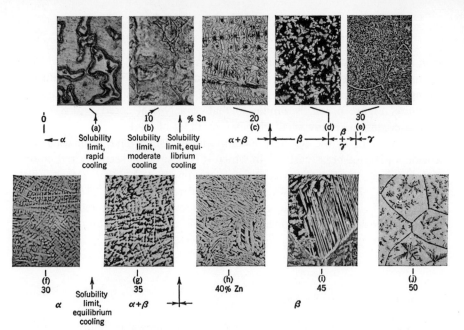

**Figure 6.15** Metallographic structures of (*top row*) copper-tin and (*bottom row*) copper-zinc alloys in the "as-cast" condition, illustrating coring and the apparent shift in the solidus line resulting from incomplete diffusion. Unless otherwise indicated, the phase fields are those existing just after solidification under equilibrium conditions. Original magnifications given, reduced approximately one-half in reproduction.

*Copper-tin alloys:* **a.** 95% copper, 5% tin. Etched with $NH_4OH + H_2O_2$ (×500). In these alloys the transformations $\gamma \rightarrow \beta$ and $\beta \rightarrow \alpha + \delta$ nearly always tend to occur in the solid alloys during cooling. [Photomicrograph by J. T. Mackenzie, Jr.] Note the appearance of very small particles of $\delta$ secondary solid solution ($Cu_{31}Sn_8$) in the dendrites richer in tin even though, after equilibrium solidification, this alloy should fall within the $\alpha$ primary solid-solution field. The presence of $\delta$ is clear evidence of the presence of some $\beta$ in the alloy just after solidification. **b.** 95% copper, 10% tin. Etched with $NH_4OH + H_2O_2$ (×500). [Photomicrograph by C. L. McVicker.] Although this alloy also should fall within the $\alpha$ field, comparatively large particles of the $\delta$ constituent can be seen readily in a cored solid-solution matrix. The rate of solidification was undoubtedly rapid enough to form some $\beta$ which then decomposed during cooling. **c.** 80% copper, 20% tin. Etched with Grard's No. 1 (×200). [Photomicrograph by G. W. Brown.] The $\alpha$ dendrites and particles of the $\delta$ constituent can be seen readily at this low magnification. Even with equilibrium solidification this alloy should contain considerable $\beta$ which then would transform to $\alpha$ and $\delta$ during cooling. **d.** 73% copper, 27% tin. Etched with Grard's No. 1 (×500). [Photomicrograph by A. J. Calpaxis.] Particles of light etching $\delta$ in an unresolved matrix composed either of $\alpha$ or of a mechanical mixture of $\alpha$ and $\delta$. This structure should correspond nearly to the eutectoid composition but undoubtedly has been modified during solidification and cooling to give the appearance of a somewhat higher tin content. **e.** 70% copper, 30% tin. Etched with 5% ferric chloride (×200). [Photomicrograph by R. F. Hancock.] Because of the transformation, $\beta \rightarrow \alpha + \delta$, which takes place after solidification, this structure is nearly normal. Excess $\delta$ constituent at the bound-

slowly, so 0.5 to 1.5% lead often is added to improve machinability. These leaded varieties are known as commercial "G" or composition "M" depending on the allowable impurities and the mechanical properties required. Typical microstructures of low-lead cast bronzes, showing the presence of δ copper-tin constituent ($Cu_{31}Sn_8$), which always forms to some extent when the zinc is low and the rate of cooling moderate, are shown in Figures 6.16*b* and *c* and 6.17*c*.

## HIGH-LEAD BEARING BRONZES

The best combination of strength, resistance to deformation by pounding, and bearing characteristics is given by the high-lead bearing bronzes. The original compositions were 80% copper, 10% tin, 10% lead, introduced in England about 1880 and the engine brass alloy, 77% copper, 8% tin, 15% lead introduced in this country about 1892. Phosphorus often is added to deoxidize these alloys, thereby improving their casting and bearing characteristics by decreasing the amount of tin oxide. Residual phosphorus generally is kept low because in the range 0.1 to 0.5% it tends to form the embrittling compound $Cu_3P$. Today numerous bearing bronze alloys are made, containing 70 to 85% copper, 5 to 10% tin and 5 to 25% lead. A few also contain some zinc. Their metallographic structure, shown in Figure 6.17*b*, is similar to that of a cast copper-tin alloy (Figure 6.17*a*) except for the globules of insoluble lead. The δ secondary solid solution ($Cu_{31}Sn_8$) can be found in practically all of these structures. In these alloys

aries, geometrically dispersed particles of light etching δ in a matrix of dark etching α within the grains.

*Copper-zinc alloys:* **f.** 70% copper, 30% zinc. Etched with Grard's No. 1 (×100). [Photomicrograph by T. S. Luerssen.] A small amount of dark etching β has been formed in cored regions of the α solid solution because of coring and the solidus displacement resulting from nonequilibrium cooling. No transformation to α on cooling is apparent at this magnification. **g.** 65% copper, 35% zinc. Etched with Grard's No. 1 (×100). [Photomicrograph by C. M. Campbell.] The amount of dark etching β has increased as the copper content decreased. No transformation to α on cooling is apparent at this magnification. **h.** 60% copper, 40% zinc. Etched with Grard's No. 1 (× 100). The β formed on solidification has transformed on cooling, precipitating large needles of light-etching α. Except for the large particles, this structure is nearly normal. **i.** 55% copper, 45% zinc. Etched with Grard's No. 2 (×100). This structure is quite similar to that of the 60:40 alloy except that the dark etching background, which is now more noticeable, is a finely dispersed mixture of α and β' formed by the reaction $β \xrightarrow{\text{cooling}} α + β'$. **j.** 50% copper, 50% zinc. Etched with $NH_4OH + H_2O_2$ (×100). [Photomicrograph by R. R. Sterner.] A few small dark etching particles of γ have precipitated during cooling, both at the grain boundaries and on a geometrical pattern within the β grains. This structure also is nearly normal, but indicates that the actual analysis is probably a little higher in zinc than the 50% shown above.

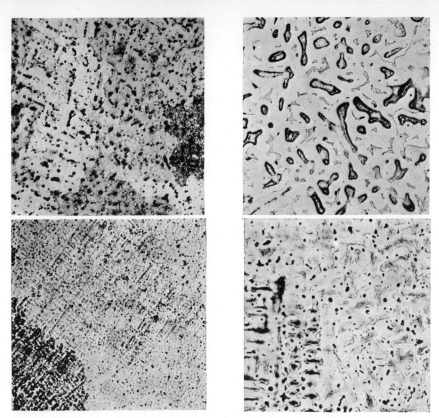

**Figure 6.16** Metallographic structures of some cast brasses and bronzes. [Photomicrographs courtesy Crane Company Research Laboratories.] **a** (*top left*). Ounce metal—cast red brass (85% copper, 5% tin, 5% zinc, 5% lead). Etched with $NH_4OH + H_2O_2$ ($\times$50). **b** (*top right*). Composition G (88% copper, 10% tin, 2% zinc). Etched with $NH_4OH + H_2O_2$ to develop cored dendrites, lightly polished and re-etched in $FeCl_3$ to increase contrast ($\times$100). **c.** Composition M (89% copper, 6% tin, 3% zinc, 2% lead). Etched with $NH_4OH + H_2O_2$ (*bottom left: $\times$25; bottom right: $\times$75*).

the tin is distributed between the copper-rich and the insoluble lead-rich phases so the microstructures are not necessarily consistent with either the copper:tin ratio or the actual percentages of this element present.

### LEAD BRONZES

The lead bronzes (Figures 1.15*a* and 6.17*d*), used extensively for steel-backed bearings made by either the direct casting or the powder metallurgy method, are not bronzes at all but mixtures of 65 to 70% copper with 35 to 30% lead. These two metals form a two-phase mixture even in the liquid state except over a narrow range of temperatures.[11] A few per cent of other elements such as tin, nickel, or silver may be added to improve dispersion.

[11] In this respect the copper-lead diagram is somewhat comparable to the iron-copper diagram in Figure 6.19*b*.

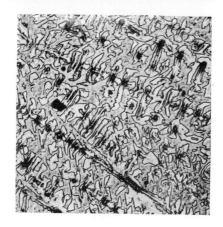 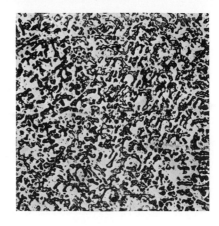

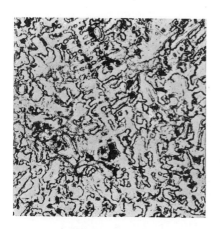 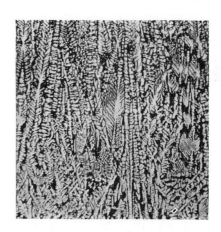

**Figure 6.17** Metallographic structures of some cast copper-base bearing alloys. **a** (*top left*). Bell metal (80% copper, 20% tin), showing particles of secondary solid solution ($Cu_{31}Sn_8$) in a matrix of cored copper-rich $\alpha$ solid solution. Etched with $NH_4OH + H_2O_2$ and Grard's No. 1 ($\times$200). [Photomicrograph by G. W. Brown.] **b** (*top right*). Bearing bronze (80% copper, 10% tin, 10% lead). Etched with $NH_4OH + H_2O_2$ ($\times$50). [Photomicrograph by L. C. Cavalier.] **c** (*middle left*). Gun metal (88% copper, 10% tin, 2% zinc). Etched with $NH_4OH + H_2O_2$ ($\times$100). [Photomicrograph by J. H. Dedrick.] **d** (*middle right*). Cross section of gravity-cast copper lead bearing alloy (70.5% copper, 28.5% lead, 1.0% silver). Unetched ($\times$100). Note the tendency for branches to develop in the wide dendrites. [Photomicrograph courtesy The Cleveland Graphite Bronze Company.] **e** (*bottom*). Graphite-bronze bearing (89% copper, 10% tin, 1% carbon) made by powder metallurgy. Etched with $NH_4OH + H_2O_2$ ($\times$200). Compare Figure 5.2.

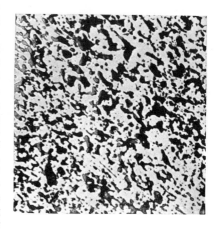

## GRAPHITE BRONZES

Likewise, graphite bronzes (Figure 6.17*e*) are made by powder metallurgy methods, with graphite as the self-lubricating phase instead of lead. These compositions largely are used for oilless bearings.

## HIGH-STRENGTH CAST NICKEL BRONZES

Higher strength castings can be secured by decreasing the amount of insoluble lead, by establishing better control of impurities, and by adding various strengthening elements. The 5:5:2 nickel bronzes containing 5.0 to 5.5% nickel, 5.0 to 5.5% tin, 1 to 2% zinc with 0.03 to 0.05% phosphorus are typical. A stronger 7.5:8:2 variety also is made. The metallographic structure, Figure 6.18*a*, is not greatly different from that of the other cast bronzes except for the absence of lead, and shows only a few particles of what probably is $\delta$ copper-tin constituent ($Cu_{31}Sn_8$) in a dendritic primary solid solution matrix of nickel and tin in copper.

These alloys can be hardened and strengthened by heat-treatment, for general reasons that are discussed in Chapter 7, with a marked improvement in properties. The usual annealing or homogenizing treatment is 5 hr at 1400 F (760 C) followed by a rapid cooling, the severity of which depends on the casting. Holding (aging) for 5 hr at 550 to 600 F (290

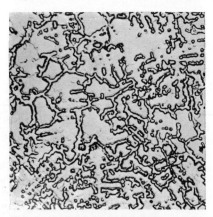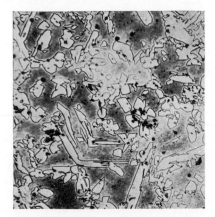

**Figure 6.18** Metallographic structures of high-strength copper-base casting alloys. **a** (*left*). Chill-cast nickel bronze (5% nickel, 5% tin, 2% zinc, remainder copper). Etched with $NH_4OH + H_2O_2$ ($\times100$). [Photomicrograph by L. Litchfield.] **b** (*right*). Cast manganese bronze (60% copper, 2% tin, 3% manganese, 1% aluminum, 1.5% iron, 0.5% lead, remainder zinc). Etched with $FeCl_3$ to darken the $\beta$ ($\times100$). [Photomicrograph courtesy Crane Company Research Laboratories.]

to 315 C) then gives the best combination of strength and ductility. However, nickel-bronzes, unlike many heat-treatable alloys, do not depend on a prior homogenizing (solution) treatment for giving a good response to aging. They can be heat-treated as-cast, to improve properties, although the effect of aging is lost if gassy castings are treated.

**TABLE 6.3   Strength Properties Typical of 5:5:2 Nickel-Bronze Castings in Various Conditions**

|  | Tensile Strength (*psi*) | Yield Strength (0.5% Elong.) (*psi*) | Elongation (% in 2 in.) | Brinell Hardness (10 mm– 1,000 Kg) |
|---|---|---|---|---|
| As-cast | 48,000 | 29,000 | 40 | 86 * |
| Cast and aged 10 hr at 550 F | 73,000 | 61,000 | 5 | 170 |
| Cast and annealed 10 hr at 1400 F, quenched, and aged 5 hr at 550 F | 87,000 | 70,000 | 10 | 190 |

* 500-Kg load.

## CAST MANGANESE BRONZES

The cast manganese bronzes are basically Muntz metals alloyed to give an excellent combination of strength, ductility, and corrosion resistance. Nominal compositions of the three commonest types are shown in Table 6.4.

**TABLE 6.4**

| Commercial Designation | % Cu | % Zn | % Sn | % Mn | % Al | % Fe | % Pb | % Ni |
|---|---|---|---|---|---|---|---|---|
| Leaded manganese bronze | 59.0 | Rem. | 0.75 | 0.50 | 0.75 | 1.25 | 0.75 | |
| No. 1 manganese bronze | 57.5 | Rem. | 1.0 * | 1.50 * | 1.00 | 1.25 | 0.40 * | 0.5 * |
| High-strength manganese bronze | 64.0 | Rem. | 0.20 * | 4.00 | 5.00 | 3.00 | 0.20 * | 0.8 * |

* Maximum.

These alloys have a high shrinkage and, because of their composition, a comparatively high tendency to become contaminated with oxide during casting. Both of these objectionable features can be overcome by proper design and casting techniques.

Metallographic structures, as shown in Figure 6.18*b*, are similar to those of a fine-grain alpha-beta brass of the Muntz metal type although the structures of some compositions may be considerably more complex. The black spots are probably an iron-bearing constituent which always is profuse in these alloys.

Typical mechanical properties are shown in Table 6.5. To secure the best properties, it is necessary to use virgin metal, ingots of controlled purity, or selected scrap.

TABLE 6.5   Strength Properties Typical of the Cast Manganese Bronzes

| Commercial Designation | Tensile Strength (psi) | Yield Strength (0.5% Elong.) (psi) | Elongation (% in 2 in.) | Brinell Hardness (10 mm– 500 Kg) |
|---|---|---|---|---|
| Leaded manganese bronze | 65,000 | 30,000 | 18 | 85 |
| No. 1 manganese bronze | 70,000 | 28,000 | 30 | 98 |
| High-strength manganese bronze | 90,000– 120,000 | 46,000– 70,000 | 15–19 | 170–210 * |

* 3,000-Kg load.

## EFFECT OF ALLOYING ELEMENTS UPON THE ALLOTROPIC TRANSFORMATIONS IN PURE IRON

Binary constitutional diagrams which involve the metal iron generally are complex because of the allotropic nature of this metal rather than because of the number of intermetallic phases which can form. In this respect they differ from the copper-zinc and copper-tin diagrams. Elements alloyed with iron affect the allotropic transformations in one of two ways.[12] Alloying elements in the first group depress the alpha-gamma transformation and raise the gamma-delta transformation, thus widening the temperature range within which gamma iron is stable. Alloying elements in the second group depress the gamma-delta transformation rapidly and either have less effect in the same direction on the gamma-alpha transformation or actually raise its temperature. Usually a continuous loop surrounding

[12] See, for a further discussion, E. C. Bain, *The Alloying Elements in Steel* (Cleveland: American Society for Metals, 1939), and Ref. 10 at the end of this chapter.

the gamma field is formed, so that the alpha and delta fields are merged. This extends the temperature range over which alpha iron is stable and decreases the composition range within which gamma iron is stable. In each of these two classes, there are two subdivisions depending upon whether intermetallic compounds or solid solutions rich in the alloying elements are formed. In each case, however, the iron-rich portion of the diagram is the most significant portion. The constitution of engineering alloys is approximated by such iron-binary diagrams only if the carbon content is relatively low, say, less than 0.10%.

The alloying metals manganese, nickel, and cobalt increase the range of stability of gamma iron. These elements are soluble in appreciable amounts in both gamma and alpha iron. The iron-nickel diagram, typical for these metals, is illustrated in Figure 6.19*a*.

The alloying elements, copper, zinc, gold, nitrogen, and carbon also increase the temperature range of stability of gamma iron. However, either compounds or solid solutions rich in the alloying elements form, and the constitutional diagram, therefore, resembles that for iron-copper shown in Figure 6.19*b*.

The elements silicon, chromium, tungsten, molybdenum, phosphorus, vanadium, titanium, beryllium, tin, antimony, arsenic, and aluminum decrease the temperature range of stability of gamma iron, and form what is known as a gamma loop, as illustrated by the iron-molybdenum diagram in Figure 6.19*c*. All of these metals, in addition, form solid solutions of appreciable extent with body-centered cubic iron. This may be considered to be either alpha- or delta-iron, depending on the temperature range considered, because the two merge and become identical once the gamma loop is closed.

The elements tantalum, zirconium, boron, sulfur, and cerium also decrease the temperature range of stability of gamma iron; but in each instance the diagram is complicated by the occurrence of compounds, as illustrated by the iron-cerium diagram in Figure 6.19*d*.

## IRON-CARBON ALLOYS

The iron-carbon diagram [13] is so important for rationalizing the structure and treatment of steels and cast irons that it will be discussed in considerable detail. In its effects on the allotropic transformations in pure iron, carbon is of the same general type as the iron-copper diagram shown in

[13] For a thorough discussion, see S. Epstein, *The Alloys of Iron and Carbon*, Vol. I—"Constitution" (New York: McGraw-Hill, 1936); also Refs. 1 and 2 at the end of this chapter.

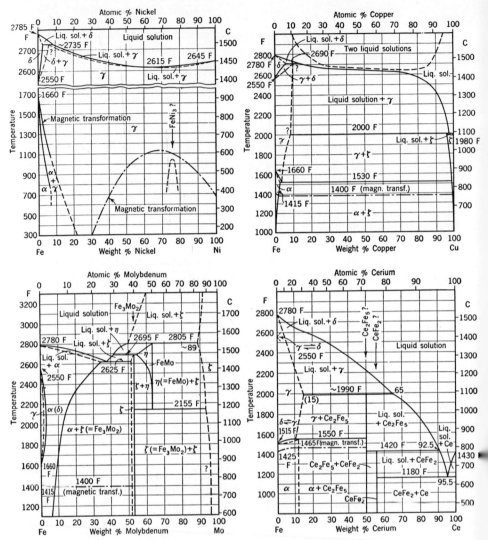

**Figure 6.19** **a** (*upper left*) and **b** (*upper right*). Constitutional diagrams typical of iron binary alloys in which the temperature range of stability of gamma iron is increased by alloying. [After F. Wever.] **a.** Iron-nickel diagram, representative of elements which are soluble both in gamma and in alpha iron. [After M. Hansen.] **b.** Iron-copper diagram, representative of elements which form either compounds or second phases—i.e., secondary or other primary solid solutions. [After M. Hansen.] The iron-iron carbide diagram (Figure 6.20) is also of this type.

**c** (*lower left*) and **d** (*lower right*). Constitutional diagrams typical of iron binary alloys in which the temperature range of stability of gamma iron is decreased by alloying. [After F. Wever.] **c.** Iron-molybdenum diagram, representative of elements which are soluble both in gamma and in alpha iron. [After M. Hansen.] **d.** Iron-cerium diagram representative of elements which form either compounds or second phases—i.e., secondary or other primary solid solutions. [After M. Hansen.]

Figure 6.19*b*. Experimental difficulties have permitted the study of the system only up to about 5% carbon, and little or nothing is known beyond 6.67% carbon, which is the composition of the metastable carbide of iron, $Fe_3C$. Actually there are two constitutional diagrams for alloys of iron and carbon. The industrially more important diagram involves the metastable iron carbide, $Fe_3C$, found in most steels and in many cast irons. In the less important stable diagram this carbide does not exist and the second phase to appear is graphite. The stable diagram is given in Figure 6.47.

From Figures 6.20 and 6.21 it can be seen that there are only three significant single-phase areas in the iron-iron carbide diagram in addition to the liquid solution of carbon in iron. Because of their industrial importance, these three phases have been given characteristic names:

1. Ferrite [14] (from the Latin *ferrum*), commercially pure alpha iron containing a maximum of approximately 0.04 to 0.05% carbon in solid solution.

**Figure 6.20** Constitutional diagram for the alloys of iron and iron carbide: the steels and white cast irons. [After M. Hansen.]

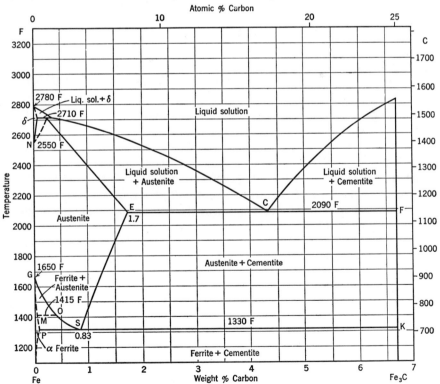

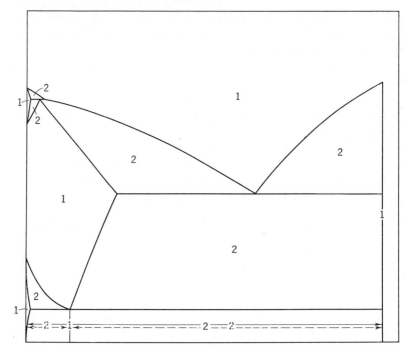

**Figure 6.21** Application of the 1:2:1 rule to the constitutional diagram for the alloys of iron and iron carbide.

2. Austenite [14] (named for the English metallurgist Sir William Roberts-Austen), an interstitial primary solid solution of carbon in gamma iron containing a maximum of approximately 1.7% carbon at 2090 F (1140 C) and of approximately 0.83% carbon at 1330 F (725 C).[15]

3. Cementite (from the Latin *caementum*), the iron carbide, $Fe_3C$, containing 6.67% carbon, which probably melts or decomposes at a temperature in excess of 3540 F (1950 C) (compare Figure 6.26), and is thermodynamically unstable below about 2200 F (1200 C).

The peritectic reaction occurring near the melting point of iron results in a fourth single-phase area called delta iron.

In addition, there is a eutectic at about 4.3% carbon and 2090 F (1140 C). The characteristic structure, known as ledeburite, which exists

[14] Common usage actually has made ferrite and austenite structural names, referring, respectively, to any body-centered cubic phase and any face-centered cubic phase based on iron.

[15] Accurate determinations have been made by R. F. Mehl and C. Wells, *Trans. A.I.M.E.*, **125** (1937), 429–69; L. S. Darken and R. W. Gurry, *ibid.*, **191** (1951), 1015–18; R. P. Smith and L. S. Darken, *ibid.*, **215** (1959), 727–28. See also Refs. 1 and 2 at the end of this chapter.

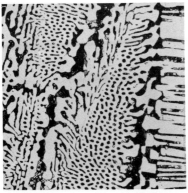 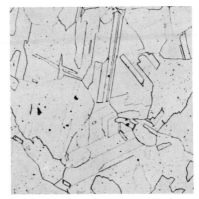

**Figure 6.22  a** (*left*). Metallographic structure, typical of the iron-iron carbide eutectic, ledeburite, produced by melting commercially pure ingot iron under graphite. Etched with nital (×500). [Photomicrograph by M. C. Fetzer.] Compare Figure 5.25*b*. The light etching regions are cementite and the dark etching regions are unresolved transformed austenite—i.e., pearlite. **b** (*right*). Metallographic structure typical of the solid solution of carbon in gamma iron, austenite (×100). In plain carbon steels this constituent is stable only above $A_1$. The structure shown is that of an 18% chromium, 8% nickel austenitic stainless steel.

at ordinary temperatures from this eutectic reaction is shown in Figure 6.22*a*. This constituent is found infrequently in industrial alloys except in some white cast irons.

### THE EUTECTOID

At a temperature of 1330 F (725 C) and a composition of approximately 0.83% carbon, the diagram has a configuration similar in appearance to that of a eutectic transformation. However, here a solid solution exists above the "V" on the diagram, whereas in the eutectic transformation it is a liquid solution which transforms at the lowest temperature into a mixture of two solid phases. This new type of transformation is known as a eutectoid.[16] It may be described either as the transformation, on cooling, of a solid solution at a constant temperature into a mixture of two other solid phases, or by the equation

$$\text{Solid I} \xrightleftharpoons[\text{heating}]{\text{cooling}} \text{Solid II} + \text{Solid III}$$

[16] Eutectoid transformations occur in many systems other than iron-carbon. For example, see W. R. Hibbard, Jr., G. H. Eichelman, Jr., and W. P. Saunders, *Trans. A.I.M.E.*, **180** (1949), 92–100; E. P. Klier and S. M. Grymko, *ibid.*, **185** (1949), 611–19; R. H. Fillnow and D. J. Mack, *ibid*, **188** (1950), 1229–36; J. S. Brett, G. L. Kehl, and E. Jaraiz F., *ibid.*, **218** (1960), 753–63.

In iron-carbon alloys, this transformation is very important. Above 1330 F (725 C), an alloy containing 0.83% carbon, with the remainder essentially iron, is composed of the stable solid solution of carbon in face-centered cubic iron, called austenite. This would have a microstructure similar to that shown in Figure 6.22*b* if it were examined in its stable temperature range. As this alloy cools through the critical temperature in the vicinity of 1330 F (725 C) a eutectoid transformation occurs which may be expressed, specifically, by the equation

$$\text{Austenite} \xrightleftharpoons[\text{heating}]{\text{cooling}} \text{Ferrite} + \text{Cementite}$$

Under equilibrium conditions this transformation takes place at a constant temperature exactly as would a comparable eutectic transformation. After transforming under equilibrium conditions, the alloy is composed of a mechanical mixture of alternate plates or lamellae of the two phases, ferrite and cementite, arranged as in the photomicrograph shown in Figure 6.23*a*. The solid solubilities of carbon in alpha iron and of iron in cementite are rather small so the structure remains practically unchanged during its subsequent cooling to room temperature. This mechanical mixture of two phases, which is readily distinguishable under the microscope even though the lamellae may not be resolved, as in Figure 6.23*b*, is so important that it frequently is considered to be a separate constituent in slowly cooled steels, purely as a matter of convenience. It was discovered by Sorby, who called it pearlite or pearly constituent, because when etched it often displays a spectrum of colors very suggestive of mother-of-pearl. The reason

**Figure 6.23**  Metallographic structures typical of the iron-iron carbide eutectoid, pearlite. Etched with nital. Compare Figure 8.6*a*. **a** (*left*). Showing its lamellar nature resolved (×250). **b** (*right*). Showing the majority of the lamellae unresolved (×100).

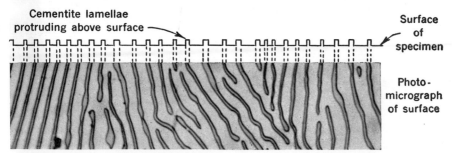

**Figure 6.24** Schematic representation of a cross section through a patch of pearlite (×2500), illustrating the relative thicknesses of the ferrite and cementite lamellae and the grating effect produced by etching, which gives this constituent its iridescent appearance.

for this can be understood from the diagram shown in Figure 6.24, in which the cross section of a patch of pearlite is idealized. The layers of either constituent are seldom more than 0.00004 in. thick, so pearlite affects light in a manner somewhat similar to a diffraction grating because of the fact that the harder carbide particles stand out in relief after polishing and etching. White light striking a surface such as this is broken up into its constituent colors, thus giving it a pearly or iridescent appearance.

Steels containing less carbon than the eutectoid composition are known as hypoeutectoid steels, whereas those containing carbon between the eutectoid composition and the limit of solid solubility in the gamma phase (approximately 1.7% carbon) are known as hypereutectoid steels. Iron-carbon alloys beyond this point usually are not classed as steels. In addition, any ferrite or cementite existing in the alloy in excess of that required to form pearlite is referred to as proeutectoid (or free) ferrite or cementite, as the case might be. The name proeutectoid arises from the fact that the "excess" phase is precipitated, during cooling, before the separation of the eutectoid.

## REACTION TO ETCHING OF CONSTITUENTS IN IRON-CARBON ALLOYS

Three etching reagents are used most commonly to delineate the constituents of the slowly cooled iron-carbon alloys.[17] These are, respectively (a) nital, a water-free solution of 2 to 4% nitric acid in either methyl or

[17] See J. R. Vilella, *Metallographic Technique for Steel* (Cleveland: American Society for Metals, 1937); also, *Trans. A.I.M.E.,* **191** (1951), 605–19. Ref. 1 (7th ed.) at the end of this chapter gives many other etchants that are used for specific purposes.

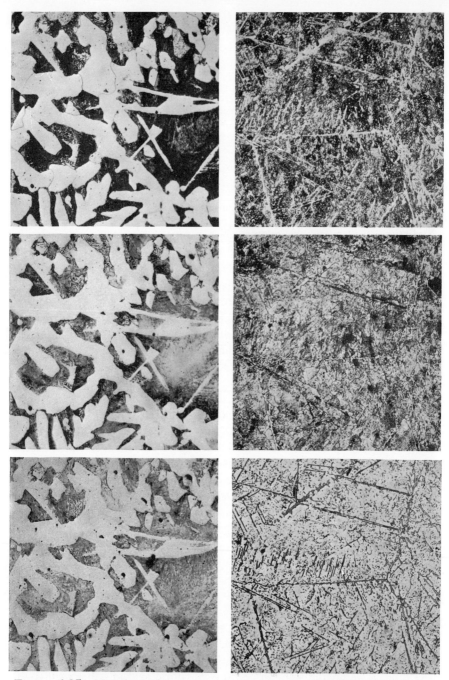

**Figure 6.25** Metallographic structures of (*left side*) a 0.5% carbon hypo-eutectoid steel and (*right side*) a 1.2% carbon hypereutectoid steel—after etching with (*top pair*) nital, (*middle pair*) picral, and (*bottom pair*) alkaline sodium picrate (×100). Portions of three very large grains are shown in the hypereutectoid steel with proeutectoid cementite appearing both at the grain boundaries and as plates precipitated within the original (austenite) grains.

ethyl alcohol; (b) picral, a solution of 2 to 5% picric acid in ethyl alcohol; (c) alkaline sodium picrate, a solution of 2 gm picric acid and 25 gm sodium hydroxide in 100 ml water.

With nital, the boundaries of cementite are outlined clearly. This has the effect of darkening pearlite when viewed at low magnifications. Nital also reveals grain boundaries in ferrite areas. Both ferrite and cementite appear white after etching.

The action of picral is similar, except that it etches fine pearlite much more uniformly than nital does. However, it does not etch ferrite so rapidly as nital, and does not indicate the ferrite grain boundaries clearly. As before, both ferrite and cementite appear white after etching, and pearlite appears dark.

Alkaline sodium picrate is used, either electrolytically or as a boiling etchant, to differentiate between cementite and ferrite. Ferrite is unattacked and, therefore, appears white after etching, whereas cementite is attacked and darkened.

The appearance of typical slowly cooled hypo- and hypereutectoid carbon steels, after etching with each of these three reagents, is illustrated in Figure 6.25.

## TRANSFORMATION NOMENCLATURE IN IRON ALLOYS

The nomenclature used for the transformations in pure iron is carried over to the steels with few changes. The $A_4$ transformation is of little industrial importance for most steels and is not discussed here. The $A_3$ transformation, during which gamma iron changes to alpha iron on cooling, becomes in the steels the line *GSK* on the diagram shown in conventional form in Figure 6.20 and, as redrawn with a distorted composition scale to enlarge the steel regions, in Figure 6.26. The line *GSK* decreases in temperature from $A_3$ for pure iron to the eutectoid composition, and then follows the eutectoid temperature. The $A_2$ transformation, during which alpha iron develops ferromagnetism on cooling, proceeds nearly horizontally from the $A_2$ transformation in pure iron until it meets and merges with the $A_3$ line, *GS*, at the point *O*. The $A_1$ transformation, which is not found in pure iron, is the eutectoid reaction, and indicates the lowest temperature at which iron-carbon austenite can exist in a stable form. It is shown as the line PSK, corresponding to the eutectoid temperature, 1330 F (725 C). The $A_0$ transformation, which is not shown but occurs at approximately 390 F (200 C), usually is considered to be caused by a magnetic change in cementite.

Only the $A_3$ and $A_1$ transformations are of real importance in most industrial steels. In addition, the line ES (Figure 6.20) which indicates the

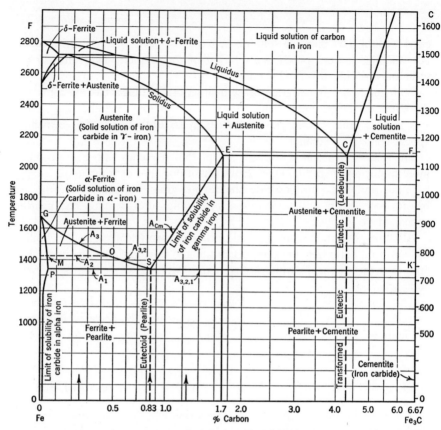

**Figure 6.26** Constitutional diagram for the alloys of iron and iron carbide drawn with a distorted composition scale in order to place greater emphasis on the constitution of the steels. [From *Metal Progress,* courtesy American Society for Metals.] The arrows on the composition axis correspond to the compositions discussed in Figures 6.27, 6.36, and 6.37.

maximum solubility of carbon in austenite and runs from the eutectic temperature to the eutectoid temperature, is known as $A_{Cm}$. Below this line cementite precipitates from austenite.

## MICROSTRUCTURAL CHANGES AS A HYPOEUTECTOID STEEL COOLS SLOWLY

Consider, for purposes of illustration, a structural steel containing 0.25% carbon and substantially no impurities (Figure 6.27). Other hypoeutectoid steels transform in a manner essentially the same although the relative amounts of different constituents vary with composition.[18] If the high-

[18] D. J. Blickwede and R. C. Hess, *Trans. A.S.M.,* **49** (1957), 427–44, discuss these cooling transformations in some 0.40% carbon constructional steels.

temperature peritectic reaction is ignored for simplicity, immediately after solidification from the single-phase liquid state, this 0.25% carbon alloy consists entirely of coarse-grained austenite, the solid solution of carbon in gamma iron, and both its composition and structure should become reasonably uniform quickly because of the comparatively rapid diffusion of carbon at the high temperatures involved. No change, except possible further homogenization, takes place in this austenite until the alloy cools to the temperature of the $A_3$ transformation, that is, until the constant composition line at 0.25% carbon intersects the line *GS* on the constitutional diagram. At this temperature a transformation begins and the steel enters a two-phase region. The austenite which is stable below this temperature contains progressively greater amounts of carbon as the temperature continues to fall, than the austenite which was stable above this temperature. To compensate for this, iron must be rejected from the austenite in the form of a second phase of very low carbon content. This

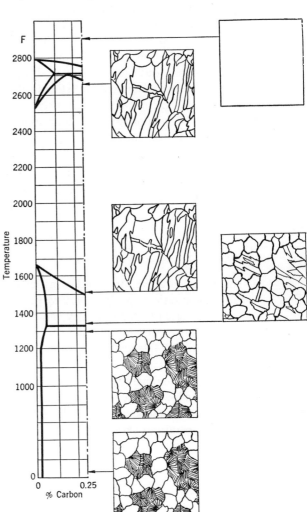

**Figure 6.27** Schematic illustration of the structural changes in a 0.25% carbon constructional steel as it cools slowly to room temperature from the liquid state.

phase, body-centered cubic ferrite, is precipitated at the grain boundaries of the austenite grains. The process of precipitation of ferrite at the austenite grain boundaries and enrichment of the remaining austenite in carbon continues until the $A_1$ transformation is reached at 1330 F (725 C). At this temperature, the remaining austenite is of eutectoid composition and contains the maximum amount of dissolved carbon, approximately 0.83%, because it has rejected or precipitated the excess iron at its grain boundaries as ferrite. Austenite of eutectoid composition then transforms into coarsely lamellar pearlite. Once the transformation is complete, the structure remains essentially unchanged down to room temperature. The fact that the free ferrite develops magnetism on passing through the $A_2$, or Curie transformation, does not affect either the structure or the mechanical properties.

Because free ferrite was formed originally at the boundaries of the austenite grains, some estimate of the sizes of these austenite grains can be made, particularly in the higher carbon hypoeutectoid alloys, by a method substantially similar to that illustrated in Figure 1.19, even though the austenite grains themselves are stable only above $A_3$.

The compositions of neither the ferrite nor the cementite change to any marked extent once they are formed, so the lever rule can be used here, with particular advantage, to estimate the carbon content of plain-carbon steels from their metallographic structures. All that is required is that the specimen be in approximate equilibrium, that is, slowly cooled from above the critical temperature range. For the 0.25% carbon alloy the constitution is, by weight

$$\% \text{ Proeutectoid ferrite} = 100 \times \frac{0.83 - 0.25}{0.83 - 0} = 70\%$$

$$\% \text{ Pearlite} = 100 \times \frac{0.25 - 0}{0.83 - 0} = 30\%$$

The metallographic structural constituents would be in nearly the same ratio because their specific volumes (1/sp gr) are comparable.

A cooling curve for this alloy can be rationalized readily on the basis of those given earlier for the simpler alloys. The rate of cooling decreases during the solidification period, and during the separation of free ferrite between $A_3$ (the line $GO$) and $A_1$; and there is a flat portion when the saturated austenite transforms to pearlite.

If this alloy is reheated, again ignoring the high temperature peritectic reaction for simplicity, essentially the same changes occur at nearly the same temperatures except in the reverse order. The pearlite transforms into austenite at approximately 1330 F (725 C); and, as the temperature increases up to $A_3$, the remaining proeutectoid ferrite redissolves in this austenite. Above $A_3$ the alloy consists entirely of fairly homogeneous austenite grains until the temperature reaches the solidus line, when melting begins.

These phase changes repeat themselves on cooling or on heating as often as the alloy is carried through the cycle, so long as the composition does not change because of oxidation or other causes, and the rates of temperature change are not too high for equilibrium to be preserved.

## MILD AND LOW-CARBON STEELS

The commercial mild steels contain up to 0.15 to 0.20% carbon [19] and the low-carbon steels up to 0.30 to 0.35% carbon, although these limits both are rather arbitrary. A "dead mild" grade of sheet steel containing around 0.07% carbon also is in common production. Typical microstructures are shown in Figures 6.28 and 6.29, respectively.[20] In each, the normal slowly cooled structure consists of ferrite (light color) and pearlite (dark color), the relative amounts depending on the carbon content. The banded structure, typical of hot-rolled material is caused by segregation of steelmaking elements and impurities.[21] Both types are made in specification grades of somewhat higher quality than the nonspecification grades used for ordinary uses, examples of which are fence wire, reinforcing bars, and machinery steels such as hot-screw stock, and hot- or cold-rolled bar stock.

Although considerable nonspecification material is used for general purpose machinery, large amounts of free-machining steel, much of it of S.A.E. 11xx or 13xx specification grade,[22] also are used. In these free-machining steels, cold work and additions of manganese (up to 1.5%) and phosphorus (up to approximately 0.13%) frequently are used to increase machinability by increasing hardness and brittleness.[23] Additions of sulfur (up to 0.25%) (Figure 6.30a), lead (up to 0.25%) or tellurium also are

[19] The 0.15 to 0.20% carbon grade often is called case-hardening steel or weldable structural steel, depending on its use.

[20] R. L. Rickett and F. C. Kristufek, *Trans. A.S.M.,* **41** (1949), 1113–41, have discussed the possible range of microstructures in detail.

[21] Banding is discussed by C. F. Jatcak, D. J. Girardi, and E. S. Rowland, *Trans. A.S.M.,* **48** (1956), 279–303; also P. Bastian, *Journ. Iron and Steel Inst.,* **187** (London: 1957), 281–91.

[22] The Society of Automotive Engineers (S.A.E.) system of nomenclature is given in the Appendix.

[23] The basic reasons for good machinability in these alloys are discussed thoroughly by M. E. Merchant and N. Zlatin, *Trans. A.S.M.,* **41** (1949), 647–72.

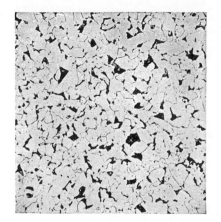

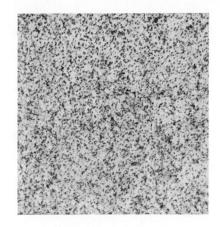

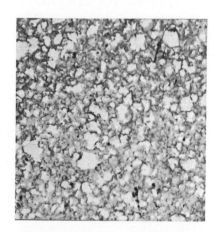

**Figure 6.28** Metallographic structures of mild steel (0.10 to 0.15% carbon). Etched with nital ($\times$100). **a.** Normalized, showing pearlitic carbides in a ferritic matrix. **b.** Process annealed, showing spheroidized carbides in a ferritic matrix. Rockwell hardness = $B$41 to $B$44. **c.** Water quenched from above $A_3$, showing martensitic regions at the ferritic grain boundaries. Rockwell hardness = $B$100 to $B$106. (See Chapter 8.) [Photomicrographs by L. Litchfield.]

**Figure 6.29** Metallographic structures of normalized low-carbon structural steels containing approximately 0.25% carbon. Etched with nital ($\times$250). **a** (*left*). Transverse section. **b** (*right*). Longitudinal section, showing banding.

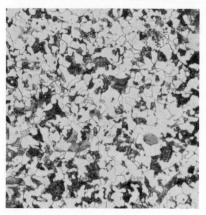

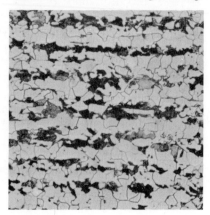

made, and in some cases special heat-treatments are used to spheroidize carbides (compare Figure 6.28$b$) or to form free graphite (Figure 6.30$b$) in the microstructure. All of these modifications are intended to facilitate chip production and hence to make it easier to remove metal from the region at which the actual machining is taking place. Leaded free-machining steels also are used commonly but the effect of lead is to lubricate continuous chips rather than to serve as a chip breaker. The addition of small amounts of tellurium to leaded steels is reported to improve machinability still more.

Mild steels used for deep-drawing operations usually are of specification grade—for example, S.A.E. 1010—particularly if the operations are severe,

**Figure 6.30** Metallographic structures of free-machining types of carbon steels. **a.** High-sulfur, showing stringer-like inclusions of FeS and MnS in both (*top left*) a process annealed and a (*top right*) normalized section. Etched with nital (×100). **b.** Graphitic, showing nodules of free graphite in both (*bottom left*) an unetched and (*bottom right*) a nital-etched ferritic matrix (×100).

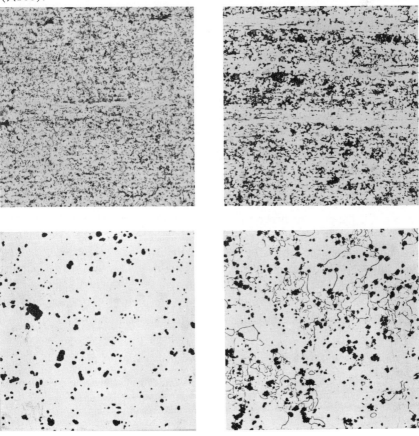

as for automobile body and fender stock. The mechanical properties and the nature of the deformations required determine the type of steel and the temper used.[24] The common tempers for strip steel, with typical mechanical properties for a thickness of 0.050 in., are shown in Table 6.6.

**TABLE 6.6**

| *Temper* | *Rockwell B Hardness* ($\frac{1}{16}$-100-B) | *Tensile Strength* (*psi*) | *Elongation* (*% in 2 in.*) |
|---|---|---|---|
| No. 1, Hard | 84–96 | 68,000–92,000 | 1–5 |
| No. 2, Half-hard | 75–85 | 56,000–72,000 | 4–14 |
| No. 3, Quarter-hard | 64–74 | 48,000–60,000 | 13–27 |
| No. 4, Soft or planished | 52–64 | 43,000–53,000 | 24–36 |
| No. 5, Dead soft | 38–52 | 40,000–48,000 | 33–45 |

In general, the harder the material, the less drawing it will stand. However, if the softness is produced by sacrificing small grain size, the surface is roughened considerably in a typical orange-peel pattern (Figure 2.19) and the ductility is lower than it would be with a fine grain.

Unless mild steels are deoxidized [25] fully, their properties tend to change spontaneously at atmospheric or moderately elevated temperatures after a final heat-treatment or a final cold-working operation. This change, known as aging, is discussed further in Chapter 10. Steels which might be susceptible to aging usually are used in the No. 3 or No. 4 temper rather than the No. 5 temper.

Low-carbon steels are made in various specification grades, depending to some extent upon the intended application. The most widely used are the structural, flange, and firebox grades, the differences between them being more in the rigidity of the specifications they are required to meet than in metallurgical characteristics of the steels themselves. If intended for riveting only, the carbon content may run as high as 0.35 to 0.40%, but the range of 0.15 to 0.25% carbon is more common today because of the wide use of welding. These steels generally are used as hot rolled, and are normalized only if necessary to meet particular requirements of specifications.

[24] R. L. Rickett, S. H. Kalin, and J. T. Mackenzie, Jr., *Trans. A.I.M.E.*, **185** (1949), 242–51.

[25] Deoxidization is done by adding controlled amounts of manganese, silicon, often aluminum, and sometimes other metals, to the liquid steel before it is cast into ingot form. Primarily, it minimizes the amount of gas released as the metal solidifies.

## USE OF LOW-CARBON STEELS AT ELEVATED TEMPERATURES

The use of low-carbon steels at elevated temperatures, particularly under pressure, is determined largely by various codes such as the Boiler and Unfired Pressure Vessel Code of the American Society of Mechanical Engineers. In most cases these codes give the temperature ranges in which steel made to a given specification can be used from a strength viewpoint and the maximum allowable design stresses which are permitted. Frequently, the same design stresses are permitted for all temperatures from −20 F to 650 F. The allowable stress values depend on the particular code but one-quarter of the minimum specified ultimate strength at room temperature is a common maximum value. Above 650 F the maximum allowable design stress decreases with increasing temperature. The stress which produces 0.01% elongation in a 1,000 hr creep test (sometimes expressed as 1% creep in 100,000 hr) frequently is the determining criterion. With time at temperature above approximately 900 F (480 C) the carbides tend to spheroidize, decreasing the strength somewhat but usually not beyond the allowable design stress. These plain-carbon steels are subject to two further types of deterioration in elevated temperature service: graphitization and hydrogen attack. There are effective methods to control both of these types of deterioration.

## GRAPHITIZATION OF LOW-CARBON STEELS

Graphitization occurs primarily because iron-carbide is only metastable and under appropriate conditions tends to decompose slowly to a mixture of iron and graphite.[26] The stable iron-graphite constitutional diagram is given in Figure 6.47. This graphite may appear, in a matrix which may be completely ferritic in extreme cases, as random nodules or with various degrees of segregation. The most serious type is that which occurs almost continuously near the low-temperature edge of weld heat-affected zones (Figure 6.31). Graphitization in steels is encouraged by additions of silicon, but opposed by manganese, molybdenum, chromium, and other elements with high affinities for carbon. It also can be inhibited by addition

[26] C. R. Austin and M. C. Fetzer, *Trans. A.S.M.*, **35** (1945), 485–535, studied graphitization in 1% carbon steels thoroughly, and G. V. Smith, J. A. MacMillan, and E. J. Dulis, *ibid.*, **43** (1951), 692–711, have done the same for lower carbon steels.

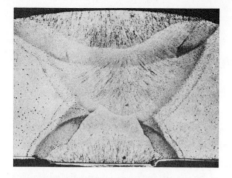

**Figure 6.31** (*left*) Segregated graphitization near low-temperature edge of weld heat-affected zones (compare Figure 3.16). Note random graphite in the parent metal also.

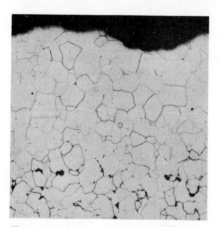 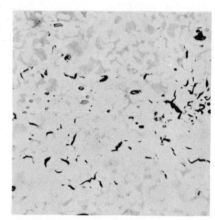

**Figure 6.32  a** (*left*). Decarburized layer at surface in early stage of attack by hot gaseous hydrogen under pressure. **b** (*right*). Internal intergranular fissures at later stage in hydrogen attack on a low-carbon steel.

of sufficient nitrogen.[27] If a steel contains more than approximately 0.7% chromium it usually is considered to be completely resistant to graphitization.

## ELEVATED-TEMPERATURE HYDROGEN ATTACK ON LOW-CARBON STEELS

Molecular hydrogen dissociates either thermally, if the temperature is high enough, or chemically; and the atomic hydrogen so formed diffuses readily through solid steel, in the ionic form. This hydrogen reacts with the carbon dissolved in the ferrite, forming methane. Decarburization is

[27] E. J. Dulis, G. V. Smith, and W. E. Dennis, *Trans. A.S.M.,* **46** (1954), 1318–28; G. V. Smith and B. W. Royle, *ibid.,* **48** (1956), 320–26.

quite slow in dry hydrogen, but much more rapid if moisture is present.

Above approximately 950 F (510 C) this reaction with carbon takes place largely at external surfaces forming a decarburized layer (Figure 6.32a). However, at lower temperatures (compare Figure 6.33), the reaction with carbon takes place largely at internal surfaces. In these regions, thermodynamic considerations indicate that hydrogen can reassociate and build up a partial pressure equal to its external partial pressure (solution pressure). In addition, any methane formed by reaction of hydrogen with dissolved carbon at internal surfaces collects in internal voids or fissures, thus increasing the total pressure indefinitely. Ultimately, this pressure becomes high enough to cause grain boundary fissuring (Figure 6.32b). The final effect is similar in many respects to the embrittlement of oxygen-bearing copper mentioned in Chapter 4 (compare Figure 4.6). Data collected from a variety of sources [28] indicate that this hydrogen attack on low-carbon steel does not occur unless both the hydrogen partial pressure and the temperature exceed certain minimum values (Figure 6.33). Hot bent elbows, regions with coarse-grains, heat-affected zones of welds are particularly susceptible. Furthermore, attack in these regions can be highly localized (Figure 6.34), so that spot checks are of questionable value. As indicated in Figure 6.33, additions of chromium and/or molybdenum impart resistance to hydrogen attack. The higher the temperature and the greater the partial pressure of hydrogen, the greater the amount of alloying element needed to provide protection.

## NOTCH-BRITTLENESS OF LOW-CARBON STEELS

For applications at normal atmospheric and lower temperatures, the notch-brittle characteristics of the low-carbon steels are of engineering significance because these materials are prone to fail by cleavage [29] at stresses of the order of the yield strength even with relatively mild notches (compare Figure 2.36). With severe notches and with changes of section, even though these may not appear to constitute severe notches, complete failure can occur under calculated stresses of the order of 10,000 psi. Many cleavage fractures in these materials are characterized by a chevron pat-

---

[28] See R. T. Effinger, M. L. Renquist, A. G. Wachter, and J. G. Wilson, *Proc. Amer. Pet. Inst., Div. of Ref.,* **31M-III** (1951), 107–30; also, G. A. Nelson (ed.), *Corrosion Data Survey,* 3rd ed. (San Francisco: Shell Development Company, 1960).

[29] See, for example, M. Gensamer, *Trans. A.I.M.E.,* **215** (1959), 2–18; also *Mechanisms of Brittle Fracture* by D. C. Drucker (Washington, D. C.: National Academy of Science, 1954).

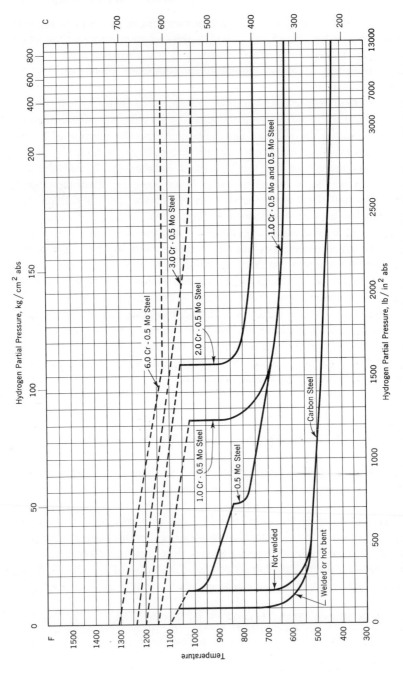

**Figure 6.33** Operating limits for carbon and alloy steels in contact with hydrogen at high temperatures and pressures. [After G. A. Nelson, courtesy Shell Development Company.]

278

**Figure 6.34** Section of 8-in. diameter carbon steel pipe that was attacked by hydrogen in petroleum refinery service and later macro-etched in hot 50:50 hydrochloric acid-water solution to disclose attacked regions. (*top*) Internal surface of pipe showing attack just beyond low-temperature edge of heat-affected zone. (*bottom*) Cross section showing weld and penetration of attacked region. The attack was highly localized and approximately one-eighth of the pipe circumference was attacked in this way. (Magnification approximately ×2.)

tern [30] which "points back" toward the origin of the fracture (Figure 2.34).

It is known that a steel is more resistant to notch-brittle failure if the ferrite grain size is small,[31] if the carbon content is low, and if it is deoxidized properly. From a practical viewpoint these objectives are achieved best by (1) making the steel to fine-grain practice, which usually means deoxidizing or killing it with aluminum; (2) maintaining a manganese to carbon ratio of at least 3:1 and preferably higher, or in other words by keeping the carbon content as low as is feasible and adding manganese to secure the strength needed; (3) giving the steel a normalizing heat-treatment (see Chapter 8) before use. Ordinarily, stress-relief heat-treatments after welding are beneficial also.[32] All of these methods add to the cost, so some judgment is required to specify only those which are most useful for a given application. Under proper manufacturing controls a premium grade of carbon steel can be made with a 15 ft-lb Charpy impact average energy absorption at −50 F (−45 C). Alloy steels of special types or nonferrous

[30] A clear explanation of this is given by G. M. Boyd, *Engineering* (Jan. 16, Jan. 23, 1953); see also C. F. Tipper, *Journ. Iron and Steel Inst.*, **185** (London: 1957), 4–9.

[31] J. M. Hodge, R. D. Manning, and H. M. Reichhold, *Trans. A.I.M.E.*, **185** (1949), 233–40.

[32] However, proper temperatures must be used. See, for example, W. C. Leslie, R. L. Rickett, and W. D. Lafferty, *Trans. A.I.M.E.*, **218** (1960), 699–709.

alloys customarily are used at lower temperatures because most carbon steels are subject to brittle failure under many operating conditions.

Other treatments would be helpful [33] but they are not always commercially practical at this time. For example, a water quench and temper treatment, which probably produces the equivalent of a very fine ferritic grain size, gives a low transition temperature for a given hardness but not many steel mills today are able to handle tonnage lots of steel plate on this basis. Such treatment increases the cost also.

## CARBON-STEEL CASTINGS

Carbon-steel castings are classified somewhat differently from wrought steels as low-carbon (less than 0.20% carbon), medium-carbon (0.20 to 0.40% carbon), or high-carbon (more than 0.40% carbon). All of these usually contain, in addition, 0.50 to 1.00% manganese, 0.20 to 0.75% silicon, and less than 0.05% phosphorus and 0.06% sulfur. Typical mechanical properties for three grades in the normalized condition are shown in Table 6.7. Unless chills [34] are used, steel castings cool rather slowly in

**TABLE 6.7**

|  | Low-Carbon | Medium-Carbon | High-Carbon |
|---|---|---|---|
| Tensile strength (psi) | 42,000–70,000 | 60,000–80,000 | 70,000–120,000 |
| Yield point (psi) | 20,000–38,000 | 30,000–40,000 | 35,000–75,000 |
| Elongation (% in 2 in.) | 35–22 | 30–20 | 25–3 |
| Reduction in area (%) | 64–30 | 40–30 | 40–2 |
| Brinell hardness (10 mm–3,000 Kg) | 90–143 | 130–325 | 156–500 |

the sand molds in which they usually are made. Because of this, the austenite grain size is coarse and influences the structure even after the austenite has transformed to pearlite and the casting has cooled to room temperature. Traces of the austenite grains can be seen readily, outlined by white ferrite, in the photomicrograph shown in Figure 6.35b. This large grain size tends to give these so-called green castings an undesirable combination of a relatively low strength, low ductility, and low toughness which makes them comparatively poor for engineering purposes.

[33] See R. H. Frazier, F. W. Boulger, and C. H. Lorig, *Trans. A.I.M.E.*, **203** (1955), 323–29.
[34] A chill is a metal insert which is embedded in the surface of a sand mold or core or placed in a mold cavity to increase the cooling rate at that point.

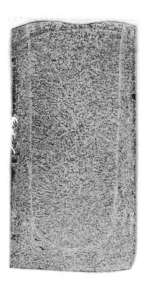

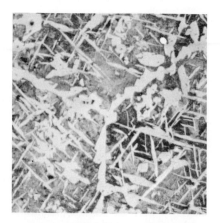

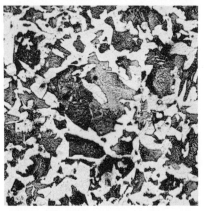

**Figure 6.35** Metallographic structure of a cast steel containing about 0.40% carbon. Etched with nital. **a** (*left*). Macroetched experimental ingot ($\times 1$), illustrating dendritic structure. [Photograph by A. J. Calpaxis.] **b** (*top right*). As cast (Widmannstaetten type of structure, $\times 100$). **c** (*bottom right*). Normalized ($\times 100$).

In fine-grained steel, the ferrite separates from the austenite, as the steel cools through the critical range, almost entirely at the grain boundaries. However, in coarse-grained castings, the ferrite separates both at the grain boundaries and along the close-packed crystallographic planes of the very coarse-grained austenite matrix, giving a characteristic geometrical structural pattern of ferrite within the pearlitic areas. This also may be seen in Figure 6.35b and is called a Widmannstaetten structure after its discoverer who first found it in meteorites.

Because of the structural changes which occur on heating through $A_3$, the coarse-grained Widmannstaetten structure, along with its deleterious effects on these materials, can be eliminated by giving a normalizing heat-treatment of air cooling from approximately 1600 F (870 C). During this additional heating, the ferrite redissolves in the now fine-grained austenite. This, when cooled, transforms to the normal structure of small grains of pearlite surrounded by ferrite which has separated at the austenite grain boundaries in the manner shown schematically in Figure 6.27, and as a microstructure in Figure 6.35c. Except for the relative amounts of the ferrite and pearlite constituents, this microstructure is substantially the same as that of the normalized 0.25% carbon structural steel in Figure 6.29a. The size of the pearlite patches or colonies, which is determined to some extent by the size of the austenitic grains at the heat-treating temperature, depends upon the temperature of normalizing; and the fineness of the lamellae of the pearlite is determined largely by the rate at which the casting cools after heat treatment. It is this fine-grained normalized structure which gives cast steel the combination of strength, ductility, and toughness for which it is noted.[35] However, steel castings, like wrought steel, still are subject to notch-brittle failure at ambient and subatmospheric temperatures. Furthermore, the quality of the casting—that is, design, soundness, content of inclusions (nonmetallic impurities), and the like—is at least as important as the metallographic structure in determining its engineering usability. This is determined chiefly by the controls used by the foundry making the casting.

## MICROSTRUCTURAL CHANGES AS EUTECTOID STEEL COOLS SLOWLY

Consider next a tool steel free from impurities and of approximately eutectoid composition, 0.83% carbon (Figure 6.36). Immediately after solidification, this steel, also, is composed essentially of a homogeneous austenite which differs only in its carbon content from that formed in the structural steel example. The microstructure at this temperature is that of a typical austenite. During slow cooling, no change takes place in the structure, except possible further homogenization, until the $A_1$ [36] transformation begins at the eutectoid temperature. At this temperature, austenite of eutectoid composition already is saturated with carbon and, therefore, transforms directly and completely, at an essentially constant temperature, into a coarsely pearlitic structure. The size of the pearlite grains need not necessarily be the same as that of the austenite grains from which they form.[37] Under some conditions the pearlite regions are larger, but usually they are smaller than the austenite grains. Essentially no change takes place in the alloy as it cools from the $A_1$ transformation to room temperature.

The cooling curve for this alloy shows, in addition to the usual trans-

[35] M. F. Hawkes and B. F. Brown, *Trans. A.S.M.*, **41** (1949), 519–56, discuss the relationship between mechanical properties and structure.

[36] This sometimes is called $A_{321}$ because $A_3$, $A_2$, and $A_1$ all merge into a single temperature.

[37] This is discussed somewhat in Chapter 8.

formation on solidification from the liquid state, only one break, a flat portion at the $A_1$ transformation.

During reheating, the changes occur in the reverse order. The pearlitic structure is essentially unchanged up to the eutectoid temperature where, at a constant temperature, it transforms into an alloy which is completely homogeneous austenite.

**Figure 6.36** Schematic illustration of the structural changes in a 0.83% carbon tool steel as it cools slowly to room temperature from the liquid state.

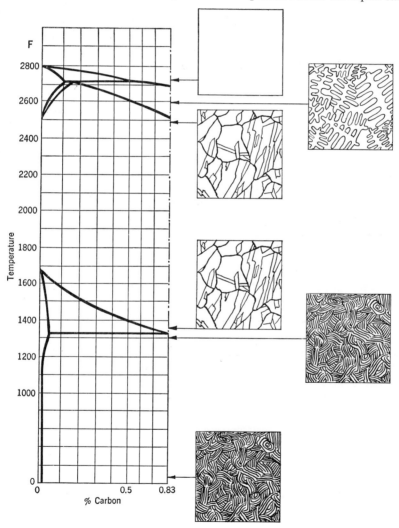

Although this eutectoid alloy at room temperature is completely pearlitic, pearlite is composed of two phases, ferrite and cementite. The relative percentages of these can be computed according to the lever rule:

$$\% \text{ Ferrite} = 100 \times \frac{6.67 - 0.83}{6.67 - 0} = 87.5\%$$

$$\% \text{ Cementite} = 100 \times \frac{0.83 - 0}{6.67 - 0} = 12.5\%$$

Because both ferrite and cementite have nearly the same specific volumes (1/sp gr), in the micrograph taken at a high magnification (Figure 6.24) the thicker lamellae in a given pearlite colony are the ferrite, and the thinner lamellae are the cementite.

## MICROSTRUCTURAL CHANGES AS A HYPEREUTECTOID STEEL COOLS SLOWLY

Next consider a hypereutectoid tool steel containing approximately 1.25% carbon and free from impurities (Figure 6.37). Although this alloy does not solidify completely until a temperature is reached which is appreciably lower than for the two preceding examples, it too solidifies into homogeneous austenite exactly like steels of lower carbon content, which do not undergo the high-temperature peritectic reaction. This austenite cools essentially unchanged until it reaches a temperature indicated by the line *ES* on the diagram in Figure 6.26. The line *ES*, known also as $A_{Cm}$, indicates the temperatures at which cementite starts to precipitate from austenite. Using a terminology similar to that used for the hypoeutectoid steels, the austenite which is stable at temperatures below the $A_{Cm}$ line can retain in solid solution smaller amounts of carbon than it holds in equilibrium above the line. Therefore, it must dispose of its excess carbon, and it does so by precipitating it as cementite, the compound $Fe_3C$, at the grain boundaries of the austenite grains. However, because there is much less cementite precipitated for a given change in carbon content than there was free ferrite in the hypoeutectoid steels, the cementite envelopes around the austenite grains are much thinner than the ferrite envelopes in the hypoeutectoid steels.

The precipitation of excess carbon as cementite continues until the $A_1$ transformation is reached at 1330 F (725 C). At this temperature the austenite contains approximately 0.83% carbon. Therefore, it transforms

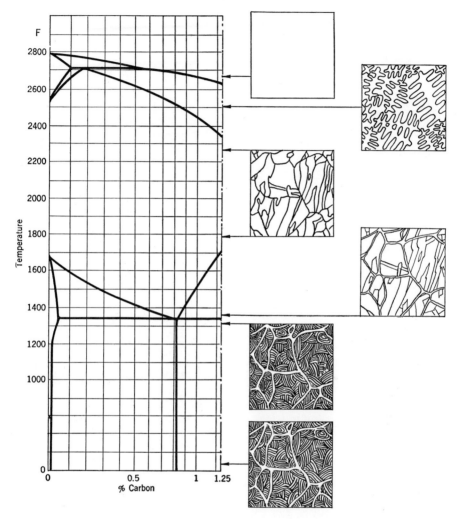

**Figure 6.37** Schematic illustration of the structural changes in a 1.25% carbon tool steel as it cools slowly to room temperature from the liquid state.

to pearlite on further cooling. The resulting structure consists of pearlitic regions outlined by envelopes of free cementite.

In these alloys the cementite formed at the grain boundaries of the former austenite grains can be used as a measure of the austenite grain size which was stable before cooling started (Figure 1.19).

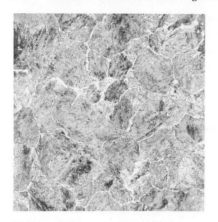 

**Figure 6.38**   Metallographic structures of a 1.25% carbon steel. **a** (*left*). Normalized, original austenite grains surrounded by envelopes of cementite and transformed to pearlite. Etched with picral (×250). **b** (*right*). Spheroidized cementite, divorced spheroids in a matrix of ferrite. Etched with picral (×500). [Photomicrograph by M. C. Fetzer.]

Application of the lever rule to the structure of a 1.25% carbon steel indicates a structural distribution of

$$\% \text{ Pearlite} = 100 \times \frac{6.67 - 1.25}{6.67 - 0.83} = 92.8\%$$

$$\% \text{ Proeutectoid cementite} = 100 \times \frac{1.25 - 0.83}{6.67 - 0.83} = 7.2\%$$

or, considering the alloy in terms of the phases ferrite and cementite

$$\% \text{ Ferrite} = 100 \times \frac{6.67 - 1.25}{6.67 - 0} = 81.2\%$$

$$\% \text{ Cementite} = 100 \times \frac{1.25 - 0}{6.67 - 0} = 18.8\%$$

Metallographic structures of alloys in each of these conditions are shown in Figure 6.38.

It should be noted that it is possible to tell (without sodium picrate etching) whether a steel is hypo- or hypereutectoid—that is, whether a boundary constituent separating pearlite areas is ferrite or cementite—by any of the following means: (1) if the constituent is cementite it is hard and therefore stands in relief on the average surface; (2) if the constituent is ferrite it commonly shows scratches which are less prominent or are not seen on the cementite; (3) if the constituent is ferrite it is seen to be continuous with the "ferrite-in-pearlite" at high magnification, whereas cementite has a boundary between it and the pearlite.

The cooling curve for an alloy of this composition shows two changes in addition to those occurring during solidification from the liquid state, a slight change of slope beginning at the temperature at which the alloy crosses the $A_{Cm}$ and a constant temperature or flat portion as the austenite transforms to pearlite at the eutectoid temperature $A_1$.

If the alloy is heated, the same changes occur, except in reverse order as has been discussed previously.

## PROPERTY CHANGES WITH PERCENTAGE CARBON IN SLOWLY COOLED STEELS

The properties of slowly cooled carbon steels also can be rationalized reasonably well from their metallographic structures. Ferrite is relatively soft with an ultimate strength of about 40,000 psi. The eutectoid, pearlite, is very much harder and stronger, its strength approximating 100,000 psi. The pearlitic structure is the strongest found in the slowly cooled alloys of iron and carbon. The compound, cementite, is hard and brittle; the contribution of free cementite to the strength of steel is negligible, probably not exceeding 5,000 psi. Furthermore, any brittle constituent such as cementite may rupture as soon as any appreciable strain occurs in the steel.

All of the carbon steels are mechanical mixtures of ferrite and cementite so their hardness [38] increases as the percentage of iron carbide increases. The hardness for any annealed, normalized, or hot-rolled carbon steel (Figure 6.39) is only slightly greater than that which is indicated by a straight-line relationship between the hardness of ferrite and cementite.

The tensile strength is affected to a greater extent than the hardness by the manner of aggregation of the ferrite and cementite particles. The eutectoid alloy, because it is composed of the finest state of aggregation in the slowly cooled carbon steels, usually has the strongest structure. The tensile strength increases rapidly with the percentage of pearlite in hypoeutectoid steels, reaching a maximum near the eutectoid composition.

The most cold-workable alloy is composed entirely of ferrite, and as the percentage of iron carbide (in the form of pearlite) increases, the cold-workability decreases appreciably. The greatest brittleness is found after the eutectoid composition is exceeded and excess iron carbide appears as a constituent surrounding the pearlite grains. On the other hand, if the cementite exists as a continuous grain boundary layer (compare Figure 6.46d), as may occur in iron with less than 0.10% carbon after suitable

[38] See F. T. Sisco, *The Alloys of Iron and Carbon,* **II** (New York: McGraw-Hill, 1937), 83–85.

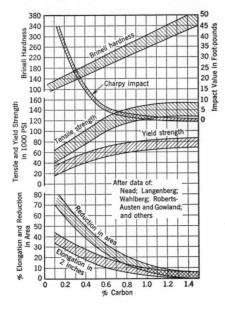

**Figure 6.39**    Effect of carbon content on mechanical properties of hot-worked steels. [From *The Alloys of Iron and Carbon,* **Vol. II,** by F. T. Sisco. New York: McGraw-Hill, 1937.]

heat-treatment, even alloys which are composed almost entirely of ferrite may crack in tension after very low deformation.

Thus, for slowly cooled carbon steels, the lower the carbon content, the softer, more workable, and weaker the alloys are; the higher the carbon content, the harder, stronger, and more brittle they are. By assuming that the variations in tensile strength proceed according to straight line relationships, depending on the percentage of ferrite, pearlite, and cementite present, reasonably close approximations to the actual tensile strengths can be secured by simple arithmetical computation.[39]

## THE EFFECTS OF ALLOYING ELEMENTS UPON IRON-CARBON ALLOYS

Steels are alloys of iron and carbon. When a third element is added to an alloy of iron and carbon, the resulting alloy may be considered either as an alloy steel, in which case the important thing is its effect on the iron-carbon diagram, or else the carbon may be considered as modifying the iron-binary alloy. The usefulness of either of these viewpoints depends upon the specific alloy concerned. In some cases, one of them may be simpler to interpret than the other.

[39] See, for example, F. M. Walters, Jr., *Trans. A.I.M.E.,* **154** (1942), 407–12, if it is desired to base the computation on chemical composition rather than structure.

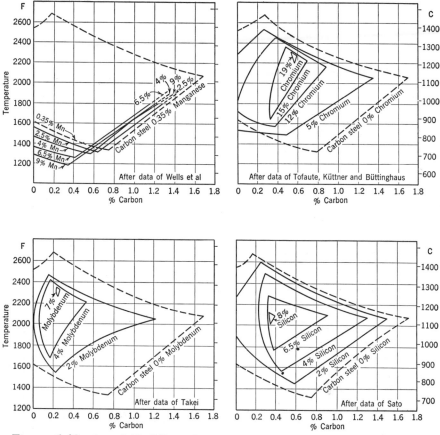

**Figure 6.40** (*top left*) Effect of several uniform manganese contents upon the carbon limitations for pure austenite at elevated temperatures. [From E. C. Bain, courtesy American Society for Metals.]

**Figure 6.41** Effects of several uniform (*top right*) chromium, (*bottom left*) molybdenum, and (*bottom right*) silicon contents upon the carbon limitations for pure austenite at elevated temperatures. [From E. C. Bain, courtesy American Society for Metals.]

In Figure 6.40 the effect of the important alloying element, manganese, upon the limits of the austenite field in the iron-carbon diagram is shown. Increasing the percentage of manganese lowers the eutectoid temperature, and decreases the percentage of carbon in the eutectoid. This means that a fully pearlitic structure can be produced containing as little as about 0.3% carbon, if the optimum manganese content is used.

In Figure 6.41, the effects of the three alloying elements, chromium, molybdenum, and silicon, upon the limits of the austenite field in the iron-carbon diagram are illustrated. These three metals behave in a different manner from manganese; the addition of any one of them decreases the extent of the austenite field instead of increasing it. This means that the addition of any of these alloying elements alone to a steel tends to make it ferritic, that is, composed essentially of body-centered cubic iron. The

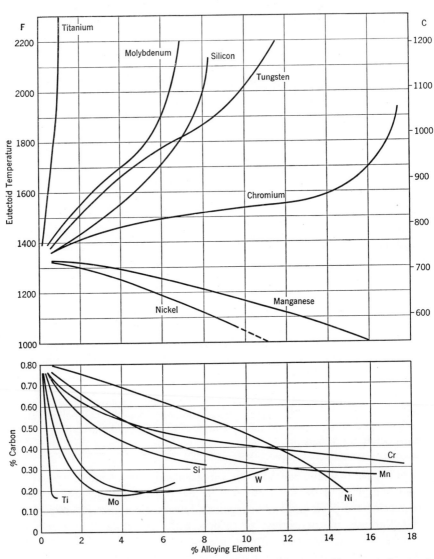

**Figure 6.42**   Eutectoid temperature and eutectoid composition as influenced by several alloying elements. [From E. C. Bain, courtesy American Society for Metals.]

constituent austenite (face-centered cubic) in these alloys is stable only within a more narrowly restricted range of temperatures and compositions, depending upon the percentage of alloying element present. In each of these examples, also, the percentage of carbon in the eutectoid decreases with increasing amounts of alloying element, as with manganese, but the temperature of the eutectoid inversion increases with increasing amounts of alloying element rather than decreasing as it did with manganese. Thus, for these three elements, a fully pearlitic structure also can be produced with appreciably less carbon than in a plain-carbon steel, but the transformation takes place at a considerably higher temperature.

This ability of alloying elements to give a fully pearlitic structure with a comparatively low carbon content is important. If such a structure is produced in an alloy steel, less iron carbide is present, and the structure tends to be softer and less brittle than a similar structure in plain carbon steel.

The effects of different percentages of the important alloying elements upon the eutectoid temperature and upon the percentage of carbon in the eutectoid are summarized in Figure 6.42. All of these alloying elements decrease the percentage of carbon in the eutectoid but, of the seven shown, only manganese and nickel decrease the eutectoid temperature.

In addition, as alloying elements are added to iron, the Curie temperature, below which the iron is strongly ferromagnetic, decreases. An alloy whose Curie temperature is below room temperature is classed as nonmagnetic for most applications.

## THE EFFECTS OF CARBON UPON IRON-BINARY ALLOYS

Where the complementary problem is considered, of the effect of carbon on an iron-binary alloy, the result may be predicted to a large extent from information already available. First, gamma iron is known to dissolve appreciable amounts of carbon, whereas alpha iron is known to dissolve only limited amounts. In either case, the carbon in excess of that held in solid solution generally appears as a carbide, either of iron or of iron plus the alloying element. Furthermore, the addition of carbon to gamma iron is known to widen the temperature range within which gamma iron is stable, and to produce an alloy, austenite, which may decompose to a mixture of ferrite and carbide by an eutectoid inversion.

The presence of carbon, in addition to an alloying element which widens the stable range of gamma iron, makes austenite stable at a lower temperature. These alloy steels eventually reach a composition at which the austenite is stable at room temperature and then are known as austenitic steels. In such alloys, the austenite can be made to decompose [40] only by cooling it to a sufficiently low temperature, such as that of liquid air, for example; and in some alloys even this is not possible. Such austenitic alloys nearly always are not susceptible to heat-treatment and thus differ from the plain-carbon steels. For this reason it often is better to consider them as iron alloys rather than as alloy steels.

When the alloying element decreases the stable range of gamma iron by forming a closed gamma loop, the added carbon can remain in solid solution only so long as the austenite remains stable. If the iron-binary alloy is ferritic, the carbon must appear as a carbide of some sort. The alloy steel then is known as a ferritic alloy steel. If such a ferritic alloy can be brought into an austenitic range by heating, it is considered best as a steel because it is susceptible to heat-treatment in the manner discussed in Chapter 8. However, if such an alloy steel remains ferritic irrespective of the temperature to which it is heated,[41] it usually is preferable to consider it as an iron alloy instead of as an alloy steel because it is not susceptible to heat-treatment.

## ALLOY DISTRIBUTION IN HEATED STEELS

In general, the alloying elements in steel can exist only in a few ways: (a) dissolved in austenite, (b) dissolved in ferrite, (c) combined as carbides, (d) combined as nonmetallic inclusions (in alloy steels, this classification may include nitrides only). The partition of a given alloying element between these four seldom is known precisely. When the alloying element goes into solid solution, its effect upon properties is similar to that found for any other solid solution—that is, it tends to increase the hardness and strength, to decrease the workability, and to raise the recrystallization temperature. However, these effects are relatively unimportant in comparison with the effects of the alloying elements upon the rate of transformation of austenite in the eutectoid inversion, which are discussed in more detail in Chapter 8. One point which often is overlooked is that only the alloying element actually in solid solution in ferrite or austenite affects the properties, not the total alloy content. Thus, if carbides (or nitrides) rich in alloying element separate from solid solution as a second phase, the effective alloy content—that is, that remaining in solid solution—is depleted so the properties change accordingly.

---

[40] This is a nonequilibrium transformation which will be discussed in Chapters 8 and 9.

[41] Banded steels, mentioned earlier in this chapter, are of this type when the ferritic regions are high in segregated phosphorus.

## IRON-NICKEL ALLOYS

The gamma-alpha transformation is very sluggish in iron-nickel alloys (Figure 6.19a). Consequently, with increasing nickel content, the true limiting temperatures for the two-phase area are known to decrease but their exact values are not known closely.[42] Many meteorites are basically iron-nickel alloys which appear to have cooled very slowly, forming very coarse grains and the typical distributions of alpha in gamma (compare Figure 6.35b) known as a Widmannstaetten structure.

## NICKEL STEELS

The only commercial low-nickel alloys are structural steels which contain, nominally, 2.25%, 3.5%, 5%, or 9% nickel with about 0.80% manganese. In the welding grades, the carbon content is kept below 0.13 to 0.20% depending on nickel content, but it may run up to 0.25% or higher if the steel is not intended for welding. Because of their nickel content, these steels all are higher priced than the carbon and low-alloy structural steels and must be heat-treated with some care.[43] This is particularly true of the 9%-nickel alloy. However, they have relatively low-notch sensitivity, so for applications at subatmospheric temperature, particularly below −50 F (−45 C), they are about the only ferritic steels which can be used satisfactorily. Some of this low notch-sensitivity probably is the result of a finer ferrite grain size than usually is found in ferritic steels but there must be other contributing factors. The 9%-nickel alloy, which is attractive economically in the temperature range −150 to −320 F (−100 to −200 C) because of its low brittle-transition temperature, is used in the double normalized (1650 F and 1450 F (900 C and 790 C)) and tempered (1050 F (565 C)) condition or the quenched (1450 F (790 C)) and tempered (1050 F (565 C)) condition. After the latter treatment the tensile strength averages 110,000 psi, with a yield strength of 99,500 psi, an elongation in 2 in. of 27%, and a reduction in area of 73%. Other newly developed alloy steels containing 18 to 25% nickel can be heat-treated to give tensile strengths approaching 500,000 psi.

[42] See also *The Alloys of Iron and Nickel* by J. S. Marsh (New York: McGraw-Hill, 1938); The "Iron-Nickel Diagram" by R. W. Floyd in *Institute of Metals Annotated Equilibrium Diagram Series, No. 11* (London: The Institute of Metals, 1955); also Refs. 1 and 2 at end of this chapter.

[43] J. P. Hugo and J. H. Woodhead, *Journ. Iron and Steel Inst.,* **187** (London: 1957), 174–88, have correlated tensile properties and microstructure for some 3%-nickel steels.

With more than about 25% nickel, austenite becomes stable at room temperature so twinned crystals typical of this constituent make up the microstructure, sometimes as a second phase in addition to ferrite. These particular austenitic alloys have peculiar thermal expansion characteristics which are associated with magnetic Curie points below, near, or somewhat above room temperature; and lead to many interesting applications.

## IRON-NICKEL ALLOYS OF CONTROLLED THERMAL EXPANSION

The range of thermal expansion coefficients possible in these iron-nickel alloys, or relatively simple modifications of them (Figure 6.43a), is so great that almost any requirement can be met. For example, the 36%-nickel alloy Invar (usually with 0.4% manganese and 0.1% carbon) has almost zero expansion at atmospheric temperatures.[44] At higher temperatures, however, its expansion is normal. In the hot-rolled or forged condition, it also has a high corrosion resistance, a hardness of about 160 Brinell, a tensile strength of 65,000 to 85,000 psi, with a yield point of 40,000 to 60,000 psi, an elongation of 30 to 45%, and a reduction in area of 55 to 70%. Fluctuations or variations in treatment result in irregular or transitory changes in dimensions over long periods of time. For the most accurate instruments, therefore, the forged bars must be cooled slowly through the range 210 to 70 F (100 to 20 C) over a period of several months and then aged for a long time at room temperature.

In commercial alloys the effects of impurities must be considered because they exert a marked influence on the expansivity. The presence of manganese, chromium, silicon, tungsten, or molybdenum causes the minimum expansion to shift toward higher nickel contents than the normal 36%, whereas copper, carbon, or cobalt cause the minimum to shift toward lower nickel contents. Consequently, the impurities either must be kept very low or else must be balanced properly. These effects are illustrated in Figures 6.43b and c.

Heat-treatment and cold work affect the expansivity (inches per inch per degree) appreciably. After cold working, the expansion increases with the temperature of subsequent annealing up to about 1100 F (600 C), the temperature for which the maximum value is attained.

The 36%-nickel alloy also has the highest thermal coefficient of elasticity of any of the iron-nickel alloys, about $278 \times 10^{-6}$ per °F ($500 \times 10^{-6}$ per °C). Two iron-nickel alloys, containing exactly 29% and 45% nickel, have zero thermoelastic coefficients at 68 F (20 C), but both compositions

[44] B. S. Lement, B. L. Averbach, and M. Cohen, *Trans. A.S.M.*, **43** (1951), 1072–97, discuss the dimensional behavior of this alloy.

are so sensitive to slight variations in nickel content that, practically, they cannot be used. However, if the composition is modified to fall within the ranges shown in Table 6.8, the resulting alloy is much less sensitive to varia-

**TABLE 6.8**

| % Fe | 61–53 |
|---|---|
| % Ni | 33–35 |
| % Cr | 4–5 |
| % W | 1–3 |
| % Mn | 0.5–2 |
| % Si | 0.5–2 |
| % C | 0.5–2 |

tions in nickel content than the straight iron-nickel alloy. Its percentage change in stiffness for a 200° F change in temperature is approximately

**Figure 6.43** **a** (*left*). Effect of composition on the coefficient of linear expansion of nickel-iron alloys (0.4% manganese and 0.1% carbon) at various temperatures in the range −150 F (−100 C) to 1650 F (900 C). **b** (*top right*). Increase in coefficient of linear expansion by the addition of other metals. **c** (*bottom right*). Change in nickel content required to retain minimum coefficient of expansion as other metals are added. [After C. E. Guillaume.]

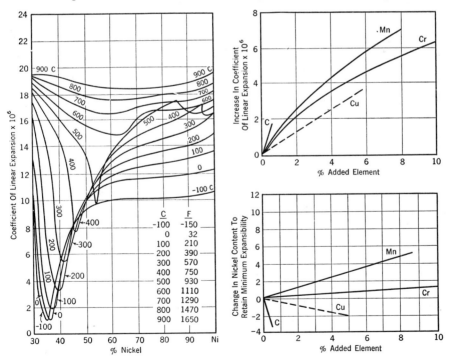

0.8, about one-quarter to one-sixth that of other commonly used spring materials.

Other iron-nickel alloy compositions find various uses because their expansion coefficients fall within a specific range. For example, the expansion of a 61% iron, 39% nickel alloy matches almost exactly that of a low-expansion glass sometimes used for radio power tubes. The 54% iron, 46% nickel composition has almost the same expansion as platinum so it can be used to replace platinum in lead-in seals for electronic tubes. The 44% iron, 56% nickel alloy is used in machines which measure the dimensions of steel gauges and machine parts because it is stable, corrosion-resistant, and has the same expansion coefficient under ambient conditions as ordinary steel so temperature corrections are unnecessary.

## MAGNETIC ALLOYS OF IRON AND NICKEL

Because iron and nickel are both ferromagnetic metals, their alloys would be expected to have magnetic properties which would be of value in special limited applications.

Annealed iron-nickel alloys have high permeabilities, although if they contain more than 50% nickel, they are sensitive to rate of cooling, as illustrated in Figure 6.44. There are different classes of these alloys, depending upon the relationship between permeability and the other electrical and magnetic characteristics.

The alloys containing 30 to 90% nickel, 0 to 4% chromium, 0 to 4% molybdenum, remainder iron, or 76% nickel, 1.5% chromium, 6% copper, remainder iron, have high permeability at low field strengths and are used principally when very high impedance characteristics are required at flux densities ($\beta_{max}$) less than 1 gauss (compare Figure 4.9). The chromium or molybdenum is added to the first of these to give higher permeability without air quenching.

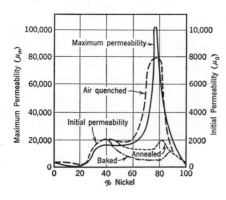

**Figure 6.44** Minimum and initial permeabilities for the iron-nickel series, illustrating the influence of various heat-treatments. [After G. W. Elmen.]

Some of the magnetic properties of these alloys in comparison with the pure irons and other materials are shown in Table 6.9.

**TABLE 6.9**

| | PERMEABILITY | | Saturation | |
| | Initial (Gauss) | Maximum (Gauss) | Value (Gauss) | Resistivity (Microhm-cm) |
|---|---|---|---|---|
| 99.95% (Puron) iron | — | 100,000 | 21,600 | 10 |
| Armco iron | 250 | 7,000 | 22,000 | 11 |
| Nickel | 110 | 600 | 6,100 | 9.5 |
| 4.5% Si–95.5% Fe | 500 | 12,000 | 19,500 | 55 |
| 45% Ni–55% Fe | 2,700 | 23,000 | 16,000 | 45 |
| 78.5% Ni–21.5% Fe, quenched | 10,000 | 105,000 | 10,700 | 16 |
| 78.5% Ni–3.8% Cr-17.7% Fe | 12,000 | 62,000 | 8,000 | 65 |
| 78.5% Ni–3.8% Mo-17.7% Fe | 20,000 | 75,000 | 8,500 | 55 |
| 76% Ni–1.5% Cr-6% Cu–16.5% Fe * | 30,000 | 100,000 | 6,500 | 60 |
| 49% Co–2% V-49% Fe | 800 | 4,500 | 24,000 | 27 |
| 35% Co–1% Cr-64% Fe | 650 | 10,000 | 24,200 | 20 |

* Annealed in a continuous stream of pure dry hydrogen at 2000 F (1100 C).

Alloys containing approximately equal parts of iron and nickel (50:50) have high permeability for high field strengths and are most useful for high-impedance designs carrying only alternating currents such as transformer cores. However, their high cost limits them to special transformers, such as current transformers. For best results they should be annealed thoroughly for several hours at 1830 to 2200 F (1000 to 1200 C) in dry hydrogen, after all fabricating operations have been completed. These alloys have an initial permeability of 4,500 to 5,000, a maximum permeability which may vary between 3,200 and 100,000 depending on the specific composition, purity, and treatment, a saturation value of 16,000 gauss, which is the highest of all iron-nickel alloys containing more than 30% nickel, and a resistivity of 45 microhm-cm. For many applications the high saturation value is a distinct advantage, even though the initial permeability is quite low. The fairly high resistivity is advantageous in limiting eddy currents.

If the 50% iron, 50% nickel alloy is annealed incompletely at temperatures below 1475 F (800 C), it has a constant permeability at low magnetizing forces. This characteristic is useful wherever a constant inductance or reactance is needed, as in filter coils for radio circuits or loading coils for telephone circuits.

In the alloys of iron with 30% nickel, and small amounts of chromium, manganese and silicon, the permeabilities vary with temperature, in some instances almost linearly within the range of $-4$ to $+140$ F ($-25$ to $+60$ C) for all values of $H$ up to 1,000. These alloys are used to compensate for the decrease of the magnetic permeability of iron and its alloys with temperature. This decrease creates an error in the readings of electrical meters, such as watt-hour meters, which depend upon the flux produced by a constant voltage supply or a definite load current. To compensate for this error, a certain amount of the magnetic flux is shunted around the moving part of the meter by an alloy which has a high magnetic temperature coefficient between 30 to 210 F (0 and 100 C). Thus, as the surrounding temperature increases, the amount of the shunted flux decreases, forcing more of the flux through the moving member than otherwise would be the case. By proper proportioning it is possible, therefore, to compensate nearly completely for the temperature changes.

In electromagnets, too, the temperature of the magnet winding fluctuates with changes in the surrounding temperature. As the temperature increases, therefore, the copper resistance increases and the current through the winding decreases. The field strength depends upon this current, so the field also must weaken as the temperature increases. This weakening of the field can be overcome by proper use of a compensating shunt which usually is attached to the core of the magnet. This type of compensation is important in voltage regulators.

### IRON-SILICON ALLOYS

The constitutional diagram for the alloys of iron and silicon (Figure 6.45) is of the same general type as the iron-molybdenum diagram (Figure 6.19c). The gamma loop closes at approximately 2.2% silicon [45] so alloys containing greater amounts of silicon are ferritic to the solidus temperature.

Silicon structural steels containing 0.25 to 1.25% silicon and 0.60 to 0.90% manganese, with 0.25 to 0.35% carbon, were developed rather early and still are used to some extent. In the hot-rolled condition they have tensile strengths of 80,000 to 95,000 psi, with yield strengths of 45,000 to 65,000 psi, elongations of 22 to 16% and notched impact values comparable to those of low-carbon structural steel. Their ductility is somewhat low for cold forming and there are some difficulties in welding. Metallographic structures are substantially the same as those of the low-carbon structural steels (compare Figure 6.29).

However, the iron-silicon alloys are best known because of their use as lamination sheets in generators, motors and transformer cores. These

---

[45] See also *The Alloys of Iron and Silicon* by E. S. Greiner, J. S. Marsh, and B. Stoughton (New York: McGraw-Hill, 1933), Chapters 14 and 15.

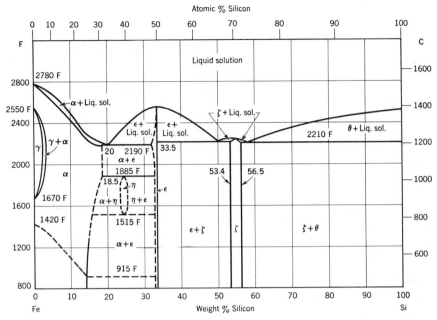

**Figure 6.45** Constitutional diagram for the alloys of iron and silicon. [After R. L. Rickett.]

alloys often are called Hadfield electrical steels after Sir Robert Hadfield, their discoverer. Silicon in solid solution increases the electrical resistance of pure iron more than any other substitutional element and promotes grain growth, but alloys containing more than about 5% silicon are not usable because they are too brittle. These steels can be made by conventional processes and are hot rolled. Impurities, particularly manganese (0.10% max), carbon (0.03% max), phosphorus (0.02% max), and sulfur 0.02% max), must be kept low. Various grades are used for specific applications (Table 6.10). The principal mechanical requirement is that the

**TABLE 6.10**

| Grade | % Si | Uses |
|---|---|---|
| Armature | 0.5 | Generators and small motors |
| Electrical | 1.0 | Generators and small motors |
| Motor | 2.5–3 | Induction motors |
| Transformer I | 3.25–4 | Generators and low-frequency transformers |
| Transformer II | 4–5 | 60-cycle transformers |

**Figure 6.46** Metallographic structures of silicon-iron transformer sheet. Full cross sections. **a** (*top row*). Hot-rolled. Etched with picral (×100). Note that the grains, possibly because of the stress distribution, occupy approximately one-half of the cross section of the sheet. **b** (*second row*). Cold-rolled. Etched with picral (×100). The grains either were comparatively small before rolling or else have been fragmented greatly during rolling. **c** (*third row*). Annealed at elevated temperatures. Etched with picral (×100). Note that the individual grains now occupy the entire cross section of the sheet. **d** (*bottom left*). Iron carbide at grain boundaries of annealed 3.5% silicon-steel transformer strip indicative of presence of carbon. Etched with nital (×500). **e** (*bottom right*). Typical as-cast structure of vacuum melted ingot of high-purity iron containing 3.3% silicon. Etched with nital (×600). Note the clear grain boundaries. [Photomicrographs *a*, *b*, *c* courtesy Research Laboratory, Westinghouse Electric Corporation; *d*, *e* courtesy Research Laboratory, General Electric Company; reduced approximately one-half in reproduction.]

sheets shear or punch without forming ragged edges. Heating to about 200 F (95 C) improves the ductility noticeably, because without this treatment, the alloyed ferrite has a high brittle-transition temperature. For best properties, transformer sheets are annealed in the range 1475 to 1650 F (800 to 900 C) using a nonoxidizing atmosphere. The rate of cooling is not important so long as the sheets remain flat, and any carbon has an opportunity to precipitate as graphite. This annealing heat-treatment gives a coarse grain size, desirable to decrease magnetic losses.[46]

A further improvement in magnetic properties is secured when as many grains as possible are oriented in such a way that a cube direction of their crystal lattice is related to the direction in which the sheets are to be used. In ferritic materials these cube directions have the highest permeability, that is, the best magnetic conductivity. The steel then can be magnetized more easily in these cube directions and its flux-carrying capacity can be increased by more than 25 to 30% with no increase in the magnetizing force or the core loss. On a development basis, single crystal sheets of 3.5%-silicon iron have been produced deliberately with the "easy-magnetization" direction in the plane of the sheets.

Metallographic structures of typical silicon electrical alloys after various treatments are shown in Figure 6.46. Note the freedom from oxide inclusions, the result of the deoxidizing effect of silicon.

## THE STABLE IRON-GRAPHITE DIAGRAM

The constitutional diagram for the stable iron-graphite system is of the same general type as that for the metastable iron-iron carbide system, but the major phase boundaries are displaced somewhat as shown in Figure 6.47. Thus the compositional limits over which austenite is stable in the presence of graphite are restricted somewhat more than in the presence of cementite. In either case, however, the carbon is in solid solution in austenite or ferrite as atomic carbon rather than one of the combined or associated forms.

From a practical viewpoint, the decomposition of cementite is used in a controlled manner in making gray, malleable and nodular cast iron and, to a limited extent, in making graphitic steels. In all of these, however, the impurities are so high that they really are alloying elements, forming rather complex alloys. Graphite also forms occasionally in low-carbon steels which are held for long times at elevated temperatures under stress, for example in certain types of steam power plant or petroleum refinery equipment, as has been mentioned earlier.

[46] Magnetic properties of the 3%-silicon steels are given by D. A. Leak and G. M. Leak, *Journ. Iron and Steel Inst.,* **187** (London: 1957), 190–94.

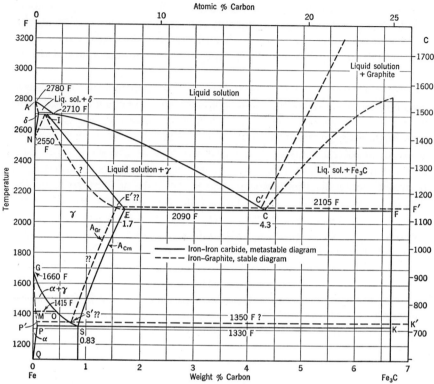

**Figure 6.47** Constitutional diagram for the stable alloys of iron and graphite and for the metastable alloys of iron and iron carbide superimposed. [After M. Hansen.]

## CAST IRONS

If the carbon content of an iron alloy is above approximately 2% there always is free iron carbide or graphite in the microstructure so the material cannot be worked satisfactorily and hence must be cast while liquid into what is essentially the final shape. Pig iron, the form in which impure iron comes from an iron blast furnace, is an impure form of cast iron which usually is purified partially before being cast into molds to make the various commercial cast irons. The name semisteel, loosely applied to some grades of cast iron, came from the practice of adding steel scrap to pig iron to reduce its carbon and silicon contents to the range more commonly used for cast irons.

All cast irons contain 1.7 to 4% total carbon either in the combined form (as a carbide) or in the free form (as graphite). The type of solid cast iron produced and its properties are determined largely by which of these forms predominates. This is controlled by varying the chemical composition, the treatment before casting, the rate of cooling, and the heat-treatment after casting. Section thickness, therefore, is an important factor. The quality of the casting, however, is determined almost entirely by the controls used by each foundry, and not by the chemical composition.

The primary cast irons—that is, those used chiefly "as cast"—are known as white, gray, and nodular (spheroidal graphite) cast iron. Malleable cast iron is the major secondary type, formed by heat-treating a properly balanced composition which, from its chemical analysis alone, would be expected to solidify as a white cast iron.

Mechanical tests on cast irons customarily are made on various separately cast test bars of standardized sections or, at best, on a prolong attached to the casting, rather than on the casting itself. The size of these test bars is intended to simulate the average section of final casting. However, the casting may have significantly different sections so its actual properties may differ appreciably from those of the test bar. Chemical analysis usually is not specified except in the alloy grades, because different foundries can produce similar properties with greatly different chemical analyses.

Several alloy cast irons, mostly of the types which can be hardened by heat-treatment are discussed later.

## WHITE CAST IRON

If most of the carbon occurs in the combined form as the hard brittle iron carbide, cementite, the fracture tends to occur through this material because of its brittleness, and the surface thus exposed has a silvery white metallic luster (Figure 6.48$b$). Such material is termed white cast iron, because of this fact.

The separation of carbon as iron carbide on solidification is favored by a low silicon content, and by rapid cooling. It is possible and, in fact, common, so to control the composition of the iron that a small or chilled section is completely white in fracture, whereas a somewhat larger one is completely gray.

The metallographic structure of white cast iron, Figure 6.49, consists of pearlite and cementite, either in the free form or as part of the structure of the solidified eutectic (ledeburite), depending largely upon the carbon and alloy content. Some austenite always is formed during solidification and this transforms to pearlite as the alloy cools slowly through $A_1$. Many white cast iron structures can be rationalized on the basis of the simple iron-iron carbide diagram but this is not always possible because of the alloy content. The coarse dendrites typical of the structure of most white cast irons can be seen readily in Figures 6.49$a$ and $b$.

**Figure 6.48  a** (*left group*). Fractures typical of gray cast irons showing how increased carbon content coarsens and darkens the fracture. The carbon contents increase as position in the group changes from lower right to upper left. [Photograph courtesy The International Nickel Company.] **b** (*right pair*). Fractures typical of an alloyed white cast iron containing 3.5% carbon, 5% silicon, 4.5% nickel, 1.5% chromium, remainder iron. (*upper*) Sand cast. (*lower*) Chill cast. [Specimens courtesy The International Nickel Company.]

In general, white cast irons are used because of their wear resistance or for primary castings which are to be transformed to malleable cast iron by heat-treatment. The use of irons which are locally "white" is discussed later under "Mottled and Chilled Irons."

## MALLEABLE CAST IRON

Malleable cast iron is made by annealing white cast iron of proper composition. Because of this there are definite size limitations on this type of cast iron. Most foundries do not produce castings more than, roughly, 1.5 in. thick. However, under special conditions a few castings as thick as 4 in. have been made satisfactorily.

Typical analyses used for ferritic-malleable automotive castings (analyzed in the white iron condition) are shown in Table 6.11. In each instance

**TABLE 6.11**

| | % C | % Si | Tensile Strength (psi) Minimum | Yield Strength (psi) Minimum | Elongation (% in 2 in.) Minimum | Brinell Hardness (10 mm– 3,000 Kg) |
|---|---|---|---|---|---|---|
| White cast iron | 2.00–2.45 | 0.95–1.35 | | | | |
| Malleable iron | | | 53,000 | 35,000 | 18 | 110–135 |
| White cast iron | 2.30–2.65 | 0.90–1.65 | | | | |
| Malleable iron | | | 50,000 | 32,500 | 10 | 110–135 |

the amounts of the other significant elements are 0.25 to 0.55% manganese, 0.18% max phosphorus, and 0.05 to 0.18% sulfur. Considerable variation in the properties of the finished castings is possible because they are affected at least as much by foundry practice as by chemical composition.

**Figure 6.49** a (*right*). Metallographic appearance of white cast iron. Etched with nital (×250). The dark regions are pearlitic. The light regions are probably free cementite and the gray regions transformed ledeburite. b (*bottom left*). Showing dendritic structure (×50). c (*bottom right*). Showing details of pearlitic background (×500). [Photomicrographs by L. Litchfield.]

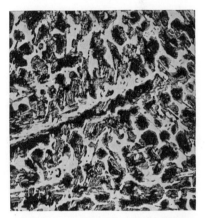

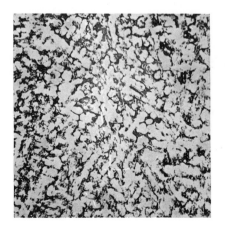

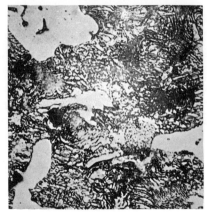

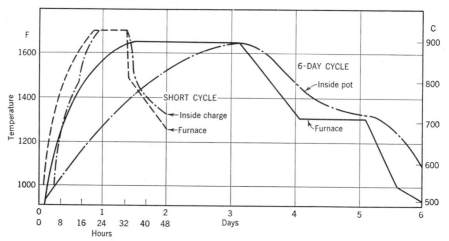

**Figure 6.50** Diagrammatic representation of former 6-day and modern controlled-atmosphere short-annealing cycles for ferritic malleable iron automotive castings. Note the short time lag between temperature of work and furnace in modern process. [From *Metal Progress*, courtesy American Society for Metals.]

Annealing cycles typical of the old 6-day cycle and the modern short cycle in a controlled atmosphere are shown schematically in Figure 6.50. Even shorter cycles are now being used on iron melted in an induction furnace and treated with addition agents just before pouring. Slow heating of white iron castings is advisable to minimize the likelihood of cracking from thermal strains. The actual transformation from cementite to temper carbon takes place in two stages: (a) holding at 1650 to 1750 F (900 to 950 C), and (b) a slow cool through the critical range just under 1400 F (725 to 750 C).

During the first of these steps the important reaction is

$$\text{Austenite I} + \text{Fe}_3\text{C} \rightarrow \text{Austenite II} + \text{Temper Carbon}$$

involving a decomposition of nearly all the free cementite.[47] The presence of two austenites is shown because the constitutional diagram indicates that austenite in equilibrium with cementite has a different composition from austenite in equilibrium with graphite. In any case, only a certain proportion of carbon can be gotten into the graphitic form by this treatment alone, because the austenite always remains saturated. The time required for this stage is shorter the higher the temperature which can be used. This is determined largely by the uniformity which can be maintained in the furnace and by the closeness of temperature control, because a temperature of

---

[47] J. Burke, *Journ. Iron and Steel Inst.,* **194** (London: 1960), 443–45, discusses the kinetics of this reaction.

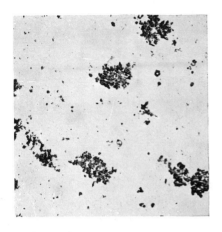

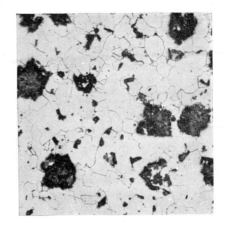

**Figure 6.51** Metallographic structures of various types of malleable cast irons. Etched with 4% nital. **a** (*top left*). Ferritic, unetched (×100). **b** (*top right*). Ferritic, etched (×100). **c** (*middle*). Pearlitic (×100). **d** (*bottom left*). Sorbitic—i.e., quenched and tempered (×100). **e** (*bottom right*). Martensitic—i.e., quenched (×1000). [Photomicrographs *c*, *d*, *e* courtesy Dr. H. A. Schwartz, National Malleable and Steel Castings Company.]

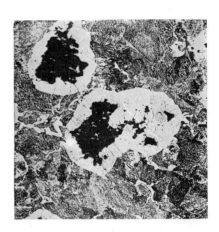

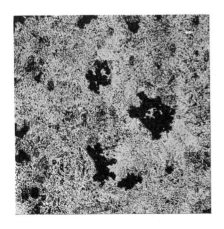

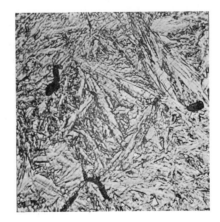

1800 to 1900 F (980 to 1040 C) causes softening if not partial melting. If after this treatment, the casting is cooled normally to room temperature, the pearlitic malleable structure, consisting of pearlite and temper carbon, results (Figure 6.51c). Pearlitic malleable irons may analyze anywhere within the range shown previously for ferritic malleables. The manganese content may run somewhat higher, however, up to 1.25%. Other matrix structures, which can be produced by heat-treatment, also are shown in Figures 6.51d and e. The mechanical properties of pearlitic malleable cast iron vary nearly linearly with the Brinell hardness. For a Brinell of 200 the material has a tensile strength of 80,000 to 90,000 psi with a yield strength of 50,000 to 70,000 psi and an elongation of 10 to 7% depending on the strength. To be machinable readily, there should be little or no residual cementite; this usually means a Brinell hardness below 200.

If a fully ferritic malleable structure is desired, a second stage of heat-treatment also must be given. During the slow cool through the critical range, the austenite tends to decompose into ferrite and cementite in the form of pearlite. However, because of the presence of existing nodules of graphite, either this decomposition does not occur or else the cementite formed decomposes fairly rapidly into the more stable phases, ferrite and graphite. The ultimate result of this treatment is to produce a structure composed only of ferrite and temper carbon, the common structure of malleable cast iron (Figure 6.51b). Sometimes the metal is reheated and recooled several times from just above to just below the critical range in order to assist the decomposition process in this second stage.

After annealing, the castings absorb shock, but they are not readily workable. Their name arises from the increased toughness given them by an essentially continuous ferrite matrix in comparison with their original high cementite structure. Malleable irons tend to fracture through the temper carbon so a typical fractured surface (Figure 6.52) is black.

**Figure 6.52**   Fracture typical of malleable cast iron. [Specimen courtesy Albany Castings Company.]

A close study of the graphite particles in malleable iron (Figure 6.51a) and in nodular (spheroidal) cast iron (Figure 6.59a) shows that they are quite different. The temper carbon in malleable iron is much more open and filigreed in texture rather than appearing as spheroids with a dense structure radiating from a central nucleus as it does in nodular cast iron. Either structure has excellent machinability.

## GRAY CAST IRON

If the majority of the carbon is in the form of the relatively soft and weak flake graphite, with less than 0.8% carbon in the combined form, the material is termed gray cast iron. Any fracture tends to occur through the weakest sections, that is, the graphite flakes, thus exposing a surface which is dull gray in color (Figure 6.48a). The graphite flakes also tend to prevent galling in applications involving wear and to improve machinability.

The separation of the carbon, as flake graphite, during solidification is favored, in general, by the high carbon content, by a high silicon content, varying from 1.25 to 3% depending on the section thickness, and by a slow rate of cooling. The thinner the section is, the higher is the silicon content required to produce a given structure, because thinner sections cool more rapidly than thicker sections.

In order to determine the characteristics of a given composition of cast iron, the step-bar test sometimes is used. In this test, the iron is cast into a mold of metal or sand which has the shape shown in Figure 6.53. Frac-

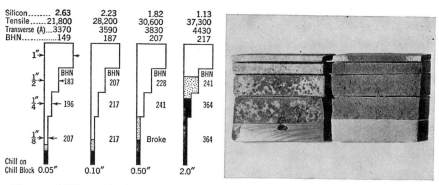

| Silicon | 2.63 | 2.23 | 1.82 | 1.13 |
| Tensile | 21,800 | 28,200 | 30,600 | 37,300 |
| Transverse (A) | 3370 | 3590 | 3830 | 4430 |
| BHN | 149 | 187 | 207 | 217 |

| | BHN 183 | BHN 207 | BHN 228 | BHN 241 |
| | 196 | 217 | 241 | 364 |
| | 207 | 217 | Broke | 364 |

Chill on
Chill Block   0.05"   0.10"   0.50"   2.0"

**Figure 6.53** **a** (*left*). Hardening gray iron by decreasing the silicon content as indicated by the step-bar test. **b** (*right*). A somewhat similar hardening effect is produced by adding nickel. This is illustrated by the fractures of ⅛-, ¼-, ½-, and 1-in. thick sections of a step bar. The 1-in. thick section at the bottom was sliced half-way through by means of a high-speed rubber-bonded abrasive wheel before being fractured. *Left,* At left is step bar cast from base analysis, 3.0% T.C., 1.5% silicon, and at right is step bar cast from same alloy after treatment with 3% nickel. [Courtesy The International Nickel Company.]

ture of the various sections shows quickly the structure which can be expected from that iron for chill cast sections of various thicknesses. The test is particularly useful for many alloy cast irons. Tapered wedges also are used widely for this purpose.

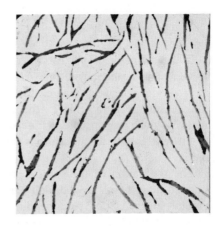

**Figure 6.54** Metallographic appearance of graphite in gray cast irons. Unetched ($\times$50). [Courtesy American Society for Testing and Materials.] These correspond approximately to the following sizes in A.S.T.M. Tentative Standard A247-T: (*top left*) Size 2, longest flake, 1–2 in. in length ($\times$50). (*top right*) Size 3, longest flake $\frac{1}{2}$–1 in. in length ($\times$50). (*middle*) Size 4, longest flake $\frac{1}{4}$–$\frac{1}{2}$ in. in length ($\times$50). (*bottom left*) Size 5, longest flake $\frac{1}{8}$–$\frac{1}{4}$ in. in length ($\times$50). (*bottom right*) Size 7, longest flake $\frac{1}{32}$–$\frac{1}{16}$ in. in length ($\times$50). The A.S.T.M. Tentative Standard also includes sizes 1, 6, and 8.

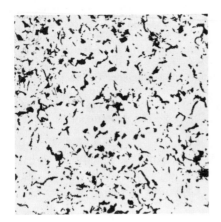

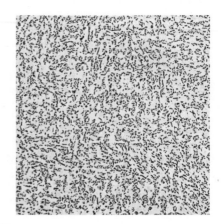

Metallographically,[48] gray iron is a mixture of four constituents:

1. The essentially flake graphite which is formed during solidification and which to a large extent determines the properties of the casting by its amount, size, shape, and distribution. Typical sizes are illustrated in Figure 6.54. Graphite flakes usually are distributed in a (a) random, (b) dendritic (compare Figure 6.56) or (c) rosette pattern.

2. Pearlite, which may vary in composition between approximately 0.5 and 0.8% carbon because of the alloy content.

3. Steadite, a hard brittle eutectic of iron (containing some phosphorus in solution) and iron phosphide ($Fe_3P$) which always can be found when much phosphorus is present. Steadite contains 10.2% phosphorus and 89.8% iron; therefore, a cast iron containing 1% phosphorus contains about 10% steadite in its structure because very little if any phosphorus is found in other forms. Steadite remains molten down to the comparatively low temperature of 1920 F (1050 C), and hence usually is found at the edges of the large grains formed on solidification. Its structure is shown in Figure 6.55*a*. The fine speckled structure inside the particles is characteristic of this eutectic.

4. Free ferrite, which usually appears only in appreciable amounts in low-strength cast irons. Ferrite etches white with nital so it sometimes is difficult to differentiate from steadite and cementite. However, the ferrite usually is more rounded in appearance than either the steadite or the cementite, because it precipitates from the solid solution (austenite) rather than solidifying directly from the liquid solution. Frequently, in addition, it is found in close association with graphite flakes, as in Figure 6.55*b*.

Free cementite seldom is found in gray irons. The light-etching steadite, which usually has a distinct fine structure because of its eutectic nature, sometimes is mistakenly identified as free cementite, however.

The general structural constituents of gray cast iron are shown in Figure 6.56 at a somewhat lower magnification than used previously. Alloy castings also may be austenitic or contain specific complex constituents in addition to those mentioned above.

The mechanical properties of gray cast iron are influenced greatly by the size, shape, and distribution of the graphite flakes and by the amount of free ferrite in the microstructure.[49] For any given section, these structural factors are controlled by varying the carbon:silicon ratio.

Ordinary gray cast iron usually is of low strength. Specification grade gray iron is made in seven classes differing in the minimum strengths required in 1-in. bars (Table 6.12). The four higher classes, sometimes called

[48] See R. M. Allen, *Microscope in Elementary Cast Iron Metallurgy* (Chicago: American Foundrymen's Association, 1939); also *Fundamentals of Iron and Steel Castings* by A. P. Gagnebin (New York: International Nickel Company, 1957).

[49] See J. F. Wallace, *Metals Engineering Quarterly*, 1 (1961), 12–23.

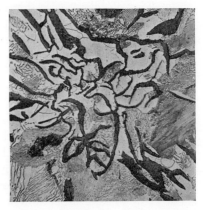

**Figure 6.55   a** (*left*). Metallographic appearance of steadite (light speckled regions) in gray cast iron. Etched with nital (×500, reduced approximately one-third in reproduction). [Photomicrograph courtesy United States Pipe and Foundry Company.] **b** (*right*). Metallographic appearance of free ferrite (white) in gray cast iron. Etched with nital (×500, reduced approximately one-third in reproduction). [Photomicrograph courtesy United States Pipe and Foundry Company.]

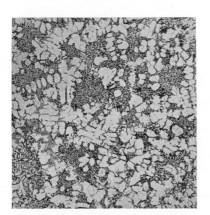

**Figure 6.56**   Metallographic appearance of general structural constituents of gray cast iron. Etched with nital (×100, reduced approximately one-quarter in reproduction). **a** (*left*). Low-strength centrifugal casting, as cast, containing large amounts of free ferrite (3.40% total carbon, 1.90% silicon, 0.50% manganese, 0.50% phosphorus, 0.07% sulfur, remainder iron). **b** (*right*). Normal sand casting, as cast (3.78% total carbon, 0.67% combined carbon, 1.09% silicon, 0.38% manganese, 0.43% phosphorus, 0.064% sulfur, remainder iron). [Photomicrographs courtesy United States Pipe and Foundry Company.]

high-test cast irons, can be produced consistently only by careful control of the charge and the melting cycle, in order to keep the total carbon low and the graphite small and uniformly distributed. This requires a high-quality foundry.

**TABLE 6.12**

| Class No. | Tensile Strength (psi), Minimum |
|-----------|-------------------------------|
| 20 | 20,000 |
| 25 | 25,000 |
| 30 | 30,000 |
| 35 | 35,000 |
| 40 | 40,000 |
| 50 | 50,000 |
| 60 | 60,000 |

In general, the lower carbon cast irons, containing the proper amounts of silicon, form fine graphite flakes and little free ferrite and hence have the higher strengths. Low-carbon cast irons also have a better combination of galling resistance and wear resistance for most applications than the high-carbon cast irons which have more graphite. The higher carbon irons with normal silicon contents are soft and have low strengths because of the presence of coarse graphite flakes and considerable free ferrite.

Gray cast iron usually has an effective modulus of elasticity in the range 12,000,000 to 18,000,000 psi, but it may approach 30,000,000 psi in alloy castings. There is no well-defined elastic limit or yield point. The fatigue endurance limit is about one-half the tensile strength and varies nearly linearly with it. Gray cast irons have a high damping capacity because of the flake graphite. They should be used above 800 F (425 C) with caution because of a tendency to oxidize internally and to grow dimensionally (compare Figure 6.64).

The transverse flexure test [50] is one of those used commonly. In this test, a standard cast arbitration test bar [51] 0.875, 1.20, or 2.00 in. in diameter or thickness is placed on corresponding supports 12, 18, or 24 in. apart, respectively, and loaded at the center. Either a specified load is applied and the deflection in inches is measured, or the specimen is loaded for deflection and the load is increased gradually until failure occurs. For this latter procedure, the modulus of rupture is found either from the equation

$$\text{Modulus of rupture} = \frac{2.546 LS}{D^3}$$

[50] See *A.S.T.M. Standard A 48;* W. R. Clough and M. E. Shank, *Trans. A.S.M.,* **49** (1957), 241–62, discuss the deformation and rupture of these materials.
[51] Reference to A.S.T.M. Standard Specifications is recommended.

for a round bar, where $L$ = distance between supports, $S$ = the breaking load, and $D$ = the diameter of the test bar; or from the equation

$$\text{Modulus of rupture} = \frac{3LS}{2BH^2}$$

for a rectangular bar, where $B$ = width, and $H$ = the height of the test bar, and $L$ and $S$ have the same significance as above.

Arbitration bars made of high-test cast iron have a transverse strength of 4,200 to 5,600 lb with a deflection of 0.15 to 0.25 in. A compressive strength of 165,000 to 190,000 psi can be produced readily in any sections 0.5 to 4 in. thick by adding controlled amounts of alloying elements. A typical base analysis for pressure iron castings contains 3.1% total carbon, 2.0% silicon. To this base may be added 0.75 to 1.5% nickel, 0.5 to 0.9% manganese, 0.30% chromium, and 0.30 or 0.60% molybdenum. The relationship between composition, strength, hardness, and section thickness for several of these cast irons, as well as for several automotive iron castings, is shown in Figure 6.57. These irons have fatigue endurance limits of 50 to 57% of the tensile strength.

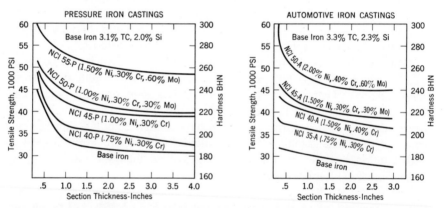

**Figure 6.57**   Influence of alloy content and section thickness on the properties of typical pressure and automotive iron castings. [Courtesy The International Nickel Company.]

Corrosion of gray cast iron under alkaline or neutral conditions—seldom, if ever, under acid conditions—removes the ferritic materials leaving behind an intermixed layer of flake graphite and insoluble corrosion products. This sometimes is called graphitization or graphitic corrosion. In some cases this layer can be so impermeable to further penetration of the corroding liquids as to form an excellent protective coating. If the layer is permeable, however, the corrosion rate may be accelerated significantly because of the galvanic effect of the cathodic graphite.

## MOTTLED AND CHILL CAST IRON

Borderline castings, in which the structure and fracture show a mixture of gray iron and white iron because of proper balancing of the factors of chemical composition and rate of cooling, are termed mottled cast irons. (Figure 6.58*a*.) Frequently it is desirable to control the structure and properties of the cast iron specifically for a definite purpose, and to secure a gray structure in one part and a white structure in another instead of the two being mixed randomly. This type of casting is known as chill casting. As the name implies, its structure is determined by the already stated fact that, for a given chemical composition, a rapid cooling rate tends to give a white structure, whereas a slow rate tends to give a gray one. Consequently, a plate of metal, or some other material with a relatively high thermal conductivity, is built into the usual sand mold in order to cool rapidly or to chill the desired section. This chilled section, therefore, has a white fracture which blends, through a mottled zone, into a region which has a gray fracture, as illustrated in Figure 6.58*b*, because the rate of cooling was slower there. The rate of cooling decreases as the distance from the chill increases, so the depth of the chill layer can be controlled to some extent by varying the composition of the alloy and the treatment given it before casting.

Irons of this type also are cast centrifugally in hard sand, ceramic, and metal molds.

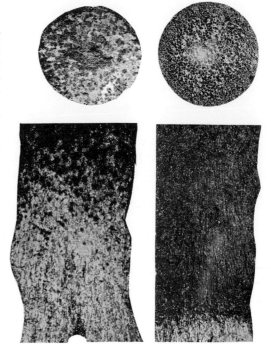

**Figure 6.58   a.** Fractures typical of mottled cast iron. (*top left*) Normal type, a white iron turning gray, as shown by graphitic spots in the structure. (*top right*) A carbidic iron containing 3.25% carbon, 2.5% silicon, 1.2% chromium, remainder iron, a gray iron turning white by forming a well-defined carbide network. [Specimens courtesy Albany Castings Company, and The International Nickel Company.] **b.** Fractures typical of chill cast iron containing about 2.8% carbon, 2.3% silicon. (*bottom left*) Uninoculated. (*bottom right*) Inoculated. [Specimens courtesy The International Nickel Company.]

## SUPERHEATING AND INOCULATION

When gray cast irons are melted at temperatures within the range 2725 to 3100 F (1500 to 1700 C), graphitization is inhibited to some extent and does not commence until the iron has cooled to some temperature which is well below the solidification zone. In addition, there is a much shorter range within which graphitization can occur so that the flakes tend to be finer. There also is some carbide stabilization.

In American superheating practice, the usual casting temperature is approximately 2750 F (1510 C); only a few automotive castings use 2800 F (1540 C) or higher consistently. Superheating usually is accomplished in an electric furnace.

When it is desired to improve the structure of the cast iron and, consequently, its mechanical properties, the metal often is inoculated just before pouring. This involves melting a white iron, which is free from the complications produced in gray iron by superheating, and then changing it into a gray iron at the last moment by introducing silicon.[52] Ferrosilicon, calcium silicide, graphite, and numerous commercial inoculants are used for this purpose. Inoculation and superheating constitute the principal reasons for most of the "trademarked" cast irons. The effects of inoculation on the macrographic structure of a chill casting also are illustrated in Figure 6.58b.

## NODULAR (SPHEROIDAL) CAST IRON

The relatively low strength and ductility of most gray cast iron is a natural result of the almost continuous network of flake graphite. These mechanical properties can be improved significantly by causing the graphite to form as spheroidal particles [53] rather than flakes, so ferrite becomes the continuous phase. This type of structure can be achieved by treating the melt properly with various materials, among which are: cerium; [54] sodium; magnesium or a magnesium-containing addition agent such as ferro-silicon-magnesium, nickel-magnesium, or copper-magnesium; various halides of alkali or alkaline-earth metals accompanied by calcium silicide as a reduc-

---

[52] This was discussed well by J. T. Eash, *Trans. Amer. Foundrymen's Assoc.* (1941), 887–910.

[53] Characteristics of these nodules have been reported by H. M. Weld, R. L. Cunningham, and F. W. C. Boswell, *Trans. A.I.M.E.,* **194** (1952), 738–42.

[54] See H. Morrogh and W. J. Williams, *Journ. Iron and Steel Inst.,* **158** (London: 1948), 306–22.

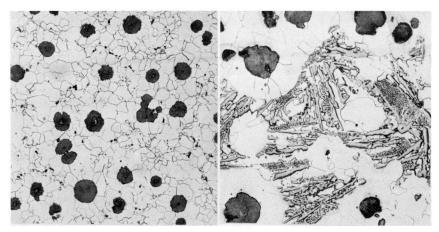

**Figure 6.59 a** (*left*). Ferritic nodular cast iron. Etched with nital ($\times$250). **b** (*right*). Nodular cast iron, as cast, with residual massive carbide that must be eliminated by subsequent heat treatment. Etched with nital ($\times$500).

ing agent; or yttrium.[55] Inoculation with ferrosilicon or calcium silicide along with this treatment often is helpful in producing well-formed spheroids and decreasing the amount of free cementite in the structure. A proprietary nickel-magnesium treatment is used most commonly in the United States today.[56] All of the process advantages of gray cast iron, such as fluidity, castability, and machinability, are retained.

Much of the effectiveness of the treatment depends on getting the sulfur content to a very low level, of the order of 0.01% or less. A typical metallo-graphic structure (Figure 6.59a) shows nodular or spheroidal graphite in a ferritic matrix. The modulus of elasticity is more like steel than cast iron and approximates 25,000,000 psi. Typical tensile properties will exceed 60,000 psi ultimate and 45,000 psi yield strength, with an elongation of 15% minimum.[57] In complicated sections there may be some free carbide (Figure 6.59b) so a final softening or annealing heat-treatment near 1300 F (700 C) often is given. Tensile strengths as high as 85,000 to 105,000 psi, and even as high as 150,000 psi with heat-treatment, also can be secured but only by sacrificing ductility, because the elongation will fall to 2 to 4%.

[55] See J. J. Kanter, J. Magos, and W. L. Meinhart in paper presented at the annual meeting of A.S.M.E. (November 28, 1961).

[56] See A. P. Gagnebin, K. D. Millis, and N. B. Pilling, *Iron Age*, **163** (1949), 76–84; there are other methods which have not been used so widely, see H. K. Ihrig, *Trans. A.S.M.*, **49** (1957), 232–40.

[57] See J. F. Wallace, *Metals Engineering Quarterly*, **1** (1961), 12–23; C. R. Wilks, N. A. Mathews, and R. W. Kraft, Jr., *Trans. A.S.M.*, **47** (1955), 611–30, give elevated temperature properties.

Various low-alloy ductile irons are made containing such elements as nickel to increase strength, and silicon to increase oxidation resistance and thereby decrease the tendency toward growth at elevated temperatures.

## WEAR-RESISTANT CAST IRONS

Wear-resistant cast irons frequently are chill cast. The hardness and wear resistance may be increased appreciably by proper alloying without interfering greatly with machinability, because machinability of cast iron is determined by microstructure rather than the Brinell hardness. Consequently, wear-resistant castings often are made as hard as the application, structure, and shape permit. This is illustrated diagrammatically in Figure 6.60. If the hardness is increased merely by increasing the amount of com-

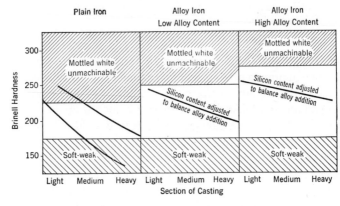

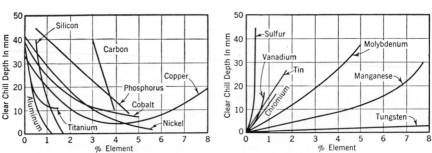

**Figure 6.60   a** (*top*). Diagrammatic presentation of general effects of alloys in widening range of mechanical properties in cast irons which are pearlitic and at the same time machinable. [From P. D. Merica, *Trans. A.I.M.E.,* **125** (1937), 2–46.] **b** (*bottom*). The comparative influence of various elements on the chill depth of a chilled iron roll. (*left*) Elements which decrease the depth of chill. (*right*) Elements which increase the depth of chill. [From *Cast Metals Handbook,* courtesy American Foundrymen's Association.]

bined carbon, the wear resistance actually may decrease, particularly if the carbide particles tend to fall out. By proper use of certain alloying elements—nickel, chromium, molybdenum, manganese, copper, vanadium, and titanium—iron can be hardened more effectively and more uniformly than is possible by the use of chills alone. The influence of various alloying elements on the depth of chill (Figure 6.60*b*) is significant in this process, which requires close control and hence can be done only by a quality foundry. The effects of some of these additions already have been shown in Figure 6.57.

The amount of the various alloying elements which must be used depends to a large extent upon the wear resistance required and the nature of the application. This can be illustrated best by some specific examples.

Castings which have a light section or an irregular shape can be hardened adequately by the use of small amounts of nickel, chromium, or molybdenum, the total of which seldom exceeds 2%. These additions serve principally to make the microstructure fully pearlitic instead of predominantly ferritic. Low-alloy cast irons comprise the greatest tonnage of castings made predominantly to resist wear. Compositions generally fall within the limits shown in Table 6.13. The alloys contain less than 0.12% sulfur and less

**TABLE 6.13**

| | |
|---|---|
| % Si | 1.5–3.0 |
| % TC * | 2.5–3.5 |
| % GC * | 2.0–3.0 |
| % CC * | 0.3–0.9 |
| % Mn | 0.5–0.9 |
| % Ni | 0–2.0 |
| % Cr | 0.1–1.0 |
| % Mo | 0.2–1.0 |
| % Cu | 0–1.0 |

\* Total Carbon, Graphitic Carbon, Combined Carbon.

than 0.20% phosphorus. Depending upon the microstructure, the tensile strengths of castings of this type may range from 30,000 to 75,000 psi. They are made to a wide range of specifications for transverse test results.

About 2 to 4% of alloying elements is required when castings with heavy sections must be modified, because of their slower rates of cooling. Increasing the nickel content for a given section makes the matrix pearlite successively finer until it becomes nearly unresolvable at a hardness of about Brinell 250 to 275 (Figure 6.61*a*.) These compositions still are machinable because the core is gray and high-speed cutting tools can be used on the chilled face. Increasing the amount of nickel above this, how-

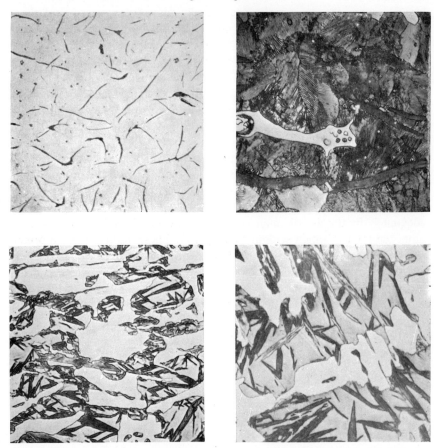

**Figure 6.61** Metallographic structures of wear-resistant irons. **a.** Moderately hardened (2.30% nickel, 0.96% chromium, 1.75% silicon, 3.09% total carbon, remainder iron). (*top left*) Unetched, showing appearance of graphite flakes. (*top right*) Etched with 2% nital, showing detail of fine pearlitic matrix (×500). **b.** Fully-hardened alloy types. Etched with nital. (*bottom left*) 4.60% nickel, 1.64% chromium, 1.28% silicon, 3.41% total carbon, remainder iron (×100). (*bottom right*) 4.55% nickel, 1.55% chromium, 0.45% manganese, 0.47% silicon, 3.48% total carbon, remainder iron (×500). [Photomicrographs courtesy The International Nickel Company.]

ever, causes martensite to form.[58] The hardness exceeds Brinell 325 and the casting may be too brittle unless it is heat-treated properly. About 0.7 to 1.0% chromium is used, largely to decrease the cost by decreasing the amount of nickel required to produce a given result, and the silicon and carbon are kept toward the low side of the limits given for castings with lighter sections.

[58] Constituents produced by heat-treatment are discussed in Chapter 8.

Heavy-duty wear-resistant castings must be made of a fully-hardened chilled or white cast iron with massive carbides in a martensitic matrix (Figure 6.61*b*). To accomplish this, nickel additions in the range 4 to 6% are used with 1.0 to 2.5% chromium and preferably with low-silicon and moderate-carbon contents to decrease the graphitic carbon. One of the better known materials of this alloy type analyzes, on the average, as shown in Table 6.14. The composition of these castings varies depending upon the section dimensions and properties desired.

**TABLE 6.14**

| | |
|---|---|
| % Si | 0.4–1.2 |
| % TC | 3.2–3.6 |
| % CC | 3.2–3.6 |
| % Mn | 0.4–1.5 |
| % Ni | 4.0–6.0 |
| % Cr | 1.0–2.5 |

With a fully white structure this alloy has a tensile strength of 35,000 to 50,000 psi, and with a gray core the strength may reach 60,000 to 80,000 psi. In the transverse test, specimens deflect 0.06 to 0.08 in. for loads of 4,500 to 6,000 lb. The Brinell hardness ranges from 600 to 650, for sand cast, to 700 to 750, for chill cast specimens. By controlling the composition for a given section, castings can be produced which are hard when sand cast, as well as those which require chills to produce a given hardness.

For applications requiring a high impact strength, or when some bending may be expected in use, castings usually are heat-treated by soaking at 1650 to 1700 F (900 to 930 C) followed by an oil quench and a draw at 400 F (200 C) with a slow cool. This toughening treatment first partially dissolves and breaks up some of the massive carbides and then, in the draw, reprecipitates them in a finely spheroidized form.

## HEAT-RESISTANT CAST IRONS

Heat resistance becomes important when cast irons are used above 800 F (425 C) in air or superheated steam. With these materials, heat resistance implies a resistance to growth, as well as retention of mechanical properties and resistance to scaling. Growth in cast irons is attributable both to graphitization and to an infiltration of gases. In severe cases, it may lead to increases in volume of as much as 50%, leaving the casting weak and brittle. Growth occurs whenever castings are reheated repeatedly to temperatures above 800 F (425 C). The amount of growth for a given iron is proportional to the heating temperature and the number of heatings, as illustrated in Figure 6.64 for both a plain and a high-alloy cast iron at 1500 F (815 C). The usual nickel-chromium cast irons would be intermediate.[59]

For resisting growth, low-silicon contents to limit the graphitizing tendency and the addition of some chromium to stabilize the carbides are generally desirable. A phosphorus content somewhat higher than normal is frequently beneficial also. Some typical analyses for specific applications are shown in Table 6.15.

**TABLE 6.15**

| *Application* | *% Si* | *% TC* | *% Mn* | *% Ni* | *% Cr* |
|---|---|---|---|---|---|
| Diesel engine cylinder heads | 1.2 | 3.2 | 0.6 | 1.5 | 0.3 |
| Grate bars | 1.5 | 3.4 | 0.7 | 1.5 | 0.6 |
| Stoker links, up to 1400 F (750 C) | 2.0 | 3.2 | 0.6 | — | 1.0 |
| Exhaust manifolds | 2.0 | 3.4 | 0.6 | — | 0.4 |

In these alloys the graphitic carbon generally ranges from 2.2 to 2.8% with the combined carbon 0.6 to 0.8%. The sulfur seldom, if ever, exceeds 0.14%, and the phosphorus usually is held at 0.40% maximum; both of these elements, however, may run appreciably lower. Molybdenum, in the range 0.35 to 1.0%, sometimes is added to improve the heat resistance.

### CORROSION-RESISTANT CAST IRONS

Corrosion-resistant cast irons usually are of the ferritic type, high in silicon, or of the austenitic type, high in nickel.

The high-silicon cast irons have a low tensile strength, averaging near 18,000 psi, and are very hard and almost as brittle as glass, but they have unusual resistance to corrosion, by both oxidizing and nonoxidizing acids, particularly the more active ones like nitric, sulfuric, and phosphoric. These alloys vary in composition within the limits shown in Table 6.16. However, the best alloys are held to the narrow range of 14.35 to 14.65 silicon because the maximum corrosion resistance corresponds to an ordered solid solution [60] containing 14.4% silicon ($Fe_3Si$).

[59] See R. J. Greene and F. G. Sefing, *Corrosion,* **11** (1955), 315t–21t.
[60] See Chapter 5. The ordering is not indicated on the constitutional diagram in Figure 6.45.

**TABLE 6.16**

| | |
|---|---|
| % C | 0.2–1.0 |
| % Si | 13–17 |
| % Mn | 0.25–0.90 |
| % S | 0.02–0.05 |
| % P | 0.02–0.05 |

The usual silicon-iron alloy does not resist too well corrosion by hydrochloric acid, hydrofluoric and other halide acids, or sulfurous acid. However, a modified alloy containing approximately 81% iron, 14.5% silicon, 3.5% molybdenum, 1% nickel corrodes at a much lower rate.

Typical metallographic structures, shown in Figure 6.62, consist of primary grains of "silicoferrite," the alpha solid solution of silicon and manganese in iron. The eutecticlike distribution of silicoferrite with flake graphite is essentially the same in both alloys. In the modified alloy the molybdenum appears as either $Fe_3Mo_2$ or $Fe_3Mo_3C$ in the eutectic constituent, and the nickel is dissolved in the silicoferrite matrix.

The two main varities of austenitic cast irons have the analyses shown in Table 6.17, the remainder being essentially iron in each case. The

**TABLE 6.17**

| | *Type 1* (Regular) | *Type 2* (Copper-free) |
|---|---|---|
| % Si | 1.0–2.75 | 1.0–2.75 |
| % TC | 1.8–3.0 | 1.8–3.0 |
| % Mn | 4–1.5 | 4–1.5 |
| % Ni | 14–17.5 | 18–22 |
| % Cr | 1.75–2.50 | 2–4 |
| % Cu | 5.5–7.5 | — |

sulfur content generally is held between 0.04 and 0.12%, and the phosphorus is kept in the range 0.04 to 0.30%. A typical microstructure is shown in Figure 6.63. Some residual carbides can be seen in the austenitic matrix in addition to the flake graphite. Types made with nodular or spheroidal graphite, instead of flake graphite have a tensile strength of 55,000 to 70,000 psi, with a yield strength of 30,000 to 40,000 psi and elongation as high as 10 to 20%.

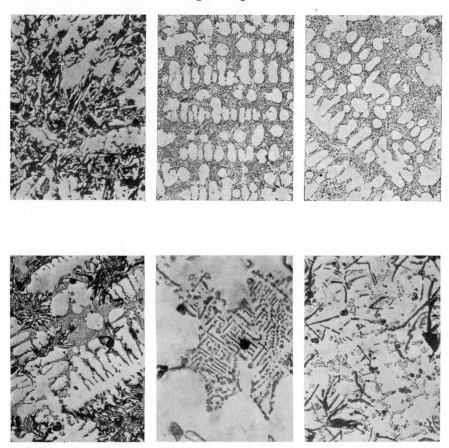

**Figure 6.62** Metallographic structures of (*top row*) plain high-silicon cast iron and (*bottom row*) the molybdenum-modified form. Etched with mixed acids in glycerol. The structure of the plain silicon alloy consists of graphite in a dendritic matrix of "silicoferrite"—i.e., iron containing silicon and manganese in solid solution. The graphite may vary in size from the coarse form shown in the left picture (×100), to the fine form shown in the right picture (×100). The middle picture (×100) shows the intermediate form which is most desirable from the viewpoint of mechanical properties. Intermediate structures which are a combination of the coarse and fine forms also may be found in the commercial product. Commercial castings are annealed 4 hr at 1660 F (905 C) to improve their strength. This does not change the microstructure, however. The effect of structure on the corrosion resistance and mechanical properties is small. The structure of the modified alloy consists of graphite in a dendritic matrix of "silicoferrite" and its eutectic with $Fe_3Mo_2$ or iron-molybdenum carbide ($Fe_3Mo_3C$). This is seen in the as-cast structure (×100, *left,* and ×500, *middle*). After annealing at 1660 F (905 C) for 24 hr, in accordance with commercial practice, the strength has been increased approximately 25% and the molybdenum constituent has been coalesced as shown (×100) at the right. [Courtesy The Duriron Company.]

These austenitic cast irons are practically free from growth, as illustrated in Figure 6.64, because they are oxidation resistant and undergo no phase changes at elevated temperatures. However, the Type 2 alloy is somewhat more stable than the Type 1 alloy. They also resist scaling very well up to 1500 F (815 C), and they are markedly superior to ordinary gray iron in resisting the action of many corrosive agents including several acids, alkalies, salts, and corrosive gases.

The chromium is added to increase the hardness and strength to values comparable with those of ordinary gray cast iron. Without chromium the

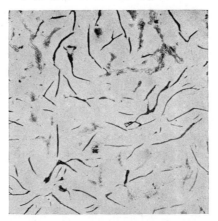

**Figure 6.63** Metallographic structure of austenitic nickel cast iron (2% silicon, 2.8% total carbon, 1% manganese, 20% nickel, 2% chromium, remainder iron). Etched with 5% picral (×100). [Photomicrograph courtesy The International Nickel Company.] The matrix is austenitic, containing graphite flakes and small residues of the eutectic, alloyed ledeburite, between iron-chromium carbides and austenite.

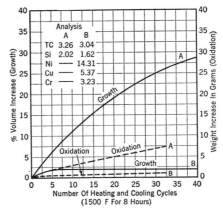

**Figure 6.64** Typical curves showing oxidation and growth of a plain cast iron (*A*) and an austenitic cast iron (*B*) at 1500 F (815 C). [Courtesy The International Nickel Company.]

Brinell hardness is about 100, and it increases approximately 20 points with each 1% chromium added. A limit of 2 to 3% chromium, however, is maintained as a rule in order to retain machinability, which is apt to be somewhat poor anyway because of the greater toughness of the austenitic matrix as compared with the usual pearlitic matrix of ordinary gray cast iron. By varying the carbon and silicon contents, mechanical properties can be secured in the range:

| | |
|---|---|
| Arbitration bar transverse strength | 1,800 to 3,000 lb |
| Arbitration bar transverse deflection | 0.2 to 1.0 in. |
| Tensile strength (1¼ in. section) | 25,000 to 45,000 psi |
| Brinell hardness | 130 to 250 |

The alloys also have fair impact values for this type of material, namely, 60 to 150 ft-lb for a 1.2-in. diameter, unnotched bar of the flake-graphite type on 6 in. supports, and 7 to 15 ft-lb Charpy V-notch for the nodular-graphite type. However, elongation of the material with flake graphite usually is quite low in a tensile test, averaging only a few per cent, despite the austenitic matrix.

Because these alloys corrode by a uniformly distributed surface oxidation, they cannot be used where this would be deleterious, as in the manufacture of high-purity sulfuric acid for example. The Type 2 (copper-free) alloy is preferred today, particularly where resistance to alkaline agents is the main consideration, and the advantages of the higher nickel content are desirable.

## QUESTIONS

1. If the $\beta$-phase in the copper-zinc system has the approximate formula CuZn and is body-centered cubic, what are the probable arrangements of atoms on the space lattice in the ordered ($\beta'$) and the disordered ($\beta$) forms? Give at least three advantages and three disadvantages of the alpha brasses in comparison with the alpha-beta brasses. Which of these two do you think would cost more?

2. The machinability of brass is increased by lead additions, by cold working, and by the presence of $\beta$-phase. Would you expect all of these methods to act in a similar manner? What would you expect their relative effects to be on cold workability, hot workability, strength, ductility?

3. Compare the three copper alloys, 70:30 cupronickel, admiralty metal, and aluminum brass, for condenser tube service. How does a stress-relief treatment act to minimize season cracking of copper alloys? Might a similar heat-treatment have any advantages in decreasing the tendency toward fire cracking?

4. In brass and bronze casting alloys, what is the element which must be controlled most carefully in making high quality castings? Suppose this element is present in more than allowable limits, can scrap or rejected castings from this metal be remelted and reused? Under what conditions? Does the presence of this element impart any advantages?

5. In formulating nonferrous casting alloys, certain characteristics should be kept under as careful control as is feasible economically. What do you think the more important of these would be, why is it desirable to control them, and what are some of the methods you think might be practicable for doing so? Are there any disadvantages to such controls?

6. From a metallurgical viewpoint, and without considering any effects of the allotropic transformation in iron, what would you expect the major differences to be between ferrite containing, say, 0.03 to 0.04 per cent carbon and copper containing 7 to 8 per cent silver? How would you expect this very low-carbon ferrite to differ metallurgically from ingot iron?

7. Inasmuch as the eutectoid composition transforms at a constant temperature, how is it possible to vary the size of the constituents in it, for example, the thickness of the lamellae? Would you expect the eutectoid and the eutectic to differ significantly in this respect, assuming the transformed structure to be lamellar in each case? Why do you think so? How do eutectoid and peritectoid transformations differ? In which of these should it be possible to get a more chemically uniform structure? Why do you think so?

8. Differentiate between eutectoid, hypereutectoid and hypoeutectoid structures and proeutectoid constituents. Can you think of any methods (other than changing composition) by which the amount of a proeutectoid constituent in the microstructure might be controllable?

9. In a 0.25% carbon steel, what complications are introduced, in discussing structural changes during cooling, by considering the peritectic reaction just below the melting point? Would you expect this transformation to introduce any problems in ingot solidification or hot rolling?

10. A low-carbon steel has graphitized in service. What are the disadvantages of this type of structure? Do you think graphitization of this type ever could be advantageous? Once graphitization has occurred, what can be done to restore the original structure? Would this be true of a structure like nodular iron or malleable cast iron also? Why do you think so?

11. Consider two forms of bimetal tubes, the first in which an admiralty metal tube is placed inside a steel tube by a slip fit followed by cold drawing and the second in which the two tubes are welded completely together throughout their surface of contact. Introduce atomic hydrogen into the outer surface of the steel either electrolytically or by a mild chemical reaction. The hydrogen then will endeavor to permeate the entire metal structure. Describe what you think will happen in the two examples of bimetal tubes cited. Will there be any difference if the admiralty is on the

outside and the hydrogen is introduced at the inner surface? Suppose the tubes are steel in the two examples?

12. Iron of reasonable purity, made by the technique used for ingot iron and containing substantially no carbon, had an unnotched impact transition temperature of −200 F. The addition of carbon is known to raise this transition temperature, so to get a quantitative measure, 0.005% of carbon was alloyed with this iron. The comparable transition temperature for this material was −250 F. Disregarding possible experimental error, what do you think might have caused the transition temperature to decrease rather than to increase as expected?

13. What are some of the advantages of carbon steel castings over nonferrous castings? If a carbon steel casting with a Widmannstaetten microstructure is normalized, how is the microstructure changed? How does this affect the properties? If the microstructure changes during normalizing, will this eliminate any defects—for example, blowholes or other unsoundness—introduced into the casting during its original solidification? How about tight cracks?

14. What are the objections to Invar as a material of low-thermal expansion (a) at atmospheric and subatmospheric temperatures, and (b) at elevated temperatures? Are these deficiencies correctable?

15. Why are cast irons used so widely? Why was the discovery of a technique for making nodular iron important? Does nodular iron have any real advantages over malleable iron? Why is an added annealing treatment frequently beneficial for nodular iron castings? What are some of the advantages and disadvantages of austenitic cast irons? In view of the austenitic matrix, is there any advantage to a nodular graphite structure in comparison to flake graphite?

## FOR FURTHER STUDY

1. *Metals Handbook,* 7th ed. (1948) and *Supplements,* and 8th ed., Vol. I (1961). Metals Park, Ohio: American Society for Metals.

2. *Constitution of Binary Alloys* by M. Hansen and K. P. Anderko. New York: McGraw-Hill, 1958.

3. *Phase Diagrams in Metallurgy* by F. N. Rhines. New York: McGraw-Hill, 1956.

4. *The Making, Shaping, and Treating of Steels.* Pittsburgh: United States Steel Co., 1951.

5. *S.A.E. Handbook.* New York: Society of Automotive Engineers, published yearly.

6. *Steel Castings Handbook,* C. W. Briggs (ed.). Cleveland: Steel Founders' Society of America.

7. *Cast Metals Handbook.* Chicago: American Foundrymen's Association.

8. *Cast Bronze* by H. J. Roast. Cleveland: American Society for Metals, 1953.

9. *Control of Steel Construction to Avoid Brittle Failure,* M. E. Shank (ed.). New York: Welding Research Council, 1957.

10. *The Alloying Elements in Steel* by E. C. Bain and H. W. Paxton. Metals Park, Ohio: American Society for Metals, 1961.

11. *Magnetic Properties of Metals and Alloys.* Cleveland: American Society for Metals, 1959.

# Principles Affecting Reactions Under Nonequilibrium Conditions

## TRANSFORMATIONS UNDER NON-EQUILIBRIUM CONDITIONS

CONSTITUTIONAL DIAGRAMS GIVE THE NUMBER AND composition of the phases stable at any temperature in an alloy of known composition, so long as it is substantially in equilibrium. However, they tell little about the distribution or state of aggregation of these phases and, generally, nothing about metastable transition phases which might form before the stable equilibrium phases under suitable conditions.

If a given alloy is displaced from equilibrium conditions in any manner, it tends to reattain equilibrium, usually by changing its microstructure, provided the energy needed is available. In some cases, however, a change toward a more stable condition takes place by a change in external shape, without any change in microstructure. Thus, a bar of metal subjected to unequal residual stresses may warp into a metastable shape for which these stresses are balanced.

The process of strain recrystallization is a change from a metastable structure, produced by deformation, toward a stable unstrained or recrystallized structure. As the structure proceeds toward the stable end-condition it may pass through intermediate or transition stages such as stress relief (recovery) and polygonization. A suitable energy, supplied usually by holding at a high enough temperature for a long enough time, is required for this change toward stable conditions to take place. Furthermore, even though the change has started, if the intensity of energy is decreased, for example by lowering the temperature, the process stops.

In discussing constitutional diagrams, several instances were noted in which structural changes took place during cooling. Typical examples are solid solubility which diminishes with temperature (for example, Figure 5.28) so the phase stable at the higher temperature must reject another phase rich in one of the components as the temperature decreases in order to remain stable, and the eutectoid inversion (Figures 6.20 and 6.36), which is the decomposition of a solid solution stable at elevated temperatures into two other phases stable at lower temperatures. For these reactions to occur, it is necessary for a single phase containing more than one component to become unstable and to tend to decompose into phases of differing compositions. This instability usually takes place because of a decrease in temperature, but it can occur, for example, because of a change in pressure, or because another component is added to the solid alloy by diffusion.

## THE PRECIPITATION PROCESS

Structural changes, in which a new phase of different composition is precipitated, take place by processes of nucleation and growth in accordance with definite patterns.[1] Whenever the composition changes, diffusion must be involved so the reaction is time dependent.

In any solid solution the composition is only uniform statistically. The occurrence by chance of small regions whose compositions fluctuate from the mean value is well recognized. Each of these is a region of short range order which, because it is a state of higher energy in a stable disordered solid solution, has a limited life and tends to disappear by diffusion in a relatively short time. However, when conditions are changed in such a way that the parent solid solution becomes unstable, the stability of these regions of composition fluctuation, sometimes called clusters, increases although their size and numerical distribution remain substantially as they were before the change in conditions occurred.

Precipitation reactions start very slowly. During this incubation period, in which nothing can be proved to happen, these small regions of short-range order which have compositions suitable for precipitation are growing in size, becoming precipitation embryos. Except in composition, however, these embryo regions still appear to be part of the parent solid solution lattice at this stage, although there may be a statistical alternation of structure between that of the matrix and that of the precipitating phase during

[1] See, for a more complete discussion, M. Cohen, *Trans. A.I.M.E.*, **212** (1958), 171–83; a good mathematical treatment is given by W. A. Johnson and R. F. Mehl, *ibid.*, **135** (1939), 416.

at least the later stages of the incubation period. At some stage in their growth these embryos become large enough to become stable and to grow under the conditions existing. They then become precipitation nuclei, with the general atomic arrangement of the precipitate. However, this atomic arrangement probably is distorted elastically if the nuclei still remain closely bonded to (coherent with) the parent lattice.[2]

When this formation of precipitation nuclei occurs by chance, with a statistically uniform distribution of particles, the precipitation is said to be uniform or continuous. This is illustrated schematically in Figure 7.1 (*top*).

It must be emphasized that the initial precipitation nuclei are stable only under the conditions of formation. For example, if the temperature is increased, it is probable that, at the higher temperature, some of the nuclei already formed become too small to remain stable, so they will redissolve. However, with increased time the precipitation nuclei grow by diffusion, so a time probably comes eventually at which they remain stable over a range of increasing temperatures.

### FORCES OPPOSING NUCLEATION

When a nucleus forms in the solid state it is subject to at least two restraints. One of these arises from the fact that the volumes of the matrix and of the precipitating phase usually are different, so the precipitating phase must work against an elastic distortion of the surrounding matrix in order to form. The second occurs because the surface atoms of the particle tend initially to be bonded both to the matrix lattice and to the precipitate lattice. This surface bonding presents no problems if the atomic spacing in the two lattices is identical, a situation which occurs rarely. In actual precipitation the surface atoms of both the precipitate and the parent lattices are strained elastically into some equilibrium relationship. These strains are known as coherency strains. So long as they exist, thereby

---

[2] The kinetics of precipitation from a supercooled solid solution are discussed thoroughly by G. Borelius, *Trans. A.I.M.E.,* **191** (1951), 477–84; the property changes accompanying precipitation are discussed well by A. H. Geisler, *ibid.,* **180** (1949), 230–54.

---

**Figure 7.1** (*opposite page*) Schematic representation of three general types of precipitation from a supersaturated solid solution by heat-treatment. (*top*) Uniform or continuous type of precipitation. (*middle*) Localized type of precipitation appearing preferentially at grain boundaries and along slip planes. (*bottom*) Nonuniform or discontinuous type of precipitation appearing preferentially at grain boundaries. [From R. F. Mehl and L. K. Jetter, courtesy American Society for Metals.]

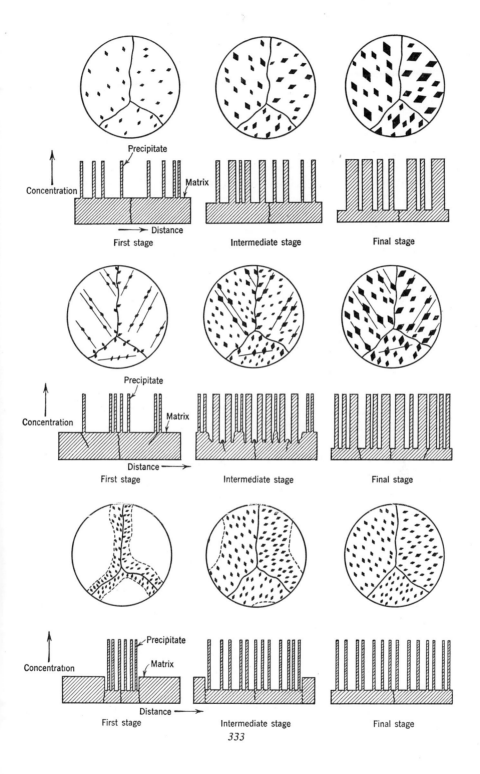

Precipitate

Concentration

Matrix

Distance

First stage          Intermediate stage          Final stage

Precipitate

Concentration

Matrix

Distance

First stage          Intermediate stage          Final stage

Precipitate

Concentration

Matrix

Distance

First stage          Intermediate stage          Final stage

333

holding the two lattices into a distorted alignment, the precipitating particle is said to be coherent.[3]

Coherency strains are a minimum for nuclei of certain shapes, as well as sizes, depending on the amount of distortion required by the two lattices involved to attain equilibrium. The nucleus, therefore, tends to assume that shape, for example, spheroid, plate, rod, or needle, which gives minimum coherency strains.

The nucleus also tends to form preferentially along those planes in the parent lattice which match best its own lattice arrangement in size and distribution,[4] because this tends to keep coherency strains to a minimum. However, because the match is almost never perfect, coherency strains increase as the nucleus grows in size until ultimately a critical size is reached at which the strain becomes too large and the particle breaks away from the matrix forming a physical interface. The strain energy in the particle and in the surrounding matrix then is changed to the energy of the dislocation array which forms the interface. Strictly, this initial formation of an incoherent particle is its first existence as a new phase but this strict interpretation is not always followed.

The nucleus which actually forms under the conditions existing, therefore, is at some period at least partially coherent with the matrix, has a preferred shape and bounding surfaces, and a definite lattice orientation with reference to the parent lattice, because all these factors tend to keep restraints to a minimum. Under some conditions these orientation relationships and preferred shapes are retained until the particles become visible metallographically. The structure then is known as a Widmannstaetten structure. Examples on almost a macroscale are shown in Figures 6.4 and 6.35. Under other conditions, however, the precipitation process can be quite complex, as will be discussed later, even when geometrical Widmannstaetten structures are formed. Also precipitation sometimes may occur in a nonhomogeneous manner rather than uniformly.

## DRIVING FORCE FOR PRECIPITATION

The driving force for the precipitation is the difference in free energy between the metastable parent lattice and the nucleus of the precipitating

---

[3] It should be noted that, if a transformation involves the production of ordering in a previously disordered solid solution, the ordered portion always is coherent with the disordered portion. Ordering, therefore, would be expected to produce marked hardening. See, for an analysis of this, D. Harker, *Trans. A.S.M.,* **32** (1944), 210–34.

[4] See, for example, the numerous papers by R. F. Mehl and co-workers in *Trans. A.I.M.E.,* starting about 1932, which show that coarse geometrically-arranged precipitates (of what are known as the Widmannstaetten type) always form with a common plane of nearest match for the precipitate and parent space lattices.

particle, but an activation energy is required to initiate the reaction. This difference depends on the amount of supercooling below the single-phase boundary at the time of nucleation. At this phase boundary or reaction temperature the driving force is low, the activation energy is high, and the size which an embryo must attain to become a stable nucleus is large, so the chance of formation is relatively small and precipitation is suppressed easily. As the solid solution alloy is supercooled into the two-phase field below the boundary the driving force increases, the activation energy decreases, and the required embryo size decreases so the likelihood of nucleation increases. However, as the temperature falls, the rate of diffusion also decreases. Consequently, the reaction rate plot of temperature versus holding time has a "C" shape (Figure 7.2) and the precipitation reaction starts most quickly and takes place most rapidly over some narrow range of temperatures at the nose of the curve.

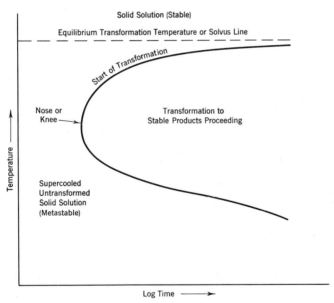

**Figure 7.2** Schematic reaction curve showing the time for precipitation to start at various temperatures.

As temperature increases above the nose, diffusion becomes more rapid, but the driving force becomes smaller and the stable nucleus becomes larger with a smaller chance of formation, so the reaction rate decreases. As temperature decreases below the nose, the driving force becomes larger and the required nucleus becomes relatively small with a large chance of formation, but diffusion is so slow that it controls the reaction rate. Presumably, also, at some temperature the critical embryo size required to form a stable nucleus may decrease to the size of a unit cell of the precipitate so that both the minimum size of embryo required to form a nucleus and therefore the number of potential nuclei approach a constant value.


## SIGNIFICANCE OF REACTION TEMPERATURE

Temperature, of course, is a relative factor, the exact level of which depends upon the characteristics of the particular alloy being considered. In some relatively high-melting alloys precipitation reactions take place only at high temperatures. Even at moderate temperatures of a few hundred degrees such reactions proceed at too slow a rate to be significant. If precipitation reactions take place below the recrystallization temperature it becomes possible to combine the effects of cold work and those of the precipitation reactions. Cold working after precipitation often is not too practical if the hardening from precipitation is great, although it is done with some alloys. In other relatively low-melting alloys, precipitation reactions may proceed at normal atmospheric temperatures and can be prevented only by cooling rapidly to subzero temperatures.

In general, if the solid solution which is stable above the solvus line or reaction temperature can be cooled to a low enough temperature faster than a certain critical rate, a precipitation reaction can be prevented completely, provided there is a composition change during the precipitation so diffusion is the controlling factor. By reheating this quenched alloy and holding at a constant temperature (sometimes called tempering, aging, or a precipitation treatment) the energy available for diffusion is supplied at a controlled level so the reaction can be made to proceed at a controlled rate. A low enough temperature is selected to permit the desired result to be secured in a reasonable time without danger of overshooting. An example of this was given in Figure 6.4.

Alternatively, the alloy can be quenched directly from the temperature range in which the parent solid solution is stable to the temperature at which it is desired to have the reaction take place. After partial or complete transformation at this temperature, the reaction can be stopped by cooling to a low enough temperature. The two methods do not always give the same results, however, possibly because greater thermal stresses are introduced by the quench-and-temper method.


## CONTROL OF QUENCHING RATE

During quenching from high temperature, heat removal is controlled by the insulating vapor film, formed on the surface of the hot metal, through which heat passes very slowly. Heat should be removed uniformly from the piece being quenched, so it is important that this gas film either be produced or be broken down almost at will. The quenching media used most commonly are: air, oil, water, and brine. Differences in quenching media are greatest for pieces of intermediate section thickness. If those thicknesses are small, say 0.25 in. or less, relatively little heat must be removed so the differences in quenching media are decreased. On the other hand, for steel masses above approximately 6 in. ruling section so much heat has to be removed that the cooling curve of the center is practically independent of the quenching medium used. Quenching also is done industrially in molten lead and molten salt baths,[5] if the final temperature desired is in the proper range. Hydrogen and helium have been used on an experimental basis.

The rates of quenching in these common media [6] are determined by the persistence with which the vapor or gas film adheres to the piece being quenched. In an air quench, the air film produced is quite persistent, and is broken away with difficulty. Hence the rate of cooling generally is comparatively slow, and about the only control over the process is given by the velocity of the blast of air. The higher the velocity, the greater the tendency for the air film to break away, and, therefore, the faster the rate of cooling.

In an oil quench, a considerable range of quenching rates can be secured by blending animal, vegetable, or mineral oils properly, sometimes with a small amount of water.[7] Preheated or precooled oil baths also can be used. The vapor pressure of the oil is particularly important, because this determines, to a great extent, the thickness of the oil vapor film produced on the surface of the piece being quenched. In Figure 7.3 is shown a series of pictures indicating the nature of film formation during the quenching of a specimen into oil. Under some conditions rates almost as slow as an air quench are possible, whereas under other conditions rates almost as fast as a water quench can be secured.

Although a water quench is usually a rather fast quench, a steam film which is comparatively difficult to break down forms on the surface of the piece. Hence, the use of water alone may give regions in which the rate of cooling is decreased considerably because of the close adherence of a portion of the steam film. If it is possible to break down this steam film readily, water quenching may be quite adequate. Pictures taken during a water quench (Figure 7.4) give some idea of the persistence of the steam film. By using rapidly flowing streams of water and by agitating

[5] See M. J. Sinnott and J. C. Shyne, *Trans. A.S.M.*, **44** (1952), 758–69.
[6] For typical values see G. Stanfield, *Second Report of the Alloy Steels Research Committee* (London: The Iron and Steel Institute, 1939), 299–318; also D. J. Carney, *Trans. A.S.M.*, **46** (1954), 882–924.
[7] G. Stolz, Jr., V. Paschkis, C. F. Bonilla, and G. Acevedo, *Journ. Iron and Steel Inst.*, **193** (London: 1959), 116–23.

**Figure 7.3**   High-speed photographs showing various stages in the quenching of a steel cylinder into oil. (*left*) Beginning of quench in transformer oil. (*middle*). 0.5 sec and 1 sec after beginning of quench in Russian oil. (*right*) 5 sec after the beginning of quench in Russian oil. Bubbles of oil vapor form quickly, but the vapor rapidly becomes a relatively thin layer which limits the rate of heat removal. [From *Technology Review,* courtesy I. N. Zavarine.]

**Figure 7.4**   High-speed photographs showing various stages in the quenching of a steel cylinder into water. (*left*) Start of 1550 F (840 C) quench. (*middle*) Types of reaction taking place within 2 sec after start of quench. (*right*) Appearance of specimen (actually quenched in 5 sec in brine) after quench is complete. Initially, a relatively thin film of steam surrounds the specimen and a few bubbles are given off. As this increases in turbulence the action becomes violent enough to tear off scale, and then gradually ceases as the heat is withdrawn. [From *Technology Review,* courtesy I. N. Zavarine.]

the work in the quenching bath, the film is broken down to a considerable extent; but the process is by no means certain because crevices and depressions in the piece may assist retention.

The addition of about 10% salt to the water-quenching bath gives a brine solution which is much more efficient than water as a quenching medium. In Figure 7.5 several pictures taken during a brine quench are shown. Apparently, during the formation of the steam film on the surface, crystals of salt, containing occluded water, tend to be deposited. As soon as these are formed on the hot surface of the specimen, they practically explode because of the rapid evolution of the water and its transformation into steam. The explosion of these crystals breaks the steam film away from the surface and, therefore, permits actual contact of the liquid and the specimen with an accompanying rapid removal of heat.

## DIFFUSIONLESS OR SHEAR TRANSFORMATIONS

If no composition change is involved in the transformation, diffusion cannot be a significant factor. However, structural changes to a more

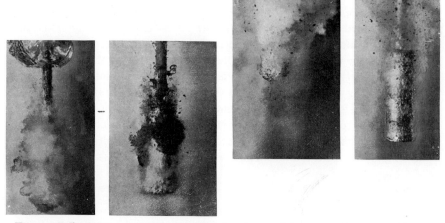

**Figure 7.5** High-speed photographs showing various stages in the quenching of a steel cylinder into brine. (*left pair*) Beginning of quench in 20% sodium chloride solution and in 5% sodium chloride solution. (*right pair*) Two-step quench. Specimen has been dropped to position shown after holding for two intervals of less than 0.25 sec in a higher position above the field of the photograph. Note the distinctive action which occurs in brine or caustic solutions. A cloud of salt crystals is thrown away from the surface with almost explosive violence. This effectively breaks down any films which have been formed. [From *Technology Review,* courtesy I. N. Zavarine.]

stable (lower free energy) configuration of the same composition still may nucleate during quenching by transformations involving shear alone.[8] These transformations can occur in pure metals, for example, at low temperatures, as well as in alloys.[9] In all cases the important factors are the increase in driving force as the material is supercooled below the equilibrium transformation temperature, and the decrease in size, and accompanying increase in number, of the nuclei required to initiate the transformation. Once initiated, the transformation proceeds rapidly, that is, the rate of growth of the new constituent is high, approximating roughly the velocity of sound or of a shear wave through the lattice. This is particularly significant because in a low temperature range other reactions which are diffusion-controlled can be initiated and can proceed only with difficulty, if at all, because of insufficient thermal energy.

These diffusionless transformations occur in many alloy systems. However, they often are called martensitic because the most important of them, and the first to be recognized, was the austenite-to-martensite reaction by means of which hardening takes place in rapidly cooled steels. Usually a new metastable crystalline constituent is formed (such as martensite in steels), by regular rearrangement of the lattice, in such a way that neighboring atoms do not change places and the relative displacements constitute uniform shears which probably do not exceed interatomic distances in magnitude.[10]

These transformations cannot be prevented below the initiating temperature, called $M_s$, which thus marks the lowest temperature to which the high-temperature phase can be supercooled. At this temperature, the combination of the available energy of thermal vibration and the difference in free energy between the old phase and the new phase (that is, the driving force resulting from supercooling) becomes sufficiently large to cause nuclei to form immediately. The higher the temperature of the quenchant, provided it is below $M_s$, the smaller is the number of nuclei and the larger is the size of the martensitic needles formed by the resulting growth. As the temperature of the quenchant or of the alloy is decreased, the number

[8] Much of the work in clarifying these transformations has been done by G. V. Kurdjumow and his co-workers; see, for example, *Journ. of Metals,* **11** (1951), 449–53, and *Journ. Iron and Steel Inst.,* **197** (London: 1961), 26–48; also B. A. Bilby and J. W. Christian in Ref. 5 at the end of this chapter; and *Journ. Iron and Steel Inst.,* **197** (London: 1961), 122–31.

[9] C. S. Barrett and his co-workers have done considerable work in this field, for example, Ref. 3 at the end of this chapter; *Trans. A.I.M.E.,* **175** (1948), 579–600; *ibid.,* **188** (1950), 1329–32; see also, *1948 Symposium on Transformations in Pure Metals,* National Research Council Committee on Solids, Cornell University; and *Trans. A.S.M.,* **49** (1952), 53–117.

[10] See P. M. Kelley and J. Nutting, *Journ. Iron and Steel Inst.,* **197** (London: 1961), 199–211.

of nuclei increases but their average temperature of growth decreases so their size tends to be smaller. Again, at some temperature the smallest nucleus which can form may become comparable in size to the unit cell. This temperature should mark the substantial end of the transformation, $M_f$, because all possible nuclei can be formed and the energy available for growth is larger than it can be at any lower temperature. The martensite transformation always extends over a temperature range, with the needles formed at each stage having a characteristic size.

As the martensitic constituent forms, it remains coherent with the lattice of the parent phase. The resulting coherency stresses increase as the particles increase in size and, with the volume change, impose elastic restraints on further transformation. When they reach some limiting magnitude, part of the coherency and of the coherency stress may be lost but enough remains to cause growth to stop even though the parent phase still may surround the growing constituent. If coherency is not lost the reaction probably is completely reversible,[11] that is, the martensitic constituent forming during cooling disappears during reheating. In some instances there is a temperature hysteresis, that is, after the reaction stops it does not start to reverse immediately, but only after there has been further reheating.

The change in free energy during cooling depends on the particular alloy system involved. If the driving force is not too large, it is possible to cool the material so rapidly that there is insufficient thermal vibration energy available and the rate of transformation approaches zero. Thus the martensitic type of transformation also has a rate curve with a nose or maximum rate even though this frequently cannot be shown experimentally in most systems of this type.

Plastic deformation and elastic stressing may initiate these transformations in some alloys at temperatures which are above $M_s$ but below a higher temperature sometimes called $M_d$, above which the parent solid solution phase is mechanically stabilized.[12] Some stabilization against transformation also can be produced by slow cooling above $M_s$, by interrupting quenching, or by holding in a suitable temperature range determined by the alloy. Essentially, this holding relieves some of the elastic coherency or transformation stresses so they no longer assist in initiating further reaction. When this type of stabilization occurs, the transformation does not initiate as soon as cooling is resumed but delays until the additional supercooling alone is sufficient to restart it.

---

[11] The formation of iron-carbon martensite is substantially irreversible so either a significant part of the coherency probably is lost or the necessary shear rearrangements are too complex to be reversible.

[12] Some aspects have been covered by L. S. Birks and E. F. Bailey, *Trans. A.I.M.E.*, **203** (1955), 179–82.

## ENERGY REQUIREMENTS FOR TRANSFORMATION

Phase transformations whether of the precipitation or the diffusionless type occur only if there is a reduction in free energy. Some of this excess free energy is needed (1) to rearrange the atoms in the nucleus into the configuration (orientation and/or spacing) of the new constituent; (2) to overcome the coherency strains at the surface of the nucleus; (3) to overcome the elastic constraints introduced by the difference in volume between equivalent regions of the matrix and the new constituent. This may be expressed by the equation

$$\Sigma F_p = V \frac{\Delta F}{N} + S\sigma + V\epsilon$$

where $\Sigma F_p$ = free energy change when a nucleus of the new constituent is formed from the matrix; $V$ = volume of the nucleus; $\Delta F$ = free energy change per gram atom of the new constituent (positive if heat is absorbed during its formation, negative if heat is given off); $N$ = Avogadro's number, atoms per gram atom; $S$ = surface area of the nucleus; $\sigma$ = interfacial energy per unit of area; $\epsilon$ = strain energy per unit of volume. The values of $V$ and $S$ vary with the size and shape of the nucleating particle but the value of $\epsilon$ is independent of the particle size.

The surface energy terms are reduced greatly if the perfection of matching between the atomic arrangements of the matrix and the precipitate is good and if coherent rather than incoherent particles are nucleated.

## EQUILIBRIUM VERSUS TRANSITION PRECIPITATES

In general, phase transformations occurring during cooling tend to give off excess free energy as heat. Hence, the equation for $\Sigma F_p$, which itself must be negative for the reaction to occur, has one negative and two positive terms. When the particle formed is so large that the last two (positive) terms approach the first (negative) term in magnitude, the stable constituent tends to form directly. This equilibrium phase usually has a structure significantly different from that of the parent solid solution and is separated from it by a high energy interface which normally is incoherent.

On the other hand the reaction follows the path of maximum net decrease in free energy so the nuclei which form in greatest abundance are those for which the sum of the free-energy contributions by all factors gives the greatest decrease. Hence, metastable constituents may form first, even though they have a higher volume free energy than the stable phase, simply because their space lattice matches better and deforms more readily to become coherent with the parent solid-solution matrix. Under these conditions the surface coherency has its lowest energy, and the transition phase is more stable when the coherent particles are small. This lower surface energy also tends to increase the rate of nucleation and hence the rate of precipitation. As the coherent particles of the transition phase increase in size, the surface energy requirements to maintain coherency increase, and the transition phase becomes less stable relative to the equilibrium phase. The equilibrium particles then tend to precipitate and the transition particles tend either to transform to the equilibrium phase or to redissolve.

The surface energy terms alone favor a spherical shape for a nucleus but a confined sphere is associated with a high volume strain energy. The volume strain energy approaches zero when the particle has the shape of a thin disc. However, such a shape has a high surface energy so its probability of formation is low unless its surface energy can be decreased by the application of coherency strains to improve the fit with the matrix lattice. The shape of an embryo thus can change as the coherent particle into which it transforms grows in size.

## EFFECT OF COLD DEFORMATION ON PRECIPITATION

If a metastable quenched alloy is cold worked before the second phase is precipitated, the reaction rate is more rapid because nuclei can form more readily in the localized strained regions in the vicinity of slip bands. This increases the number of nuclei and decreases the distance across which an atom must diffuse to reach a nucleus. Such localized precipitation is illustrated schematically in Figure 7.1 (*middle*). In addition, diffusion should be accelerated because of the internal stress gradients. If material in which there is a coherent precipitate is cold worked, there may be sufficient added strain introduced because of the slip to cause coherency to be lost and an actual physical interface to form. Under these conditions small particles of precipitate appear along the active slip planes. Later discussions on yield point and strain aging of low-carbon steels also illustrate examples of this.

## PRECIPITATION AT INTERNAL SURFACES

Precipitation also tends to be more rapid at other internal surfaces or discontinuities, such as grain boundaries or twin boundaries. This is generally the case because boundary energy is released by the formation of an embryo or nucleus at a boundary. Solute atoms also can diffuse more readily to a nucleus in a grain boundary than to one in the grain, and transformation stresses can be released more readily at the boundaries than within the grains so they do not constrain the reaction. Although less is known about this aspect than about precipitation within the grains it also is probable that, in some alloys at least, the concentration of solute atoms may be greater in the grain boundaries than elsewhere in the grains and there may be impurities in these regions which could either accelerate or retard nucleation. The nonuniform or discontinuous type of precipitation which may occur at internal surfaces for any of these reasons also is illustrated schematically in Figure 7.1 (*bottom*).

## HOMOGENEOUS VERSUS HETEROGENEOUS PRECIPITATION

In general, nucleation is said to be homogeneous when no foreign particles, surfaces, or other lattice irregularities are involved, so pure chance is the significant factor. Imperfections are higher energy arrangements and thus a type of instability in the perfect lattice. Consequently, they generally accelerate nucleation. This imperfection-accelerated nucleation is said to be heterogeneous, along with the cases of nucleation at internal surfaces, discussed above.

## QUESTIONS

1. Why do you think an alloy in a nonequilibrium condition tends to change its microstructure in an effort to reattain equilibrium? Do you think this is basically the same as, or different from, the warpage which often occurs when a bar with unequal residual stresses is heated? Can you give a simple method of producing unequal stresses in such a bar and causing warpage simultaneously?

2. Why isn't diffusion always the controlling step in a solid-state precipitation or decomposition reaction? Under what conditions is diffusion apt to be the controlling step?

3. Differentiate between short-range and long-range order. Does either occur in the liquid state? How about the solid state? Is the life of short-range order apt to be relatively long or short? Why? Under what conditions does the life of short-range order increase?

4. What probably happens during the incubation period of a precipitation reaction? Why is the effect on properties so small? When precipitation occurs, why is it noticed first at grain boundaries, regions of plastic deformation, and similar regions of imperfection?

5. What is meant by restraints to the formation of a precipitation nucleus? What does this mean from the viewpoint of energy? Compare a congruent and an incongruent transformation from the solid to the liquid state with a coherent and an incoherent transformation in the solid state.

6. Explain the factors determining the formation of a Widmannstaetten-type precipitate. Why isn't all precipitation of a Widmannstaetten-type? What do you think the present knowledge of this type of precipitation tells about the probable cooling cycle of meteorites, in which this type of precipitation first was found?

7. How does an activation energy for a reaction differ from the energy difference between the original stable parent lattice and the combination of the new stable matrix lattice and a precipitated particle, that is, of the structures before and after transformation?

8. Why do precipitation reactions in high-melting alloys seldom take place at moderate temperatures? In relatively low-melting alloys—for example, aluminum-base—why does precipitation sometimes occur during quenching? The statement sometimes is made that the hardness of a given alloy can be increased only so much regardless of whether the hardening is done by cold working, by precipitation, or by a combination of the two. What would be your opinion?

9. A reaction vessel, say 6 ft diameter, 15 ft long and 1 in. thick, with hemispherical heads and top and bottom manways, must be quenched from 2000 F to below 1000 F within 2 min. Calculations show that the water required to fill it is sufficient to remove the sensible heat of the metal. Do you think the quenching operation will be a success? Why? What other problems than heat removal might arise during such a quenching operation?

10. Why is quenching into a low-temperature molten salt bath less drastic than, say, quenching into water? Is heating by immersion in a high-temperature molten salt bath probably less drastic or more drastic than putting the part into a hot furnace? Why?

11. When a diffusionless shear transformation occurs, why can't it be stopped by more rapid quenching? By considering the factors responsible for this type of transformation, can you think of any way in which it might be stopped, at least in some regions? Why?

12. Why is the $M_d$ temperature higher than $M_s$? What would you expect to happen if an alloy which undergoes a diffusionless transformation is cooled rapidly to just above $M_s$ and then is cooled slowly? Why?

13. Why do transition precipitates occur under some conditions? What factors favor their formation? Are transition precipitates apt to occur under equilibrium conditions? Why?

14. In certain slowly cooled alloys, heterogeneous precipitation occurs first at the grain boundaries. At a somewhat lower temperature, homogeneous precipitation occurs randomly throughout the grain except in a band adja-

cent to the grain boundary where no precipitation at all occurs. What do you think is the reason for this lack of precipitation?

15. Random precipitation of oxides in copper occurs within the grains. When the metal is exposed to hydrogen at elevated temperatures, water vapor forms at the internal grain boundaries. How could the hydrogen and oxygen get together in these regions to react? Why doesn't the reaction take place at the edges of the oxide particles in situ?

## FOR FURTHER STUDY

1. *Age Hardening of Metals.* Cleveland: American Society for Metals, 1940.
2. *Precipitation from Solid Solution.* Cleveland: American Society for Metals, 1959.
3. *Phase Transformations in Solids.* New York: John Wiley & Sons, 1951.
4. *The Physical Chemistry of Metallic Solutions and Intermetallic Compounds,* Vols. I and II. London: Her Majesty's Stationery Office, 1959.
5. *The Mechanism of Phase Transformations in Metals.* London: The Institute of Metals, 1956.
6. *Thermodynamics in Physical Metallurgy* by L. S. Darken and R. W. Gurry. New York: McGraw-Hill, 1953.
7. *Thermodynamics in Physical Metallurgy.* Cleveland: American Society for Metals, 1950.
8. *Metal Interfaces.* Cleveland: American Society for Metals, 1952.
9. *Strengthening Mechanisms in Solids.* Metals Park, Ohio: American Society for Metals, 1961.
10. *Defects in Crystalline Solids.* London: The Physical Society, 1955.
11. *Metals Handbook,* 7th ed. Cleveland: American Society for Metals, 1948.

# 8 *Heat-Treatment of Steels*

## COMMERCIAL HEAT-TREATMENTS FOR STEELS

Heat-treatment is used to homogenize, to soften, or to harden steels. Except for the process annealing of cold-worked steel, which is comparable to the recrystallization annealing discussed in Chapter 3, each of these treatments starts with conversion of the structure to austenite. The temperature ranges used for austenitizing in each case are shown in Figure 8.1. In general, heating into the completely austenitic range is used to make the structure and composition more uniform but, the temperatures used must be kept as low as possible to avoid grain coarsening. For this reason the preferred annealing and hardening ranges are just above $A_3$.

**Figure 8.1** Critical-range diagram for iron-carbon alloys, showing normalizing, annealing, and hardening ranges. [From *Metals Handbook*, courtesy American Society for Metals.]

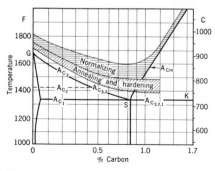

Heating hypoeutectoid steels just above $A_3$ produces a uniform austenite structure with minimum tendency toward grain growth. Lower temperatures in the $A_1$ to $A_3$ range should be avoided because the mixed structure of low-carbon (unhardenable) ferrite and higher-carbon austenite does not harden uniformly and hence has undesirable properties.

Heating hypereutectoid steels only above $A_3$ produces a mixed structure of uniform austenite and some spheroidized carbides, depending in amount on the carbon content. These steels would have to be heated above $A_{Cm}$ to dissolve all the carbides but this has two serious disadvantages. First, the high temperatures required coarsen the grain size once the restraining influence of the dissolved carbides is removed; such grain-coarsened steels harden deeply when quenched but also tend to crack. Second, the presence of free spheroidized carbides is desirable for increasing the wear resistance.

Annealing produces both homogenization and softening. As shown schematically in Figure 8.2a there are three stages to a full anneal: (a) reasonably slow heating to the austenitizing temperature; (b) holding to be sure of temperature uniformity (the empirical rule is not less than 1 hr for each inch of thickness); (c) slow cooling, usually in a furnace or a protected and insulated container. The metallographic structure produced contains ferrite and coarsely lamellar pearlite in substantially equilibrium proportions.

Normalizing is basically a standardizing treatment with softening incidental. The austenitizing temperature for normalizing is higher than is used for annealing, as indicated in Figure 8.1. The added homogeneity from heating hypereutectoid steels above $A_{Cm}$ outweighs the disadvantages. In addition, as shown schematically in Figure 8.2b, the heating rate is more rapid and the holding time at temperature somewhat shorter than in annealing; cooling is in still air and hence also is more rapid than in annealing. In careful practice, normalizing precedes hardening.

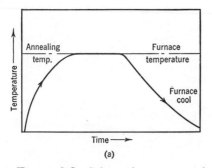 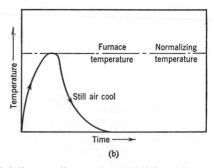

**Figure 8.2**   Schematic representation of full annealing and normalizing heat-treatments. **a.** Full annealing. **b.** Normalizing. In actual heat-treating the normalizing temperature would be higher than the annealing temperature (compare Figure 8.1).

The austenitizing ranges for hardening and annealing are roughly the same, but cooling for hardening must be rapid enough to harden to the depth required for the particular engineering application. Usually this produces a hardness level, with accompanying brittleness, greater than that needed so the part is tempered or drawn until the hardness reaches the range desired. This is indicated schematically in Figure 8.31. Cooling after tempering usually is not critical so far as the hardness is concerned.

In some instances tempering is carried to the point of complete softening by heating just below the critical range ($A_1$) in order to produce a structure composed of ferrite and spheroidized carbides. Such a softening heat-treatment often is called a process anneal, although this term usually means annealing cold-worked steel below $A_1$.

Hardening heat-treatments are most important, in industry, with automotive steels and tool steels both of which are discussed briefly later.

## TRANSFORMATION OF AUSTENITE AT A CONSTANT SUBCRITICAL TEMPERATURE

The eutectoid transformation of austenite in iron-carbon alloys to two-phase mixtures of ferrite and cementite is one of the most important metallurgical precipitation reactions both from a scientific and from a commercial viewpoint.[1] Understanding of this reaction was facilitated greatly by the thorough work of Davenport and Bain [2] using a method involving transformation at constant temperatures below the one at which the reaction takes place under equilibrium conditions, that is, according to the constitutional diagram.

As already has been pointed out, if an alloy of eutectoid composition (approximately 0.83% carbon) is held above $A_1$, it becomes entirely a homogeneous solid solution of carbon in gamma iron known as austenite. If this austenite is permitted to transform slowly on cooling, it changes to a lamellar mixture of ferrite and cementite known as pearlite. On the other hand, if it is cooled rapidly enough it tends to remain as supercooled austenite without transforming.

Davenport and Bain took advantage of this fact. Specimens first were held at a temperature above the critical range until they reached essential equilibrium as austenite. This sometimes is called austenitizing or an austenitizing treatment. Several specimens then were cooled to some temperature below the eutectoid temperature, and held at that constant temperature

---

[1] J. C. Fisher, *Trans. A.S.M.,* **42A** (1950), 201–41.
[2] E. S. Davenport and E. C. Bain, *Trans. A.I.M.E.,* **90** (1930), 117; see also E. S. Davenport, *Trans. A.S.M.,* **27** (1939), 837–86.

until transformation had proceeded for a variety of times and hence to a variety of degrees of completion. Other series were treated similarly at other isothermal holding temperatures, before finally quenching to atmospheric temperatures. Microscopical examination then allowed varied degrees of isothermal transformation to be recognized in the specimens, and the isothermal transformation diagram to be assembled. This type of heat-treatment, now sometimes known as austempering, is illustrated schematically in Figure 8.3. At any of these subcritical temperatures, the process of transformation could be followed either by microstructure, as illustrated schematically in Figure 8.4, or by the change in some other property, such as hardness, volume, magnetization, or resistivity (with the advantage that a continuous isothermal transformation record might be obtained from one experimental run on a single specimen). In any case, for each temperature a curve of per cent transformation versus time, similar to that shown in Figure 8.4 could be plotted.

By assembling the data from all of these curves, a plot of the temperature of transformation against the time, indicated on a logarithmic scale, of holding at that temperature can be made, as in Figure 8.5. Such curves are known as TTT curves, or because of their shape as S curves. For times to the left of the left-hand curve the austenite has transformed less than 1%, for times between the two curves it is in process of transformation, and for times to the right of the right-hand curve the transformation is more than 99% complete.

## AUSTENITE TRANSFORMATION PRODUCTS

The data contained in such a TTT curve for a 0.83% carbon eutectoid steel show, first of all, that any one of three different types of microstructures may be formed, depending upon the actual temperature at which the decomposition of austenite takes place.

1. The first is a lamellar mixture of ferrite and cementite, which has been named, in general, pearlite. This constituent forms at temperatures between the eutectoid temperature and approximately 1025 F (550 C), the knee of the TTT curve.

2. The second is a featherlike constituent, which is known as bainite after its discoverer. This constituent, often subdivided as upper bainite and lower bainite (which is more feathery) is formed when 0.83% carbon austenite decomposes at temperatures between approximately 1025 F (550 C) and 350 F (180 C).

3. The third is a needlelike constituent, martensite, the hardest constituent in heat-treated steels. It forms during cooling, at temperatures below

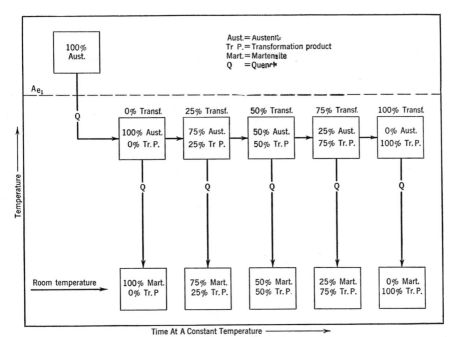

**Figure 8.3** Schematic representation of the progress of transformation of austenite at a constant subcritical temperature. Note how quenching to follow the course of the transformation changes any untransformed austenite into martensite.

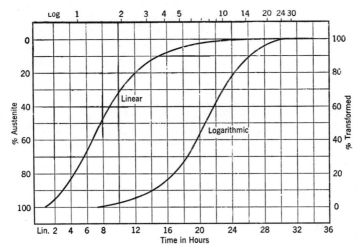

**Figure 8.4** Typical curve showing progress of transformation of austenite as plotted both on linear and on logarithmic scales. Note that the reaction starts slowly and dies out slowly, attaining its maximum rate near the 50:50 range. [From E. C. Bain, *Trans. A.I.M.E.*, **100** (1932), 2–27.]

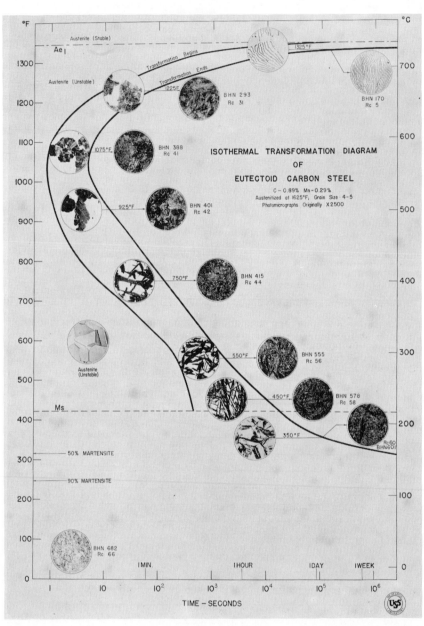

**Figure 8.5**  The S-curve of Davenport and Bain, as modified by later developments. [From *Atlas of Isothermal Transformation Diagrams,* copyright 1951 by United States Steel Corporation.]

$M_s$, approximately 350 F (180 C) for a 0.83% carbon steel, in increasing amount as the temperature is decreased to $M_f$.[3] Martensite is a transition phase between austenite and ferrite (plus cementite) produced by a diffusionless shear-type transformation in which the dissolved carbon does not have time enough to separate.[4] The heat-treatment capacity of steels depends on their ability to be cooled to $M_s$ as austenite and thus to avoid the isothermal transformation to pearlitic or bainitic structures. As discussed later, this is the basis of hardenability.

## PEARLITE

The generic name pearlite covers a wide range of austenite transformation structures, all of which are lamellar in nature. Those formed just below the eutectoid temperature, 1325 F (720 C), form very slowly, and are composed of coarse lamellae, as illustrated in Figure 8.6a. The hardness is low—for example, Rockwell C5. As the transformation temperature decreases, the rate at which the transformation occurs increases, and the thickness of the layers decreases. This decrease in thickness is accompanied by an appreciable increase in hardness to a maximum of approximately Rockwell C42. The most rapid rate of transformation occurs near 1025 F (550 C), the knee of the TTT curve. Transformation at this knee produces a nodular pearlite, which has the finest lamellae in a radiating or fan-like arrangement (Figure 8.6b), and is the hardest form. Pearlite lamellae always tend to contract to a roughly spherical form when held at a high enough temperature, so steels may show a marked tendency to yield spheroidized structures directly as an isothermal transformation product from austenite at temperatures approximately 50° to 100° F (25° to 50° C) below $A_{e_1}$.

The following statements are in general accord with the principles which have been given previously for reactions of this sort.

1. Transformations occurring under limited conditions of supercooling tend to produce relatively few nuclei. Because of the comparatively large amount of atomic mobility resulting from the high transformation temperature, each of these nuclei grows into comparatively large particles, resulting in coarse lamellae in the case of a eutectoid reaction. The reasons why a lamellar structure is formed are related to the fact that the austenite

---

[3] See A. B. Greninger and A. R. Troiano, *Trans. A.S.M.*, **28** (1940), 537–74.

[4] The over-all transformation characteristics of the steel may complicate this simplified picture. So long as there is austenite present it is at best only metastable and hence often can transform isothermally to bainite in some alloy steels if it does not transform to martensite. For example, see Figure 8.15.

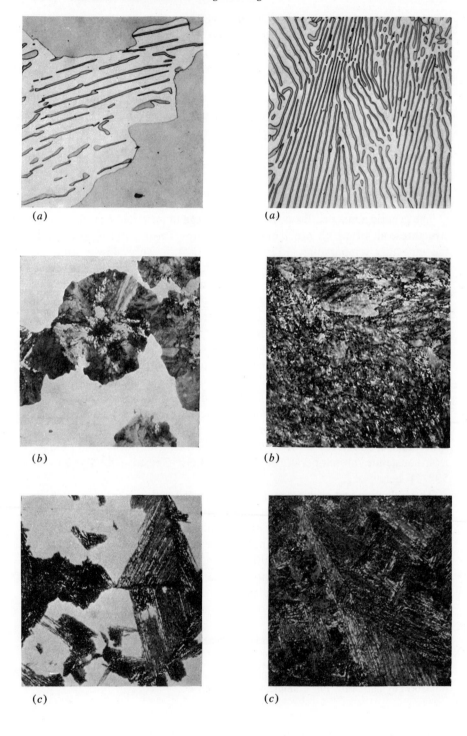

(a)                                    (a)

(b)                                    (b)

(c)                                    (c)

(*d*)

(*d*)

**Figure 8.6** Metallographic structures produced by decomposing a eutectoid steel (0.89% carbon, 0.29% manganese, remainder iron) at several different subcritical temperatures. (*left side*) Decomposed 50%. (*right side*) Decomposed 100%. All etched with saturated picral. (Original magnification ×2500; reduced approximately one-half in reproduction.) **a.** Coarse lamellar pearlite, transformed isothermally at 1325 F (720 C). **b.** Very fine nodular pearlite, transformed isothermally at 1075 F (580 C). **c.** Coarse feathery bainite, transformed isothermally at 850 F (455 C). **d.** Fine bainite, transformed isothermally at 550 F (290 C). **e.** Martensite, formed by quenching into brine. [Photomicrographs courtesy United States Steel Corporation Research Laboratory.]

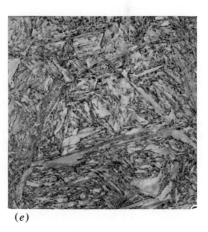

(*e*)

which is transforming is saturated in both carbon and iron, and hence reacts by getting rid of the carbon as cementite and the iron as ferrite, alternately.[5] In a sense, this is a supersaturation by compositional change which is just as powerful a producer of nuclei or of growing regions of a new phase as a supersaturation by temperature supercooling.

2. As the amount of supercooling increases, that is, as the transformation temperature decreases, the number of nuclei increases. Further, because of the lower atomic mobility, the size to which any nucleus can grow in a given time becomes less so the thickness of the lamellae produced tends to decrease. As the amount of supercooling increases, the reaction tendency

[5] This reaction has been studied thoroughly by R. F. Mehl and co-workers, for example, R. F. Mehl, *Trans. A.S.M.,* **29** (1941), 813–62; and R. F. Mehl and W. C. Hagel, *Progress in Metal Physics,* **6** (New York: Pergamon Press, 1959).

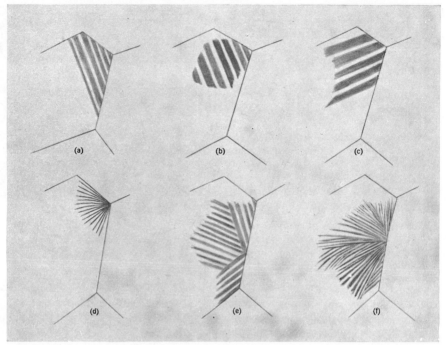

**Figure 8.7**   Possible modes of formation of pearlite as suggested by H. C. H. Carpenter and J. M. Robertson, and by H. Jolivet in *Journ. Iron and Steel Inst.,* **140** (London: 1939), 95. [Courtesy The Iron and Steel Institute, London.]

is favored, and this also decreases the time required for the reaction to start.

3. At still lower temperatures, diffusion becomes the controlling factor and the reaction rate again decreases.

The formation of pearlite from austenite by several possible methods is indicated schematically in Figure 8.7. Pearlite nucleates at the grain boundaries of homogeneous austenite;[6] probably the cementite layer forms first. If the austenite grains are large, several pearlite colonies may nucleate and grow in a single grain.

## BAINITE

The most rapid rate of formation of the constituent bainite occurs just below the knee of the TTT curve. The so-called upper bainite formed in

[6] Some kinetics aspects are given by J. W. Cahn, *Trans. A.I.M.E.,* **209** (1957), 140–44; see also J. H. Frye, Jr., E. E. Stansbury and D. L. McElroy, *Trans. A.I.M.E.,* **197** (1953), 219–24.

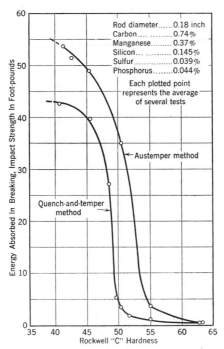

**Figure 8.8** Comparison of impact strengths at various hardnesses of quenched-and-tempered and austempered steels. [From E. S. Davenport, E. L. Roff and E. C. Bain, courtesy American Society for Metals.]

this temperature range in eutectoid plain-carbon steel is the coarsest form (Figure 8.6c) with a structure which is definitely acicular for ferrite but is granular for cementite. As the transformation temperature decreases, the fineness of the bainite increases (Figure 8.6d), and the rate of its formation decreases markedly.[7] Lower bainite sometimes is difficult to distinguish from tempered martensite in appearance.

The hardness of the bainite also tends to increase as the transformation temperature decreases, Figure 8.11. For a given hardness, bainite generally has poorer impact strength than tempered martensite of the same hardness, except in high-carbon steels in which the martensite contains cracks, for example, Figure 8.8. Even here bainite is inferior to martempered material,[8] which is discussed later. Bainite structures are only

[7] P. Vasudevan, L. W. Graham, and H. J. Akon, *Journ. Iron and Steel Inst.*, **190** (London: 1958), 386–91, discuss the kinetics for plain-carbon steels, and S. V. Radcliffe and E. C. Rollason, *ibid.*, **191** (1959), 55–65, discuss the kinetics for pure iron-carbon alloys.

[8] See N. P. Allen, L. B. Pfeil, and W. T. Griffiths, *Second Report of the Alloy Steels Research Committee* (London: The Iron and Steel Institute, 1939), 369–90.

practical for commercial applications when a small cross section (less than approximately 0.25 in. for a plain-carbon steel) permits isothermal heat-treatment to be used.

The formation of upper bainite probably starts with the separation of acicular ferrite, followed or accompanied by granular cementite, and that of lower bainite with the separation of supersaturated ferrite from which the carbon has not had time enough to separate.[9] The subsequent carbide rejection then gives lower bainite its feathery appearance. The rate of transformation is determined, to some extent at least, by the diffusion of carbon. This decreases markedly with a decrease in transformation temperature so the rate of the reaction also becomes appreciably slower. Nucleation is not restricted to grain boundaries, and the rate of transformation is nearly independent of grain size.[10]

## MARTENSITE

When plain-carbon or low-alloy austenite is cooled rapidly enough to prevent the nucleation of either pearlite or bainite it tries to transform to ferrite (plus cementite) but can only proceed part way because there is insufficient time available for the carbon to separate by diffusion. Hence nucleation of the diffusionless shear-type tranformation to the hard brittle constituent known as martensite takes place.[11] The needlelike product grows primarily during cooling.[12] When this martensite is prepared freshly, by cooling to a low enough temperature to prevent thermal decomposition, it etches light gray in color, Figures 8.6*e* and 8.9*a*, and usually is called white martensite. However, if it is quenched too slowly or is reheated even moderately it etches darker, because of some decomposition to ferrite and minute particles of carbide, and is known as black martensite (Figure 8.9*b*).

[9] This bainite reaction was reviewed by O. Krisement and F. Wever, pp. 253–63, Ref. 3 at the end of this chapter; see also R. F. Hehemann and A. R. Troiano, *Trans. A.I.M.E.*, **200** (1954), 1272–80, and *Metal Progress* (August 1956), 97–104; N. P. Allen, L. B. Pfeil, and W. T. Griffiths, *Second Report of the Alloy Steels Research Committee* (London: The Iron and Steel Institute, 1939), 369–90; and G. R. Speich and M. Cohen, *Trans. A.I.M.E.*, **218** (1960), 1050–59.

[10] J. Barford and W. S. Owen, *Journ. Iron and Steel Inst.*, **197** (London: 1961), 146–51.

[11] See, for example, M. A. Jawson, pp. 173–85, in Ref. 3 at the end of this chapter; also M. Cohen, E. S. Machlin, and V. G. Paranjpe, *Trans. A.S.M.*, **42A** (1950), 242–70; A. B. Greninger and A. R. Troiano, *Trans. A.I.M.E.*, **185** (1949), 590–98; J. C. Fisher, J. H. Holloman, and D. Turnbull, *ibid.*, 691–700; M. Cohen, *1962 Howe Memorial Lecture, A.I.M.E.*

[12] In certain alloy steels there is some evidence of isothermal martensite formation; see C. H. Shih, B. L. Averbach, and M. Cohen, *Trans. A.I.M.E.*, **203** (1955), 183–87; also B. L. Averbach and M. Cohen, *Trans. A.S.M.*, **41** (1949), 1024–57.

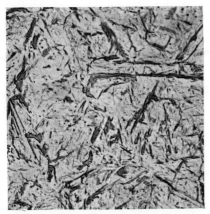

**Figure 8.9**   Metallographic appearance of various types of martensite. **a** (*left*). White, as freshly transformed by quenching. **b** (*right*). Black, after tempering at a low temperature. Etched with picral (×500).

The amount of martensite formed increases as the temperature to which the metal is cooled decreases within the temperature range $M_s$ to $M_f$. Thus, if a given piece of steel is quenched only to 200 F (95 C), a definite percentage of martensite forms. If it is quenched to 100 F (40 C), a greater percentage of martensite forms, and if it is quenched to room temperature, a still greater amount results. The martensite needles are appreciably harder than the layers in the bainite constituent. The hardness of a sample with a martensitic structure increases as the transformation temperature decreases,[13] probably because of the finer structure formed at the lower temperatures and the absence of accidental tempering effects. However, the hardness of martensite also decreases markedly, in both plain-carbon and low-alloy steels, as the carbon content decreases,[14] because with the high $M_s$, automatic tempering and carbide precipitation occurs even with the fastest cooling rates. This lower hardness, with the accompanying increase in ductility, is made use of in industry; for example, it permits weldments of many of these alloys to be used as welded—a post-weld softening treatment is not required.

The temperature over which austenite transforms to martensite, $M_s$ to $M_f$, is affected markedly by the carbon content (Figure 8.10) so it is not possible to retain untransformed austenite at room temperature for steels with the lowest carbon contents. The martensite transformation for these steels is completed at higher temperatures. However, with hypereutectoid

---

[13] See K. J. Irvine, F. B. Pickering, and J. Garstone, *Journ. Iron and Steel Inst.,* **196** (London: 1960), 66–81.

[14] R. H. Aborn, *Trans. A.S.M.,* **48** (1956), 51–85.

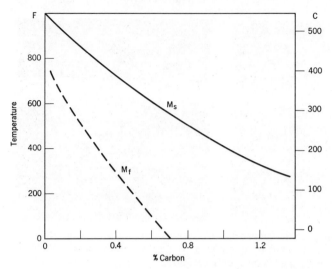

**Figure 8.10** Change in $M_s$ and $M_f$ temperature of carbon steels with carbon content. [After A. R. Troiano and A. B. Greninger in *Metals Handbook*, courtesy American Society for Metals.]

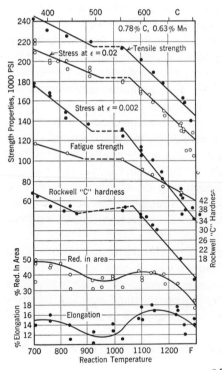

**Figure 8.11** Mechanical properties of decomposition products of austenite as a function of their temperature of formation for a plain-carbon eutectoid steel (0.78% carbon, 0.63% manganese, 0.014% phosphorus, 0.030% sulfur, 0.18% silicon, remainder iron), austenitic grain size before quenching 8 to 9. All specimens furnace cooled after reaction. [From M. Gensamer, E. B. Pearsall, W. S. Pellini, and J. R. Low, Jr., courtesy American Society for Metals.]

carbon steels or with low-alloy steels, it is not difficult to retain small amounts of austenite at room temperature, and in fact, cooling below room temperature often must be resorted to if complete transformation to martensite is desired.

## THE HARDNESS OF THE PRODUCTS OF AUSTENITE TRANSFORMATION AT CONSTANT TEMPERATURE

In Figure 8.11 are plotted several mechanical properties of the various constituents into which austenite transforms directly, as a function of the transformation temperature at which they are produced. Although, in general, the hardness and strength of the constituents increases as the transformation temperature decreases, the curve is by no means a smooth one. The properties involving ductility also vary markedly with transformation temperature and attain an optimum value for a specific range of reaction temperatures for both the pearlite and bainite reactions.[15]

## THE EFFECT OF CARBON CONTENT ON THE TRANSFORMATION OF AUSTENITE

The simple TTT diagram in Figure 8.5 is valid only for a eutectoid steel. More complicated diagrams result whenever the carbon content decreases below or increases above the eutectoid composition, because of the separation of proeutectoid ferrite (Figure 8.12) or cementite (Figure 8.13).

In general, the knee of the curve is shifted somewhat toward shorter times (that is, to the left) if the carbon content is either lower or higher than the eutectoid composition. This decreases the time available to cool below the knee of the curve. In other words, a faster cooling rate is required to miss the knee of the curve entirely. Also, above the knee an additional line appears on the diagram to indicate the precipitation of the proeutectoid constituent from austenite.

The initial separation of the proeutectoid constituent occurs at the austenite grain boundaries. Carbon diffusion, either toward the remaining austenite, if ferrite precipitates, or away from the remaining austenite, if carbide precipitates, must accompany this separation.

Below the knee of the curve the initial formation of a proeutectoid constituent is suppressed except in alloys containing less than 0.5% car-

[15] See also E. S. Davenport, *Trans. A.I.M.E.,* **209** (1957), 677–88.

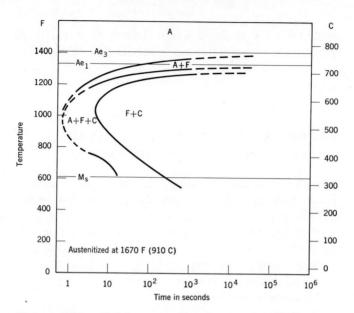

**Figure 8.12** TTT-Curve typical of a hypoeutectoid steel containing 0.50% carbon, 0.91% manganese. [From *Atlas of Isothermal Transformation Diagrams,* copyright 1951 by United States Steel Corporation.]

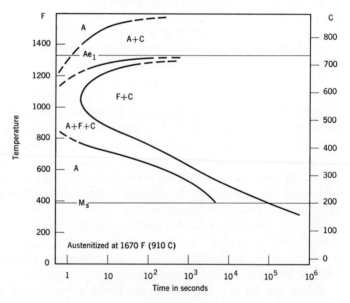

**Figure 8.13** TTT-Curve typical of a hypereutectoid steel containing 1.13% carbon, 0.30% manganese. [From *Atlas of Isothermal Transformation Diagrams,* copyright 1951 by United States Steel Corporation.]

362

bon.[16] Instead the austenite transforms isothermally directly to bainite.

In addition (Figure 8.10), the martensite transformation $(M_s)$ is depressed in almost a linear manner from near 940 F (505 C) for a 0.10% carbon steel to roughly 250 F (120 C) for a 1.4% carbon steel.[17] Likewise, the temperature at which the transformation is substantially complete $(M_f)$ decreases in a similar manner. For example, in a 0.20% carbon steel the $M_f$ temperature probably is above 650 F (345 C), and in a 0.50% carbon steel above 210 F (100 C), whereas in a high-carbon steel it may be even a little below room temperature. For this reason, in the lower carbon steels the martensite formed usually is tempered significantly during the quenching cycle itself. This is one reason why the ductility of martensite increases so markedly as the carbon content is decreased.[18]

## AUSTENITE STABILIZATION

In high-carbon steels, as well as in many alloy steels, it is possible to stabilize some of the austenite and thus to get only incomplete transformation to martensite.[19] This stabilization occurs when the cooling of austenite is halted within the temperature range of martensite transformation. After stabilization occurs, the remaining austenite does not start to transform immediately to martensite when cooling is resumed but instead must be cooled to a lower temperature. Thus, in high-carbon steels, or in alloy steels in which the normal $M_f$ is not greatly above room temperature, interrupted cooling may result in retained (stabilized) austenite when the alloy finally reaches ambient temperature.[20]

It is known that stabilization produces no compositional change in the austenite. Consequently, it seems probable that it is largely the result of the relaxation of the elastic stresses produced in the austenite by the earlier formation of martensite needles. It is known that these elastic stresses favor nucleation of new martensite needles when the temperature is lowered normally. Therefore, their relaxation would remove favored

[16] See O. Krisement and F. Wever, Ref. 3 at the end of this chapter.

[17] See A. R. Troiano and A. B. Greninger, pp. 263–66, in Ref. 1 at the end of this chapter; also W. Steven and A. G. Haynes, *Journ. Iron and Steel Inst.*, **183** (London: 1956), 349–59. Martensite transformation versus temperature can be calculated with reasonable accuracy; see R. A. Grange and H. M. Stewart, *Trans. A.I.M.E.*, **167** (1946), 467–91.

[18] R. H. Aborn, *Trans. A.S.M.*, **48** (1956), 51–85.

[19] See S. G. Glover and T. B. Smith, pp. 265–76, in Ref. 3 at the end of this chapter; also W. J. Harris, Jr., and M. Cohen, *Trans. A.I.M.E.*, **180** (1949), 447–76.

[20] M. Cohen, *Trans. A.S.M.*, **41** (1949), 35–94, has discussed retained austenite thoroughly.

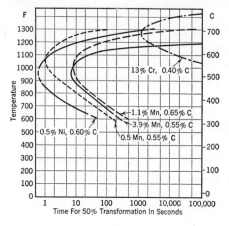

**Figure 8.14** Comparative time intervals for 50% transformation in steels containing different amounts of nickel, manganese, and chromium. Note that a shift of the curve toward the right indicates a slower rate of transformation and hence a greater tendency for an austenitic or a martensitic structure to be produced. [From *U.S.S. Carilloy Steels*, copyright 1948 by United States Steel Corporation.]

nucleation sites and make additional subcritical cooling necessary before other less-favored sites could become operative.

## EFFECT OF ALLOYING ELEMENTS ON AUSTENITE TRANSFORMATION

Alloying elements, except cobalt,[21] dissolved in austenite shift the nose of the TTT curve toward the right, that is, toward longer times. This is illustrated in Figure 8.14 for different amounts of nickel, manganese,[22] and chromium in steels containing 0.40 to 0.65% carbon. Thus, the rate of transformation of austenite, on cooling, to mixtures of ferrite and cementite is slower in a typical alloy steel than in a plain carbon steel. This effect is in addition to the effects of the alloying elements on the eutectoid composition and temperature which were mentioned in Chapter 6.[23]

The temperature of the knee of the curve, in relation to the equilibrium transformation temperature, usually is changed very little by the addition of moderate amounts, up to 5%, of alloying elements. However, the $M_s$ temperature, at which martensite starts to form on cooling, may be affected appreciably, usually being lowered.[24] The TTT curve itself also may become more complex because of the occurrence of additional reactions or because some alloying elements have a much greater effect on the rate of

[21] The effects of cobalt were studied by E. Davenport, *Trans. A.S.M.*, **27** (1939), 837–86; and by M. Hawkes and R. F. Mehl, *Trans. A.I.M.E.*, **172** (1947), 457–92.

[22] See also M. L. Picklesimer, D. L. McElroy, T. M. Kegley, Jr., E. E. Stansbury, and J. H. Frye, Jr., *Trans. A.I.M.E.*, **218** (1960), 473–80.

[23] See also, R. A. Grange, P. T. Kilhefner, and T. B. Bittner, *Trans. A.S.M.*, **51** (1959), 495–513.

[24] For example, the effect of chromium is discussed by J. B. Bassett and E. S. Rowland, *Trans. A.I.M.E.*, **180** (1949), 439–46; and the effect of nickel by C. A. Clark, *Journ. Iron and Steel Inst.*, **193** (London: 1959), 11–12. This subject is discussed more generally by R. Brook, A. R. Entwisle, and E. F. Ibrahim, *Journ. Iron and Steel Inst.*, **195** (London: 1960), 292–98.

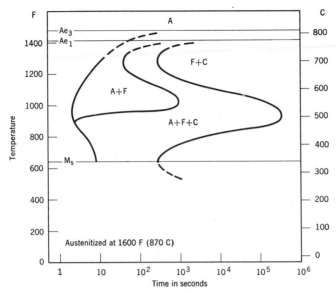

**Figure 8.15** TTT-Curve typical of a hypoeutectoid steel containing 0.33% carbon, 0.45% manganese, 1.97% chromium. [From *Atlas of Isothermal Transformation Diagrams*, copyright 1951 by United States Steel Corporation.]

formation of pearlite [25] than on the rate of formation of bainite. Thus an alloy steel often can be cooled at such a rate that the austenite has no tendency to transform to pearlite and instead transforms to bainite either partially or completely. This is illustrated in Figure 8.15 for a steel containing 0.33% carbon, 0.45% manganese and 1.97% chromium.

### AUSTENITIC STEELS

In addition, some transformable alloy steels can be cooled to room temperature without even transforming to martensite. Such steels then are austenitic at room temperature and would behave more like a nonferrous than a ferrous alloy. However, austenitic steels often are not truly stable and transform to martensite during cold working or during cooling to subatmospheric temperatures. In iron-base alloys the face-centered cubic austenitic structure usually is nonmagnetic, so the possibility arises of such a steel developing magnetic properties at low temperatures, step-by-step with transformation, instead of progressively by passing through a Curie point.

[25] Both the rate of nucleation and the rate of growth may be affected; R. W. Parcel and R. F. Mehl, *Trans. A.I.M.E.,* **194** (1952), 771–80, discuss this for molybdenum and nickel.

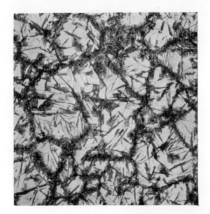

**Figure 8.16** Metallographic structures typical of a Hadfield high-manganese steel (13% manganese, 1.3% carbon, remainder iron), used for wear resistance. **a** (*top left*). Cooled slowly from 1850 F (1010 C). Etched with saturated picral (×500). Structure predominantly martensitic with some carbides occurring both at the grain boundaries and as needles within grains. **b** (*top right*). Water-quenched from 1850 F (1010 C). Etched with picral (×500). Structure completely austenitic. **c** (*bottom*). Water-quenched from 1850 F (1010 C) and cold-reduced 25%. Etched with picral (×1000). Strain or deformation lines in work-hardened austenite. Original magnifications are given, photomicrographs reduced approximately one-half in reproduction. [Photomicrographs courtesy United States Steel Corporation Research Laboratory.]

For example, Figure 8.16, shows various structures of a high-manganese wear-resisting steel. If the composition is within the range: 0.95 to 1.40% carbon, 10 to 14% manganese, 0.3 to 1.0% silicon, remainder iron, the steel is substantially austenitic between 1830 and 1920 F (1000 to 1050 C) and remains austenitic when water quenched, with considerable strength and toughness. When cooled slowly, or when reheated above about 750 F (400 C) the structure becomes predominantly martensitic with some free carbides. When the structure is completely austenitic, the alloy work-hardens readily, with the formation of the usual strain or deformation lines and also probably with some transformation of the austenite to martensite.[26] It is these work-hardening characteristics which give it its excellent resistance to abrasion under heavy loading. Under light loading it is not significantly better than the lower alloy steels. The carbon helps to retain and stabilize the austenite; decarburization gives a hardened surface in this alloy.

Fully austenitic steels are desirable at room temperature only for a few wear- or corrosion-resisting applications and for parts demanding extremely low notch-sensitivity in impact, a category which increases in importance where service is below room temperature. For many applications, however, like ball-bearings, case-hardened gears, and high-speed tool steels, it may be desirable to retain some austenite after quenching. Consequently, the mechanical properties of the austenite decomposition products generally are of more interest in engineering than those of austenite itself.

The main effect of moderate amounts of alloying elements, from the practical viewpoint, is to permit a given structure or property to be produced by a slower rate of cooling and by a lower carbon content than could be used with a plain-carbon steel.[27] This is of considerable importance because the more drastic the rate of cooling and the higher the carbon content, the greater are the internal stresses produced by cooling, and hence the greater the tendency for the piece to crack during quenching. The use of a slower rate of cooling tends to decrease the possibility of failure by cracking, and gives a greater leeway in quenching time to produce a given structure.

## EFFECT OF GRAIN SIZE ON AUSTENITE TRANSFORMATION

The grain size of austenite affects the rate at which it transforms, even though identical quenching temperatures are used. This effect is illustrated in Figure 8.17, in which the initial rates of transformation at the knee of the curve are indicated for both coarse-grain and fine-grain steels. A fine-grain steel (G.S. 8 to 9) transforms much more rapidly at the knee of the curve than a coarse-grain steel of identical composition. This may be explained by the greater amount of grain boundary material in a given volume of the fine-grain steel as compared to a coarse-grain steel, as illustrated in Figure 8.18. Such internal surfaces produce regions favorable for trans-

---

[26] K. R. Buhr, S. L. Gertsman, and J. Reekie, *Trans. A.S.M.,* **49** (1957), 706–17.
[27] For example, the effects of the important alloying element, molybdenum, are discussed well by J. M. Hodge, J. L. Giove, and R. G. Storm, *Trans. A.I.M.E.,* **185** (1949), 218–27.

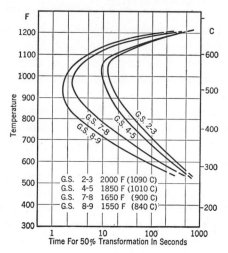

**Figure 8.17** Comparative time intervals for 50% transformation in a single steel as heated to four different temperatures in the austenitic range prior to transformation, with corresponding difference in austenitic grain sizes (G.S.). Note how the curve for the finest grain steel (G.S. 8 to 9) is displaced to the left, thus indicating a greater tendency to transform to pearlite than that of the coarsest grain steel (G.S. 2 to 3). Compare Figure 8.27. [From *U.S.S. Carilloy Steels,* copyright 1948 by United States Steel Corporation.]

formation from which the new phase can grow. In a fine-grain steel, therefore, not only are there more centers at which the new phases can start to grow, but also less material in a given grain to be consumed. Both of these conditions increase the rate of transformation at the knee of the curve. This is not true at lower temperatures in the bainite region.

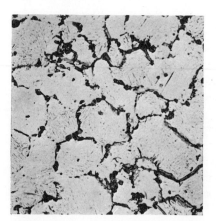
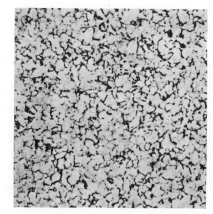

**Figure 8.18** (*left*) Coarse and (*right*) fine austenitic grains delineated by nodular pearlite as a result of quenching at a rate just slower than the critical cooling rate. Etched with picral (×100). [Photomicrographs courtesy United States Steel Corporation Research Laboratory.]

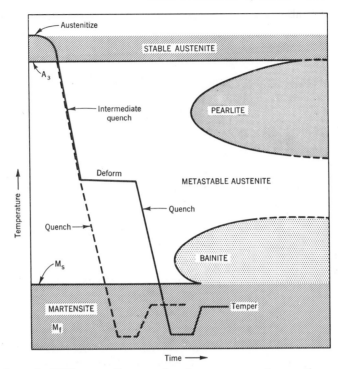

**Figure 8.19** Schematic TTT-curve diagram showing sequence of operations in ausforming (solid line) and in conventional heat-treatment (dashed line). [From D. V. Gullotti, *Materials in Design Engineering,* September 1960, with permission.]

## AUSFORMING

An excellent combination of strength and ductility can be secured by deforming austenite plastically before it transforms to martensite (or bainite). This is known as ausforming.[28] Two requirements must be met for ausforming to be possible. First, the TTT diagram for the steel must have a deep "bay" region between the pearlite and bainite knees. Second, these knees must be displaced toward longer times so no isothermal transformation takes place during the process. It then is possible to quench steels of this type to an intermediate temperature at which austenite is metastable, to deform the austenite mechanically at this temperature, and finally to quench the deformed austenite to a martensite structure. These requirements and steps are illustrated schematically in Figure 8.19.

[28] See D. J. Schmatz, J. C. Shyne, and V. F. Zackey, *Metal Progress,* **76** (1959), 66–69; D. V. Gullotti, *Materials in Design Engineering,* **52** (1960), 16–18; R. A. Grange and J. B. Mitchell, *Metals Engineering Quarterly,* **1** (1961), 41–53.

As compared to a conventional quench-and-temper treatment, the ausforming treatment produces a very fine highly strained martensitic structure. With some steels, tensile strengths of the order of 450,000 psi have been produced with a yield strength near 350,000 psi and an elongation near 10%.[29] In general, the strength properties produced by ausforming are about 35% higher than those produced by the conventional quench-and-temper method and even greater improvement may be possible ultimately.

## TRANSFORMATION OF AUSTENITE DURING CONTINUOUS COOLING

Although TTT curves give information on austenite transformation at constant temperatures, austenite usually is transformed industrially during some sort of cooling cycle,[30] compare Figures 8.20 and 8.21. This cooling is secured by using various types of media—for example, air, oil, water, brine, molten salt, or molten metal. Some of the complications which may arise were discussed briefly in Chapter 7.

The TTT curve cannot be used directly to predict, with any reliability, what will happen during cooling unless only the sensible heat of the specimen has to be removed so the cooling can be continuous, producing a fully martensitic or austenitic structure, depending on the alloy. The sizable amount of heat evolved when austenite transforms to pearlite and the much smaller amount given off by the bainite transformation are sufficient to interrupt the quench, if not to increase the temperature somewhat if these reactions start during cooling. Consequently, large sections which contain considerable heat, steels which transform rapidly and hence have limited time for heat removal, and quenching media which produce insulating layers of vapor on the surface of the quenched part and have limited ability to remove heat for other reasons—for example, because their own temperature is too high—all can introduce complicating factors into the quenching of steels by making it more difficult to remove heat and so to control the structural transformations. Interruptions in quenching which occur in the bainite transformation region may be enough to stabilize the austenite and to stop the bainite reaction completely, and possibly the martensite reaction as well, depending on the alloy composition and the transformation conditions.

[29] J. C. Shyne, V. F. Zackey, and D. J. Schmatz, *Trans. A.S.M.,* **52** (1960), 346–61.

[30] For a discussion of various aspects, see R. A. Grange and J. M. Kiefer, *Trans. A.S.M.,* **29** (1941), 85; C. A. Liedholm, *Trans. A.S.M.,* **38** (1947), 180–208; W. I. Pumphrey and F. W. Jones. *Journ. Iron and Steel Inst.,* **159** (London: 1948), 137–44.

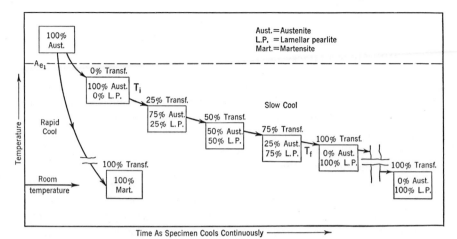

**Figure 8.20** Schematic representation of transformation of austenite during continuous cooling at a given rate. Transformation does not begin until temperature $T_i$ is reached. A certain amount of austenite transforms at each temperature, as it is reached during cooling, to a pearlite of corresponding fineness, the entire transformation being complete by the time temperature $T_f$ is reached. The course of the transformation can be followed by quenching to change any untransformed austenite into martensite. Note that a rapid cool, faster than the critical cooling rate, completely prevents the formation of lamellar pearlite, producing martensite instead. [After R. A. Grange and J. M. Kiefer.]

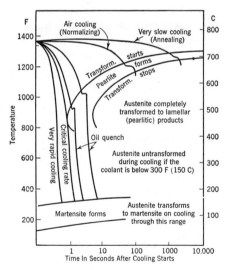

**Figure 8.21** Schematic representation of the relation between cooling rate and temperature of initial transformation of cooling as indicated by the TTT-curve. [From *U.S.S. Carilloy Steels,* copyright 1948 by United States Steel Corporation.]

## EFFECT OF RATE OF COOLING ON AUSTENITE TRANSFORMATION

The changes taking place in austenite for various rates of cooling are summarized in relation to the TTT curve for a eutectoid steel by Figure 8.21. Application of the concepts to other TTT curves should be straightforward. Strictly, relationships between cooling rate and microstructure can be deduced only for specimens which cool essentially uniformly throughout the entire section.

When the rate of cooling is very slow, such as would result from cooling in a furnace or in some insulating material during annealing, the rate of energy removal from the specimen is low so transformation tends to begin at a comparatively high temperature. Austenite, in this range of temperature, transforms to a structure which is essentially all coarse pearlite. The transformation itself also gives off a sizable amount of heat energy so this slows up the rate of cooling even more, and therefore tends to give a fairly uniform structure.

As the rate of cooling is increased, as by cooling in air during normalizing for example, the transformation tends to begin more quickly and at a lower temperature. Both of these conditions result in a finer pearlitic structure, but again the evolution of heat energy slows up the reaction to some extent.

As the rate of cooling is increased further, by liquid quenching, the transformation tends to take place still more rapidly and at a still lower temperature. Metallographic structures typical of these intermediate stages for oil quenching are illustrated in Figure 8.22. If the rate of cooling is increased to such an extent that the austenite is cooled below the knee of the curve, approximately 1025 F (550 C), in a shorter interval of time than is required for the transformation to begin, the austenite does not transform to pearlite at all but is carried to the much lower $M_s$ temperature before transformation (to martensite) begins.

### CRITICAL COOLING RATE

The rate of cooling which is just fast enough to avoid the formation of any lamellar constituent is known as the critical cooling rate. For rates of cooling just slower than this rate, a certain amount of very fine or nodular pearlite is produced; but the entire alloy may or may not transform to the lamellar constituent depending upon the exact rate of cooling and the energy released by the portion which transforms. For rates of cooling faster than the critical cooling rate there is no transformation until the region

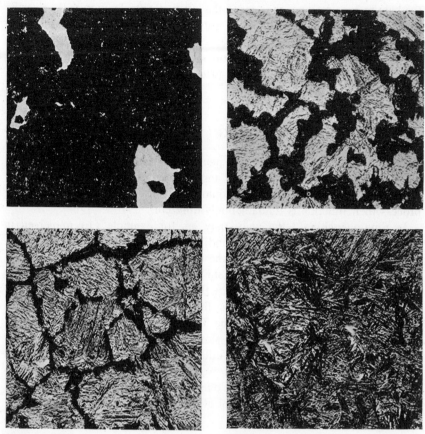

**Figure 8.22** Photomicrographs of eutectoid iron-carbon alloys which have transformed partly to dark-etching nodular pearlite and partly to light-etching martensite during direct oil-quenching to room temperature. Etched with picral (×500). Increased cooling rates give decreased amounts of nodular pearlite.

of initial martensite formation, $M_s$, is reached, at approximately 350 F (180 C) for a eutectoid steel, unless the specimen is quenched into a bath held at a temperature higher than this and held in that bath until transformation to bainite is complete. It must be remembered, of course, that the rate of removal of heat always is greater at the surface than in the interior of the piece and that for this reason the thickness of the section must be considered in applying these concepts, particularly if the depth of martensitic hardening is to be more than a thin skin.

Because of the shape of the TTT curve in plain-carbon steels, no continuous cooling schedule can cause the initial stage of transformation of austenite to result in the formation of bainite. Some form of interrupted cooling must be used in order to produce it. In some alloy steels, however, the bainite knee may occur so far to the left that a steel can miss the pearlite transformation during cooling and still transform partially or completely to bainite (compare Figure 8.15), depending largely on how much the heat evolved by the initial transformation slows down the cooling and allows stress relief to occur, to stabilize the austenite.

## INTERRUPTED QUENCHING

Certain methods of interrupted quenching, notably time-quenching and martempering, have been developed and are used to some extent in industry. Although they are actually developments from the basic austempering process their function is fundamentally different.

In time-quenching [31] the piece may be, for example (1) immersed in water for a definite period of time and then allowed to cool in air or transferred to an oil bath to complete the quench, or (2) immersed in water for a definite time, removed and held in air for a definite time, and then returned to the water bath to complete the quench.

The purpose of such treatment is, first, to cool the specimen quickly to a temperature below the knee of the TTT curve, thus retaining austenite, and then to allow it to cool more slowly so stresses are reduced and/or portions of it can transform to bainite as well as to martensite. By this means, combinations of mechanical properties can be secured which otherwise would not be obtainable. The dimensions and shape of the piece determine how deeply these structural effects penetrate.

## MARTEMPERING

Martempering is a somewhat similar process indicated schematically in Figure 8.23, which was placed on a practical commercial basis by the development of a molten salt bath [32] which cools the piece rapidly to the temperature range of 400 to 500 F (200 to 250 C), where metastable austenite can remain longest without starting to transform, and holds it there in the austenitic form until the thermal gradients are eliminated. The temperature of formation of martensite is not influenced by the rapidity of the quench, provided the austenite reaches $M_s$ untransformed, so the piece can be made completely martensitic merely by cooling it from the

[31] See J. L. Burns and V. Brown, *Trans. A.S.M.*, **28** (1940), 209–29.
[32] The quenching characteristics of a salt bath are discussed by M. J. Sinnott and J. C. Shyne, *Trans. A.S.M.*, **44** (1952), 758–69.

**Figure 8.23** Schematic representation of the interrupted quenching process of martempering. The steel is quenched from above its critical range into a salt bath held at the temperature of greatest subcritical austenite stability (compare Figure 8.5). When the temperature has equalized, air-cooling to room temperature causes complete strain-free transformation to martensite.

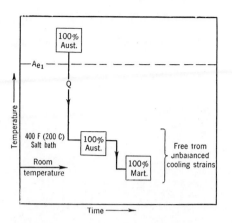

salt bath to as low a temperature as is necessary. By this means high thermal strains are eliminated, leaving in the piece only those unavoidable strains which result directly from the austenite-to-martensite transformation. Full martensitic hardnesses can be secured in this manner with a greatly decreased danger of cracking or distortion,[33] and combinations of properties can be achieved after tempering which are superior to those secured by austempering.

## FACTORS AFFECTING COOLING RATE DURING HEAT-TREATMENT OF PLAIN-CARBON STEELS

In practical heat-treating many factors determine the microstructure and properties of quenched parts. In general, if moderately thin sections of plain-carbon steels are being considered, cooling in the furnace or in still air may be classified as slow rates of cooling; air- and oil-quenching as intermediate rates of cooling; and water- and brine-quenching as rapid rates of cooling. The first two therefore tend to lead to a pearlitic structure in plain-carbon steels, varying from coarse to fine. The second two probably would result in a pearlitic structure varying from fine to very fine or nodular, with the possibility of producing some martensite near the faster end of the range. Water- and brine-quenching almost invariably exceed the critical cooling rate in a plain-carbon steel with a relatively thin section, and, therefore, should result in an almost completely martensitic structure. The effects of different cooling rates on the structure of a 0.70% carbon steel with a 0.5-in. section are illustrated in Figure 8.24.

[33] C. M. Carman, D. F. Armiento, and H. Markus, *Trans. A.S.M.,* **46** (1954), 1500–20, have analyzed the influence of the conditions on hardening.

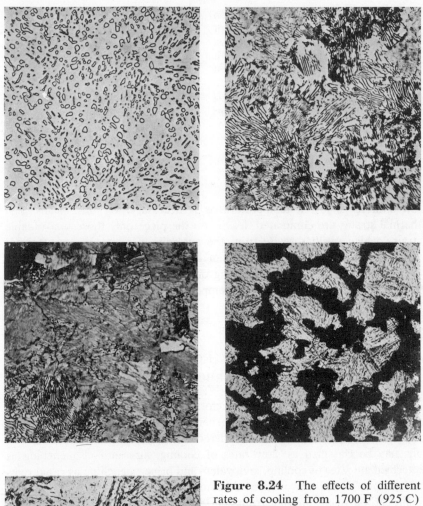

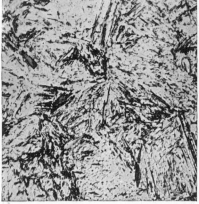

**Figure 8.24**  The effects of different rates of cooling from 1700 F (925 C) on the metallographic structure of a ½-in. diameter 0.70% carbon steel bar. Etched with picral (×500). **a** (*top left*). As-received, spheroidized. **b** (*top right*). Annealed. **c** (*middle left*). Normalized. **d** (*middle right*). Oil-quenched. **e** (*bottom left*). Water-quenched. [Photomicrographs by M. C. Fetzer.] Figure 8.22 shows some of the variations in structure which may arise as the result of oil-quenching.

The structure produced by quenching also depends upon the shape [34] and the dimensions or the mass of the piece being quenched, because a balance is being reached between two opposing tendencies. On the one hand the austenite tends to transform to pearlite, a reaction which proceeds at a rate dependent on the temperature. Opposing this is the tendency for heat to flow from the specimen being quenched to the quenching medium; this is controlled, to a certain extent, by the surface and the temperature of the piece. The greater the mass of the piece the greater the amount of heat to be removed, and the slower the cooling rate resulting from a given quench. However, to a close approximation, all heat-treatable steels have the same heat-transfer characteristics so that, apart from effects produced by transformation itself, the same quenching medium gives substantially the same cooling schedules for geometrically similar specimens of any heat-treatable steels.

If the critical cooling rate is exceeded throughout, the piece becomes entirely martensitic. However, the quenching rate required to produce this structure depends upon the rate of transformation of the steel, particularly as affected by alloy content and austenitizing temperature, and thus tends to define the appropriate quenching medium. In other words, a steel which transforms very slowly can be made completely martensitic by an air quench, whereas one that transforms very rapidly might require a brine quench or an even faster rate of cooling in order to achieve the same result. Likewise, a small enough section might become martensitic with an air quench, whereas a heavy section of the same steel might not harden throughout in a brine quench.

## INTERNAL STRESSES AND CRACKING DURING QUENCHING

As a rule, the more rapid the rate of cooling used, the greater are the internal stresses produced inside the piece being quenched. This is almost invariably true, even when the section is quite symmetrical, simply because the entire piece cannot be introduced into the quenching medium at exactly the same instant. There always must be some time lag. For this reason, the direction in which a given section is quenched may be extremely important when possible internal stresses are considered. For instance, if a solid cylinder is quenched, the stresses are much less harmful when it enters the quenching bath vertically than they are when it enters the quenching bath horizontally.

[34] A shape factor of the type (area/volume)$^2$ affects cooling rate; see D. J. Carney and A. D. Janulionis, *Trans. A.S.M.*, **43** (1951), 480–93.

In addition, the surface always cools more rapidly than the interior, thereby setting up thermal strain gradients. When a steel goes through the $M_s/M_f$ range, the expansion of the inside occurs after the outside has transformed and "set." The transformation of the inside then produces residual compressive stresses inside the piece and tension stresses in the outer material.[35] If the tension forces are large enough, the piece may crack during quenching. In some alloy steels and some welds and large sections of dies, for example, cases are known where parts apparently were quenched without difficulty but then cracked at some later time—that is, delayed cracking. Usually this is the result of a low martensite transformation range or a sluggish transformation rate. Thus, the part did not crack immediately after quenching because the stresses then present were essentially those from thermal gradients from quenching. However, when these stresses later were reinforced by the austenite-to-martensite transformation stresses, cracking occurred. This type of cracking can be minimized by not letting the part cool below 200 to 250 F (95 to 120 C) before tempering. Above this range most steels retain enough ductility to resist cracking.

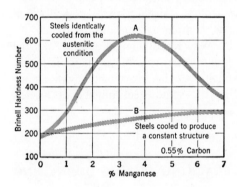

**Figure 8.25**  Effect of manganese upon the hardness of 0.55% carbon steels when identically cooled from the austenitic condition, Curve *A*. Curve *B* indicates similar data when secured on steels so cooled as to have constant structures. [From E. C. Bain, courtesy American Society for Metals.]

## RELATIONSHIP BETWEEN MICROSTRUCTURE AND PROPERTIES OF HEAT-TREATED STEELS

In comparing steels of low- to medium-alloy content with plain-carbon steels, it is not feasible to compare the properties produced by cooling at given constant rates, because of the differences in transformation rates in the two materials. A much more logical method is to quench at those rates which produce identical structures in the two steels, and then to compare their properties. This is done in Figure 8.25 for hardness, with medium-manganese and plain-carbon steels. In curve *A*, the hardnesses are com-

[35] See, for example, G. Sachs and K. R. Van Horn, Chapter 5 in *Practical Metallurgy* (Cleveland: American Society for Metals, 1940).

pared for similar rates of cooling; marked differences in hardness result. In curve *B*, on the other hand, they are compared after cooling at rates which produce similar structures. The hardnesses are much more consistent under these conditions.

In Figure 8.26 the effects of various small amounts of manganese upon the mechanical properties of 0.55%-carbon steels, cooled to similar structures, are shown. Although the additional amounts of manganese tend to increase all the strength properties and to decrease the elongation, these changes are by no means so great as might have been anticipated. This emphasizes the point that the most important effects of alloying elements,

**Figure 8.26** Effect of dissolved manganese in strengthening the ferrite of a 0.55% carbon series of uniform, lamellar structures. [From E. C. Bain, courtesy American Society for Metals.]

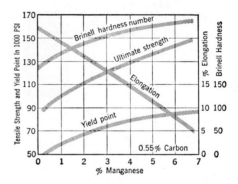

in the small amounts customarily used, are to decrease the rate of transformation of the austenite, and to permit the use of slower rates of cooling to secure given structures and properties, rather than to modify very extensively the properties resulting from a given structure. Furthermore, by decreasing the rate of transformation it becomes possible to harden larger sections without increasing the severity of quench. This increase in the hardenability of the steel is discussed later.

## HARDENABILITY

The most important objective in the industrial heat-treatment of steel is to harden in a controlled manner to whatever depth is desired and, frequently, to harden throughout. In order to do this in the most favorable manner, the mildest possible quenching bath should be used in order to keep the quenching stresses to a minimum. A more severe quench than is necessary also may be objectionable in some cases because of excessive austenite retention. Hence, it is important to know, or at least to have a close idea of, the severity of quench which is required. Information of this

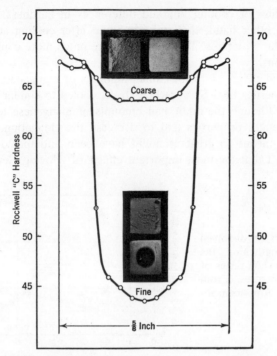

**Figure 8.27** Hardness distribution across two ⅝-in. specimens of a single steel as affected by coarsening treatment. G.S. of 5 (coarse) in the deep-hardened specimen established at 1800 F (980 C); G.S. of 8 (fine) in shallow-hardened specimen established at 1550 F (840 C); both quenched from 1375 F (745 C). Compare Figure 8.17. [From E. S. Davenport and E. C. Bain, courtesy American Society for Metals.]

sort is secured by determining the hardenability or depth of reaction to heat-treatment of the steel. Essentially the methods used involve two factors: (a) the austenitic grain size for a given prequenching or austenitizing temperature, and (b) the tendency of austenite of a particular composition and grain size to transform.

The effect of grain size, as illustrated in Figure 8.27 already has been mentioned in the discussion of the TTT curve (Figure 8.17). A coarse grain size shifts the nose of the curve to the right, indicating thereby a decreased tendency to initiate the transformation of the austenite to pearlite or, conversely, an increased tendency for the austenite to remain untransformed until it reaches the martensite range. Clearly, the greater the tendency to transform to martensite, or the greater the amount of time available for cooling below the knee of the curve, the greater the hardness penetration. Basic knowledge concerning the factors affecting the tendency of the austenite within the grains to transform to pearlite, in contradistinction to the effect of the grain boundaries in initiating the transformation, is determined most readily by one of the experimental methods given below.

## THE CRITICAL DIAMETER

From any given steel a series of specimens can be made with a range of diameters. Each of these then can be quenched from the selected hardening temperature into a given quenching medium, and the diameter which just hardens through to the center—that is, hardens to 50%-martensite 50%-pearlite by definition—can be determined by trial and error. A plot of depth of penetration versus diameter, similar to that in Figure 8.28, then gives the critical diameter, by definition the maximum diameter which can be hardened for a given quenching bath.

For comparison, or for use with pieces actually being quenched, such as gears for example, the rate of cooling at the center of each of these test pieces can be measured by an inserted thermocouple, and the critical cooling rate for this section of the material determined. The critical cooling rate for the important section of the piece being heat-treated can be determined in a similar manner by quenching a trial specimen with a thermocouple inserted in the desired position. Comparison of the two sets of data then shows which rate of cooling must be used to harden the desired specimen completely. The most complete information can be secured by heat-treating a prototype of the part made of a steel of known moderate or low-hardenability. Hardness tests then identify cooling rates at strategic points and a steel can be chosen which gives the desired hardness values when cooled at these rates.

The concept of "critical diameter" has been extended to include "critical ruling section," with agreed conversion charts covering equivalence in quenching of different noncircular shapes.

**Figure 8.28**   The hardenability of a 0.45% carbon steel, S.A.E. 1045, as indicated by a plot of the thickness of the hardened exterior rim, after a vigorous water quench, against the diameter of round, and illustrating the significance of the critical diameter. [After M. A. Grossman, courtesy American Society for Metals.]

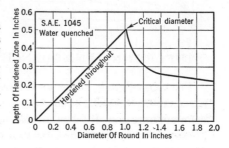

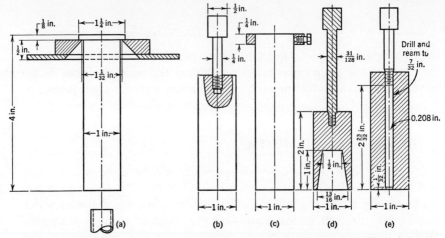

**Figure 8.29** Various types of test bars used in the end-quench or Jominy hardenability test. **a.** Preferred test specimen, showing also a schematic representation of a holding jig and quenching orifice. **b** and **c.** Optional types of standard bar. **d.** Drilled L-bar specimen for shallow-hardening steels. **e.** Drilled bar specimen for steel available only in small sizes. [After *A.S.T.M. Tentative Standard A255-T,* courtesy American Society for Testing and Materials.]

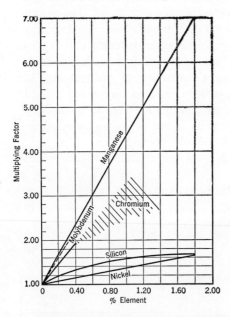

**Figure 8.30** Assembly of multiplying factors representing the effects of varying alloying elements upon hardenability. [From M. A. Grossman, *Trans. A.I.M.E.,* **150** (1942), 227–55.]

## THE JOMINY END-QUENCH TEST

The type of gradient test used most frequently today for determining the hardenability of steels is the one developed by W. E. Jominy.[36] A bar of definite dimensions is taken, heated to a definite temperature, and quenched by water impinging against one end with a definite velocity (Figure 8.29). The hardness penetration then can be measured and compared with the known rates of cooling of points at various distances from this end. These

[36] W. E. Jominy, pp. 66–94, Ref. 11 at the end of this chapter.

rates are determined, either by placing a thermocouple at various positions along the bar or by correlating the hardnesses or the metallographic structures in the end-quenched bar with those in specimens of various diameters whose cooling rates have been determined by the method mentioned before.[37]

Under certain conditions, especially when the steels are comparatively shallow-hardening—that is, when the rate of transformation is comparatively fast for the given quenching medium—some modification of the usual Jominy bar is desirable; and the use of the L-bar,[38] also shown in Figure 8.29, is recommended. Likewise, special bars have been proposed for deep-hardening steels,[39] and for carburized steels.[40]

## EFFECTS OF ALLOYING ELEMENTS ON HARDENABILITY

The effects of small amounts of some of the various alloying elements generally found in alloy steels upon the hardenability, as evaluated by M. A. Grossman, are shown in Figure 8.30.[41] These effects multiply rather than add. This is just one of several methods which may be used to estimate the quantitative effects of various elements on hardenability.[42]

In the formula derived by Grossman, carbon content and grain size give a basic factor which is multiplied by factors for each of the other elements, yielding a product called $D_I$, the "ideal critical diameter." This quantity is a mathematical abstraction which happens to be convenient to use. It represents the diameter of a hypothetical bar which would attain a 50% martensite structure at the center, when subject to an "ideal quench," that is, one which cools the surface instantaneously to that of the quenching medium so that internal heat-transfer alone delays the center cooling. This quench also can be described as one for which the surface exchange factor, $H$, is infinite.

If it is assumed that the basic figure for grain size and carbon content is found to be $D_I = 1$ in. for the material on hand and, then, 0.3% of some

[37] A correlation of this type has been made by E. W. Weinman, R. F. Thomson, and A. L. Boegehold, *Trans. A.S.M.,* **44** (1952), 803–34.

[38] W. E. Jominy, *Trans. A.S.M.,* **27** (1939), 1072–85.

[39] G. DeVries, *Trans. A.S.M.,* **41** (1949), 678–88; and W. Wilson, Jr., *Trans. A.S.M.,* **43** (1951), 454–73.

[40] F. X. Kayser, R. F. Thomson, and A. L. Boegehold, *Trans. A.S.M.,* **45** (1953), 1056–72.

[41] See M. A. Grossman, *A.I.M.E. Tech. Pub. No. 1437* (1942) (Metals Technology, June 1942), 1–29.

[42] See, for example, J. L. Burns, T. L. Moore, and R. S. Archer, *Trans. A.S.M.,* **26** (1938), 1; J. L. Burns and G. C. Riegel, pp. 262–301 in Ref. 11 at the end of this chapter; and, for hypereutectoid steels, C. F. Jatczak and D. J. Girardi, *Trans. A.S.M.,* **51** (1959), 335–49; E. J. Whittenberger, R. R. Burt, and D. J. Carney, *Trans. A.I.M.E.,* **206** (1956), 1008–16.

other element, say chromium, is added to the standard composition, the diameter of 1 in. is multiplied by the factor for 0.3% chromium, which is 1.7, and the resulting alloy, therefore, hardens completely through in a bar 1.7 in. in diameter—that is, $1.7 \times 1$. Similarly the effect of every alloying element present, including the so-called incidental elements which usually are considered only as impurities, must be evaluated, and the effects multiplied together to give the diameter of the bar of that composition which will harden as desired. Correlation charts then may be used to derive the sections which will half-harden at the center (or mid-radius, etc.) in practical quenches with known values of $H$. Of course, such a calculation involves many assumptions, including one that the effective composition of the austenite throughout the section corresponds to the average analysis of the steel. In the circumstances, considerable experience and study are necessary before the method can be applied successfully.

It is noted that in the low percentage ranges, a given increment of alloying element is more effective than it is in the high-percentage ranges. For this reason, equivalent hardenabilities can be produced much more readily by adding small amounts of several alloying elements than they can by adding

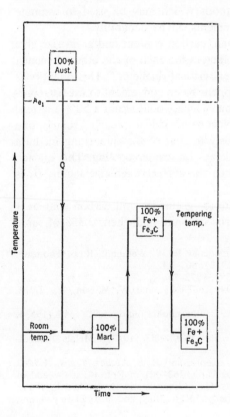

**Figure 8.31**   Schematic representation of the conventional method of heat-treating a eutectoid or hypereutectoid steel. The steel first is heated above its critical range $A_1$ ($A_3$ for a hypoeutectoid steel) in order to make it completely austenitic. Then it is quenched into water or oil, depending on the mass and composition, to secure an extremely hard martensitic structure. Finally, the desired structure and mechanical properties are secured by tempering, that is, reheating, at the proper temperature between 375 and 1000 F (190 and 540 C). During tempering, control of properties is secured by varying either the temperature or the time or both. The rate of cooling following tempering is not important.

comparatively large amounts of only one or two. This fact was extremely important in the conservation of critical alloying elements by the development of the so-called National Emergency Steels during the period of World War II. Small additions of boron also were found at that time to be particularly effective in increasing hardenability,[43] primarily by decreasing nucleation rates of pearlite and bainite. The popularity and use of boron steels, however, decreased greatly after other alloying elements became available again.

## REHEATING OR TEMPERING

The final stage in the conventional method of improving the properties of steel by heat-treatment (see Figure 8.31) is a tempering or drawing treatment applied to the martensitic steel.[44]

## DECOMPOSITION OF MARTENSITE DURING REHEATING

Although the constituents pearlite, bainite, and martensite remain essentially unchanged at any temperature below their temperature of formation, during reheating to any higher temperature they tend to change to a granular or spheroidal structure, that is, the cementite tries to assume the form of small globules rather than the lamellar form it has in pearlite.[45] This commonly is found to be the tendency in any constituent as it approaches complete equilibrium, because a spherical shape includes the greatest possible volume within the smallest possible surface. Very fine cementite granules often are difficult to resolve under the microscope (Figure 8.32) whereas more coarsely aggregated cementite spheroids are resolved readily.

In general, the higher the temperature to which a given carbon-bearing constituent is heated, the larger the cementite granules produced in it. However, there is a limiting size of particle which is some function of the reheating temperature for times of the order of magnitude most commonly used. If the particles can be resolved readily under moderate magnifica-

[43] See, for example, A. R. Elsea and G. K. Manning, *Trans. A.I.M.E.*, **203** (1955), 193–200; and R. A. Grange, W. B. Seens, W. S. Holt, and T. M. Garvey, *Trans. A.S.M.*, **42** (1950), 75–105; also J. C. Shyne, E. R. Morgan, and D. N. Frey, *ibid.*, **48** (1956), 265–71, for more specific information on optimum boron levels.

[44] J. H. Hollomon and L. D. Jaffe, *Trans. A.I.M.E.*, **162** (1945), 223–49, discuss the relationship between time and temperature for steel.

[45] B. S. Lement, B. L. Averbach, and M. Cohen, *Trans. A.S.M.*, **46** (1954), 851–77, have discussed this for carbon steels; and P. Payson, *ibid.*, **51** (1959), 60–93, has done the same for low-alloy steels.

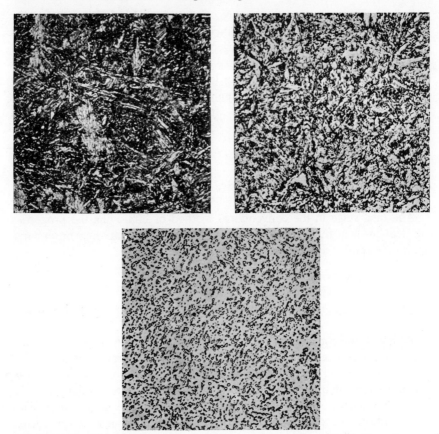

**Figure 8.32** Metallographic appearance of granular structures produced by tempering martensite. Etched with picral (×500). [Photomicrographs by M. C. Fetzer.] **a** (*top left*). Very fine spheroidized cementite (troostite). **b** (*top right*). Fine spheroidized cementite (sorbite). **c** (*bottom*). Coarsely spheroidized cementite (sometimes called spheroidite).

tions, the structure sometimes is called spheroidite or spheroidized cementite or, where the starting point was pearlite, divorced or spheroidized pearlite. Because of this possibility that nearly identical end structures of spheroidized carbides can be produced in different ways it is nearly impossible to tell, from microscopic examination alone, how such a structure was produced. Its carbon content also is difficult to estimate in this way.

The change of hardness with tempering temperature of the various initial constituents is shown in Figure 8.33.[46]

[46] More complete information is given by R. A. Grange and R. W. Baughman, *Trans. A.S.M.*, **40** (1956), 165–92; see also A. M. Turkalo and J. R. Low, Jr., *Trans. A.I.M.E.*, **212** (1958), 750–58.

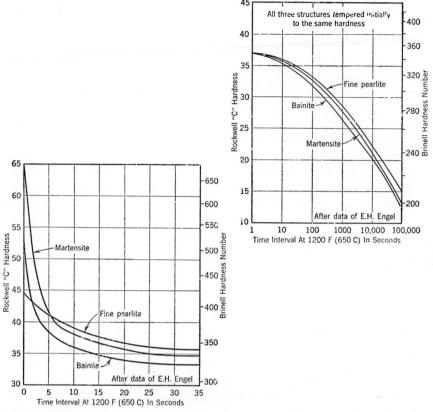

**Figure 8.33** The softening, at 1200 F (650 C), in three characteristic structures of carbon steel, (*left*) with increase of short-time interval, (*right*) with increase of long-time interval after first softening all three to the same hardness by tempering the martensite 16 sec, the bainite 7 sec, and the fine pearlite 20 sec. [From E. Engel, courtesy American Society for Metals.]

## CHANGE IN ALLOY CONTENT OF CARBIDES DURING TEMPERING

During the tempering of alloy steels the first stage probably is the precipitation of an iron carbide. This may be either epsilon carbide (general type $Fe_2C$, a metastable form) at lower temperatures or cementite ($Fe_3C$), at the higher temperatures used more commonly with alloy steels. These carbides may or may not contain dissolved alloying elements depending on the composition of the steel, the original structure, and the conditions of tempering. With increased tempering time other changes may occur, again depending on the alloy.

Alloying elements like manganese and nickel do not tend to nucleate alloy carbides. Hence, the major changes in alloys containing these elements are an increase in the size of the cementite particles and a change in their composition determined by the relative solubility of the alloying element in the cementite under the transient conditions of initial precipitation as compared to the more stable conditions produced by tempering. In general, the alloy content of the carbides tends to increase as the tempering time and temperature increases.[47]

With alloying elements which nucleate alloy carbides the initial particles of iron carbide first tend to redissolve during tempering. The rate at which this occurs depends somewhat on the original microstructure. For example, particles precipitated from martensite usually are smaller than those precipitated from bainite so they tend to redissolve more rapidly. The next stage is the nucleation and precipitation of an alloy carbide. This may be followed, at a later time, by precipitation of a more stable alloy carbide. For example, in carbon steels containing 0.50% molybdenum the initial precipitate is $Mo_2C$ and the later precipitate $Mo_{23}C_6$. Tungsten and vanadium behave in a somewhat similar manner. Some elements, such as chromium, appear to act in both ways, at early stages in the tempering dissolving in the initial or secondary carbides and at later stages nucleating its own carbide, usually $Cr_7C_3$ in low-alloy steels.

The effect of these various types of precipitates on strength properties depends largely on whether or not they form in coherent form and on how long coherency is retained. The initial iron carbide usually is not coherent but the alloy carbides usually are (chromium seems to be the major exception). Coherency frequently is retained long enough to give significant strength increases in a short-time tensile test and with many elements, molybdenum, tungsten, and vanadium for example, the retention is good enough to affect long-time creep and rupture properties significantly. In many cases, however, it is difficult to establish these points completely because the elements which form alloy carbides also seem to produce significant solid-solution strengthening.[48]

So far as long-time properties are concerned, it has been suggested, with considerable supporting evidence,[49] that nitrides such as silicon nitride ($Si_3N_4$) may exert a significant effect.

[47] Several aspects of this are discussed by J. B. Austin, *Trans. A.S.M.,* **38** (1947), 28–69.

[48] See C. R. Austin, C. R. St. John, and R. W. Lindsay, *Trans. A.I.M.E.,* **162** (1945), 84–105.

[49] See the series of papers by J. Glen and his co-workers, for example, in the *Journ. Iron and Steel Inst.,* London, starting in 1958.

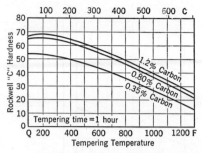

**Figure 8.34** The softening of quenched carbon steels by tempering for 1 hr at indicated temperatures. [From E. C. Bain, courtesy American Society for Metals.]

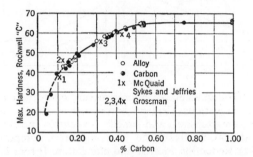

**Figure 8.35** Maximum hardness of quenched alloy and carbon steels versus carbon content. [From J. L. Burns, T. L. Moore, and R. S. Archer, courtesy American Society for Metals.]

## EFFECT OF CARBON CONTENT ON THE HARDNESS OF TEMPERED STEEL

The amount of iron carbide in any ferrite-cementite structure is proportional to the carbon content so the hardness of a spheroidized steel should be affected by the carbon content as well as by the tempering temperature. In Figure 8.34 this relationship is shown for steels containing 0.35, 0.80, and 1.2% carbon, starting with a structure which was martensitic originally.

The hardness of the fully-hardened martensitic structure—that is, of the mixture of martensite and possible other constituents—also depends upon the carbon content.[50] This relationship (Figure 8.35) shows that a carbon content of approximately 0.55% must be exceeded in the quenched steel

[50] The effect of lower carbon contents on ductility is discussed by R. H. Aborn, *Metal Progress* (December 1955), 112; see also *Trans. A.S.M.*, **48** (1956), 51–85. In these alloys, however, $M_s$ is so high that it is almost impossible to prevent some tempering of the martensite from occurring during cooling after transformation.

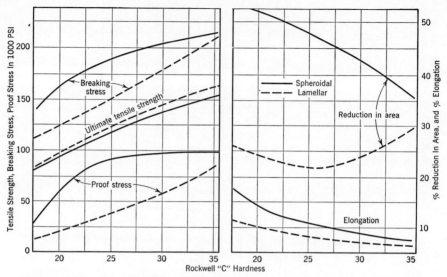

**Figure 8.36** The influence of microstructure upon the tensile properties of a eutectoid steel at various identical hardnesses as shown for spheroidal structures (tempered martensite), and lamellar structures (pearlitic). (*left*) Ultimate tensile strength, proof stress, and breaking stress computed on the reduced section. (*right*) Reduction in area and elongation. [From E. C. Bain, courtesy American Society for Metals.]

if a fully-hardened (Rockwell *C*65) structure is to result.[51] If the structure is not hardened fully, the hardness level is lower, although for each level of martensite produced a certain carbon content must be exceeded to give full hardness for that martensite level.[52]

## COMPARATIVE PROPERTIES OF LAMELLAR AND SPHEROIDAL STRUCTURES

Although identical hardnesses can be secured with either lamellar or spheroidal structures, the other mechanical properties are not always similar. The relationship between them is shown in Figure 8.36 for the most common properties.[53] With the exception of ultimate tensile strength, the spheroidal type of structure is superior.

[51] In opposition to this, K. J. Irvine, F. B. Pickering, and J. Garstone, *Journ. Iron and Steel Inst.*, **196** (London: 1960), 66–81, indicate a rapidly increasing hardness up to about 0.7% carbon, on the basis of diamond pyramid hardness readings, followed by a more slowly increasing hardness up to about 1.2% carbon.

[52] J. M. Hodge and M. A. Orehoski, *Trans. A.I.M.E.*, **167** (1946), 627–38; also Ref. 1 at the end of this chapter, 8th ed., Vol. I (1961), 189–216.

[53] G. E. Dieter, R. F. Mehl, G. T. Horne, *Trans. A.S.M.*, **47** (1955), 423–39, give statistical fatigue properties for a eutectoid steel.

## EFFECT OF CARBON CONTENT ON MACHINABILITY

Whether a lamellar or spheroidal structure has the better machinability is determined largely by the carbon content. Steels with less than 0.15% carbon are so soft in the annealed or normalized condition that they tend to stick to the cutting tool. Hence, the machinability can be increased significantly by using a quench-and-temper heat-treatment to raise the strength level and lower the ductility. In the 0.15 to 0.30% carbon range the machinability of a pearlitic structure (annealed or normalized) is satisfactory. The strength of a pearlitic structure in steels of 0.30 to 0.55% carbon is somewhat high, however, and machinability can be improved by partially spheroidizing the carbides. If the steel contains more than 0.55% carbon a fully-spheroidized structure has the best machinability.

Free-machining steels, containing sulfur or lead, and sometimes other elements like tellurium as well, also are made.

## CARBURIZING

Case carburizing is a process for increasing the hardness of steel by diffusing carbon into the surface at temperatures above the critical range and usually within the range 1600 to 1800 F (870 to 980 C). Typical curves showing the change in carbon content with case depth for S.A.E. 1020 steel are given in Figure 8.37. The resulting variation in composition from case to core is illustrated by the metallographic structure of the normalized specimen shown in Figure 8.38a.

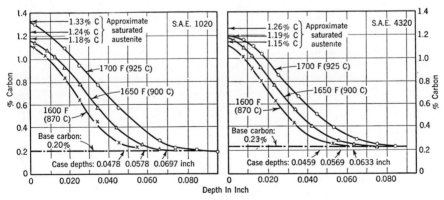

**Figure 8.37** Carbon-penetration curves for S.A.E. 1020 and 4320 (0.20% carbon, 1.65 to 2.00% nickel, 0.40 to 0.60% chromium, 0.20 to 0.30% molybdenum) steels after 7.5 hr at heat in a mixture of 55 parts Drycolene and 8 parts natural gas. [From *Metal Progress,* courtesy American Society for Metals.]

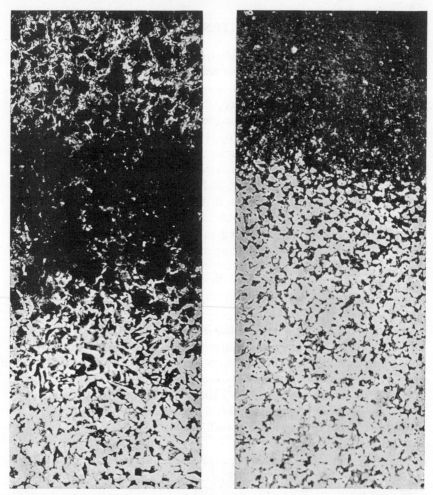

**Figure 8.38** Metallographic structures of two different case-carburized steels, showing variation in structure from case (*top*) to core (*bottom*). Etched with nital. **a** (*left*). Normalized (×50). In this specimen the case is hypereutectoid on the surface and eutectoid (dark zone) farther in. **b** (*right*). Oil quenched (×100). The case is much thinner than in *a*, probably because of different carburizing conditions and, because of the heat-treatment, has a finer structure. [Photomicrographs by L. Litchfield.]

Either solid, liquid, or gaseous carburizers may serve as the source of carbon.

A commonly used solid carburizer is a mixture of hardwood charcoal with about 20% of a metallic carbonate which acts as an "energizer." Many different types of commercial carburizing compounds are sold under various trade names, but their composition is usually of this general type.

Solid carburizers are used in a process known as pack- or box-carburizing, because the pieces to be carburized are packed into sealed heat-resistant alloy boxes along with the carburizing agents. All of the solid carburizers depend on the formation of carbon monoxide gas, which does the actual carburizing. Because of the mass of metal and compounds which must be heated to the carburizing temperature, pack-carburizing usually takes several hours and gives a comparatively thick case.

Liquid carburizers are chemical salts of the cyanogen radical type which yield carbon by direct or indirect action when heated in contact with the steel. These salts are solid at room temperature, but liquid at the temperature of use.

Gaseous carburizers, such as carbon monoxide and the hydrocarbons— methane, ethane, propane, and butane—are used widely. Some of the higher hydrocarbons are cracked in preheating furnaces and the products of this reaction are used for the actual carburizing. A typical relationship for an S.A.E. 3115 steel between carburizing time and carbon penetration is shown in Figure 8.39 for several carburizing temperatures. Likewise, typical carbon contents at various depths are shown in Figure 8.37 for S.A.E. 1020 and 4320 steels after carburizing at several temperatures.

**Figure 8.39** Relation between time and carbon penetration for several carburizing temperatures. Carburized in vertical gas retort using natural gas (90 to 98% methane). Measurements made on a triangular test specimen. S.A.E. 3115 steel. Note that both the case depth and the time have been plotted on logarithmic scales. [After data of R. W. Schlumpf.]

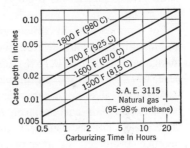

A carbonitriding process also is used extensively in which both the carbon and the nitrogen contents of the case are increased by heating in a suitable gaseous atmosphere (containing some ammonia) and then cooling at a rate favorable for producing the properties desired.[54] The nitrogen serves chiefly to reduce the critical cooling rate of the case.

## AUTOMOTIVE STEELS

Automotive steels are of specification quality because of the high degree of dependability and reproducibility required in properties and hardenability. All of these are covered by Society of Automotive Engineers

[54] G. W. P. Rengstorff, M. B. Bever, and C. F. Floe, *Trans. A.S.M.*, **43** (1951), 342–71, 378–98.

(S.A.E.) [55] and American Iron and Steel Institute (A.I.S.I.) Specifications. The *S.A.E. Handbook* also gives recommended heat-treatments for all of these grades.

Automotive steels are of two main types, carburizing and heat-treating. These steels can be purchased today with a Jominy hardenability which falls within specified limits.[56] Such steels are designated by the letter *H* after the S.A.E. numerical symbol, for example, 4140*H*. With carburizing types the core hardenability is the controlled one.

## CARBURIZING GRADES OF AUTOMOTIVE STEELS

The standard plain-carbon case-carburizing steel is S.A.E. 1020. Typical curves showing the change in carbon content with case depth for S.A.E. 1020 steels are shown in Figure 8.37. The higher manganese variation *X*1020 (0.70 to 1.00% manganese) also is used because of its better machinability. In addition, the better hardenability of the higher manganese grade when carburized gives it less tendency to form soft spots than the 1020 grade. Grades as high as 1040 are carburized when a harder core is required.

For applications in which good combinations of strength, toughness, and machinability are desired, the free-cutting grades 1115 (0.70 to 1.00% manganese, 0.075 to 0.15% sulfur), and *X*1314 (1.00 to 1.30% manganese, 0.075 to 0.15% sulfur) are used.

Although, if enough care were taken, almost any carburized part could be made of plain-carbon steel, frequently it is more convenient to use an alloy steel. This is usually a question of the heat-treating or quenching practice preferred in any particular plant. Alloy price may affect the selection of a particular alloy steel, but obviously it cannot be the determining factor in eliminating plain-carbon steel from consideration. However, total cost, including labor and overhead charges, might do this, because so many different operations must be considered for each particular application.

The alloy carburizing grades generally contain about 0.15 to 0.20% carbon with varying amounts of nickel (up to about 5%), chromium (up to 1.75%) and molybdenum (up to 0.30%) depending upon the particular application. In general the alloy grades are oil-hardening when carburized and hence distort less and have better hardenability than the

---

[55] The S.A.E. numerical designation system for steels is given in the Appendix.

[56] Ref. 1 at the end of this chapter, 8th ed., Vol. I (1961), pp. 189–216, gives many of these curves.

plain-carbon grades.[57] Increasing nickel content increases toughness and strength but also increases the tendency toward retained austenite. Such steels sometimes must be given subzero "cold-treatments" to transform retained austenite to martensite before tempering, although for some applications, for example, ball bearings, up to 30% retained austenite is preferred. Chromium improves hardness, strength, and wear resistance, especially in heavier sections. Molybdenum is added to increase core strength, wear resistance and hardenability. Typical carbon penetration curves for a 4320 steel (0.20% carbon, 1.65 to 2.00% nickel, 0.40 to 0.60% chromium, 0.20 to 0.30% molybdenum) are given in Figure 8.37, in comparison with similar data for a S.A.E. 1020 steel.

The selection of the proper carburizing steel composition, case depth, and heat-treatment can be a far more complex problem than would be anticipated even within the required limits of a hard, wear- or fatigue-resistant surface on a lower carbon core. When bending stresses are involved, both core hardness (strength) and case depth are related so directly that they must be considered simultaneously if premature failure from fatigue is to be prevented.

The more important factor is selection of the proper core strength to resist the service conditions. The minimum suitable case depth then should be used with it. In general, thicker cases are less desirable than thinner cases because they require much longer times to produce and are apt to lead to greater internal stresses after hardening and to a greater tendency to spalling of the case. This is important in all service involving rolling contact under stress.

Strengthening of the core can be secured by increasing the carbon content, the alloy content, or both. Many automotive and other carburized parts are made to withstand higher stresses by the use of steels containing up to 0.40% carbon,[58] frequently with moderate alloying because carbon alone does not give high core properties except with rapid quenching and then only in small sections, such as 1 in. and below. Rapid quenching leads to high internal stresses and heavy distortion so it is avoided whenever possible. The higher carbon cores are given a gas carburizing case of 0.005 to 0.010 in. depth with a surface carbon content of about eutectoid concentration. The light case provides a high surface hardness to resist wear whereas the high core hardness supplies the carrying capacity for compressive loads and the necessary resistance to alternate bending. In addition to these advantages, the higher carbon content of the core improves the machinability, if proper heat-treatment is used, over that of the mild-carbon carburizing grades.

[57] See Ref. 12 at the end of this chapter.
[58] This assumes that high core toughness is not required.

## HEAT-TREATMENT AFTER CARBURIZING

Certain difficulties may arise in the heat-treatment of steels after carburizing because of the different carbon contents of the case and the core. The lower carbon core should be heated above the upper critical temperature $(A_3)$ before cooling, whereas the higher carbon case need only be heated above the lower critical temperature $(A_1)$. There is an appreciable temperature difference between these two critical temperatures, and the use of the lower one often does not give a homogeneous core. Grain-size control is important in the carburized case because of its effect upon wear resistance. The optimum wear-resisting characteristics result from the presence of excess carbides in the case—that is, a hypereutectoid case. However, if these carbides are present in a coarse network, this region tends also to be comparatively brittle. Hence, the best combination of properties is secured by keeping the grain size small and the carbides well dispersed in a relatively thin grain-boundary network.

Either a single or a double heat-treatment can be used, depending upon the steel, its grain-size characteristics, and whether or not it is necessary to refine the grain size and harden both the case and the core or merely the case alone. Some of the methods of heat-treatment used for various types of steels, with respect to inherent grain-size characteristics, are indicated schematically in Figure 8.40. The use of alloying elements not

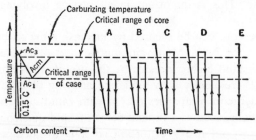

**Figure 8.40** Diagrammatic representation of various hardening treatments for carburized steels and summary of case and core properties. (1) Best adapted to fine-grained steels: **A.** Case refined without dissolving excess carbides; core unrefined, soft and machinable. **B.** Case slightly coarsened with some solution of excess carbides; core partially refined, stronger and tougher than **A.** **C.** Case somewhat coarsened with solution of excess carbide favored and austenite retention promoted in highly alloyed steels; core refined to maximum strength and hardness and better combination of strength and ductility than in previous treatments. (2) Best treatment for coarse-grained steels. **D.** Case refined with solution of excess carbide favored and austenite retention minimized; core refined and made soft and machinable with maximum toughness and resistance to impact. (3) Adapted to fine-grained steels only: **E.** Case unrefined with excess carbide dissolved, austenite retained and distortion minimized; core unrefined but hardened. [From *Nickel Alloy Steels*, courtesy The International Nickel Company.]

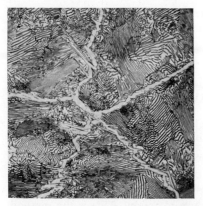 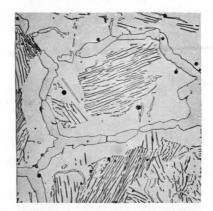

**Figure 8.41** Metallographic structures of typical examples of (*left*) normal and (*right*) abnormal steels after standard McQuaid-Ehn treatment. Etched with picral (×1000 originally, reduced approximately one-half in reproduction). [Photomicrographs courtesy United States Steel Corporation Research Laboratory.]

only tends to keep the core grain size fine, but also permits somewhat greater leeway in the selection of type and temperature of heat-treatment and in the rate of quenching of the case to secure a definite hardness. The metallographic structure of an oil-quenched carburized low-carbon steel is shown in Figure 8.38 (*right*).

### THE McQUAID-EHN TEST

Steels of almost identical chemical analyses do not necessarily behave similarly when case carburized. The McQuaid-Ehn test is used to determine "inherent" grain size and to show what the reaction of the final carburized product to heat-treatment would be. The test is carried out by carburizing at 1700 F (925 C) for a time necessary to produce a case, approximately 0.050 in. thick, which can be studied metallographically, at 100 diameters magnification, to determine the austenitic grain size of the material at the carburizing temperature, and the nature of the cementite and pearlite formation in the hypereutectoid zone. These factors tell whether the steel is *normal* or *abnormal*,[59] as illustrated in Figure 8.41. However, the McQuaid-Ehn test gives the grain size only under definite case-car-

[59] In the *normal* steel, pearlitic "grains" are outlined by thin cementite films, whereas in the *abnormal* steel pearlite occupies a smaller portion of the structure and ferrite bands tend to separate the pearlite from the cementite rims and masses in the thicker boundaries. The names actually were designated more or less arbitrarily and it is not known specifically which are truly "normal" structures. The "abnormal" steels failed to harden uniformly when treated after carburizing in accordance with standard quenching practice, and even when they were recarburized they failed to respond normally and to harden without soft spots. In general, the "abnormal" steels tend to be fine-grained and the "normal" steels coarse-grained.

burizing conditions, and actually gives comparatively little information concerning the grain size of the steel under conditions other than those covered by the test.

## HEAT-TREATING GRADES OF AUTOMOTIVE STEELS

In the heat-treating grades, hardenability, which is affected by the shape of the piece being hardened as well as by its section or composition, is very important. This is especially true of parts like gears in which all the wearing surfaces must be hardened properly if a satisfactory life is to result. On the more complicated shapes, only experiments in actual hardening can give the most satisfactory procedure to follow. This is the method usually used for the majority of parts regardless of their shape. The use of *H*-steels with an established procedure then gives highly reproducible results.

The heat-treating grades may contain from 0.30 to 1.00% carbon because of the wide range of properties required of them. However, in general, alloys containing less than 0.50% carbon are used largely for forgings and those containing more than this for springs, bearings and similar applications.

The plain-carbon grades contain 0.40 to 1.20% manganese, and may contain small amounts of nickel, chromium and molybdenum as well. These additional elements have a marked effect on hardenability so they either are specified or kept at a low level. The steels in the 0.70 to 1.20% manganese range have moderate machinabilities and fair deep-hardening characteristics and harden during water quenching, but in thin sections or small diameters water quenching is not advisable because of the dangers of cracking. Lower manganese (0.40 to 0.70%) varieties are made with less hardenability as well as manganese steels (1.60 to 1.90%) which are oil-hardened readily.

The commonest alloy grades contain various combinations of nickel, chromium, molybdenum, and vanadium. For the higher-carbon spring grades a combination of 1.80 to 2.20% silicon with 0.70 to 0.90% manganese is used widely.

In the heat-treated condition, all low-alloy steels of a given carbon content, such as 0.40% carbon, have quite similar properties if they have comparable metallographic structures, even though they apparently react quite differently when tempered at the same temperature.[60] Because of their different compositions, partially hardened steels react differently to tempering from the essentially completely martensitic structure secured by

[60] K. J. Irvine and F. B. Pickering, *Journ. Iron and Steel Inst.,* **194** (London: 1960), 137–83, discuss the tempering characteristics of low-carbon low-alloy steels.

hardening the section throughout during quenching.[61] Also partially hardened structures always temper less readily than fully martensitic structures. Although the trend is the same in each case, as illustrated in Figure 8.42*a* for several oil- and water-hardening varieties, some of the steels may have to be tempered as much as 200 F (95 C) higher than others in order to reach the same tensile strength and hardness.

However, if the steels are compared when tempered to a constant tensile strength [62] (or hardness), by individual adjustment of tempering temperature, instead of on the basis of a constant tempering temperature, it is found that a close relationship exists between them. This is illustrated in Figure 8.42*b* for the common mechanical properties with the exception of the notched-bar impact values. The agreement is satisfactory except for the reduction in area data in the higher hardness ranges, where tensile strengths exceed 200,000 psi. Even when the alloy, section dimensions, and quenching medium are so selected that complete hardening throughout the cross section is not secured during quenching, the properties of one steel can be approximated well by those of another, provided the most suitable, rather than an identical, tempering temperature is used.

For these reasons there are few parts of moderate section size that cannot be made equally as well from a plain-carbon steel as from a low-alloy steel. All that is required is a proper appreciation by the design engineer of the metallurgical factors involved, and possibly a more rigid control of the heat-treating procedures. Selection of the alloy S.A.E. grades is dictated more by convenience than by any superiority of the properties considered above. The economics require, as a rule, that the cheaper alloys receive more careful treatments than the more expensive alloy grades and vice versa. The selection, therefore, is not entirely arbitrary, but rather one of adaptability to specific manufacturing procedures.

If the application requires a large section, however, or if it involves stress conditions conducive to brittle failure, the use of alloy steels may become mandatory. Often the desired properties and depth of hardening can be secured only in this manner. Likewise, when the very highest combination of properties is required the choice of possible materials usually is limited to a relatively few alloy steels. Such steels often must be free of temper brittleness [63] as well as being through-hardened by a mild quench.

It also is feasible to utilize the quantitative aspects of hardenability, and to secure the properties desired, by keeping the content of any particular alloying element in the range 0.15 to 0.50% and using a greater number of elements. Such a procedure is especially desirable in times of national

---

[61] See J. M. Hodge and M. A. Orehoski, *Trans. A.I.M.E.,* **167** (1946), 627–38; also Ref. 1 at the end of this chapter, 8th ed., Vol. I (1961), 189–216.

[62] Note that this is equivalent to tempering to a similar metallographic structure.

[63] Discussed later in Chapter 9.

emergency when more scrap must be used in steelmaking and scrap segregation becomes a significant problem. Likewise, the beneficial effects on hardenability of small additions of boron can be utilized. However, both of these methods have been accepted only moderately by industry since

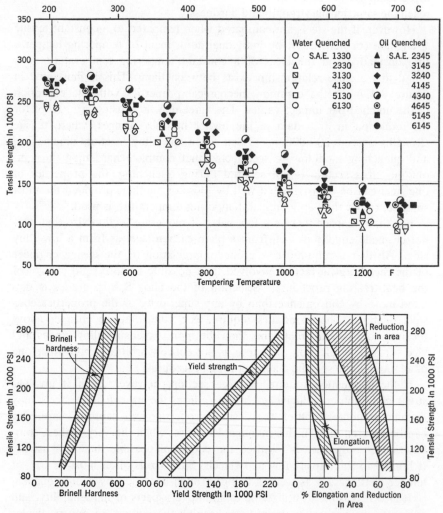

**Figure 8.42   a** *(top).* Change in tensile strength with increase in tempering temperature for water- and oil-hardening steels. The specimens were held at temperature for 30 min. **b** *(bottom).* Change in Brinell hardness, yield strength, elongation, and reduction in area with tensile strength. Round bars of 1-in. diameter were normalized, quenched in oil or water according to S.A.E. recommendations, then tempered at various temperatures from 400 to 1300 F (200 to 700 C). [From E. J. Janitsky and M. Baeyertz, *Metals Handbook,* courtesy American Society for Metals.]

World War II even though they were used successfully at that time. It is inherent in modern steel-making processes that some alloying elements are decreased in amount or eliminated when scrap is remelted whereas others are diluted, at most. Under such conditions it is easy to see why control might be difficult if small amounts of several of these alloying elements were present.

Some of the highest strengths in engineering materials are being secured routinely in these heat-treating grades of automotive steels, or the cleaner equivalent aircraft steels. The 4130 alloy in particular can be treated in small sections to give tensile strengths in excess of 300,000 psi, and full development of the ausforming treatment (Figure 8.19) should raise this limit appreciably.

## ALLOYING ELEMENTS IN TOOL STEELS

Tool steels generally contain carbon (2.45%) and one or more of the elements: manganese (1.75%), silicon (2.25%), vanadium (2.50%), nickel (4.25%), molybdenum (9%), cobalt (12%), chromium (18%), tungsten (21%). In each case the number in parentheses indicates the maximum amount of this element ordinarily used.[64] Each of these elements has a specific influence in determining the basic characteristics of the tool, the six most important of which are: wearing ability, mechanical strength and shock resistance, formability, hardness or cutting ability, hardenability, and heat resistance.[65] Depending upon its size, shape and alloy content, a tool may be hardenable, to a desired depth, by cooling in water (brine), oil or air. The alloy content and cooling rate required also markedly affect the dimensional stability and the tendency of the tool to crack during heat-treatment.

Carbon is the essential element because it makes hardening possible. Tool steels are generally either eutectoid or hypereutectoid although some carbon contents are as low as 0.6%, usually in conjunction with alloys which lower the carbon content of the eutectoid significantly; an exception is for percussion tools which generally are hypoeutectoid.

Silicon may dissolve in the ferrite or the austenite depending upon the temperature. This element is found in all tool steels as a deoxidizer. As an alloying element, it increases the depth of hardening slightly. However, it almost never is used alone because of its deleterious effect on the uniformity

---

[64] The subject of tool steels is discussed well in Ref. 1 at the end of this chapter, 8th ed., Vol. I (1961), 637–54.

[65] Steels which retain desirable tool properties at an elevated temperature (red heat) are said to be red-hard.

of hardness penetration. In high-carbon steels which have been cold worked, the presence of 0.50% silicon alone causes graphite to form during process annealing. To prevent this, small amounts of chromium generally are added to stabilize the carbides, or the manganese to silicon ratio is made at least 2. The addition of silicon also increases the wear resistance of the alloy, but with an accompanying increase in brittleness, and in combination with manganese improves the fatigue resistance appreciably, a characteristic which is especially valuable in tools subject to batter.

Manganese is found in all tool steels because of its deoxidizing and desulfurizing properties. Although it dissolves chiefly in the iron, hardening and strengthening it at all temperatures, it has some tendency to combine with carbon and to be found in the carbides in the heat-treated steel. It decreases both the carbon content and the temperature of the eutectoid, thereby decreasing the brittleness for an equivalent hardness; and it increases the hardenability appreciably, thereby permitting larger sections to be hardened without excessive deformation.

Chromium dissolves in both the ferrite and the carbides. It refines the grain and strengthens the ferrite, and it increases the hardness and stability of the carbides. Thus, the hardness of the steel is increased without an accompanying increase in brittleness. Chromium makes the austenite transformation more sluggish and modifies the iron-carbon constitutional diagram as has been mentioned already.

The principal effects of vanadium are somewhat similar to those of chromium. In addition, it serves as a strong scavenger (deoxidizer), and inhibits austenitic grain growth. This latter effect permits a broader safe-hardening range but increases the possibility of soft spots because of the lower-hardenability of a fine-grained structure. The steels containing 0.25% vanadium are the shallowest hardening of all the water-hardening carbon tool steels. Consequently, it is essential that drastic quenching methods be employed. In oil- and air-hardening alloys both vanadium and chromium generally are added.

Tungsten is essentially a carbide-former, increasing the hardness and wear resistance of the steel as well as inhibiting its grain size. If enough tungsten is added, it imparts great stability under heat, giving what is termed red-hardness, a particular form of heat resistance found in tools. Tungsten almost always is used in conjunction with other alloying elements.

Molybdenum dissolves in the ferrite, as well as combining with carbon to form a carbide and with iron to form an intermetallic compound. It is a stronger carbide-former than chromium but not so strong as tungsten. In solid solution in the ferrite it increases the hardness and affects the critical temperatures. In percentages much greater than 2% it tends to volatilize from the steel as the oxide at rolling, forging, and heat-treating temperatures unless salt baths, controlled-atmosphere furnaces, or some protective coating such as borax is used. Molybdenum can be used as at least a partial substitute for tungsten in case of a shortage of that element. Only about half as much molybdenum as tungsten is required in a tool steel to produce comparable properties. However, the resulting molybdenum tool steels tend to be susceptible to decarburization and to be sensitive to grain growth in both manufacture and heat-treatment so temperature control must be precise. The most marked characteristic imparted by molybdenum is reaction to heat-treatment; it produces a greater tendency to air-harden than any other alloying element. Its full benefits are not evident unless it is used in combination with other elements.

Cobalt dissolves in the ferrite or the austenite, depending on the temperature. It is used in tool steels, principally of the red-hard type, because of its beneficial effects on the cutting ability at elevated temperatures; and is used, generally, only in combination with other alloying elements.

Despite their differences in alloy content, the metallographic structure of heat-treated tool steels consists basically of very hard carbides in a background of tempered martensite.[66] The alloying elements are distributed between these two constituents.

There are three general types of tool steels, depending on whether the tools are intended primarily for (a) general purposes, largely cold cutting and forming; (b) die work; or (c) hot-work. The types of tool steel for different applications differ mostly because of the varying emphasis which has to be placed on toughness, wear resistance (cutting edge), and softening at service temperature.[67] Where resistance to the last of these is the important factor, a high content of highly alloyed, refractory carbides is sought. Otherwise the varied properties are not indicated much by microstructure.

## GENERAL-PURPOSE TOOL STEELS

The plain-carbon steels are the best general-purpose tool steels although they have no red-hardness and tend to warp during heat-treatment. They may be used for any type of cutting tool or for any die for which the size, or the necessity for securing nondeforming,[68] heat resisting, or other special

[66] P. Payson, *Trans. A.S.M.*, **51** (1959), 60–93, has discussed this well.

[67] *The Steel Products Manual on Tool Steels,* issued by American Iron and Steel Institute (New York), gives rather complete information on the different types of tool steels; refer also to the various manufacturers of these materials, and to Ref. 1 at the end of this chapter.

[68] Nondeforming characteristics are the result of decreasing martensitic expansion by using partial hardening. See Ref. 14 at the end of this chapter.

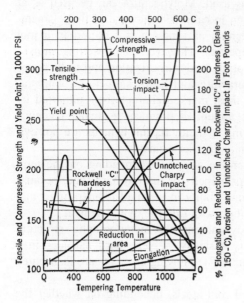

**Figure 8.43** Effect of tempering temperature on some mechanical properties of a medium-hardening carbon tool steel, containing approximately 1.10% carbon, 0.25% manganese, 0.25% silicon, remainder iron, after water quenching from 1425 F (775 C).

characteristics, does not require the use of alloying elements. The carbon content, which may range from 0.65 to 1.30% depending on the intended application, is very important in determining the properties of these steels. By increasing the carbon content, both hardness and wearing ability usually are increased. However, if the carbon content is increased above the eutectoid range (approximately 0.80 to 0.90%) the wearing ability is increased appreciably because of the proeutectoid carbides although the hardness remains essentially unchanged.

Most general-purpose plain-carbon tool steels contain 0.80 to 1.10% carbon. If the tool does not harden clear through, and this is frequently the case except in small sections, these steels generally consist of a comparatively hard and brittle case with a core which is significantly softer and more shock resistant. The major constituent of the case is martensite and of the core a very fine or nodular pearlite. Some control of the hardenability [69] or depth of hardness penetration for a given quenching rate is necessary if reproducible results are to be secured.

The change in mechanical properties of a medium-hardening 1.10% carbon tool steel with increasing tempering or drawing temperature is indicated in Figure 8.43.

[69] Hardenability of these tool steels is discussed by N. J. Culp, *Trans. A.S.M.*, **47** (1955), 769–83.

Various alloy modifications also are made which differ somewhat in hardenability and reaction to tempering. Typical properties are given in Figures 8.44, 8.45, and 8.46. Most steels of this type are water-hardening although some (Figure 8.45, for example) can be hardened in oil.

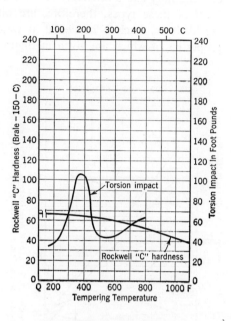

**Figure 8.44** Effect of tempering temperature on some mechanical properties of a high-carbon low-tungsten type tool steel, containing approximately 1.25% carbon, 1.50% tungsten, 0.25% silicon, 0.25% manganese, 0.70% chromium, 0.25% molybdenum, 0.20% vanadium, remainder iron, after water quenching from 1475 F (800 C).

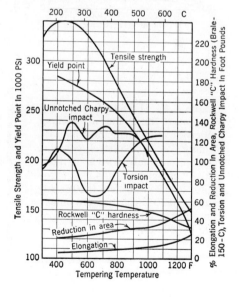

**Figure 8.45** Effect of tempering temperature on some mechanical properties of a silicon-manganese type tool steel, containing approximately 0.60% carbon, 2.25% silicon, 0.50% molybdenum, 0.80% manganese, 0.25% vanadium, remainder iron, after oil quenching from 1600 F (870 C).

## DIE STEELS

Die steels, in general, should have nondeforming characteristics, good hardenability and a relatively low tendency to crack during heat-treatment. Most of these types, therefore, are oil-hardening or air-hardening; they are likely to crack if hardened in water. The low-alloy varieties, typical properties of which are given in Figure 8.47, have a low wear resistance,

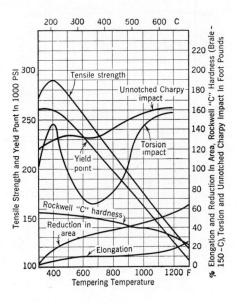

**Figure 8.46** Effect of tempering temperature on some mechanical properties of a low-chromium-vanadium type tool steel, containing approximately 0.50% carbon, 1.45% chromium, 0.20% vanadium, 0.25% manganese, 0.25% silicon, remainder iron, after water quenching from 1575 F (860 C).

**Figure 8.47** Effect of tempering temperature on some mechanical properties of a manganese nondeforming type of tool steel, containing approximately 0.90% carbon, 1.10% manganese, 0.45% chromium, 0.45% tungsten, 0.20% vanadium, 0.30% silicon, remainder iron, after oil quenching from 1475 F (800 C).

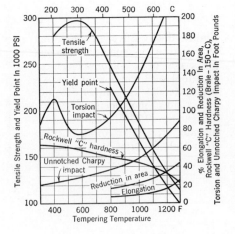

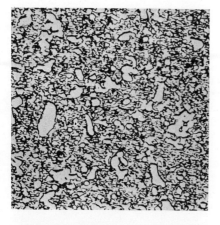

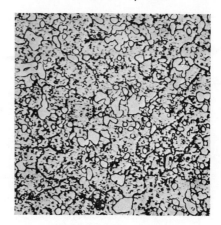

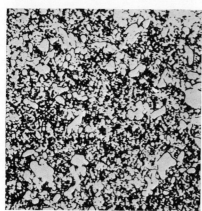

**Figure 8.48**  Metallographic structures typical of the high-carbon high-chromium tool steels. Etched with nital (×500). [From *Bethlehem Tool Steels,* courtesy The Bethlehem Steel Company.] **a** (*top left*). Annealed by very slow cooling from 1650 F (900 C). **b** (*top right*). Pack hardened from 1850 F (1010 C) and tempered at 400 F (200 C). **c** (*bottom*). Pack hardened from 1850 F (1010 C) and tempered at 900 F (480 C).

medium shock resistance, and little red-hardness. High-alloy varieties, containing 12 to 17% chromium and 1.10 to 2.35% carbon, have increased wear resistance because of the presence of chromium carbides in the microstructure (Figure 8.48). They may be either oil- or air-hardening depending upon the exact composition and are deep-hardening with a low warpage.[70] However, these materials have a relatively low impact resistance and also have limited red-hardness. Typical properties of one of the air-hardening varieties are given in Figure 8.49.

Because of their high-chromium content these steels differ from the usual structural pattern of tool steels. As cast, they are composed of a heavy segregate of iron-chromium carbides, surrounded by, or imbedded

[70] K. Sachs and G. T. F. Jay, *Journ. Iron and Steel Inst.,* **191** (London: 1959), 353–60, have discussed distortion in these die steels.

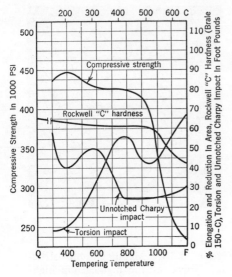

**Figure 8.49** Effect of tempering temperature on some mechanical properties of a high-carbon high-chromium type of tool steel, containing approximately 1.60% carbon, 12.90% chromium, 0.75% molybdenum, 0.25% vanadium, 0.35% manganese, 0.45% silicon, remainder iron, after cooling in still air from a 3-hr pack-hardening treatment at 1850 F (1010 C).

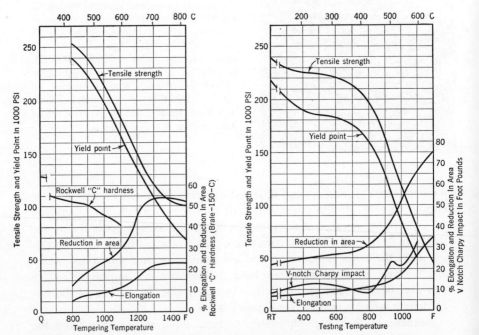

**Figure 8.50 a** (*left*). Effect of tempering temperature on some room-temperature mechanical properties of a chromium die steel, containing approximately 0.90% carbon, 3.60% chromium, 0.25% silicon, 0.25% manganese, remainder iron, after oil quenching from 1650 F (900 C). **b** (*right*). Elevated temperature properties after oil quenching from 1650 F (900 C) and tempering at 900 F (480 C) to a Rockwell hardness (measured at room temperature) of *C*50.

in, a ferrous matrix containing dissolved chromium and carbon. The amount of segregate, which can be broken up only by mechanical work, is dependent on both the chromium and carbon contents. The high-carbon content is essential, so finished tools frequently are packed in carburizing compounds during the austenitizing part of the hardening cycle to avoid surface decarburization.

For dies used in hot-working operations, additions of tungsten and/or chromium may be used depending on the expected operating temperatures. Alloys containing approximately 4% chromium may be either air-hardening or oil-hardening, depending on the section, if they contain approximately 0.90% carbon, and are oil-hardening if the carbon content is approximately 0.70%. The lower carbon alloy also has lower resistance to deformation at about 500 F (260 C). Mechanical properties typical of the chromium die steels without molybdenum or tungsten are shown in Figure 8.50. Because they can be air-cooled, are deep-hardening, and show a considerable rigidity if deformed at moderate temperatures, they are well suited for dies which do not become heated to more than about 500 to 600 F (260 to 315 C) in use. They have medium wear resistance and strength, and low warpage both on oil-quenching and on air-cooling. In the range in which they often are used—namely, hardnesses in the vicinity of 400 Brinell (Rockwell *C*41)—they can be machined, but with some difficulty. In the spheroidized condition machinability is much better.

Steels of this type are not suitable for dies which involve more than a relatively small amount of shock or which may become heated to a visible red heat in operation. Their largest use is for gripper dies for hot-heading round-headed rivets or bolts, for compression and hydraulic riveters, or for many types of bending dies for hot work up to 600 F (315 C).

The addition of tungsten increases red-hardness characteristics appreciably, although more than 12% must be added if the tool is to be used above 1000 F (540 C). Some properties of a common analysis containing 9.75% tungsten and 3% chromium are given in Figure 8.51.

## HIGH-SPEED TOOL STEELS

Many high-speed tool steels are of the high-alloy 18:4:1 type. They usually contain 0.55 to 0.75% carbon, 17 to 19% tungsten, 3.5 to 4.5% chromium and 0.75 to 1.25% vanadium. The best combination of hardness, cutting ability, strength and shock resistance is given by a carbon content of 0.67 to 0.73%.[71] Lower carbon alloys have greater shock re-

---

[71] The effects of vanadium and carbon on constitution are discussed by D. J. Blickwede, M. Cohen, and G. A. Roberts, *Trans. A.S.M.*, **42** (1950), 1161–90; see also A. H. Grobe and G. A. Roberts, *ibid.*, **45** (1953), 475–91.

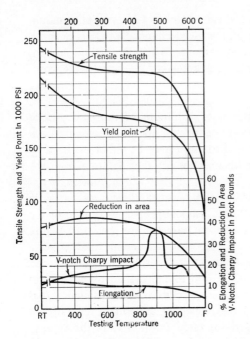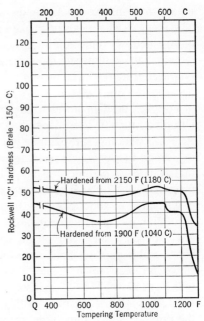

**Figure 8.51** **a** (*left*). Effect of temperature of testing on some mechanical properties of a tungsten die steel, containing approximately 0.30% carbon, 9.75% tungsten, 3.00% chromium, 0.50% vanadium, 0.30% manganese, 0.30% silicon, remainder iron, after oil quenching from 2150 F (1175 C) and tempering to a Rockwell hardness of about C50. **b** (*right*). Effect of tempering temperature on the surface hardness after oil quenching from 1900 F (1040 C) and 2150 F (1175 C).

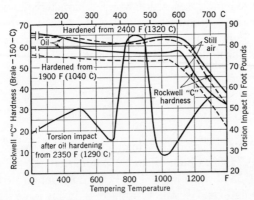

**Figure 8.52** Effect of tempering temperature on some mechanical properties of an 18:4:1 high-speed steel, containing aproximately 0.70% carbon, 15.50% tungsten, 4.0% chromium, 1% vanadium, 0.25% manganese, 0.25% silicon, remainder iron, after quenching in oil or in still air from 1900 F (1040 C), 2350 F (1290 C), or 2400 F (1320 C) as indicated.

sistance and higher carbon alloys have greater wear resistance and cut better. The effect of tempering temperature on the hardness and shock resistance of a typical 18:4:1 high-speed steel is given in Figure 8.52 for several different quenching treatments.

Molybdenum can be substituted for tungsten successfully, either entirely or partially. Only about half as much molybdenum need be used in comparison with tungsten. These molybdenum high-speed steels have largely displaced the tungsten alloys in the United States in recent years although they are not used so widely elsewhere. The two types have comparable properties if they are heat-treated properly. However, each has its own optimum heat-treatment and the molybdenum-types, in particular, are rather sensitive to any variations from this optimum.

The 18:4:1 high-speed steel is heat-treated by presoaking at 1550 to 1650 F (840 to 900 C) followed by a rapid heat to a hardening temperature, at least above 2000 F (1100 C) and often above 2300 F (1260 C), where it is held just long enough to secure adequate solution of the alloy carbides and still avoid excessive grain growth.[72] It then is quenched in oil, salt baths, or air depending upon the particular type of steel. Tempering usually is carried out twice in the range 1000 to 1100 F (540 to 590 C), with a quench to room temperature in between. The initial quench from the hardening heat retains considerable austenite although much of it transforms to martensite. The first tempering treatment tempers the martensite and conditions the retained austenite so it transforms isothermally to bainite or to fresh martensite during cooling. The second tempering treatment then tempers this fresh martensite.[73] To minimize the possibility of cracking complex tools, the technique also is used of quenching from the hardening heat into a salt bath at 1100 F (590 C) and subsequently quenching to room temperature followed by either a single or a double temper at 1000 to 1100 F (540 to 590 C).

The metallographic structures of all high-speed steels in the "as-cast" condition show considerable segregation (illustrated in Figure 8.53a) although higher carbon contents accentuate this difficulty. The properties are dependent to a large extent on the effects of the added elements and heat-treatments in breaking up the segregate to give a matrix of the more homogeneous type shown in the quenched structure in Figure 8.53b. The steels are air- or oil-hardening and have a high wear resistance combined with deep-hardening characteristics, some shock resistance, low warpage, and high red-hardness. These characteristics make them useful for cutting tools of all types, and especially for those intended for severe hot-work

[72] T. Malkiewicz, Z. Bojarski, and J. Foryst, *Journ. Iron and Steel Inst.,* **193** (London: 1959), 25–31, discuss the carbides in high-speed steels.
[73] C. H. White and R. W. K. Honeycombe, *Journ. Iron and Steel Inst.,* **197** (London: 1961), have studied this tempering with an electron microscope.

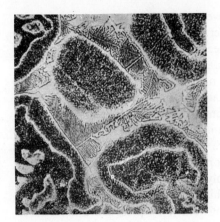

**Figure 8.53** Metallographic structures of an 18:4:1 type high-speed steel. Etched with nital. **a** (*left*). As cast, showing eutectic segregate high in tungsten and carbon (×300). [Photomicrograph by C. L. McVicker.] **b** (*right*). After quenching, showing free complex-carbides in a martensitic background (×500). [Photomicrograph by R. P. Stemmler.]

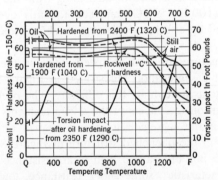

**Figure 8.54** Effect of tempering temperature on some mechanical properties of a cobalt-type high-speed steel, containing approximately 0.75% carbon, 18.80% tungsten, 4.50% chromium, 1.50% vanadium, 5.20% cobalt, 0.60% molybdenum, 0.35% manganese, 0.35% silicon, remainder iron, after quenching in oil or in still air from 1900 F (1040 C), 2350 F (1290 C), or 2400 F (1320 C) as indicated.

*412*

such as blanking dies and similar dies for hot-work. Heating 50° F above the preferred austenitizing temperature would cause a eutectic to melt, giving the characteristic "butterfly wing" appearance seen in the as-cast material. High-speed steel showing this structure is not suitable for tools and must be reforged or scrapped.[74]

The cutting properties of high-speed steels increase with additions of up to 12% cobalt, although because of the tendency of cobalt to decrease hardenability the carbon must be increased somewhat (to 0.65 to 0.80%) as a compensating factor. The cobalt types have increased brittleness, a finer grain when hardened and a greater tendency to crack in larger sections than the standard types. However, they usually are less susceptible to grain growth than regular 18:4:1 and hence can be hardened from a higher temperature. Mechanical properties typical of the popular 5%-cobalt type are given in Figure 8.54.

## QUESTIONS

1. Why is the cooling rate after tempering unimportant whereas the cooling rate during the original quench before tempering is extremely important? What is the basic difference (a) in properties, and (b) in microstructure between quenched-and-tempered and isothermally-transformed eutectoid steels which have the same hardness?

2. Differentiate between austenitizing, ausforming, austempering, and martempering. In each case what is the microstructure like after the specimen reaches low temperature?

3. What determines whether or not any residual austenite in a martensitic structure will transform to bainite? In a crack-sensitive material—for example, a weld in a low-alloy chromium-molybdenum steel—why is it usually recommended that the alloy not be permitted to cool below, roughly, 200 F without tempering?

4. Proeutectoid constituents form primarily at the austenite grain boundaries. Why? In coarse-grained material proeutectoid constituents also form within the grains in a Widmannstaetten pattern. What do you think is the reason for this? Why does the rate of cooling affect the formation of proeutectoid constituents?

5. Why do you think the $M_s$ temperature decreases so much with increasing carbon content? If elastic stress relaxation is the primary reason for austenite stabilization, why is it easier to stabilize austenite as the alloy content of the steel is increased? Would you expect the nature of the alloy-

[74] G. Hoyle and E. Ineson, *Journ. Iron and Steel Inst.*, **193** (London: 1959), 254–69.

ing elements to have an effect? Should an increase in carbon content increase the likelihood of austenite stabilization?

6. Why do you think the temperature of the knee of the TTT curve for carbon steel is so little affected by moderate additions of alloying elements? Does it appear likely that different alloying elements would have different effects on the pearlite, bainite and martensite transformations? Why do you think so?

7. In a fully austenitic alloy steel, is it necessary to quench the material drastically to retain the austenite? Why do you think so? How can you tell whether or not such an austenite will transform to martensite at lower temperatures, for example, subatmospheric? Suppose it does undergo a martensite transformation at subatmospheric temperatures—in what sort of an application might this be important?

8. Why does ausforming give much higher strengths than are possible with heat-treatment alone? Does the temperature at which ausforming takes place have a significant effect? Can plain-carbon steels be ausformed? Why do you think so? What are some of the problems involved in trying to utilize TTT-curve data to predict what will take place during a continuous-cooling cycle? Can any data on a TTT curve be used advantageously for predicting continuous-cooling transformation? Why?

9. Can a bainitic structure be produced in a plain-carbon steel by direct quenching? Why do you think so? What kind of alloying elements, from the viewpoint of their effects on the TTT curve, are used for steels in which a bainitic structure is desired? Can you see any objections to using interrupted quenching as a method for producing a bainitic structure?

10. A part which must be heat-treated distorts badly when given a conventional direct quench-and-temper treatment. Can you suggest two or more methods for producing the desired hardness with a decreased chance of distortion? A part, reportedly made of a shallow-hardening steel, tends to crack in the quenching bath. Give some reasons to explain the cracking and what can be done to decrease the likelihood of cracking. How would your analysis and recommendations change if the cracking did not occur in the bath but sometime later, after the steel had apparently been quenched successfully?

11. Controlled hardenability is extremely important to many high-production American industries. Why? Of what value do you think it would be to the steel industry? To the automotive industry? Does hardenability control imply grain size control also? Why? How is controlled hardenability applied to a part being made for the first time? What are the advantages of the Jominy test which have caused it to be adopted so widely? Why are special specimens needed for variations such as shallow-hardening, deep-hardening, and carburizing steels?

12. Give some reasons why epsilon carbide ($Fe_2C$) does not appear on the iron-carbon constitutional diagram? When any carbide forms during tem-

pering, what are some of the factors which determine its type, composition, and the partitioning of alloying elements between the carbide and the matrix? Is it possible to have more than one type of carbide formed by tempering an alloy steel? What are some of the factors which must be considered in selecting (a) the steel, and (b) the method of carburizing for making a given carburized steel part? What factors must be considered in selecting the heat-treatment to follow carburization?

13. What does the McQuaid-Ehn test tell about the inherent austenitic grain size of a steel? Will it tell whether or not the grain size will coarsen when the steel is austenitized at a certain temperature? Why do you think so? What do you think determines whether the structure of a steel is normal or abnormal after a McQuaid-Ehn test (from the viewpoint of what happens during the transformation rather than from the microstructure)?

14. What are some of the special problems which arise for tools which either are used at elevated temperatures or at such high loadings that the cutting edge reaches elevated temperatures? What limits the maximum temperature at which a cutting tool can be used? If such a tool later must be used at still higher temperatures, what can be done about it?

15. What is meant by a nondeforming tool steel? Do you think that both composition and heat-treatment would have to be controlled carefully to achieve this? Why do you think such steels frequently crack when water quenched? Would you expect such steels to be shallow-hardening or deep-hardening? Why? How would you expect them to rate as cutting tools?

## FOR FURTHER STUDY

1. *Metals Handbook,* 7th ed. (1948) and *Supplements,* and 8th ed., Vol. I (1961). Metals Park, Ohio: American Society for Metals.

2. *Phase Transformations in Solids.* New York: John Wiley & Sons, 1951.

3. *The Mechanism of Phase Transformation in Metals.* London: The Institute of Metals, 1956.

4. *Thermodynamics in Physical Metallurgy* by L. S. Darken and R. W. Gurry. New York: McGraw-Hill, 1953.

5. *Alloying Elements in Steel* by E. C. Bain and H. W. Paxton. Metals Park, Ohio: American Society for Metals, 1961.

6. *Decomposition of Austenite by Diffusional Processes.* New York: Interscience Publishers, 1961.

7. *Atlas of Isothermal Transformation Diagrams.* Pittsburgh: United States Steel Company, 1951. This book contains an excellent selected bibliography also.

8. *Supplement to Atlas of Isothermal Transformation Diagrams.* Pittsburgh: United States Steel Corp., 1953.

9. *Atlas of Isothermal Transformation Diagrams.* London: The Iron and Steel Institute, 1956.

10. *Ferrous Metallurgical Design* by J. H. Hollomon and L. D. Jaffe. New York: John Wiley & Sons, 1949.

11. *Hardenability of Alloy Steels*. Cleveland: American Society for Metals, 1939.

12. *Atlas of Hardenability of Carburized Steels*. New York: Climax Molybdenum Company, 1960.

13. *Principles of Heat-Treatment* by M. A. Grossman. Cleveland: American Society for Metals, 1957.

14. *Distortion in Tool Steels* by B. S. Lement. Metals Park, Ohio: American Society for Metals, 1960.

15. *S.A.E. Handbook*. New York: Society of Automotive Engineers, published yearly.

# 9 Chromium Steels and Stainless Steels

## IRON-CHROMIUM ALLOYS

THE CONSTITUTIONAL DIAGRAM FOR THE ALLOYS OF the two body-centered cubic metals iron and chromium [1] is relatively simple (Figure 9.1), especially above 1500 F (815 C). With increasing chromium content, the temperature of the $A_4$ transformation decreases whereas that of the $A_3$ transformation first decreases (up to approximately 8% chromium) and then increases until the two meet, forming a closed gamma loop (austenite field) at approximately 13% chromium. In this respect the diagram is similar to that for iron and molybdenum (Figure 6.19c).

## SIGMA PHASE IN FERRITIC ALLOYS

The sigma ($\sigma$) phase is an intermetallic compound (FeCr) containing approximately equal parts of iron and chromium. [2] Like most intermetallic

[1] See Ref. 1, 7th ed., at the end of this chapter. N. J. Grant and his co-workers—for example, D. S. Bloom and N. J. Grant, *Trans. A.I.M.E.,* **191** (1951), 1009–14; also C. Stein and N. J. Grant, *ibid.,* **203** (1955), 127–34—have reported that pure chromium is face-centered cubic above 3345 F (1840 C); but the effects of this allotropic change on the chromium-rich iron alloys, which are of relatively minor industrial importance at present, have not been investigated.

[2] Phases of the sigma-type are found in many binary and ternary systems involving transition elements. See A. H. Sully, *Journ. Inst. Metals,* **80** (London: 1951), 173–79; and the numerous papers by P. A. Beck and his co-workers, for example, P. Greenfield and P. A. Beck, *Trans. A.I.M.E.,* **20** (1954), 253–57.

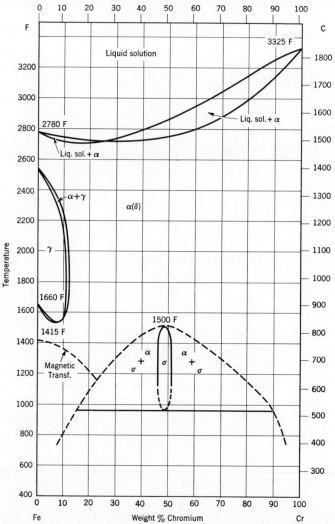

**Figure 9.1** Constitutional diagram for the alloys of iron and chromium. [After M. Hansen, and A. J. Cook and F. W. Jones.]

compounds it has a complex crystal structure and is hard and brittle. The diagram indicates that a wide range of compositions can become partially or completely transformed to sigma by heating in the proper temperature range.[3] However, if alloys containing sigma then are heated at a higher

[3] On the high-iron side, the limits of sigma precipitation from ferrite in alloys of industrial purity were studied by F. J. Shortsleeve and M. E. Nicholson, *Trans. A.I.M.E.,* **43** (1951), 142–56; compare Figure 9.15.

temperature in the alpha solid solution field the sigma redissolves and the alloy becomes completely ferritic. It has been suggested [4] that sigma phase undergoes a eutectoid transformation, at approximately 970 F (520 C), into two body-centered cubic solid solutions, one $(\alpha_1)$ rich in iron and the other $(\alpha_2)$ rich in chromium.

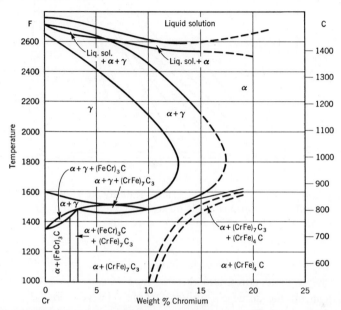

**Figure 9.2** Effect of 0.1% carbon in modifying constitutional relationships in iron-chromium alloys. [After K. J. Irvine, D. J. Grove, and F. B. Pickering, *Journ. Iron and Steel Inst.*, **195** (London: 1960), 386–405. Courtesy Iron and Steel Institute, London.]

## EFFECT OF CARBON ON IRON-CHROMIUM DIAGRAM

The addition of 0.1% carbon extends the gamma loop and modifies the diagram as indicated in Figure 9.2.[5] The extent of the fields of carbide stability at 1290 F (700 C) for various chromium and carbon contents is given in Figure 9.3. As with iron, carbides are formed when carbon is added to these alloys beyond the limit of solid solubility. In industrial alloys containing less than approximately 15% chromium these carbides are of the cementite type (Fe, Cr)$_3$C, or of the trigonal chromium-carbide

[4] See R. O. Williams and H. W. Paxton, *Journ. Iron and Steel Inst.*, **185** (London: 1957), 358–74; also R. O. Williams, *Trans. A.I.M.E.*, **212** (1958), 497–502.

[5] A great deal of additional constitutional information on these alloys is given in *The Alloys of Iron and Chromium*, Vols. I and II, by A. B. Kinzel and W. Crafts (New York: McGraw-Hill, 1937).

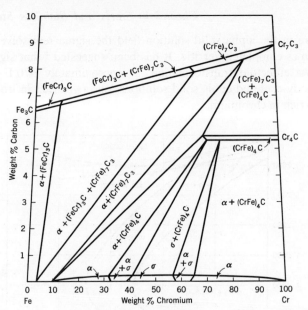

**Figure 9.3** Extent of fields of carbide stability at 1290 F (700 C) in iron-chromium alloys for various levels of carbon content. [From *Metals Handbook*, courtesy American Society for Metals.]

type $(Cr, Fe)_7C_3$. In alloys richer than 15% chromium they may be of either the trigonal chromium-carbide type $(Cr, Fe)_7C_3$, containing up to 40% iron, or the cubic chromium-carbide type $(Cr, Fe)_{23}C_6$,[6] containing up to 30% iron. There are also several three-phase fields where two of these carbides appear. Because of the high-chromium content of these carbides the effective chromium content of the solid solution matrix is depleted whenever carbides precipitate. This depletion may be significant in high-temperature service, where holding times are long enough to get almost complete precipitation, because when chromium carbides form by tempering martensite they increase in alloy content as tempering proceeds.[7]

## HARDENABLE IRON-CHROMIUM STEELS

As a usable approximation, the compositions of any chromium steels for which

$$\%Cr - 17 \times \%C \leqslant 12.5\%$$

[6] Sometimes, for simplicity, this carbide is referred to as $Cr_4C$ or $(Cr, Fe)_4C$ in these steels.

[7] See, for example, K. J. Irvine, D. J. Crowe, and F. B. Pickering, *Journ. Iron and Steel Inst.*, **195** (London: 1960), 386–405.

fall within the gamma loop and hence can be hardened by heat-treatment. The transformation reactions for such alloys are similar to those for carbon steels. That is, they are pearlitic when cooled slowly, martensitic when quenched, and a mixture of ferrite and spheroidal carbides when quenched and tempered. As suggested in Figure 8.14, the effect of adding chromium to steels is to displace the knee of the TTT curve toward longer times and thus to make the alloys hardenable by relatively slow rates of cooling. If the carbon content is kept below 0.10%, or preferably below approximately 0.06% which is more difficult to do on a production basis, the tendency to air-harden is decreased and any hardening which occurs is of decreased significance because of the greater ductility of the low-carbon martensite formed.

## EFFECT ON WELDING OF THE AIR-HARDENING OF CHROMIUM STEELS

These air-hardening characteristics are deleterious in welding because the relatively brittle martensite in the weld metal and heat-affected zones tends to crack if it is subjected to a combination of the differential cooling stresses and the shrinkage stresses inherent to most welding operations as well as the additional stresses which are produced by the austenite-to-martensite transformation. Cracking may be prevented by using preheat and controlling the interpass temperatures to maintain a minimum metal temperature in the range 200 to 300 F (95 to 150 C). This is low enough to permit complete transformation to martensite and yet high enough to remain above the ductile-brittle transition temperature of the steel [8] and thus to minimize differential cooling effects and take advantage of all the ductility available. After welding, the material then is post-heated immediately at a suitable temperature, for example, 1200 to 1375 F (650 to 750 C), and for a time suitable for tempering the martensite to a stable mixture of ferrite and spheroidal carbides. This type of thermal treatment for weldments is particularly important for complicated assemblies or for closure welds made under restraint conditions. For simpler nonrestrained welds it often is not essential although it may be required by the applicable construction codes.

For many of these hardenable chromium steels even the cooling during normalizing does not produce a soft stable structure so normalizing is followed by a tempering treatment in the range 1250 to 1350 F (675 to 730 C) to produce a spheroidized carbide structure.

[8] See Chapter 2.

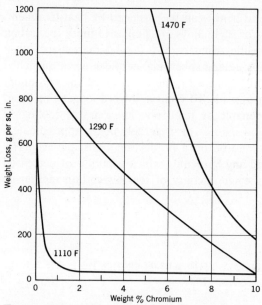

**Figure 9.4** Effect of chromium content on oxidation of steels at various temperatures. [After H. Jungbluth and F. Mueller.]

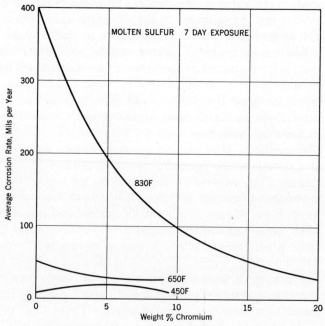

**Figure 9.5** Effect of chromium content on corrosion of steels by molten sulfur.

## LOW- AND INTERMEDIATE-CHROMIUM STEELS

The low-chromium (0.5 to 3.25% chromium) and intermediate-chromium (4 to 9% chromium) steels find numerous applications at elevated temperatures and pressures in the process (for example, petroleum) and steam-power industries. Resistance to oxidation (Figure 9.4) and to sulfidation (Figure 9.5) increase with increasing chromium content. Chromium additions in this range, however, are not particularly effective in increasing resistance to corrosion by hydrogen sulfide, particularly in the presence of hydrogen (Figure 9.6).[9]

If more than 0.7% chromium is present, the carbides become stable enough to make the alloys resist graphitization [10] during long time exposures in the range 750 to 1050 F (400 to 565 C).

The stabilizing effects of chromium additions also are shown by the resistance imparted to high-temperature attack by pressurized hydrogen. As shown in Figure 6.33, for each chromium content there is a definite empirical relationship between temperature and hydrogen partial pressure for determining whether or not hydrogen attack will occur. For each chromium content there is no attack if conditions are to the left of or below the applicable curves, that is, hydrogen diffuses through the steel without difficulty but there are no significant internal reactions (for example, with dissolved carbon to form methane). On the other hand, if the conditions are such as to fall above or to the right of the curve there is attack—that is, reaction with dissolved carbon at internal surfaces, forming methane.

All of the low- and intermediate-chromium steels also contain either 0.5% or 1% molybdenum to improve high-temperature strength and to inhibit temper embrittlement.[11] In the absence of molybdenum, these chromium steels become notch sensitive and, therefore, brittle [12] in the presence of surface defects, after they have been heated in the range of 750 to 1000 F (400 to 540 C). The rate of embrittlement depends on the exact

[9] See A. Dravnieks and C. H. Samans, *Journ. Electrochem. Soc.,* **105** (1958), 183–91.
[10] See Chapter 6.
[11] A. E. Powers, *Trans. A.S.M.,* **48** (1956), 149–64, discusses the beneficial effects of molybdenum (and tungsten) additions. See also, G. Bhat and J. F. Libsch, *Trans. A.I.M.E.,* **203** (1955), 330–35. Temper brittleness also occurs in plain-carbon steels, see L. D. Jaffe and D. C. Buffum, *Trans. A.I.M.E.,* **180** (1949), 513–18; *Trans. A.S.M.,* **42** (1950), 604–14.
[12] This is shown best by measuring one property such as impact resistance over a range of temperatures, that is, by determining the notch-brittle transition curve (compare Figure 2.36). As embrittlement occurs, the brittle-transition range shifts to a higher temperature. However, temper brittleness usually causes intercrystalline fractures rather than the cleavage fractures of the brittle transition discussed in Chapter 2.

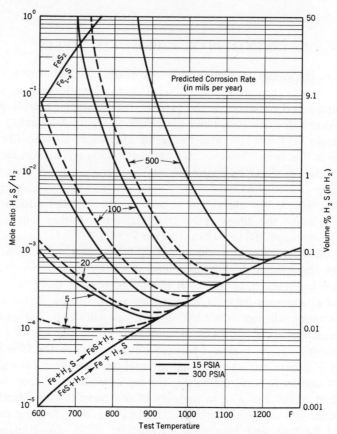

**Figure 9.6** Diagram for predicting corrosion rates of low-carbon and chromium steels by mixtures of hydrogen sulfide and hydrogen at total pressures of 1 atmosphere and 20 atmospheres. Corrosion rates are substantially the same for chromium contents from 0 to 9%. [After A. Dravnieks and C. H. Samans.]

composition of the steel.[13] Temper embrittlement may be sufficiently rapid to occur during slow cooling from above 1100 F (595 C), or it may be relatively slow, requiring a long-time exposure to elevated temperatures. In general, embrittlement occurs most rapidly near 950 F (510 C) and its effects can be removed entirely by heating to and cooling rapidly from above 1125 F (605 C). Carbon and nitrogen probably are the principal elements responsible for temper brittleness although the effect of phosphorus also may be significant.[14]

[13] A. P. Tabor, J. F. Thorlin, and J. F. Wallace, *Trans. A.S.M.*, **42** (1950), 1033–55, give data on this point.

[14] W. Steven and K. Balajiva, *Journ. Iron and Steel Inst.*, **193** (London: 1959), 141–47, maintain that phosphorus, arsenic, antimony, and tin are responsible rather than carbon, nitrogen or other elements.

The strongest of the low- and intermediate-chromium steels, from the viewpoint of both short-time and long-time (creep-rupture) strength properties at elevated temperatures are those containing, nominally, 1.25% chromium, 0.75% silicon, 0.5% molybdenum, and 2.25% chromium, 1.0% molybdenum.[15] Silicon additions increase oxidation resistance. The

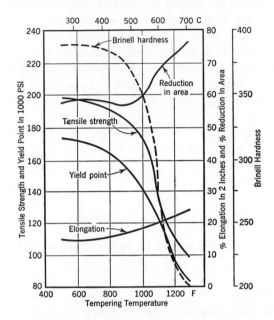

**Figure 9.7** Effect of tempering temperature on the tensile properties of a 1-in. round of 4 to 6% chromium steel, containing 0.19% carbon and 0.5% molybdenum, after oil quenching from 1700 F (930 C). [Courtesy The Carpenter Steel Company.]

stresses allowable for design purposes at elevated temperatures with these alloys are specified by the relevant constructional codes—for example, the Boiler and Pressure-Vessel Code of the American Society of Mechanical Engineers and the American Standards Association Code for Pressure Piping.

The oldest alloy of this type is the 4 to 6% chromium, 0.5% molybdenum composition originally developed for use in the petroleum-refining industry. This alloy hardens readily during oil-quenching, and air-hardens to some extent, depending largely on the carbon content. Typical effects

[15] The strength properties of these alloys have been compiled in *Special Technical Publications No. 100* and *No. 151* (Philadelphia: American Society for Testing Materials, 1950 and 1953, respectively). J. D. Murray, J. S. B. Pair, G. G. Foster, H. W. Kirkby, and J. Blackhurst, *Journ. Iron and Steel Inst.*, **193** (London: 1959), 354–59, give considerable data on the 2.25%-chromium alloy.

of various tempering temperatures on tensile properties are given in Figure 9.7 for an alloy containing 0.19% carbon (rather high for modern alloys of this type). Also shown are some elevated temperature properties (Figure 9.8). The practice today is to keep the carbon content below 0.10%, where possible, in order to minimize hardening during welding. As shown in Figure 9.9, the normal structure of this alloy is ferritic with the carbides spheroidized. During welding the structure becomes largely martensitic in both the weld metal and the heat-affected zone. Post-weld heat-treatment then returns it to nearly the annealed structure.

The 6 to 8% chromium, 0.5% molybdenum alloy, and the 9% chromium, 1% molybdenum alloy have replaced the 4 to 6% chromium, 0.5% molybdenum steels where additional resistance to oxidation or sulfidation is required.

Steels containing 3.25 to 4.25% chromium, 0.65 to 1.00% carbon are typical die steels and have been mentioned previously with the tool steels (compare Figure 8.50).

## THE 12%-CHROMIUM STEELS

The alloys containing 11 to 14% chromium with less than 0.15% carbon (A.I.S.I. Type 410) are the least expensive of all stainless steels.

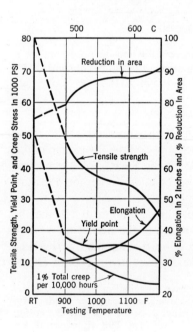

**Figure 9.8**  Tensile properties at elevated temperatures of an annealed 4 to 6% chromium steel containing 0.19% carbon and 0.5% molybdenum. [Courtesy The Carpenter Steel Company.]

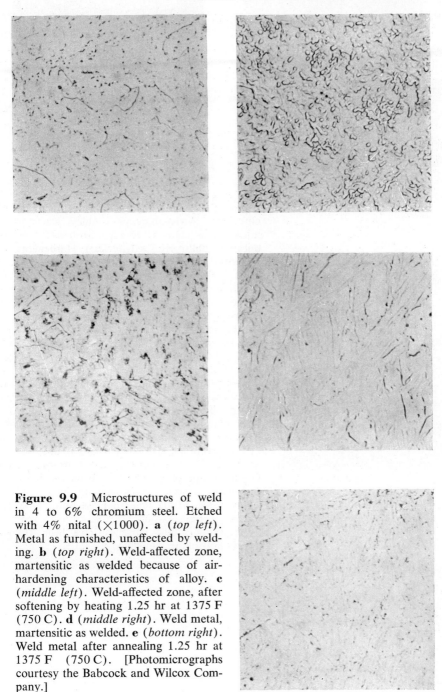

**Figure 9.9** Microstructures of weld in 4 to 6% chromium steel. Etched with 4% nital (×1000). **a** (*top left*). Metal as furnished, unaffected by welding. **b** (*top right*). Weld-affected zone, martensitic as welded because of air-hardening characteristics of alloy. **c** (*middle left*). Weld-affected zone, after softening by heating 1.25 hr at 1375 F (750 C). **d** (*middle right*). Weld metal, martensitic as welded. **e** (*bottom right*). Weld metal after annealing 1.25 hr at 1375 F (750 C). [Photomicrographs courtesy the Babcock and Wilcox Company.]

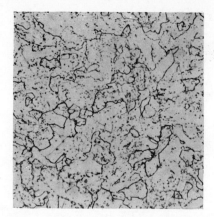

**Figure 9.10** Metallographic structures of the 13% chromium hardenable-type stainless steels. [Photomicrographs courtesy Rustless Iron and Steel Corporation, Baltimore.] **a** (*top left*). Hardenable stainless iron (12% chromium, 0.12% carbon, remainder iron), annealed. Carbides of iron and chromium in a ferritic matrix. Hardness approximately 160 Brinell. Etched with hydrochloric-picric acid reagent (×500). **b** (*top right*). Hardenable stainless iron (12% chromium, 0.12% carbon, remainder iron), hardness approximately 400 Brinell. Martensitic. Etched with hydrochloric-picric acid reagent (×500). **c** (*middle*). Standard cutlery-type stainless steel (13% chromium, 0.35% carbon, remainder iron), annealed. Carbides of iron and chromium in a ferritic matrix. Hardness approximately 180 Brinell. Etched with hydrochloric-picric acid reagent (×500). **d** (*bottom left*). Standard cutlery-type stainless steel (13% chromium, 0.35% carbon, remainder iron), hardened. Carbide particles in a martensitic matrix. Hardness approximately 555 Brinell. Etched with hydrochloric-picric acid reagent (×500). **e** (*bottom right*). Free-cutting type stainless iron (12% chromium, 0.10% carbon, 0.30% sulfur, remainder iron). Gray sulfide particles have been elongated during hot-rolling. Unetched (×250).

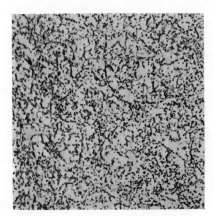

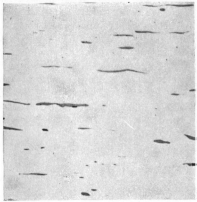

*428*

However, their chromium content is the minimum for resisting many types of mild corrodants or for resisting scaling in continuous operation at temperatures up to 1200 F (650 C). Microstructures of industrial alloys consist of iron-chromium carbides in a ferritic matrix if annealed (Figure 9.10*a*) or in a martensitic matrix if quenched (Figure 9.10*b*).[16] The machinability of these alloys is poor because the chips tend to gall and seize on the tool. However, free-machining varieties, with about 0.30% sulfur or selenium and, sometimes, up to 0.60% molybdenum, contain stringers of a second phase (Figure 9.10*e*) and machine somewhat better than the standard varieties.

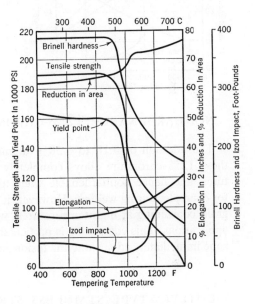

**Figure 9.11** Effect of tempering temperature on the tensile properties of a 1-in. round of 13%-chromium steel containing 0.1% carbon, after oil quenching from 1700 F (930 C). [Courtesy The Carpenter Steel Company.]

The effects on the tensile properties of tempering after oil quenching from 1700 F (930 C) are shown in Figure 9.11. Tensile properties decrease with increasing temperature (Figure 9.12) in the manner typical for ferritic steels. However, this alloy is not used commonly for high-temperature applications. Even for many applications involving corrosion at atmospheric temperatures it has limited application because of its tendency to embrittle and crack when exposed to conditions which liberate atomic hydrogen, particularly in the presence of applied stresses or residual stresses such as result from hardening to above Rockwell *C*20 by heat-treatment or cold work.

[16] K. J. Irvine, D. J. Crowe, and F. B. Pickering, *Journ. Iron and Steel Inst.*, **195** (London: 1960), 386–405, describe the physical metallurgy of the 12%-chromium steels.

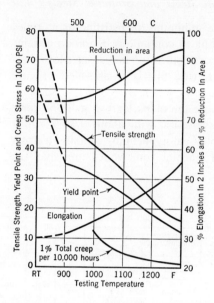

**Figure 9.12** Tensile properties at elevated temperatures of an annealed 13%-chromium steel containing 0.1% carbon. [Courtesy The Carpenter Steel Company.]

## NONHARDENABLE 12%-CHROMIUM STEELS

The addition of 0.10 to 0.30% aluminum (A.I.S.I. Type 405) makes these 12%-chromium alloys completely ferritic to their melting temperatures, and hence nonhardenable when air-cooled from high temperatures, for example, during welding. However, it also introduces a tendency toward grain coarsening at high temperatures, which may be undesirable in some applications. This coarsening is particularly serious in the high-temperature zone immediately adjacent to the fusion zone of a weld.

### CUTLERY-TYPE STAINLESS STEELS

Cutlery-type stainless steels are made with 11 to 13% chromium content but with a carbon content of 0.25 to 0.35% to give a greater hardness. However, blades made of this alloy still have only moderate wear resistance and do not hold an edge too well. Because corrosion resistance is lost by chromium depletion when carbides are precipitated during annealing, these steels preferably should be used only in the hardened condition, although they may be used in other conditions if necessary. Properties will be somewhat higher than those shown in Figure 9.11. For example, after oil quenching or air cooling from 1825 F (1000 C), in moderate sections because hardenability is high, hardness is approximately 512 Brinell or Rockwell C52. Tempering at 1000 F (540 C) drops these values to 401 and C43, and complete annealing, by furnace cooling from 1400 F (790 C), gives

*430*

196 and C20.[17] Typical metallographic structures, shown in Figures 9.10c and d, differ from those for the lower-carbon alloy largely in the greater amount of free carbides in the annealed structures. Free-machining modifications of these steels also are made.

A modified cutlery steel containing about 16.5% chromium and 0.60% to 1.00% carbon (A.I.S.I. Type 440) gives a more intense hardness than the standard cutlery grade. As shown in Figures 9.13c and d, the higher carbon content gives these steels a greater amount of free carbide in their microstructures. Consequently, wear resistance is improved and they hold an edge better than the lower-carbon types.

The still higher alloy varieties, containing 1.10 to 2.35% carbon with 12 to 17% chromium have been mentioned earlier with the tool steels (Figures 8.48 and 8.49).

## UNHEAT-TREATABLE STAINLESS IRONS

As a usable approximation, alloys for which

$$\%Cr - 17 \times \%C \geqslant 12.5\%$$

fall outside the gamma loop and cannot be hardened significantly by heat-treatment although a small amount of martensite may form in segregated areas (Figure 9.13b).[18] Industrial alloys are magnetic at room temperature with an annealed structure of ferrite and iron-chromium carbides (Figure 9.13a). They range from the 17%-chromium, 0.10% carbon (A.I.S.I. Type 430) composition, which is comparable to the hardenable 13%-chromium alloy in corrosion resistance but with a greater factor of safety, to the 27%-chromium alloy (A.I.S.I. Type 446), Figure 9.13e, which may contain as much as 0.35% carbon. Scaling resistance increases with chromium content and is adequate, for continuous service, to 1500 F (815 C) for the 17%-chromium steel or to 1900 F (1040 C) for the 27%-chromium steel. However, particularly in the higher chromium alloys of this type—for example, 27% chromium—there will be a progressive embrittlement and loss of corrosion resistance (that is, of effective chromium content) during continued exposure at elevated temperatures because of the formation of the sigma phase.

[17] R. L. Rickett, W. F. White, C. S. Walton, and J. C. Butler, *Trans. A.S.M.,* **44** (1952), 138–68, discuss isothermal transformation, hardening, and tempering for these alloys.

[18] J. J. Gilman, *Trans. A.S.M.,* **43** (1951), 161–87, shows, however, that under proper conditions significant hardening can result from the precipitation of sigma phase.

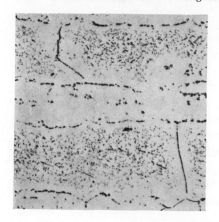
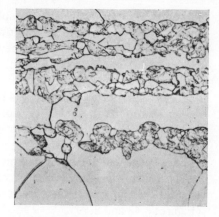

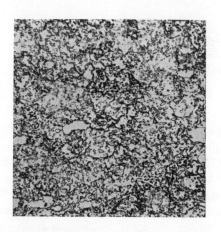

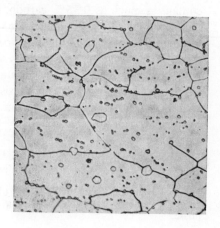

**Figure 9.13** (*opposite page*) Metallographic structures of the higher-chromium types of stainless steels, both ferritic and hardenable. [Courtesy Rustless Iron and Steel Corporation, Baltimore.] **a** (*top left*). Ferritic stainless iron (18% chromium, 0.10% carbon, remainder iron), annealed. Carbides of iron and chromium in a ferritic matrix. Hardness approximately 170 Brinell. Etched with hydrochloric-picric acid reagent (×500). **b** (*top right*). Ferritic stainless iron (18% chromium, 0.10% carbon, remainder iron), hardened. Dark martensitic areas in a ferritic matrix. Hardness approximately 255 Brinell. Etched with hydrochloric-picric acid reagent (×500). The amount of martensite formed is so small that its hardening effect is negligible. **c** (*middle*). Modified cutlery-type stainless steel (17% chromium, 1.0% carbon, remainder iron), annealed. Large carbide particles in a ferritic matrix. Hardness approximately 200 Brinell. Etched with hydrochloric-picric acid reagent (×500). **d** (*bottom left*). Modified cutlery-type stainless steel (17% chromium, 1.0% carbon, remainder iron), hardened. Large carbide particles in a martensitic matrix. Hardness approximately 627 Brinell. Etched with hydochloric-picric acid reagent (×500). **e** (*bottom right*). Ferritic stainless steel (27% chromium, 0.20% carbon, remainder iron), annealed. Carbides of iron and chromium in a ferritic matrix. Hardness approximately 170 Brinell. Etched with hydrochloric-picric acid reagent (×500).

---

In the annealed condition these ferritic stainless irons have ultimate strengths of 70,000 to 85,000 psi, with yield strengths of 45,000 to 55,000 psi, elongations of 20 to 30% in 2 in., reductions of area of 30 to 40%, and a hardness near 150 Brinell or Rockwell $B$80. They work-harden only moderately and in the hard-rolled condition reach tensile strengths of 110,000 to 120,000 psi, with yield points of 106,000 to 112,000 psi, and an accompanying Rockwell hardness of $B$98 to $B$105. They undergo no phase change so can be recrystallized only by annealing following cold work. This is a distinct disadvantage when welding is used because of the grain coarsening which occurs at high temperatures.

## HIGH-TEMPERATURE DISABILITIES OF FERRITIC STAINLESS ALLOYS

The ferritic stainless steels and irons have only fair high-temperature properties, as indicated somewhat schematically in Figure 9.14, and hence should not be used for load-carrying service much above about 1000 F (540 C), the usual limit for most ferritic steels.

The chief disabilities of these alloys for elevated temperature use are the susceptibility of alloys containing more than about 14% chromium to sigma-phase embrittlement [19] and to "885 F embrittlement." [20] As shown in Figure 9.15, the iron-rich limit of the two-phase (ferrite-plus-sigma)

[19] See A. J. Lena, *Metal Progress,* **66** (1954), 122–26, 128.
[20] See A. J. Lena and M. F. Hawkes, *Trans. A.I.M.E.,* **200** (1954), 607–15.

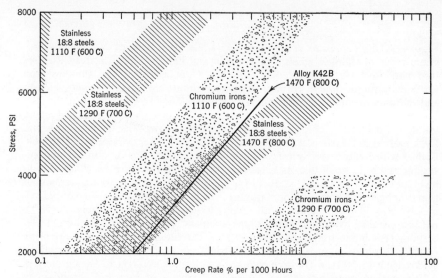

Figure 9.14 Comparative effects of temperature on the approximate distribution of the stress-deformation relationship for 18:8 stainless steels and chromium irons (8.5 to 24.5% chromium, low nickel). A curve for the heat-resisting alloy K42B (46% nickel, 25% cobalt, 19% chromium, 7.5% iron, 2.5% titanium) also is shown for comparison. [From C. R. Austin and H. D. Nickol, *Journ. Iron and Steel Inst.,* **137** (London: 1938), 177–221. Courtesy The Iron and Steel Institute, London.]

Figure 9.15 A comparison of the phase boundary for industrial-purity alloys with the boundary for high-purity alloys. [After A. J. Cook and F. W. Jones.] The area at the right actually is two-phase, ferrite-plus-sigma.

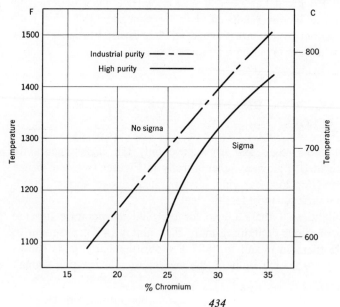

field for sigma-phase formation is different for alloys of industrial purity than for the high-purity materials covered by the binary constitutional diagram (Figure 9.1). As is the case with other precipitation reactions, the time-temperature-transformation (TTT) curve for sigma formation from ferrite solid solution has a C-shape as illustrated for the 24%, 31%, and 33%-chromium alloys in Figure 9.16. These formation times become relatively long for the lower-chromium alloys so they are important largely in applications, like those in the process industries, which may require holding in a sigma-forming range for periods of thousands of hours. However, the higher-chromium alloys transform relatively rapidly. Strain-hardening any of these alloys speeds up sigma formation greatly.

The embrittling effects of sigma-phase formation are much more pronounced at normal atmospheric temperatures than at the temperature of formation. Hence, the embrittlement may not be a significant factor while the metal is hot. Sigma phase can be redissolved by reheating the alloy to the single-phase field, but, unless this reheating is for a long enough time and at a high enough temperature to cause significant chromium diffusion also, there still is enough residual chromium segregation to renucleate sigma phase relatively quickly when the alloy again is held at service temperatures.

When ferritic steels containing more than about 14% chromium are heated in the range 700 to 1050 F (370 to 570 C) they harden and embrittle with time. The effect is greatest near 885 F (475 C), as indicated in Figure 9.17, so it usually is termed "885 F (or 475 C) embrittlement." The hardening action apparently continues indefinitely, although at a decreasing rate because it approaches a limiting value for each alloy and, probably, each hardening temperature. No evidence has been reported of

**Figure 9.16** Time-temperature-transformation curves of the ferrite to ferrite-plus-sigma transformation in 24, 30, and 35%-chromium steels.

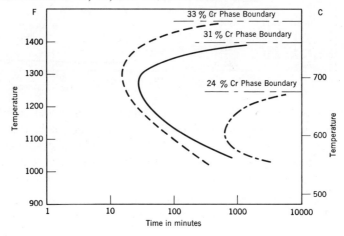

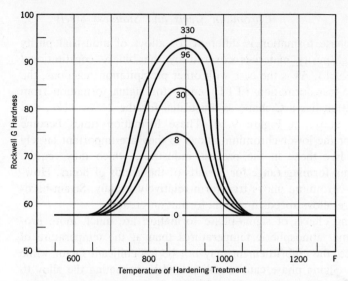

**Figure 9.17** Effect of temperature and holding time (hr) on the 885 F (475 C) embrittlement of a 27%-chromium steel.

**Figure 9.18** Relative locations of some of the important A.I.S.I. stainless steel compositions with respect to the limits of the sigma regions at 1200 F (650 C). [After M. E. Nicholson, C. H. Samans, and F. J. Shortsleeve.]

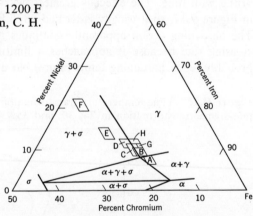

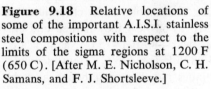

| | Per Cent Cr | Per Cent Ni | AISI Spec. No. |
|---|---|---|---|
| A | 16–18 | 6–8 | 301 |
| B | 17–19 | 8–10 | 302,303 |
| C | 18–20 | 8–11 | 304 |
| D | 19–21 | 10–12 | 308 |
| E | 22–24 | 12–15 | 309 |
| F | 24–26 | 19–22 | 310 |
| G | 17–19 | 8–11 | 321 |
| H | 17–19 | 9–12 | 347 |

a peak hardness followed by softening as is often the case in reactions of this general type. After several thousand hours of heat-treatment, a very fine spheroidal precipitate of a chromium-rich body-centered cubic phase has been separated and identified. This and other data have led to an explanation [21] based on a belief that two body-centered solid solutions are

[21] See R. M. Fisher, E. J. Dulis, and K. G. Carroll, *Trans. A.I.M.E.*, **197** (1953), 690–95; also R. O. Williams and H. W. Paxton, *Journ. Iron and Steel Inst.*, **185** (London: 1957), 358–74.

the stable constituents in this temperature range rather than sigma phase. In any case, the embrittlement can be removed by rapid cooling from above 1125 F (605 C). This is the usual method of identifying it and of providing an intermittent softening treatment where this is desirable.

Chromium, like silicon, also increases greatly the inherent brittleness of these alloys by raising their notch-brittle transition temperature. For example, in the 17%-chromium ferrite, this transition is above 200 F (100 C), even in the absence of any complications caused by heat-treatment.[22]

## IRON-CHROMIUM-NICKEL ALLOYS

If more than approximately 2% nickel is added to the ferritic stainless steels, nonmagnetic austenite ($\gamma$) becomes stable along with magnetic ferrite ($\alpha$), at some elevated temperature determined by the exact composition, and can be retained at atmospheric temperatures by rapid cooling. For example, the iron-rich portion of the ternary constitutional diagram at 1200 F (650 C) for alloys of industrial purity is shown in Figure 9.18. Increasing the nickel content beyond 2% increases the amount of austenite until the alloy ultimately becomes completely austenitic. The nickel content required to accomplish this is dependent on the chromium level, but the effect of nickel in stabilizing austenite out-weighs (on a weight percentage basis) that of chromium in stabilizing ferrite.[23]

## SIGMA PHASE IN AUSTENITIC ALLOYS

In Figure 9.18 the chromium limit of the ternary sigma phase ($\sigma$) is shown as substantially constant at 42%, suggesting that nickel substitutes for iron in the crystal structure.[24] The diagram also shows sigma phase to be capable of dissolving up to about 6% nickel, although in the iron-chromium system sigma is almost invariable in composition. In alloys containing between 42% and 16 to 18% chromium the sigma phase forms rel-

---

[22] W. O. Binder and H. R. Spendelow, Jr., *Trans. A.S.M.*, **43** (1951), 759–72, show that this embrittlement is much less if the total carbon plus nitrogen content, regardless of distribution, is less than 0.035%.

[23] L. Pryce and K. W. Andrews, *Journ. Iron and Steel Inst.*, **195** (London: 1960), 415–17, give a method for estimating ferrite content from composition.

[24] Phases with crystal structures isomorphous with sigma phase also occur in many other ternary alloy systems. See, for example, A. H. Sully, *Journ. Inst. Metals*, **80** (London: 1951), 173–79, and P. Greenfield and P. A. Beck, *Trans. A.I.M.E.*, **200** (1954), 253–57, as well as many subsequent papers by P. A. Beck and co-workers.

atively slowly so, for short heating times, a pseudoequilibrium structure is formed with ferrite and austenite as the only phases present. However, as the holding time at 1200 F (650 C) increases, the equilibrium structures indicated in Figure 9.18 are approached.

Sigma phase forms much faster from ferrite than from austenite, so in the two-phase $(\alpha + \gamma)$ structures, sigma is detected metallographically in

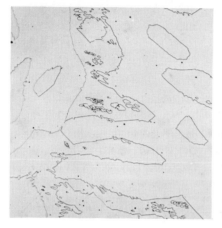

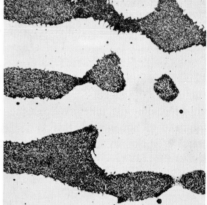

**Figure 9.19** Two phase $(\alpha + \gamma)$ structure in a stainless steel before (*left*) and after (*right*) sigma has formed in the ferritic regions.

**Figure 9.20** Sigma phase in a completely austenitic stainless steel.

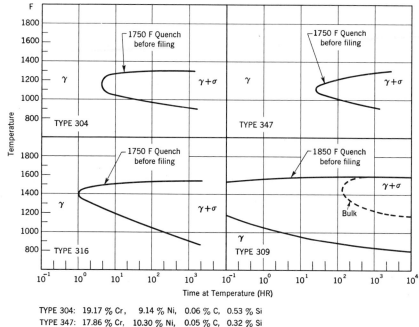

TYPE 304:  19.17 % Cr,   9.14 % Ni,   0.06 % C,  0.53 % Si
TYPE 347:  17.86 % Cr,  10.30 % Ni,   0.05 % C,  0.32 % Si
TYPE 316:  17.27 % Cr,  11.96 % Ni,   0.04 % C,  0.58 % Si,  2.47 % Mo
TYPE 309:  23.21 % Cr,  13.40 % Ni,   0.13 % C,  0.39 % Si

**Figure 9.21** Effect of temperature on sigma-formation times in $-120$ mesh filings of (a) Type 304, (b) Type 347 and (c) Type 316 stainless steels. [After G. F. Tisinai, J. K. Stanley, and C. H. Samans.]

**Figure 9.22** Effect of sigma on impact values of nickel-chromium-iron alloys, as determined on Charpy-keyhole specimens. [From F. B. Foley and V. N. Krivobok in *Metal Progress,* courtesy American Society for Metals.] The alloys studied varied between 20% nickel, 25% chromium and 35% nickel, 30% chromium, and were in both the cold-worked and the annealed conditions initially.

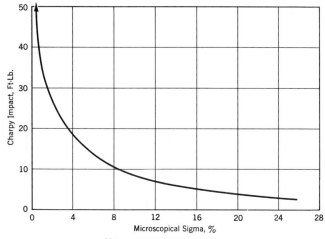

the ferrite (Figure 9.19) rather than in the austenite. However, sigma forms even in a completely austenite alloy (Figure 9.20) although the times required may be of the order of hundreds or thousands of hours. The rate of nucleation is increased significantly by cold working [25] but even for heavily deformed filings it is rather slow, as indicated for three types of stainless steels in Figure 9.21.[26]

The chromium level beyond which sigma phase is not stable is shown to decrease initially from approximately 21% chromium in the nickel-free alloys (compare Figure 9.18) to approximately 16% chromium at the 3% nickel level and then to increase to approximately 17.5% chromium at the 8% nickel limit of the two-phase field ($\alpha + \gamma$) and to 20% chromium at the 25% nickel level for alloys which are completely austenitic. It should be noted in particular that these composition limits are the maximum chromium contents which can be used for alloys in continuous service at 1200 F (650 C) [27] if sigma-phase embrittlement is to be avoided. Alloys lower in chromium than these composition limits have decreased oxidation resistance. In alloys higher in chromium, sigma phase (containing 42% chromium) precipitates slowly as the holding time at 1200 F (650 C) increases.[28] The matrix composition thereby becomes successively depleted in chromium until it reaches the composition limit already mentioned. Thus, any increased oxidation resistance resulting from the initially higher chromium content is only a transient advantage which disappears with increased service time as the alloy embrittles by forming sigma. The typical effect of increasing amounts of sigma phase on the impact resistance of some completely austenitic alloys is shown in Figure 9.22.[29]

## COMMON AUSTENITIC STAINLESS STEELS

Also shown in Figure 9.18 are the nickel and chromium specification limits for nine of the most commonly used A.I.S.I. types of austenitic stainless steels. All of these fall at least partially in the field of sigma-phase formation and hence certain compositions of each type will embrittle to some extent if the holding time at 1200 F (650 C) is long enough.

[25] A. J. Lena and W. E. Curry, *Trans. A.S.M.,* **47** (1955), 193–210.

[26] See G. F. Tisinai, J. K. Stanley, and C. H. Samans, *Trans. A.I.M.E.,* **206** (1956), 600–04.

[27] The composition limits are somewhat different at other temperatures.

[28] Regardless of whether or not the alloys are fully austenitic; see R. C. Frerichs and C. L. Clark, *Trans. A.S.M.,* **46** (1954), 1285–96.

[29] A. M. Talbot and D. E. Furman, *Trans. A.S.M.,* **45** (1953), 429–40.

## EFFECT OF CARBON AND NITROGEN CONTENT ON STRUCTURE OF AUSTENITIC STAINLESS STEELS

Carbon and nitrogen are soluble in these alloys up to limits which depend on the alloy composition and the temperature. If enough carbon and nitrogen are added (the specific amount needed depends on the chromium level) it is possible to secure completely austenitic structures in alloys containing little or no nickel.[30] However, in most industrial stainless steels the carbon content is controlled but the nitrogen content is the level which results from the steelmaking process without special attention, usually about 0.04 to 0.06%. The presence of this amount of nitrogen has been found to be quite important for stabilizing austenite when the materials are cooled to room temperature. In completely nitrogen-free alloys the structure tends to become at least partially ferritic in certain border-line compositions such as 18:8.[31] In most alloys this is the result of the $M_s$ temperature of the austenite being above atmospheric temperature. As a result, even during rapid cooling some austenite transforms to martensite and the quenched alloys are somewhat magnetic. Nitrogen lowers the $M_s$ temperature so this does not happen unless the alloy is cooled to below atmospheric temperatures.[32]

## SOLUTION AND PRECIPITATION OF CARBIDES IN AUSTENITIC STAINLESS STEELS

The approximate solid solubility of carbon in an alloy containing, nominally, 18% chromium, 8% nickel, remainder iron, is shown in Figure 9.23.[33] The exact values depend to some extent on the specific composition of the matrix. Holding within the solid solubility (austenite) field dissolves carbides. The resulting single-phase (austenitic) structure, illustrated in Figure 9.24a, then is retained if the alloy is quenched rapidly enough. With these materials this is known as annealing or solution heat-treatment because it produces the softest structure.[34]

[30] See G. F. Tisinai, J. K. Stanley and C. H. Samans, *Trans. A.S.M.,* **49** (1956), 356–67; *ibid.,* **51** (1959), 589–608.

[31] See, for example, H. H. Uhlig, *Trans. A.S.M.,* **30** (1942), 947–79.

[32] G. H. Eichelman, Jr., and F. C. Hull, *Trans. A.S.M.,* **45** (1953), 77–95, discuss the effects of composition on the spontaneous transformation of austenite to martensite in these steels.

[33] See also the determination of S. J. Rosenberg and C. R. Irish, *Journ. Res., Nat. Bur. Stand.,* **48** (1952), 40–48.

[34] Care must be used not to overheat or serious grain coarsening may occur; see B. Cina, *Journ. Iron and Steel Inst.,* **193** (London: 1959), 18–28.

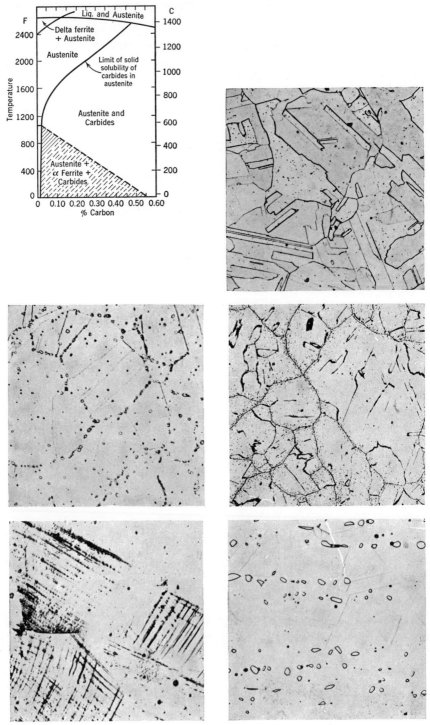

If the solid-solution structure is cooled to a temperature in the two-phase field—austenite and chromium-iron carbides, $(Cr, Fe)_{23}C_6$—or if the quenched alloy is reheated to a temperature in this field, carbides precipitate. If the reheating temperature is just below the solvus line,[35] these carbides precipitate, primarily at the grain boundaries, in a relatively coarse and well separated form, giving what sometimes is called a thermally-stabilized structure (Figure 9.24b). As the precipitation temperature decreases, the carbides formed are successively finer although they still precipitate at grain boundaries and at other internal surfaces such as the edges and ends of annealing twin bands (Figure 9.24c). If the annealed alloy is cold worked before reheating, the carbides precipitate within the grains but along deformation lines from the cold work (Figure 9.24d).[36]

Carbide precipitation in these alloys also follows a C-shaped TTT curve so ultimately a temperature is reached, in the range 800 to 1000 F (425 to 535 C), below which the austenite is metastable and no carbides precipitate even after very long holding times.

[35] The temperature, therefore, depends on the carbon content.

[36] The carbides in stainless steels have been discussed thoroughly by E. M. Mahla and N. A. Nielsen, *Trans. A.S.M.,* **43** (1951), 290–319; and by A. B. Kinzel, *Trans. A.I.M.E.,* **194** (1952), 469–88.

---

**Figure 9.23**   (*opposite page, top left*) Probable nature of solid solubility limits (solvus line) in steels alloyed with 18% chromium and 8% nickel. [After R. H. Aborn, E. C. Bain, and others.] The more recent data of S. J. Rosenberg and C. R. Irish indicate an appreciably lower solid solubility—e.g., 0.02% carbon at 1500 F (815 C).

**Figure 9.24**   (*opposite page*) Metallographic structures of 18:8-type austenitic stainless steels. **a** (*top right*). After quenching from 2100 F (1150 C). Etched electrolytically with 2.5% oxalic acid (×100). **b** (*middle left*). After quenching from 1950 F (1065 C) and reheating 15 min at 1725 F (940 C). Coarse carbides precipitated at grain boundaries by heating just under solvus temperature. Etched electrolytically with 2.5% oxalic acid (×750). **c** (*middle right*). After quenching from 1950 F (1065 C) and reheating 1900 hr at 1300 F (705 C). Fine carbides precipitated near grain boundaries and the edges of annealing twin bands. Etched electrolytically with 2.5% oxalic acid (×100). **d** (*bottom left*). After quenching from 1950 F (1065 C), cold working, and reheating 1 hr at 1000 F (540 C). Carbides have precipitated along slip planes. Etched with mixed acids in glycerol (×500). **e** (*bottom right*). Free ferrite formed by the addition of molybdenum to the 18:8 alloy. Etched with mixed acids in glycerol (×500). [Photomicrographs *d* and *e* courtesy Rustless Iron and Steel Corporation, Baltimore.]

## EFFECT OF CARBON CONTENT ON THE PROPERTIES OF 18:8 STAINLESS STEELS

Increasing the carbon content increases the tensile strength of the solution-treated material (Table 9.1). Higher carbon alloys also work-harden to a greater extent than lower carbon alloys. The improved strength from carbon additions is retained to some extent at elevated temperatures, even when the carbides precipitate at the grain boundaries in a finely divided form. Oxidation resistance at temperature is not affected significantly by carbon content.

**TABLE 9.1   Effect of Carbon Content on the Nominal Strength Properties of Annealed 18:8 Stainless Steels**

| % Carbon | Tensile Strength (psi) | 0.2% Yield Strength (psi) | Elongation (% in 2 in.) | Reduction in Area (%) | Brinell Hardness (10 mm– 3,000 Kg) |
|---|---|---|---|---|---|
| 0.03 * | 80,000 | 30,000 | 55 | 65 | 140 |
| 0.07 | 85,000 | 35,000 | 55 | 65 | 150 |
| 0.11 | 85,000 | 37,000 | 55 | 65 | 156 |
| 0.17 | 93,000 | 40,000 | 50 | 65 | 165 |

* Maximum. This extra low carbon (L) grade now is produced commonly.

## SENSITIZATION

In the austenitic solid-solution form, stainless steels are resistant to a large number of aqueous corroding media, although they are by no means uncorrodable, especially where the medium contains nitric acid together with chlorides or hydrochloric acid. The precipitation of grain-boundary carbides causes the alloys to become sensitized and to lose a large part of their corrosion resistance by becoming extremely susceptible to grain-boundary attack. This susceptibility can be shown readily by boiling in Strauss solution, composed of 47 ml $H_2SO_4$ (sp gr 1.84) and 13 gm $CuSO_4 \cdot 5H_2O$ per 1000 ml of water solution. The treatment causes no loss in weight with normal (unsensitized) metal, but produces severe intergranular attack upon sensitive material, as illustrated metallographically

**Figure 9.25** Microstructure of disintegrated metal after sensitization and corrosion ($\times 100$ originally, reduced approximately one-third in reproduction). [Photomicrograph courtesy United States Steel Corporation Research Laboratory.]

in Figure 9.25. The Huey test, boiling in 65% nitric acid, also is used to study sensitization. However, loss of weight in this test may occur following sigma formation as well as following carbide precipitation so the results may not be completely definitive.

The idealized diagram shown in Figure 9.26 gives a reasonable explanation for this susceptibility to intergranular attack.[37] According to this explanation, a minimum of about 12% chromium is needed to impart corrosion resistance to the alloy. The austenitic structure, before precipitation of carbides at grain boundaries, has a chromium content well above this limit and resists corrosion either by the formation of a very thin protective oxide film or by passivation.[38] However, when carbide precipitation occurs, the particles are predominantly chromium-iron carbide, $(Cr, Fe)_{23}C_6$, so the regions adjacent to these particles are depleted both in carbon and, more important, in chromium, thereby becoming susceptible to corrosive attack. Carbides precipitate predominantly at the grain boundaries so the grain-boundary regions are depleted to the greatest extent and are attacked most rapidly. When the alloy is held at a high enough precipitation temperature for longer times two things occur:

[37] There also is a reasonable possibility of electrochemical acceleration of attack, either of the carbides or of the depleted grain boundary regions, with reference to the remainder of the grain.

[38] Passivation probably results from the formation of an almost monomolecular film of oxygen atoms on the surface. This layer is not thick enough to have the crystal structure of an oxide. The passivating effect is not permanent unless a passivating agent is present. Any oxidizing agent—for example, air—passivates stainless steels fairly rapidly.

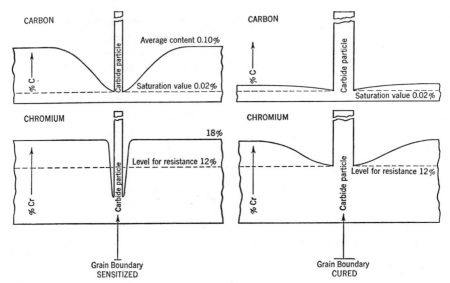

**Figure 9.26** Idealized diagram showing probable distribution of carbon and chromium concentrations (ordinate) in the vicinity of a carbide particle. Abscissa is distance on either side of the grain boundary. (*left*) Soon after precipitation, the alloy is sensitized. (*right*) After sufficient approach to equilibrium to restore grain-boundary corrosion-resistance. [Courtesy American Society for Metals.]

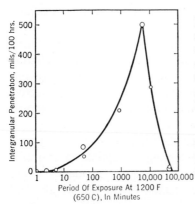

**Figure 9.27** Sensitization and restoration at 1200 F (650 C) in 18:8 containing 0.08% carbon. Different specimens of the alloy were held at temperature for the times shown and then corrosion tested, intergranular penetration being measured. Note that after about 100 hr (6,000 min) at 1200 F (650 C) the subsequent penetration begins to decrease. This brings out clearly the important fact that sensitization inevitably is followed by restoration if enough time is given at constant temperature. [Courtesy American Society for Metals.]

1. The carbides grow in size, removing carbon from the surrounding regions and thereby preventing carbide precipitation in them. In addition, the larger carbides often become well separated, giving a discontinuous, and thus less injurious, rather than a continuous zone of possible susceptibility.

2. Chromium diffuses from the surrounding regions to the grain-boundary regions thus tending to equalize the concentration and possibly to

*446*

restore the chromium concentration needed for corrosion resistance.

As a consequence of these factors, the resistance to corrosion is returned if the heating is carried out long enough at the proper temperatures, as illustrated for 1200 F (650 C) by Figure 9.27.

## PREVENTION OF SENSITIZATION

There are five known methods for preventing the selective corrosive attack resulting from sensitization:

1. Reduce the carbon content to below the solubility limit.

2. Restrict the use of the alloy to temperature ranges in which carbide precipitation does not occur during the anticipated periods of exposure, and make certain that a solution heat-treatment is given before use if the manufacture has involved unsuitable times and temperatures.

3. Disperse the carbides throughout the grains by causing precipitation to occur along deformation lines, within the grains, instead of at grain boundaries. This is done by cold working before heating to the sensitizing range.

4. Cause the carbide precipitation to take place under controlled conditions by heating at a high enough temperature and for a long enough time to restore the chromium content of the depleted zones; this sometimes is called thermal stabilization.

5. Add carbide-forming elements which will substitute for chromium in the carbide, and thus not disturb the corrosion resistance.

The first of these is being used in the industrial extra low carbon (ELC or L) grades. Alloys with a carbon content of 0.03% max [39] seem to be sufficiently free from intergranular precipitation and deterioration.[40]

The second would mean elimination of the alloy from many applications in which it has enjoyed widespread use as a result of the successful operation of the other methods. Many fabricated structures cannot be fully annealed. However, types of welding have been developed (for example, shot welding) which avoid exposure of sensitized material at the surface of material which might suffer dangerous combinations of time and temperature during fabrication.

The use of cold work to disperse the carbides throughout the grains, by precipitation along deformation lines as shown in Figure 9.24*d*, instead of at the grain boundaries, is feasible so long as the temperature of subsequent

[39] This is considered to mean less than 0.035% when stainless steels are sold.
[40] W. O. Binder, C. M. Brown, and R. Franks, *Trans. A.S.M.*, **41** (1949), 1301–46.

heating or use is in the range within which the precipitated carbides do not redissolve to any marked extent—namely, up to approximately 1400 F (760 C). It has been used to only a limited extent, however, largely because it can be applied only to a limited number of products and fabricated shapes.

Thermal stabilization (at 1600 ± 25 F for a minimum of 4 hr) has been used successfully for 18:8 steels, A.I.S.I. 304, in the petroleum-refining industry in order to eliminate intergranular stress corrosion cracking from polythionic acids (Figure 9.32*b*) when the normally high-temperature units are off stream. For many applications, however, the increased general corrosion rate that results from the two-phase (austenite-plus-carbides) structure is undesirable.[41] The precipitation of coarse carbides at grain boundaries also increases the notch sensitivity of the materials significantly.

The most successful method of controlling sensitization has been to add strong carbide-forming elements such as titanium (A.I.S.I. Type 321)[42] or columbium (A.I.S.I. Type 347) to the base alloy.[43] The amount added should be at least five times the carbon content for titanium additions and at least ten times the carbon content for columbium additions. Welding rod always is of the columbium-stabilized type. In these chemically stabilized alloys, carbide precipitation still occurs but as a random precipitate within the grains instead of as a continuous pattern at the grain boundaries, as illustrated in Figure 9.28 for an alloy stabilized with columbium. This method of protecting against sensitization is the preferred one except where a highly polished finish is desired.

## WORK-HARDENING CHARACTERISTICS OF 18:8 STAINLESS STEELS

Work-hardening is the only means available for producing the high strengths needed for many of the engineering applications of the sheet and strip forms of the 18:8-type stainless steels. Some typical effects of various degrees of cold working on mechanical properties are given in Figure 9.29.

Because the austenitic stainless steels are marginal in composition, minor

[41] S. J. Rosenberg and J. H. Darr, *Trans. A.S.M.*, **41** (1949), 1261–88, have done considerable work in this field.

[42] T. V. Simpkinson, *Trans. A.S.M.*, **49** (1957), 721–46, discusses the metallography of this modification.

[43] Because of the difficulty of separating columbium (niobium) and tantalum chemically, alloys containing both of these elements now are used industrially. Tungsten also has been used for stabilization and other additions undoubtedly would be used if they were attractive economically.

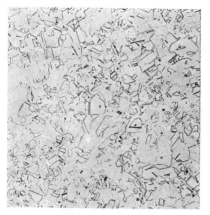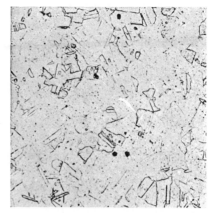

**Figure 9.28** Metallographic structure of a columbium-stabilized 18:8 stainless steel which contains a maximum of 0.08% carbon and at least ten times as much columbium as carbon. Etched with oxalic acid to bring out both carbides and grain boundaries (*left,* ×100; *right,* ×500). The carbides occur as a very light-etching general precipitate throughout the structure.

alterations which move the alloys in or out of the stable austenite field strongly affect the hardness and other properties.

Nickel has the greatest effect upon the strength characteristics and their increase by work-hardening. For example, in a series of low-carbon (0.05%) annealed alloys containing 17% chromium, the use of 7% nickel gives a tensile strength of approximately 130,000 psi and of 9%

**Figure 9.29** Influence of cold working on some mechanical properties of an 18:8 type stainless steel.

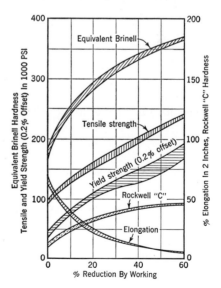

nickel approximately 85,000 psi. After cold working to a 60% reduction, the difference between the two does not change materially, the 7% nickel alloy reaching approximately 210,000 psi and the 9% nickel alloy 175,000 psi. Increasing the chromium content to 18% or 19%, on the other hand, has only a slight effect on strength although it does increase the elongation appreciably for the lower reductions.

The effect of increased carbon content in increasing the rate of work-hardening is striking. For example, after a cold reduction of approximately 55%, a 17% chromium, 7% nickel alloy containing 0.14% carbon has a strength near 255,000 psi, appreciably higher than that secured with the lower carbon alloy. In these higher carbon alloys, also, an increase in the chromium content, in the range 17 to 20% chromium, results in a pronounced drop in the tensile strength, the decrease sometimes being as much as 25% in the heavier cold-work reductions, and a somewhat smaller drop in the elongation. This is particularly important in the use of cold-rolled sheet because some bending or other forming operation frequently is necessary.

The differences resulting from changing the chromium, nickel and carbon contents have been attributed to the effects of these elements on the stability of austenite in this type of alloy. It appears likely that in the so-called borderline alloys—that is, those near the boundary of the austenitic field, like the 7%-nickel alloys—there is some transformation of the austenite to martensite by cold working and that this is the real explanation of the high work-hardening capacities of these alloys. Depending upon the exact composition, the amount and rate of this effect of cold working can vary over relatively wide ranges.

In using these alloys a proper balance must be maintained between the workability required for the fabrication of the rolled material and the strength needed for the design. Usually, therefore, a moderate tensile strength—that is, 150,000 to 175,000 psi—is all that can be secured if the elongation is to be reasonably good. The 17:7 type alloy (A.I.S.I. Type 301) is superior to the others in this respect.

## SHOT WELDING OF 18:8 STAINLESS STEEL

The high strength of cold-rolled stainless steel combined with its corrosion resistance and high modulus of elasticity (26,000,000 psi) has broadened its applications as a structural material. Use for extended periods at temperatures as high as 800 F (425 C) is feasible. Built-up sections to give high rigidity (an early design is shown in Figure 9.30) can be made entirely of thin sheet if properly controlled localized spot welding, some-times called shot welding, is used for joining. Although during shot welding, the temperature at the weld itself is well over 2000 F (1100 C) the com-bination of the low thermal conductivity of austenitic stainless steel and the short heating time definitely limits the extent to which the heat can flow away from the weld. The presence of cold metal around the weld also cools it rapidly, and thus prevents the precipitation of carbides.

The appearance of properly and improperly made shot welds of stainless steel is shown in Figure 9.31. In the properly made weld (third picture from the top) there are three distinct zones: (a) the weld zone itself, which has the characteristic dendritic structure of a casting; (b) the sensitized zone, where heat penetration from the weld into the base metal has caused carbide precipitation, with accompanying decrease in resistance to corrosion; (c) the unchanged base metal which should surround the weld on all sides and thus protect it from the corroding medium. In the weld which has been made improperly by using too high a temperature—that is, too high a current and/or too long a time—the sensitized zone penetrates to the surface, thus exposing the sheet to corrosion. Properly made spot welds are tough and ductile, and may be twisted through nearly 90 deg without shearing.

**Figure 9.30** Beams, drawn to scale, with same moments of inertia. The box girder at left is welded of 18:8 strip, weighs 38% as much as the 5-in. I-beam of structural steel at right, and has an ultimate strength 2.5 times as great. Even when figured with factors of safety of 6 and 4 respectively it will carry a 50% greater bending moment.

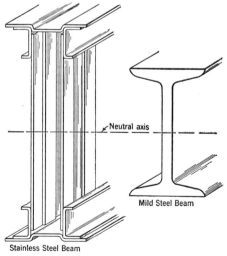

Neutral axis

Mild Steel Beam

Stainless Steel Beam

**Figure 9.31** a (*top group*). Welded areas between two 0.010-in. sheets of 18:8 stainless steel, cross sectioned. Slightly etched (×38). Two samples at top had insufficient heat and are brittle; third sample is correctly made "Shotweld"; bottom sample had too much heat and the surface has been impaired to an extent where corrosion would result. b (*bottom group*). Metallographic structures of metal in each of the three zones of the correctly made spot weld. (*left*) Weld zone. (*middle*) Heat-affected, sensitized zone. (*right*) Unaffected zone. Etched electrolytically with 2% oxalic acid (×750). [Photomicrographs courtesy E. G. Budd Manufacturing Company.]

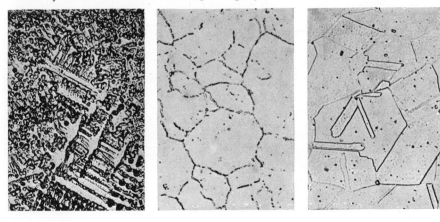

## EFFECT OF LOW TEMPERATURE ON MECHANICAL PROPERTIES OF 18:8 STAINLESS STEELS

When tested at low temperatures, 18:8 stainless steel shows the increase in tensile strength found with most steels but also retains considerable ductility rather than becoming brittle as most ferritic steels do. For example, at a temperature as low as $-425$ F ($-254$ C) an 18:8 stainless steel had a tensile strength of 263,000 psi, with a yield point of 122,700 psi, an elongation of 25%, a reduction in area of 30.5%, and excellent V-notch Charpy impact strength.

When carbide or ferrite is precipitated at the grain boundaries, the austenitic steels may show evidence of notch sensitivity in the impact test as the temperature is decreased. The fracture in such lower ductility alloys, however, is intergranular rather than of the transgranular cleavage-type found in ferritic steels.

## STRESS-CORROSION CRACKING OF AUSTENITIC STAINLESS STEELS

Austenitic stainless steels are susceptible to stress-corrosion cracking in chlorides and in caustic [44] and should be used with caution under these conditions particularly where the chlorides can concentrate and build up to relatively high values locally.[45] The transgranular branched-type of crack pattern shown in Figure 9.32*a* is typical. Plant experience with this type of cracking does not always correlate with laboratory test data.

After they have been sensitized by intergranular carbide precipitation austenitic stainless steels also are susceptible to intergranular stress-corrosion cracking (like that shown in Figure 9.32*b*) if exposed to certain media. A common one is a solution of polythionic acids ($H_2S_xO_6$) such as is formed when water and sulfidic corrosion products (or hydrogen sulfide) are exposed to air. These conditions may be encountered, for example, when some petroleum-refining units are shut down and opened for inspection and repair.

## AUSTENITIC CHROMIUM-MANGANESE STAINLESS STEELS

Completely austenitic stainless steels (either nickel-free or low in nickel) also can be produced by using sufficient carbon and nitrogen with chro-

---

[44] P. P. Snowden, *Journ. Iron and Steel Inst.*, **194** (London: 1960), 181–89, shows that level of stress, temperature, and solution strength are the important variables.
[45] See, for example, Refs. 9, 10, and 11 at the end of this chapter.

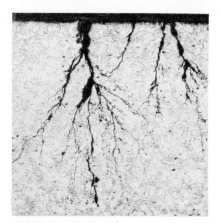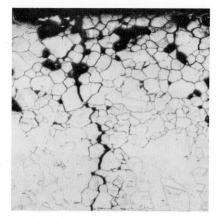

**Figure 9.32**   **a** (*left*). Typical transgranular stress-corrosion crack produced in austenitic stainless steels in chloridic media. **b** (*right*). Typical intergranular stress-corrosion crack produced by polythionic acids in sensitized austenitic stainless steel in aqueous sulfidic media.

mium.[46] However, from an industrial viewpoint it has been simpler to substitute manganese for the nickel, keeping carbon low and nitrogen at the level desired.[47] The A.I.S.I. grades 201 and 202 are of this type. These alloys have good corrosion resistance at atmospheric or moderately elevated temperatures. However, they are of questionable value for service above 750 F (400 C) because of precipitation of carbides and nitrides from solid solution. The accompanying decrease in effective chromium content decreases corrosion resistance markedly.

### SURFACE-HARDENING OF STAINLESS STEELS

The surface hardness of austenitic stainless steels can be increased significantly by nitriding. The passive surface layer is removed and the alloy is exposed, at 930 to 1000 F (500 to 540 C), to an atmosphere of dissociated ammonia, usually in a sealed container. The activated nitrogen produced by ammonia dissociation is the nitriding agent. Any chromium nitride formed in this manner will tie up a certain amount of chromium and thus reduce the effective chromium content of the austenitic matrix. This also reduces the corrosion resistance to most media.

[46] G. F. Tisinai, J. K. Stanley, and C. H. Samans, *Trans. A.S.M.*, **48** (1956), 356–65; G. F. Tisinai and C. H. Samans, *ibid.*, **49** (1957), 747–58.

[47] See V. F. Zackay, J. F. Carlson, and P. L. Jackson, *Trans. A.S.M.*, **48** (1956), 509–20; also C. M. Hsiao and E. J. Dulis, *ibid.*, **49** (1957), 655–77, and **50** (1958), 773–99. The constitution of these alloys is discussed thoroughly by R. Franks, W. O. Binder, and J. Thompson, *Trans. A.S.M.*, **47** (1955), 231–85.

## PRECIPITATION-HARDENING STAINLESS STEELS

Austenitic chromium-nickel stainless steels can be hardened by heat-treatment if the chemical composition is adjusted properly and if substantial amounts of alloying elements like aluminum, copper, molybdenum, or titanium are added. The four general types: (1) single-treatment martensitic, (2) austenitic-martensitic, (3) austenitic, and (4) austenitic-ferritic, have different microstructures in the hardened condition. These are all proprietary alloys, and are classed as precipitation-hardening.[48]

Typical wrought single-treatment martensitic alloys are shown in Table 9.2. These are austenitic solid solutions at the annealing temperature which transform to martensite and harden to about Rockwell $C30$ when cooled below approximately 300 F (150 C). During the subsequent hardening treatment, submicroscopic precipitation of the hardening constituents increases the hardness to Rockwell $C40$ to $C45$.

**TABLE 9.2**

|  | % C | % Cr | % Ni | % Cu | % Al | % Other |
|---|---|---|---|---|---|---|
| *Stainless W* * | 0.07 | 17 | 7 | — | 0.2 | Ti 0.7 |
| *17-4 PH* † | 0.04 | 17 | 4 | 4 | — | Cb 0.3 |

\* Solution anneal 1900 F (1040 C), harden 950 to 1050 F (510 to 565 C).
† Solution anneal 1900 F (1040 C), harden 900 to 1100 F (480 to 595 C).

Two wrought austenitic-martensitic types are shown in Table 9.3. These sometimes are called "semiaustenitic" because their structure is fully austenitic after the first heat-treatment (although alloys containing aluminum may contain some delta ferrite), making them relatively soft and ductile and hence readily formable. This austenite can be transformed to martensite either (a) by heating near 1400 F (760 C) to make the austenite unstable so it transforms during cooling, (b) by a refrigeration treatment below the $M_s$ point and possibly as low as $-100$ F ($-75$ C), or by cold working, if other conditions are suitable. The martensitic matrix then is hardened to approximately Rockwell $C50$ by precipitating another constituent during heat-treatment in the range 750 to 1100 F (400 to 595 C).

The wrought austenitic types like those shown in Table 9.4 always have a completely austenitic matrix with a hardness of approximately Rockwell $B90$. Precipitation of carbides and/or phosphides during the subsequent heat-treatment then increases the hardness to Rockwell $C28$.

[48] See Refs. 15 and 16 at the end of this chapter.

**TABLE 9.3**

|          | % C  | % Cr | % Ni | % Mo | % Al |
|----------|------|------|------|------|------|
| 17-7 PH * | 0.07 | 17   | 7    | —    | 1.2  |
| A M 350 † | 0.08 | 17   | 4    | 2.8  | —    |

* Solution anneal 1950 F (1065 C), transform 1400 F (760 C), harden 1050 to 1100 F (565 to 595 C); or anneal 1750 F (955 C), transform −100 F (−75 C), harden 950 F (510 C).

† Solution anneal 1725 F (940 C), transform −100 F (−75 C), temper 750 to 900 F (400 to 480 C); or anneal 1700 to 1950 F (925 to 1065 C), age 1350 F (730 C), age 800 to 900 F (425 to 480 C).

**TABLE 9.4**

|          | % C  | % Cr | % Ni | % P  | % Al |
|----------|------|------|------|------|------|
| 17-10 P * | 0.12 | 17   | 10   | 0.25 | —    |
| 3311 †    | 0.17 | 22   | 23   | —    | 3.25 |

* Solution anneal 2050 F (1120 C), harden 1200 to 1300 F (650 to 700 C).
† Solution anneal 2200 F (1200 C), harden 1200 to 1400 F (650 to 760 C).

**TABLE 9.5**

|        | % C  | % Cr | % Ni | % Si | % Cu | % Mo | % Be |
|--------|------|------|------|------|------|------|------|
| V2B *  | 0.07 | 19   | 10   | 3    | 2    | 3    | 0.15 |

* Solution anneal 2000 F (1095 C), harden 925 F (495 C).

A typical austenitic-ferritic type like that shown in Table 9.5 is used only for castings because of poor hot-working characteristics. By adjusting the composition, the microstructure contains both austenite and delta ferrite, sometimes in about equal amounts. Solution annealing dissolves the minor elements, giving a hardness near Rockwell $C28$. The hardening treatment then hardens the ferrite quickly and the austenite more slowly to Rockwell $C38$.

## QUESTIONS

1. In iron-binary-alloy constitutional diagrams in which a closed gamma loop appears, what should be the effect of increasing the carbon content? Why? What effect should this have on whether or not the steel is hardenable by heat-treatment? In an iron-chromium alloy which is to be fusion welded, do you think it would be preferable to keep the carbon "on the high side" or "on the low side"? Why? What approximate ranges of carbon are being considered in this case?

2. A 27%-chromium steel is susceptible to embrittlement by sigma phase when heated for a long time at 1200 F. What can be done to slow down this embrittlement? The sigma phase is redissolved by heating 1 hr at 1700 F and the part is re-exposed at 1200 F. Would you expect sigma to form during this second exposure at 1200 F at approximately the same rate as during the first exposure, at a faster rate, or at a slower rate? What reasons do you have for this belief?

3. Consider an intermediate-chromium steel, like the 5% chromium, 0.5% molybdenum alloy, which is to be fusion welded. The recommended pre-heat and interpass temperature is 200 to 300 F. If the weldment is sub-jected to severe restraint is it preferable to stress relieve at 1250 to 1350 F immediately after welding or to let the weldment cool to atmospheric temperatures first? Why? Suppose there are substantially no restraints? Can you see any disadvantages to using a higher preheat temperature, say 600 F, if the weldment is to be postheated immediately? How about if it is to be cooled to atmospheric temperatures first?

4. How does elevated-temperature hydrogen attack on carbon steel compare with hydrogen embrittlement of tough-pitch copper? Above approximately 1000 F, hydrogen decarburizes low-carbon steel entirely at the outer sur-face; there is no internal fissuring. What do you think is responsible for this?

5. Why is it advisable to use a notch-brittle transition curve to evaluate sensi-tivity to or the effects of temper embrittlement rather than a single room-temperature impact test?

6. Why is grain coarsening near the fusion line of welds a much more serious factor in Type 405 nonhardenable stainless steel than in the Type 410 hardenable type?

7. Why do the modified cutlery steels (Type 440) hold an edge much better than the 13% chromium, 0.30% carbon steels do? Applying this same reasoning to plain-carbon steels, how could you improve the edge reten-tion of a eutectoid composition alloy? What are the advantages of vanadium steels over plain-carbon steels for cutting tools such as knives?

8. What are some of the advantages and disadvantages of austenitic stainless steels over ferritic stainless steels for elevated temperature use? Carbon strengthens 18:8 type austenitic steels for elevated-temperature applica-

tions. If they are so used, when must appropriate precautions be taken to prevent deterioration from intergrannular corrosion? What are the objections to the extra low carbon grades of austenitic stainless steels for elevated temperature use?

9. Furnace tubes of 0.08% carbon (max) 18:8-type stainless steel 6 in. diameter and 0.5 in. thick are cold worked as a final stage of manufacture before being installed in a furnace in which the expected metal temperature is 1300 F. What can you say about the likelihood of service embrittlement by carbide precipitation or sigma formation? What is the probability of grain-boundary sensitization leading to intergranular corrosion when the furnace is cold? If this procedure should work, what would be the disadvantages from a purchasing agent's viewpoint?

10. Why does it take so long for the matrix of an austenitic stainless steel to recover from the effects of sensitization? Can anything be done to speed up this recovery? Would you expect the higher alloy (for example, 25:12 or 25:20) austenitic stainless steels to be as susceptible as 18:8 to sensitization by carbide precipitation? Would there be any advantage to adding, say, approximately 1% columbium to these higher alloy grades, as is done in Type 347 stainless steels? What would be accomplished?


## FOR FURTHER STUDY

1. *Metals Handbook,* 7th ed. (1948) and *Supplements,* and 8th ed., Vol. I (1961). Metals Park, Ohio: American Society for Metals.

2. *The Elevated-Temperature Properties of Chromium-Molybdenum Steels, S.T.P. No. 151.* Philadelphia: American Society for Testing Materials, 1953.

3. *Digest of Steels for High-Temperature Service.* Canton, Ohio: The Timken Roller Bearing Co., 1957.

4. *High-Temperature Alloys* by Claude L. Clark. New York: Pitman Publishing Corp., 1953.

5. *High Temperature Materials* by R. F. Hehemann and G. M. Ault. New York: John Wiley & Sons, 1959.

6. *Stainless Steels* by C. A. Zapffe. Cleveland: American Society for Metals, 1952.

7. *Stainless Steels in Industry,* 3rd ed. by J. H. G. Monypenny. London: Chapman and Hall, Ltd., 1951.

8. *Stainless Steel Tubing.* Beaver Falls, Pa.: The Babcock and Wilcox Co., 1959.

9. *Physical Metallurgy of Stress Corrosion Fracture.* New York: Interscience Publishers, 1959.

10. *Stress-Corrosion Cracking of Austenitic Chromium-Nickel Stainless Steels, S.T.P. No. 264.* Philadelphia: American Society for Testing Materials, 1960.

11. *N.A.C.E. Technical Report on Stress Corrosion Cracking (Publ. 59–4)*. Houston, Tex.: National Association of Corrosion Engineers, 1959.

12. *Data on Corrosion- and Heat-Resistant Steels and Alloys—Wrought and Cast, S.T.P. No. 52-A*. Philadelphia: American Society for Testing Materials, 1950.

13. *The Elevated Temperature Properties of Stainless Steels, S.T.P. No. 124*. Philadelphia: American Society for Testing Materials, 1952.

14. *Symposium on High Temperature Steels and Alloys for Gas Turbines*. London: Iron and Steel Institute, 1951.

15. *Physical Metallurgy of Precipitation Hardenable Stainless Steels* by D. C. Ludwigson and A. M. Hall. Washington, D. C.: Office of Technical Services, Department of Defense, 1959 (Code PB 15 1067).

16. *Physical and Mechanical Properties of Precipitation Hardenable Stainless Steels* by D. A. Roberts, D. B. Roach, and A. M. Hall. Washington, D. C.: Office of Technical Service, Department of Defense, 1959 (Code PB 15 1068).

# 10 Aging and Precipitation-Hardening

## AGING IN IRONS AND LOW-CARBON STEELS

IRONS AND LOW-CARBON STEELS ARE SUBJECT TO time-dependent hardening because of reactions involving the interstitial elements carbon and nitrogen,[1] even though the solid solubility of these elements is relatively small. If the precipitation is from supersaturated ferrite the hardening is known as quench aging.[2] If it follows some sort of plastic deformation or straining it is known as strain aging.

The solubility of carbon in alpha iron is approximated in Figure 10.1.[3] The maximum solubility of nitrogen is somewhat greater, approximately 0.11 wgt %, and the nitrogen eutectoid temperature is only 1080 F (580 C). Even though these solid solubilities are low, they decrease so much as the temperature decreases that a large supersaturation results from quenching from near the eutectoid temperature. Near atmospheric temperatures the solubility of carbon is believed to be approximately $10^{-7}\%$ and that of nitrogen $2 \times 10^{-4}\%$. When the quenched alloy is reheated at temperatures

---

[1] H. W. Paxton has reviewed this subject recently in Ref. 3 at the end of this chapter; see also L. J. Dijkstra, *Trans. A.I.M.E.,* **185** (1949), 252–60.

[2] This was discussed thoroughly by R. L. Kenyon and R. S. Burns in Ref. 5 at the end of this chapter; see also G. Lagerberg and B. S. Lement, *Trans. A.S.M.,* **50** (1958), 141–61.

[3] L. S. Darken and R. W. Gurry (Ref. 9 at the end of this chapter) give this accurately as

$$\text{Wgt } \% \text{ C} = 2.55e^{\frac{-9,700}{RT}}$$

*460*

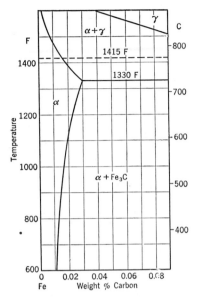

**Figure 10.1** Constitutional diagram for the alloys of carbon and alpha ferrite, the deep-drawing steels. [After J. H. Whiteley.]

in the range of, say, 32 to 210 F (0 to 100 C) carbon precipitates [4] first as disc-shaped platelets of the epsilon ($\epsilon$) carbide, $Fe_{2.4}C$, simply because this phase has the greatest probability of nucleating. The arrangements of atoms, and their spacing, in the $\epsilon$-carbide lattice and in the ferrite lattice are so similar that it does not require much strain energy to form a coherent nucleus. As the temperature increases, the tendency to form the stable precipitate, cementite ($Fe_3C$), increases. However, aging times of the order of 30 min at 570 F (300 C) are required before cementite can be detected by electron diffraction.

The $\epsilon$-carbide also shows a large solubility for nitrogen whereas cementite dissolves relatively little nitrogen. Nitrogen alone precipitates first as $Fe_{16}N_2$, an ordered body-centered cubic nitride, and later as the face-centered cubic, $Fe_4N$, but usually only in very low-carbon alloys. Here again the ferrite and $Fe_{16}N_2$ lattices match quite well so it does not require much strain energy to form a coherent nucleus.

Typical hardness changes with aging time for a low-carbon (0.06%) deep-drawing steel are shown in Figure 10.2. Note that there is ample evidence of (a) the overaging or softening which occurs after the precipitate loses coherency, and (b) a higher maximum hardness as the aging temperature decreases. Quench aging lowers the impact resistance but seldom results in actual brittleness. Any tendency toward quench aging

---

[4] See also R. H. Doremus and E. F. Koch, *Trans. A.I.M.E.*, **218** (1960), 590–605.

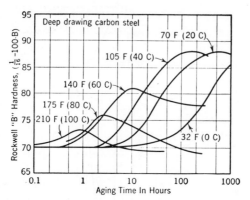

**Figure 10.2** Change in Rockwell *B* hardness, with time, of deep-drawing carbon steel after quenching from approximately 1300 F (700 C) and aging at the temperatures indicated. A logarithmic time scale has been used for convenience and economy of space. [From J. Johnston, *Trans. A.I.M.E.*, **150** (1942), 1–29.]

can be eliminated by cooling slowly enough to approximate equilibrium, after the final heat-treatment.

Strain aging is more complicated than quench aging.[5] Strain aging is related to the yield-point phenomenon which is particularly noticeable in steels.[6] The relation between yield-point elongation, the stress-strain curve, and the surface appearance of the test specimen is shown in Figure 10.3a. When the yield point is present, the metal first deforms elastically to a higher stress than that needed to continue plastic deformation. Once this upper yield stress is exceeded, the metal flows discontinuously (actually, the flow is merely more rapid than the testing machine can maintain), in localized regions known as stretcher strains or Lueder's lines, until work-hardening strengthens these deformed regions sufficiently, or until the entire gauge length has been involved in the block deformation process; then plastic deformation continues in a uniform manner. It is shown clearly in Figure 10.3a (*A* through *E*) that the more pronounced the yield point discontinuity is, the greater and more localized is the yield-point deformation. If annealed sheet is given a light rolling and tested at once, the discontinuous yield point first decreases and then disappears (Figure 10.3b). However, as shown in Figure 10.4, during aging following the cold rolling the discontinuous yield point returns, the aging time required to do this being shorter the higher the aging temperature.[7]

[5] J. D. Lubahn, *Trans. A.S.M.*, **44** (1952), 643–64, has shown that strain aging occurs more generally than in mild steels.

[6] Methods of control are known. See, E. R. Morgan and J. C. Shyne, *Trans. A.I.M.E.*, **209** (1957), 65–69.

[7] P. Garofalo and G. V. Smith, *Trans. A.S.M.*, **47** (1955), 957–83, have determined some of these time and temperature effects.

Where it is encountered at elevated temperatures, strain aging usually is referred to as blue brittleness. This is the direct result of the specimen going through repeated yielding, leading to a higher ultimate strength and a lower ductility than is found at nominal atmospheric temperatures.

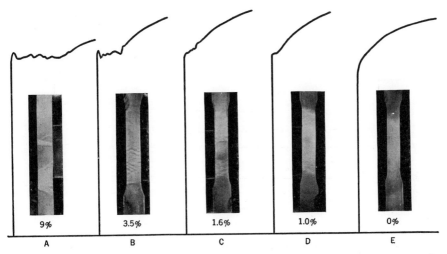

**Figure 10.3  a** (*top*). Five stress-strain curves showing different amounts of elongation at yield point, together with photographs of the corresponding tensile specimens. Yield point elongations are indicated in each instance, higher values indicating a greater tendency to produce stretcher strains, as shown in the photographs. [From R. L. Kenyon and R. S. Burns, courtesy American Society for Metals.] **b** (*bottom*). Stress-strain curves of normalized, box-annealed, mild-steel sheets, temper cold rolled 0, 0.5, 1, 2, and 3% and tested fresh. Note absence of marked yield point in materials subjected to about 1% or more cold reduction. [From *Metals Handbook,* courtesy American Society for Metals.]

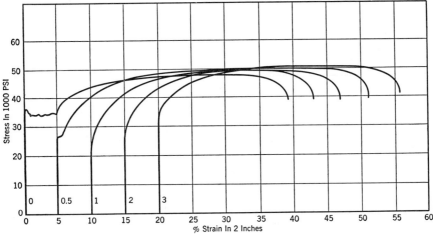

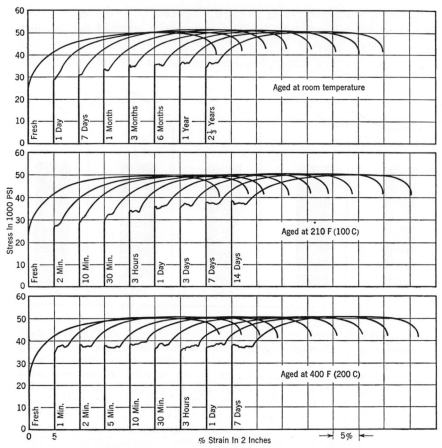

**Figure 10.4** Stress-strain curves of mild-steel sheets, temper cold rolled 1% and aged for the indicated times at three different temperatures, showing the more rapid return of the yield point at higher aging temperatures. [From R. L. Kenyon and R. S. Burns, courtesy American Society for Metals.]

## DISLOCATION EXPLANATION OF AGING IN IRON AND STEELS

All of these strain-aging effects in iron and steel are explained by dislocation theory.[8] Small interstitial atoms like carbon and nitrogen (also hydrogen and boron) are most stable in solid solution in ferrite if they are located at regions of lattice misfit. Thus they tend to collect as an "atmosphere" at the tension side of line dislocations. If subjected only

[8] See A. H. Cottrell and B. A. Bilby, *Proc. Phys. Soc.,* **62A** (1949), 49.

to small displacements, a dislocation tends to return to its atmosphere of interstitials. However, after a high enough stress has been applied, it breaks away and moves more easily the farther away from its interstitial atmosphere it gets. The break-away stress corresponds to the upper yield point. This is followed by relatively easy flow because the dislocations no longer are pinned by an atmosphere of interstitials, until, ultimately, the moving dislocations start to pile up and slow down as work-hardening occurs. The same effects do not occur in face-centered cubic austenite largely because the tendency for interstitial atoms to remain randomly dispersed in solid solution is greater than their tendency to condense as an atmosphere around dislocations. Thus, the change in free energy of the dislocation is not great enough to lock it into position.

After deformation, there is a redistribution of interstitials, by diffusion to the regions of greatest stability as atmospheres around the greatly increased numbers of dislocations in their new positions. This again anchors the dislocations in position, and increases the stress required for flow because of the larger number of dislocations. Diffusion takes time [9] so, until the atmospheres reform and reanchor the dislocations, the stress required to move them is relatively low and the stress-strain curve shows no yield-point effect. The higher the aging temperature the more rapid the diffusion so the more quickly the discontinuous yield point returns. Because it is more soluble than carbon, has a higher diffusion coefficient, and precipitates less completely in slowly cooled steels, nitrogen probably is the main cause of strain aging in commercial steels.

The blue-brittle effect is simply the result of the increased diffusion rate of carbon and nitrogen at higher temperatures. Although the dislocation breaks away from its atmosphere at the initial yielding, the interstitials diffuse after it so rapidly that a new atmosphere quickly reforms. The tensile test thus is a series of dislocation break-aways and atmosphere reformations, each one at a somewhat higher stress because of the effect of work-hardening. In order to explain all the effects of strain aging it is necessary to introduce also an influence of residual stresses.[10]

Strain aging can be controlled most readily by treating the steel with strong carbide and nitride formers such as aluminum, vanadium or titanium, while it still is molten. If substantially all of the carbon and nitrogen can be combined as stable carbides and nitrides, there will be no significant interstitials left to condense on dislocations.

---

[9] The presently accepted constants for the diffusion of carbon in alpha iron are $A = 0.02$ sq cm/sec, $Q = 20{,}100$ cal/mol, and for nitrogen $A = 0.003$ sq cm/sec, $Q = 18{,}200$ cal/mol; hydrogen is several orders of magnitude faster. These constants vary with concentration; for carbon in austenite, for example, see C. Wells, W. Batz and R. F. Mehl, *Trans. A.I.M.E.,* **188** (1950), 553–60.

[10] This is summarized by H. W. Paxton in Ref. 3 at the end of this chapter.

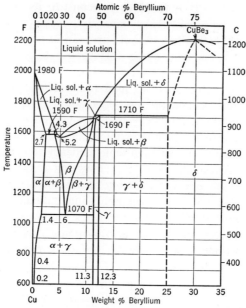

**Figure 10.5** Constitutional diagram for the alloys of copper with up to 35% beryllium, the beryllium bronzes. [After M. Hansen.]

## BERYLLIUM-COPPER ALLOYS

The copper-rich end of the constitutional diagram for the alloys of beryllium and copper (Figure 10.5) indicates a diminishing solubility of beryllium in copper with decreasing temperature, suggesting that the alloys might be subject to precipitation-hardening.[11] The beta phase in this system also decomposes as a eutectoid but these alloys are not industrially important.

The commonest commercial alloy, copper alloy No. 172, containing 1.80 to 2.05% beryllium,[12] with 0.25% (max) iron and 0.50% (max) nickel or cobalt, often is known as beryllium bronze. The iron and nickel or cobalt largely serve to inhibit grain growth although their presence also reduces the rate of precipitation significantly, thereby giving more uniform hardening. The addition of a very small amount of tin increases the precipitation rate and so permits required hardnesses to be reached with lower beryllium contents.

---

[11] W. D. Robertson and R. S. Bray discuss these and other precipitation-hardenable copper-base alloys in Ref. 3 at the end of this chapter. The decomposition of the eutectoid is described by R. H. Fillnow and D. J. Mack, *Trans. A.I.M.E.*, **188** (1950), 1229–36; and by J. S. Brett, G. L. Kehl, and E. Jeraiz, *ibid.*, **218** (1960), 753–63.

[12] An alloy, with 1.60 to 1.80% beryllium also is sold. It has lower strength and hardness than the 2% beryllium alloy and is somewhat less brittle. Because of the lower beryllium content it also is less expensive.

Water quenching from 1425 to 1475 F (775 to 800 C) both anneals cold-worked material and provides a suitable solution treatment before precipitation-hardening. No evidence has been found of any precipitation during this quenching treatment. If maximum properties are not needed, however, annealing temperatures as low as 1200 F (650 C) can be used. A typical microstructure for the quenched alloy is given in Figure 10.6a. After slow cooling, sometimes called a homogenizing heat-treatment for these alloys, precipitation is complete (Figure 10.6c) and the alloy can be cold worked but not precipitation-hardened.

**Figure 10.6** Metallographic structures of beryllium copper (2.0% beryllium, 0.25% nickel, remainder copper). Etched with FeCl$_3$ to blacken the beta phase ($\times$75). **a** (*top left*). Quenched after solution heat-treatment. At this magnification the structure would be essentially the same after a precipitation heat-treatment to maximum hardness. **b** (*top right*). Quenched, rolled 4 B. & S. No. hard, and precipitation heat-treated. [Photomicrographs courtesy Technical Department, The American Brass Company.] **c** (*bottom*). Slowly cooled, showing coarse particles of the beta phase. This structure never is encountered industrially if the alloy is to be heat-treated. Etched with NH$_4$OH + H$_2$O$_2$ ($\times$300).

Hardness changes with time of aging at 660 F (350 C), for alloys of several beryllium contents, are shown in Figure 10.7.

Precipitation-hardening temperatures usually are in the range 480 to 620 F (250 to 325 C), the exact time and temperature depending on the properties desired. Typical mechanical properties are shown in Table 10.1.

**TABLE 10.1**

|  | Tensile Strength (psi) | Yield Strength (0.75% Elongation) (psi) | Elongation (% in 2 in.) | Brinell Hardness (10 mm– 3,000 Kg) | Rockwell Hardness |
|---|---|---|---|---|---|
| Soft, quench-annealed | 70,000 | 31,000 | 45 | 110 | B68–B73 |
| Quenched, heat-treat-hardened | 175,000 | 134,000 | 6 | 340 | C38 |
| Quenched, cold-rolled 4 B. & S. No. | 118,000 | 105,000 | 4 | 220 | C24 |
| Quenched, cold-rolled, and heat-treat-hardened | 193,000 | 138,000 | 2 | 365 | C41 |

The temperature of the precipitation heat-treatment is below the recrystallization temperature for the 2.0%-beryllium composition. Therefore, the effects of precipitation-hardening can be superimposed on those of work-hardening, the total effect being nearly the sum of the increments produced by each. Tensile strengths higher than 200,000 psi can be produced in this way. If maximum properties are not required with this alloy, much greater toughness can be secured, without serious loss in strength, by overaging rather than underaging. This can be accomplished more easily by aging at a temperature in the vicinity of 750 to 800 F (400 to 425 C) than by the alternate method of greatly increasing the aging times in the usual range, 480 to 620 F (250 to 325 C).

The 2.0%-beryllium alloy has a higher fatigue resistance than any other copper-base alloy and a better wear resistance than phosphor bronze when run against any grade of steel, especially under light loading and without lubrication. The alloy also is used for nonsparking tools.

Precipitation in these alloys starts by the formation of thin beryllium-rich coherent plates parallel to the cube planes of the matrix.[13] The extent and

[13] The mechanism of precipitation is described by A. H. Geisler, J. H. Mallery, and F. E. Steigert, *Trans. A.I.M.E.,* **194** (1952), 307–16.

thickness of these plates depends on the aging time, the aging temperature and the composition. There is at least one transition phase formed, of uncertain structure. This seems to cause most of the hardening rather than the ordered body-centered cubic gamma phase. However, if the solution-annealed alloy is cold worked before it is aged below 615 F (325 C), the stable gamma phase precipitates and the hardening is more rapid. If the aging is carried out above 1070 F (575 C) the precipitate is the body-centered cubic beta phase.

A microstructure typical of the cold-worked-and-aged alloy is shown in Figure 10.6b. The striated pattern is typical of aged material. Cold working encourages a uniform or continuous precipitation (compare Figure 7.1). If the alloy is annealed before aging instead of being cold worked, there often is also a lamellar discontinuous precipitate, the distribution of which is nonuniform, occurring primarily at the grain boundaries, and sometimes

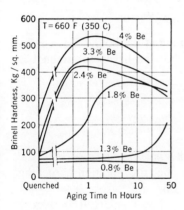

**Figure 10.7** Change in Brinell hardness, with time, of copper alloyed with different amounts of beryllium, during aging at a constant temperature of 660 F (350 C). The equilibrium solubility at this temperature is about 0.4% beryllium. A logarithmic time scale has been used for convenience and economy of space. [After G. Masing and O. Dahl.]

**Figure 10.8** Constitutional diagram for the alloys of aluminum and copper, the duralumin-type alloys. [After M. Hansen.]

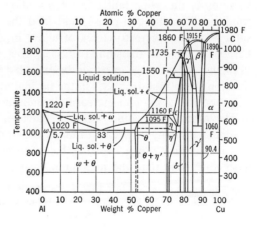

**Figure 10.9** (*opposite page*) Changes in the metallographic structure of an aluminum bronze (90% copper, 10% aluminum) as a result of heat-treatment (×100 originally, reduced about one-third in reproduction). The effect of composition on some properties of the solid solution alloys also is shown. [Courtesy Bridgeport Brass Company.] **a.** Water quenched from 1650 F (900 C). Etched with $NH_4OH + H_2O_2$. [Photomicrograph by S. J. MacMullan, Jr.] Needlelike structure is shown in portions of two grains. The grain size is very coarse because of the high heat-treating temperature. **b.** Reheat *a* to 1470 F (800 C) for 2 hr, cool slowly. Etched with Grard's No. 1. [Photomicrograph by C. T. Stott.] Coarse needles of $\alpha$ in a finely dispersed eutectoid of $\alpha$ and $\delta$ are shown in portions of two grains. **c.** Reheat *a* to 1290 F (700 C) for 2 hr, cool slowly. Etched with $NH_4OH + H_2O_2$. [Photomicrograph by J. H. Dedrick.] The "needles" of $\alpha$ are somewhat finer than in *b* because of the lower reheating temperature. Portion of a single grain is shown. **d.** Reheat *a* to 1110 F (600 C) for 2 hr, cool slowly. Etched with Grard's No. 1. [Photomicrograph by H. D. Nickol.] The "needles" of $\alpha$ are noticeably finer than in *b* or *c* and the geometrical nature of their occurrence is very striking in the portion of a single grain shown. This is also a Widmannstaetten-type structure.

---

spreading into the grain. In such cases, hardening at the boundaries occurs more rapidly than in the center of the grain but the hardness attained is not so great.

### ALUMINUM-COPPER ALLOYS

The system aluminum-copper (Figure 10.8) has examples of both the eutectoid-transformation (copper-rich) and the precipitation-hardening (aluminum-rich) types of hardening mechanisms.

The copper-rich portion of the diagram is shown enlarged in Figure 10.9.[14] As with the copper-zinc and copper-tin systems discussed in Chapter 6, the important engineering alloys are confined to the primary solid solution, the two-phase field, and the first (copper-rich) secondary solid solution. Microstructures of alloys in either of these fields are comparable to those of the similar brasses. The strength properties, also shown in Figure 10.9, change as would be expected for a solid solution except that the elongation first decreases in the normal manner to about 3% aluminum and then increases with increasing aluminum content.

The eutectoid decomposition of the beta ($\beta$) phase during quenching is similar in many respects to that of the iron-carbon eutectoid except that it is somewhat simpler because the substitutional aluminum atoms diffuse more sluggishly than the interstitial carbon atoms. It also is different be-

[14] This system was studied before the phase designation convention was adopted so the $\alpha$-solid solution is the copper-rich primary solid solution, although, by modern convention, alpha should designate the aluminum-rich primary solid solution.

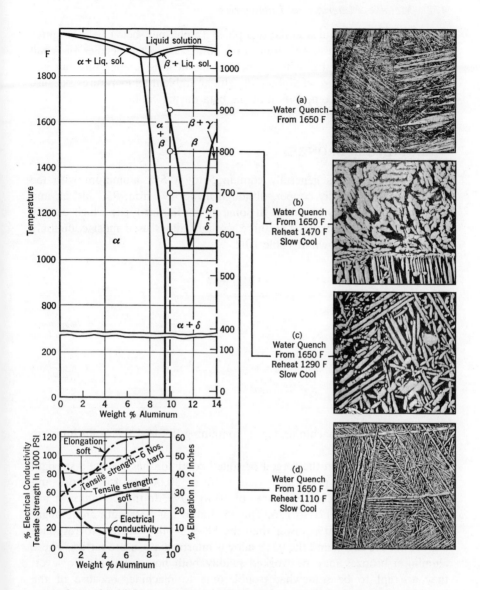

(a) Water Quench From 1650 F

(b) Water Quench From 1650 F Reheat 1470 F Slow Cool

(c) Water Quench From 1650 F Reheat 1290 F Slow Cool

(d) Water Quench From 1650 F Reheat 1110 F Slow Cool

cause here the high-temperature solid solution is body-centered cubic and the principal low-temperature constituent is face-centered cubic.[15]

As shown by the metallographic structure in Figure 10.9a, the beta phase decomposes martensitically during water quenching. Reheating an alloy, after it is quenched from a high temperature at which it had a beta

[15] Isothermal transformation of the eutectoid has been studied by E. P. Klier and S. M. Grymko, *Trans. A.I.M.E.*, **185** (1949), 611–19; also A. H. Krasberg, Jr., and D. J. Mack, *ibid.*, **191** (1951), 903–08.

structure, to temperatures in the two-phase (alpha-plus-beta) field (Figures 10.9*b, c,* and *d*) causes the alpha to separate as coarse needles or small narrow plates in a matrix which is beta at the heating temperature but is a finely dispersed mixture of alpha and delta at ambient temperatures because of the eutectoidal decomposition of the beta during cooling.

## ALUMINUM BRONZES

Aluminum bronzes generally contain 5 to 10.5% aluminum with the remainder substantially copper, although up to 4% iron, 9% nickel, and 10% manganese may be added in some of the harder types which usually are made only as castings. The three wrought alloys used most commonly in this country are shown in Table 10.2.

**TABLE 10.2**

| Type | Copper Alloy No. | % Cu | % Al | % Fe (max) | % Other Additions (Ni, Si, Sn, Mn) (max) | % Impurities (Zn, Cd, Pb) (max) |
|---|---|---|---|---|---|---|
| 88:9:3 | 628 | Rem | 8–11 | 1.5–3.5 | 4–7 Ni, 0.5–2 Mn | 0.50 |
| 95:5 | 606 | 92–96 | 4–7 | 0.50 | — | 0.50 |
| 92:8 | 612 | 90–93 | 7–9 | 0.50 | — | 0.50 |

In addition, free-machining types, containing 0.5 to 1.0% tellurium, are made in some forms.

The 88:9:3 type in the forged or rolled condition has a tensile strength of 70,000 to 95,000 psi, with a yield point of 30,000 to 45,000 psi, and an elongation and reduction in area of 10 to 30%. In this condition it has a Brinell hardness of 120 to 135. The 95:5 alloy has a strength and elongation approximately 20% lower than the 88:9:3 alloy, with a correspondingly lower hardness; and the 92:8 alloy is intermediate in properties. These aluminum bronzes may be worked readily both hot and cold. However, they are apt to be somewhat troublesome to machine, because of the presence of small inclusions of aluminum oxide.

Alloys of copper with 7% aluminum also can be precipitation-hardened [16] if they contain 0.5 to 1% titanium or zirconium or 1 to 2% cobalt, with approximately 1% iron or 5% nickel, but these alloys are not yet available for general use.

[16] See J. P. Dennison, *Journ. Inst. Metals,* **82** (London: 1953), 117; *ibid.,* **83** (1955), 564; *ibid.,* **84** (1955–56), 115.

## ALUMINUM ALLOYS CONTAINING COPPER

At the aluminum-rich end of the diagram the solubility of copper decreases from about 5.7% at the eutectoid temperature, 1020 F (550 C), to less than 0.1% at room temperature.[17] The equilibrium second phase, $\theta$, is the intermetallic compound $CuAl_2$. The microstructure of a slowly cooled alloy (Figure 10.10) shows coarse particles of this phase in a solid-solution matrix.

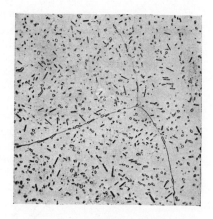

**Figure 10.10** Metallographic structures of duralumin-type precipitation-hardenable alloy showing coarse particles of a second phase precipitated during slow cooling from the primary solid solution field. Etched with ½% HF (×100). [Photomicrograph courtesy Aluminum Research Laboratories.]

Impure aluminum-copper alloys were the first in which precipitation-hardening was recognized, by Alfred Wilm in 1906. Since then both impure and high-purity alloys have been studied extensively in order to clarify the precipitation and hardening mechanisms.[18] Impure aluminum-copper alloys (containing iron and silicon) do not age-harden at room temperature, unless some magnesium is added. During natural aging of high-purity alloys, at atmospheric temperatures, the hardness and strength properties increase slowly with holding time and the elongation decreases slowly. During artificial aging, at elevated temperatures, the rate of change of these properties is greater than during natural aging, and the maximum values usually are greater also. Typical aging curves are shown in Figure 10.11. Likewise, because the rate of the hardening reactions is governed by an activation

[17] L. F. Mondolfo, *Trans. A.I.M.E.*, **215** (1959), 289–94.
[18] This has been discussed in detail by A. H. Geisler in Ref. 4 at the end of this chapter; and by W. A. Anderson in Ref. 3 at the end of this chapter. See also A. Guinier, *Journ. of Metals,* **8** (1956), 673–82, and G. C. Smith in *Progress in Metal Physics,* **1** (New York: Interscience Publishers, 1949), 162–234.

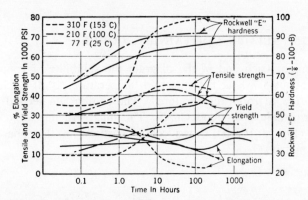

**Figure 10.11** The effect of different aging temperatures on the Rockwell *E* hardness, the tensile and yield strengths, and the elongation of a wrought aluminum alloy (approximately 4% copper) quenched into oil from 16 hr at 975 F (525 C). [From W. L. Fink and D. W. Smith, *Trans. A.I.M.E.,* **128** (1938), 223–33.]

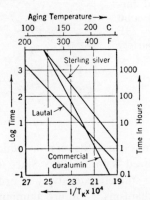

**Figure 10.12** Rates of aging at different temperatures for the alloys: Lautal, containing 4.5% copper, 0.75% silicon, 0.75% manganese, remainder aluminum [after C. H. M. Jenkins and E. H. Bucknall], duralumin, containing 4.19% copper, 0.58% magnesium, 0.14% silicon, 0.65% manganese, 0.32% iron, 0.08% chromium, remainder aluminum [after M. Cohen], and sterling silver, containing 8.71% copper, 91.28% silver [after M. Cohen], as measured by the times to attain maximum tensile strength.

energy, a plot of log time to reach maximum hardness against the reciprocal of the absolute temperature gives a straight line (Figure 10.12).

The entire hardening process is complex, but all steps do not take place under all conditions. Four stages

$$\text{G. P. Zones (1)} \rightarrow \text{G. P. Zones (2) or } \theta'' \rightarrow \theta' \rightarrow \theta(\text{CuAl}_2)$$

are recognized between the first significant change in the statistically-homogeneous metastable solid solution and the equilibrium precipitate, $\theta(CuAl_2)$, although all of them are not indicated clearly by property changes.

The initial stage, G. P. Zones (1),[19] is the formation of copper-rich regions of plate-like shape on the cube planes of the solid-solution matrix. In material aged at room temperature, the coherent platelets have a size of approximately 50 Å. In the second stage, G. P. Zones (2) or $\theta''$, the copper and aluminum atoms arrange themselves in a definite ordered pattern based on CuAl. This stage may coexist with either the first or the third stage. Throughout the first three stages, the nuclei probably are coherent with the cube planes of the matrix. The $\theta'$ constituent is tetragonal with the approximate formula $Cu_2Al_{3.6}$. The tetragonal equilibrium precipitate phase $\theta$ usually is referred to as $CuAl_2$ although this stoichiometric composition actually is just outside the field in which the $\theta$ phase is stable. Under certain conditions of supersaturation and aging both the $\theta'$ and the $\theta$ constituents can nucleate independently from the solid solution.

At lower aging temperatures, the formation of the G. P. Zones (1) is the predominant hardening mechanism. Although the other constituents may form if the aging time is long enough, they have not been detected after aging from the quenched state at substantially room temperature (compare Figure 10.13a). However, as the aging temperature is raised (compare Figure 10.13b and c), the other two metastable constituents and the stable constituent can be detected, particularly if the temperature is high enough and the time long enough. In each case an incubation period is noted. When overaging and softening occur, coherency has been lost and particles of the stable precipitate $\theta$ form.[20]

If the alloy is cold worked the formation of the $\theta'$ and the $\theta$ phases along the deformation lines is accelerated, to such an extent that $\theta$ has been observed after room temperature aging, as well as after elevated temperature aging (compare Figure 10.13d).

Most of the existing theory of precipitation-hardening was derived from careful studies on the aluminum-copper system so it is not surprising that there is good agreement between theory and experiment. For example, it can be shown readily that an alloy which has been hardened at room temperature first softens somewhat when heated to a higher temperature, say 210 F (100 C). This is the natural result of some nuclei returning into solid solution and thus disappearing as hardening agents. The nuclei stable at 210 F (100 C) are significantly larger than those stable at room tem-

[19] The Guinier-Preston (G.P.) name derives from the simultaneous X-ray diffraction studies of A. Guinier in France and G. P. Preston in England, first announced in 1938.

[20] Note, however, that dispersed hard particles alone also strengthen metals. See, for example, N. J. Grant and O. Preston, *Trans. A.I.M.E.*, **209** (1957), 349–57.

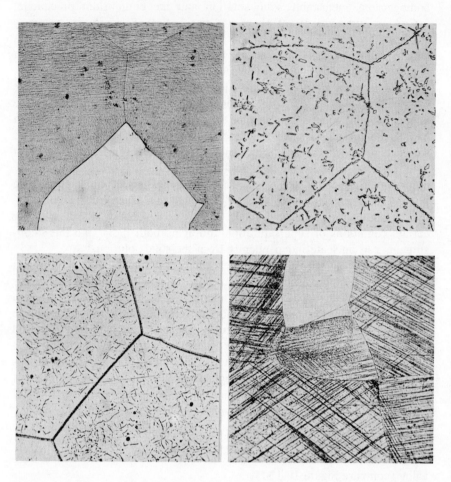

**Figure 10.13**   Typical metallographic structures of a 96% aluminum, 4% copper alloy showing the various types of precipitate formation. Etched with Keller's reagent. Compare this with the coarse uniform precipitation characteristic of the fully annealed condition (Figure 10.10). [Photomicrographs courtesy Aluminum Research Laboratories.] **a** (*top left*). As quenched, no precipitation (×500). **b** (*top right*). Localized precipitation both at grain boundaries and within the grains (×100). **c** (*bottom left*). Fine uniform precipitation on a geometrical pattern throughout the grains. (Widmann-staetten-type.) (×500.) **d** (*bottom right*). Localized precipitation along deformation lines (×100).

perature. Also, the thermal stresses introduced by a drastic quench may be high enough to reach the relatively low yield strength of these aluminum alloys. This tends to give discontinuous hardening, the reaction proceeding more rapidly in the deformed regions than in the undeformed material.

## PRECIPITATION-HARDENABLE ALUMINUM STRUCTURAL ALLOYS

The precipitation-hardenable aluminum structural alloys [21] usually are of one of three basic types (1) alloys with copper and magnesium, (2) alloys with magnesium and silicon or (3) alloys with copper, magnesium, and zinc.

### ALUMINUM-COPPER-MAGNESIUM ALLOYS

Industrial alloys of the copper-magnesium group contain 2.2 to 6.0% copper, up to 1.8% magnesium, up to 1.2% manganese, and up to 1.2% silicon, remainder aluminum plus normal impurities. The two most important have the nominal compositions shown in Table 10.3. Duralumin

**TABLE 10.3**

| Designation * | % Cu | % Mg | % Mn | % Si |
|---|---|---|---|---|
| 2014 | 4.4 | 0.4 | 0.8 | 0.8 |
| 2024 | 4.5 | 1.5 | 0.6 | † |

\* See Appendix for more information on these alloy symbols.
† Present but not specified.

(2017), containing 4.0% copper, 0.5% magnesium, 0.5% manganese, remainder aluminum, the original precipitation-hardening alloy, still is made but only in limited amounts, largely because for most applications its properties are not so good as those of 2024 for a comparable cost. Typical microstructures for 2017 in the annealed and in the fully age-hardened conditions are shown in Figure 10.14. A free-machining variety (2011) containing 5.5% copper and 0.5% each of lead and bismuth, remainder aluminum, also is made. The lead and bismuth appear as insoluble constituents in the microstructure (Figure 10.15); these act as chip breakers.

The addition of magnesium makes possible the natural aging of impure (containing iron plus silicon) aluminum-copper alloys at atmospheric

[21] D. Peckner, *Materials in Design Engineering,* **53** (1961), 133–40, gives a good discussion of high-strength aluminum alloys which comprise about 10% of aluminum alloy production.

**Figure 10.14** Metallographic structures typical of aluminum alloy, 2017 (4% copper, 0.5% manganese, 0.5% magnesium, remainder aluminum), sheet. Etched with Keller's reagent (×100). **a** (*left*). Annealed: -O temper. **b** (*right*). Fully heat-treated and age-hardened: -T4 temper. [Photomicrographs courtesy Aluminum Research Laboratories.]

**Figure 10.15** Metallographic structure of free-cutting aluminum alloy, 2011-T3, rod (5.5% copper, 0.5% lead, 0.5% bismuth, remainder aluminum). Etched with Keller's reagent (×100). [Photomicrograph courtesy Aluminum Research Laboratories.]

temperature. Manganese is added to improve both the strength and the corrosion resistance. Silicon in excess of approximately 0.5% increases the strength secured with elevated temperature aging, if the magnesium is less than 1%. This may be the result of precipitating the compound $Mg_2Si$. In higher magnesium alloys such as 2024, however, increasing the silicon tends to reduce the strength in both the naturally-aged and the artificially-aged conditions. The major hardening reaction is essentially that outlined already for the aluminum-copper alloys.[22]

Typical properties after various aging treatments [23] are shown in Table 10.4.

[22] See, P. R. Sperry, *Trans. A.S.M.*, **48** (1956), 904–18.
[23] The significance of various temper designations also is given in the Appendix.

**TABLE 10.4**

| Properties | 2014 | | | 2024 | | | |
|---|---|---|---|---|---|---|---|
| | -O | -T4 | -T6 | -O | -T3 | -T4 | -T36 |
| Tensile strength (psi) | 27,000 | 62,000 | 70,000 | 27,000 | 70,000 | 68,000 | 72,000 |
| Yield strength (0.2% offset) (psi) | 14,000 | 42,000 | 60,000 | 11,000 | 50,000 | 47,000 | 57,000 |
| Elongation (% in 2 in.) | 18 | 20 | 13 | 22 | 18 | 20 | 13 |
| Brinell hardness (10 mm–500 Kg) | 45 | 105 | 135 | 47 | 120 | 120 | 130 |
| Fatigue endurance limit ($5 \times 10^8$ cycles) (psi) | 13,000 | 20,000 | 18,000 | 13,000 | 20,000 | 20,000 | 18,000 |

The fatigue strength of the hardened conditions is not as great, in comparison with the annealed condition, as would be expected from the difference in strength. This may be because the coarser precipitate in the annealed material provides regions of internal stress concentration.

The Alclad forms [24] of both alloys have properties about 10% lower than those shown unless special heat-treatments are used. This form should be used if there is to be extended exposure to the weather.

Natural aging (at atmospheric temperature) requires approximately one day to reach 90% of maximum hardening and four days to reach substantial completion, but the hardening can be delayed by holding at 32 F (0 C) or lower temperatures. This low-temperature holding sometimes is used in industry for rivets or other parts which must be formed after quenching.

By artificial aging (at elevated temperatures) the strength and the ratio of yield to ultimate strength is increased but the elongation is lower than with natural aging. However, the properties obtained by elevated temperature aging are dependent on both the temperature and the time, the time required to reach maximum strength decreasing approximately exponentially with increasing temperature.[25]

[24] The Alclad forms are made with a thin integral surface (one or both) layer of an aluminum alloy which is anodic to the base aluminum alloy and thus protects it electrochemically. See article by E. M. Dix in *Engineering Laminates* (New York: John Wiley & Sons, 1949), pp. 282–302.

[25] Considerable specific data are given by W. A. Anderson in Ref. 3 at the end of this chapter; see also Ref. 1.

For the 2014-T4 temper, the preferred solution heat-treatment is a rapid water quench from a soak at 940 F (505 C) for 2014 and from 920 F (495 C) for 2024, followed by natural aging. These solution heat-treatment temperatures are not far below the eutectic temperature. Hence they must not be exceeded or partial melting will occur. If quenching is not rapid enough, coarse grain-boundary precipitates form and properties are generally lower. For artificial aging to the -T6 temper, 2014 should be heated 8 to 12 hr at 340 F (170 C). For 2024 several -T8 tempers also are used, involving 5 to 6% cold working followed by artificial aging for various times (in the range 7 to 13 hr) at 375 F (190 C).

Metallographic structures typical of 2014 (Figure 10.16a) and 2024 (Figure 10.17) show little detail at low magnifications. Most of the particles which can be seen are compounds characteristic of the impurities, chiefly iron, rather than of the alloying elements. In the naturally aged condition none of the hardening constituents can be detected even under high magnifications (compare Figure 10.13a).

The corrosion resistance of 2014 and 2024 is affected markedly by the specific heat-treatment used. Artificial aging is beneficial if it is for a long enough time and at a high enough temperature. This presumably is the result of composition homogenization. Natural aging gives good corrosion resistance only if preceded by very rapid rates of quenching, for example, thin sections quenched in cold water. During slow quenching, such as would result from quenching thick sections or from using warm or hot liquids, a highly selective grain boundary precipitation occurs. This leads to alloy depletion near the grain boundaries and hence to intergranular

**Figure 10.16** Metallographic structures typical of two aluminum forging alloys in the fully heat-treated and age-hardened condition (×100). **a** (*left*). 2014-T6 (4.4% copper, 0.8% silicon, 0.8% manganese, 0.4% magnesium, remainder aluminum). Etched with Keller's reagent. **b** (*right*). 6151-T6 (1% silicon, 0.6% magnesium, 0.25% chromium, remainder aluminum). Etched with ½% HF. [Photomicrographs courtesy Aluminum Research Laboratories.]

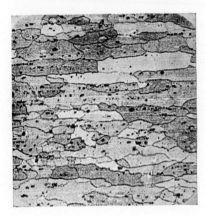
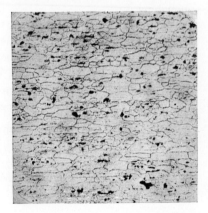

corrosion because the depleted metal is anodic to the rest of the grain and corrodes preferentially. Such intergranular attack reduces the strength of thin sheet rapidly and hence is objectionable. For this reason Alclad forms of both 2014 and 2024 are made to provide sacrificial electrochemical protection.

## ALUMINUM-MAGNESIUM-SILICON ALLOYS

Industrial aluminum alloys of the magnesium-silicon group contain enough of these elements, and in the proper ratio, to form 1 to 2% $Mg_2Si$. They usually contain small amounts of chromium, manganese or copper also, although the manganese content may not be specified. Both chromium and manganese improve strength and corrosion resistance, and inhibit grain growth and grain-boundary precipitation. Copper is added primarily for strength. However, these three elements may be omitted if an alloy that extrudes better and gives a better finish electrochemically is desired; an example is alloy 6063 which contains only 0.7% magnesium and 0.4% silicon, remainder aluminum.

The hardening effect of $Mg_2Si$ precipitation also appears to be of the coherency type with an intermediate transition phase forming before the equilibrium compound. The precipitate first appears in a needle-like form with only one major direction. This then grows laterally, forming platelets whose greatest dimension in less than 100 Å. The equilibrium precipitate, $Mg_2Si$, finally forms as three-dimensional particles.

**Figure 10.17** Metallographic structures typical of aluminum alloy 2024 (4.5% copper, 1.5% magnesium, 0.6% manganese, remainder aluminum), sheet ($\times$100). **a** (*left*). Annealed: -O temper. Etched with Bossert's reagent. **b** (*right*). Solution heat-treated and naturally aged to maximum hardness: -T4 temper. Etched with Keller's reagent. [Photomicrographs courtesy Aluminum Research Laboratories.]

Some typical compositions of alloys of this type are shown in Table 10.5.

**TABLE 10.5**

|  | % Cu | % Mg | % Si | % Cr |
|---|---|---|---|---|
| 6053 | — | 1.3 | 0.7 | 0.25 |
| 6061 | 0.25 | 1.0 | 0.6 | 0.25 |
| 6151 | — | 0.6 | 1.0 | 0.25 |

Typical metallographic structures for annealed tempers are shown in Figure 10.18 for the alloy 6053, used mostly for wire and rivets, and the alloy 6061, used for a variety of structural purposes in bus, truck, railway and ship building as well as for architectural hardware. The structure for the forging alloy 6151 in the -T6 temper is shown in Figure 10.16*b*. In all these structures the particles which can be seen at low magnification are largely those of iron-bearing impurity phases. In the two annealed structures there is some precipitated $Mg_2Si$ in addition. No evidence of this would be seen in the -T6 temper except possibly at very high magnifications.

**Figure 10.18**  Metallographic structures of annealed aluminum alloys (*left*) 6053-O (0.7% silicon, 1.3% magnesium, 0.25% chromium, remainder aluminum) and (*right*) 6061-O (0.6% silicon, 1.0% magnesium, 0.25% copper, 0.25% chromium, remainder aluminum) in sheet form. Etched with ½% HF (×100). [Photomicrographs courtesy Aluminum Research Laboratories.]

Typical room temperature mechanical properties for the important alloy 6061, in various tempers are shown in Table 10.6.

**TABLE 10.6**

|  | -O | -T4 | -T6 |
|---|---|---|---|
| Tensile strength (psi) | 18,000 | 35,000 | 45,000 |
| Yield strength (0.2% offset) (psi) | 8,000 | 21,000 | 40,000 |
| Elongation (% in 2 in.) | 30 | 25 | 17 |
| Brinell hardness (10 mm–500 Kg) | 30 | 65 | 95 |
| Fatigue endurance limit (5 × 10⁸ cycles) (psi) | 9,000 | 14,000 | 14,000 |

All of these alloys customarily are used in the artificially aged (-T6) condition to take advantage of the higher properties. Highest strengths are obtained with low-temperature—for example, 225 F (105 C)—long-time aging treatments.

The tensile properties of 6151-T6 are about 3,000 psi higher than the properties given for 6061-T6 with approximately the same elongation and hardness, and an endurance limit lower by 3,000 psi. In the -T4 temper the tensile properties of alloy 6053 are only a little lower than those of 6061 but they are appreciably lower in the -T6 temper, indicating a poorer response to artificial aging. All three alloys can be worked easily and formed readily in either the annealed or solution-heat-treated condition although 6061 work-hardens somewhat less rapidly than the other two.

For the -T4 temper these alloys should be cold-water quenched following a soak at 960 to 980 F (515 to 525 C). This is well below the eutectic melting temperature. In alloy 6061 some increase in strength can be secured by going to higher temperatures, up to approximately 1025 F (550 C).[26] These alloys appear to harden almost indefinitely during natural aging although the rate decreases significantly with time. Artificial aging to the -T6 temper requires 6 to 8 hr at 350 F (175 C) for 6053, 16 to 20 hr at 320 F (160 C) for 6061, or 8 to 12 hr at 340 F (170 C) for 6151. All three alloys can be fully annealed (-O temper) by holding for 2 hr at 750 to 800 F (400 to 425 C) followed by a furnace cool to at least 500 F (260 C).

[26] R. C. Lemon and H. Y. Hunsicker, *Trans. A.S.M.*, **42** (1950), 357–72, discuss these factors more thoroughly.

## ALUMINUM-COPPER-MAGNESIUM-ZINC ALLOYS

The highest strength aluminum structural alloys today are those with 0.6% to 2.0% copper, 1.5 to 3.4% magnesium, 4.0 to 7.5% zinc, and approximately 0.25% chromium,[27] remainder aluminum. The most widely used of these is 7075, containing 1.6% copper, 2.5% magnesium, 5 to 6% zinc and 0.25% chromium, remainder aluminum. The main hardening phase appears to be $\beta$-($MgZn_2$). The first stage of precipitation is the formation of G. P. Zones on the octahedral (body-diagonal) planes, followed by a transition phase, and ultimately by the equilibrium precipitate. Small amounts of the compounds $CuAl_2$ and $CuMgAl_2$ also have been detected. Copper is added to increase strength, although both copper and chromium improve resistance to corrosion and stress-corrosion cracking. In the absence of chromium the highly selective grain-boundary precipitate formed is anodic to the body of the grain so rapid intergranular attack occurs in corrosive environments. The chromium apparently forms another compound, $Al_{12}Mg_2Cr$, which may nucleate general precipitation of the hardening phase.

Typical mechanical properties for 7075 are shown in Table 10.7. The properties of as-extruded alloys are about 10% higher than those for the -T6 temper, and the properties of Alclad products are about 10% lower than those given.

TABLE 10.7

|  | -O | -T6 |
|---|---|---|
| Tensile strength (psi) | 33,000 | 83,000 |
| Yield strength (0.2% offset) (psi) | 15,000 | 73,000 |
| Elongation (% in 2 in.) | 16 | 11 |
| Brinell hardness (10 mm–500 Kg) | 60 | 150 |
| Fatigue endurance limit ($5 \times 10^8$ cycles) (psi) | — | 23,000 |

The marked increase in tensile strength (85,000 psi versus 72,000 psi) of 7075-T6, over 2024-T3, for example, is not accompanied by a cor-

---

[27] E. H. Dix, Jr., *Trans. A.S.M.*, **42** (1950), 1057–1127, discusses these alloys in detail, particularly the ways to control their susceptibility to stress-corrosion cracking and to secure optimum properties.

responding increase in fatigue endurance limit (23,000 psi versus 20,000 psi). This must be taken into account in many aircraft structural designs. The alloy 7075 also is somewhat more notch-sensitive than the other strong alloys.

The 7075 alloy should be solution heat-treated (-W temper) at 870 F (465 C) although sheet can be heat-treated safely as high as 920 F (495 C) because, unlike forgings and extrusions, it generally is free of low-melting (890 F) segregate phases. A rapid quenching rate is essential if maximum properties are to be secured as the strength of 7075 falls off more rapidly with decreasing quenching rate than those of either 6061 or 2024. Natural aging continues at an appreciable although decreasing rate almost indefinitely. It can be retarded by refrigeration but cannot be suppressed entirely even at 0 F (−18 C). However, natural aging requires so long to attain maximum properties that the alloy is only used in the artificially aged (-T6) temper. A treatment of 24 to 28 hr at 250 F (120 C) usually is recommended. Even this is a relatively long-time treatment, so cold-worked 7075 alloy is given shorter-time more complicated treatments, for example 4 hr at 212 F (100 C) plus 8 hr at 315 F (155 C), or 3 hr at 250 F (120 C) plus 3 hr at 350 F (175 C). These shorter-time treatments are not recommended for hot-worked products or for any of the other alloys of this group. Regardless of the artificial aging treatment, however, it is necessary to start the treatment immediately after quenching if maximum properties are to be secured. If this is not possible, the natural aging should be for several days rather than for a shorter time.

The 7075 alloy is fully annealed (-O temper) by heating for 2 to 3 hr at 775 F (415 C) followed by air cooling. It forms best in this condition. It then is solution heat-treated and aged to the strength desired. Although freshly-quenched sheets can be used if only moderate formability is desired, these alloys are not readily formable so forming often is done at elevated temperatures.

The corrosion resistance of 7075 is comparable with that of 2024 and there is a tendency toward intergranular attack if quenching is not rapid enough. For that reason Alclad materials with anodic surface layers often are used. With such materials, heat-treating times should be kept as short as possible to minimize interdiffusion between the coating and the alloy.

## PRECIPITATION-HARDENABLE MAGNESIUM-ALUMINUM ALLOYS

In the magnesium-aluminum alloys (usually containing some zinc) discussed briefly in Chapter 5 the compound $Al_{12}Mg_{17}$ precipitates from the magnesium-rich primary solid solution, at all temperatures below the eutectic temperature, without the formation of any transition structure. This precipitation is not affected significantly by the zinc and manganese usually found in commercial alloys. The precipitation of $Al_{12}Mg_{17}$ may be either discontinuous, forming nodules of a pearlite-like constituent at the grain boundaries (see Figure 5.59), or general, as fine discrete particles throughout the grains. The discontinuous precipitation involves formation of alternate plates of magnesium-aluminum primary solid solution and $Al_{12}Mg_{17}$. The nodules nucleate at the grain boundaries and grow into the grains with a sharp boundary between the growing nodule and the untransformed matrix. The matrix portion of the nodule usually is strained sufficiently to recrystallize into a new orientation. Both discontinuous and continuous precipitation can occur simultaneously in the same grain. The ratio between the two is determined by the aluminum content, the rate of cooling from the solution heat-treating temperature and the temperature at which the precipitation is taking place.[28] For optimum properties after subsequent aging, all of the $Al_{12}Mg_{17}$ must be dissolved, so it is desirable to solution heat-treat at as high a temperature as possible without melting. Any zinc-enriched areas have a low melting point so these must be homogenized before solution heat-treating.

In general, the pearlite-like nodules are less strengthening and somewhat more embrittling than the continuous precipitation. Hence, the less the discontinuous precipitation the higher are the strength and the ductility. For example, air cooling (190 sec) the AZ92A alloy (9% aluminum, 2% zinc, 0.1% manganese, remainder magnesium) from 770 F (410 C) to 370 F (185 C) followed by aging for 18 hr at 350 F (175 C) gives a tensile strength of 40,000 psi, with a yield strength of 24,100 psi and 2% elongation in 2 in. However, if a water quench (0.5 sec) is used, the same aging treatment gives a tensile strength of 48,200 psi, with a yield strength of 29,900 psi and an elongation of 3.5%.

Castings of alloys AZ92A and AZ63A (6% aluminum, 3% zinc, 0.15% manganese, remainder magnesium) often are used in the -T5 condition after an artificial aging treatment of 4 hr at $500 \pm 10$ F (260 C). However, they also are used in the solution-heat-treated (-T4) condition or after further artificial aging (-T6). The temperatures recommended are shown in Table 10.8.

The wrought alloy AZ80A (8.5% aluminum, 0.5% zinc, remainder magnesium) is used only in the extruded or forged (-F temper) condition or in the -T5 temper because the solution heat-treating step required for the -T6 temper causes grain coarsening and lower properties. Artificial aging raises the tensile strength of this alloy from 49,000 psi to 55,000

[28] See also R. S. Busk and R. E. Anderson, *Metals Technology* (Feb. 1945); and T. E. Leontis and C. E. Nelson, *Trans. A.I.M.E.,* **191** (1951), 120–24.

**TABLE 10.8**

|        | -T4 | | -T6 | |
|--------|-----|--------|-----|--------|
| AZ91C  | 18 hr | 775 F (410 C) | 16 hr | 335 F (168 C) |
| AZ92A  | 18 hr | 765 F (405 C) | 4 hr  | 500 F (260 C) |
| AZ63A  | 12 hr | 725 F (385 C) | 5 hr  | 425 F (218 C) |

psi and the tensile yield strength from 36,000 psi to 40,000 psi. However, it raises the compressive yield strength much more, from 25,000 psi to 35,000 psi, largely because the precipitated $Al_{12}Mg_{17}$ platelets inhibit mechanical twinning in the solid solution matrix. It is this twinning which causes the as-extruded (-F temper) material to have a lower compressive than tensile yield strength.

## MAGNESIUM-ZINC ALLOYS

There are four industrial precipitation-hardenable [29] magnesium-zinc alloys but castings made from them have relatively poor properties, because of their coarse grain size, unless about 0.7% zirconium is present. Because of poor fluidity, high cracking tendency and high dross formation they are used largely for simple highly stressed parts of uniform cross-section.

Hardening in magnesium-zinc alloys is caused by the continuous-type precipitation of a transition lattice MgZn' which has a structure identical with that of $MgZn_2$. This transition lattice has been shown to be stable for as long as 5,000 hr at 400 F (205 C). The precipitate is extremely fine and is not resolved clearly even in electron micrographs at a magnification of 9,600× except after long-time holding at an aging temperature. After a sufficiently long time, the transition precipitate, MgZn', transforms into the equilibrium compound, MgZn, the stable second phase at all temperatures below 615 F (325 C).

The ZK51A alloy (4.6% zinc, 0.7% zirconium, remainder magnesium) is modified by adding 1.2% mischmetal.[30] The resulting alloy, ZE41A, has

---

[29] See T. E Leontis, *Trans. A.I.M.E.,* **180** (1949), 287–321; also T. E. Leontis and C. E. Nelson, *ibid.,* **191** (1951), 120–24.

[30] Mischmetal is a mixture of rare-earth elements of the lanthanide group (atomic numbers 57 through 71) in metallic form. It contains approximately 50% cerium, the remainder being principally lanthanum and neodymium. Another somewhat similar mixture is known as didymium.

improved casting characteristics and weldability, but at some sacrifice of mechanical properties.[31] Likewise, alloy ZK61 (6.0% zinc, 0.7% zirconium, remainder magnesium), is modified by adding 1.8% thorium. The resulting alloy, ZH62A, is weldable and has better casting characteristics than ZK51A with approximately the same mechanical properties. These alloys can develop a tensile strength of approximately 40,000 psi, with a yield strength of 26,000 psi and elongation of 4 to 8%. Properties are lower than this for ZE41A and for all the alloys in the as-cast (-F temper) condition. Alloy ZK61 develops a tensile strength of 47,000 psi, with a yield strength of 32,000 psi and an elongation of 9% in 2 in. if it is aged for 2 hr at 930 F (500 C) followed by 12 to 24 hr at 300 F (150 C).

One wrought alloy of this type, ZK60A (6% zinc, 0.7% zirconium, remainder magnesium) is used for extrusions and forgings.[32] The alloy as-extruded (-F temper) has a tensile strength of 50,000 psi with a yield strength of 30,000 psi and an elongation of 13%. These values can be increased by aging, for example for 48 hr at 250 F (120 C), to a tensile strength as high as 54,900 psi, with a tensile yield strength of 46,000 psi, a compressive yield strength of 42,500 psi and an elongation of 10% in 2 in. Unfortunately, it has not been possible to solution heat-treat extrusions of this alloy at a high enough temperature to secure complete solution without destroying the desirable fine grain size, so the properties which can be developed are limited. However, forgings do not have so fine a grain size so solution treatment followed by aging (-T6 temper) can be used effectively. For example, by quenching at 930 F (500 C), followed by artificial aging at 275 F (135 C) for 48 hr (-T6 temper), a tensile strength of 50,000 psi can be developed in forgings, with a tensile yield strength of 42,000 psi, a compressive yield strength of 25,000 psi and an elongation of 9% in 2 in.

## ALLOYS OF MAGNESIUM AND RARE-EARTH METALS

Two types of magnesium-base engineering alloys have been developed with improved high-temperature properties. The first of these [33] takes advantage of the strengthening effect caused by grain-boundary precipitation of an intermetallic compound between magnesium and a lanthanide rare-earth metal when the alloy is stressed at elevated temperatures. Three

[31] Properties of sand-cast alloys are given by T. E. Leontis, *Trans. A.I.M.E.,* **180** (1949), 287–321.

[32] See J. P. Doan and G. Ansel, *Metals Technology,* **13** (1946), 18.

[33] See T. E. Leontis, *Trans. A.I.M.E.,* **185** (1949), 968–83; *ibid.,* **191** (1951), 987–93.

commercial casting alloys have been developed; no wrought alloys are available commercially.

1. EK30A (2.5 to 4.4% rare-earth metals, 0.3% max zinc, 0.2% min zirconium, remainder magnesium)

2. EK41A (3.0 to 5.0% rare-earth metals, 0.3% max zinc, 0.40 to 1.0% zirconium, remainder magnesium)

3. EZ33A (2.5 to 4.0% rare-earth metals, 2.0 to 3.5% zinc, 0.50% min zirconium, remainder magnesium)

The lanthanide rare-earth metals are used in their most available forms, as mischmetal or didymium.

Zirconium is added as a grain-refining agent and zinc is added to increase the stability of these alloys during long exposures to high temperatures. The higher zinc content in EZ33A facilitates formation of precipitate at the grain boundaries by a low-temperature anneal without requiring a high-temperature solution heat-treatment. The alloys EK30A and EK41A are solution-treated at 1050 F (565 C) for 18 hr and then are aged for 16 hr at 400 F (205 C) to develop optimum properties. The solution-treatment sometimes is omitted with EK41A and only the aging treatment is used. However, without a solution heat-treatment, EZ33A can be given only the simpler heat-treatment of 5 hr at 420 F (215 C).

Typical short-time properties after these treatments are shown in Table 10.9.

**TABLE 10.9**

| Temperature | | Tensile Strength | Yield Strength | Elongation |
| F | C | (psi) | (psi) | (% in 2 in.) |
|---|---|---|---|---|
| 70 | 20 | 23,000 | 16,000 | 1–3 |
| 400 | 205 | 21,000 | 12,000 | 12–20 |
| 600 | 315 | 12,000 | 8,000 | 50–70 |

## MAGNESIUM-THORIUM ALLOYS

The second group of magnesium alloys with improved high-temperature properties takes advantage of the fact that about 4 to 5% thorium is soluble in magnesium at the eutectic temperature of 1080 F (580 C). This decreases to about 1% at 570 F (300 C), precipitating $Mg_4Th$ or $Mg_5Th$

in a continuous fashion, with some preference for grain boundaries, in a manner similar to the rare-earth metal alloys.[34]

There are three commercial magnesium alloys of this type.

1. HM21XA (2% thorium, 0.6% manganese, remainder magnesium)
2. HK31A (2.5 to 4.0% thorium, 0.5 to 1.0% zirconium, remainder magnesium)
3. HZ32A (2.5 to 4.0% thorium, 1.7 to 2.5% zinc, 0.5% min zirconium, 0.10% rare-earth metals, remainder magnesium)

The first two of these three are used in the wrought form and the last two in the cast form.[35] Zirconium is added to refine the grain size of these normally coarse-grained alloys. Precipitation in the wrought alloys is dependent upon the amount of cold work given between the solution heat-treatment and the aging steps. A typical solution heat-treatment (-T4 temper) is 2 hr at 1050 F (565 C), with artificial aging for 16 hr at 400 F (205 C) for either the -T5 or -T6 tempers.

Typical short-time tensile properties are somewhat higher than for the rare-earth metal alloys (Table 10.10).

**TABLE 10.10**

| Temperature | | Tensile Strength | Yield Strength | Elongation |
|:---:|:---:|:---:|:---:|:---:|
| F | C | (psi) | (psi) | (% in 2 in.) |
| 70 | 20 | 29,000–37,000 | 15,000–29,000 | 6–10 |
| 400 | 205 | 17,000–24,000 | 10,000–21,000 | 17–33 |
| 600 | 315 | 12,000–20,000 | 7,000–12,000 | 15–70 |
| 700 | 370 | 10,000–13,000 | 7,000– 8,000 | 26–50 |

## PRECIPITATION-HARDENABLE NICKEL-BASE ALLOYS

Reactions in the precipitation-hardenable nickel-base alloys tend to be rather sluggish. Consequently, these alloys may respond to hardening heat treatments after either rapid or slow cooling from the solid-solution range. Furthermore, the properties secured by aging are not affected adversely by prolonged heating at the hardening temperature. When over-heated for short times there is a limited loss of properties at temperature but this

---

[34] See T. E. Leontis, *Trans. A.I.M.E.,* **194** (1952), 287–94; *ibid.,* **194** (1952), 633–42.
[35] See K. E. Nelson, *Trans. A.I.M.E.,* **197** (1953), 1493–97.

loss can be recovered to a considerable extent by recooling to the optimum aging temperature. This recovery suggests that the loss in properties during overheating is caused by the smaller particles going back into solution rather than by agglomeration from overaging. Recooling to the correct temperature then merely reestablishes coherency. If the overheating is for too long a time, or if cooling rates are very slow, overaging and agglomeration of the usual type occur. This can be corrected only by another solution heat-treatment.

Industrial precipitation-hardenable nickel alloys usually contain titanium or aluminum or both and the precipitating phase is known to be the ordered $Ni_3Al$ phase (with partial replacement of aluminum by titanium) even when titanium predominates in the alloy. The loss of properties on reheating then could be considered as a sluggish disordering reaction which reverses to reform the ordered phase on cooling to the proper temperature. Too long an overheating produces some sort of segregated condition which must be restored to substantial homogeneity by another solution-treatment before the alloy can be rehardened.

There are three general types of alloys depending upon whether the base composition is largely: (a) nickel, (b) nickel-copper, or (c) nickel-chromium.[36]

## AGE-HARDENABLE NICKELS

The age-hardenable nickels are known as Duranickel alloy 301® [37] (93 min % nickel, 4.00 to 4.75% aluminum, 0.25 to 1.00% titanium) and Permanickel alloy 300® (97 min % nickel, 0.20 to 0.50% magnesium, 0.20 to 0.60% titanium). In each alloy the elements copper, manganese, iron, silicon, carbon, and sulfur are kept below specified maximum values; any cobalt present is considered as nickel.

Largely because of its aluminum content, Duranickel alloy 301® has a lower thermal conductivity, a higher electrical resistivity and a higher temperature coefficient of electrical resistivity than Permanickel alloy 300® and it becomes nonmagnetic on heating at a much lower temperature—namely, above about 120 to 200 F (50 to 95 C) as compared to 600 to 565 F (315 to 295 C)—the second temperature indicating the precipitation-hardened condition in each instance. The corrosion resistance of both alloys is comparable to that of nickel.

Duranickel alloy 301® softens when water quenched from temperatures above 1350 F (730 C). Heating times should be as short as possible—

[36] W. A. Mudge, *Metal Progress,* **59** (1951), 529–36.
[37] Trademarks of The International Nickel Company.

for example, 2 to 5 min at 1600 F (870 C) or 1 to 3 min at 1800 F (980 C)—in order to limit grain growth. To insure freedom from surface contamination, complete cleanliness and a controlled reducing atmosphere are essential. Partial age-hardening occurs during slow cooling through the 1200 to 900 F (650 to 480 C) range. However, to secure optimum properties, hardening should be for 8 to 16 hr at 1080 to 1100 F (580 to 595 C), the longer times being used for softer material and the shorter times for harder material. For fully cold-worked material (250 to 340 Brinell) the preferred treatment is 6 to 10 hr at 980 to 1000 F (525 to 535 C). The hardening treatment must be followed by controlled slow cooling. Typical properties for Duranickel alloy 301℗ strip after aging are shown in Table 10.11. Still higher values can be secured by proper control of temperature and time. Short-time tensile data at elevated temperatures for both soft and heat-treated Permanickel alloy 300℗ are given in Figure 10.19. Typical metallographic structures in the quenched, slowly cooled, and precipitation-hardened conditions are shown in Figure 10.20. The hardening precipitate is submicroscopic unless overaging occurs.

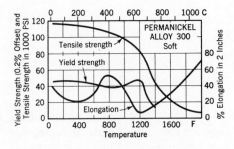

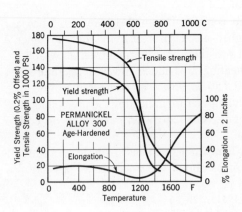

**Figure 10.19**   Short-time tensile properties of Permanickel alloy 300℗ at elevated temperatures. (*top*) Soft. (*bottom*) Precipitation-hardened. [Courtesy The International Nickel Company.]

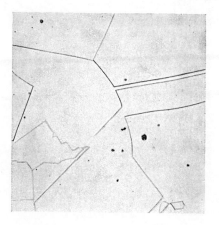

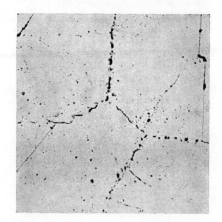

**Figure 10.20** Metallographic structures of Permanickel alloy 300ⓡ. Etched with nitric and acetic acids (×250). **a** (*top left*). As quenched from 1975 F (1080 C). **b** (*top right*). Slowly cooled from 1975 F (1080 C). **c** (*bottom*). Quenched, and aged to maximum hardness. [Photomicrographs courtesy The International Nickel Company.]

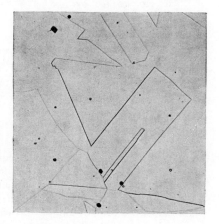

**TABLE 10.11**

| Original Condition | Tensile Strength (*psi*) | Yield Strength (0.2%), *psi* | Elongation (% *in 2 in.*) | Rockwell Hardness |
|---|---|---|---|---|
| Annealed (soft) | 104,000 | 47,000 | 42 | C4 |
| Annealed * | 159,000 | 105,000 | 33 | C30 |
| Cold-rolled 10% * | 171,000 | 124,000 | 24 | C34 |
| Cold-rolled 50% * | 208,000 | 186,000 | 14 | C41 |

* And aged for 2 hr at 1100 F (595 C).

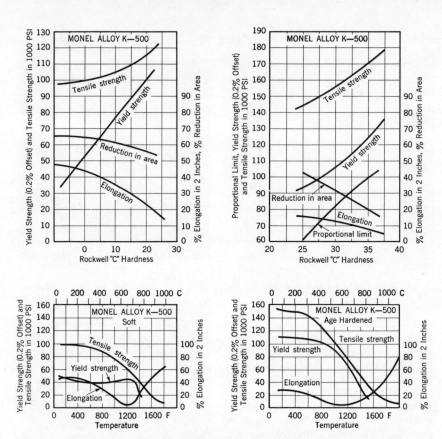

**Figure 10.21** Relationships between average tensile properties of Monel alloy K-500⑬ and Rockwell *C* hardness or test temperature. **a** (*top left*). Hot-rolled and cold-drawn rod, tested at room temperature. **b** (*top right*). Cold-drawn rod, heat-treated (properties for both hot-rolled and forged rod, heat-treated, are roughly similar to these), tested at room temperature. **c** (*bottom left*). Soft (hot-rolled and quenched), tested at elevated temperatures. **d** (*bottom right*). Hot-rolled and age-hardened, tested at elevated temperatures. [Courtesy The International Nickel Company.]

## AGE-HARDENABLE NICKEL-COPPER ALLOYS

Wrought Monel alloy K-500⑬ (65% nickel, 29.5% copper, 0.50% titanium, 2.80% aluminum, 1.0% iron, 0.15% max carbon) is a commercial example of the nickel-copper type of age-hardenable alloy. A free-machining variety, Monel alloy 501⑬,[38] which contains higher carbon (0.23%) than the wrought variety, and cast varieties, in which silicon (to 4.5%) replaces some nickel to improve fluidity, are made.

Monel alloy K-500⑬ has a corrosion resistance and cold-working characteristics similar to those of Monel alloy 400⑬ although somewhat more

[38] Trademarks of The International Nickel Company.

power is required to deform it because of the greater hardness and the greater rate of work-hardening of the hardenable alloy. Machinability is fair up to a hardness of about 275 Brinell. The alloy softens when water quenched from moderate holding times above approximately 1400 F (760 C) but the recommended heat-treatment is 2 to 5 min at 1600 F (870 C) or 0.5 to 2 min at 1800 F (980 C). A single heat-treatment of 10 to 16 hr at 1080 to 1100 F (585 to 595 C) in air or in a reducing atmosphere, followed by controlled slow cooling, age-hardens the alloy; no preliminary quenching treatment is needed to accomplish this hardening. Both temperature and time vary with the initial hardness of the alloy so this must be known for optimum results. In general, however, the higher the initial hardness the shorter the time and the lower the hardening temperature. Typical relationship between tensile properties and Rockwell hardness for Monel alloy 500® rods in the hot-rolled, cold-drawn, and heat-treated conditions are shown in Figure 10.21. Even in the hot-worked condition this alloy has excellent strength properties, and its combination of strength and ductility in the fully heat-treated condition is excellent.[39] A stress-equalizing thermal treatment of 3 hr at 525 F (275 C) often is used if fully-hardened material must be straightened or otherwise deformed. Typical properties for strip are shown in Table 10.12. Still higher values can be secured by proper control of temperature and time.

**TABLE 10.12**

| Original Condition | Tensile Strength (psi) | Yield Strength (0.2%) (psi) | Elongation (% in 2 in.) | Rockwell Hardness |
|---|---|---|---|---|
| Annealed (soft) | 100,000 | 50,000 | 39 | C3 |
| Annealed * | 142,000 | 90,000 | 31 | C24 |
| Cold-rolled 10% * | 155,000 | 122,000 | 23 | C31 |
| Cold-rolled 50% * | 179,000 | 166,000 | 12 | C38 |

* And aged for 2 hr at 1100 F (595 C).

Typical metallographic structures are shown in Figure 10.22 for the quenched, precipitation-hardened, and slow-cooled conditions. The precipitate is the ordered $Ni_3Al$ phase. It can be resolved only with the electron microscope.

[39] See, for example, W. A. Mudge and P. D. Merica, *Trans. A.I.M.E.*, **117** (1935), 265–76; also W. O. Alexander, *Journ. Inst. Metals,* **4** (London: 1937), 602; *ibid.,* **5** (1938), 773; *ibid.,* **7** (1940), 106.

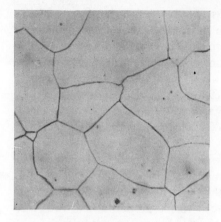

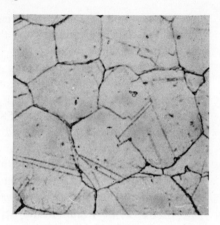

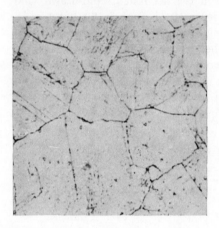

**Figure 10.22** Metallographic struc- tures of Monel alloy K-500 ℗. Etched electrolytically with 10% $H_2SO_4$ (×1000). **a** (*top left*). As quenched from 1600 F (870 C). **b** (*top right*). Quenched and aged to maximum hard- ness. **c** (*bottom*). Slowly cooled from 1600 F (870 C). [Photomicrographs courtesy The International Nickel Com- pany.]

## AGE-HARDENABLE NICKEL-CHROMIUM ALLOYS

The nickel-chromium types of age-hardenable alloys are modifications of the corrosion- and oxidation-resistant alloy Inconel alloy 600℗ [40] (72% min nickel, 14 to 17% chromium, 6 to 10% iron) and its higher silicon (3%) casting variety, Inconel alloy 610℗, or of the Nimonic alloy 80A℗ type (20.5% chromium, 0.55% iron, 2.35% titanium, 1.25% aluminum, remainder nickel).

One modification, Inconel alloy X-750℗ (70% min nickel, 14 to 17% chromium, 5 to 9% iron, 2.25 to 2.75% titanium, 0.7 to 1.2% colum- bium, 0.4 to 1.0% aluminum), was developed primarily to have a low creep rate under high stresses (for example, 1000 hr resistance to a load

[40] Trademarks of The International Nickel Company, Inc.

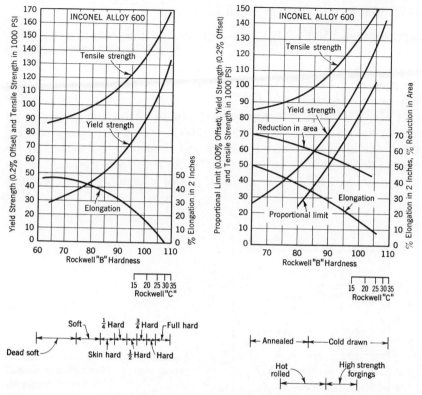

**Figure 10.23** Relationships between average tensile properties of Inconel alloy 600Ⓡ and Rockwell hardness. **a** (*left*). Sheet and strip. **b** (*right*). Hot-rolled and cold-drawn rod. [From *Engineering Properties of Inconel Alloy 600*, courtesy The International Nickel Company.]

of 30,000 psi) at 1200 to 1500 F (650 to 815 C) in the heat-treated form.[41] Although the precipitation reactions have not been studied thoroughly, the constituent $Ni_3(Al, Ti)$ is known to form in resolvable size over the range 1400 to 1700 F (760 to 925 C) from material previously solution-treated at approximately 2100 F (1150 C). Solution heat-treatment for good creep resistance has to be of much longer duration than that needed for age-hardening, presumably to secure the best possible— that is, most uniform—dispersion of the hardening phase. The columbium functions either as a carbide stabilizer or, in solid solution, to strengthen the matrix.

Average tensile properties for Inconel alloy 600Ⓡ are given in Figure 10.23. These properties are retained well at elevated temperatures up to

[41] See, for example, C. C. Clark and J. S. Iwanski, *Trans. A.I.M.E.*, **215** (1959), 648–55; also N. E. Rogen and N. J. Grant, *ibid.*, **218** (1960), 180–82.

approximately 950 F (510 C), as indicated by the short-time high-temperature tensile test data in Figure 10.24. The creep strength (satisfactory long-term behavior at 2,000 psi) and resistance to progressive oxidation are good up to 2000 F (1100 C); and even in oxidizing sulfur-bearing atmospheres Inconel alloy 600⊕ can be used safely to about 1500 F (820 C). The range 1850 to 2300 F (1000 to 1250 C) is recommended for hot working. Work done below 1200 F (650 C) is classed as cold work. The alloy has reduced ductility and should not be worked in the range 1200 to 1600 F (650 to 870 C). A stress-relief treatment in the range 1000 to 1400 F (540 to 760 C) often is used after cold working.

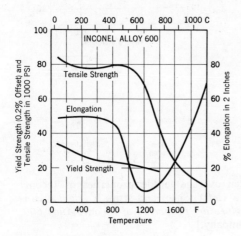

**Figure 10.24**   Short-time tensile properties of hot-rolled Inconel alloy 600⊕ at elevated temperatures. [From *Engineering Properties of Inconel Alloy 600,* courtesy The International Nickel Company.]

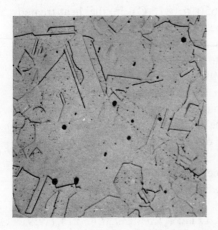

**Figure 10.25**   Metallographic structure of rolled and annealed Inconel alloy 600⊕. Etched with HF and HNO₃ (×100). [Photomicrograph by L. Litchfield.]

Softening by annealing begins at about 1600 F (870 C) and is reasonably complete in about 15 min at 1800 F (980 C), giving material with a characteristic microstructure (Figure 10.25); rate of cooling is not important. At higher temperatures undesirable grain coarsening occurs.

Inconel alloy X-750® is solution-treated by heating 2 to 4 hr at 2100 ± 25 F (1150 ± 15 C). Air cooling is rapid enough to give optimum creep properties but water or oil quenching must be used if softness is needed for fabrication. After solution-treatment, as an essential step, a high-temperature aging treatment of 24 hr at 1500 ± 25 F (815 ± 10 C) is used, always followed by low-temperature aging for 20 hr at 1300 ± 25 F (705 ± 10 C) and air cooling. The preaging heat-treatment at 1500 F (815 C) causes precipitation to occur near the grain boundaries. This is favorable to ductility in the range 1200 to 1400 F (650 to 760 C) where ductility is quite low if only the 1300 F (705 C) aging is used. This grain-boundary precipitate probably is $Ni_3(Al, Ti)$, possibly accompanied by the carbide or carbonitride of columbium also.[42]

A stress-equalizing heat-treatment of 24 hr at 1625 ± 25 F (885 ± 10 C) sometimes is given with parts intended for use, after aging, at temperatures up to 1100 F (595 C). However, it is not recommended for components intended for use at 1200 to 1500 F (650 to 815 C); these require a full solution heat-treatment.

Typical short-time tensile properties of Inconel alloy X-750® when given the recommended double-aging heat-treatments are shown in Table 10.13. These are appreciably higher than those secured with Inconel alloy 600®.

**TABLE 10.13**

| Test Temperature F | C | Tensile Strength (psi) | Yield Strength (0.2% offset) (psi) | Elongation (% in 2 in.) | 1000 hr Stress-Rupture (psi) |
|---|---|---|---|---|---|
| Room | | 162,000 | 92,000 | 24 | — |
| 600 | 315 | 154,000 | 88,000 | 28 | — |
| 1000 | 535 | 140,000 | 84,000 | 22 | 108,000 |
| 1200 | 650 | 120,000 | 82,000 | 9 | 68,000 |
| 1500 | 815 | 52,000 | 44,000 | 22 | 18,000 |

[42] See W. C. Bigelow, J. A. Amy, and L. O. Brockway, *Trans. A.S.M.E.,* **212** (1950), 543–49.

Several other age-hardening varieties of Inconel alloy 600Ⓣ have been developed for elevated-temperature service. Molybdenum sometimes is added in amounts of approximately 3% as a matrix strengthener although such alloys may be susceptible to internal oxidation during long-time exposures. Because aluminum gives better oxidation resistance than titanium it generally is used preferentially, in amounts up to approximately 3%, in alloys intended for higher service temperatures. Minor components may include boron, to give better workability in the temperature range 1350 to 1500 F (730 to 815 C), zirconium, which acts in a similar manner, and magnesium and calcium, as strong deoxidizers and desulfurizers.

Wrought Nimonic alloy 80AⓉ [43] contains, nominally, 20.5% chromium, 0.55% iron, 2.35% titanium, and 1.25% aluminum, with the remainder nickel and normal impurities.

In Nimonic alloy 80AⓉ the main precipitating phase, $Ni_3(Al, Ti)$, dissolves above 1610 F (875 C), and nearly the same results are secured, after hardening at lower temperatures, by using any solution treatment in the range 1650 to 2190 F (900 to 1200 C). Heat-treatment in air is recommended, with an allowance of 0.003 in. for scale. Optimum creep and stress-rupture properties of the matrix are produced by solution-treating at 1975 F (1080 C) for 8 hr, air cooling and hardening for 16 hr at 1240 F (700 C).

Because of the impurity content, however, there are other precipitates in this alloy, chromium carbide for example, which have a significant effect on properties. To dissolve all of these precipitates a temperature in excess of 2100 F (1150 C) is required. At this temperature there is considerable grain growth. The resulting structure has a low creep rate but may have a very short life because grain-boundary rupture occurs at relatively small elongations. The rupture life can be extended significantly by solution-treating within the range 1830 to 1920 F (1000 to 1050 C) in order to precipitate chromium carbides at the grain boundaries to strengthen them. As a final step a precipitation-treatment should be given at a temperature no higher than that at which optimum creep properties are needed.

An alloy to be cold worked should be annealed at 1825 F (955 C) and water quenched. After cold working, solution- and precipitation-treatments should be given to develop full properties.

The tensile strength of Nimonic alloy 80AⓉ decreases nearly linearly from 155,000 psi at room temperature to 120,000 psi at 1200 F (650 C). Over the same range the 0.1% yield strength remains substantially constant at 80,000 psi. At higher temperatures both properties decrease

[43] W. Betteridge and A. W. Franklin, *Journ. Inst. Metals,* **85** (London: 1956–57), 473–79; see also Refs. 1 and 16 at the end of this chapter.

rapidly. The elongation in 2 in. and the reduction of area are approximately 40% up to 1000 F (535 C) and then decrease to a minimum of 20% in the range 1200 to 1500 F (650 to 815 C) before increasing at higher temperatures. In the hardened form, the stress for 1,000 hr rupture life is approximately 15,000 psi at 1500 F (815 C) and 4,000 psi at 1700 F (925 C). General usage of the Nimonic alloys has been in the range 1300 to 1500 F (705 to 815 C).

## AGE-HARDENABLE IRON-NICKEL ALLOY

A low-carbon (0.06% max) iron-base alloy of this general type, Ni-Span-C alloy 902®, contains 41.0 to 43.5% nickel, 4.90 to 5.75% chromium, 2.20 to 2.75% titanium, 0.80% max manganese, 1.0% max silicon, and 0.30 to 0.80% aluminum. With proper choice of cold working and heat-treatment the thermoelastic coefficient (microin. per in. per °C) can be controlled over the temperature range of $-50$ F to 150 F ($-45$ C to 65 C). With this alloy the required solution-treatment is 20 to 90 min at 1750 to 1830 F (950 to 1000 C) followed by rapid cooling in oil or water. The material then usually is cold worked (50% reduction) and aged at 1100 to 1350 F (600 to 730 C) for periods of 48 hr to 3 hr, respectively. This produces a tensile strength of 200,000 psi, with a yield strength (0.2% offset) of 180,000 psi, an elongation of 7% in 2 in., and a modulus of elasticity of $27 \times 10^6$ psi. Somewhat lower strength properties and higher ductilities can be secured by modifying the combinations of cold work and aging treatments. The hardening compound is $Ni_3Ti$.

### QUESTIONS

1. Why are carbon and nitrogen so effective in causing precipitation-hardening in iron? What must be done to avoid hardening from quench aging? What is the mechanism by which the hardening is prevented?

2. Why can the yield-point discontinuity in iron be eliminated by giving sheet a light skin pass? Why does the discontinuity reappear after aging at a somewhat higher temperature?

3. What is meant by a dislocation being pinned by an atmosphere of interstitial atoms? Why is similar interstitial-atom pinning found much less frequently in face-centered cubic metals than in body-centered cubic metals? What is the difference between (a) interstitial atoms in solid solution, and (b) interstitial atoms as an atmosphere around a dislocation? Why are hydrogen atoms not as effective as nitrogen and carbon atoms for pinning dislocations?

4. In beryllium copper much greater toughness can be secured by overaging rather than underaging. Why do you think this occurs? Do you think it should be a general characteristic of precipitation-hardening alloys or is there some characteristic which makes it particularly true with beryllium copper alloys?

5. Give at least two ways to explain the occurrence of small inclusions of aluminum oxide in aluminum bronzes. What methods could be used to prevent the occurrence of such inclusions? What would be the objections to these methods? If you wished to develop a precipitation-hardenable aluminum bronze (as a typical alloy) what general procedure would you follow?

6. Aluminum-rich alloys with copper follow very closely the usually accepted theory of age-hardening or precipitation-hardening alloys. Is this good evidence that this theory is correct? Why do you take this position? Why do industrial aluminum-copper alloys age-harden at room temperature only when some magnesium is present?

7. Why are aluminum alloys of the 2017 type seldom if ever used in modern aircraft? Why have the 7075 alloys largely replaced the 2024 alloys? What do you think would be the major objections to aluminum alloys for aeronautical uses as aircraft speeds increase?

8. In the Alclad types of aluminum alloys, how much would you expect the strength to be reduced? Why? Would you expect that the same Alclad coating could be used for all such alloys or would this depend on the specific base alloy? Why?

9. Why does quenching to a subzero temperature delay natural aging in aluminum alloys? Can aging be delayed indefinitely by this method? Why do you think artificial aging (elevated temperature) tends to give different properties from natural aging?

10. In quenching any age-hardening alloy, and particularly those of the light-metal types, what would you expect to happen to the microstructure and properties if (a) the quenching is too slow, and (b) the quenching is too drastic? Why?

11. In age-hardening alloys in general, would the solution-quenched structure be expected to have better corrosion resistance than the aged structure? Why? Would the aging temperature used have any effect on this? Would the specific alloy be important?

12. Why is the control of solution-treatment temperature frequently much more critical in castings and extrusions than in wrought materials? What is the purpose of using the fastest possible quenching rate following a solution-treatment? What difficulty can be anticipated if Alclad materials are solution-treated? What can be done to minimize such difficulties?

13. Why do you think additions of 0.7% zirconium are effective in controlling the grain size of magnesium-zinc alloys? If you were doing research on other ways of controlling this grain size, what methods would you suggest trying?

14. Why is a rapid quench following a solution-treatment frequently not necessary with nickel-base alloys? Can you think of any types of alloys (general, not specific) or circumstances when it might be essential to quench rapidly? Why is a solution-treatment required before precipitation-hardening again can occur if many nickel alloys are overheated for too long a time? Would you expect that the holding time for such a solution-treatment should be relatively long or relatively short? Why?

15. Why do the age-hardenable iron-nickel alloys of the Ni-Span-C alloy 902® type have such special thermal expansion characteristics? In age-hardening nickel alloys intended for elevated-temperature use, would you expect the improved properties to last indefinitely? Why? Will this have any effect on the useful life of the material in this type of application? In what form does carbon tend to precipitate in nickel alloys? Does this have any effect on machinability? Why?

## FOR FURTHER STUDY

1. *Metals Handbook,* 7th ed. (1948) and *Supplements,* and 8th ed., Vol. I (1961). Metals Park, Ohio: American Society for Metals.

2. *Constitution of Binary Alloys* by M. Hansen and K. P. Anderko. New York: McGraw-Hill, 1958.

3. *Precipitation from Solid Solution.* Cleveland: American Society for Metals, 1959.

4. *Phase Transformations in Solids.* New York: John Wiley & Sons, 1951.

5. *Age Hardening of Metals.* Cleveland: American Society for Metals, 1940.

6. *The Physical Chemistry of Metallic Solutions and Intermetallic Compounds,* Vols. I and II. London: Her Majesty's Stationery Office, 1959.

7. *The Mechanism of Phase Transformation in Metals.* London: The Institute of Metals, 1956.

8. *Strengthening Mechanisms in Solids.* Metals Park, Ohio: American Society for Metals, 1961.

9. *Thermodynamics in Physical Metallurgy* by L. S. Darken and L. W. Gurry. New York: McGraw-Hill, 1953.

10. *Thermodynamics in Physical Metallurgy.* Cleveland: American Society for Metals, 1950.

11. *Defects in Crystalline Solids.* London: The Physical Society, 1955.

12. *Metal Interfaces.* Cleveland: American Society for Metals, 1952.

13. *Physical Metallurgy of Stress Corrosion Fracture.* New York: Interscience Publishers, 1959.

14. *The Physical Metallurgy of Magnesium and Its Alloys* by G. V. Raynor. London: Pergamon Press, 1959.

15. *Magnesium and Its Alloys* by C. S. Roberts. New York: John Wiley & Sons, 1960.

16. *Nimonic Alloys* by W. Betteridge. London: Edward Arnold, 1959.

# APPENDIX A

# *Basic Numbering System for S.A.E. Carbon and Alloy Steels (After 1961 S.A.E. Handbook)*

The first two (or three) numbers indicate the alloy content. The last two numbers indicate the nominal carbon content in units of 0.01%.

Carbon Steels
| | |
|---|---|
| Plain-carbon | 10xx |
| Free-cutting | 11xx |

Manganese Steels
| | |
|---|---|
| Mn 1.75 | 13xx |

Nickel Steels
| | |
|---|---|
| Ni 3.50 | 23xx |
| Ni 5.00 | 25xx |

Nickel-Chromium Steels
| | |
|---|---|
| Ni 1.25; Cr 0.65 | 31xx |
| Ni 3.50; Cr. 1.57 | 33xx |
| Corrosion- and heat-resisting | 303xx |

Molybdenum Steels
| | |
|---|---|
| Mo 0.25 | 40xx |

Chromium-Molybdenum Steels
| | |
|---|---|
| Cr 0.50 and 0.95; Mo 0.25, 0.20 and 0.12 | 41xx |

Nickel-Chromium-Molybdenum Steels
| | |
|---|---|
| Ni 1.82; Cr 0.50 and 0.80; Mo 0.25 | 43xx |
| Ni 1.05; Cr 0.45, Mo 0.20 | 47xx |
| Ni 0.55; Cr 0.50 and 0.65; Mo 0.20 | 86xx |
| Ni 0.55; Cr. 0.50; Mo 0.25 | 87xx |
| Ni 3.25; Cr 1.20; Mo 0.12 | 93xx |
| Ni 1.00; Cr 0.80; Mo 0.25 | 98xx |

*504*

Nickel-Molybdenum Steels

    Ni 1.57 and 1.82; Mo 0.20 and 0.25            46xx

    Ni 3.50; Mo 0.25            48xx

Chromium Steels

    Low Cr 0.27, 0.40 and 0.50            50xx

    Low Cr 0.80, 0.87, 0.92, 0.95, 1.00 and 1.05    51xx

    Low Cr (bearing) 0.50           50100

    Med Cr (bearing) 1.02           51100

    High Cr (bearing) 1.45           52100

    Corrosion- and heat-resisting        514xx and 515xx

Chromium-Vanadium Steels

    Cr 0.80 and 0.95; V 0.10 and 0.15 min       61xx

Silicon-Managanese Steel

    Mn 0.65, 0.85, 0.87 and 0.85; Si 1.40 and 2.00;

    Cr none, 0.17, 0.32 and 0.65          92xx

Low-Alloy High-Tensile Steel           950

Boron-Intensified Steels           xx*B*xx

Leaded Steels           xx*L*xx

Steels Subject to Controlled Hardenability-Band * Limits    xxxx*H*

   * See Chapter 8.

# APPENDIX B

# *Aluminum Association Designations for Wrought Aluminum and Wrought Aluminum Alloys*

Basic Alloy Designations

The first digit indicates specific alloy groups.

| | |
|---|---|
| 1xxx | Aluminum content 99.00% min and greater |
| 2xxx | Copper as major alloying element |
| 3xxx | Manganese as major alloying element |
| 4xxx | Silicon as major alloying element |
| 5xxx | Magnesium as major alloying element |
| 6xxx | Magnesium and silicon as major alloying elements |
| 7xxx | Zinc as major alloying element |
| 8xxx | Elements other than above as major alloying addition |
| 9xxx | Unused series |

The third and fourth digits indicate the aluminum purity or identify the aluminum alloy. The second digit indicates a modification of the original alloy or impurity limit.

# APPENDIX C

# *A.S.T.M. Recommended Codification of Light Metals and Alloys* *

The designations for alloys and unalloyed metals are based on the chemical composition limits in A.S.T.M. Specifications using the following letters to represent various alloying elements:

| | | |
|---|---|---|
| A—Aluminum | G—Magnesium | P—Lead |
| B—Bismuth | H—Thorium | Q—Silver |
| C—Copper | K—Zirconium | R—Chromium |
| D—Cadmium | L—Lithium | S—Silicon |
| E—Rare Earth | M—Manganese | T—Tin |
| F—Iron | N—Nickel | Y—Antimony |
| | | Z—Zinc |

Designations for alloys consist of not more than two letters representing the alloying elements specified in the greatest amount, arranged in order of decreasing percentages, or in alphabetical order if of equal percentages, followed by the respective mean percentages rounded off to whole numbers and a serial letter arbitrarily assigned in alphabetical sequence starting with A (omitting I and O). For example, the magnesium alloy ZK51A contains, as principal alloying elements, zinc (Z) and zirconium (K) in approximate amounts of 5% and 1% respectively; the A indicates that this is the first of these alloys, there might also be ZK51B, ZK51C, etc., modifications.

* See A.S.T.M. Designation B275, latest revision, for further details.

# A.S.T.M. Recommended Temper Designation of Light Metals and Alloys, Cast and Wrought

The temper designation, used for all metal forms except ingot, follows the alloy designation and is separated from it by a dash. The following temper designations are used.*

-F    As-fabricated

-O    Annealed, recrystallized (wrought products only)

-Hxx    Strain-hardened only (-12, quarter hard; -14, half hard; -18, full hard; -19, extra hard)

-H2x    Strain-hardened to harder temper and then partially annealed to strength indicated (second digits have same significance as in -H1x series)

-H3x    Strain-hardened to temper indicated (same as -H1x series) and then stabilized by low-temperature heating to increase ductility.

-W    Solution heat-treat (an unstable temper), used only with those alloys which age spontaneously at room temperature after solution heat-treatment.

-T    Treated to produce stable tempers, other than -F, -O, or -H, with or without supplementary strain-hardening (followed by one or more digits).

-T2    Annealed (casting products only).

-T3    Solution heat-treated, and then cold worked, then naturally aged.

-T4    Solution heat-treated and naturally aged to a substantially stable condition.

-T5    Artificially aged only (without prior solution heat-treatment).

-T6    Solution heat-treated and then artificially aged.

* See A.S.T.M. Designation B296, latest revision, for further details.

-T7    Solution heat-treated and then stabilized (aged beyond the point of maximum hardness to control growth or residual stress).

-T8    Solution heat-treated and cold worked, then artificially aged.

-T9    Solution heat-treated and artificially aged, then cold worked.

-T10   Artificially aged and then cold worked (castings only).

*Note:* For various -H and -T tempers the use of a third following digit (for example, -T36) indicates a special set of properties. In such cases the alloy manufacturer should be consulted.

# Index

$A_c$, 16
$A_e$, 16
$A_r$, 16
$A_{C_m}$, 268, 348
$A_0$, 267
$A_1$, 15, 16, 267, 348
$A_2$, 15, 267
$A_3$, 15, 16, 106, 108, 267, 3⸱ 417
$A_4$, 15, 16, 107, 108, 267, 417
Abnormal grain growth, 102–03, 105
  steels (McQuaid-Ehn), 397
Acid copper sulfate test for stainless steels
  (*see* Strauss test)
Activation energy, for diffusion, 34; for
  precipitation, 335
Admiralty metal, 243, 245
Age-hardening (*see* Precipitation-hardening)
Aging, 336, 460–501
  in low-carbon steels, 274, 460–65;
  quench-, 460–61; strain-, 462–63,
  control of, 465
Air quenching, 337
Air-hardening die steels, 406–09; effect on
  welding of chromium steels, 421;
  high-speed tool steels, 411
Alclad, 479, 481, 485
Allotriomorphic grains, 6
Allotropic transformation
  crystallographic relationships, 107
  effect of cooling rate, 108–09
  iron, 14; effect of alloying elements,
    258
  property changes from, 108
  recrystallization by, 106
Allotropy, 14–16; in metals, 14
Allowable stresses, A.S.M.E. Code, 275
Alloy brasses, cast, 249–58; wrought,
  243–47
Alloying elements, 9, 16–17
  distribution in heated steels, 292
  effect on allotropic transformation in
    iron, 258–59; on bainite transforma-
    tion in steels, 365; on brasses, 243–
    47; on cast irons, 318–26; on eutec-
    toid transformation in steels, 290; on
    grain size, 100–02; on hardenability,
    383–85; on iron-carbon alloys, 288–
    91; on pearlite transformation in
    steels, 364; on recrystallization of
    copper, 96; on resistivity of alumi-
    num, 129–30, of copper, 130; on
    tool steels, 401–03
  methods of combining, 159
  nucleation of carbides by, 388
  partitioning of, in carbides during tem-
    pering, 387–88
Alloy types, 157–230, 232–326
  commercially pure metal, 128–55, 167–
    68
  complete solid solubility, 174–78
  eutectic, 191–93, 211–16, 221–30

Alloy types (*cont.*)
  eutectoid, 191, 211
  intermediate solid solution, 171–72, 213–30
  intermetallic compounds, 169–71, 213–30
  mechanical mixtures, 172–74
  partial solid solution, 189
  peritectic, 169, 216–18
  peritectoid, 216
  primary solid solution, 16, 168–69
  secondary solid solution, 171–72, 213–30
  terminal solid solution, 16, 168–69
Aluminum, 1, 12, 128–31
  Alclad, 211
  alloy designation, 506, 507
  coating on iron or steel, 143
  effect on stability of gamma iron, 259
  imperfections in, produced by radiation, 28
  temper designation, 508–09
Aluminum alloys
  **A214**, 225; **A132**, 209–10
  **EC**, 128, 130–31
  free-machining, 477
  high-strength, 477–81
  nomenclature, 506
  precipitation-hardenable, 473–85
  structural, 477
  temper designations, 508–09
  with copper, 194; copper and magnesium, 477–81; copper, magnesium, and zinc, 484–85; iron, 139; magnesium, 221–30; magnesium, and silicon, 481–83; silicon, 173, 207–11; zinc, 154, 211–13
  **13**, 210
  **43**, 210; **45**, 210; **47**, 207
  **214**, 223–24; **218**, 223–24; **220**, 223–24
  **356**, 209; **360**, 210
  **1060**, 128
  **1100**, 128–29, 211, 223
  **2011**, 477–78; **2014**, 477–81; **2017**, 477–78; **2024**, 477–81, 484
  **3003**, 222–23
  **5052**, 222–23; **5083**, 222; **5154**, 222
  **6053**, 482–83; **6061**, 482–83; **6151**, 480–83
  **7072**, 211; **7075**, 484–85
Aluminum Association designation for wrought aluminum alloys, 506
Aluminum brass, 245
Aluminum bronze, 470–72
American Society for Mechanical Engineers (*see* A.S.M.E.)

American Society for Testing and Materials (*see* A.S.T.M.)
American Standards Association (*see* A.S.A.)
Anchored dislocations, 65–66
Annealing
  after cold work, 91
  austenitic stainless steels, 441
  during hot work, 113
  for maximum ductility, 114
  full, for steels, 348
  process, for steels, 347, 349
  temperature ranges for steels, 348
  twins, 117; effect on carbide precipitation in austenitic stainless steels, 442
Antimony, 1, 8, 11
  alloys with lead, 145, 173, 204–07; with tin, 205–07, 216–17
  as dezincification inhibitor in brass, 241
  effect on stability of gamma iron, 259
Arbitration bars, cast iron, 314–26
Arrest, thermal, 15, 16; heating, 5, 16; cooling, 5, 16
Arrhenius relationship, 34
Arsenic, 2
  alloys with lead, 145
  as dezincification inhibitor in brass, 241
  effect on stability of gamma iron, 259
Artificial aging, alumin. alloys, 473, 479
A.S.A. Code for Pressure Piping, 425
A.S.M.E. Boiler and Unfired Pressure Vessel Code, 275, 425
A.S.T.M.
  Recommended Codification of Light Metals and Alloys, 507
  Recommended Temper Designation of Light Metals and Alloys, Cast and Wrought, 508–09
Atmosphere of interstitial alloying elements, 464
  furnace, for heat-treating nickel alloys, 189, 492, 495, 498
Atomic
  binding forces, 3, 10, 11
  mobility, 34
  number, 10
  per cent composition, conversion to weight per cent, 166
  weight, 10
Ausforming, 369–70
Austempering, 350–58
Austenite, 14, 262
  carbon limitations, effects of alloying elements, 289
  cast irons, 322–26
  decomposition during malleablizing, 306–08

Austenite (*cont.*)
grain size, 24–25, 108
stabilization, 363; by nickel, 437
stainless steels, 437, 440–54; chromium depletion, by carbide precipitation, 445, by sigma formation, 440; chromium-manganese, 453–54; chromium-nitrogen, 441; extra low carbon, 447; nitriding, 454; precipitation-hardening, 455–56; properties, effect of carbon content, 444, of low temperatures, 453; sensitization, 444–48; stabilized, with columbium or titanium, 448–49, thermally, 443, 449; stress corrosion cracking, 452; structure, effect of carbon and nitrogen, 441; welding, 450–52; work-hardening, 448–50
transformation, at constant subcritical temperature, 349–58; by ausforming, 369–70; by direct quench-and-temper, 375–78, 385–87; by interrupted quenching, 374; during continuous cooling, 370–72; effect of alloying elements, 290, 364–65, of carbon content, 361–63, of cold work, 365–67, of cooling rate, 372, of grain size, 367–68, of subatmospheric cooling, 365; in eutectoid steels, 282–84, hypereutectoid steels, 284–87, hypoeutectoid steels, 268–70; to bainite, 350, 356–58, 365, martensite, 358–61, pearlite, 353–56
Austenitizing heat treatments, 347–49
Autofrettage, 93
Automotive steels, carburizing grades, 394–95; heat-treating grades, 398–401

Babbitts (*see* Bearings)
Bainite, 354, 356–58
from austenite transformation, 350
lower, 354, 356
TTT curve, 365
upper, 354, 356
Banded structure, in hot-rolled steels, 271
Base box, terne plate, 146; tin plate, 150
Bearings
bronze, leaded, 253–55; graphite, 256
hard babbitts, 221
lead-alkali metal, 215; -alkaline earth metal, 215; -antimony, 204; -base, 206–07; -tin-antimony, 205–07
oilless, 160, 256
tin-base, 218–21
soft babbitt, 220

steel-backed, 254
Bell metal, 255
Beryllium, 1, 14
alloy with copper, 466–69
bronze, 249, 466–69
effect on stability of gamma iron, 259
Binary alloys, 159, 162, 165–68; interpretation of constitutional diagrams, 198
Bismuth, alloys with lead, 145; with aluminum, 477
Blue brittleness, 463, 465
Body-centered cubic space lattice, 11–14
-diagonal planes, 55
Boiler and Pressure-Vessel Code (*see* A.S.M.E. Boiler and Unfired Pressure-Vessel Code)
Boiling nitric acid test for stainless steels (*see* Huey test)
Boron, for hardenability, 385; effect on stability of gamma iron, 259
Boundary energy, 344–45
Brale hardness indenter, 42–43
Brass, 234–37
alloy, 244–47
alpha, 23, 234–37
beta, 23, 234–37
cartridge, 242
cast, 249–51, 252–53, 257
color change with composition, 239
commercial bronze, 241
common high, 242
constitution, 234–37
dezincification, 241–43
drawing, 242
etching, 23, 241
extruded, 23
gilding metal, 241
heat-treatment, 238–39
high, 242
leaded, 243–44
low, 242
manganese bronze, 245, 256–58
Muntz metal, 242
nickel, 246–47
properties, 242
recrystallization, 96–97, 101
red, rich-low, 241
season cracking, 247–48
wrought, 240–41
Bright annealing, 115; cupronickel, 186
Brinell hardness, 41, 44
Brine quenching, 337–39
Brittle materials, 39, 73
transition range, 81, 82, 423, 437
Bronze, 173, 234–37
aluminum, 471–72
bearing, 253–56

Bronze (*cont.*)
beryllium, 249, 466–69
cast, 249–58
commercial, 241
constitution, 234, 236–37
graphite, 255–56
lead, 254
manganese, 245, 256–58
nickel, 256–57
phosphor, 248–49
porous, 161
powder metal, 160–61
properties, 237
wrought, 248–49
zinc, 251
Bubble rafts, 30; critical shear stress, 59
Bulk modulus, 49–50
Burgers vector, 67
Burning, 184

Cadmium, 1, 14; alloy with zinc, 152
Calcium, alloy with lead, 145; with magnesium, 147; deoxidizer for copper, 134
Capped steel, 86
Carbides
austenite stainless steels, precipitation, 441–43; solution, 441; stabilization, 447–49
carbon and alloy steels, 385–92, 407–09; change in alloy content during quenching, 387–88
ferritic stainless steels, 419–33
Carbon (*see also* Graphite), 16
deoxidizer for copper, 134
effect on aging in iron, 460–65; on austenite transformation, 361–63; on fracture of gray cast iron, 304, 309; on hardness of quenched steel, 389–90; on iron-chromium diagram, 419–21; on machinability of steel, 391; on martensite transformation in steel, 359–60, 363; on properties of 18:8 stainless steels, 441; on stability of gamma iron, 259; on work-hardening of 18:8 stainless steels, 450
extra low, in austenitic steels, 447
solubility, in alpha iron, 461–62; in 18:8 stainless steels, 441
tool steels, 404
Carbonitriding, 393
Carbonyl iron, 137
Carburizing, 391–93
heat treatment after, 396
grades of automotive steels, 394–95

steels, effect of heat-treatment on grain size, 25
Cast brass, 249–51; high-strength, 257–58; red, 249–50, 254; yellow, 251
Cast bronze, 249–51, 253–58; aluminum, 472; bearing, 253–56; graphite, 255–56; leaded, 253–56; manganese, 257–58; nickel, 256–57; steam and structural, 251–53; zinc, 251
Cast irons, 20, 302–26; austenitic, 325–26; chilled, 304, 315–16; corrosion-resistant, 322–26; gray, 309–15; heat-resistant, 321–22; malleable, 304–08; mottled, 315; nodular, 316–18, 323; wear-resistant, 318–21
Castings
aluminum-base, 223–24
chilled-iron, 304, 315–16
cast-iron, 302–26
copper-base, 249–58
corrosion-resistant, iron, 322–26
gray-iron, 309–15
heat-resistant iron, 321–22
magnesium-base, 227–29
malleable-iron, 304–08
mottled-iron, 315
nickel-base, 187–88
nodular-iron, 316–18
recrystallization, 109–10
stainless-steel, structure, 451
steel, 280–82
wear-resistant, 318–21
zinc-base, 212
C-curve
explanation of shape, 335
for carbide precipitation, austenitic stainless steels, 443
for sigma formation, austenitic stainless steels, 439; ferritic steels, 443
Cementite, 262
decomposition to graphite, 275, 301, 306
in cast iron, 302–04, 311, 315; hypereutectoid steels, 284–86; iron-chromium alloys, 419
properties, 287
Cerium, alloys with iron, 259–60; effect on stability of gamma iron, 259
Cesium, 3
Chemical
activity, grain boundaries, 31
elements, metallic, 1; nonmetallic, 1; transuranium, 1
lead, 143–44
potential, 163
Chevron pattern, cleavage fracture of low-carbon steels, 277
Chill cast iron, 304, 315–16

Chinese-script eutectic structure, 191

Chip breakers to improve machinability, 243–44, 273, 477

Chloride stress-corrosion cracking, austenitic stainless steels, 453

Chromium, 1, 12
 aluminum alloys, 481, 484–85
 automotive steels, 394–95, 398–99
 cementite stabilization, 275–76, 423
 depletion by carbide precipitation, stainless steels, 445–46
 die steels, 408, 426
 effect on austenite transformation, 364; on carbide limitations of austenite, 289; on general precipitation in **7075** aluminum, 484; on hardenability, 384; on stability of gamma iron, 259
 electrodeposited over copper and nickel, 136
 face-centered cubic, 417
 iron alloys, 417–37
 low- and intermediate-, steels, 423–27
 nickel alloys, 496–501
 stainless steels, austenitic, 437–56; ferritic, 417–37
 steels, resistance to hydrogen attack, 277–78; to hydrogen sulfide, 423–24; to oxidation, 422–23; to sulfidation, 422–23
 tool steels, 401–02, 406–13
 welding, steels, 421–23, 450–52

Cleavage fracture, 77, 80; low-carbon steel, 277; velocity, 80

Climb of dislocations, 65, 68–69; during creep, 120

Close-packed directions, 56, 61
 planes, 55, 56, 61
 space lattices, 12, 13

Clusters, atomic, in solid solutions, 331

Coarse grains, 7, 61, 102–05, 116; in tin coatings, 154; in zinc coatings, 153–54

Coarsening temperature, 102, 105

Cobalt, 1, 14
 effect on stability of gamma iron, 259
 in beryllium bronze, 466; high-speed tool steels, 413

Coercive force, 138

Coherency
 carbide precipitation in steels, 388, 461; annealing twins, 117; loss by cold deformation, 343; nitride precipitation in steels, 461; ordering, 334
 strains, 332, 334, 343; ordered structures, 334; diffusionless transformations, 341; precipitation reactions,

342–43, 475; Widmannstaetten precipitates, 338

Coherent boundaries, 117

Cold deformation (cold work), 59–61
 ausforming of metastable austenite, 369–70
 compared to hot work, 113–14
 effect on carbide precipitation in stainless steels, 442–43, 447; on martensite transformation in austenitic steels, 341, 365–67, 450; on precipitation, 336, 343; on subsequent recrystallization, 91–99

Color changes with zinc in brass, 239

Columbium, 1, 2, 12
 as carbide stabilizer in stainless steels, 447–49
 in nickel-chromium alloys, 497

Commercial
 bronze, 241
 G bronze, 253
 red brass, 251

Commercially pure metal, 167–68

Components in alloys, 158, 162

Composition
 brass, 249–50
 effect on properties, aluminum bronzes, 470–71; brasses, 236–37; bronzes, 236–37; carbon steels, 387–88; austenitic stainless steels, 441, 448–50
 G bronze, 251, 254
 M bronze, 253–54
 plane, in twinning, 117
 rule for constitutional diagrams, 176
 supersaturation, 331, 355

Compound, chemical, 18; intermetallic, 18, 169–71

Compressibility, 50

Concentration gradients during diffusion, 33–34; during solidification, 182

Condensed systems, 164–65

Condenser tubes, 245

Conductivity
 electrical, 9; change during crystallization, 97; of aluminum, 128–31; of copper, 131–32; of iron, 139; of silicon transformer sheets, 299–301
 magnetic, 138–39
 metallic, 9
 thermal, 9

Congruent melting, 169

Constituents, micro, 199

Constitutional diagrams, 165–67
 aluminum-copper, 469, 470
 aluminum-magnesium, 222
 aluminum-silicon, 208
 aluminum-zinc, 211

Constitutional diagrams (*cont.*)
   antimony-lead, 204
   antimony-tin, 216
   beryllium-copper, 466
   carbon-chromium-iron, 419, 420
   carbon-iron, 261, 268, 302; carbon solid
      solubility, 461
   cerium-iron, 260
   chromium-iron, 418
   chromium-iron-nickel, 436–38; carbon
      solubility in 18:8, 442–43
   complete liquid and partial solid solu-
      bility, 192; and complete solid solu-
      bility, 174
   copper-iron, 260
   copper-magnesium, 215
   copper-nickel, 176
   copper-silver, 192–93
   copper-tin, 236–37
   copper-zinc, 235, 237
   eutectic, simple, 197
   eutectoid, 261
   interpretation, lever rule, 178–80; phase
      rule, 162–65; 1:2:1 rule, 197–99
   iron-graphite, 301
   iron-nickel, 260
   iron-molybdenum, 260
   iron-silicon, 299
   lead-magnesium, 214
   lead-tin, 200
   limitations, 174
   nomenclature, 234
   peritectic, 216
   plotting, 166–67
   tin-zinc, 197
Constructional   Codes,   A.S.A.,   425;
   A.S.M.E., 275, 425
Continuous precipitation, 195, 332–33; in
   aluminum-copper alloys, 476
Cooling
   continuous, transformation of austenite,
      370–72
   curves, 4, 5, 15; apparatus to determine,
      5; copper-nickel alloys, 175; copper-
      silver alloys, 190; eutectic, 190; eu-
      tectoid steels, 282–83; hypereutectoid
      steels, 287; hypoeutectoid steels, 270–
      71;   intermetallic compound, 169;
      pure metal, 174, 189; solid solubility,
      174–75
   rate, critical, 372–74; during quench-
      ing, 336–39; effect on allotropic re-
      crystallization,   106,   108–09;   aus-
      tenite transformation, 372; grain
      size, 106; microstructure, 375–76;
      factors affecting, during heat treat-
      ment, 375–77

Copper, 1, 7, 12, 18, 131–38
   billet, 7
   conductivity, 130–31
   deoxidized, 134–35
   effect on stability of gamma iron, 259
   electrodeposited, 136–37
   embrittlement by hydrogen, 133
   free-machining, 135
   grain size, 61
   oxygen-free, 59, 60, 61
   recrystallization, 96, 98
   tough-pitch, 131–32
   wire bar, 7
   work-hardening, 61
Copper alloys, aluminum, 194–95
   beryllium, 466–69
   iron, 143, 254, 259–60
   lead, 254–55
   magnesium, 214–16
   nickel, 174–89
   silver, 189–90, 192–95
   tellurium, 244
   tin, 173, 234–37, 248–49
   zinc, 152–53, 234–48
   **No. 102,** 131; **No. 110,** 131; **No. 113,**
      131; **No. 114,** 131; **No. 116,** 131;
      **No. 120,** 135; **No. 122,** 135; **No.
      145,** 135; **No. 147,** 135; **No. 172,**
      466
   **No. 210,** 240; **No. 220,** 240; **No. 230,**
      240; **No. 240,** 241; **No. 260,** 241;
      **No. 268,** 241; **No. 270,** 241; **No.
      280,** 241
   **No. 442,** 245; **No. 443,** 245; **No. 444,**
      245; **No. 445,** 245; **No. 462,** 245;
      **No. 464,** 245; **No. 465,** 245; **No.
      466,** 245; **No. 467,** 245
   **No. 510,** 249; **No. 521,** 249; **No. 524,**
      249
   **No. 606,** 472; **No. 612,** 472; **No. 628,**
      472; **No. 670,** 245; **No. 675,** 245;
      **No. 687,** 245
   **No. 704,** 185; **No. 706,** 185; **No. 710,**
      185; **No. 715,** 185; **No. 720,** 185;
      **No. 752,** 246
Coring, 150; effect on liquation, 184; in
   brasses and bronzes, 249, 252–53; in
   cupronickel, 186
Corrosion
   dezincification, 241–43, 245
   fatigue, 87
   Huey test, 444
   of sensitized stainless steels, 444–45
   graphitic, 314
   resistance of solid solutions, 17
   -resistant cast iron, 322–26
   season cracking, of brasses, 247–48

Corrosion (*cont.*)
  Strauss test, 444
  stress-, 248, 453, 484
Cracking, cleavage, 77–80
  during quenching, 367, 377–78; welding chromium steels, 421
  fire, 186
  intergranular, 80–81, 423–24, 453
  season, of brasses, 247–48
  shear, 74–77
  stress-corrosion, 248, 453, 484
  velocity, 79
Creep, 119–21
  parameter for predicting, 125
  some high-temperature alloys, 434
Critical
  cooling rate, 372–74, 377
  diameter, 381; for through hardenability, 381–82; ideal, 383
  range, for steels, 347
  ruling section, for hardenability, 381
  shear stress, for slip, 58
Crystallization, metal, as a factor in fatigue failure, 87
  nucleus, 6–9
Crystallographic planes, 54–55
Cube structure in copper, 104–05; in iron-silicon alloys, 301
Cupping tests, 115
Cupronickel, 185–86
Curie point, 15, 365
Cutlery-type stainless steels, standard, 428; modified, 431

Damping capacity, gray cast iron, 313
Dealuminification, of alloy brasses, 242
Decarburization, 137, 140, 276–77; effect on high-manganese steel, 367
Deep drawing, 61, 115–16; steels, 273, 461–62
Defect
  Frenkel, 26
  lattice, 26, 28–32
  propagation, 38–39
  radiation produced, 31
Deformation
  as a factor in precipitation, 442–43, 447, 475–76
  at fracture, 39–40, 74–77
  by movement of defects, 65–70
  cold, 59
  effects of grain size, 60–62
  elastic, 49, 57
  geometrical, 61–64
  grain-boundary, 70
  hot, 113
  mechanical, 9, 38

  metallic, 38
  nonmetallic, 38
  permanent, 51
  plastic, 38
  resistance to, strength, 47
  shear, 48
Deformation lines in bronze, 72; precipitation on, in aluminum-copper alloys, 476; in austenitic stainless steels, 442–43, 447
Degrees of freedom, 163–65
Dendritic structure, 150, 182, 186, 252–53, 281
Denickelification, of alloy brasses, 242
Deoxidation of copper, 131, 134–35, 248; of steels, 274
Deuteron, 29
Dezincification, of brasses, 241, 243, 245
Diamagnetism, 138
Diamond pyramid hardness, 41
Didymium, 487, 489
Die-castings, aluminum-base, 223–24
  magnesium-base, 228–29
  zinc-base, 212
Die steels, 406
Diffusion, 32–34
  as a factor in hydrogen embrittlement, 133; in eutectoid decomposition, 356; in peritectic reaction, 216–18; in redistributing interstitials after deformation, 465; in precipitation reactions, 331–32, 335–36; in separation of proeutectoid constituents, 361; in solidification, 176–78, 182; in zone melting, 184–85
  carbon in alpha iron, 465; in gamma iron, 465
  carburizing, 391–93
  coefficient, 33–34
  decarburization, 140, 276–77
  dislocation climb by, 68
  grain boundary, 34
  hydrogen in alpha iron, 465
  interatomic, 33
  nitrogen in alpha iron, 465
  surface, 34
  thermal, 4
  volume, 35
Diffusionless shear transformation, 339–41, 353, 358
Direct-quench transformation, 336
Discontinuous precipitation, 195, 332–33
  yield point, in steels, 462, 465
Dislocations
  destruction of, 69–70
  disappearance during recrystallization, 95

Dislocations (*cont.*)
  edge, 29, 30
  explanation of aging in iron and steel,
    464–65; of creep, 120–21
  movement of, 65; during polygoniza-
    tion, 94–95; during recovery, 93
  negative, 30
  pile ups, 69, 73
  positive, 30
  screw, 29–31
Displacement spikes, 29
Distortion control
  by martempering, 374–75
  during quenching, 377
  from imperfections, 26, 65; unbalanced
    stresses, 330
Dodecahedral planes, 55
Driving force, for precipitation, 334–35
Drop-of-the-beam yield point, 51
Ductile-brittle fracture transition, in
    steels, 81
Ductility, 54
  changes by annealing, 91–100, 113–15;
    by recrystallization, 95
  of materials, 39, 51, 52
  tests for, 115–16
Duralumin-type aluminum alloys, 469,
    473–76

Eddy current loss, 139
Edge dislocation, 29, 30; anchored, 66;
    climb, 68; propagation, 65
Elastic deformation, 48, 57–59
  distortion, during precipitation, 332;
    during quenching, 377
  energy, decrease during polygonization,
    95
  limit, 48, 51
  moduli, 49, 51
  properties, 47, 48
  stresses, effect on austenite stabiliza-
    tion, 363
Electrical resistivity
  effect of alloying elements, on alumi-
    num, 129, 130; on copper, 130, 131;
    on iron, 139
  steels, silicon, 298–301
Electroforming, 136
Electrolytic
  deposition of aluminum, 129; of cop-
    per, 136–37; of iron, 137; of nickel,
    150, 151; of tin, 150, 151; of zinc,
    155
  polishing, of lead, 143
Electromagnets, 298
Electron, 9–10, 29
  compounds, 169

concentration, 169
  energy levels, 9
  excited, 29
  free, 10
  spin, 10, 15
  tightly bound, 9, 10
Electrotin, 150–51
  -typing, 136
  -zinc, 155
Elongation, 50, 53
Embrittlement
  copper, by hydrogen attack, 133–34
  iron, by hydrogen, 276–78; by low-
    temperature, 77–82
  orientation, hexagonal metals, 75
  stainless steels, by carbide precipitation,
    453; inherent, 437; by hydrogen, 429;
    by sigma phase precipitation, 433–
    37; by 885 F embrittlement, 433,
    435–37
  temper, 423–24
  welds, by hydrogen, 110; by hardening,
    chromium steels, 421
Embryo, 331, 335–36, 344
End-quench test, 382–83
Energy
  levels, 9; electron, 9, 10
  requirements for transformation, 342
  thermal, effects on cold worked mate-
    rial, 91–98
Engine brass, 253
Engineering metals, 1, 128–55
Epsilon carbide, $Fe_{2.4}C$, 461
Equiaxed grain, 6
Equilibrium diagram (*see* Constitutional
    diagram)
  state, 162
Erichsen ductility tester, 115–16
Etching, 20–22
  brasses, 241
  carbon steels, 265–67
  contrast, 21–23
  heavy, 21, 22
  light, 21
  pits, 22
Eutectic, 191–92
  constitutional diagrams with, 192–93,
    197
  copper-cuprous oxide, 133
  high-speed steels, 413
  iron-carbon, 262–63
  lead-tellurium, 144
  occurrence of, 196
  structures, typical, 191, 263
Eutectoid, 331
  aluminum-copper, 470–71
  beryllium-copper, 466

Eutectoid (*cont.*)
 continuous cooling transformation, 370–72
 iron-carbon, 263–64, 282–83
 iron-nitrogen, 460
 isothermal transformation, 352–58
 microstructural changes in steels from transformation, 282–84
 other systems, 263
 reaction, 331
 sigma phase decomposition in iron-chromium alloys, 419
Expansion, thermal, iron, 108; iron-nickel alloys, 294–96
Explosive shock loading, 39
Extra low carbon grade, austenitic stainless steels, 447
Extrapolation parameters for stress-rupture, 123–24
Extrusion, 145

Face-centered cubic space lattice, 11–14
Face-diagonal plane, 55
Fatigue strength, 85
 effect of imperfections, 87; of notches, 87; of metal crystallization, 87; of residual stresses, 88; of surface finish, 87
 testing, 85; times for various materials, 86
Ferrite, 14, 261
 aging of, 460–65
 grain size, 108
 in cast iron, 311; in 18:8 stainless steels containing molybdenum, 443
 nucleation of bainite, 358
 precipitation in hypoeutectoid steels, 268–71
 properties, 287
 stabilization by chromium, 457; by other elements, 259
 Widmannstaetten, in cast steel, 281
Ferromagnetism, 138
Fibrous fracture, 74
Fick's laws, for diffusion, 33
Fine grain, 7, 102, 116; for ductility, 114; for increasing resistance to notch-brittleness, 279
Firebox quality steels, 274
Fire cracking, 186
Flange quality steels, 274
Forces, binding, 11
 cohesive, 11
 electrostatic, 11
 external, 11
 interatomic, 11, 57–58
 repulsive, 11

Fracture, 73
 brittle, 53, 73, 77–79
 cleavage, 77
 cup-and-cone, 75–76
 ductile, 53, 74
 effect of impurities, 74
 fatigue, 86
 fibrous, 74
 high-ductility, 74, 76
 initiation of, 73
 intergranular, 80–81, 247, 453, 484
 low-ductility, 74, 76
 notch, 78
 shear, 74, 76
 stress-corrosion, 247–48, 448, 453, 484
 stress-rupture, 122
 transgranular, 453
 transitions, 81
Frank-Read sources, 66–67; spirals, 65
Free
 electrons, 10
 energy, 34, 335, 342–43
 -machining aluminum bronze, 472; aluminum-copper alloys, 477; brass, 243–44, 251; bronze, 249, 253, 254; copper, 135–36; nickel alloys, 187, 494; nickel silvers, 247; stainless steel, 428–29; steel, 271, 273, 391, 394
Freezing point, 4; for iron, 14
Frenkel defects, 26
Fusion, latent heat of, 3, 5, 9
 welding, structural changes during, 110–13

Gallium, 3
Galvanized coatings, 153–55
Gamma loop in iron alloys, 259–60, 292, 298; in iron-chromium alloys, 417, 421
Gases, 3
General-purpose tool steels, 403–05
Gibbs' phase rule, 162–65
Gilding metal, 241
Glide (*see also* Slip)
 of dislocations, 65
Gold, 2, 12
 effect on stability of gamma iron, 259
Government bronze, 251
Grain
 allotriomorphic, 6; coarse, 7, 61, 102–05, 116, 153–54; columnar, 6; equiaxed, 6, 26; fine, 7, 102, 114, 116, 279; idiomorphic, 8
 boundary, 21–22, 25, 28; carbide precipitation, austenitic stainless steels,

442–43; constituents in steels, identification, 286; corrosion, in stainless steels, 445–47; deformation, 70; depletion in chromium, in stainless steels, 445; diffusion, 34; etching, 22, 32; fracture in stainless steels, 453; in stress corrosion cracking, 248, 453; in stress-rupture, 122, in temper embrittlement, 423–24; misfit, 31; nucleation of transformation, 358; precipitation, 332–33

coarsening, during heat-treatment of steels, 347

growth, 91, 100–01; abnormal, 102–03, 105; after recrystallization, 100; inhibition, 100–02; effect critical strain, 104, of furnace atmosphere, 64, of temperature, 98–103, 111; in welding, 110–13, 430, 433

refinement, by allotropic transformation, 107, by recrystallization, 95–98

size, 8, 23–25; austenitic, 24–25, 108; by direct comparison, 24; change during welding, 111; effect of hot work, 114; ferritic, 108; effect on austenite transformation, 367–68, on hardenability, 380; idealized, 25; inherent, McQuaid-Ehn, 397; in hypereutectoid steel, 285; Jeffries, 24; measurement, 23, 24; nonferrous, 27; solidification, 8; standard, 25, 27

Granular eutectic, structure, 192

Granular transformation products of austenite, 385–87

Graphite
bronze, 255–56
in gray cast iron, 20, 304, 309–13; malleable iron, 308; nodular iron, 316–17; transformer steel, 301
corrosion of cast iron, 314
steels, 273

Graphitization (*see also* Graphite corrosion)
effect of chromium in resisting, 423
elevated temperature, of low-carbon steel, 275–76

Gray cast iron, 301, 309–14

Green castings, 280
water trouble, 241

Griffith theory, brittle fracture, 78; Orowan modification, 78; with prior plastic deformation, 78

Grossman formula, for hardenability, 383–85

Growth
cast irons, 313, 321–22, 325
grain, 91, 100–01; abnormal, 102–03,

105; after recrystallization, 100; inhibition, 100–02; effect of critical strain, 104, furnace atmosphere, 104, temperature, 98–103, 111

precipitation embryos, 331

Guinier-Preston zones (*see* G.P. zones)

Gun metal, 255

Hadfield steel, electrical, 298–301; manganese, 366–67; silicon, 298–301; wear-resisting, 366–67

Hardenability, 353, 379–81
automotive steels, carburizing grades, 394–95; heat-treating grades, 398–401
critical diameter, 381–82
effect of alloying elements, 383–85; of grain size, 380
Jominy end-quench test, 382–83
tool steels, 401–13

Hardening
precipitation, 460–501
range for steels, 347–49
steels, by heat-treatment, 347–413
surface, 391–93, 396, 454
work-, 38–40, 59–61, 69–70

Hard lead, 144–45

Hardness, 39–46
Brinell, 41, 44
changes by annealing, 91; by deformation, 38, 40; by heat-treatment, steels, 347–413; by precipitation-hardening, 460–501; by recrystallization, 95
diamond pyramid, 41
Meyer, 40–41
microhardness, 41
Monotron, 41
Rockwell, 41–43
scales, relationship, 46
Shore scleroscope, 41, 45
Tukon, 41
ultimate Meyer, 41
Vickers, 41, 44

Heat
-affected zone, of welds, 112, 451–52
energy, given off by austenite transformation, 372
latent, 3, 5
-resistant cast iron, 321–22
specific, 3
-treatment, after carburizing, 396; annealing, 91, 113–14, 348; of commercial steels, 347–413; effects on microstructure of brass, 238–39, of section size, 399, of hardenability,

379–81; of high-speed tool steels, 411; precipitation, 334–36, 443–47, 460–501; to constant microstructure instead of hardness, 378–79, 399; normalizing, 347–48, 372; solution, 336, 441; tempering, 385–90; tool steels, 401–13

Heterogeneous precipitation, 344

Hexagonal close-packed space lattice, 12, 13

High
  brass, 241
  -carbon tool steels; high-chromium, 407–08; low-tungsten, 405
  -ductility shear fracture, 74
  -purity aluminum, 128; copper, 131; iron, 137, 140; zinc, 152
  -speed tool steels, 409–13
  -strength aluminum alloys, 477–81

Homogeneous precipitation, 344

Homogenizing treatment, beryllium copper, 467

Hooke's law, 48, 49, 58

Hot
  -dip coatings, aluminum, 143; lead, 145; terne, 145; tin, 143, 150–51; zinc, 143, 153–54
  rolling, iron, 115
  -screw stock, 271
  -shortness, 135
  tears, during welding, 112
  work, 113–15, 121
  -working die steels, 409

Huey test (boiling nitric acid), 444–45

Hydrogen, 3, 16
  attack on steels, 276–79; carbide stabilizing effects of chromium, 423
  decarburizing of iron, 140
  embrittlement of copper, 133–34, 277
  pick-up during welding, 110
  sulfide corrosion of steels, 424

Hypereutectoid steels
  application of lever rule, 286
  heat-treatment, 348, 359–61
  identification of grain-boundary constituents, 286
  microstructural changes during cooling, 284–87

Hypoeutectoid steel
  application of lever rule, 270
  heat-treatment, 348
  identification of grain-boundary constituents. 286
  microstructural changes during cooling, 268–71

Hysteresis, 138–41

I.A.C.S., 131

Idiomorphic crystals, 8

Impact
  strength, 82; nickel, 149; nickel-chromium-iron alloys, effect of sigma phase, 439
  tests, 82; Carpenter, 84; Charpy, 82–84; cleavage fracture in, 78; intergranular fracture in, 423–24, 453; Izod, 83–84; keyhole specimen, 83; Luerssen-Greene, 84; notch sensitivity, 82; tensile, 83–84; torsion, 85

Imperfections, 22, 26, 59
  diffusion of, 32
  dislocation, 29–31
  distortion from, 26, 65
  effect on fatigue life, 87
  lattice, 26
  line, 29
  point, 26
  production by irradiation, 28
  surface, 28, 31

Impurities, 9
  effect on conductivity of aluminum, 129–31; of copper, 130–31; on copper deposition, 137; on fracture, 74; on workability, 54
  inhibition of grain growth by, 100–02
  in iron, 139; in lead, 143; in magnesium, 146; in nickel, 148; in tin, 154; in zinc, 152–55

Inclusions, 8; nonmetallic, 16

Incoherent boundaries, 117

Incongruent melting, 169, 216

Incubation period, 96, 331

Index of relative hardness, 41; of strain hardening, 41

Ingot, 7
  iron, 139–41

Inherent grain size, McQuaid-Ehn, 397

Inherent brittleness of chromium stainless steels, 437

Inhibitors of dezincification in brasses, 241, 245

Inoculation of cast iron, 315–16

Interatomic diffusion, 11, 13

Intercrystalline fracture
  aluminum alloys, stress cracking, 484
  austenitic stainless steels, polythionic acid stress corrosion, 448, 453; at low temperature, from intergranular carbides, 453
  creep-rupture, 80–81
  season cracking of brass, 247–48
  temper embrittlement, 423

Intermediate-chromium steels, 423–27
  solid solutions, 167, 170–72

Intermetallic compounds, 18, 158, 167, 169–71

  AlMg, 222, 224; $Al_3Mg_2$, 222, 224; $Al_{12}Mg_2Cr$, 484; $Al_{12}Mg_{17}$, 222, 225–26, 228, 230, 485–86

  $CaPb_3$, 215

  CuAl, 475; $Cu_2Al_{3.6}$, 475; $CuAl_2$, 473, 475, 484; CuAu, 169; $Cu_3Au$, 169; $CuMgAl_2$, 484; $Cu_6Sn_5$, 218–21; $Cu_3P$, 253; $Cu_{31}Sn_8$, 235, 249, 253, 255–56; $Cu_4Sn$, 235, 240

  $(Cr, Fe)_7C_3$, 420; $Cr_7C_3$, 388; $(Cr, Fe)_{23}C_6$, 420, 443, 445; $(Cr, Fe)_4C$, 420; $Cr_4C$, 420

  $Fe_2C$, 387; $Fe_{2.4}C$, 461; $Fe_3C$, 169, 261, 262, 284, 387, 461; $(Fe, Cr)_3C$, 419; FeCr, 417; $Fe_3Mo_2$, 323–24; $Fe_3Mo_3C$, 323–24; $Fe_{16}N_2$, 461; $Fe_4N$, 461; $Fe_3Si$, 322; $FeSn_2$, 151; $FeZn_3$, 154; $FeZn_7$, 157

  $Mg_2Pb$, 213–14; $Mg_2Si$, 230, 478, 481; $MgZn_5$, 152; $MgZn_2$, 484, 487; MgZn, 487; MgZn', 487; $Mg_4Th$, 489; $Mg_5Th$, 489

  $Mo_2C$, 388; $Mo_{23}C_6$, 388

  $Ni_3Al$, 491, 495; $Ni_3(Al, Ti)$, 497, 499, 500; $Ni_3Ti$, 501; $NiSi_3$, 210

  SbSn, 8, 218–21; $Si_3N_4$, 388

Internal stresses, 93

  decrease by heat-treatment, 92–93

  during quenching of steels, 377–78

  shape changes from unbalanced, 330

Internal surfaces as a factor in hydrogen attack, 133–34, 276–79; in precipitation, 343–44

International Annealed Copper Standard (*see* I.A.C.S.)

Interrupted quenching, 341, 374

Interstitial atoms, 16, 28–29

  anchors for dislocations, 465

  diffusion of, 32–33

  in iron, strain aging, 464–65

  solid solution of, 16, 18, 168

Invar, 294–95

Ions, positive, metals as, 10

Iridium, 2, 12

Iron, 1, 12, 14, 137–43

  aging in, 460–65

  allotropic recrystallization in, 106–07

  allotropy, 14

  alpha, 14

  carbide, 169, 282–88, 303, 311, 315, 460–61

  cooling curves, 15

  Curie point, 15, 365

  delta, 14

  effect on aluminum, 129–30; on alumi-num bronze, 472; on beryllium bronze, 466; on cupronickel, 186; on manganese bronze, 258

  gamma, 14

  grain size, 108, 115; refinement during welding, 112

  heating curves, 15

  latent heats, 15

  mechanical twins in, 72

  Neumann bands in, 72

  recrystallization, 99

Iron alloys

  aluminum, 259

  antimony, 259

  arsenic, 259

  beryllium, 259

  binary alloys, types, 259–60; effect of carbon on, 291–92

  boron, 259

  carbon (iron carbide), 259, 261, 268; effect of alloying elements, 288–91

  castings, 302–26

  cerium, 259–60

  chromium, 259, 417–37; chromium-nickel-, 437–56

  copper, 143, 254, 259–60

  gold, 259

  graphite, 301–02

  heat-treatment, 347–413

  molybdenum, 259–60

  nickel, 259–60, 293–98; precipitation-hardenable, 501

  nitrogen, 259, 461

  phosphorus, 259

  silicon, 259, 298–301

  sulfur, 259

  tantalum, 259

  tin, 259

  transformation nomenclature, 267–68

  tungsten, 259

  vanadium, 259

  zinc, 259

  zirconium, 259

Irradiation

  interstitial atoms from, 28–29

  producing imperfections, 28

Isothermal transformation of austenite, 349–58

Isotopes, 10

Jominy end-quench test, 382–83

K42B, high-temperature alloy, 434

Killed steel, 86

Knee of TTT curves

  bainite, 365, 369

  effect of alloying elements, 364–65,

421; of carbon content on, 361–63; of grain size, 367–68
pearlite, 352–53, 365, 369
relation to critical cooling rate, 372–74, 380

L grade, austenitic stainless steel (*see* Extra low carbon grade)
Lake copper, 131
Lamellar eutectic structure, 191
transformation products of austenite, 353–56, 390
precipitate in beryllium copper, 469; in magnesium alloys, 229–30, 586
Larson-Miller parameter for correlating stress-rupture, 123–24; creep, 125
Latent heat, 3, 5–6, 9, 15
Lattice imperfection, 26, 28
Lautal, 474
Lead, 1, 12, 143–46
burning, 144
effect on copper, 131, 135–56; on aluminum-copper alloys, 477; on cupro-nickel, 186; on zinc, 152
grain size, effect of impurities, 100–01
hot work, 113
quenching in, 337
Lead alloys
antimony, 173, 204–05
babbitt bearings, 205–07
brasses, 243–44
bronze, 254
copper, 254–55
magnesium, 213–14
silver, 203–04
tin, 200–01, 205–07
Ledeburite, 191, 262–63
Le Chatelier principle, 16
Leveling, zone, 185
Lever rule, 178–79
application to eutectoid steels, 284; to hypereutectoid steels, 286; to hypoeutectoid steels, 270; to low-carbon steels, 270; to tool steels, 284, 286
Line dislocations, 464–65; imperfection, 29
Liquation, 184
Liquid solutions, 158
Liquid state, 3–4
Liquidus, 75
Lithium, as deoxidizer for copper, 134
Load versus elongation curves, 47, 48; after aging, for steels, 460–65
Localized precipitation, 332–33; in aluminum-copper alloys, 476; in austenitic stainless steels, 442–43
Logarithmic creep, 121

Long-range order (*see* Ordered structure)
Low
-carbon steels, aging in, 460–65; carburizing, 391–93; castings, 280–82; decarburization, 276–77; graphitization, 275–76; hydrogen attack, 276–77; martensitic, 359–63; notch-brittleness, 277; wrought, 271–74
-chromium steels, 423–27; vanadium-type tool steels, 406
-ductility shear fracture, 74
-temperature, effect on mechanical properties of 18:8 steels, 453; nickel steels for, 293; notch-brittleness at, 277; properties of Monel alloy at, 189, 400
Lower yield point, 77
Lueder's lines, 462
Luster, metallic, 9

$M_d$, 341
$M_f$, 341, 353, 359
effect of carbon content, in steels, 359–60, 363
relation to retained austenite, 363
$M_s$, 340, 353, 359, 373
effect of alloying elements, in steels, 364; of carbon content, 359–60, 363; in austenitic stainless steels, 441
Machinability
aluminum-copper alloys, effect of lead and bismuth, 477
copper alloys, effect of lead, 135–36, 243–44, 247, 249, 251, 253–54, 472
nickel alloys, 187, 494
stainless steel, 428–29
steel, 271, 273, 391, 394
Macrosegregation, 182–83
Magnesium, 1, 14, 146–47
Magnesium alloys
aluminum, 130, 221–30, 485–87
copper, 214–16
lead, 213–14
nomenclature, 507
precipitation-hardenable, 485–90
rare earth metals, 488–89
thorium, 489
zinc, 152
**AM100A**, 228; **AZ31B**, 225–26, 228; **AZ61A**, 225–26, 228; **AZ63A**, 228–30, 486–87; **AZ80A**, 225–27, 486; **AZ81A**, 228; **AZ91C**, 228–29, 487; **AZ92A**, 228–30, 486–87
**EK30A**, 489; **EK41A**, 489; **EZ33A**, 489
**HK31A**, 490; **HM21XA**, 490; **HZ32A**, 490

Magnesium alloys (*cont.*)
  **M1A,** 146–47
  **ZE41A,** 487–88; **ZK51A,** 487–88; **ZK60A,** 488; **ZK61,** 488; **ZK62A,** 488
Magnetic alloys
  iron-nickel, 296–98
  properties, iron, 138–41
Magnetism, 138
  Curie point, 15, 365
  development, in austenitic steels, by transformation, 365
  iron-nickel alloys, 296–98; -silicon alloys, 297–301
Magnetization curve, 138
Malleability, 54
Malleable cast iron, 301, 304–08
Manganese, 1, 11, 12
  alloys with aluminum, 223; with aluminum bronze, 472; with cupronickel, 186; with magnesium, 147, 225; with nickel, 187, 501
  austenitic nickel cast irons, 325; stainless steels, 453–54
  automotive steels, 394, 398
  bronze, wrought, 245; cast, 256–58
  change of content of carbides during tempering, 388
  effect on austenite transformation in steels, 364; on carbon limitations of austenite, 289; on austenite eutectoid composition and temperature, 290; on properties of 0.55% carbon steel, 378–79; on stability of gamma iron, 259
  nondeforming tool steels, 406
  wear-resisting steels, 366–67
Manson-Haferd parameter for stress-rupture, 124
Martempering, 357, 374–75
Martensite
  black, 358–59
  effect of carbon content, 359
  formation by ausforming, 369–70
  from austenite transformation, 350–53, 355, 358–61
  precipitation-hardening stainless steels, 455–56
  tempering, 385–87
  transformation, 339–41; of austenite by cold work, 365, by subatmospheric cooling, 365; in aluminum bronze, 471–72; in high-manganese steel, 366–67; in low-carbon steel, 272; in austenitic stainless steels, 441, 450
  white, 358–59
McQuaid-Ehn test for carburized grain size, 397–98

Mechanical
  deformation, 9, 38–73; mixtures, 19, 172–74
  polishing, 19, 21, 71–72, 118; of lead, 143
  properties of cast iron, effect of alloying elements, 318
  twinning, 71–72; as a factor in deformation, 75–76
Medium red brass, 251
Melting, 9, 169
  congruent, 169
  for alloying, 159
  in eutectic alloys, 191–92; liquation, 184; lead-silver solders, 203; soft solder, 201
  incongruent, 169, 216
  partial, in solid solution alloys, 175–78
  zone, 184–85
Mercurous nitrate test for copper alloys, 248
Mercury, 1, 3, 14
Metallic characteristics, 9
  space lattices, 11–13
  states, 3–4
Metallography, 18–19
  specimen mounting, 19; preparation, 19–22
Metal-arc inert-gas welding, 110
Metals
  allotropic, 14
  engineering, 1, 128–55
  ferrous, 3
  mechanical stability, 11
  monatomic, 3
  noble, 2
  polymorphic, 14
  precious, 2
Metal whiskers, 59
Metastable
  austenite, 349, 363, 365–66, 441, 450, 455; as a factor in ausforming, 369, in martempering, 374–75
  iron carbide (*see* Intermetallic compounds, $Fe_3C$)
  transition phases, 330, 461, 469, 474–75, 481, 487
Meyer hardness, 40–41
Microconstituents, 22, 199–200
Microsegregation, 17, 184
Microstructure, 21, 268–71, 282–87
  annealed, 92, 97, 101, 105
  changes by annealing, 92; by cold working, 60–61; by recovery, 93; by recrystallization, 97; by welding, 112, 450–52
  cold deformed, 60, 72
  engineering metals, 128–55

Microstructure (*cont.*)
  eutectic, 191–92, 263; eutectoid, 264
  for grain size, 25, 27, 103
  heat-treatment to constant, 378–79, 399
  intermetallic compound, 170
  peritectic, 218
  relationship to properties for heat-treated steels, 378–79
  solid solutions, 18, 170, 183
  stainless steels, austenitic, 442; ferritic, 428, 432–33
  steels, hypereutectoid and hypoeutectoid, 266
  transformed austenite, 354–55, 373
  two-phase mechanical mixtures, 23, 173, 201, 273
Microtome, for lead alloys, 143
Mild steels, 271–74
Mischmetal, 487, 489
Misfit, grain boundary, 31
Modified structures, aluminum-silicon alloys, 207–08
Modulus of elasticity, 49, 51, 313; of rigidity, 49; of rupture, gray cast iron, 313–14
Molten salt quenching, 337
Molybdenum, 1, 12
  alloys, with iron, 259–60
  effect on chromium steels, 423; on stability of gamma iron, 259; on temper embrittlement, 423–24
  high-speed tool steels, 411–13
  stainless steels, 439–40, 443
Monel metal (*see* Nickel alloys)
Monkman-Grant relationship, parameter for stress-rupture, 122
Mottled cast iron, 315–16
Muntz metal, 240–41, 256–58
  dezincification, 241, 243

National Emergency Steels, 385
Natural aging, aluminum alloys, 473, 479
Naval brass, 245
Necking, in tensile test, 52
Negative climb of dislocations, 69
Nelson curves for hydrogen attack on steels, 278
Neodymium, 487
Neutron, 10; produced imperfections, 28
Nickel, 1, 12, 18, 147–50
  effect on austenite transformation, 364; on graphite in cast iron, 322–26; on stability of gamma iron, 259
  electrodeposited over copper, 136
  precipitation-hardenable, 490–501
Nickel alloys
  bronze, 256–57
  cast irons, 309, 318–26

chromium, 496–500
copper, 174–89; precipitation-hardenable, 494–96
iron, 259–60, 293–98, 501
Duranickel alloy **301**, 148, 491–92
Inconel alloy **600**, 496–500; alloy **610**, 496; alloy **X-750**, 496, 498
Invar, 294
Monel alloy **400**, 186–89; alloy **R-405**, 187–88; alloy **410**, 187; alloy **K-500**, 187, 494–95; alloy **K-501**, 187, 494–95; alloy **505**, 187; alloy **506**, 187
Nickel **200**, 149; **201**, 149; **210**, 150
Nimonic alloy **80A**, 496, 500
Ni-Span-C, 501
Permanickel alloy **300**, 491–93
Silvers, 246–47
Niobium (*see* Columbium)
Nital etchant, 265
Nitriding, 393; stainless steels, 454
Nitrogen, 16
  effect on carbonitriding, 393; on stabilizing austenitic stainless steels, 441, 453–54; on stability of gamma iron, 259; on strain aging in iron, 465
  solubility in alpha iron, 460
Nondeforming tool steels, 301
Nodular cast iron, 301, 316–18, 323
  pearlite, 372–73
Nomenclature
  allotropic changes in iron, 14–15
  Aluminum Association, for aluminum alloys, 506
  A.S.T.M., for light metals and alloys, 507–09
  S.A.E. steels, 504–05
  tempers of light metals and alloys, 508–09
  transformation, in iron alloys, 267–68
Nonequilibrium
  cooling, brasses and bronzes, 252–53
  reactions, 330–31; peritectic, 217–18; steels, 370–74, 375–77
Nonmetallic materials, characteristics, 9, 10
Nonuniform precipitation (*see also* Discontinuous precipitation), 332–33
Normalizing
  carburized steels, 392
  effect on grain size, 103
  heat-treatment for steels, 348, 372
  ranges for steels, 347
Normal steels (McQuaid-Ehn), 397
  structure, aluminum-silicon alloys, 207–08
Nose of TTT curve (*see* Knee of TTT curve)

Notch brittleness, 81; chromium stainless steels, 437; low-carbon steels, 277–80; steel castings, 282; stainless steels, from grain-boundary carbide precipitation, 453; temper embrittlement, 423
Nucleation
  aging of iron, 461
  allotropic transformation, 109
  alloy carbides by alloying elements, 588
  aluminum-copper alloys, 473–76
  carbide, stainless steels, 443–48
  driving force, 97
  elastic stresses, effect, 363
  forces opposing, 331–32
  frequency, 98
  general precipitation, by $Al_{12}Mg_2Cr$, 484
  lower bainite, 358
  martensite, 358, 363
  pearlite, 353–58
  recrystallization, 96–97
  sigma phase, iron-chromium alloys, 435, 437–40
  stability, aluminum-copper alloys, 475
  solidification, 6
Nucleus
  atomic, 10
  crystallization, 6–9
  precipitation, 332, 334, 335–36, 344
  recrystallization, 96
  solidification, 5, 8

Octahedral plane, 55; as composition plane in twinning, 127
O.F.H.C. copper, 132
Oilless bearings, 256
Oil quenching, 337–38
Olsen ductility tester, 115–16
Orange-peel surface, 61, 70, 104, 274
Ordered structures, 170, 475, 491, 493
Orr, Sherby, and Dorn, parameter for stress rupture, 124
Orowan modification of Griffith theory, 78
Osmium, 2, 14
Ounce metal, 249–50, 254
Overloading, effects of, on engineering metals, 39
Oxidation
  effect of chromium in steels, 422–23, 431
  internal, of gray cast iron, 313, 321–22, 325
Oxygen
  as impurity in copper, 131–34; in iron, 139–41

-bearing copper, 131–34
-free copper, 131
Oxide inclusions, in iron, 21; in tough-pitch copper, 134

Pack-hardening, tool steels, 407–08
Palladium, 2, 12
Paramagnetism, 138
Partitioning of alloying elements in steel during tempering, 387–88
Passivation of austenitic stainless steels, 445
Pearlite, 264–65, 353–56, 372
  austenite transformation to, 349–50
  formation, during cooling, in eutectoid steels, 282–84; in hypereutectoid steels, 284–87; in hypoeutectoid steels, 268–71; in gray cast iron, 311; in low-carbon steel, 311
  modes of formation, 356
  nodular, 353–54
  properties, in steels, 287
Periodic table of the chemical elements, 1
Peritectic reaction, 216–17
  antimony-tin alloys, 216–18
  iron-carbon alloys, 262
  under nonequilibrium conditions, 217–18
Peritectoid reaction, 216
Permanent magnet alloys, 139
Permanent set, after deformation, 48
Permeability, 139
  iron-nickel alloys, 297; -silicon alloys, 301
Phase, 162–65, 167
  diagrams (*see* Constitutional diagrams)
  rule, Gibbs, 163–65
Phosphor bronzes, 248–50
Picral etchant, 267
Plumber's brass, 251
Powder metallurgy, 159–62; bearings, 254–56
Phosphorus
  deoxidizer for copper, 134–35
  effect on stability of gamma iron, 259
  impurity in iron, 139–41
  inhibitor against dezincification in copper-zinc alloys, 241
Plastic properties, 47
Platinum, 2, 12
Plutonium, 1, 11
Polygonization, 91, 94–95, 120
Poisson's ratio, 49, 50, 79
Polishing, metallographic, 19; relief, 20
Polycrystalline, 70
Polymorphic metals, 14 (*see also* Allotropy)

Polythionic acid stress cracking of austenitic stainless steels, 448, 453
Positive climb of dislocations, 69
Post-weld heat-treatments, low-carbon steels, 359
Precipitation, 331–33
  -hardening, 460–501; in aluminum alloys, 473–485; in antimony-lead alloy, 145; in beryllium bronze, 466–72; in magnesium alloys, 485–90; in nickel alloys, 490–501; stainless steels, 455–56
  treatment, 336
Preferred orientation, in silicon transformer steels, 301
Primary solid solution, 167–69
Process annealing, steels, 347, 349
Proeutectoid constituent, 265
  cementite, separation during cooling, 284–87, 361–63
  ferrite, separation during cooling, 268–71, 361–62
Proof stress, 51
Proportional limit, 49
Proton, 10, 29
*p-T-x* diagram, 164

Quaternary alloy, 159
Quench-aging, iron and low-carbon steels, 460–62
Quench-and-temper transformation, 336
Quenching
  control of rate, 336–37
  cracking during, 377–79
  internal stresses during, 377–79
  interrupted, 341, 374–75
  media, 337–39
  microstructure produced by, in steels, 376–77; austenitic stainless steels, 441–42
  of steels, 370, 375
  volume changes during, 377–79

Reaction kinetics, "C" curve, 335
  for sigma precipitation in stainless steels, 435, 437–40
  TTT curve for steels, 350, 352, 362, 365
  temperature, 335; eutectic, 191–92; eutectoid steels, 262; peritectic, 216–17
Recalescence, 15
Recovery, 91, 92–94
Recrystallization, 9
  allotropic, 106
  aluminum, 129
  cast structures, 109–10

copper, 133
diagrams, 99
during welding, 112–13
effect of alloying elements on, 96; of prior cold work, 98; of time, 95
iron, 141
lead, 143–44
lowest temperature of, 95
magnesium, 146–47
strain, 330; primary, 91, 95–98; secondary, 91, 104–05; tertiary, 104
temperature, 336
zinc, 152
Red-hardness, 401, 409–13
Reduction in area in tensile test, 53
Reheating (*see also* Tempering, Aging, Precipitation-treatment)
  effect on structure, in quenched aluminum bronze, 471–72; steels, 385
Relaxation, 123
Remanent magnetism, 138
Residual stress, 93
  effect on austenite stabilization, 363; on cracking during quenching, 377; on fatigue life, 88
  removal by martempering, 374; during recovery, 91, 92–94
  in strain aging, 465
Resistance to penetration, 39–46
Restoration of corrosion resistance by heat-treatment of austenitic stainless steels, 446
Restraints to precipitation, 332
Retained austenite
  stabilization, 363
  by alloying, 365–67
  carburizing grades of automotive steels, 395
  hypereutectoid steels, 359–61
Retrograde solubility, 331
Rhodium, 2, 12
Rimmed steel, 86
Rockwell hardness, 41–43; superficial, 43
Rolled zinc, 152–53
Rubidium, 3
Rupture (*see also* Fracture), 74
  stress-, 121–22; parameters for extrapolating, 123–25
Ruthenium, 2, 14

S.A.E. numbering system for steels, 504–05
  steels (*see* Automotive steels)
Sand casting, 304, 315
Scleroscope hardness, 41
Screw dislocations, 29, 30–31; motion of, 65

S-curve (*see* TTT curve)
Season cracking of brass, 247–48
Secondary creep, 121
    solid solution, 167, 170–72
Section size, effect on heat-treatment, 381, 399
Segregation, 180–85; calculation of, 184
    in hot-rolled steels, 271
Selective attack
    dezincification in brasses, 241–43
    on sensitized grain boundaries in aluminum alloy, 484
    in austenitic stainless steels, 444–48
Selenium, 2
    free-machining alloy with copper, 135–36; with ferrite stainless steels, 429
Self diffusion, 33; during creep, 121
Semired brass, 251
Sensitization of austenitic stainless steels
    from carbide precipitation, 444–52
    prevention of, 447
Shape of precipitate, effect on coherency strains during precipitation, 334, 343
Shear, 57, 74
    fracture, 74, 76
    lip, in cleavage fracture, 80
    modulus, 49, 58–59, 67
    transformation, 339–41, 353, 358
Shore hardness, 41, 45
Short-range order, 331
Shot welding of 18:8 stainless steels, 450–53
Shrinkage in castings, 180
Sigma phase
    effect of temperature on stability, 435
    in stainless steels, austenitic, 437–40, ferritic, 417–19; transition-element alloys, 417
Silicon, effect on austenite transformation in steels, 289; on stability of gamma iron, 259; on cast irons, 303, 309–10; on eutectoid composition and temperature, 290; on low- and intermediate-chromium steels, 425
Silicon alloys
    aluminum, 129, 130, 173, 207–11
    cast irons, 322–24
    iron, 104, 139, 259, 298–301
    manganese tool steels, 401
    nickel-copper, 187
Silver, 2, 12; as impurity in Lake copper, 131, 133
Silver alloys
    copper, 189–90, 192–95
    lead, 203–04
Simple-cubic space lattice, 11, 12, 13
Sintering, powder metallurgy, 159

Slag, in wrought iron, 141
Slip, 59, 61, 65, 74
Society of Automotive Engineers (*see* S.A.E.)
Sodium picrate etchant, 267
Soft lead, 143–44
Solders, dip, 200; lead-silver, 203–04; sweating, 200; tin-lead, 200–02; wiping, 201–02
Solid-solubility limit, 193, 194–95, 199, 336; for carbon in ferrite, 443; for 18:8 austenitic stainless steels, 461
Solidification, 4–6
    equilibrium, 177, 179
    nonequilibrium, of solid-solution alloys, 180–84
    normal, 176–79, 181
    shift in apparent solidus, 182
Solid phases
    types in binary alloys, 167–68
    solubility, 193; changes with temperature, 194, 196
    solutions, 16–18, 73, 162, 167
    state, 3
Solidus, 175
Solute, 16
Solution
    liquid, 158; solid, 162
    heat-treatment, austenitic stainless steels, 441
Solvent, 16
Solvus line (*see* Solid solubility)
Sorbite, 386
Space lattice, 3, 10–13, 17–18, 54; deformation, 61
Specific heat, 3, 4
Specimen mounting, metallographic, 19
Spheroidal graphite, 303
    structures from austenite transformation, 385–87; in steels, properties compared to lamellar structures, 390
Spheroidized carbides
    heat-treatment to produce, 348–49, 353
    in low-carbon steels, 272
Spheroidite, 386
Spot welding, 18:8 stainless steels, 451–53
Stabilization
    austenite, 363; by nitrogen in chromium-nickel steels, 441, 453–54
    carbides in austenitic stainless steels, chemical, 447–48; thermal, 442–43, 447
Stacking sequences, 118
    faults, 118–19

Stainless irons, hardenable-type, 426–30
high-temperature properties, 434
unheat-treatable, 431–33
Stainless steels, 7; austenitic, 437–56; ferritic, 420–22, 426–37
carbide precipitation in, austenitic, 194, 441, 444–48
precipitation-hardening, 455–56
sensitization, austenitic, 444–48
surface-hardening, 454
work-hardening, 448–50
Standard electrical resistance, 186
Steadite, in cast iron, 311–12
Steam bronze, 251
Steel, 14
annealing, 348, process-, 347, 349
austenitic, 365–67; stainless, 440–56
automotive, 393–96, 398–401
carburizing, 391
castings, 280–82
chromium, 417–37
coarsening temperature, 105
commercial heat-treatment, 347–413
constitution, 261, 268; effect of alloying elements, 288
deep-drawing, 273
etching, 265–67
eutectoid, 263–65, 282–84
fracture, low-carbon, 77
free-machining, 271
graphitic, 273
hardening, 347–49
heat treatment, 347–413
hypereutectoid, 284–87
hypoeutectoid, 268–71
machinability, 271, 391
mild and low-carbon, 271–80
manganese, 365–67
nickel, 293
properties, effect of carbon content, 287–88; of microstructure, 378
silicon, 298–301
spheroidized, 173
structural, 268–71
tempers for strip, 274
tool, 401–**13**
transformation nomenclature, 267
TTT curves, 352, 362, 365
Single crystals, by annealing, 104
Step-bar test, for cast iron, 309
Stereoscopic microradiography, 20
Sterling silver, 190–95, 197, 474
Strain-aging in irons and low-carbon steels, 460–62, 464–65; control, 465
Strain-hardening (*see also* Work-hardening)
exponent, 53

recrystallization, 91, 95–98, 104–05, 330
Strauss test (acid copper sulfate), 444
Strength, 9, 39, 47
coefficient, 53
changes by annealing, 91; by recrystallization, 95, 97; by deformation, 38
engineering metals, relative, 47
tensile, 47–48
theoretical, 57
ultimate, 52
-weight ratio, 47
yield, 51
Stress-corrosion
cracking of, aluminum alloys, 484; austenitic stainless steels, intergranular, 448, 453, transgranular, 453; brasses, 247–48
-relief, 92–94
-rupture, 119, 121; extrapolation parameters, 123–25
-strain curves, 47, 48, 51, 52; effect of strain-aging, 465
Stretcher strains, 462–63
Strip steel, tempers, 274
Structure beams, stainless steel, built-up, 451
Structural bronze, 251
steels, carbon, 268–71, 274; nickel, 293–98; silicon, 298
Subatmospheric cooling, effect on austenite transformation, 365, 395
Subcritical temperature, effect on austenite transformation, 349–58
Subgrains, 26, 95
Submerged arc welding, 110
Substitutional solid solution, 16–18
Sulfur
as alloy in copper, 135–36; in steel, 271, 273
corrosion of steels, effect of chromium, 422–23
effect on stability of gamma iron, 259
print, 183
Sunburst structure, 7
Supercooling, 5
effect on diffusionless transformations, 341; on eutectoid transformation in steel, 353, 355; on precipitation, 335
Superheating, 9
cast iron, 316
Supersaturation by cooling, 331, 335, 336; by compositional change, 331, 355; by pressure change, 331
Surface diffusion, 34
imperfections, 28, 31

Surface diffusion (*cont.*)
  energy, 342–43; around recrystalliza-
    tion nuclei, 97–98

Tantalum, 1, 12
  effect on stability of gamma iron, 259
Tapered wedge test, for cast iron, 309
Tellurium, 2
  as alloy in copper, 135–36, 244; in lead,
    144
Temper
  by cold rolling, 463–64
  embrittlement, 423–24
  for light metals and alloys, nomencla-
    ture, 508
Temperature
  annealing, 91, 114
  effect on grain size, 98–103, 114
  relationship to hot work, 113–14
  significance of reaction, 336
  subcritical, transformation of austenite,
    349
Tempering, 336
  change of alloy content of carbides
    during, 387–88
  effect on carbon steels, 349, 370, 384–
    85; on martensite, 358–59, 385–87;
    on 4 to 6%-chromium, 0.5%-molyb-
    denum steel, 425; on 12%-chromium
    stainless steels, 429
  softening during, 387, 389
Tensile strength, 47–48; ultimate, 52
Terminal solid solution, 167–69
Ternary alloy, 159, 166–67
Terne coatings, 145–46
Thermal diffusivity, 4, 6
  expansion, iron, 108; iron-nickel alloys,
    294–96
  spikes, from irradiation, 29
  stabilization, of carbides in austenitic
    stainless steels, 442–43, 447–48
Time
  effect on recrystallization, 98–99
  quenching, 374
  -temperature-transformation curve (*see*
    TTT curve)
Tin, 1, 7, 11, 150–52
  coating on iron, 143, 154
  effect on stability of gamma iron, 259
Tin alloys
  antimony, 205–07, 216–17
  bearings, 218–21
  copper, 173, 234–37, 248–49
  cupronickel, 186
  lead, 145, 200–01, 205–07
  zinc, 197

Titanium, 1, 14
  alloy with zinc, 152; with nickel, 491–
    501
  carbide stabilization, austenitic stain-
    less steels, 448
  control of strain aging in low-carbon
    steel, 465
  effect on stability of gamma iron, 259
Tool steels, 401–13; microstructural
    changes during slow cooling, 282–87
Tough
  materials, 39, 54
  -pitch copper, 131–34
Transformation
  allotropic, 14, 107–09, 258
  ausforming, 369–70
  austempering, 350
  austenite, at constant subcritical tem-
    perature, 349–58; during continuous
    cooling, 370–72; effect of alloying
    elements, 364, of carbon, 361–63, of
    cold work, 365–67, of cooling rate,
    372, of grain size, 367–68, of sub-
    atmospheric cooling, 365; mechani-
    cal properties of products, 360–61
  diffusionless, 350–53
  high-manganese steel, 366–67
  latent heat of, 3
  nuclei, 353
  shear-type, 350–53
  to bainite, 350, 354, 356–58, 365; pearl-
    ite, 349–56; martensite, 350–53, 357–
    58
  TTT curve, for eutectoid steel, 352
  under equilibrium conditions, 234–326,
    342; nonequilibrium conditions, 330–
    31
Transformer sheet, 298–301
Transgranular stress-corrosion cracking,
    stainless steels, 453
Transition curve
  notch-brittle, 81, 423, 437, 453
  precipitate, 342–43
Transverse contraction
  tensile test, 50
  flexure test, 313
Triaxial tension, 39
Trigonal carbides, in iron-chromium al-
    loys, 420
Troostite, 386
True unit stress, 52, 53
TTT curve, 350
  carbide precipitation in austenitic stain-
    less steels, 443
  comparison with continuous cooling,
    371

TTT curve (*cont.*)
  direct transformation of austenite to bainite, 365
  eutectoid steel, 352–58
  hypereutectoid steel, 361–62
  hypoeutectoid steel, 361–62
  knee, 353, 356, 361
  sigma formation, from chromium ferrite, 435; from chromium austenite, 439
Tungsten, 1, 12
  -arc inert-gas welding, 110
  effect on stability of gamma iron, 259
Twin bands, 26; etching and repolishing, 73
Twinning
  annealing, 70, 117
  composition plane, 71
  dislocation explanation, 73
  mechanical, 26, 62
  recrystallization, 117
*T-x* diagram, 164–66, 168; from cooling curves, 175–76, 192–93

Ultimate strength, 52
Uniform precipitation (*see* Continuous precipitation)
Upper yield point, in body-centered cubic metals, 77
Uranium, 11; corrugated crystallographic planes, 54

Vacancy, 26–28
  from irradiation, 29
  -interstitial pairs, 26
Valence, chemical, 18
  electrons, 169
Valve composition, 251
Vanadium, 1, 12
  effect on stability of gamma iron, 259
  in high-speed tool steels, 409–13
Vapor deposition
  aluminum, 129
  pressure, as a factor in constitutional diagrams, 164
  state, 3
Vaporization, latent heat of, 3
Vickers hardness, 41, 44
Volume
  changes during quenching, 377–79; during allotropic change in iron, 108
  diffusion, 34
  energy, 342–43

Water quenching, 337–38
Wear-resisting cast irons, 318–21; steels, 366–67

Welding
  air-hardenable chromium steels, 421
  fusion, structural changes during, 110-13
  hardenable 12%-chromium steels, 426
  nonhardenable 12%-chromium steels, 426
  shot-, austenitic stainless steels, 451–53
  tungsten-arc inert-gas, 120
  4 to 6%-chromium steels, microstructure, 427
White cast iron, 301, 303–05
Weight per cent composition, conversion to atomic per cent, 166
Whiskers, metal, 59
Widmannstaetten structure, 334; aluminum-copper alloys, 476; brasses, 239; cast steels, 281; copper-aluminum alloys, 470–71; nickel steels, 293
Wiping solders, 202
Wire bar, copper, cast, 7
Workability, 9, 54
Work-hardening, 38, 39, 51, 52, 59
  austenite in high-manganese steel, 365–66; in chromium-nickel stainless steel, 448–50
  before fracture, 76
  copper, 61
  dislocation explanation, 68
  during tensile test, 51–52; during ausforming, 369–70
  effect on sigma formation, 435, 439–40; on precipitation, 341, 442, 475–76
  18:8 stainless steels, 448–50; to prevent sensitization, 442, 447
Wrought iron, 141–42; slag, 20

Yield
  in tensile test, 57
  nonhomogeneous, 77
  point, dislocation explanation, 465; relation to strain aging in low-carbon steels, 462–64
  strength, 51
  theoretical, 57
Young's modulus, 49, 50, 79; for engineering metals, 50
Yttrium, as nodularizing agent in cast iron, 317

Zinc, 1, 14, 152–55
  bronze, 251
  coating on iron, 143, 153–55
  effect on cupronickel castability, 186; on stability of gamma iron, 259
  hot working, 113

Zinc (*cont.*)
  mechanical twins in, 72
  rolled, 152–53, 234–48
Zinc alloys
  die-casting, 212, 213
  with aluminum, 211–13; with copper,
    152–53, 234–48
  **AG40A,** 212–13; **AC41A,** 212–13
Zirconium, 1, 14
  effect on stability of gamma iron, 259
Zone leveling, 185
  melting, 184–85
  refining, 185
  4 to 6%-chromium steels, 425–27
  12%-chromium steels, hardenable,
    426–30; nonhardenable, 430–33
  18:4:1-type high-speed steel, 409–13

18:8 stainless steels, carbon content,
  effect on properties, 444; high-temperature properties, 434; low-temperature, effect on properties, 453;
  microstructure, 442–43; nitrogen, effect on austenite structure, 441; sensitization, 444–52; shot-welding, 451–
  53; solubility of carbon in, 441;
  work-hardening, 448–50
1:2:1 rule, 197; application to constitutional diagrams, 199, 214, 262
80:10:10 bronze, 253, 255
85:5:5:5 brass, 249–50, 254
88:10:2 bronze, 251, 255
885 F (475 C) embrittlement, iron-
  chromium alloys, 433, 435–37